Contemporary
Literary and Cultural Theory

Contemporary Literary & Cultural Theory

THE JOHNS HOPKINS GUIDE

Edited by

MICHAEL GRODEN

MARTIN KREISWIRTH

AND IMRE SZEMAN

THE JOHNS HOPKINS UNIVERSITY PRESS | Baltimore

© 2012 The Johns Hopkins University Press
All rights reserved. Published 2012
Printed in the United States of America on acid-free paper
9 8 7 6 5 4 3 2 1

The Johns Hopkins University Press
2715 North Charles Street
Baltimore, Maryland 21218-4363
www.press.jhu.edu

Library of Congress Cataloging-in-Publication Data
Contemporary literary and cultural theory : the Johns Hopkins guide / edited by
Michael Groden, Martin Kreiswirth, and Imre Szeman.
      p. cm.
   Includes bibliographical references and indexes.
   ISBN 978-1-4214-0638-1 (hdbk. : acid-free paper) — ISBN 978-1-4214-0639-8
(pbk. : acid-free paper) — ISBN 978-1-4214-0705-0 (electronic) — ISBN 1-4214-0638-1
(hdbk. : acid-free paper) — ISBN 1-4214-0639-X (pbk. : acid-free paper) — ISBN
1-4214-0705-1 (electronic)
   1. Criticism—Bio-bibliography.   2. Literature—History and criticism—Theory,
etc.—Bio-bibliography.   I. Groden, Michael.   II. Kreiswirth, Martin.   III. Szeman,
Imre, 1968–
   PN81.C744 2012
   801′.950922—dc23   2012002228

A catalog record for this book is available from the British Library.

Special discounts are available for bulk purchases of this book. For more information,
please contact Special Sales at 410-516-6936 or specialsales@press.jhu.edu.

The Johns Hopkins University Press uses environmentally friendly book materials,
including recycled text paper that is composed of at least 30 percent post-consumer
waste, whenever possible.

For Molly (M.G.)

For Pearl Kreiswirth (M.K.)

For Max (I.S.)

CONTENTS

PREFACE

Over the course of the past three or four decades, literary and cultural theory have come to play a central role in the academic study of the humanities and social sciences. The diverse, often apparently competing or incompatible approaches, perspectives, and modes of inquiry that continue to flourish today under the generic label "theory" have brought most scholars to a welcome awareness of the importance of attending to methodological concerns in critical practice. Moreover, criticism as it is currently understood no longer confines itself to the study of literature: its discourses now extend well beyond literature to intersect with anthropology, philosophy, psychology, linguistics, political science, and much else besides, even as the objects of critical analysis that "literary" scholars attend to encompass all forms of cultural production, literary and nonliterary.

The first (1994) and second (2005) editions of *The Johns Hopkins Guide to Literary Theory and Criticism* responded in part to the growing sense among specialists that by the early 1990s a watershed had been reached in the great literary theoretical adventure. In the ensuing two decades, work in literary theory and criticism has multiplied exponentially, both in terms of the quantity of writing produced and the new theoretical directions taken. Figures and approaches that once occupied a prominent place on the critical horizon have faded, especially those critics and theories of the immediate post–World War II period from which literary "theory" as such often sought to distinguish itself. Other theorists and approaches just emerging in the early 1990s have now become centrally important to the endeavor of criticism and theory. As an outgrowth of the 1994 and 2005 editions, as well as the annually updated online version, *Contemporary Literary and Cultural Theory* is intended to make some of the most important entries of the first two editions—along with a number of new entries—available in a usable, easy to access desktop edition.

As with the other editions, the aim of this volume is to make accessible in clear and concise form a body of material that has become overwhelming. We hope it will have a wide audience in the academy, an audience composed not only of professors and graduate students in literary studies but also of many others working in adjacent fields that have been significantly influenced by recent developments in literary theory and criticism. Intended for use by scholars as well as by students and others seriously interested in theoretical issues but who do not have specialized knowledge, the volume endeavors to act as an informative, reliable introduction to the principal manifestations of this large and challenging area of inquiry. Our hope is that it will answer most of the questions that occur to teachers, students, and others as they traverse the contemporary critical and theoretical landscape and that it will show them where to turn for instruction beyond the range of the book itself.

As evidence of the widespread interest in literary theory and criticism, there has been a proliferation of study aids, tools, and reference guides that either touch on or deal extensively with the subject. Valuable as many of them are, these books—anthologies of primary texts, dictionaries, narrative surveys of one sort or another—nonetheless do not offer readers an accessible means of establishing a context broad, deep, and flexible enough to engage directly the many definitional difficulties and discursive complexities that abound in literary theory and criticism. One of the merits of this volume is that its extended, detailed entries furnish readers with the means to establish just such a context.

This edition consists of eighty alphabetically arranged entries on individual critics and theorists, critical and theoretical schools and movements. It also treats figures who did not explicitly deal with but who still deeply affected literature and also literary and cultural theory, as well as figures and kinds of inquiry from other fields that have been shaped by or have themselves shaped literary and cultural theory. Each entry includes a selective bibliography and there is extensive cross-referencing both within and at the conclusion of each entry. The entries that originally appeared in the second edition of *The Johns Hopkins Guide to Literary Theory and Criticism* have been shortened, and only the primary bibliographies have been included here. (Secondary texts that are quoted or cited directly in an entry are listed, however.) The indexes are designed to allow readers to locate substantive discussions of people and topics wherever they occur. Given the multiplicity of access points provided—alphabetically arranged entries, ample cross-referencing, bibliographies, indexes—the reader should be able to make use of what the book offers in a variety of ways. An online version of the second edition of *The Johns Hopkins Guide to Literary Theory and Criticism* is also available (http://litguide.press.jhu.edu), and much more extensive and precise searching is possible there.

Mindful of the political, if not polemical, cast of contemporary literary and cultural studies, we face squarely the question of bias. Entry topics have been selected as objectively as possible, with the benefit of a great deal of outside advice, and we are convinced that the editorial contours of the volume do indeed accurately reflect the coverage and focus described above. We have tried to be as inclusive as possible in the range of topics that we have chosen to cover. The guiding motive behind all the editions has been to provide readers with informed access to the field as a whole rather than to present the field through any one critical or theoretical lens. Although no principle of organizing information is altogether theoretically or ideologically innocent, we have attempted to make this volume open and useful to all critical and theoretical purposes and have avoided imposing a theoretically prejudiced view of the whole.

Representing the combined effort of over a hundred contributors, the book is multivocal and inclusive. As was the case with the selection of entry topics, the selection of contributors reflects the advice of hundreds of scholars and experts. We sought specialists who were able to place their subjects in the context of the larger intellectual environment, and ideally their entries provide reliable, accurate, and also interesting accounts in which their own positions neither dominate nor are obscured. We read and assessed all the completed entries, which were also appraised by external readers chosen by the publisher. Entries are all signed by their authors, and a complete list of contributors precedes the indexes.

Using the Book

To make the volume as convenient to consult as possible, we have adopted throughout certain uniform conventions:

- Cross-references are indicated by caps and SMALL CAPS (hypertext links in the online version), but only when the name or phrase exactly matches an entry title (for example, JACQUES DERRIDA is cross referenced, while "Derridean" is not).
- Parenthetical "see" references within entries and more general "see also" indications at the end of each entry direct readers to related discussions elsewhere in the volume.
- A cross-reference is provided only at the first appearance in each entry of another entry title.
- Translations of non-English texts are by the entry authors unless a parenthetical reference points to a published translation listed in the bibliography.
- For non-English titles, we give the translated title in the entries themselves and both the original and an English title in the bibliographies.
- To save space in the references, we call attention to italics only where the author of an entry has introduced them into a quotation; where no indication follows italicized words in a quotation, the italics appear in the original text.
- Quotations are referenced in accordance with the system adopted by the Modern Language Association of America.
- Abbreviations are the conventional ones or are otherwise self-evident.

The bibliographies that appear immediately after the body of each entry offer selected lists of sources and also include sources for quotations that appear in the entries. The indexes that follow these lists reference names and topics treated at substantial length within one or more entries (we mean by "substantial" a full paragraph or the equivalent). The indexes list names and topics that are not discussed so often that their inclusion would be meaningless. Topics in SMALL CAPS are themselves full entries. Finally, the indexes direct readers to entries by title.

A huge thanks to Sarah Blacker, Paula Derdiger, Matthew MacLellan, and Justin Sully. Each put an enormous amount of work into this project and played a significant role in the making sure the book came together. We're indebted to you not only for your keen editorial eyes but for suggestions that made this book better than it might otherwise have been.

Thanks as well to the staff at the Johns Hopkins University Press, especially our editor Matt McAdam, who encouraged us to undertake this project and showed faith that we'd manage to eventually complete it.

Contemporary
Literary and Cultural Theory

Adorno, Theodor W.

Theodor W. Adorno (1903–1969) began his intellectual career in Frankfurt and Vienna during the Weimar Republic, continued his work in American exile during the fascist era, and returned to West Germany after World War II to reconstitute the FRANKFURT SCHOOL of neo-Marxist critical theory with Max Horkheimer. Adorno was a capacious European intellectual of universal interests whose writings address an astonishing variety of disciplines: philosophy and sociology, psychology and social research, aesthetics, literary and music criticism, and the philosophy and sociology of music. While his essays in literary criticism form a relatively small part of his oeuvre, they presuppose a philosophical position that can best be understood through a discussion of his central works: *Dialectic of Enlightenment* (1947), *Negative Dialectics* (1966), and *Aesthetic Theory* (1970).

Dialectic of Enlightenment, coauthored with Horkheimer, proposes an overarching philosophy of history based on the notion of the domination of nature, arguing that the Western world, impelled by the instinct of self-preservation, overcame the terrors of nature through magic, myth, and finally the Enlightenment but that this rational and technological Enlightenment then reverted to myth and barbarism (the historical reference point is German fascism). Reason became instrumental and technocratic, and humans repressed their imbrications with the natural environment. The theme of the domination of nature, with nature conceived as both outer and inner nature, is thus combined with the Weberian motif of rationalization and disenchantment of the world to produce a "concept of Enlightenment" (the title of the first, programmatic chapter) that betrays its own original liberating impulse. For Horkheimer and Adorno, idealism's project to instrumentalize nature, that is, to relegate nature to the status of object, is implicated in historical phenomena such as the Holocaust that demonstrate that not only animals and nature but also humans can be manipulated as objects. In order to avoid this less than enlightened consequence of idealist thinking, Adorno proposes that rather than being suppressed or ignored, nature should be acknowledged.

Adorno's argument about nature and instrumental reason in *Dialectic of Enlightenment* stages a much larger concern that he elaborates in *Negative Dialectics*: what happens when an antagonistic concept—for example, nature for enlightened society—is suppressed? The question is vital for Adorno, for he is always concerned with the analysis and critique of power, domination, and violence. As he puts it, "History stays alive, not despite antagonism, but by means of it" (*Negative Dialectics* 320). Following G. W. F. Hegel, Adorno proposes a dialectical model that examines these antagonisms. However, he argues that when Hegel resolves antagonisms in the name of a salvational model—that is, when he dismisses nature in favor of the progression of the world spirit—he exhibits latent strands of idealist thinking. Rather than suppress the antagonisms of history and philosophy as idealism did when it created universalizing and totalizing narratives, Adorno seeks to come to terms with them. The redemptive moment of his thinking resides in an examination of the negative or suppressed aspect of the dialectic, which he also calls a "utopian negativity."

Rather than address power positively and explicitly, Adorno analyzes its implicit repression. This he carries out by "immanent critiques," that is, by pursuing the inner logic of the works he examines—philosophical, literary, musical, or other. He seeks out their implied structure and sheds light on the contradictory elements. In this way Adorno never explicitly or prescriptively states how one ought to live but instead offers immanent critiques of "damaged life" (see, e.g., Minima Moralia, Adorno's collection of aphoristic cultural analyses written while he was in American exile during Germany's fascist era and not published until 1951).

This negative form of critique manifests itself, too, in one of the most vital concepts he proposes in the Negative Dialectics: the defense of nonidentity. Again taking his cue from Hegel, Adorno examines identity thinking. In order for us to understand the being of something, we must designate what it is. But precisely here the problem in understanding the being or the identity of something begins. A concept never really covers the object. There is always a remainder, something that contradicts the traditional norm of adequation. Furthermore, in order to define the subject, one has to turn for its identity to other predicates. This is the nonidentity of identity in Adorno: the thing never quite matches up with the identification.

These are some of the thematic preoccupations of Adorno's Negative Dialectics, but the work also enacts Adorno's concerns in its very form. In the German original Negative Dialectics does not include chapters, nor is the work broken down into paragraphs as it is in the English version. Negative Dialectics is structured as a constellation. Even if the reader moves through the book in a linear fashion, understanding is not arrived at by progressing through Adorno's argument. Instead, Adorno presents the reader with a number of concerns between which the reader must constantly weave back and forth. The model is that of a constellation or a force field that was first proposed by WALTER BENJAMIN in Origin of German Tragic Drama (1928). The constellatory form, which forces the reader to construct meaning out of a multiplicity of concerns, finds its variation in the three "models" with which Adorno concludes Negative Dialectics.

The three closing chapters of Negative Dialectics, monograph-length studies of practical reason in Immanuel Kant, of history in Hegel, and of metaphysics, are explicitly designated as models. Adorno appropriates the term "model" from Arnold Schoenberg, for whom it refers to the endless permutation and variation on an initial arrangement. In this Hegelian manner of sublation (Aufhebung), the three models

Adorno offers us toward the end of *Negative Dialectics* simultaneously cancel out and preserve the preceding argument.

A distrust of logical rigor or Cartesian clarity and distinctness informs the structure not only of Adorno's *Negative Dialectics* but also of *Aesthetic Theory*. Published posthumously in 1970, *Aesthetic Theory* stages its argument in its very structure: it is paratactic, placing words, clauses, and arguments next to one another without indicating coordination or subordination.

Aesthetic Theory addresses classical themes of aesthetics—the autonomy of the work of art and its status as sociohistorical phenomenon, the beauty of nature and of art, *schöner Schein* (beautiful semblance)—insisting that philosophical aesthetics must come to grips with (not necessarily "beautiful") modernist art and its persistent negation of society as part of the post–World War II struggle to resist a recurrence of fascism.

For Adorno, who had gone to Vienna to study music with Alban Berg in 1925 and 1927, the paradigmatic innovation of modernist art is the atonal music of the Vienna school, led by Schoenberg. Yet he also examines its merits in literary texts—for example, in the writings of Samuel Beckett, Franz Kafka, and Marcel Proust. (Most of Adorno's literary criticism is contained in the volumes *Notes to Literature* [1958], *Prisms* [1955], and *Critical Models* [1963].) As Adorno argues in "Trying to Understand *Endgame*," what Beckett's drama *Endgame* stages, and this it holds in common with Kafka, is the hollowness of gesture and being. Rather than refer us to something, the characters in *Endgame* and their nervous ticks refer us to a lack. Kafka's writing, Adorno argues in his "Notes on Kafka," "expresses itself not through expression but by its repudiation, by breaking off. It is a parabolic system the key to which has been stolen. . . . Each sentence says 'interpret me,' and none will permit it" (*Prisms* 246). Like Beckett's, Kafka's writing operates on the basis of absence. The meaning of the symbolic is either withheld or does not exist. What both stage, according to Adorno, is a "trial run of a model of dehumanization" (*Notes* 254). In Kafka, particularly in his animal parables, this is the moment when humans realize that they are no longer humans. According to Adorno, Beckett stages what little remains of humans: "Spirit . . . is pitiful imitation; . . . soul . . . dramatizes itself; and the subject is its most abstract characteristic" (*Notes* 251). Beckett's *Endgame* shows what pathetic fragments of language and subjectivity remain to truncated humans but contains no vision of reconciliation, insisting instead on the negative.

Adorno's political and philosophical concerns motivate his literary criticism. Whether in his thematic focus or in the staging of his own writing, Adorno lingers on fragments and shuns closure. In all his essays Adorno juxtaposes fragments without hierarchy or synthesis. In an emblematic manner, each interpretive "vignette" is equal to the others, and together they constitute a new constellation. Such essays cannot be summarized, for they are not organized as "thesis" and "demonstration."

In order to achieve the effect of fragmentation, Adorno implicitly uses or explicitly studies tropes or structures that impede closure or linearity at the level of the book, essay, or sentence, such as the constellation model (*Negative Dialectics*), aphorism (*Minima Moralia*), essay ("Essay as Form"), and parataxis ("Parataxis"), to name only a few examples. At the level of the book, essay, or sentence each of these forms of writing synecdochically encapsulates the project of a larger whole in a moment without sacrificing the moment to the larger whole. They are structurally what Adorno advocates both explicitly and implicitly in his texts: he shuns a structure that would demand that the part be subsumed by or identical with the whole.

At the level of the sentence, Adorno stages or enacts his point through his very syntax. For this reason his work is notoriously difficult. It pushes German syntax to its limits: articles are deleted; the antecedent of pronouns is consistently obscure and on occasion irreducibly ambiguous; prepositional objects are as a rule elliptical; the subject of a clause may be deleted and reappear in the form of a relative clause; the reflexive pronoun is deferred until the end of the sentence; the negating *nicht* may appear, atypically, at the beginning of a sentence; foreign, classical, and archaic terms are constantly used; adverbs are positioned ungrammatically and accordingly accented. These techniques are specific to German syntax and frequently untranslatable.

The preeminent challenge of Adorno's aesthetics of negativity, and of his writings on literature and music, is the Marxist project of relating not only themes but also technique—not only content but also the intricacies of artistic form—to general social and historical development while avoiding the familiar dead ends of orthodox Marxist criticism. For this reason, the works of high modernism that have been such a bane for orthodox Marxism (GEORG LUKÁCS's analyses, which tend to favor referential realism) are of particular interest to Adorno, even as his treatment is nonetheless recognizably materialist and Marxist (see MARXIST THEORY AND CRITICISM).

The last decade has witnessed a proliferation in Adorno scholarship. While Susan Buck-Morss's *Origin of Negative Dialectics: Theodor W. Adorno, Walter Benjamin, and the Frankfurt School* (1977), FREDRIC JAMESON's *Late Marxism: Adorno; or, The Persistence of the Dialectics* (1990), and Martin Jay's *Adorno* (1984) are still invaluable introductions to Adorno's life and works, new volumes—such as J. M. Bernstein's *Adorno* (2001), Peter Hohendahl's *Prismatic Thought: Theodor W. Adorno* (1995), and Simon Jarvis's *Adorno: A Critical Introduction* (1998)—update Adorno scholarship. In 2003, the centennial of Adorno's birth, two new biographies of the great thinker appeared.

CHRISTINA GERHARDT

See also FRANKFURT SCHOOL.

Theodor W. Adorno, *Ästhetische Theorie* (1970, *Aesthetic Theory*, trans. Robert Hullot-Kentor, 1997), *Eingriffe: Neun kritische Modelle* (1963, *Critical Models*, trans. Henry W. Pickford, 1998), *Minima Moralia: Reflexionen aus dem beschädigten Leben* (1950, *Minima Moralia: Reflections from Damaged Life*, trans. Edmund Jephcott, 1978), *Negative Dialektik* (1966, *Negative Dialectics*, trans. E. B. Ashton, 1973), *Noten zur Literatur* (1958–1960, *Notes to Literature*, trans. Shierry Weber Nicholsen, 1991–1992), *Philosophie der neuen Musik* (1949, *Philosophy of Modern Music*, trans. Anne G. Mitchell and Wesley V. Bloomster, 1973), *Prismen* (1955, *Prisms*, trans. Samuel and Shierry Weber, 1981); Theodor W. Adorno et al., *Aesthetics and Politics* (trans. Anna Bostock et al., 1977); Andrew Arato and Eike Gebhardt, eds., *The Essential Frankfurt School Reader* (1978); Max Horkheimer and Theodor W. Adorno, *Dialektik der Aufklärung* (1947, *Dialectic of Enlightenment*, trans. John Cumming, 1972).

African American Theory and Criticism

1. Harlem Renaissance to the Black Arts Movement

A central concern in African American literary criticism prior to the 1970s is the relationship between the literary arts and developing conceptions of African American culture. Many of the major critical texts from the first six decades of the twentieth century advance our understanding of African American literary production, among them Sterling Brown's *The Negro in American Fiction* (1937), Hugh Gloster's *Negro Voices in American Fiction* (1948), and Robert Bone's *The Negro Novel in America* (1958). For all the considerable value of their local insights, however, these works now appear methodologically outdated, relying as they do too heavily on unreflective sociological or formalist perspectives. The pronouncements of writers themselves, rather than critical surveys, offer the best introduction to early African American literary criticism.

Grounded in a representationalist and moralistic "reading" of literature dependent on a Christian humanist ideology, African American literary criticism in the early twentieth century expressed a vision of cultural formation not significantly different from that of Victorian literary critics. The major venue for this early criticism was *Crisis*. Established by the National Association for the Advancement of Colored People (NAACP), this journal first appeared in 1910 under the editorial direction of W. E. B. Du Bois.

The early editorial position of *Crisis* owed much to the political and social aims of the NAACP, particularly its emphasis on racial uplift and social development. For *Crisis*, art properly considered was a merging of aesthetics and politics. In 1921, Du Bois argued that "we want everything that is said about us to tell of the best and highest and noblest in us. We insist that our Art and Propaganda be one" (55). *Crisis* consistently attempted to position literature as a tool in the struggle for political liberation while equally emphasizing the need for "Beauty." The fundamental defects of the journal's early criticism stemmed precisely from this attempt to mediate the opposition between an aesthetic and instrumental conception of literature. Frequently, the view of literature as a source of aesthetic pleasure conflicted with the view of art as a political tool, since "truth" understood aesthetically tended to be idealized while "truth" understood politically tended to be pragmatic.

Complicating this opposition was *Crisis*'s unqualified acceptance of a class-based interpretation of artistic production. From this perspective, art was clearly the province of the more "intelligent" and "advanced" classes, a view encapsulated by Du Bois's well-known faith in natural elites or "the talented tenth." (*Souls of Black Folk* [1903]). The question of whether beauty or truth was paramount was made more difficult by antecedent questions concerning the nature of black culture: which class best represented "the Negro"? In his anthology entitled *The New Negro* (1925), Alain

Locke assembled the work of scholars and artists alike in order to exhibit what he viewed as an emerging world historical phenomenon, the development of modern black culture. The list of contributors includes Du Bois, William Stanley Braithewaite, Countee Cullen, Jessie Fauset, Rudolph Fisher, E. Franklin Frazier, Melville Herskovitz, Langston Hughes, Zora Neale Hurston, Claude McKay, Jean Toomer, and Walter White.

In the lead essay of this volume, Locke outlines the critical transformation of mass black consciousness into a more heightened sense of itself as a "progressive" force (3). Rather than characterizing the post–World War I black demographic shift northward as exclusively a response either to extreme poverty or racial violence, Locke describes it primarily as a function of an emerging affirmative sense of a "common consciousness" (7). Harlem, then, becomes a progressive "race capital" for the black masses (7). Locke slightly modifies Du Bois's vision of the "talented tenth," giving a less prominent role to the "intelligentsia": "In a real sense it is the rank and file who are leading, and the leaders who are following" (7). Yet, for all its nationalist implications, this emerging collective consciousness is not to be confused with separatism (here Locke's target is clearly Marcus Garvey). Rather, Locke sees this nationalism as a constructive phase of development toward democracy, an eclectic engagement with "white" culture.

George S. Schuyler similarly takes up the issue of African American artistry in "The Negro-Art Hokum." Schuyler's skepticism, clearly indicated by his title, finds its source in a "historical" reading of cultural development, one that privileged the nation-state as the basis for cultural formation. Citing a long list of "Negro" artists, including Claude McKay, Edward Wilmot Blyden, Alexander Pushkin, Paul Laurence Dunbar, James Weldon Johnson, and Charles Chesnutt, Schuyler argues that "their work shows the impress of nationality rather than race. They all reveal the psychology and culture of the environment—their color is incidental" (663). Schuyler's perspective brings the idea of culture into contact with the idea of race. In doing so, he problematizes both concepts by suggesting the possibility of a more fluid notion of identity (and cultural production) than the idea of race alone would allow. Further, by framing identity as emerging out of commingled sources, Schuyler also anticipates the similar dismantling of the idea of "race" undertaken by some postmodern commentators.

Unfortunately, Schuyler's analysis operates out of largely underdeveloped conceptions of race, culture, and nationality. Revealingly, his analysis alternately separates and conflates all three categories. While Schuyler is assuredly aware of the limitations of a concept such as race, his devaluation of color as a signifier of difference depends on the substitution of the idea of "nation," a concept no less insubstantial. Furthermore, although "The Negro-Art Hokum" tries to locate the source of human consciousness in some form of "history," it ultimately offers an unapologetically classist reading of artistic creation. What passes for Negro art is either indistinguishable in all respects from other forms of "high" art (i.e., "it shows more or less evidence of European influence") or is the product of "the peasantry of the South," whose skin color is mere "coincidence" (662).

One of the more powerful voices rising in opposition to this form of class-based interpretation belonged to Langston Hughes. His early critical statements in particular proposed explicit revisions of African American gentility. One week after the publication of Schuyler's "Negro-Art Hokum," Hughes responded in the *Nation* with a different reading of African American art. Hughes's "The Negro Artist and the Racial Mountain" plays off of Du Bois's conception of the double consciousness outlined in *Souls of Black Folk*. From Hughes's perspective, the problem for the Negro artist was not so much the need to balance African and American identities within this double consciousness as the need to emphasize a Negro cultural integrity out of which might rise an authentic conception of African American art.

For Hughes, the racial mountain, or "the urge within the race toward whiteness," obstructs this effort (692). The flight from race not only robs the Negro artist of his or her cultural perspective but also distances the artist from the most fertile source of material: working-class Negro life. Hughes views the working class as a locus of cultural integrity, a realm untouched by the urge toward whiteness and uninfected by a suspicion of "play." Hughes's insistence on the legitimacy of "racial" art prefigures not only Richard Wright's (and to some extent Ralph Ellison's) engagement with a nationalistic perspective on art but also that of the black arts movement of the 1960s. In many respects, however, both Hughes's championing of lower-class black life and his excoriation of the black middle classes and their desire for an "Episcopal heaven" seems oversimplified and unreflective. The characterization of lower-class black life as playful, direct, unmediated, and somehow more natural than the world of the middle class is overly romantic at best and at worst a simple inversion of the traditional racist stereotype that figures African Americans psychologically as children.

Richard Wright's criticism and that of the black arts movement forty years later extend the idea of nationalism, but both attempt to define this idea in a more problematic and complicated form. In "Blueprint for Negro Writing," Wright tries to balance two different and competing claims regarding the relation of the artist to the community. Wright was sympathetic to the nationalist position articulated by Hughes in "Negro Artist," but he was far too cognizant of the reality of racism to allow for a valorizing of the idea of play. His chief criticism of Zora Neale Hurston's *Their Eyes Were Watching God*, for example, is that she "voluntarily continues in her novel the tradition that was forced upon the Negro in the theater, that is, the minstrel technique that makes the 'white folks' laugh" ("Between" 25).

Despite his wariness of constructions of blackness that resemble stereotypes, Wright nevertheless seeks other grounds for a rehabilitated version of nationalism, convinced of the integrity of African American culture. Wright maintains that racism tended to fashion a collective experience that contributed heavily to the formation of a nationalist perspective ("Blueprint" 57) and, hence, a culture. And African American writers played a significant role within the project of cultural transmission. At their best, they conceive of themselves as summary figures, encapsulating and communicating the entire historical range of African American cultural life. Having gained this historical view, black writers may then "stand shoulder to shoulder with Negro workers in mood and outlook" (55). In Wright's view this solidarity would significantly lessen the distance between the masses and the typically middle-class literary artist.

At this point in his life, Wright's nationalistic posture was complicated by his allegiance to doctrinaire Marxism (see MARXIST THEORY AND CRITICISM). Marxist class analysis reads history in a different fashion than does the racial and cultural analysis favored by black nationalism, rendering problematic the Marxist insistence on solidarity across racial lines. Wright tries to mediate these two competing perspectives by affirming African American cultural integrity while simultaneously warning against a "specious" nationalism. For Wright at this time, nationalism was an intermediate rather than final goal. The primary job of the Negro artist remained the unmasking of previously hidden class conflict and the location of that conflict within the arena of economic oppression. This imperative required the artist to forsake a vision of literature either as primarily aesthetic or as a vehicle by which one might gain entrance into white society or petition that society for justice.

In order to achieve this revisionist and revolutionary posture, Wright argues, the Negro writer must turn his or her attention to the material conditions of black life and, further, embrace the proletarian perspective held by black laborers, who were freer from the bonds of bourgeois values than the artist. Wright rejects the bourgeois conception of the artist as isolated individual; his sense of nationalistic imperative instead locates the act of writing as a publicly committed, socially conscious act. Two facts, however, complicate this synthesis. First, precisely how the writer makes the transition from a nationalist perspective focusing on African American cultural life to a more full-fledged revolutionary solidarity remains unexplained. Further, Wright himself admits that the nationalistic aspects of African American culture are largely a function of segregation's "warping way of life" (54). His recognition of this distortion leads Wright to insist on the need to transcend nationalism, but even the affirmative aspects of this nationalism become vexed by virtue of their origins in segregation. African American culture, then, emerges less a self-generating phenomenon and more a function of a racist society.

In her review of Wright's Uncle Tom's Children, Zora Neale Hurston praises Wright's capacities as a writer of fiction but wonders "what he would have done had he dealt with plots that touched the broader and more fundamental phases of Negro life instead of confining himself to the spectacular" ("Stories" 32). Hurston argues that Wright's fiction tended to reduce African American characters to mere products of racial animosities, thereby turning the work of art into little more than a chronicle of crime and outrage. Like Hurston, but two decades later, James Baldwin sees profound limitations in such naturalistic "protest" fiction, particularly of the sort practiced by Wright. For Baldwin, the evolution of African American fiction from a body of literature emphasizing uplift and affirmation to one emphasizing protest and degradation results finally in a highly reductive and monolithic form. What is worse, Baldwin maintains, "the 'protest' novel, so far from being disturbing, is an accepted and comforting aspect of the American scene, ramifying that framework we believe to be so necessary" ("Everybody's Protest Novel," *Price* 31). Moreover, the protest novel can mask, as it did for Wright from Baldwin's perspective, "an almost ineradicable self-hatred" and a fundamental ignorance of black life ("Alas, Poor Richard," *Price* 287, 285–86).

Eschewing the bankrupt form of the "protest novel," Baldwin posits a vision of fiction in which the work of art not only engages but also transcends the problems of race and democracy. For Baldwin, America itself is a kind of fiction in the making: a text not fully cognizant of its own power or nature. Additionally, Baldwin sees literature within the context of alienation and expatriation, in terms of both race and sexuality. For him, there is no home for the black writer anywhere.

While Ralph Ellison's most important contribution to African American literary study is undoubtedly *Invisible Man* (1953), his contributions to African American literary criticism have been only slightly less significant. His most important volumes of literary and cultural essays are *Shadow and Act* (1966) and *Going to the Territory* (1986). Overall, Ellison's writing attempts to reintroduce the work of literary art into the context of the national debate concerning democracy and, more specifically, to address the place of African Americans within that discourse. For Ellison, the novel is the venue in which the struggle for individual and collective freedom implied by the issue of race ought to be explored. The work of art, in this view, refuses to provide specific answers but instead provides an arena for a complex meditation on the informing social conflict of the day.

In his acceptance speech for the National Book Award, printed as "Brave Words for a Startling Occasion," Ellison advances an unvarnished criticism of naturalism, envisioning a fiction "leaving sociology to the scientists" (105). Instead of the "final and unrelieved despair" (105) of naturalism, Ellison urges a more magical and expansive form of writing, the sort of prose more characteristic of late modernism or early postmodernism. Such literature, for Ellison, reveals a more pronounced authorial intention to foreground the power of the work of art over and against the power of an intractable experience. Central to Ellison's critical position is the insistence on treating African American art with the same sophistication as other kinds of art. Equally, Ellison avoids reductionist sociological readings of the sort offered by Irving Howe in his famous "Black Boys and Native Sons" (1963). Yet while emphasizing the role of the text as text and not simply as a sign of a particular political position, Ellison never removes the literary work of art from its cultural grounding. For Ellison, the work of art is significant only insofar as it engages the central issues of the time. Ellison reads the African American fictional character (his central example is, naturally enough, Jim from Mark Twain's *Huckleberry Finn*) as signifying the informing drama of American cultural life, the conflict between the professed ideals of democracy and the real practice of slavery in its past and present forms. This role confers on African American characters an "irrepressible moral reality" (*Shadow and Act* 51).

Supporting this reading of the centrality of the African American character and of the equivalent value of the novel to democracy is Ellison's attempt to rehabilitate liberalism. His criticism and fiction may be understood as themselves embodying the kind of paradox and ambiguity outlined in the pages of *Invisible Man*. On the one hand, Ellison was convinced that the "invisibility" of African Americans stemmed from specific historical causes, namely racism and classism. Yet in advocating what Thomas Hill Schaub has termed a "psychologized Marxism" (111), Ellison uses language that seems of a piece with the liberalism of his time. This conflation tends to "universalize," "existentialize," and therefore "whiten" the condition of African Americans, making it nearly identical with what might be called the "modern condition." Further, Ellison sees a principle of freedom at work in liberalism, a principle worth saving not only because it acts as a bulwark against despair, but also because it leaves room to recognize "the invented character of identity and social institutions" (Schaub 109). Ellison's affirmation of liberalism, however, seems no less visionary and ephemeral than Wright's interest in Marxism and existentialism, particularly since Ellison's language allows him to be constructed as a liberal centrist. Criticizing Ellison's privileging of the principles of democracy over and against the practices enacted in the name of those principles (as in *Invisible Man*), later commentators, especially members of the black arts movement, read Ellison's advocacy of democratic virtues as fundamentally naïve and assimilationist.

The core ideological basis for the black arts movement was its conviction in the reality of black nationhood and its connection with the black power movement (Neal, "Black" 257). The movement recognized racism as perhaps the most significant force in the construction of African American culture, a conviction that led the group to venerate Wright and particularly his *Native Son* (1940). As a result of persistent racism, African Americans become alienated from white American culture (Baraka 114–15; Fuller, "Towards" 9). But instead of arguing for a trajectory that required a synthesis of two different selves as Du Bois does in *Souls of Black Folk* or for a trajectory inscribed by Ellison's sense of ambiguity, the theorists of the black arts movement held that recognition of this fundamental alienation should lead the black artist to embrace a fervent nationalism. "Implicit in the Black Arts movement is the idea that Black people, however dispersed, constitute a nation within the belly of white America" (Neal, "Black" 257). Notable works that advocate this sentiment include Addison Gayle's *Black Aesthetic* and LeRoi Jones and Larry Neal's *Black Fire* (1968).

The movement espoused that art must necessarily shape the contours of the black nation and reveal it to the world. This imperative inclined black arts criticism and theory to advance an instrumental view of artistic production. Validity becomes a primary artistic criterion, a validity indicated not so much by idealized truth as by political efficacy. "Black art, like everything else in the black community, must respond positively to the reality of revolution. . . . What is needed is an aesthetic, a black aesthetic, that is a criteria [sic] for judging the validity and/or the beauty of a work of art" (Karenga 31). The forces motivating validity are two: the need to represent the truth concerning the black community and the need to "reflect and support the Black revolution" (31)—rather than simply "protest" conditions as in previous schools of African American literature (Fuller, "New" 335; Neal, "Black" 258). According to this schema, validity requires a form of art that immerses itself in the concrete particulars of black life rather than in "abstractions" (Neal, "Black" 260). All aesthetic choices derive from the centering of a black audience and a black artist operating in a black world—from the choice of aesthetic materials to problems of evaluation and judgment. As Don L. Lee puts it in his poem "The New Integrationist," "We seek the integration of Negroes with black people."

Examined in retrospect, however, the literary criticism of the black arts movement nevertheless seems in many respects hopelessly dated and profoundly romanticized. While the movement's willingness to expose the degrading conditions of some parts of black life shows that it did not wholly reject literary realism, the visionary character of the black arts movement inclined it to advance a view of "blackness" that was fundamentally essentialized, monolithic, and ahistorical. Rather than opposing the West, therefore, the movement too often employed categories of analysis rooted firmly in Western sociocultural perspectives (especially but not exclusively the homophobia and sexism of the fiction, poetry, and prose). In fact, the sexism of the black arts movement became a target of the feminist revisions of African American critical discourse common since the 1980s.

THEODORE O. MASON JR.

Houston Baker, "Discovering America: Generational Shifts, Afro-American Literary Criticism, and the Study of Expressive Culture," Blues, Ideology, and Afro-American Literature: A Vernacular Theory (1984); James Baldwin, The Price of the Ticket: Collected Nonfiction, 1948–1985 (1985); Imamu Amiri Baraka, Home: Social Essays (1966); W. E. B. Du Bois, "Negro Art," Crisis 22 (1921); Ralph Ellison, Shadow and Act (1964); Dexter Fisher and Robert Stepto, eds., Afro-American Literature: The Reconstruction of Instruction (1979); Hoyt Fuller, "The New Black Literature: Protest or Affirmation" (Gayle), "Towards a Black Aesthetic" (Gayle); Addison Gayle, ed., The Black Aesthetic (1972); Stephen Henderson, Understanding the New Black Poetry: Black Speech and Black Music as Poetic References (1973); Langston Hughes, "The Negro Artist and the Racial Mountain," Nation, 23 June 1926; Zora Neale Hurston, I Love Myself When I Am Laughing . . . And Then Again When I Am Looking Mean and Impressive: A Zora Neale Hurston Reader (ed. Alice Walker, 1979), "Stories of Conflict," Saturday Review of Literature, 2 April 1938; LeRoi Jones and Larry Neal, Black Fire (1968); Ron Karenga, "Black Cultural Nationalism" (Gayle); Don L. Lee, "Toward a Definition: Black Poetry of the Sixties (after Leroi Jones)"

(Gayle); Alain Locke, *The New Negro* (1925); Larry Neal, "The Black Arts Movement" (Gayle); Larry Neal, "Some Reflections on the Black Aesthetic" (Gayle); J. Saunders Redding, *A Scholar's Conscience: Selected Writings of J. Saunders Redding, 1942–1977* (1992, ed. Faith Berry), *To Make a Poet Black* (1939); Thomas Hill Schaub, *American Fiction in the Cold War* (1991); George S. Schuyler, "The Negro-Art Hokum," *Nation*, 16 June 1926; Richard Wright, "Between Laughter and Tears," *New Masses* 25 (1937), "Blueprint for Negro Writing," *New Challenge* 2 (1937), "Literature of the Negro in the United States," *White Man, Listen!* (1957).

2. 1977 to 1990

Two major developments marked the history of African American literary theory and criticism between 1977 and 1990: the appearance of more theoretically grounded approaches to African American literary production and the emergence of a vigorously feminist African American literary theory and criticism. The inclination toward more consciously literary and theoretically based analyses of African American literature appears most famously in the seminar titled "Afro-American Literature and Course Design" held at Yale University in June 1977. Funded by both the Modern Language Association of America and the National Endowment for the Humanities, the seminar was led by Robert Stepto and published as *Afro-American Literature: The Reconstruction of Instruction* (1978). From the perspective of those involved, the field of African American criticism and pedagogy required reconstruction because it had become dominated by fundamentally ideological or sociological methodologies that tended toward the naïvely reductive. As Stepto writes in his introductory essay, "Teaching Afro-American Literature," the contemporary fashion of teaching and thinking about African American literature was to treat it as merely "an agreeable entrée to black history, sociology, and politics" (9). In his "Preface to Blackness: Text and Pretext," HENRY LOUIS GATES JR. extends this sentiment by decentering the consideration of "blackness . . . [as] a material object or an event" (67) and turning the critic's "attention to the nature of black figurative language, to the nature of black narrative forms, to the history and theory of Afro-American literary criticism, to the fundamental unity and form of content, and to the arbitrary relations between the sign and its referent" (68). The decentering of simplistic sociological approaches to literature meant, in the words of Robert Hemenway, a "concentration . . . on the aesthetic forms, linguistic constructions, and imaginative patterns" of African American literature (123). While the idea of an African American literary tradition remained important to all the contributors to this volume, tradition was to be established not by the "race" of the author but rather by a consideration of intertextuality. Fundamentally, *The Reconstruction of Instruction* aimed to outline the forms that intertextuality might take in both theory and practice.

To those taking an instrumental view of the content of the work of art, *Reconstruction of Instruction* seemed to reinvoke "art for art's sake" rather than constructing art as a weapon in a social and political struggle for liberation. Further, the theoretical language adopted by many of the contributors seemed to some unnecessarily inflated and elitist. Finally, the critics of *Reconstruction* saw the general movement as attacking the fundamentally reflectionist ethos of earlier criticism on which this instrumental reading of literature was based. Clearly, the renewed emphasis on language use owed much to the criticism of Ellison, who earlier had insisted on the distinction between sociology and literature in "Brave Words for a Startling Occasion" (113). Like Ellison, the two most important theorists of African American literature during this period, Henry Louis Gates Jr. and Houston Baker Jr., emphasized the central importance of language. At times, however, Gates and Baker could be seen as antagonists in the developing contest over the direction of African American letters. Early on, Gates contended that Baker's work seemed to emphasize the extraliterary, arguing that his "criticism teaches us more about his attitude toward being black in white America that it does about black literature" (Stepto and Fisher 65). Over time, however, the opposition between the two was bracketed by their growing agreement about many of the principles articulated in *Reconstruction*. For example, they agreed that African American literary criticism required some sort of reform and that formal consideration of literature was not necessarily apolitical or antipolitical.

Initially, Gates's critical position shared close ties with traditional academic "high theory." In "Criticism in the Jungle" (1984), Gates outlines a theoretical basis for the initial development of an African American literary canon and for the study of African American literature as a form of language use rather than as a form of unmediated social practice. The development of an African American tradition by means of a "synthesis" of African American vernacular and the language of theory is further articulated in *"Race," Writing, and Difference* (1986) and is given fullest expression in *The Signifying Monkey* (1988) and *Figures in Black: Words, Signs, and the "Racial" Self* (1987). Gates defines the central term "signifyin(g)" as both a linguistic process, the vernacular improvising on formal critical speech by way of a "double-voicedness" and a metaphor indicating a larger cultural practice (*Signifying* 44–51).

The significant motives driving Gates's paradigm were: (1) the need to reform the study of African American literature; (2) the positioning of this reform as an explicit "signifyin(g)" revision of dominant critical theory; and (3) the development of a culturally specific theory of African American literature and criticism. Over time, Gates's work came to emphasize the third principle over and against the other two. Having "signified" on "high academic theory," Gates moved on to a revised form of criticism that talked "that talk, the language of black difference" ("Authority" 46). For Gates, such a critic "signified" and thus moved from being simply a trickster figure to being something more in the way of a culture worker in a field with nationalist overtones.

The career of Houston Baker has run parallel to that of Gates, though in a somewhat opposite direction. While Gates can be seen as having moved from theory toward literary nationalism, Baker can be seen as having moved from a profoundly nationalistic cultural base toward a revision of that position complicated by an engagement with language and with theory. Consequently, by the end of the period in question, both Gates and Baker could be described as occupying relatively similar positions at opposite ends of their careers. In his early work, such as *Long Black Song*, Baker took as his chief task the defining of African American literature within a cultural setting. In "Completely Well," he tries to outline the contours of a distinctly African American notion of culture based on the idea of the whole life of a people. He juxtaposes this version of culture with a more Victorian or Arnoldian vision that fetishizes the best products of the best classes. This interest in African American cultural formation remerges in Baker's *Blues, Ideology and Afro-American Literature, Modernism and the Harlem Renaissance* (1987), and *Afro-American Poetics: Revisions of Harlem and the Black Aesthetic* (1988). The central aim of these works is to establish a connection between the African American cultural past and current African American discursive and cultural practice. Over time, Baker's focus shifted more to language use and its relation to culture. In "Discovering America," Baker distances himself from the "race and superstructure" criticism and "romantic Marxism" of the early black arts movement (*Blues* 81) while retaining and revising their emphasis on cultural anthropology (105). Additionally, he moved away from the concept of "repudiation," in which black culture was marked by a rejection of things "white" (*Long* 13) toward a recognition of cultural "hybridity."

Just as Gates, Baker, and other African American theorists have claimed Ralph Ellison as one of their precursors, so too have the recent generation of African American feminist critics located Zora Neale Hurston as a progenitor. And just as the opposition between Ellison and Richard Wright seemed informing for the theorists, so too was the opposition between Hurston and Wright for the feminist critics after 1977. Hurston's feminist-centered fiction, with its emphasis on female intersubjectivity, contrasts with Wright's emphasis on the construction of an embattled masculinity within a racist environment. Giving impetus to this view was the publication of two volumes by Alice Walker. Her edition of writings by Hurston, *I Love Myself When I Am Laughing*, concludes with "Looking for Zora," an account of her discovery of Hurston's grave. Hurston's rediscovery became a metonym for the archaeological act of another form of reconstruction, the recovery of the trajectory of African American women's literary and cultural tradition.

To establish this trajectory required a distancing from both masculinist writing and white academic feminism. Two essays in Elaine Showalter's *The New Feminist Criticism: Essays on Women, Literature and Theory* (1985) explicitly signal this break. In "Toward a Black Feminist Criticism," Barbara Smith points to the virtual invisibility of black women writers generally (and black lesbian writers specifically) and calls for a counteracting mode of criticism that would open up the space needed for the exploration of black women's lives and the creation of consciously black woman-identified art. At the same time, a redefinition of the goals and strategies of the white feminist movement would lead to much-needed change in the focus and content of what is now generally accepted as women's culture (169). Smith furthers this claim by suggesting that the general opposition to white patriarchy voiced in African American women's writing demonstrates its fundamentally "lesbian" nature (175). In a companion essay, "New Directions for Black Feminist Criticism," Deborah McDowell takes exception to this view as dangerously reductive and essentialist and demonstrates important connections between African American women's and men's writing by focusing on language.

The period after 1977 witnessed the publication of a number of works furthering the general aims outlined by Smith and McDowell. Toni Cade Bambara's *The Black Woman: An Anthology* (1970) was one slightly earlier precursor to this movement. Later anthologies include Roseann P. Bell, Bettye J. Parker, and Beverly Guy-Sheftall's *Sturdy Black Bridges: Visions of Black Women in Literature* (1979), Gloria Hull, Patricia Bell Scott, and Barbara Smith's *All the Women Are White, All the Blacks Are Men, But Some of Us Are Brave: Black Women's Studies* (1982), Barbara Smith's *Home Girls: A Black Feminist Anthology* (1982), Marjorie Pryse and Hortense Spillers's *Conjuring: Black Women, Fiction, and Literary Tradition* (1985), Joanne M. Braxton and Andrée McLaughlin's *Wild Women in the Whirlwind* (1990), and Henry Louis Gates Jr.'s *Reading Black, Reading Feminist* (1990). Each of these volumes undertakes, in Braxton's words, "an exploration of intertextuality, not only within Black female literary tradition, but also within the Black and female experience which has given rise to this tradition" (xxiv).

Like any critical movement, however, African American literary feminism was fraught with internal divisions. Smith's claim that African American women's writing is inherently lesbian ("Black Feminist" 175 ff.) threatened to create more problems than it solved, ironically marginalizing literature focusing on explicitly eroticized relations between women. Conversely, texts such as Smith's own *Home Girls* or Audre Lorde's *Sister Outsider* (1984), with their important assertion of lesbian difference made even more problematic, if not impossible, a stable and uniform representation of African American woman as oppositional other.

Further complicating the development of African American literary feminism was its position inside the academy, a locale consistently pictured as antithetical to any significant concentration on African American women's expressivity. Hazel Carby's influential *Reconstructing Womanhood* (1987) advocates "that black feminist criticism be regarded as a problem, not a solution" (15). Carby's work complicated matters further by interrogating the neglect of middle-class African American writers such as Jessie Fauset and Nella Larsen, pointing to the romanticization of "the folk" and the construction of African American identity as fundamentally rural (175). Similarly complicating was the work of bell hooks (Gloria Watkins). Her *Talking Back: Thinking Feminist, Thinking Black* (1979), *Feminist Theory: From Margin to Center* (1984), and *Yearning: Race, Gender, and Cultural Politics* (1990) aimed to not only engage the construction of an African American feminist discursive practice but also to make that practice more attuned to questions of class and postmodern critical practice (see POSTMODERNISM). In "Feminist Theory: A Radical Agenda," she advances the notion that theorizing activity is indispensable to a feminist practice (in direct opposition to Barbara Christian) and locates the animus against theory as a form of anti-intellectualism (*Talking Back* 38–39). hooks launches a postmodern attack on essentialism within African American feminist discourse, even as she emphasizes the significance of African American women's experiences and criticizes the shortcomings of postmodernism. Similarly, hooks sees value in interrogating the relation between African American literary feminism and the academy.

Developments in literary feminism also worked to reconstruct literary history by filling in heretofore unrecognized gaps. In *Color, Sex, and Poetry* (1987), Gloria Hull treats the work of Harlem Renaissance writers Alice Dunbar-Nelson, Angelina Weld Grimké, and Georgia Douglas Johnson with the goal of revaluating their work and centering their contributions to this formative moment in African American literary and cultural history. More importantly, Hull interrogates the implicit masculinist bias of key figures such as Alain Locke and shows how the question of sexuality becomes especially problematic for the writers covered in *Color, Sex, and Poetry* (7). Furthermore, Hull's work opens up a neglected area of concern by exploring the way in which women's sexualities that did not conform to traditional social patterns seem to largely disappear from literature.

While Hull's work helps refigure Harlem Renaissance literary history, its conspicuous weakness is an undertheorized representation of subjectivity and a reliance on "experience" as a central term of analysis. The end of the 1980s saw the emergence of a set of powerful female voices seeking to more explicitly theorize black female subjectivity while continuing to situate that subjectivity in the realm of politics. Cheryl Wall's influential anthology, *Changing Our Own Words: Essays on Criticism, Theory, and Writing by Black Women* (1989) focuses on the development of more sophisticated approaches to African American women's literature undertaken by women themselves. The larger goal of the collection is transformation. In Wall's language, "changing words means transforming words." The last decade of the twentieth century and the first decade of the twenty-first witnessed not only the transformation of the criticism of black women's writing but the transformation of other critical discourses in response to black women's writing. "The extent to which feminist and Afro-Americanist writing and, yes, even centrist criticism are more inclusive than they were twenty years ago owes much to black women's writing and its critics changing as many words as they pleased" (15).

Such a changing of words brings with it a certain destabilization of familiar categories. Essays such as Claudia Tate's "Allegories of Black Female Desire" (1989) or Hortense Spillers's " 'The Permanent Obliquity of an In(pha)llibly Straight': In the Time of the Daughters and the Fathers" (1989) or her well-known "Mama's Baby, Papa's Maybe: An American Grammar Book" (1987) threaten conventional dominant and oppositional understandings of gender, family, and race in ways that are uncomfortable to many. While not denying the distinctiveness of black female identity, these thinkers represent this identity as less transparent and less immediately available than previously thought.

The problems posed by *experience* as an analytical term became the focus of an important exchange between Deborah Chay and Barbara Smith in a 1993 issue of *New Literary History*. While acknowledging Smith's contributions to contemporary African American feminist criticism particularly and literary study generally, Chay draws attention to the limitations of experience: "Hypostasizing experience to secure her claims, Smith is prevented from making distinctions among categories such as 'black men' and 'white *feminists*' which might otherwise allow her to pursue her analysis and critique of black women's social conditions in a less deterministic fashion" (638–39). Experience bodies forth as a naturalized given, even as it is cited by Smith and others as political. Moreover, rarely, if ever, had black women's experience been interrogated as at least in part a product of hegemony. Citing the work of Valerie Smith and Barbara Christian, Chay praises the movement toward more theoretical versions of black feminist criticism, precisely because the variety of critical interventions comprehended under that heading cannot be accounted for by a homogenizing category such as experience. Barbara Smith's rejoinder to Chay in the same volume of *New Literary History* rephrases the defense of experience and attacks Chay's criticisms as "profoundly apolitical" (655), arguing that Chay is positioning "identity as an intellectual construct with insignificant political or material consequences within a white supremacist, misogynist, capitalist and patriarchal *state*" (655). This opposition anticipates controversies over the dislocations in identity resulting from the interrogations undertaken by black British cultural studies in the 1990s (see CULTURAL STUDIES: 1. UNITED KINGDOM).

By the end of the 1980s, the critical and theoretical concerns about the nature of African American literary discourse remained for the most part unresolved. Even if it was clear that postmodernism and academic feminism had value for a consideration of African American literature, the nature and the extent of that value were not clear. Equally unclear was the relation between the ideology of the academy and the scholarly consideration of African American discursive practice. Assuredly clear, however, was that African American literary criticism and theory promised considerable intellectual richness, in addition to fruitful controversy, with implications for the general study of literature as well.

THEODORE O. MASON JR.

Molefi Kete Asante, *The Afrocentric Idea* (1987); Houston A. Baker Jr. "Belief, Theory, and Blues: Notes for a Post-Structuralist Criticism of Afro-American Literature," *Belief vs. Theory in Black American Literary Criticism* (ed. Joe Weixlmann and Chester J. Fontenot, 1986), *Blues, Ideology, and Afro-American Literature: A Vernacular Theory* (1984), "In Dubious Battle," *New Literary History* 18 (1987), *The*

Journey Back: Issues in Black Literature and Criticism (1980), Long Black Song: Essays in Black American Literature and Culture (1972), Singers of Daybreak: Studies in Black American Literature (1974); Houston A. Baker Jr. and Patricia Redmond, eds., Afro-American Literary Study in the 1990s (1989); Joseph Beam, ed., In the Life: A Black Gay Anthology (1986); Joanne M. Braxton and Andrée Nicola McLaughlin, eds., Wild Women in the Whirlwind: Afra-American Culture and the Contemporary Literary Renaissance (1990); Hazel Carby, Reconstructing Womanhood: The Emergence of the Afro-American Woman Novelist (1987); Deborah G. Chay, "Rereading Barbara Smith: Black Feminist Criticism and the Category of Experience," New Literary History 24 (1993); Barbara Christian, Black Feminist Criticism (1985), "The Race for Theory," Cultural Critique 6 (1987); Michael Cooke, Afro-American Literature in the Twentieth Century: The Achievement of Intimacy (1984); Ralph Ellison, "Brave Words for a Startling Occasion," Shadow and Act (1964); Mari Evans, ed., Black Women Writers (1950–1980): A Critical Evaluation (1984); Dexter Fisher and Robert Stepto, eds., Afro-American Literature: The Reconstruction of Instruction (1979); Henry Louis Gates Jr., "Authority, (White) Power and the (Black) Critic; It's All Greek to Me," Cultural Critique 7 (1987), Black Literature and Literary Theory (1984), The Signifying Monkey: A Theory of Afro-American Literary Criticism (1988), " 'What's Love Got to Do With It?': Critical Theory, Integrity, and the Black Idiom," New Literary History 18 (1987); bell hooks, Yearning: Race, Gender, and Cultural Politics (1990); Gloria Hull, Color, Sex, and Poetry: Three Women Writers of the Harlem Renaissance (1987); Zora Neale Hurston, I Love Myself When I Am Laughing . . . And Then Again When I Am Looking Mean and Impressive: A Zora Neale Hurston Reader (ed. Alice Walker, 1979); Joyce A. Joyce, "The Black Canon: Reconstructing Black American Literary Criticism," New Literary History 18 (1987), " 'Who the Cap Fit': Unconsciousness and Unconscionableness in the Criticism of Houston A. Baker and Henry Louis Gates Jr.," New Literary History 18 (1987); Deborah McDowell, "New Directions for Black Feminist Criticism," The New Feminist Criticism: Essays on Women, Literature, and Theory (ed. Elaine Showalter, 1985); Theodore O. Mason Jr., "Between the Populist and the Scientist: Ideology and Power in Recent Afro-American Literary Criticism; or, 'The Dozens' as Scholarship," Callaloo 11 (1988); R. Baxter Miller, "Baptized Infidel: Play and Critical Legacy," Black American Literature Forum 21 (1987); R. Baxter Miller, ed., Black American Literature and Humanism (1981); Toni Morrison, "Unspeakable Things Unspoken: The Afro-American Presence in American Literature," Michigan Quarterly Review 28 (1989); Winston Napier, ed., African American Literary Theory: A Reader (2000); Barbara Smith, "Reply to Deborah Chay," New Literary History 24 (1993), "Toward a Black Feminist Criticism" (Showalter); Valerie Smith, Self-Discovery and Authority in Afro-American Narrative (1987); Hortense Spillers, "The Permanent Obliquity of an In(pha)llibly Straight: In the Time of the Daughters and the Fathers" (Wall); Robert Stepto, From Behind the Veil: A Study of Afro-American Narrative (1979); Claudia Tate, "Allegories of Black Female Desire; or, Rereading Nineteenth-Century Sentimental Narratives of Black Female Authority" (Wall); Alice Walker, In Search of Our Mothers' Gardens: Womanist Prose (1983); Cheryl Wall, ed., Changing Our Own Words: Essays on Criticism, Theory, and Writing by Black Women (1989); Susan Willis, Specifying: Black Women Writing the American Experience (1987).

3. The 1990s

Following the lead of Dexter Fisher's and Robert Stepto's The Reconstruction of Instruction, African American literary criticism of the 1980s began to define itself through patently theoretical principles emphasizing the discursive complexities of African American literary production. Extending this critical platform, African American criticism of the 1990s took the theoretical initiative in several directions, bearing witness to the expanding influence of CULTURAL STUDIES, feminism, psychoanalysis, and QUEER THEORY AND CRITICISM. Additionally, the long-standing tensions between the sociological and discursive extremes of African American criticism increasingly came to be seen as an enabling point of critical practice rather than a disabling zero-sum paradigm.

During this time, critics began to interpret African American literary production as one index of the spectrum of responses and accommodations to the hostile disposition of African-derived populations in the modern West perpetuated in the histories of enslavement, segregation, and other routines of racialization. The prevailing effort was to clarify the imbrications of the sociological and discursive aspects of African American literatures and cultures so as to yield critical orientations that questioned the limits of literary textuality.

Cultural studies played an important role in this reformulation. Relying fundamentally on critical templates established by Michel Foucault and Raymond Williams, cultural studies queries symbolic transactions as never merely or finally textual. It questions the practices and assumptions of civic, legal, and social power, taking up literary texts insofar as they make available the social and psychic schemes of the cultures they record. The intellectual movement known as critical race theory, which investigates the complicity of U.S. law, jurisprudence and its legal archive in the definition and maintenance of the inequalities defined by race, gender, class, and sexual orientation, underscored the broad disciplinary range of this version of cultural studies. The legal scholar Kimberlé Crenshaw, for example, in "Mapping the Margins: Intersectionality, Identity Politics, and Violence Against Women of Color" (1991) articulates the erasure of African American women from the separate legal rubrics of "woman" and "African American." In another influential legal essay, "Whiteness as Property" (1993), Cheryl Harris defines the cultural location of African American communities as "where white supremacy and economic domination meet," and, conversely, the cultural location of white racial dominance as where social and economic supremacy are conflated and finalized as property; so that the "fact" of racial whiteness (to use her term), an ambiguous phenotypical ideal, amounts to the reification of the expectation of privilege.

Two influential examples of literary orientations developed along the terms of cultural studies are the critical writings of Toni Morrison and the Oxford University Press series Race and American Culture. In *Playing in the Dark* (1992), Morrison argues that canonical American literature presents itself as virtually uninfluenced by the four-hundred year physical and figurative Africanist presence in the United States and demonstrates the existence of that gap through an analysis of cultural absence. In *Race-ing Justice, En-gendering Power* (1992), Morrison relies on the full interdisciplinary range of cultural studies, bringing together historians, literary critics, legal scholars, and political scientists, to analyze the national spectacle of the U.S. Supreme Court confirmation hearings of Clarence Thomas, a spectacle fully invested in the mythical predilections of African American bodies. In *Birth of a Nation'hood* (1997), Toni Morrison and coeditor Claudia Brodsky Lacour consider the exponentially greater national and interracial spectacle of the murder trial and acquittal of O. J. Simpson. A comparison of the various public representations of O. J. Simpson to that of Melville's "Benito Cereno" is particularly telling. The critical orientation underpinning the juxtaposition of the canonical literary text, the mass media of late capital, and attention to representational structures proposes the diffuse meaningfulness of race in the United States—psychic, narrative, historical.

The series "Race and American Culture" similarly imbricates literature with the broader culture. In *Scenes of Subjection: Terror, Slavery, and Self-Making in Nineteenth-Century America* (1997), Saidiya Hartman considers the epistemological underpinnings and consequences of nineteenth-century representations of African Americans. Examining textual representations of African Americans by agents of the dominant culture as well as by African Americans themselves, Hartman explores racial power as well as the limits of the legal and narrative representability of African American "humanity" within epistemological and rhetorical schemes discounting that possibility. In order to expose race in the fabric of nineteenth-century forms of knowledge and perception, Hartman draws on a wide range of disciplinary discourses in addition to literary analysis.

In *"Who set you flowin'?" The African American Migration Narrative* (1995), Farah Jasmine Griffin examines the narrative construction of "safe spaces" in the literary record of the African American migration to urban landscapes, undertaking analyses drawn across musical, novelistic, and photographic texts. In *Race, Rape, and Lynching: The Red Record of American Literature 1890–1912* (1996), Sandra Gunning proposes the intersection of race, political agency, and the discourses of heterosexual masculinity as the interpretative ground for reading texts by Charles Chesnutt, Thomas Dixon Jr., Mark Twain, Ida B. Wells, and others.

Broadly speaking, the change in emphasis enacted in the 1990s was from structuralist and poststructuralist interrogations of linguistic events and paradigms to an emphasis on the dynamics of racialization and symbolization evident across more widely conceived textual and extratextual points of analysis. The considerations of ex-slave narratives exemplify this shift. Samira Kawash, in *Dislocating the Color Line: Identity, Hybridity, and Singularity in African American Narrative* (1997), reconsiders the developing body of criticism on slave narratives, particularly the governing assumptions concerning the representation of racial subjectivity. This analysis supplements a line of investigation that highlights the construction of liberal subjectivity in the narrative without interrogating the ways "in which the relations of mastery and possession that define the relation between master and slave also define the relation of the sovereign subject to itself" (35). Kawash's discussion proposes that the conditions of enslavement and liberal subjectivity invert but nonetheless hold in place the set of relations that co-implicate property and personhood. Kawash delineates racial subjectivity beyond the opposed terms of enslavement and freedom by considering in several slave narratives the dynamics of fugitivity and self-purchase—concepts that confound the property-holding basis of the liberal subject. Insofar as earlier lines of investigation query literacy, the paramount technology of the liberal subject, as the point of denial or acquisition crucial to African American self-representation, the earlier body of criticism understands the issues of representation as more closely linguistic and more closely textual.

The broader disciplinary imperatives of the study of African American literature in the 1990s investigated the questions of representation, narrative authority, and the inherent complexities of discourse. One important feature was the turn to psychoanalytical paradigms and the examination of the uncertain congruity of psychoanalysis with African American cultural organization (see PSYCHOANALYTIC THEORY AND CRITICISM). In "'All the Things You Could Be by Now If Sigmund Freud's Wife Was Your Mother': Race and Psychoanalysis" (1996), Hortense Spillers stages a confrontation between race and psychoanalysis. Defining psychoanalysis in terms of its interests in locating "interior intersubjectivity," Spillers details its diacritical relation to race by arguing that the primary template for psychoanalysis is a sexuality that is intrinsically linked to concealment, whereas the primary symbolics of race and racialization rest on visibility. This diacriticism persists further, Spillers argues, since race is conceptualized as a collective enterprise, whereas psychoanalysis focuses on the individual.

Claudia Tate, in *Psychoanalysis and Black Novels* (1998), posits a more integrated relation for psychoanalysis and African American expressivity. In readings of five novels—Emma Kelley's *Megda*, W. E. B. Du Bois's *Dark Princess*, Richard Wright's *Savage Holiday*, Nella Larsen's *Quicksand*, and Zora Neale Hurston's *Seraph on the Suwannee*—Tate taps "the critical potential of psychoanalysis to demonstrate how a black text negotiates the tension between the public, collective protocols of race and private, individual desire, thereby forming an enigmatic surplus" (11). Tate draws on Freudian, Lacanian, and object-relations theories to facilitate her "analysis of unconscious textual desire" (13) while equally recognizing the conceptual oppositions of psychoanalysis and race: "Instead of regarding individuals and their stories as products of a dialectic of material circumstances and their internalization of them, psychoanalysis, as it generally operates, centers the individual's primary nurturing environment, not the external circumstances that precondition that environment" (16). In other words, by the methodological curiosity of attenuating the question of race in the choice of literary material, the study pursues the rapprochement, rather than confrontation, between psychoanalysis and race.

If the turn to explicit paradigms of political or psychic agency provided new dimensions to African American literary study, the leading role of African American literary feminism in redefining the field marked a point of continuity with the criticism of the previous decade. For example, Frances Smith Foster's *Written by Herself: Literary Production by African American Women, 1746–1892* (1993) outlines a distinctive African American women's literary tradition, while Ann duCille's *The Coupling Convention* (1993) examines the distinctive use of the marriage plot employed by the women writers of the Harlem Renaissance. Similarly, Cheryl Wall in *Women of the Harlem Renaissance* (1995) provides biographical, historical, and textual analyses of leading women figures of the same period, particularly Jessie Fauset, Nella Larsen, and Zora Neale Hurston. In short, much of the focus of African American literary feminism turned to detailing the tradition and contexts of the literature, to, as Mary Helen Washington puts it, "record[ing] the thoughts, words, feelings, and deeds of black women" (35). In this way, critics came to focus more directly on the literary discourses themselves and less on enabling claims for the (in)visibility of some social identities, the incongruities of race and gender, or the other conceptual reorientations described by the study of African American women's literature.

Still, Deborah G. Chay carefully reviewed some of the metacritical aspects of African American literary feminism in "Rereading Barbara Smith: Black Feminist Criticism and the Category of Experience" (1993). This essay queries the indeterminacies of the appeals to "experience" as a fundamental literary focus—the indeterminate relation between what experiences the text makes available and what experiences make the text available—in order to demonstrate some ironies of "the use of experience to ground claims about difference and to establish cultural legitimacy" (648), and offers more historicist definitions of "experience."

The emergence of the study of black masculinities responded to and extended the attention given to gender by African American literary feminism. In *Representing Black Men* (1996), Marcellous Blount and George P. Cunningham collect the work of cultural analysts of film, literature, and racial discourse in order to outline "the complexity and diversity of African American men's agency in the production of ideology and culture" (xi). Highlighting some of the unexplored intersections of gender studies, studies of sexuality, and race, Dwight McBride in "Can the Queen Speak?" (1998) questions the implied libidinal normativity of the most established African American appeals to race. The elaboration of the fields of black masculinity studies and African American queer theory pursue the constitutive role of sexuality in the scripting and execution of racial protocols, representations, and logic.

More particularly, beyond pointing to the enforced absence of diverse sexual communities in the comprehension of U.S. racialization, African American queer theory uncovered the ideological impress. In *Blues Legacies and Black Feminism* (1998), for example, Angela Davis posits the emancipation of African Americans and the subsequent development of African American civic culture as a single historical and sexual episode. Emancipation, Davis argues, led to cultural transformations in three primary respects: travel, education, and ostensible sexual freedom. By considering the ways in which domesticity and public life are consolidated by industrial capitalism and by examining the ideological constraints of marriage, Davis reiterates the sexual rebellions of Gertrude "Ma" Rainey, Bessie Smith, and Billie Holiday in their constructions of personal and public identities. Similarly, Phillip Brian Harper, in "Private Affair: Race, Sex, Property, and Persons" (1994), examines how the possible similarities of heterosexual and gay public practices "metaphorically represent the possible encroachment of 'foreign' interests on the conventional domestic economy" (128). These analyses foreground sexual practices in order to clarify further the complexities of African American identities, expressivities, and relations to civic agency.

The metacritical gestures of African American literary criticism in the 1990s were more settled than the similar gestures of the 1980s, pursuing a historicist rather than polemical orientation. Sandra Adell, in *Double Consciousness/Double Bind* (1994), examines "the extent to which twentieth-century black literature and criticism are implicated in the ensemble of Western literature and philosophy" (3) by considering African American critical thought, ranging from W. E. B. Du Bois to 1980s poststructuralist theorizing. Ronald Judy, in *(Dis)Forming the American Canon* (1993), examines the slave narrative and, more generally, the "African American canon . . . [as] desediment[ing] the logic of cultural literacy . . . in the intellectual trajectory that runs from the eighteenth century . . . to the poststructuralist theorizing of the influential Yale School" (42). And, in the introduction to the collection *Borders, Boundaries, and Frames: Cultural Criticism and Cultural Studies* (1995), Mae Henderson identifies the preeminent critical transformation of African American literary studies in the 1990s, developments "redefining the boundaries traditionally delineating disciplinarities . . . constructing a broader framework in which to pursue alternate modes of inquiry" (23).

LINDON BARRETT

Marcellous Blount and George P. Cunningham, eds., *Representing Black Men* (1996); Devon Carbado, *Black Men on Race, Gender, and Sexuality: A Critical Reader* (1999); Deborah G. Chay, "Rereading Barbara Smith: Black Feminist Criticism and the Category of Experience," *New Literary History* 24 (1993); Kimberlé Crenshaw, Neil Gotanda, Gary Peller, and Kendall Thomas, eds., *Critical Race Theory: The Critical Writings that Formed the Movement* (1995); Angela Davis, *Blues Legacies and Black Feminism* (1998); Madhu Dubey, *Black Women Novelists and the Nationalist Aesthetic* (1994); Shelley Fisher Fishkin and Arnold Rampersad, foreword, Thomas F. Gossett, *Race: The History of an Idea in America* (1997); Frances Smith Foster, *Written by Herself: Literary Productions by African American Women, 1746–1892* (1993); Henry Louis Gates Jr., ed., *Reading Black, Reading Feminist: A Critical Anthology* (1990), Farah Jasmine Griffin, "Who Set You Flowin'?: The African American Migration Narrative* (1995); John Cullen Gruesser, ed., *The Unruly Voice: Rediscovering Pauline Elizabeth Hopkins* (1996); Sandra Gunning, *Race, Rape, and Lynching: The Red Record of American Literature, 1890–1912* (1996); Phillip Brian Harper, "Private Affair: Race, Sex, Property, and Person," *GLQ* 1 (1994); Saidiya Hartman, *Scenes of Subjection: Terror, Slavery and Self-Making in Nineteenth-Century America* (1997); Mae Henderson, ed., *Borders, Boundaries, and Frames: Cultural Criticism and Cultural Studies* (1995); Ronald Judy, *(Dis)Forming the American Canon: African-Arabic Slave Narratives and the Vernacular* (1993); Samira Kawash, *Dislocating the Color Line: Identity, Hybridity, and Singularity in African American Narrative* (1997); Alycee J. Lane, foreword, *Loving Her* (1997); Dwight McBride, "Can the Queen Speak?" *Callaloo* 21 (1998); Toni Morrison, *Playing in the Dark: Whiteness and the Literary Imagination* (1992); Toni Morrison, ed., *Race-ing Justice, En-gendering Power: Essays on Anita Hill, Clarence Thomas, and the Construction of Social Reality* (1992); Toni Morrison and Claudia Brodsky Lacour, eds., *Birth of a Nation'hood: Gaze, Script, and Spectacle in the O. J. Simpson Case* (1997); Hortense Spillers, "All the Things You Could Be by Now, If Sigmund Freud's Wife Was Your Mother: Psychoanalysis and Race," *Critical Inquiry* 22 (1996); Claudia Tate, *Psychoanalysis and Black Novels: Desire and the Protocols of Race* (1998); Mary Helen Washington, "The Darkened Eye Restored: Notes Toward a Literary History of Black Women" (Gates).

Agamben, Giorgio

The author of a number of books and articles on aesthetics, poetics, philology, the philosophy of language, and the relation between literature and philosophy, Giorgio Agamben (b. 1942) is one of the most insightful commentators on the aesthetic theories of MARTIN HEIDEGGER and WALTER BENJAMIN. He is a gifted writer with broad interests, nuanced ideas, and vast erudition. These elements help explain why literary critics have dedicated such attention to Agamben, particularly given that it is from his work in political philosophy that he is best known. The works that brought Agamben fame as a political thinker—and, eventually, as an aesthetic one—form a series named for the book which began it, *Homo Sacer*, in which Agamben advances a number of controversial theses, chief among that "the concentration camp is the biopolitical paradigm of the modern age" (181).

Agamben grew up and studied in Rome where, in the mid-1960s, he became close to a number of prominent artists such as Elsa Morante and Pier Paolo Pasolini. While intensely drawn to the arts and even publishing some of his own verse, Agamben elected to study law at university. This course was radically altered following an encounter in the summer of 1966. While visiting a friend in the south of France, he was invited to one of the most singular philosophical seminars of the century—one made possible by René Char and conducted by Heidegger. For Agamben, the experience proved decisive. He described the seminars as a "constellation": a coming together of elements resulting in something truly unexpected. As he would later remark, it was at this point that, for him, "philosophy became possible" (Marongiu ii).

During the same years when he came to know the person and works of Heidegger, he first read Benjamin. Heidegger and Benjamin would exert the most profound influence on Agamben's work, from his first essays on art in the 1960s to those that appeared forty years later. Given this intellectual trajectory it should come then as little surprise that Agamben's first work treats the relation between art and the discipline that studies it: aesthetics. *The Man without Content* (1970) is an investigation of both the conceptual and the historical underpinnings of aesthetics. By "aesthetics" Agamben means the formalized discipline arising in the eighteenth century and centered on what Immanuel Kant famously called "disinterested judgment." Setting a pattern for many later works, *The Man without Content* couples a Foucauldian historical genealogy with an ontological reflection reminiscent of Heidegger's analyses.

While *The Man without Content* is an inquiry into the nature and function of art, it is not a neutral inquiry. The book does not engage in aesthetic inquiry for the sake of aesthetic inquiry and is not written from the distanced perspective of a historian of ideas. It is instead a response to what Agamben sees as an alarming state of contemporary affairs. For Agamben, the nature and function of art in our culture has been obscured. Art has come to resemble, in his words, "a planet which turns towards us only its dark side" (43). With the enlightening role that art had played for earlier eras waning, Agamben tries to understand *how* and *why* art's illuminating face has turned away from us and what we might do to bring about its return. *The Man without Content* retells the history of Western art from the Greeks to the present, attempting to revive art's original stature and structure, trace the progressive obscuration of the original space that art offered, and restore art to its former status as a true shaper of actions and beliefs. For Agamben, a watershed moment in this history is recorded by G. W. F. Hegel who, writing in 1829, stated that, "art no longer provides for the satisfaction of those spiritual and intellectual needs that earlier peoples and times found in art and in art alone." This conviction led Hegel to the extreme conclusion that "in all of these [cultural and spiritual] relations, art, in its highest vocation, is for us a thing of the past" (13:24–25). In Agamben's view, it was precisely the rise of "taste" and the discipline of aesthetics that effected this change: it froze art in its time, made it a thing of the past with no living, shaping, or original relation to the present. Taking a page from Heidegger's typography, Agamben writes, "if we wanted to express this characteristic with a formula, we could write that critical judgment thinks art as ~~art~~" (42).

Agamben's next book *Stanzas* (1977) is equally concerned with art and its alienations. *Stanzas* is a collection of four long essays treating four separate topics: melancholy, fetishism, images, and semiology. While in each essay a single topic guides Agamben's investigations, all the other topics are present and play a role. The problem that lies at the heart of *Stanzas* is what Plato referred to as an "ancient enmity" opposing "philosophy and poetry" (*Republic* 607b–c). Already entrenched enough by Plato's time to be described as "ancient," this enmity has shaped the relationship between truth and beauty, thought and language, and criticism and creation up to the present day. In *Stanzas*, Agamben also rejects the claims made by many as "to the 'creative' character of [contemporary] criticism," which he rather sees as "a form of negativity" (xv–xvi).

The critical element of so many works of art, exemplified in the ironic display of Marcel Duchamp's "readymades" and the indifferent surfaces of Andy Warhol's pop art, is something that interested Agamben during these years. The alleged creative character of criticism was, according to Agamben, not the result of criticism becoming more creative, but, on the contrary, *of artistic creation becoming more critical*. As Agamben writes, because "art itself has renounced nearly all pretense to creativity" (*Stanzas* xvi), criticism has no difficulty in identifying with it. The creative criticism that Agamben is asking his reader to envision is thus not one that would be deemed creative by the false standards of the day but one that would have its forgotten creative rights restored and that would be liberated from the negative critical function Agamben argues it had increasingly been inclined to adopt. Eight years later Agamben's *Idea of Prose* (1985) attempts to fulfill this promise in its fusion of creative and critical elements.

Agamben's works after *Stanzas* are less directly focused on literary questions. Nevertheless, literary figures continue to play a prominent role in them—beginning with *Infancy and History* (1978), which appeals to a host of creative writers from Michel de Montaigne to Franz Kafka. Continuing in this vein, *Language and Death* (1982), a study of negativity and negation in philosophical thought, conducts its inquiry through ample consideration of poets and poetics, from the troubadours to Giacomo Leopardi and beyond. The omnipresence of literary figures and questions in Agamben's writing is also seen in *Potentialities* (2005) where readers find abundant references to a wide range of literary figures from Guido Cavalcanti to E. E. Cummings. The essays gathered together in *The End of the Poem* (1995) treat a host of poetic topics, from the familiar, such as Dante's choice of the title *Commedia*, to the more arcane, such as the scabrous Provençal word "corn." Figures from the distant past such as the biblical Nimrod are treated alongside twentieth-century poets such as Paul Celan and Giorgio Caproni. While this volume (as elsewhere) treats Italian writers with a certain pride, writers from other literary traditions also figure prominently. German literary figures such as Johann Wolfgang von Goethe and Ingeborg Bachmann and French writers from Arnault Daniel to Charles Baudelaire to Victor Segalen are frequently cited as are anglophone writers such as Charles Dickens, John Keats, and Herman Melville, if to a lesser extent.

Agamben's abundant references to literary figures are not casual allusions and are not merely presented to adorn arguments. On the contrary, many of Agamben's most fundamental political and philosophical ideas are expressed through literary figures, from Arthur Rimbaud and Keats, whom he draws on in his consideration of language and subjectivity, to Kafka and Robert Walser, whom he appeals to in his discussions of theology. Agamben even describes his most fundamental methodological principles through literary figures, such as the idea of dynamic reversibility, which he articulates through Friedrich Hölderlin's "Patmos" and of the paradigm, which he explains through Wallace Stevens's "Description Without Place." While the five volumes in the *Homo Sacer* series (1995–2008) mark a definite shift in Agamben's thought from aesthetic to political questions, his interest in literature and his use of literary figures continues undiminished, as does his conviction that literary questions can never be fully separated from philosophical ones.

LELAND DE LA DURANTAYE

Giorgio Agamben, *L'aperto: L'uomo e l'animale* (2002, *The Open: Man and Animal*, trans. Kevin Attell, 2004), *Categorie italiane: Studi di poetica* (1996, *The End of the Poem: Studies in Poetics*, trans. Daniel Heller-Roazen, 1999), *Che cos'è il dispositivo?* (2006, *What is an Apparatus*, trans. David Kishik and Stefan Pedatella 2009), *La comunità che viene* (1990, *The Coming Community*, trans. Michael Hardt, 1993), *Homo Sacer: Il potere sovrano e la nuda vita* (1995, *Homo Sacer: Sovereign Power and Bare Life*, trans. Daniel Heller-Roazen, 1998), *Idea della prosa* (1985, *Idea of Prose*, trans. Michael Sullivan and Sam Whitsitt, 1995), *Infanzia e storia: Distruzione dell'esperienza e origine della storia* (1978, *Infancy and History: The Destruction of Experience*, trans. Liz Heron, 1993), *Il linguaggio e la morte: Un seminario sul luogo della negatività* (1982, *Language and Death: The Place of Negativity*, trans. Karen E. Pinkus with Michael Hardt, 1991), *Mezzi senza fine: Note sulla politica* (1996, *Means without End: Notes on Politics*, trans. Vincenzo Binetti and Cesare Casarino, 2000), *La potenza del pensiero: Saggi e conferenze* (2005, *Potentialities:*

Collected Essays in Philosophy, ed. and trans. Daniel Heller-Roazen, 1999), *Profanazioni* (2005, *Profanations*, trans. Jeff Fort, 2007), *Quel che resta di Auschwitz: L'archivio e il testimone* (1998, *Remnants of Auschwitz: The Witness and the Archive*, trans. Daniel Heller-Roazen, 2002), *Il regno e la gloria: Per una genealogica teologica dell'economia e del governo* (2007), *Signatura rerum: Sul metodo* (2008), *Stanze: La parola e il fantasma nella cultura occidentale* (1977, *Stanzas: Word and Phantasm in Western Culture*, trans. Ronald L. Martinez, 1992), *Stato di eccezione* (2003, *State of Exception*, trans. Kevin Attell, 2005), *Il tempo che resta: Un commento alla "Lettera ai Romani"* (2000, *The Time That Remains: A Commentary on The Letter to the Romans*, trans. Patricia Dailey, 2005), *L'uomo senza contenuto* (1970, *The Man without Content*, trans. Georgia Albert, 1999); G. W. F. Hegel, *Werke* (1970).

Badiou, Alain

In a French milieu already mistaken abroad for senseless rebellion and obscurity, Alain Badiou (b. 1937) is arguably the most counterintuitive and controversial thinker of his generation. Not only does Badiou eschew every spontaneous morality—declaring again, against any nascent spiritualism, the permanent death of God, refusing the equation of politics with tolerance, "consensus," or efficient "administration," and denying outright any natural preciousness of the individual—he challenges simultaneously, and with a rigor perhaps not seen in France since Jean-Paul Sartre or Gilles Deleuze, all of the dominant strains of contemporary thought at once, including CULTURAL STUDIES, neo-Kantian liberalism, analytic philosophy, German hermeneutics, and DECONSTRUCTION (*Metapolitics* 18, 73; see GILLES DELEUZE AND FÉLIX GUATTARI). For many, Badiou remains genuinely unintelligible, not because his writings are especially ludic or inscrutable—on the contrary, they are almost classically rationalist in style—but because his positions are so foreign to the conceptual habits and tastes of postmodernity. Badiou argues directly for a return to the category of truth, albeit one wholly devoid of reference, necessity, objectivity, or foundation. Though not primarily a literary theorist (and opposed on principle to every "philosophy of literature"), Badiou has shown a great deal of interest in poetry (particularly Stéphane Mallarmé and Fernando Pessoa), the prose of Samuel Beckett and Marcel Proust, and in the work of art more generally conceived. Literature, for Badiou, is (or can be) a mode of truth, a formulation (despite first appearances) unlikely to bolster the traditional humanist equation of literature with enlightened spiritual essence or moral *Bildung*.

Truth, for Badiou, is transcendental, not in the sense implied by religious revelation, nor by way of a Kantian (or even structuralist) subjective infrastructure, but in its powers of rupture. Badiou emphatically distinguishes truth from the rule of thumb or apothegm; it shares nothing in common with pragmatic customary wisdom. Instead, truth is the prerogative of a radical subjective break with the normative parameters of the world as it is. Though every situation (and all being is comprised of situations) presents itself as comprised of internally consistent elements and relations—the atoms that explain the material composition of physical objects, the individuals that condition our notions of civil society—the ensemble of things taken to exist in any given context relies entirely on the discriminating social efficacy of the criteria used to distinguish what is from what is not. Badiou insists that what is (in the most general sense) is nothing but multiples of multiples—pure, disseminating, inconsistent multiplicity, a wholly secularized concept of infinity—which, he argues, is best articulated by the discipline of mathematics. Periodically, at intervals that cannot be predicted or induced, something happens to disturb the ordered quantities and relations that structure a status quo; this event, testified to by a subject that draws from it a passionate conviction without certainty or comfort, functions as the birthplace of a truth: mysterious and perplexing, it can be affirmed as having happened only on the basis of a decision and by an investigative intensity undertaken in direct contravention of existing knowledges and distinctions. Truth, in this sense, is always an affirmation, always an active, polemical, self-founding (and selfless) phenomenon that is at once powered by and enslaves a subject. The subject only comes to exist in the aftermath of a truth; in what is surely one of the most controversial aspects of his philosophy, Badiou suggests that though every human has the capacity for thoughtful subjectivation, most people will spend their lives mostly circulated by the domain of routinized common sense. The task of philosophy is not a strictly generative one, says Badiou, but rather a procedure through which truths are curated or procured. These rare, exceptional occurrences of thought—the work of an Alfred Einstein, SIGMUND FREUD, or Virginia Woolf—occur in one of four domains of human being: politics, art, science, and love. Because "procedures" of truth (Badiou uses this word to emphasize the sequential, workerly nature of their composition and to fully delink it from reflexive or idealist subjectivity) often refuse to articulate themselves as such—think of the notorious inability of artists to speak about why they do something—philosophy works to isolate and arrange all that is "eternal" in the thought of an age—all of the ideas that existed on the side of the formless or inarticulable for previous generations.

Within this general metaontology of truth, Badiou argues that our ways of thinking about art have been characterized by three dominant modes (Handbook of Inaesthetics 5). Didacticism, born with Plato's proscription of poetry, sees in art a semblance of the true; such a didacticism substitutes a facile immediacy for the rigor and duration of the dialectic. Art, in this context, is to be governed by a good—be it Man, Reason, Society, Truth, and so forth—it lacks and fatally enervates. This first mode indexes the fundamental blindness of socialist realisms but also, says Badiou, the civic-minded cultural policies of liberal democracies still limited by a paradigm of "cultivation." Romanticism, linked by Badiou to the post-Hegelian denigration of mathematics, instead sees in art not mere semblance but truth itself. Perception and expression, the tortured finitude of the embodied self, are here installed to replace the arid theoreticism of concepts: art, in an inversion of the didactic schema, comes to exhaust the domain of the true, its closeness to sensation and the world an enigmatic key to the very heart of being. Classicism, meanwhile, found in Aristotle, René Descartes, and also, argues Badiou, in Lacanian psychoanalysis (see JACQUES LACAN), designates a kind of peace between art and thought: the former does not perturb the latter and is instead reconfigured as therapy or catharsis, a playground of the emotions without consequence for truth. What these three approaches share is an inability to pronounce together both the immanence and singularity of aesthetic invention. It is with this limit in mind that Badiou introduces a fourth option: a genuine aesthetic procedure is *a* (rather than *the*) truth. It is not the whole of truth (an oxymoron for Badiou), just as it is nothing like a relativist affirmation of eclecticism or artistic whim: rather, like all truth, artistic labor is a courageous, self-founding attempt to formalize the formless, a way of taking seriously the rigorous consequences of an encounter with the impossible or hitherto never experienced. Aesthetic process is not anarchic expressivity but a thinking that attempts to solve problems of form that cannot be solved within the existing aesthetic codes. Though art is henceforth inaccessible to any overarching social project, delinked, as it were, from the prerogatives of the good, this principle runs backward as well, freeing the specificity of the political (but also philosophy itself) from an aesthetic thinking that sometimes attempts to denigrate the political as "reductive" or utilitarian.

According to Badiou, true poetry withdraws language from the inherited protocols of reference and function. The everyday linguistic felicity of the human—engaged cleverly in countless acts of communication as well as complex orienting processes and exchanges—remains, for Badiou, of a kind with the skillful hums of bees; however resourceful or "meaningful" these actions may be, they are in the last instance little more than extensions of the logic of the signal and in this sense largely articulable within the structure of existing knowledges. Badiou is thus at odds with an entire cohort of postmodern and neopragmatist philosophies of language interested in eliminating precisely the distinction between *poesis* and speech, invention and the mundane. Furthermore, Badiou refuses the notion that it is the objective of the poem to sensually reflect a reality thought to predate the poetic utterance. Though the poem attests to a certain bare sensorial consistency, it does so away from any organized distribution of the relation between subject and object as well as every integrating legality of society or nature. True poetry is "subtractive" rather than unambiguously negative; instead of simply abolishing form (a move that risks succumbing to the self-consuming dialectic of modernist novelty), the thinking poem meticulously withdraws objects from the jurisdiction of relation and identity, breaking free on the basis of binding criteria for action generated by the poetic subject itself (though these criteria are in no way reducible to the poetic subject's self-consciousness) (*The Century* 54–57). This formulation immediately places the poetic operation into a parallelism with the role played by mathematics in Badiou's ontology (*Handbook of Inaesthetics* 22). Whereas mathematics presents that which defies all presentation, indicating via its minimal notation the bare multiplicity of being qua being, the poem operates within the domain of that which appears—the locus of sensations—safeguarding the openness of thought in the same way set theory does for being itself.

The appearing presence attested to by the poem is not part of a totality nor is it an extension populated by empiricist objects. Rather, it is the momentary result of a poet's subjectivating encounter with the multiplicity and force of language, an "operation" justified entirely on the basis of its own axiomatic power (29). Interestingly, like all truth, the poem is paradoxically eternal not just by virtue of the subjective intensity with which it claims the writing poet but also in its seemingly infinite accessibility to readings grouped unpredictably across time and space. For some critics, this places Badiou squarely within the tradition of canonical Great Books humanism; if there is some resonance in this claim, however, it is largely offset by Badiou's suggestion that true poetry never edifies, soothes, or socializes but instead unfolds at an angle radically indifferent (even hostile to) the human. The poem is not addressed to those deemed proficient in the art of reading, nor to some imagined average that is thought to designate the popular. It is neither the historically dominant taste of the many nor the refined delectation of the few that commands the poetic utterance; rather, it is to everyone, everybody, "the Crowd," that the poem's sparse and fragmented universality is addressed (31). In a suggestion that echoes Descartes's insistence on the radically shared capacity of the human to think, the poetic utterance is here deemed universal insofar as the most and least one can say about the human is that it has the abstract potential for thought. The Crowd, then, confounded together by the enigma of the poem, convokes a universality that is also always an egalitarianism. Clearly, Badiou's work here departs unreservedly from the historical materialist underpinnings of most contemporary criticism; feminist and critical race theorists have found in him a nuanced variation on a masculinist modernism they have seen before, while Marxist sociologists of literature are sure to see his indifference to "field" analysis as well as his insistence on the equalizing power of literary confusion disturbingly aspecific (if not openly idealist). Badiou, however, would rejoin that he is really the only theorist of his generation to remain faithful to a properly atheist materialism: his proscription of structure in this context simply ensures that nothing intercedes between the human subject and a genuinely secularized infinity.

Badiou's tendency to read literature through the lens of his system will certainly frustrate critics invested in a notion of constitutive textual polyvalence or "open," "ethical" forms of reading. Badiou's theory of the poem, however, does not in any way attempt to ground a program of literary analysis. This is in part because interpretation as a practice already presumes the consistency of its object, taking for granted the social intelligibility of the relation between a text and its reader. It is also because Badiou's is a philosophy of affirmation, of precarious action and exigency, one explicitly hostile to the mood and temporality of hermeneutics. The poem is a happening, a work of subjectivation linked to an undecidable or obscure event that ultimately can be understood only from within its own process: what it "means" is less important than what it does for the subject it is composed by—and that it (de)composes.

ANDREW PENDAKIS

See also FRENCH THEORY AND CRITICISM: 1945 AND AFTER
and MARXIST THEORY AND CRITICISM 3: 1989 AND AFTER.

Alain Badiou, *Abrégé de métapolitique* (1998, Metapolitics, trans. Jason Barker, 2005), *Beckett: L'incrévable désir* (1995, On Beckett, ed. and trans. Nina Power and Alberto Toscano and Bruno Bosteels, 2003), *L'ethique: Essai sur la conscience du mal* (1993, Ethics: An Essay on the Understanding of Evil, trans. Peter Hallward, 2001), *L'être et l'événement* (1988, Being and Event, trans. Oliver Feltham, 1996), *Gilles Deleuze: "La clameur de l'être"* (1997, Deleuze: The Clamor of Being, trans. Louise Burchill, 2000), *L'hypothése communiste* (2008, The Communist Manifesto, trans. David Macey and Steve Corcoran, 2010), *Manifeste pour la philosophie* (1989, Manifesto for Philosophy, trans. Norman Madarasz, 1999), *Le nombre et les nombres* (1990, Number and Numbers, trans. Robin Mackay, 2008), *Petit manuel d'inesthétique* (1998, Handbook of Inaesthetics, trans. Alberto Toscano, 2005), *Saint-Paul: La fondation de l'universalisme* (1997, Saint Paul: The Foundations of Universalism, trans. Ray Brassier, 2003), *La siècle* (2005, The Century, trans. Alberto Toscano, 2007), *Théorie du sujet* (1985, Theory of the Subject, trans. Bruno Bosteels, 2009).

Bakhtin, Mikhail

Mikhail Bakhtin (1895–1975), arguably the most original thinker in the humanities to emerge from twentieth-century Russia, achieved most of his fame posthumously. Known primarily during his lifetime for an unconventional book on Fyodor Dostoevsky, numerous other writings published in his last years and after his death revealed a major thinker concerned with questions of language, culture, society, interpretation, time, and ethics. His best-known works survive both as studies of particular authors or genres illuminated by unusual philosophical concepts and as treatises primarily about those concepts, illustrated by literary works. Bakhtin's influence has extended in both directions, with some thinkers continuing his combination of literary criticism and philosophy.

Bakhtin studied classics and philology at Petrograd University. In 1929, after he finished *Problems of Dostoevsky's Poetics* but before it appeared in print, he was arrested and sentenced to ten years in a labor camp, a certain death sentence. In 1936 Mordovia State Teachers College hired Bakhtin to teach Russian and world literature, but he resigned among rumors of purges. A debilitating bone disease (osteomyelitis) led in 1938 to the amputation of his right leg. In 1946 he successfully defended as his doctoral dissertation a lengthy study of Rabelais—in its original form it did not mention "carnival," but its use of ostensibly crude language caused an academic scandal. Bakhtin retired in 1961, so obscure that when interest in his work revived in Moscow in the late 1950s, his young admirers were amazed to discover that he was still alive.

In the early 1960s Bakhtin was persuaded to expand his 1929 Dostoevsky study for a second edition (published 1963). A streamlined (and sanitized) monograph on Rabelais and Renaissance popular culture followed in 1965. During his final decade Bakhtin became a cult figure among post-Stalinist Russian intellectuals. His disciples began to unearth his early philosophical manuscripts and working notebooks. In 1975, the year of his death, and then in 1979, volumes of Bakhtin's writings from 1919 through the 1970s appeared in Russian; few of those texts had been prepared for print by their author, and some were wholly private jottings. A public canon began to accumulate that would have astonished its highly private creator.

By the 1990s Bakhtin had come to be treated as a classic author. Bakhtin's ideas cover such a wide range of topics and are so remarkably diverse that numerous schemes have been developed to provide an overview. Gary Saul Morson and Caryl Emerson's *Mikhail Bakhtin: Creation of a Prosaics* (1990) starts with the "global concepts" of unfinalizability, prosaics, and dialogue; Katerina Clark and Michael Holquist begin their biography *Mikhail Bakhtin* (1984) with the problematic of the early studies of "answerability"; others have focused on his theories of language, culture, and the novel.

In the early 1920s Bakhtin devised a three-part model of the human psyche based on perception and point of view. At any given moment each of us is a person in two senses: an "I-for-myself" (how I feel from inside to my own consciousness) and an "I-for-the-other" (how I look from outside to someone else). Although both perspectives are real, only the latter is articulate and palpable. Identity—concrete, historical, and inevitably shared—belongs not to individuals but to the boundary between them.

Each of us remains "outside" others, and this "outsideness" is essential to the architectonic model of the self. Because the self is in part the gift of the other, Bakhtin questions the idea that mirrors can offer us a true view of ourselves: they deceive by giving rise to the illusion that I can see myself as others see me. I can never really see myself, although I can see an authentic image of myself reflected in your eyes. If we are inclined to consider the "gaze" of another as inevitably reifying and constituting a form of violence, Bakhtin sees the other's look as necessary to my having a self at all.

If the architectonic self is the earliest but least known of Bakhtin's models, the carnivalized self was the first to be widely appreciated outside Russia. Elaborated in the 1930s, developed in *Rabelais and His World*, and incorporated into the chapter on Menippean satire in the second edition of the Dostoevsky book, this concept of the self focuses on the body, that is, on a robust, curious, fertile, grotesque body "on holiday." It craves the physical warmth of others; it can communicate without having to learn a complex verbal language; it is cheerful and free from shame and embarrassment; it opens itself to every new experience. It is not in a rush to get anything done, and its maintenance requires neither discipline nor self-control. Crucially for Bakhtin, it laughs, expressing a philosophy of life that is irreverent, radically skeptical, and distrustful of all hierarchies, certainties, or theories. Carnival laughter is fearless, indifferent to death, and enthusiastically obscene. The laughing face becomes all mouth, with barely any eyes; the carnivalized body is all lips, cheeks, breasts, and buttocks. Like these protuberances, it is outward- and other-oriented. This self remembers little, and regrets little, so why or whether it needs any *specific* other at all, as do the architectonic and dialogic selves, is difficult to say. Others simply pass through the carnival body, or gestate and are born, because it is above all a conduit, leaving us, paradoxically, with a swollen yet somehow impoverished self, a mass of interchangeable sensations and impulses that neither learns nor ages. In times of terror and famine such a generous, open-ended, well-fed self must have been an inspiration. Bakhtin was deeply enamored of carnival selves throughout his life and valued them for their courage, perseverance, optimism, and lack of ego.

Bakhtin's carnival self—the vigorous, immortal, responsive, collective body— has appealed most powerfully to political radicals, feminist scholars, and psychoanalytic critics in investigations of his self-other ideas. Such interpreters have seen a spirit of rebellion against all that is established, against constraining structures, both political and literary-theoretical. In the late 1960s JULIA KRISTEVA, Tzvetan Todorov, and other French theorists found in Bakhtin's thought a humanizing antidote to the bloodless abstractions of STRUCTURALISM, but certain concepts were perhaps too liberally adapted in their explications, as dialogue was reduced to intertextuality and the spiritual-Christian aspects of carnival were ignored or reduced. So were the dangers of finding violence attractive.

Bakhtin's third, also highly influential model of the self is the dialogic, which he developed in the 1920s and tinkered with throughout his life. In this model, consciousness is our inner conversations with the significant voices that figure for us; in a sense, we are the voices that inhabit us. As in life, each voice is capable of making a new and surprising response, so selves develop by an internal as well as an external dynamic. No self is ever complete, nor is its development ever predictable. Because the exchange of language is essential to a dialogic self, psychology requires the tools Bakhtin develops in his "metalinguistics," which, in turn, displays a psychological dimension. This model's great strength is that the self listens, remembers, and discriminates. It can hear a dozen voices embedded in every utterance and a personality behind each voice. Dialogic selves are above all conscious and laden with memory; their spiritual task is to increase the amount of consciousness in the world. The primary obligation of the dialogic self is to fulfill, console, and supplement others by seeing or hearing what they cannot hear for themselves.

The term "dialogue" has at least three distinct meanings for Bakhtin. He sometimes uses it to refer to a kind of "truth" that cannot be adequately comprehended abstractly and that cannot be grasped by a single consciousness. It requires multiple, discrete, specific consciousnesses (or "voices") in interaction. The thesis-antithesis-synthesis dialectic is thus a kind of reduced dialogue, like projecting a three-dimensional object onto a two-dimensional surface, an error analogous to trying to view oneself in the mirror as if one were another. Likewise, disagreement, a dialogic relation requiring two consciousnesses, is not logical contradiction, which at best provides material for a disagreement, and agreement, also dialogic, is not logical identity.

The term "dialogue" also refers to an approach to language as a whole that proceeds not from disembodied words or sentences but from concrete utterances—something specific that someone says to someone else on some occasion. Sentences provide the material for utterances, as logic does for disagreements, but by themselves sentences lack the crucial component of "addressivity": they become utterances only when they are actually *said* to someone. Sentences are infinitely repeatable, but each utterance, spoken at a specific moment in time, is unrepeatable. And an utterance, as opposed to a sentence, is always shaped by the listener *as* it is being made, not just (as in some models of reader-reception theory [see READER-RESPONSE CRITICISM]) after it has been completed. Words, phrases, and styles come "already populated" with the voices of others on the same topic. Some, but by no means all, utterances foreground their other-directedness and the ways in which they recall and anticipate other utterances. Such utterances are dialogic in a third sense of the term: they become "double-voiced." They may engage in parody or take a "sidelong glance" at potential utterances to come, or they may engage in many other interactions in which the presence of more than one voice in a single utterance becomes essential to what the utterance is doing. Even before they are answered, such utterances are "internally dialogized." Bakhtin offers a fascinating catalog of such dialogues and uses them to understand psychological, novelistic, and cultural phenomena.

Though deeply interested in formal problems of language and literature, Bakhtin differed from the Russian formalists in insisting that forms themselves were always the consequence of a "form-generating ideology." Such an "ideology," which he would compare to a kind of energy, is not a system of thought but a specific take on experience, a congealed set of habits of interpreting and evaluating certain aspects of life. For example, language is crisscrossed with countless changing ways of speaking—characteristic of professions, generations, circles, and other categories—and a panoply of speech genres, each of which reflects, in its tonality and forms, a way of understanding some aspect of experience. The heteroglossia of language (its many ways of speaking, each characteristic of some group) may become the basis of a peculiar self-consciousness when one way of speaking encounters another way of thinking and speaking about a given topic. The two ways may then interact with each other in unforeseeable ways, and out of that encounter, new insights may emerge. As a result of this process of dialogization, these two ways of speaking may even give birth to new ways of speaking. In this way, Bakhtin's metalinguistics is a kind of sociolinguistics.

One of Bakhtin's theories of the novel, as developed in his essay "Discourse in the Novel," argues that the novel as a genre is characterized by an intensification of "dialogized heteroglossia." Bringing worldviews and senses of experience into dialogue with each other and then exaggerating the resulting interactions and imagining ones that have never happened is, viewed in terms of language, the central task of the novel. Crucially, the main locus for these dialogic interactions is not in the exchanges between characters but in the apparently straightforward sentences of the commenting narrator, whose discourse Bakhtin sees as shot through with alien and diverse voices brought into complex interactions. From a strictly literary point of view, this theory of language and the novel, along with its specific techniques of analysis, may be Bakhtin's most enduring contribution.

If the real action of novels takes place in the narrator's orchestration of voices, then the novel as a genre will be characterized by the sense that no absolute truth is available, that every truth, including the author's, is one truth among many—perhaps preferable to others but never truly certain. The novel's skepticism reflects its debt not only to the concept of dialogue without a final word but also to the irreverent attitude toward hierarchies and absolutes characteristic of carnival. More than once in human experience, the spirit of carnival has invaded high culture and become the form-shaping ideology for a literary genre, most crucially Menippean satire, whose development Bakhtin traces from antiquity to the present. (Bakhtin's work has substantially influenced the study of the classics in America.) If epic locates its readers at maximal distance from the "firsts and greats" of the characters' world, then Menippean satire situates its readers at maximal proximity to the represented world. This "zone of familiar contact" eventually shaped the novel as a genre. What others thought of as realism, Bakhtin thought of in terms of proximity of worlds. Critics have long argued that the novel owes a debt to epic, but Bakhtin stresses its debt to the anti-epic sensibility of Menippean satire and carnival.

As the dialogic sense of self is reflected in the discourse theory of the novel, and the carnivalized self in the Menippean theory, so the architectonic self finds expression in the "chronotopic" approach to the novel. Bakhtin attempts to describe the field that makes specific experiences of a given kind possible. His idea is that each narrative genre implicitly incorporates a sense of how events happen: what possibilities time offers, how social space shapes likely and unlikely actions, and what sort of agency, if any, human beings have. That is why the plots of given genres differ, and since moral judgment depends on what actions are possible, the moral sensibility of genres varies accordingly. A genre's complex of possible or likely actions constitutes its chronotope, and Bakhtin analyzes and traces the history of diverse generic chronotopes, which are themselves always becoming and changing. His favorite genre, the novel, shows the fullness of time and renders human life as a realistic process of gradual, daily becoming.

The architectonic model of the self also gave rise to Bakhtin's theory of polyphony, a notion he claims applies not to all novelists but only to Dostoevsky and perhaps a few (unnamed) writers since. In a nonpolyphonic work, authors maintain a radical "surplus" of meaning with respect to their characters. Authors know everything about the character, including all choices and events to come, because they know and have determined in advance the structure and closure of the work itself. This "aesthetic necessity" therefore makes it ultimately impossible to represent human freedom. But Dostoevsky (like Bakhtin) believed that freedom was genuine and therefore found a way around structure itself. In the polyphonic work there is no overall structure or pregiven outcome. The author surrenders the "essential surplus" of meaning over the characters and lets the work develop as it may. As in life, each moment has radical presentness, and no future toward which events are tending limits present options. Authors, readers, and characters therefore experience genuine "surprisingness." Although such a work risks being too chaotic to be readable at all, it can allow the palpableness of free choice to be experienced. We sense that the work as we have it could have been other, just as each of our lives could have been other.

As practiced by Dostoevsky, polyphony makes use of the overturning of all structures characteristic of Menippean satire, and to dramatize the openness of time, Dostoevsky develops techniques to maximize the openness of dialogue (in the third sense). He is therefore able to draw on both the carnivalized self and the dialogic self, and the emphasis on presentness draws on ideas developed in Bakhtin's essay on the chronotope. The second edition of *Problems of Dostoevsky's Poetics* develops each of these strands of Bakhtin's thought and therefore is often considered the best introduction to his work as a whole.

Bakhtin's stress on freedom looks back to ideas present in his earliest work, particularly his essay "Toward a Philosophy of the Act," in which he stresses the primacy of ethical choice at every moment of our lives, explores the various ways in which we try to avoid responsibility for signing our acts, and insists that in spite of all theories that displace our "oughtness" onto other people, social forces, or various abstractions, there is never "an alibi" for our responsibility. This ethical aspect of Bakhtin's thought may seem less exciting than the body warmth of carnival and the oscillating flow of dialogue, but it is arguably his most "responsible" and balanced concept. After recognizing one's ineluctable duty to sign on to responsibility, one can partake in carnival and dialogue with less risk. An integral self is made up not of qualities and "givens" but of responses and tasks.

Such integrity also permits the growth of "creative understanding." Bakhtin thought that all great works, which survive over "great time," contain rich "potential." If approached from a new dialogic angle given by a different epoch or culture, the work can become an active partner in creating new meanings. Judging from the numerous fields and schools of thought that have discovered new ideas in dialogue with Bakhtin, his work also seems to contain the sort of potentials he admired.

CARYL EMERSON AND GARY SAUL MORSON

See also LINGUISTICS AND LANGUAGE and SPEECH ACTS.

Mikhail M. Bakhtin, *Art and Answerability: Early Philosophical Essays* (ed. Michael Holquist and Vadim Liapunov, trans. Liapunov, 1990), *The Dialogic Imagination: Four Essays* (ed. Michael Holquist, trans. Caryl Emerson and Michael Holquist, 1981), *Problemy tvorchestva Dostoevskogo* (1929, 2nd ed., 1963, *Problems of Dostoevsky's Poetics*, ed. and trans. Caryl Emerson, 1984), *Speech Genres and Other Late Essays* (ed. Caryl Emerson and Michael Holquist, trans. Vern W. McGee, 1986), *Tvorchestvo Fransua Rable i narodnaia kul'tura srednevekov'iai Renessansa* (1965 [wr. 1946], *Rabelais and His World*, trans. Hélène Izwolsky, 1968), *Toward a Philosophy of the Act*, ed. Michael Holquist and Vadim Liapunov, trans. Vadim Liapunov, 1993); Viktor D. Dukavin, *M. M. Bakhtin: Besedy s V. D. Duvakinym* [M. M. Bakhtin: Conversations with V. D. Duvakin] (2002).

Balibar, Étienne

Étienne Balibar (b. 1942) became a member of a close circle of students at the École Normale Supérieure associated with Louis Althusser, including JACQUES RANCIÈRE, ALAIN BADIOU, and Pierre Macherey. He completed his *diplôme d'étude supérior* in 1963 and received his doctorate in philosophy in 1987. Among that of his cohort of post-1968 French Marxist philosophers, Balibar's thought is distinguished first, during the 1970s, by its comparatively late "break" with the philosophy of Althusser and with the French Communist Party. Since the 1980s, he has sought to resituate his earlier engagement with Karl Marx and Marxism within a longer tradition of political philosophy and in response to the changed transnational frame of political philosophy. Far from a retreat to philology, however, Balibar's more recent writing directly engages concrete social, political, and economic conditions, thus sharply contrasting with the work many of his French contemporaries. In this respect, his thought has tended to be more amenable to adoption within Anglo-American political theory and the sociology of culture. His work has had a profound impact on literary and cultural criticism, particularly through his early collaboration with Pierre Macherey and his later writing on race, nationalism, and transnational citizenship.

Balibar's first significant published work emerged from his participation in Althusser's seminars on Marx's *Capital* during the mid-1960s. The collection of essays collectively produced by this group, *Reading Capital* (1965), included Balibar's essay "On the Basic Concepts of Historical Materialism." In this essay, he elaborates the specificity of Marx's conception of "modes of production" in the philosophy of history. In line with the Althusserian thesis of the "epistemological break" enacted in Marx's mature, economic writing, Balibar's essay provides a means of thinking the philosophical import of *Capital*, particularly its significance for philosophy of history. The project of assessing the precise nature of Marx's "break" with Western philosophical tradition has occupied Balibar's writing throughout his career.

Balibar's collaboration with the *Reading Capital* group continued through his coauthorship, with Pierre Macherey, of "Literature as an Ideological Form." Widely read and anthologized in Anglo-American literary criticism, this essay represents Balibar's most direct engagement with literary criticism. Arguing for a reconception of the object of literary study, Balibar and Macherey advance a theory of "literary production" as a corrective to what they read as the sterility of both formalist and orthodox Marxist modes of literary analysis. Rejecting both the political naïveté of strict formalist attention to the text and the narrowness of a vulgar "materialist" approach to literature as an epiphenomenal reflection of "objective" conditions, Balibar and Macherey call for the movement of literary criticism beyond the false dilemma of reading literature *either* formally, "on its own terms," *or* historically in terms of its reflection of something external to itself (e.g., the author's class position or characters' reenactment of capitalist social relations). Instead, Balibar and Macherey argue that literature should be read as part of a broader "ensemble of social practices," not only as a text reflecting external conditions or the ideas of the ruling class but also as a "privileged agent of ideological subjection." Attacking the assumption of a transhistorical essence, or "literariness" of the literary text, Balibar and Macherey outline how the idea (or ideology) of literature disguises its own "production." They point to the way in which the practice of teaching and reading literature reproduces historically specific modes of identification, aesthetic sensibility, and linguistic affiliation that align with the interest of the ruling order. Among the most definitive statements of a structural Marxist literary criticism, Balibar and Macherey's essay also demonstrates a clear correspondence with PIERRE BOURDIEU's sociology of culture and was an important text for the formation of British Cultural Studies.

During the mid-1970s, Balibar published *Five Studies on Historical Materialism* (1974) and *On the Dictatorship of the Proletariat* (1976), two texts that together exemplify his ongoing commitment to Marxism at the level of theory and political praxis. *On the Dictatorship of the Proletariat* was written in the context of the fractious debate taking place at the time within European communism and the French Communist Party, of which Balibar remained an active member from the early 1960s until his expulsion in 1981. A scathing response to the events of the twenty-second meeting of the party, this text offers a complex polemic against the party's removal of the concept of the dictatorship of the proletariat from its platform and constitution. The book represents Balibar's most substantial engagement with the idea of Euro-communism that was circulating at that time.

The effect of Balibar's expulsion from the French Communist Party is apparent in the direction of his subsequent writing. Over the 1980s, he produced two book length studies in political philosophy. First, *Spinoza and Politics* (1985), a notable contribution to the widespread revival of Spinoza within the European "pensée du '68"; and, second, a study of John Locke's political writing (*Identity and Difference: The Invention of Conscience* [1998]). While these texts suggest a departure of Balibar's work from its earlier, more narrowly Marxist alignment, there is an equally clear continuity in Balibar's historical materialist or conjunctural approach to the history of philosophy. Thus, in *Spinoza and Politics* Balibar reads Spinoza's *Tractatus Theologio-Politicus* through a rigorous analysis of the local conflicts and contradictions present in the Dutch Republic during the latter part of the seventeenth century.

The most recent period of Balibar's thought can be dated from 1988, the date of the publication of *Race, Nation, Class*, a collection of essays he coauthored with Immanuel Wallerstein. In three of the essays collected in this volume—"Is there a Neo-Racism?," "The Nation Form: History and Ideology," and "Racism and Nationalism"—Balibar elaborates a critique of "culturalist" discourses of race against the concrete backdrop of new forms of racialized violence and exclusion that he interprets as manifestations of a postcolonial and increasingly globalized world order. Diagnosing a broad shift from a biological to a "cultural" discourse of race in academic theories of race, on one hand, and a parallel shift in the rhetoric of racist social movements, on the other, Balibar's essays offer a sustained attempt to critically interrogate this double aspect of a cultural, or "differentialist," neoracism. Comparing these new, cultural discourses of race with the earlier social Darwinist and biological racist discourses that they ostensibly overcome, Balibar identifies the fundamentally shared project of both in the production of the "fictive ethnicities" that structure the racist imagination. For Balibar, the historical relationship of such "fictive ethnicities" to political categories as "the people" and "the masses" exposes the ambivalent relationship of racism, nationalism, and the nation form. He argues that racism and nationalism exist in a historically reciprocal relationship, wherein racism functions as an inherent *"supplement of nationalism or more precisely a supplement internal to nationalism, always in excess of it, but always indispensable to its constitution and yet always still insufficient to achieve its project"* (54). Anticipating dominant themes in his subsequent writing, he insists that only through an "international politics of citizenship" can an effective antiracism be achieved. Published during the height of critical race theory and POSTCOLONIAL STUDIES in the Anglo-American academy, Balibar's thinking in *Race, Nation, Class* engages these theoretical discourses but also diverges significantly and critically from their mainstream. His broadly Marxist emphasis on the role of capitalist social relations in shaping racial discourse and practice was, in particular, an exception to the relative marginalization of this perspective in progressive theories of racial difference at that time.

Balibar's essays collected in *Masses, Classes and Ideas* (1994), *Politics and the Other Scene* (2002), and *We the People of Europe?* (2004) reposition the problem of race and racism within the context of the "new Europe" and fuse these concrete sociopolitical problems with the more formally philosophical preoccupations of his work during the 1980s and early 1990s. With its increasing focus on questions of citizenship, immigration, democracy and the changed subject/object of emancipatory politics, Balibar's most recent writing also demonstrates a more definitive distancing from the adherence to the categories of Marxist analysis present in his earlier work. He locates the emergent fault lines of power in the struggle, both ideological and concrete, over citizenship and borders. The ambiguous claims to universalism, civility, and radical "equaliberty" institutionalized in the Western democratic tradition become privileged vectors along which to specify the contradictions of democracy and the nation form in a new, globalized order and to forge alternative forms of citizenship and civility. Like numerous other leading voices in contemporary French philosophy (such as Rancière), the immigrant noncitizen or *sans-papiers* acquires decisive importance for Balibar as the bearer and model of a new post- or transnational citizenship. Losing none of his awareness of the extent to which these problems are conditioned by a system of capitalist social relations, Balibar exemplifies his commitment to a philosophy that remains directly engaged with its historical conjuncture through his commitment to questions of citizenship.

JUSTIN SULLY

See also MARXIST THEORY AND CRITICISM 2: STRUCTURALIST MARXISM, MARXIST THEORY AND CRITICISM 3: 1989 AND AFTER, and RACE AND ETHNICITY.

Étienne Balibar, Cinq études de materialisme historique (1974), Identité et différence: L'invention de la conscience (1998), Masses, Classes and Ideas (1994, trans. James Swenson), Nous, citoyens d'Europe? Les frontières, l'état, le peuple (2001, We the People of Europe? Reflections in Transnational Citizenship, trans. James Swenson, 2004), La philosophie de Marx (1993, The Philosophy of Marx, trans. Chris Turner, 1995), Politics and the Other Scene (2002, trans. Christine Jones, James Swenson, and Chris Turner), Spinoza et la politique (1985, Spinoza and Politics, trans. Peter Snowdon, 1998), Sur la dictature du proletariat (1976, On the Dictatorship of the Proletariat, trans. Grahame Lock, 1977); Louis Althusser, Étienne Balibar, et al., Lire le "Capital" (1965, Reading Capital, trans. Ben Brewster, 1970); Étienne Balibar and Immanuel Wallerstein, Race, nation, classe: Les identity ambiguës (1988, Race, Nation, Class: Ambiguous Identities, trans. Chris Turner, 1991); Pierre Macherey and Étienne Balibar, "Sur la littérature comme forme idéologique: Quelques hypothèses marxistes" (1974) ("Literature as an Ideological Form: Some Marxist Propositions," trans. James H. Kavanagh, Praxis 5 [1981]).

Barthes, Roland

Some critics—for example Susan Sontag—have pictured Roland Barthes (1915–1980) as more of a virtuoso of the essay in the tradition of Michel de Montaigne and André Gide than as a theoretician of literary studies. A retrospective overview of his writings would, however, tend to stress an impressive and systematic body of critical work that, to a great extent, has molded our contemporary understanding of textuality.

Barthes is sometimes seen primarily as a promoter of a French brand of STRUC-TURALISM. Yet such a label proves extremely misleading if we identify it with the "hard" and scientific version of structuralism developed in the 1950s, a school Barthes helped launch but whose limitations he soon perceived. A better way to approach Barthes's writings is to get an idea of the various trends he found himself engaged in. If we historicize him in this manner, several periods can be distinguished. The first phase corresponds to a meditation on History, always written with a capital H. This meditation takes a double form: an almost psychoanalytic analysis (albeit in a Bachelardian mode that is still very close to thematic analysis) of the work of Jules Michelet, the great poet of history (*Michelet* [1954]), and a systematic study of the concepts of language, style, and writing in *Writing Degree Zero*. As Barthes recalled his beginnings in the lecture he gave to the Collège de France when he was admitted to it" in 1978, he started his career by combining the influences of Jean-Paul Sartre, Bertolt Brecht, and FERDINAND DE SAUSSURE (*Barthes Reader* 471). The early and groundbreaking *Writing Degree Zero* provides an answer to Sartre's *What Is Literature?* whose neo-Marxist analysis of committed literature is countered and complicated through the introduction of the notion of "writing." For Barthes, three elements are brought into play: language, the general code of signs never to be directly modified by literature; style, enclosing each writer in a kind of idiolect and determined by his or her private history, a sort of writerly body; and finally writing, which transcends individual styles and appears as the locus of both personal freedom and social determinism.

With this new concept of writing, Barthes clears the ground for its history, a history of literary language that is never reduced to the history of language or to the history of styles but instead explores the historicity of the signs of literature. In Barthes's view, the modern period, initiated by Gustave Flaubert and Stéphane Mallarmé, announced the end of classical writing; thereafter, literature turned into a problematics of pure language. Hence the concept of "writing degree zero," exemplified by writers such as Albert Camus and the novelists of the *nouveau roman*, a neutral literary style deprived of all traditional markers that heralds an encounter with language as such while stressing the gap between language and the world.

Such a gap is not to be dialectically overcome, via, for example, Sartre's duality of form and content, for Barthes is primarily interested in literary form: literature cannot be reduced to communication or expression. Insofar as it is made up of language, communication is presupposed, but this particular language often has the effect of erasing intentions, private meanings, and all claims to propriety. Literature is a form-making activity, not just one case of social communication. It is from this strategic standpoint that Barthes engages in a systematic criticism of the misunderstandings deriving from the naturalization of form. When form is taken for content, history is reduced to nature, production reverts to ideological consumption, and myth covers all facts with an illusory transparent gauze. This denial of history corresponds to the world of myth.

Barthes's well-known "readings" of today's myths criticize the self-deluding tactics of contemporary ideology from a position that allows the active audience to judge and understand instead of passively identifying with represented people or events. His provocative, at times offhand, thematic treatment of Racine in *On Racine* (1963) sparked a controversy with Raymond Picard that eventually turned into a replay of the seventeenth- and eighteenth-century quarrel between the ancients and the moderns (see also *Criticism and Truth*, 1966). By the end of the 1960s it was clear that the moderns had won the day and completely redefined the map of contemporary literary studies in France, even if the academics remained somewhat skeptical.

The originality of Barthes's approach is more clearly apparent in the second phase of his career, in which the main object of inquiry is the mythology of everyday life in the context of a general analysis of codes. This originality lies in the linking of Brecht's distanciation with the linguistic analysis of Russian formalism and of Roman Jakobson, for if the gap between signifier and referent has a critical function—namely, that of compelling us to question representations that are taken for granted and to destroy the habitual link we tend to establish between nature and culture—this gap is constitutive of poetic language as such. Literary language is intransitive; it functions in a realm of its own, independent of any reference to reality. Denotation is merely the lure whereby language attempts to hide the interplay of connotations that constitutes its codes.

Barthes's second phase thus deploys a linguistic strategy in order to engage with the universe of signification, and here he indeed appears as the founder of French semiology. The first text to find immediate acclaim was *Mythologies* (1957), a witty exploration of contemporary idols and clichés. Myth is defined as a "semiological system" in the fashion of Saussure, who had heralded the birth of semiology as the general science of signs. Myth is made up of the three Saussurean components—signifier, signified, and sign—but it is a secondary system in which what is a sign in the language becomes a signifier in myth. Hence the following scheme, later to be exploited for the analysis of fashion (115):

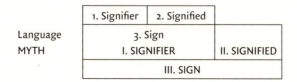

	1. Signifier	2. Signified	
Language	3. Sign		
MYTH	I. SIGNIFIER	II. SIGNIFIED	
	III. SIGN		

Language becomes the object of a metalanguage that connotation keeps redoubling. The arbitrary nature of the linguistic sign receives a purely cultural motivation in the mythological system. The bogey to destroy is always the irrepressible ghost of a naturalization of signs.

Myth is the direct inversion of poetry: myth transforms a meaning into form, whereas poetry is a regressive semiological system that aims at reaching the meaning of things themselves. According to Barthes, "The subversion of writing was the radical act by which a number of writers have attempted to reject Literature as a mythical system" (*Mythologies* 135). Barthes's study of Philippe Sollers follows these principles (*Writer Sollers*, 1979). Yet for a time Barthes also seemed to believe in the possibility of a science valid for all possible narratives, as seen in "An Introduction to the Structural Analysis of Narrative" (1966), where he manages to combine the approaches of Algirdas Julien Greimas, Claude Bremond, Vladimir Propp, Jakobson, and Russian formalism by distinguishing between the level of functions (such as "request," "aid," and "punishment" in the logic of the plot), the level of actions (characters are "actants" in a literary praxis that questions the status of subjectivity), and the level of narration (or discourse, implying a narrator and an addressee).

An even more systematic treatment of semiology is provided in the two essays *Elements of Semiology* (1964) and *The Fashion System* (1967): fashion, for instance, is analyzed not sociologically but in terms of language—"written fashion"—and the corpus is limited to a few women's magazines. Here, Barthes draws on Louis Hjelmslev, André Martinet, Nicolas S. Troubetskoy, Saussure, and Sartre to formulate a vertiginous nesting of signifying systems (in which E stands for "plane of the expression" and C, "plane of the content") (293):

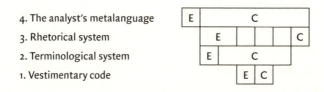

Nevertheless, the conclusion of this brilliant if rather heuristic analysis opens out onto a reiterated assertion of death: the eternal present of fashion rhetorics supposes a repression of their own futility and therefore of their death-haunted mutability, whereas "the semiologist is a man who expresses his future death in the very terms in which he has named and understood the world" (294).

Barthes's decision to focus on written or described fashion may correspond to a reversal of priorities. Whereas Saussure believes that linguistics is only a part of a wider science of signs (semiology), Barthes tends to think that semiology is only a part of the science of linguistics: human language is not merely a model, a pattern of meaning, but its real foundation. If everything is always caught up in the nets of a discourse already spoken by other subjects, it is only another step to JACQUES LACAN's formula that "there is no metalanguage." This emphasis on a discourse already spoken may describe the move to a third phase in Barthes's career, a phase in which a scientific language is not abandoned but remultiplied, pluralized, in order to reach beyond the object (such as text or myth or fashion) to the activity that produces it as such (textuality as textualization).

This third phase corresponds to the primacy of the notion of text over that of signifying system. The influence of the avant-garde represented by the *Tel Quel* movement becomes more conspicuous, and Barthes abandons semiology as a rigid scientific discourse in order to promote a new science, that of the production of signs. The key publication of this period is probably *S/Z* (1970), an exhaustive reading of Balzac's story "Sarrasine." The essay, which owes a lot to JULIA KRISTEVA's influential collection of essays *Desire in Language* (1969), stresses plurality and combines all possible semiological approaches, finally reading like a musical score and creating a work of art of its own kind. Central here is the notion of textuality understood as a weaving of codes: "*text, fabric, braid*: the same thing" (160). Barthes distinguishes five codes, corresponding to sequences of actions or behavioral patterns (proairetic codes), to the disclosure of the truth (hermeneutical codes), to descriptions of significant features (semic codes), to quotations from scientific or cultural models (cultural codes), and to the symbolic architecture of language (symbolic codes).

"The five codes create a kind of network, a *topos* through which the entire text passes (or rather, in passing, becomes a text)" (20). In an earlier essay, "The Death of the Author" (1968), which took its cue from an ambiguous sentence in "Sarrasine," textuality is defined as an interplay of codes that negates any origin: "Writing is the destruction of every voice, of every point of origin. Writing is that neutral, composite, oblique space where our subject slips away, the negative where all identity is lost, starting with the very identity of the body writing" (*Image* 142). And the essay tantalizingly concludes with the reader's new active role: "The birth of the reader must be at the cost of the death of the Author" (148).

When Barthes visited Japan, he himself became that ideal reader facing a writing that covers the world in order to cover up for the absence of the author. Japan is the happy utopia of a country in which everything is sign. But signs do not refer; they only exhibit their fictive, indeed fabricated, nature. Influenced by JACQUES DERRIDA's powerful meditation on writing as the ruin of presence and of origin, *The Empire of Signs* (1970) sees Japan as the necessary healing (and disturbing) experience of a culture that has done away with any naturalization of signs.

Japan also opens up a space of the erotic enjoyment of signs; it is, in fact, in his study of Japan that the very important motif "pleasure" first appears in Barthes's texts. The "erotic grace" of Japanese hypercodified attitudes finds its European equivalent in the Marquis de Sade's seemingly boring descriptions of sexual orgies and perversions, in Ignatius Loyola's mental exercises teaching the soul how to approach

God, or again in Charles Fourier's ritualized catalogs of passions. *Sade/Fourier/Loyola* (1971) takes a semiological approach to textuality but resolutely centers around three deviant writers who are all "logothetic": they stand out as "founders of languages" precisely because they intrepidly systematize a strategy of excess, an excess that becomes identical with writing as such (3). The introduction to the work coins for the first time the expression "the pleasure of the Text," which is taken up in the collection of maxims and aphorisms entitled *The Pleasure of the Text* (1973). Instead of asking what we know about texts, Barthes now asks only how we enjoy them?

In this last phase of his literary career, Barthes rewrites a distinction elaborated earlier in S/Z between "writerly" (*scriptible*) and "readerly" (*lisible*) texts (4), or between texts that merely obey a logic of passive consumption and texts that stimulate the reader's active participation, as an opposition between textual *plaisir* and textual *jouissance*. *Jouissance* calls up a violent, climactic bliss closer to loss, death, fragmentation, and the disruptive rapture experienced when transgressing limits, whereas *plaisir* simply hints at an easygoing enjoyment, more stable in its reenactment of cultural codes.

In this period of his "moralities," as Barthes himself called it, no pretense of scientificity hinders the direct encounter with cultural and literary signs, which are organically related to the body of their "scriptor." In *Roland Barthes by Roland Barthes* (1975), he produces a stimulating work of autobiographical criticism that tries to take into account his own subjectivity as a whole. But, the closest Barthes comes to writing pure fiction is in *A Lover's Discourse* (1977), which opts for a "dramatic" method of presentation by varying the voices and blending quotations, personal remarks, and subtle generalizations. The fictive character who enounces all the utterances is an archetypal lover—at times Johann Wolfgang von Goethe's Werther, at times Barthes himself—who comments on the ineluctable solitude of love.

The increasingly sentimental drift of these last works is counterbalanced by the sweeping and majestic summary of Barthes's beliefs about theory in his inaugural lecture, the speech he gave when he was elected to the Collège de France, the crowning of his academic career. Enunciation is alluded to as the exposure of the subject's absence to him or herself, semiotics becomes a DECONSTRUCTION of linguistics, and the main adversary is the power of language seen as a totalitarian structure: language, according to one daring formula, is always fascistic (*Barthes Reader* 461). Literature condenses all the forces of resistance to such a reactionary power, thanks to its hedonistic capacity for transforming knowledge into play, pleasure, and enjoyment. Barthes sees himself as Hans Castorp in Thomas Mann's *Magic Mountain* and finally claims his hope of achieving a possible wisdom, a *sapientia* linking knowledge and taste—in short, a whole *art de vivre*.

Camera Lucida (1981), Barthes's last book before the many posthumous collections of essays, is a moving autobiographical disclosure of his love for his mother under the guise of a study of photography that recants all previous semiological approaches. Whereas in many former essays Barthes had stressed the artificial nature of such a medium and its ideological power, he now identifies photography as pure reference; it immediately bespeaks a past presence, and its ultimate signifier is the death and absence of the loved mother. The last conceptual couple invented by Barthes opposes *studium*, a scientific approach that is ultimately boring and misses the main point, and *punctum*, the point or small detail that catches the eye of the beholder (26–27). This dualism justifies an apparently subjective selection of photographs, all chosen and lovingly described because of some minor but revealing element that varies from picture to picture. This Zen-like meditation on the illusions of appearance and the triumph of death is a fitting testament to Barthes as a writer of an almost magical power of analysis and utterance.

JEAN-MICHEL RABATÉ

See also NARRATOLOGY, FERDINAND DE SAUSSURE, SEMIOTICS, and STRUCTURALISM.

Roland Barthes, *L'aventure sémiotique* (1985, *The Semiotic Challenge*, trans. Richard Howard, 1988), *A Barthes Reader* (ed. Susan Sontag, 1982), *Le bruissement de la langue* (1984, *The Rustle of Language*, trans. Richard Howard, 1986), *La chambre claire: Note sur la photographie* (1980, *Camera Lucida: Reflections on Photography*, trans. Richard Howard, 1981), *Critique et vérité* (1966, *Criticism and Truth*, ed. and trans. Katherine Pilcher Keuneman, 1987), *Le degré zéro de l'écriture* (1953, *Writing Degree Zero*, trans. Annette Lavers and Colin Smith, 1967), "Éléments de sémiologie" (1964, *Elements of Semiology*, trans. Annette Lavers and Colin Smith, 1967), *L'empire des signes* (1970, *Empire of Signs*, trans. Richard Howard, 1982), *Essais critiques* (1964, *Critical Essays*, trans. Richard Howard, 1972), *Fragments d'un discours amoureux* (1977, *A Lover's Discourse: Fragments*, trans. Richard Howard, 1978), *Le grain de la voix: Entretiens, 1962–1980* (1981, *The Grain of the Voice: Interviews, 1962–1980*, trans. Linda Coverdale, 1985), *Image—Music—Text* (ed. and trans. Stephen Heath, 1977), *Leçon* (1978, "Inaugural Lecture, Collège de France," trans. Richard Howard, *A Barthes Reader*), *Michelet par lui-même* (1954, *Michelet*, trans. Richard Howard, 1987), *Mythologies* (1957, *Mythologies*, ed. and trans. Annette Lavers, 1972, *The Eiffel Tower and Other Mythologies*, trans. Richard Howard, 1979), *Nouveaux essais critiques* (1972, *New Critical Essays*, trans. Richard Howard, 1980), *L'obvie et l'obtus: Essais critiques III* (1982, *The Responsibility of Forms: Critical Essays on Music, Art, and Representation*, trans. Richard Howard, 1985), *Le plaisir du texte* (1973, *The Pleasure of the Text*, trans. Richard Miller, 1975), *Roland Barthes par Roland Barthes* (1975, *Roland Barthes by Roland Barthes*, trans. Richard Howard, 1977), *Sade, Fourier, Loyola* (1971, *Sade/Fourier/Loyola*, trans. Richard Miller, 1976), *Sollers écrivain* (1979, *Writer Sollers*, trans. Philip Thody, 1987), *Sur Racine* (1963, *On Racine*, trans. Richard Howard, 1964), *Système de la mode* (1967, *The Fashion System*, trans. Matthew Ward and Richard Howard, 1983), *S/Z* (1970, *S/Z*, trans. Richard Miller, 1974).

Bataille, Georges

Within the history of the avant-garde in France few twentieth-century writers have left a more far-reaching legacy than Georges Bataille (1897–1962). Librarian, libertine, radical thinker, author of erotic fictions, Bataille in life and in writing traversed disparate institutions, identities, and discourses. In his twenties Bataille rejected Catholicism and began to became an active participant in the Parisian avant-garde literary scene. Objecting to what he saw as the aestheticism and potential sentimentality of the surrealists, he rapidly became André Breton's most forceful antagonist of the intellectual ultraleft. After the war, as founding editor of the journal *Critique* and author of transgressively "philosophical" books—*Inner Experience* (1943), *Guilty* (1944), *On Nietzsche* (1945), *The Accursed Share* (1947)—Bataille emerged as a visible alternative to Jean-Paul Sartre and existentialism; he was to become, posthumously, an exemplary figure for the next generation of avant-garde writers centered around *Tel Quel*. Bataille's friendship with MAURICE BLANCHOT became a touchstone for French post-Heideggerian discussions of friendship and community.

Bataille's work transgresses disciplines and genres so frequently and radically that capsule accounts of his oeuvre contain misleading abstractions. If his thought consists in a meditation on, and performance of, "transgression," such a project is necessarily antimeditative and nonphilosophical, committed to a principled, violent specificity. His erotic fictions (*Story of the Eye* [1928]; *Madame Edwarda* [1941]), for instance, are as "theoretical" as his writings on society, economics, and history. Such generic transgressions form part of a critical project that frequently entails an appropriation and disarticulation of certain themes of G. W. F. Hegel, for whom humanness and history come into being through humanity's deathlike power to negate what exists, via consciousness (the power of abstraction) and labor. Bataille, drawing on Friedrich Nietzsche (and SIGMUND FREUD, Stéphane Mallarmé, Marcel Mauss, the Marquis de Sade), insists on this negative power's disruptive, excessive character. All philosophical, social, and psychological sublimations (language, consciousness, social forms, genital sexuality, etc.) are inhabited by an excess that at once makes sublimation possible and threatens its stability. For Bataille in "The Notion of Expenditure" (*Visions* 116–29) and *The Accursed Share*, any "restricted economy"—any putatively closed, reciprocal system, such as an identity, a concept or structure, marketplace, ecosystem, and so forth—produces more than it can account for. Any restricted economy is fractured by its own unacknowledged excess and in seeking to maintain itself will, against its own logic, crave expenditure and loss (hence Bataille's interest in sacrifice and automutilation). Any restricted economy is thus situatable in a "general economy" irreducible to proper conceptualization.

Like Blanchot, Bataille is frequently cited as a precursor for much so-called French theory. JACQUES DERRIDA and MICHEL FOUCAULT have documented their investment in Bataille, while libidinal theorists such as GILLES DELEUZE AND FÉLIX GUATTARI and JEAN-FRANÇOIS LYOTARD and post-Marxist sociologists such as JEAN BAUDRILLARD have pursued Bataillean themes (eroticism, transgression, expenditure) even more explicitly. Bataille's influence on contemporary critical thought would thus be difficult to overestimate. In the English-speaking world this influence for a long time tended to be covert (the term "general economy" is still often employed with little sense of its history or import) or restricted to particular confluences of high theory and avant-gardism. In the last decade or so of the twentieth century, however, Bataille became an increasingly visible figure in Anglo-American theoretical writing: almost all of his major work has been translated into English, and the list of books partly or wholly on him has grown impressively long.

MARC REDFIELD

Georges Bataille, *The Bataille Reader* (ed. Fred Botting and Scott Wilson, 1997), *Le coupable* (1944, Guilty, trans. Bruce Boone, 1988), *The Cradle of Humanity: Prehistoric Art and Culture* (ed. Stuart Kendall, trans. Michelle Kendall and Stuart Kendall, 2005), *L'érotisme* (1957, Death and Sensuality, trans. Mary Dalwood, 1962), *L'expérience intérieure* (1943, Inner Experience, trans. Leslie Anne Boldt, 1988), *Oeuvres complètes* (12 vols., 1970–1988), *La part maudite* (1949, The Accursed Share, trans. Robert Hurley, 1988), *Sur Nietzsche* (1945, On Nietzsche, trans. Bruce Boone, 1992), *The Unfinished System of Non-knowledge* (ed. Stuart Kendall, trans. Michelle Kendall and Stuart Kendall, 2001), *Visions of Excess: Selected Writings, 1927–1939* (trans. and ed. Allan Stoekl, 1985); Georges Bataille and Michel Leiris, *Correspondence* (ed. Louis Yvert, trans. Liz Heron, 2008).

Baudrillard, Jean

Jean Baudrillard's (1929–2007) name is synonymous with the flowering of interest in postmodern theory that occurred in the 1980s. "Simulacrum" is the buzzword of a "Baudrillard scene" reminiscent of an earlier pop intellectual cult of McLuhanatics that twenty years earlier had formed around Canadian media theorist Marshall McLuhan. Baudrillard's four volumes of fragments and aphorisms *Cool Memories* borrow "cool" from McLuhan's concept of low definition, participatory media. "Simulation" has also been influential in science fiction studies and literary criticism focused on postmodern novels.

The first and second comings of Baudrillard were modest. In 1974–1975 his *Mirror of Production* (1973) appeared in English translation within the eclectic mix of New Leftism sponsored by the *Telos* collective; the same group later sponsored a translation of his *For a Critique of the Political Economy of the Sign* (1972). It was with the publication of his travelogue *America* (1986) that Baudrillard's reputation went global.

Young Baudrillard squirreled away in obscure lycées teaching language arts for a decade and then emerged in the 1960s as a translator (German-French) of social anthropology, theater (minor Bertolt Brecht and major works by Peter Weiss), and political theory and as a book reviewer of German, Italian, and American literature in French translation. Baudrillard's work of the late 1960s is not unusual in its engagement with critical theory. Noteworthy are essays in the journal of urban sociology *Utopie* (*Utopia Deferred: Writings from "Utopie"* [2006]) treating Herbert Marcuse's meditations on repression in an affluent consumer society, Henri Lefebvre's sociology of the everyday through the myths of system and technique, and the emerging field of media studies. Baudrillard developed interests in urban and product design, as well as architecture, during his *Utopie* period, and these interests resurface in his return to architectural theory in dialogue with French practitioner Jean Nouvel in *The Singular Objects of Architecture* (1999).

The period from 1968 to 1976 was highly productive. The structuralism of *The System of Objects* (1996) took an aberrant turn by bringing forward the cultural backwash of the accessory, secondary meanings corresponding to speech, and the drift of objects toward the cultural system, away from their so-called objective, technical structuration and the stable determinations of language. This psycho-social reorientation of structuralism in the accommodation of the reflux of what would otherwise be considered external to the system allows Baudrillard to refigure consumption as an active process that confers social rank through the code of status provided by advertising, which is itself an object to be consumed. Objects dematerialized into signs are consumed and manipulated in their systematic differences with other signs, entailing the abolition of a lived, nonarbitrary, visceral human relationship with objects, from which these signs escape.

The analysis Baudrillard develops in *The System of Objects* is deepened in *Consumer Society* (1998), shedding its structuralist shell with a more pronounced return to Marxist theories of alienation and reification (see MARXIST THEORY AND CRITICISM), heavily augmented by German film and literary sources, especially doppelgänger fantasies that demonstrate capitalist mystifications and introduce how objects take revenge in an extreme fetishism, a reversal of the subject-object pole he later explores in *Fatal Strategies* (1983).

In *Consumer Society* the influence of anthropology begins to loom large in Baudrillard's thinking. His turn to so-called primitive societies of the gift, which were truly affluent, whose temporality was the rhythm of collective activity before time became money, and whose metabolic communion was not asepticized into cold, clinical communication, provides the groundwork for his theory of symbolic exchange. By contrast, consumer societies are characterized by a massive prophylactic deployment of signs that simultaneously conjure up—and away—the real so desperately evoked by all media.

In *For a Critique of the Political Economy of the Sign*, Baudrillard exposes the ideological dimension of use value, repository of the true idealism in Marxism, exposing it as an abstraction that is hidden under the cloak of immediacy and particularity and, despite Marx, already infused with equivalence. He shows that Roman Jakobson's poetic model of communication is perfused with metaphysical presumptions as a result of the terror of the code that privileges the sender over the receiver. The most important demonstration is the homology between the sign and commodity forms (exchange value is to signifier as use value is to signified) and the limited convertibility between logics of value (use value, exchange value, sign exchange value, and symbolic exchange). Symbolic exchange emerges as the heterogeneous other of homogeneous political economy and semiology and is subversive of both of these logics of value.

The themes of the critique of categories of political economy and the symbolic find their application in Baudrillard's reading of certain strains of Marxism in *The Mirror of Production*. The fatal malady of capitalism is its inability to reproduce itself symbolically, the relations of which it instead simulates; the failure of historical materialism is that it cannot escape the categories of political economy but instead holds up an insufficiently analyzed productivity and labor as the mirrors of all social activity. As an alternative, Baudrillard proffers symbolic exchange, an incessant agonistic cycle as well as the anti-utilitarian sumptuary destruction of goods (potlatch).

The two pillars of *Symbolic Exchange and Death* (1976) are named in its title. Baudrillard's radical anthropology attempts to recover death and use it as a symbolic countergift that compels modern institutions, which unilaterally give the gifts of work as a slow death, social security, and maternal ambiance of consumption, to receive and respond to in kind with their own deaths. Summoning the code or the system to receive the countergift makes it strange to itself, having been drawn into the symbolic field in which exchange is a circuit of giving, receiving, responding in kind and with interest. The failure to receive the countergift and repay in kind is loss of face—spirit, wealth, health, rank and power.

Simulacra and Simulation (1981) and *Simulations* (1983) contain Baudrillard's best-known theory of the order of simulacra:

Law	Form	Sign	Machine
1. natural	counterfeit	corrupt symbol	automaton
2. market	production	icon	robot
3. structural	simulation	two-sided psychical	android
4. fractal	proliferation	metonym/index	virtual

The first order of the counterfeit and theatrical automaton emerges in the Renaissance with the emancipation of otherwise static social rank (caste system). The second order of production arises with the Industrial Revolution and production, perfect for worker robots, and serial signs of sameness (iconic simulacra). The third order is postindustrial in which mechanical reproduction is transcended, conceived strictly in terms of reproducibility such that representation itself is commodified (genome hypothesis). In *The Transparency of Evil* (1990) Baudrillard adds a fourth level involving aleatory dispersion by infection, contiguity, and viral metonymy of theories of value, giving rise to the absorption of virtual media technologies (protheses) by human beings without shadows, a topic explored in *The Illusion of the End* (1992).

Baudrillard elaborates new forms of symbolic resistance by emphasizing the potlatch-like behaviors of the masses in *The Beaubourg Effect* (1977) and *In the Shadow of the Silent Majorities* (1978) and by drawing on an antiproductivist conception of agonistic, senseless, seduction in *Seduction* (1979), in addition to turning symbolic reversibility and cancelation against Michel Foucault in *Forget Foucault* (1977). He seeks symbolic yields in *Transparency of Evil* from an inexchangeable hostage form and the power to designate evil in order to reintroduce this accursed share into the artificially positive paradise of a society that can no longer tolerate negativity.

The Vital Illusion (2000) reveals traces of the need for a symbolic principle by another name by taking refuge in singularity (as in *Paroxysm* [1997], an eccentric, antagonistic, self-destructing, anomalous figure, irreducible to individuality) in a world of cloning, by valorizing imperfection (vernacular language resists universal digitization), and the beautiful frailty of never being fully present to ourselves. These antidotes to nihilism are perhaps best expressed in the idea that the murder of the real, the perfect crime—simulation of the world—of *The Perfect Crime* (1995), is never perfect. Respite is found in a passionate appreciation of the world's illusoriness. The circle of symbolic exchange threatens to collapse in *The Impossible Exchange* (1999), since now exchange is impossible, the general equivalent has been displaced, otherness becomes incomparable and the condition of thought is stuck in a paradoxical inability to confirm itself against any principle in the reigning speculative disorder.

Baudrillard's controversial response to the events of 11 September 2001 in *The Spirit of Terrorism* (2001) rehearses his theory of symbolic exchange: the suicide planes that embedded themselves in the twin towers of the World Trade Center are symbolic forces of disorder issuing countergifts of mass death against a system whose ideal is "zero death," as Baudrillard puts it, and that tries to neutralize the symbolic stakes of reversibility and challenge. What makes Baudrillard's short essay on 9/11 so controversial is the very thing that makes it stand out from the pack of intellectual pundits assaying the event: his excessive, poetic anthropology suggests that the challenge of the symbolic countergift obliges the global superpower, through its emblematic twin towers, to provide an appropriate acknowledgment. The towers collapsed by themselves as if responding in kind to the challenge of the suicide planes. The register in which this claim is made remains elusive.

GARY GENOSKO

Jean Baudrillard, *Amérique* (1986, America, trans. Chris Turner, 1988), *L'autre par lui-même: Habilitation* (1987, *The Ecstasy of Communication*, trans. Bernard and Caroline Schutze, 1988), *Cool Memories, 1980–1985* (1987, trans. Chris Turner, 1990), *Cool Memories II, 1987–90* (1990, trans. Chris Turner, 1996), *Cool Memories IV, 1995–2000* (2000, trans. Chris Turner, 2003), *Le crime parfait* (1995, *The Perfect Crime*, trans. Chris Turner, 1996), *De la séduction* (1979, Seduction, trans. Brian Singer, 1990), *L'échange impossible* (1999, *The Impossible Exchange*, trans. Chris Turner, 2001), *L'échange symbolique et la mort* (1976, Symbolic Exchange and Death, trans. Iain Hamilton Grant, 1993), *Écran total* (1997, *Screened Out*, trans. Chris Turner, 2002), *L'esprit du terrorisme* (2001, *The Spirit of Terrorism*, trans. Chris Turner, 2002), *Fragments: Cool Memories III, 1991–1996* (1995, trans. Emily Agar, 1997), *La gauche divine* (1985), *La guerre du golfe n'a pas eu lieu* (1991, *The Gulf War Did Not Take Place*, trans. Paul Patton, 1995), *L'illusion de la fin* (1992, *The Illusion of the End*, trans. Chris Turner, 1994), Jean Baudrillard: Photographies, 1985–1998 (2000), *Le miroir de la production* (1973, *The Mirror of Production*, trans. Mark Poster, 1975), *A l'ombre des majorités silencieuses* (1978, *In the Shadow of the Silent Majorities*, trans. Paul Foss, John Johnston, and Paul Patton, 1983), *Oublier Foucault* (1977, Forget Foucault, 1987), *Pour une critique de l'économie du signe* (1972, *For A Critique of the Political Economy of the Sign*, trans. Charles Levin, 1981), *Simulacres et simulations* (1981, Simulacra and Simulation, trans. Sheila Faria Glaser, 1994), Simulations (trans. Paul Foss, Paul Patton, and Philip Beitchman, 1983), *La société de consommation* (1970, *The Consumer Society*, trans. Chris Turner, 1998), *Les stratégies fatales* (1983, Fatal Strategies, trans. Philip Beitchman and W. G. J. Niesluchowski, 1990), *Le système des objets* (1968, *The System of Objects*, trans. James Benedict, 1996), *La transparence du mal* (1990, *The Transparency of Evil*, trans. James Benedict, 1993), *The Uncollected Baudrillard* (ed. Gary Genosko, 2001), *The Vital Illusion* (2000); Jean Baudrillard and Jean Nouvel, *Les objets singuliers: Y-a-t-il une vérité de l'architecture* (1999, *The Singular Objects of Architecture*, trans. Robert Bononno, 2002).

Beauvoir, Simone de

Simone de Beauvoir (1908–1986) was born in Paris and spent her childhood on the Boulevard Raspail and the Rue de Rennes. After attending the Cours Désir, and the Institut Sainte-Marie, she studied at the Sorbonne and, in 1929, became a candidate for the *agrégation de philosophie* alongside Claude Lévi-Strauss, Maurice Merleau-Ponty, and Jean-Paul Sartre. During this time, she began a lifelong love affair and partnership with Sartre. Together, the pair developed existentialism, a philosophy concerned with the exercise of human freedom in a world where existence has no transcendent purpose or essence to give it meaning.

Beauvoir and Sartre define a human as that being whose being is not to be. They clarify this paradox by distinguishing between "being-for-itself," which is conscious, and "being-in-itself," which is unconscious. Consciousness, they argue, implies a being other than itself that enables the for-itself to be at once a revelation, negation, desire, and choice of being only because it is *not* being. Although Beauvoir and Sartre both define humans in terms of what they lacked, Sartre is more pessimistic, emphasizing the "useless passion" and anguish of human beings.

Beauvoir finds in human lack the promise of imaginative possibilities. In *The Ethics of Ambiguity* (1947), she argues that humans must choose themselves as a lack and assume the responsibility of their ambiguous situation by rejecting authorities and absolutes and creating meaning through ethical acts. Denying that existentialism results in nihilism, Beauvoir declares that "if God does not exist, man's faults are inexpiable" (16). She forwards a model of here-and-now accountability in which humans must choose freedom as their chief end. Although she would later criticize *The Ethics of Ambiguity*, her reflections on morality in this work presage her subsequent efforts to understand structures of oppression. As cofounder and a principal editor of *Les temps modernes*, she shaped the political and cultural awareness of French intellectuals for more than forty years.

Beauvoir described herself as a literary rather than philosophical writer. Concerned with concrete experience, Beauvoir valued fiction as the mode of communication that most fully conveyed lived realities. In addition to her philosophical and autobiographical works, she wrote one play, two collections of short stories, and five novels, the most celebrated of which is *The Mandarins*, which won her the Prix Goncourt in 1954. Although Beauvoir did not write extensive literary theory, she reflects in "Literature and Metaphysics" (1946) on what it means for literature to be philosophical and on the relationship between the novel and metaphysics. Opposing philosophical literature on the grounds that a novel should not be reducible to abstract concepts or formulas, she argues that the meaning of a novel cannot be detached from it: in some respects, the meaning of a novel always exceeds and escapes its readers. Furthermore, meaning also escapes the author.

Yet, for Beauvoir, it is due to metaphysics that authors of philosophical novels should not begin with an a priori theory or formula. Importantly, metaphysics is *not* a system, but rather an attitude philosophers take by placing their total being up against the totality of the world. Beauvoir's emphasis on metaphysics as discoverable through lived experience reflects the debt existentialism owes to PHENOMENOL-OGY, a philosophy that stressed the observation of phenomena. This emphasis also underscores the existentialist idea that existence precedes essence and that the temporal and the historical are the matter from which meanings and essences are created. Thus, for Beauvoir, the temporal lived-through quality of literature is well suited to taking up the metaphysical process. The philosophical novel discovers the thickness, opacity, and rich ambiguity of the world.

Although Beauvoir contributed, in a limited way, to a theory of the philosophical novel, her continued relevance to literary theory lies in her trail-blazing study of the existential situation of women in *The Second Sex*. Here, Beauvoir argues that prevailing concepts of "the feminine" are not natural to women but instead imprison women and relegate them to a secondary status. Following G. W. F. Hegel's master-slave dialectic, Beauvoir shows how man defines woman as an "Other" who is relative and subordinate to him. She also examines women's complicity in accepting the status of objectified "Other" and argues that social, legal, and economic inequalities worked against women's ability to claim their position as autonomous subjects. Some have labeled Beauvoir's claim that "one is not born, but rather becomes, a woman" (267, Parshley trans.) as extreme, positing that her focus on the oppressive socialization of women denies any positive value to sexual difference. French literary theorists of the 1970s and 1980s, such as HÉLÈNE CIXOUS, LUCE IRIGARAY, and JULIA KRISTEVA, have argued instead that it is in women's difference that women may find the source of liberation from a phallocentric discourse.

In agreement with Beauvoir, however, some feminists have warned that the emphasis on woman's difference, either as an essentializing concept or as a political category, forestalls the dissolution of the binary oppositions between "men" and "women." Beauvoir's provocative notion that women have no natural essence challenges theorists to interrogate normative claims about women as the subject of feminism. By returning feminists to the question "what is a woman?" Beauvoir demonstrates that one cannot "be" a woman. As JUDITH BUTLER states in *Gender Trouble*, "If there is something right in Beauvoir's claim that one is not born, but rather *becomes* a woman, it follows that *woman* itself is a term in process, a becoming, a constructing that cannot rightfully be said to originate or end. As an ongoing discursive practice, it is open to intervention and resignification" (43).

Arguing that *The Second Sex* confounds efforts to place it in history or to present the truth of its history, Ruth Evans calls it a postmodern work that "produces the uncanny effect of belatedness that Freud called *Nachträglichkeit* (deferred action), as new events and new knowledge endow the text with 'untimely' meanings" (1). This anachronistic claim for postmodernity could apply to all of Simone de Beauvoir's works. Writing literature as philosophy, philosophy as autobiography, autobiography as cultural critique, Simone de Beauvoir evolved a style that resisted systems. By interrogating the self, contemporary theorists extend Beauvoir's insight that the personal is political while arguing that the self can also be a naturalized and regulating notion. As contemporary theorists explore the self that is "Beauvoir," they read across her works to create a personal genealogy of liberation (Toril Moi), or they read Beauvoir's self-representations against the "Beauvoir" narratives of others to chart just how restrictive the self can be (Nancy Fraser). Whether Beauvoir's becoming will be a legacy of freedom or a record of erasure, it will have been productive.

SUSAN R. CARLTON

Simone de Beauvoir, Le deuxième sexe (1949, The Second Sex, trans. H. M. Parshley, 1953, trans. Constance Borde and Sheila Malovany-Chevallier, 2009), "Littérature et métaphysique" (1946, L'existentialisme et la sagesse des nations, 1963), Les mandarins (1954, The Mandarins, trans. Leonard M. Friedman, 1956), Pour une morale de l'ambiguité (1947, The Ethics of Ambiguity, trans. Bernard Frechtman, 1948); Ruth Evans, ed., Simone de Beauvoir's The Second Sex: New Interdisciplinary Essays (1998).

Benjamin, Walter

A principal preoccupation of the theory and criticism of Walter Benjamin (1892–1940) is criticism itself. In its broadest sense critique means that nothing can simply be taken as given. Any text or artifact always demands something more, exceeds itself, in a movement that structures not only literature and culture but also history itself.

As early as his dissertation, "The Concept of Criticism in German Romanticism" (1920), Benjamin had explored the notion of critique as *Ergänzung* (fulfillment, completion), claiming with the Romantics, primarily Friedrich Schlegel, that critique was immanent to the movement of art itself and thus less something contingent to art than its necessary supplement. There would be no art without critique, not because critique has priority over art but because the artifact is itself, despite appearances, unfinished as well as already critical from the start. In an essay on Johann Wolfgang von Goethe's *Elective Affinities* (1922) that Hugo von Hofmannsthal called "epoch-making," Benjamin insists on the difference between critique and commentary, the former concerned with "truth content," the latter with "subject matter."

Benjamin investigates this enigmatic historicity of art and critique in a series of early essays on language, notably "On Language as Such and the Language of Man" (1916) and "The Task of the Translator" (1923). Translation, insofar as it is a relation between one language and another, exemplifies a mode of critique to the extent that it resists imitating the original and instead reveals what in that original cannot become fixed but remains in motion or incomplete (*Selected* 1:255–56). As in "Critique of Violence" (1921), Benjamin here suspends thinking in an economy of ends and means (the transmission of information for and between subjects) and tries instead to understand the sheer materiality—of language, historical survival, violence—that makes possible and renders permanently precarious the institutions of culture, politics, and economics.

The arcane corpus of German baroque drama, the *Trauerspiel*, furnishes the occasion for a more pointedly materialist but largely pre-Marxist criticism in *The Origin of the German Mourning Play* (1928). Rejected as a thesis by the University of Frankfurt, the text articulates a curiously Platonic epistemology of criticism with a reflection on the materiality of "things" and of language. Departing from the idealist promotion of the organic and totalizing symbol, Benjamin rehabilitated the discontinuous and arbitrary model of allegory, together with an enigmatic theory of critique as "mortification" (182).

During the composition of the *Trauerspiel* book, Benjamin began to engage Marxist theory and practice, primarily in a reading of Karl Marx and GEORG LUKÁCS. He met THEODOR W. ADORNO in 1923 and later became affiliated with the Institute for Social Research (the FRANKFURT SCHOOL), publishing some of his most important essays in its journal and becoming a member in 1935. He cultivated connections with agitprop theater and leftist intellectual culture generally, and in the winter of 1926–1927 he journeyed to Moscow, wondering whether he should join the Communist Party. This intense political engagement pushed Benjamin to new thinking about the relation of theory and critique, exemplified by his desire "to write a description of Moscow at the present moment in which 'all factuality is already theory'" (*Moscow Diary* 132).

A Jew born in Berlin, Benjamin studied Hebrew and considered leaving Germany to teach in Jerusalem but decided against it. Without academic employment, he wrote extensively for German newspapers and magazines well into the 1930s. He published reviews, autobiographical texts, literary studies, studies of cities, and hybrid works of social commentary and cultural theory, such as the aphoristic *One-Way Street* (1928). He was also constantly at work on the Arcades project, a vast assemblage of quotations and commentary on Paris, Charles Baudelaire, architecture, Marx, and commodity culture of the nineteenth century. This work, along with separate studies on Baudelaire and "Paris, Capital of the 19th Century" (*Arcades*), scrutinizes the new media of reproduction and representation and explores the implications of "technical reproducibility" in film and photography for an understanding of aesthetics in general and for the task of criticism. In "The Work of Art in the Age of Mechanical Reproduction" (1935) and "Eduard Fuchs, Collector and Historian" (1937) Benjamin demonstrates the necessity of reading aesthetics and politics together in a method derived from the dialectical materialism of Marx and Friedrich Engels and yet transformed by his own heterodox vision of history (in its suspicion of the myth of progress and its resistance to narrative) and his special attention to allegory as a structuring principle of language and history. In "The Work of Art in the Age of Mechanical Reproduction," Benjamin charts the "loss of aura" effected in high commodity culture, whereby the onset of the technical reproduction of the work of art on a mass scale, exemplified most spectacularly by film, signals a massive change from an older aesthetics of presence—aura being the sign of what is unique in time and space—and its attendant values of authenticity, creativity, and the like to a world of overdetermined reproductions now based primarily on politics, broadly understood and narrowly. If the aura entails the object's ability to look back at us, that amounts to a more benign, disappeared, or disappearing version of the commodity, after Marx's analysis, taking on a life of its own, which is itself the converse of the human being's becoming, via the relentless sway of commodity relations, something like a thing.

In these later works, including the unfinished Arcades project, Benjamin offers one of the most powerful examples of an engaged critique, joining close reading, informed historical study, and a philosophically rigorous thinking of representation and its technologies—articulations that remain one of the principal burdens for literary theory and criticism's future.

IAN BALFOUR AND THOMAS KEENAN

See also FRANKFURT SCHOOL and MARXIST THEORY AND CRITICISM.

Walter Benjamin, *Berliner Kindheit um neunzehnhundert* (1987, *Berlin Childhood around 1900*, trans. Howard Eiland, 2005), "Central Park" (trans. Lloyd Spencer with Mark Harrington, in Smith), *Charles Baudelaire: Ein Lyriker im Zeitalter des Hochkapitalismus* (1955, *Charles Baudelaire: A Lyric Poet in the Era of High Capitalism*, trans. Harry Zohn, 1973), *Einbahnstrasse* (1955, *One-Way Street and Other Writings*, trans. Edmund Jephcott and Kingsley Shorter, 1979), *Gesammelte Schriften* (ed. Rolf Tiedemann et al., 7 vols. to date, 1972–), *Illuminations* (ed. Hannah Arendt, trans. Harry Zohn, 1968), *Moskauer Tagebuch* (1980, *Moscow Diary*, ed. Gary Smith, trans. Richard Sieburth, 1986), "N (Theoretics of Knowledge; Theory of Progress)" (trans. Leigh Hafrey and Richard Sieburth, in Smith), *On Hashish* (trans. Howard Eiland et al., 2005), *Das Passagen-Werk* (ed. Rolf Tiedemann, 1982, *The Arcades Project*, trans. Howard Eiland and Kevin McLaughlin, 1999), *Reflections: Essays, Aphorisms, Autobiographical Writings* (ed. Peter Demetz, trans. Edmund Jephcott, 1978), *Selected Writings: 1913–1926* (ed. Marcus Bullock and Michael W. Jennings, 1996), *Selected Writings, 1927–1934* (ed. Michael W. Jennings, Howard Eiland, and Gary Smith, 1999), *Selected Writings, 1935–1938* (ed. Howard Eiland and Michael W. Jennings, 2002), *Selected Writings, 1938–1940* (ed. Howard Eiland and Michael W. Jennings, 2003), *Der Ursprung des deutschen Trauerspiels* (1928, ed. Rolf Tiedemann, 1963, *The Origin of German Tragic Drama*, trans. John Osborne, 1977), *Versuche über Brecht* (1966, *Understanding Brecht*, trans. Anna Bostock, 1973), *Walter Benjamins Archive: Bilder, Texte und Seichen* (2006, *Walter Benjamin's Archive: Images, Texts, Signs*, ed. Ursula Marx et al., trans. Esther Leslie, 2007), *The Work of Art in the Age of Its Technological Reproducibility, and Other Writings on Media* (ed. Michael W. Jennings, Brigid Doherty, and Thomas Y. Levin, trans. Edmund Jephcott et al., 2008), *The Writer of Modern Life: Essays on Charles Baudelaire* (2006, ed. Michael W. Jennings 2006); Gary Smith, ed., *On Walter Benjamin* (1988), "Thinking through Benjamin" (Smith).

Bhabha, Homi K.

Homi K. Bhabha (b. 1949) has become one of the highest-profile figures within POST-COLONIAL STUDIES. Brought up and educated in India, he migrated from Bombay to England in the early 1970s where he received a DPhil in English literature from Oxford University in 1990. After lecturing at the University of Sussex, Bhabha moved to the University of Chicago and then, in 2001, to Harvard University. His influence is out of proportion to the volume of his published work. His only single-authored text to date is *The Location of Culture* (1994), a collection of mostly previously published essays, sometimes heavily rewritten. While he began his career as a critic of literary forms of "colonial discourse," Bhabha has since become one of the most cited theoreticians of diasporic culture, of contemporary "multiculturalisms" in the West, and a respected commentator on postcolonial visual culture.

During the 1980s, Bhabha's work was distinctive for its challenge to the accounts of colonial relations provided by FRANTZ FANON's *Wretched of the Earth* (1961) and EDWARD W. SAID's *Orientalism* (1978). Bhabha argued that the tensions, contradictions, and polarities that *Orientalism* detects in colonial relations were in the end illegitimately resolved by Said's insistence on the unidirectionality and intentionality of colonial knowledge as will to power. Meanwhile, he suggested that Fanon's later work relied too much on psychically and phenomenologically fixed models of colonial identity. For Bhabha, such models problematically replicate the Manichean divisions between colonizer and colonized on which imperial discourse itself relied.

Bhabha's conception of the colonial relationship is more complex and ambiguous than that of his predecessors, primarily because of his insistence on the contradictory play of psychic affect and identification between colonizer and colonized. In this respect, his main methodological source is JACQUES LACAN, whose radical revisions of Freudian models of identity formation are echoed in one of Bhabha's foundational premises, namely, that "identity is only ever possible in the *negation* of any sense of originality or plenitude, through the principle of displacement and differentiation . . . that always renders it a liminal reality" ("Remembering" xvii–xviii). The application of Lacanian theory to analysis of colonial relations had been anticipated in Fanon's *Black Skin, White Masks* (1952), whose lead Bhabha follows in focusing on the intersubjective realm of relations between colonizer and colonized, which is conceived in hybrid and dynamic rather than binary and static terms. Bhabha argues that while psychic "ambivalence" on the part of both "partners" in the colonial relationship suggests an important degree of complicity between them, it also opens up unexpected and hitherto insufficiently recognized ways through which colonial power is circumvented by the native. Thus he argues that not only can the colonized subject return—and consequently (at least potentially) directly challenge—the colonizer's disciplinary "gaze" but he or she can also refuse to return that "gaze." Such a refusal to satisfy the colonizer's "narrative demand" for "recognition" suggests to Bhabha how psychic resistance can be politically effective (*Location* 98ff.).

For Bhabha, colonial power is immanently liable to destabilization, or what might be termed "resistance from within," for three principal reasons. First, following MICHEL FOUCAULT's *History of Sexuality* (1976), Bhabha suggests that colonial authority, like all forms of power, in Foucault's words, "unintentionally" incites "refusal, blockage, and invalidation" in its attempts at surveillance and can thus never completely fulfill its project of control (11). Second, following Lacan's *Four Fundamental Concepts of Psychoanalysis* (1973), Bhabha suggests that the "gaze" of colonial authority is always troubled by the fact that colonial identity is partly dependent for its constitution on a colonized Other and therefore can never be fully self-present. Both kinds of destabilization are further explored in Bhabha's discussion of "mimicry" and "hybridization," at least insofar as these are understood as colonial strategies that attempt to consolidate power by inducing colonized subjects to imitate the forms and values of the dominant culture. For Bhabha, such strategies can never fully succeed because they also always require the subordinate to remain at least partially different from the dominant in order to preserve the structures of discrimination on which the latter's power is based. Finally, following JACQUES DERRIDA's *Writing and Difference* (1967), Bhabha asserts that "immanent" resistance derives in part from the vicissitudes to which all language, including the language of power, are intrinsically liable, through the play of "repetition" and the structure of *différance*.

Since the beginning of the 1990s Bhabha has devoted himself primarily to the legacies of colonial history, and to the analysis of traditional discourses of race, nation, and ethnicity, in contemporary intercultural relations in the post- or neocolonial era (see RACE AND ETHNICITY). Bhabha's work preoccupies itself with questions of cultural exchange and identification determined by the contiguity of cultures (characteristically from the former colonial "peripheries") sharing the same (usually metropolitan) space within the former *imperium* and by relations of ostensible, if often illusory, equality. While at times conceptualizing modernity as a continuing, unfinished project through which new sites, times, and kinds of enunciation are made possible for the formerly colonized, Bhabha scrupulously avoids reinscribing it teleologically, as a progression toward a synthesis or sublation of historical and cultural differences and tensions. Bhabha proposes instead a conception of "cultural difference" that respects and preserves the peculiar and multiple histories and identities of the historically marginalized. "Cultural difference" is not, however, to be understood simply as that which resists the effort of one culture to "integrate" or "translate" another; he stresses that the relationship of postcolonial or migrant experience to the dominant culture of the "host" society is not simply antagonistic. For this reason he strongly opposes what he calls the doctrine of "cultural diversity," which, as in the regime of apartheid, seeks to inscribe absolute, ontologically grounded relations of difference between cultures. Equally, Bhabha seeks to "revise those nationalist or 'nativist' pedagogies that set up the relation of Third World and First World in a binary structure of opposition" (173).

Productive though Bhabha's work has undoubtedly proved, both phases of his career have excited considerable criticism. Bhabha has been accused of undervaluing material forms of resistance to colonial rule and even of implying that the (postcolonial) critic who unpicks the symbolic and narrative ordering of the hegemonic order is the privileged locus of opposition to the dominant. Bhabha's reliance on psychoanalytic theory raises other difficult questions. First, he does not really consider that psychoanalysis may be a specifically "First World" form of knowledge that may not be unproblematically translatable to analysis of (post)colonial problematics. Second, Bhabha has been accused of illegitimately conflating the psychic identities of the colonizer and colonized to produce a unitary model of the colonial subject that discounts the crucial material differences in their situations. Finally, while Bhabha claims to "provide a form of the writing of cultural difference in the midst of modernity that is inimical to binary boundaries" (*Location* 251), his key concepts often rely on the very structures he is trying to undermine for their effectivity. "Hybridity," for example, obviously depends upon a presumption of the existence of its opposite for its force. The danger is that the "hybrid" may itself become essentialized or fixed as the exclusive property of postcolonialism. In fact, Bhabha characteristically presents the "non-hybrid," notably Western (neo)colonialism and Third World nationalism, in largely unitary terms that do not do justice to their manifest internal contradictions and differentiated histories. For all these objections, the extraordinary degree to which Bhabha's work has been cited attests to the undoubted significance of his interventions in the field of postcolonial studies.

BART MOORE-GILBERT

See also MULTICULTURALISM and POSTCOLONIAL STUDIES.

Homi K. Bhabha, "Anish Kapoor: Making Emptiness," *Anish Kapoor* (by Anish Kapoor, 1998), "Anxious Nations: Nervous States," *Supposing the Subject* (ed. Joan Copjec, 1994), "Cosmopolitanisms," *Public Culture* 12 (2000), "Day by Day . . . with Frantz Fanon," *The Fact of Blackness: Frantz Fanon and Visual Representation* (ed. Alan Read, 1996), *The Location of Culture* (1994), "On Cultural Choice," *The Turn to Ethics* (ed. Marjorie Garber et al., 2000), "On the Irremovable Strangeness of Being Different," *PMLA* 113 (1998), "The Other Question: Difference, Discrimination, and the Discourse of Colonialism," *The Politics of Theory* (ed. Francis Barker et al., 1983), "Remembering Fanon," foreword to Frantz Fanon, *Black Skin, White Masks* (1986), "Representation and the Colonial Text," *The Theory of Reading* (ed. Frank Gloversmith, 1984), "The Third Space," *Identity: Community, Culture, Difference* (ed. Jonathon Rutherford, 1990), "The White Stuff," *Artforum* 36 (1998); Homi K. Bhabha, ed., *Nation and Narration* (1990); Michel Foucault, *History of Sexuality*, vol. 1 (1976).

Blanchot, Maurice

The fiction and philosophical-literary essays of Maurice Blanchot (1907–2003) form one of the most influential and elusive oeuvres in modern French letters. He was born in Quain, a village in Burgundy, in 1907, and studied at Strasbourg, where he met and befriended the future philosopher of ethics, EMMANUEL LEVINAS. During the war years he formed an important friendship with GEORGES BATAILLE and may have very nearly been shot by a German squadron near the end of the war, if one takes as biographical his *The Instant of My Death* (1994). In the 1930s he contributed articles to right-wing journals, most notably to the Maurassian periodical *Combat*; during the occupation his political views changed radically, and after the end of the war he became a disembodied but unambiguous presence on the left: he was a cosigner of the "Declaration of the 121" (1960), a call to resist French intervention in Algeria, and an active member of the Comité d'Action Étudiants-Écrivains during the student and working-class protests of May 1968. Blanchot's political turn coincided with the inauguration of a literary project that was to help shape French literary modernity. His novels and *récits* (*Thomas the Obscure* [1941]; *Aminadab* [1942]; *Death Sentence* [1948]) are significant contributions to twentieth-century French literature; meanwhile, his review of Jean Paulhan's *The Flowers of Tarbes*, "How Is Literature Possible?" (1941), opened theoretical questions that achieved definitive formulation a few years later in "Literature and the Right to Death" (1949) and in the collection of essays bearing the title *The Space of Literature* (1955).

The topical book review served as the vehicle for Blanchot's thought throughout most of his career, and his late work has explored other genres evocative of contingency or incompletion: the fragment in *The Writing of the Disaster* (1980) and gestures of dialogue or commemoration in *The Unavowable Community* (1983) and "Michel Foucault as I Imagine Him" (1986). Blanchot's loyalty to occasional forms is consonant with his understanding of "literary space," as is his double engagement with fiction and criticism—a difference that his oeuvre at once maintains and subverts: the fictions are "philosophical" and the essays possess a "literary" quality. Literary space, for Blanchot, is the locus of an anonymous, unmasterable, unspeakable experience, and his patient attention to this experience imparts to his own writing a curious difficulty.

Blanchot's work frequently takes the form of a meditation inspired by one of a select number of exemplary writers (Friedrich Hölderlin, Franz Kafka, Stéphane Mallarmé, Rainer Maria Rilke, the Marquise de Sade) and often articulates itself thematically as a critique of dialectical and existential thought. His work, particularly through the 1950s, resembles that of a number of Alexandre Kojève's "auditeurs assidus" (GEORGES BATAILLE, JACQUES LACAN, Raymond Queneau) in the intensity with which it examines a relatively narrow spectrum of Hegelian themes and metaphors: work, death, consciousness, history. For Hegel—particularly as mediated by Kojève—humans and consciousness come into being as action, with action defined as an essentially positive power of negation. The negation of natural desire (i.e., the willingness to risk death) produces humans as self-consciousness, the negation of particularity produces the concept, and so forth. Blanchot intervenes at the level of the dialectical mechanism itself, suggesting that the positivity of negation conceals a fundamental neutrality and passivity. Death, the engine of the dialectic, harbors a more absolute death; action masks a more radical passivity. The approach of "literary space" registers the proximity of this irrecuperable death (Blanchot's terms vary: other metaphors that characterize literary space include "the neutral," "desoeuvrement," "the outside," "essential solitude," and "the other night"). Literature, in its ontological inessentiality, cannot be mastered by a concept or a desire; literature names the unthinkable burden of what Blanchot in a counter-Heideggerian formulation calls "the very being of . . . concealment: dissimulation itself" (The Space of Literature 253). To write is to submit to an inexhaustible exhaustion, an endless dissolution of the "I" that cannot even be known as such: the writer betrays the literary experience in remaining true to it, producing an oeuvre by remaining blind to its necessary failure. The oeuvre, similarly, dissimulates as aesthetic unity its essential specificity, contingency, and incompletion.

Blanchot's later work has tended to shift its focus from literature to ethics and politics, though it is important to stress that for Blanchot the question of literature, as formulated in the great essays of the 1940s and 1950s, already involved questions of communication and community. In a late text, when Blanchot describes "dissimulation" as an "effect of disaster" (The Writing of the Disaster 6), he displaces a privileged term but retains the logic of its formulation. The extermination camps are the disaster of history: they are the realized nightmare of an aesthetic and utilitarian ideology that, unwilling to confront its own impossibility, transforms this impossibility into horror. In response, Blanchot pursues the elusive ontologies of friendship, conversation, and community: intersubjective themes that repeat, in a text like The Unavowable Community, some of the characteristic detours of the "literary" experience. The community, like literary space, is "unavowable" and impossible, founded on the anonymity of an endless, impersonal death rather than on the redemptive generality of Hegelian negation or Christian sacrifice. The possibility of ethics, meanwhile, turns out to reside not merely in the self's recognition of the other, but in the self's being "put into question by the other to the point of not being able to respond except by a limitless responsibility" (The Unavowable Community 73).

Blanchot's importance for a certain element in contemporary criticism would be hard to overestimate but is also hard to assess. Though his essays are in many ways foreign to the academic institution and its discourses, few critics writing at the intersection of philosophy and criticism in postwar France have failed to pay homage to Blanchot, and if anything his oeuvre has struck many serious commentators as being uncannily, disempoweringly infectious. Critics as different as Jean Starobinski and MICHEL FOUCAULT have remarked on their inability to move from paraphrase or repetition to a genuine exegesis of Blanchot's work. The careful circularity with which JACQUES DERRIDA and post-Heideggerian philosophers such as Philippe Lacoue-Labarthe and JEAN-LUC NANCY approach his oeuvre constitutes a similar, more elaborate act of homage.

MARC REDFIELD

Maurice Blanchot, *The Blanchot Reader* (1995, ed. Michael Holland), *La communauté inavouable* (1983, *The Unavowable Community*, trans. Pierre Joris, 1988), *L'écriture du désastre* (1980, *The Writing of the Disaster*, trans. Ann Smock, 1986), *L'entretien infini* (1969, *The Infinite Conversation*, trans. Susan Hanson, 1993), *L'espace littéraire* (1955, *The Space of Literature*, trans. Ann Smock, 1982), *The Gaze of Orpheus and Other Literary Essays* (1981, ed. P. Adams Sitney, trans. Lydia Davis), *L'instant de ma mort* (1994, *The Instant of My Death*, trans. Elizabeth Rottenberg, 1998), *The Siren's Song: Selected Essays of Maurice Blanchot* (1982, ed. Gabriel Josipovici, trans. Sacha Rabinovitch).

Bourdieu, Pierre

Pierre Bourdieu (1930–2002) worked in and influenced a remarkably broad range of disciplines, including philosophy, anthropology, education, sociology, and politics, as well as literary and cultural theory. Bourdieu was a sociologist of culture, but he in no way reduced culture to society. Rather, he was interested in the ways in which social struggles are played out in the apparently disinterested realms of, for instance, an art gallery, an opinion poll, a literary salon, or an academic journal. He insisted that critics are always invested in struggles and should take account of their investments accordingly. In short, Bourdieu's importance for theory and criticism rests above all on his reconfiguration of theories of culture and power and on his injunctions to critical self-reflexivity.

Bourdieu's theoretical positions undoubtedly owe something to a series of geographical and social displacements. He was born and brought up in a rural community in southwestern France and studied philosophy at the prestigious École Normale Supérieure in Paris (like Louis Althusser, he was a student of Georges Canguilhem). After a brief period as a secondary-school teacher, he was drafted into military service and saw the effects of the Algerian War of Independence firsthand. He stayed on in Africa as an anthropologist and conducted fieldwork among Algeria's various indigenous populations, particularly the Kabyles, before returning to Paris in 1960.

From the beginning, Bourdieu's work concerned itself with the contradictory unity and interdependence of apparently very distinct domains of experience. Bourdieu's first published book was The Algerians (1958), followed, upon his return to France, by Work and Workers in Algeria (1963) and The Uprooting (1964, coauthored with Abdelmalek Sayad). Though he would soon turn to the sociological dilemmas of contemporary France, which would occupy him for the rest of his career, Algeria remained a presence within his work, as counterpoint, complement, or confirmation, for at least the next two decades. The Kabylia became Bourdieu's explicit focus once more in his Outline of a Theory of Practice (1972) and The Logic of Practice (1980), and played a significant part in his later turn to questions of gender in Masculine Domination (1998). Through his description and theorization of Kabyle society, Bourdieu offers an ambitious critique both of structuralist anthropology (typified by Claude Lévi-Strauss) and the existentialist philosophy of Jean-Paul Sartre. Claiming to go beyond the traditional dichotomy between structure and agency, or between objective conditions and subjective self-determination, Bourdieu draws attention to the role of time, the interval between condition and action that allows for differential strategies to emerge. In societies in which a monetary economy is not dominant, the exchange of gifts often secures services or goods and thereby defines and secures social relations. Whereas Mauss had emphasized the subjective experience of gift giving (as a voluntary expression of a social relation) and Lévi-Strauss had stressed its structural reciprocity, Bourdieu intervenes by pointing out that a gift given in return is always delayed, and it is due to this delay that the gift giving is experienced as free. Though a gift must be reciprocated, this reciprocation takes place in due time and perhaps in a different location. But herein lies the (social) artistry: the whole exchange depends on timing, on the counter-gift's coming neither too soon nor too late, for fear of making explicit the otherwise implicit unarticulated rules of social interaction.

In modern, Western societies, according to Bourdieu, the field of culture likewise operates according to a disguised logic of deferred interest. The "market of symbolic goods" assigns cultural value to those works, and those authors, that defer immediate returns: "high" art is differentiated from "low" culture by the former's distance from, and apparent denial of, temporal rewards. In *The Rules of Art* (1992), Bourdieu's most sustained examination of literature, he shows how the novelist Gustave Flaubert, among other late nineteenth-century writers, sought to constitute a literary field whose autonomy was defined by its "rupture with the economic order" (121). A chiasmic pattern is established: those who have symbolic power or cultural status reject economic reward—and accumulate cultural status as a result—while those whose production is more attuned to economic profit find that their cultural standing slips accordingly. To emphasize that cultural autonomy inevitably has its limits and, more importantly, that cultural status can be converted into financial rewards and vice versa (albeit neither automatically nor immediately), Bourdieu designates the medium of cultural and economic valorization with the same word: they are both forms of "capital," respectively cultural or financial.

The concept of "cultural capital," which has attracted more attention from literary critics and theorists than any other concept introduced by Bourdieu, allows new ways of discussing high and low or "elite" and "mass" cultures without prioritizing either—in other words, it prevents both elitist defenses of high culture and populist celebrations of low culture. The opposition between high and low within the field of culture replicates, or is homologous to, a wider opposition that pits the holders of cultural capital against the holders of financial capital. The latter are, overall, dominant; however, the former are also considered part of the dominant class but constitute its dominated fraction. This antagonism often leads the dominated fraction of the dominant class—teachers, professors, artists, intellectuals—to ally themselves with the dominated class and thereby to articulate a distinction between forms of capital in ideological terms. However, Bourdieu insists that rather than taking either aesthetic or ideological statements on their own terms, we should look first at the composition and forms of capital structuring a given field and then at the competition between agents aiming to secure or maintain their capital. For Bourdieu, modern society is composed of a series of more or less autonomous fields, and each field displays its own strategies for consecration or dissent. Bourdieu often uses metaphors or analogies drawn from sports to describe the conflicts that structure each of these fields, arguing, for instance, that there is a difference between the explicit rules operative in a particular social space and the internalized, implicit rules that determine the better player in any given contest. Participants tend to internalize and embody these rules—what Bourdieu terms a "habitus," which operates beneath the level of ideology—such that the difference between subjectivity and objectivity as social agents play the game of culture is as ineffable as the question of whether a skilled player follows or controls the ball in a game of tennis.

Among literary critics and theorists, Bourdieu's most widely read work is *Distinction* (1979), which maps out the division between the holders of cultural and financial capital and outlines the distinctive (class) habituses that embody different dispositions toward culture. Holders of cultural capital, according to Bourdieu, embody an aestheticizing disposition that emphasizes (apparent) disinterest by subordinating function to form: they "introduce a distance, a gap . . . by displacing the interest from the 'content,' characters, plot, etc., to the form, to the specifically artistic effects which are only appreciated relationally, through a comparison with other works which is incompatible with immersion in the singularity with the work immediately given" (*Distinction* 34). They tend to prefer abstraction and formal complexity to the realism or romanticism of bourgeois and mass market culture. However, the most salient distinction made by Bourdieu is that between the *dominant* class and a *dominated* class that does not have the luxury of such distance from a world full of real needs and real exigencies. On these grounds, Bourdieu conducts an assault on the Kantian aesthetic and its radical separation of the "beautiful" from the "useful." Immanuel Kant's notion of "pure" taste confuses the social relationship that, ironically, the notion itself institutes in distinguishing between those who can afford to defer social interest and those who cannot. Aesthetic "disinterest," however, is anything but: it is a reflex of a horror of the masses, "nothing other than a refusal, a disgust—a disgust for objects which impose enjoyment and a disgust for the crude, vulgar taste which revels in this imposed enjoyment" (*Distinction* 486). It is on similar grounds that Bourdieu also criticizes the work of JACQUES DERRIDA and, by implication, poststructuralism more generally. In the 1990s, Bourdieu became associated with the so-called antiglobalization movement, wielding his by then significant academic and social standing to voice concerns about the impact of the United States on European political and cultural traditions. At a time when political engagement was unfashionable, Bourdieu was more political than ever (*Acts of Resistance* [1998]).

While Bourdieu is often criticized for his supposed "hyperfunctionalism," it would be more accurate to understand his work as premised on social change, on the emergence of new fields, and on the diverse and changing strategies that specific agents employ to maintain, convert, or exploit their reserves of cultural or financial capital. Bourdieu describes cultural fields in terms of a perpetual and multivalent agonism, as agents play the game of cultural distinction and capital accumulation in conditions that are always subtly different from the conditions under which agents' habituses were formed. The expectations generated (and frustrated) by this "hypostasis" of habitus set the scene for more generalized social conflict and unrest: most notably, for Bourdieu, the events of May 1968 should be understood in terms of an expanding educational system's inability to reciprocate the investments of upwardly mobile students. However, this notion of cultural conflict rarely conforms to the simpler class antagonism that other social critics may discern; indeed, it may seem frustrating in that the essence of the game is that the goalposts keep moving.

The theoretical tools that Bourdieu provides—concepts such as "field," "symbolic power," "cultural capital," "habitus" and its "hypostasis," and so on—are immensely powerful and flexible. His approach to the dichotomy between structure and agency, as well as the associated injunction that critics must also situate themselves as interested players in the game of cultural distinction, are invaluable contributions to problems that have bedeviled literary and cultural theory. At the same time, Bourdieu's work can be peculiarly dogmatic and strangely underdetermined, and it is thus unclear what a Bourdieuian reading of a specific text would entail. Yet insofar as such problematics can be analyzed fruitfully with tools that Bourdieu himself gives us, this is simply to say that there is room for a "Bourdieu beyond Bourdieu."

JON BEASLEY-MURRAY

Pierre Bourdieu, Contre-feux (1998, Acts of Resistance, trans. Richard Nice, 1999), La distinction: Critique sociale du jugement (1979, Distinction: A Social Critique of the Judgement of Taste, trans. Richard Nice, 1987), La domination masculine (1998, Masculine Domination, trans. Richard Nice, 2001), Esquisse d'une théorie de la pratique (1972, Outline of a Theory of Practice, trans. Richard Nice, 1977), The Field of Cultural Production: Essays on Art and Literature (1993), Homo academicus (1984, Homo Academicus, trans. Peter Collier, 1988), Meditations pascaliennes (1997, Pascalian Meditations, trans. Richard Nice, 2000), Raisons pratiques: Sur la theorie de l'action (1994 Practical Reason: On the Theory of Action 1998), Les règles de l'art (1992, The Rules of Art, trans. Susan Emanuel, 1996), Le sens pratique (1980, The Logic of Practice, trans. Richard Nice, 1990), Sociologie de l'Algérie (1958, The Algerians, trans. Alan C. M. Ross, 1962), Sur la télévision (1996, On Television, trans. Priscilla Parkhurst Ferguson, 1999); Pierre Bourdieu, ed., La misère du monde (1993, The Weight of the World, trans. Priscilla Parkhurst Ferguson et al., 1999); Pierre Bourdieu and Alain Darbel, L'amour de l'art, les musées d'art et leur public (1966, 2nd ed., 1969, The Love of Art, trans. Caroline Beattie and Nick Merriman, 1990), Travail et travailleurs en Algérie (1963); Pierre Bourdieu and Jean-Claude Passeron, Les héritiers (1966, The Inheritors, trans. Richard Nice, 1979), La reproduction: Eléments pour une théorie du système d'enseignement (1970, Reproduction in Education, Society, and Culture, trans. Richard Nice, 1977); Pierre Bourdieu and Abdelmalek Sayad, Le déracinement (1964).

Butler, Judith

Judith Butler (b. 1956) holds the Maxine Elliot Chair in the Rhetoric and Comparative Literature Departments at the University of California, Berkeley. Her work has had its primary impact on literary theory and criticism in its offering the means to rethink the identity categories that are so crucial to contemporary literature and literary criticism. In the late 1980s, those studying minorities in the humanities found themselves mired in an unproductive essentialism/social constructionism debate: are gender and racial identities innate, or are they socially constructed? The appearance of *Gender Trouble* in 1990 decisively changed the terms of these debates in the humanities by introducing the concept of "performative" identity—an identity that is neither simply determined by essentialist categories nor simply volunteristic ("socially constructed").

Within the discipline of literary criticism, by far and away the concept most readily identified with Butler's work is the "performativity" of identity, first introduced in *Gender Trouble* by way of a quotation from Friedrich Nietzsche's *Genealogy of Morals*: "There is no 'being' behind doing, acting, becoming: the 'doer' has simply been added to the deed by the imagination—the doing is everything" (178–79). Much of Butler's written work is devoted to explaining, refining and extending this notion of performativity and correcting misreadings that surround it. As Butler writes in *Bodies that Matter* (1993), if she were arguing that gender simply was a kind of theatrical performance, "that could mean that I thought that one woke in the morning, perused the closet or some more open space for the gender of choice, donned that gender for the day, and then restored the garment to its place at night" (x). But as Butler makes clear time and again throughout her work, "the reduction of performativity to performance . . . would be a mistake" (234).

Drawing widely from Nietzsche, MICHEL FOUCAULT on discursive formation, J. L. Austin and JACQUES DERRIDA on speech act theory and iterability, Louis Althusser on interpellation, JACQUES LACAN on subjective foreclosure, and EVE KOSOFSKY SEDGWICK's work on queer performativity, Butler fashions a notion of performative identity that "must be understood not as a singular or deliberate 'act,' but, rather, as the reiterative and citational practice by which discourse produces the effects that it names" (2; see QUEER THEORY AND CRITICISM). According to Butler, because the subject is the product of specific constraining normative frames, it cannot simply choose its gender as actors pick parts in plays. At the same time, because these compulsory normative frames never merely determine a subject without simultaneously opening spaces of resistance (in other words, because interpellation sometimes fails), agency is made possible and efficacious precisely because of and within these frames. "If there is agency," Butler writes, "it is to be found, paradoxically, in the possibilities opened up by that constrained appropriation of the regulatory law, by the materialization of that law, the compulsory appropriation and identification with those normative demands . . . [and] this act is not primarily theatrical" (12). The subject, in other words, is itself a product of interpellating codes, and hence it cannot enforce a critical distance between itself and these codes. If there is to be subversion of identities, it must be subversion from within.

Butler's theoretical apparatus is specifically constructed out of a consideration of the binary, male-female category of "sex" as it is understood within the normative frames of compulsory heterosexuality. Biological notions of "sex," Butler argues, are themselves performative or citational practices, which suggests that the discourse of essentialism is always already social. As Butler's reading of speech act theory shows, performatives pretend to found a situation that they merely cite: although the judge's "I now pronounce you man and wife" or the midwife's "It's a girl" may seem to be the "legal incarnation of the divine utterance," on further examination, these speech acts turn out to be "a form of cultural iterability." Such performatives are the iteration of an interpellating code rather than the metaphysical founding of a wholly new state. A subject is, then, always cited into an identity, but, in what is only a seeming paradox, it is precisely the necessity of repeating these interpellating citational codes—of identifying oneself before the law—that offers possibilities for subverting or rearticulating identity, the possibility of repeating them with a difference: for instance, "I now pronounce man as wife" or "It's a lesbian."

Butler's work on performativity has been particularly crucial in recent political criticism and its project of rethinking of so-called identity politics. While collective identification under common-cause signifiers ("woman," "queer," "African-American") is crucial for the project of recognition within a conflicted democracy, Butler argues that "the persistence of disidentification is equally crucial to the rearticulation of democratic contestation" (4). Butler's work emphasizes the importance of a kind of double movement: the necessity of identification coupled with the necessity that this identificatory movement be open to reinscription. Crucial to feminist and queer body politics is the multiplicity of sites of identification. As she writes, "One might be tempted to say that identity categories are insufficient because every subject position is the site of converging relations of power that are not univocal. But such a formulation underestimates the radical challenge to the subject that such converging relations imply" (230). This radical challenge to any essentialist notion of subjectivity is the important ethico-political legacy of Butler's scholarship and informs other of her works, including *Excitable Speech: A Politics of the Performative* (1997), *The Psychic Life of Power* (1997), and *Antigone* (2000). Within the broad coordinates of the themes and concepts that have animated her work throughout her career, in recent books such as *Undoing Gender* (2004), *Giving an Account of Oneself* (2005), and *Frames of War: When Is Life Grievable?* (2009), Butler continues to make major contributions to debates and discussions in literary and cultural theory.

JEFFREY T. NEALON

Judith Butler, Antigone's Claim: Kinship between Life and Death (2000), Bodies That Matter: On the Discursive Limits of "Sex" (1993), Excitable Speech: A Politics of the Performative (1997), Frames of War: When Is Life Grievable? (2009), Gender Trouble: Feminism and the Subversion of Identity (1990, anniv. ed. 1999), Giving an Account of Oneself (2005), The Judith Butler Reader (ed. Sara Salih, 2004), Precarious Life: Powers of Mourning and Violence (2004), The Psychic Life of Power: Theories in Subjection (1997), "Recovery and Invention: The Projects of Desire in Hegel, Kojève, Hyppolite, and Sartre" (PhD diss., 1984), Subjects of Desire: Hegelian Reflections in Twentieth-Century France (1987, new intro. 1999), Undoing Gender (2004); Judith Butler, Ernesto Laclau, and Slavoj Žižek, Contingency, Hegemony, Universality: Contemporary Dialogues on the Left (2000); Judith Butler and Joan W. Scott, eds., Feminists Theorize the Political (1992); Judith Butler and Gayatri Chakravorty Spivak, Who Sings the Nation-State? Language, Politics, Belonging (2007); Friedrich Nietzsche, On the Genealogy of Morals (1956, trans. Francis Golffing).

Certeau, Michel de

Michel de Certeau (1925–1986) worked across a wide range of academic and sociocultural terrains. Principally a cultural historian specializing in religious history, the historiography of colonial encounters, and the philosophy of history, he also wrote commentaries on contemporary life and participated in a number of European cultural policy initiatives. Plurality will provide a key to understanding Certeau's "heterological" practice (*Heterologies* 67–79). Heterology—the science of otherness, attention to what has been remaindered when categories have been named, established, and policed—is premised on the understanding that "plurality is originary" and unmanageable (*Practice* 133).

In a number of essays, particularly those collected in *The Writing of History* and *Heterologies*, Certeau focuses on texts' operations and performances (an approach partly indebted to Ludwig Wittgenstein, who insists that meaning derives from the use of language rather than from any inherent qualities within language). Certeau treats the writing of history, for instance, as a rhetorical operation that strives to make its rhetorical performance invisible. Rhetorical strategies are used to persuade the reader of the account's authenticity and to mask the constructedness of the written account. Written history also carries an authority tied to the institutional places from which it emerges (universities, for instance). Certeau sees the writing of culture, in the form of historiography, ethnology, and so on, as an activity that seeks to manage the wayward plurality—the living actuality—of culture within a series of institutional practices that both contain it and, necessarily, eradicate it. The institutional writing of culture authoritatively instills meaning by displacing culture's unmanageable, wayward plurality and replacing it with a writing animated by the institution's own desires and anxieties. Certeau's reading of ethnological accounts of the "New World" in the sixteenth century make this process particularly vivid.

From 1964 to its dissolution in 1981, Certeau was a member of the Lacanian École Freudienne de Paris. Psychoanalysis is an implicit resource in the majority of Certeau's work, made most explicit in his works on religious history, *The Possession at Loudun* (1970) and *The Mystic Fable* (1982). For both psychoanalysis and Certeau, repression always establishes the possibility of a return of the repressed. For Certeau, such returns are to be found as textual traces that cannot be managed within the economy of the text and that point to culture's unmanageable actuality (e.g., the endless variety of everyday practices). Certeau's psychoanalytic orientation is not geared toward psychopathology (the diagnosis of neurosis, paranoia, narcissism, and so on). Instead, the psychoanalytic dimension of his work is evident in his insistence on the necessity of studying the mechanisms of repression while at the same time seeking out those points within culture that allow glimpses of what has been repressed. The cultural theorist or critic's challenge is thus unerringly practical. Attention must be paid not to the meaning of a text but to its operative procedures (whence it speaks, which forms of legitimation guarantee meaning, which acts of repression it performs, etc.). Also, the traces of an unmanageable heterogeneity that institutionally sanctioned writing seeks to control and erase must be recovered.

In *The Practice of Everyday Life* (1980) the themes of repression (by an institutionally authorized practice of writing) and the originary though repressed plurality of practical life come together as Certeau turns his attention explicitly toward walking, reading, telling stories, dwelling, and so forth. In many ways this continues his practice of contemporary social commentary—*The Capture of Speech and Other Political Writings* (1968) and *Culture in the Plural* (1974)—but it also develops the theoretical implications of his archival work. *Practice* does not seek to establish the inherent meaning of the practices of everyday life but instead investigates the forms these practices take, the *manner* of reading, for instance. The book highlights a potential ethical aporia in Certeau's work: if the writing of culture represses its object, how, then, can Certeau's attention to the everyday, materialized as an institutionally legitimated practice of writing, escape a similarly repressive effect? The solution to this problem, ambitious and modest, suggests an entire refashioning of the poetics of cultural writing, a pluralizing of writing that would allow the myriad voices of others more registers for speaking. *Practice* is logically connected to the idea of the return of the repressed: if the obliteration of heterogeneous everyday life is rarely total, practices can be judged to be more or less successful in erasing the everyday. Instead of demanding a practice adequate to the wayward plurality of the everyday, Certeau gives voice to a more circumspect desire to privilege practices that are less inadequate in their attempt to register this wayward plurality. *Practice* can thus be seen as a compilation of attempts to register the everyday, from novels to sociological studies, with the caveat that no single attempt is likely to be adequate. It should also be noted that the book does not establish a method for registering the everyday; it merely intends to lay the foundations for such a possibility (or possibilities) and stands as a challenge to inventively continue the job of bringing the everyday into the foreground of the study of culture.

At the time of his death (at sixty) Certeau was embarking on a number of projects that suggest that the critical architecture of his work would likely have received sustained development: a heterological account of the "New World," a social commentary on issues involving immigration, and an anthropology of belief. Although Certeau was ordained as a Jesuit priest in 1956, his interest in belief was not confined to religious belief. (He remained a committed Christian all his life, but his work on religious history is focused almost entirely on those who were considered heretical by the church.) The anthropology of belief can already be seen in an embryonic form in *The Practice of Everyday Life*, which sees belief and its lack as a central secular element

of the modern everyday. In an age when faith and belief (in science, religion, super-
stition, emancipation, revolution, etc.) have taken on a global urgency, Certeau's
thought remains both unfinished and resolutely current.

BEN HIGHMORE

Michel de Certeau, *The Certeau Reader* (ed. Graham Ward, 2000), *La culture au pluriel* (1974, *Cul-
ture in the Plural*, trans. Tom Conley, 1997), *L'écriture de l'histoire* (1975, *The Writing of History*, trans.
Tom Conley, 1988), *La fable mystique, XVIe–XVIIe siècle* (1982, *The Mystic Fable*, vol. 1, *The Sixteenth and
Seventeenth Centuries*, trans. Michael B. Smith, 1992), *Heterologies: Discourse on the Other* (trans. Brian
Massumi, 1986), *L'invention du quotidien*, vol. 1, *Arts de faire* (1980, *The Practice of Everyday Life*, trans.
Steven Rendall, 1984), *Le lieu de l'autre: Histoire religieuse et mystique* (ed. Luce Giard, 2005), *La posses-
sion de Loudun* (1970, *The Possession at Loudun*, trans. Michael B. Smith, 2000), *La prise de parole, et autres
écrits politiques* (ed. Luce Girard, 1994, *The Capture of Speech and Other Political Writings*, trans. Tom
Conley, 1997), *La prise de parole, pour une nouvelle culture* (1968); Michel de Certeau, Luce Giard, and
Pierre Mayol, *L'invention du quotidien*, vol. 2, *Habiter, cuisiner* (1980, *The Practice of Everyday Life*, vol. 2,
Living and Cooking, trans. Timothy J. Tomasik, 1998); Michel de Certeau, Dominique Julia, and
Jacques Revel, *Une politique de la langue: La révolution française et les patois—L'enquête de Grégoire* (1975).

Cixous, Hélène

Hélène Cixous (b. 1937), whose formidable production includes twenty-nine works of poetry and fiction, seventeen plays, several collections of essays, and numerous articles, is best known in the United States for "The Laugh of the Medusa" and *The Newly Born Woman*. In France, however, she has been a far more politicized and controversial figure. In May 1968, she emerged as a radical academic in the "revolutionary" university of Vincennes, a theorist writing for the Women's Press, and an avant-garde fiction writer. Through her innovative reading and writing, she tries to dismantle patriarchal authority in the academy, including the institution of cultural criticism and theory. She attacks the binary system to which logocentrism subjects thought in the Western world and questions the solidarity between logocentrism and phallocentrism that posits woman as the repressed and ensures the system's functioning.

Cixous's discourse focuses on *écriture féminine* ("feminine writing"), a project begun in the highly politicized context of cultural revolution and DECONSTRUCTION in mid-1970s France when Cixous, LUCE IRIGARAY, JULIA KRISTEVA, and Catherine Clément, among others, began reading texts in the particular contexts of women's experience. Theories of *écriture féminine* explore major philosophical questions: how does "writing" deploy power? How does one read a feminine (nonpatriarchal) text? And, with even greater urgency, what is the "feminine"? Against biologically based readings of SIGMUND FREUD, *écriture féminine* understands femininity and feminine writing as based not on a "given" essence of male and female characteristics but on culturally achieved conventions, such as "openness" in feminine texts as a lack of repressive patterning.

"The Laugh of the Medusa" and "Castration or Decapitation?" present Cixous's case for the reading of feminine writing against psychoanalysis. Writing, she argues in "Laugh," is structured by a "sexual opposition" favoring men, one that "has always worked for man's profit to the point of reducing writing . . . to his laws" (883). Writing is constituted in a "discourse" of social, political, and linguistic relations that are characterized in a masculine or feminine "economy." In this model, patterns of linearity and exclusion (patriarchal "logic") require a strict hierarchical organization of (sexual) difference in discourse and give a "grossly exaggerated" view of the "sexual opposition" actually inherent to language (879). The exclusion of women from writing (and speaking) depends on the traditional separation of the body from the text. The female body entering the text—via closeness with the maternal body—disrupts the masculine economy of superimposed linearity and tyranny: the feminine is the "overflow" of "luminous torrents" ("Laugh" 876), a margin of "excess" eroticism and free play not directly attributable to the fixed hierarchies of masculinity.

When Cixous speaks of women's writing—or, as she later said in *Illa*, of women's search for a *langue maternelle*—she speaks in the future tense: she sets out not to say what it is but to speak "about *what it will do*" (875). Indeed, she is most influential in the apocalyptic scenario that she envisions as preparatory to the *venue à l'écriture* of woman:

> When the "repressed" of their culture and their society returns, it's an explosive, utterly destructive, staggering return, with a force never yet unleashed and equal to the most forbidding of suppressions. For when the Phallic period comes to an end, women will have been either annihilated or borne up to the highest and most violent incandescence. ("Laugh" 886)

The "openness" and possibility of such writing is evident in Cixous's own style both in fictional texts such as *Breathes* (1975) and *Angst* (1977) and in "Laugh," where she writes that "we the precocious, we the repressed of culture, our lovely mouths gagged with pollen, our wind knocked out of us, we the labyrinths, the ladders, the trampled spaces, the bevies—we are black and we are beautiful" (878). For Cixous, as for Kristeva, the feminine economy of excess does not need re-creation because it persists in the margins and gaps (as the repressed, the unconscious) of male-dominated culture. As a characteristically deconstructive reader, she understands texts as built on a system of cultural contradictions, especially concerning values. She focuses on those contradictions and finds the channels of "excess" and violation, accidents of meaning and perversities of signification, through which texts inscribe a feminine writing that goes beyond and escapes the masculine economy of texts.

Cixous's post-Lacanian discourse has been indicted for supporting patriarchal and psychoanalytic norms. Ann Rosalind Jones and others have charged that underlying Cixous's feminine economy is the assumption of an "essential" femininity in texts, the identifiable quality that allows feminine discourse to be named as such in relation to Oedipus. More recently, however, other critics such as Christiane Makward have emphasized Cixous's production as creative writer and argued that while most of her readers are determined to neglect her creative work and to see "Laugh of the Medusa" as encapsulating her thinking, Cixous's work continues to change and so to avoid the trap of essentialism (2). Anu Aneja, moreover, has suggested that the case against *écriture féminine* results from a desire "to locate *l'écriture féminine* within a definite category, a desire to co-opt into a literary theory that which always exceeds it" (195). Aneja's observations clarify the trajectory of Cixous's most recent work, which has moved away, as Cixous herself claims, from "work on the ego" (Jardine and Menke 236).

Recently, Cixous has explored the political circumstances that shape social relationships. Often treating historical figures or social realities through a style of creative poetics, Cixous investigates the powerful role that human relationships play in surviving political repression, imprisonment, social unrest, and revolution. With texts such as the fictional *Manna for the Mandelstams for the Mandelas* (1994) and in her personal essays, Cixous stresses a "more immediate" way of experiencing historical circumstances (*Stigmata* 172). As many recent postcolonial writers have done, Cixous explores in her essays about growing up in Algeria the slip between self and other that occurs when negotiating a complex network of affiliations facing people within a country struggling for independence.

These thematic developments in Cixous's later writings also emerge through her plays, including *The Terrible but Unfinished Story of Norodom Sihanouk, King of Cambodia* (1985) and *Indiada; or, The India of Their Dreams* (1978). In the theater, Cixous has found a new freedom from her own voice and from the self, claiming that the theater allows her to "step out of [her] own language, and borrow the poorest of languages" (166), to forget Hélène Cixous, French intellectual, and become a peasant woman. Time is not artificially elongated in the theater as it is in fiction, she argues; the theater, therefore, is better equipped to capture a precise moment in human destiny (170)— for Cixous, this is the theater's greatest advantage over fiction. In her plays she considers most poignant the pauses that she imposes on events, scenes that stop history and become the moments, political and personal, when "we interrogate ourselves and we say our fear and our indecision" (152).

SHARLA HUTCHISON, CHIARA BRIGANTI,
AND ROBERT CON DAVIS-UNDIANO

Hélène Cixous, "The Character of 'Character,'" trans. Keith Cohen, *New Literary History* 5 [1974]), *"Coming to Writing" and Other Essays* (ed. Deborah Jensen, trans. Sarah Cornell, Deborah Jensen, Ann Liddle, and Susan Sellers, 1991), *The Hélène Cixous Reader* (ed. Susan Sellers, 1994), *Illa* (1980), *Manne aux Mandelstams aux Mandelas* (1988, *Manna for the Mandelstams for the Mandelas*, trans. Catherine A. F. MacGillivray, 1994), "Mon Algériance" (1997, "My Algeriance, in Other Words: To Depart Not to Arrive from Algeria," trans. Eric Prenowitz, *TriQuarterly* 100 [1997]), *Photos de Racine* (1994, *Rootprints: Memory and Life Writing*, trans. Eric Prenowitz, 1997), *Portrait de Jacques Derrida en Jeune Saint Juif* (2001, *Portrait of Jacques Derrida as a Young Jewish Saint*, trans. Beverley Bie Brahic, 2004), *Readings: The Poetics of Blanchot, Joyce, Kafka, Kleist, Lispector, and Tsvetayeva* (trans. Verena A. Conley, 1991), "Le rire de la Méduse" (1975, "The Laugh of the Medusa," trans. Keith Cohen and Paula Cohen, *Signs* 1 [1976]), "Le sexe ou la tête?" (1975, "Castration or Decapitation?," trans. Annette Kuhn, *Signs* 7 [1981]), *Stigmata: Escaping Texts* (1998), *Three Steps on the Ladder of Writing* (trans. Sarah Cornell and Susan Sellers, 1993), *Vivre l'orange/To Live the Orange* (bilingual ed., trans. Ann Liddle and Sarah Cornell, 1979), "Voile Noire Voile Blanche/Black Sail White Sail" (trans. Catherine A.F. MacGillivray, *New Literary History* 25 [1994]); Hélène Cixous and Catherine Clément, *La jeune née* (1975, *The Newly Born Woman*, trans. Betsy Wing, 1986); Hélène Cixous and Jacques Derrida, *Voiles* (1998, *Veils*, trans. Geoffrey Bennington, 2001); Hélène Cixous, Madeleine Gagnon, and Annie Leclerc, *La venue à l'écriture* (1977); Anu Aneja, "The Mystic Aspect of *L'Écriture féminine*: Hélène Cixous's *Vivre l'Orange*," *Qui parle* 3 (1989); Catherine Anne Franke, "Interview with Hélène Cixous," *Qui parle* 3 (1989); Alice Jardine and Anne Menke, "The Politics of Tradition: Placing Women in French Literature," *Yale French Studies* 75 (1988); Christiane Makward, "Hélène Cixous and the Myth of 'Feminine Writing,' or 'Hélène in Theoryland'" (unpublished paper, 1990).

Cultural Studies

1. United Kingdom

What is British cultural studies? Although British cultural studies tends to be associated with the work of Richard Hoggart, RAYMOND WILLIAMS, E. P. Thompson, and STUART HALL, the various "appropriations" of work from outside the United Kingdom make this position less straightforward than it might at first appear. Cultural studies works with an inclusive definition of culture. It encompasses a "democratic" project in the sense that rather than studying only what Matthew Arnold called "the best which has been thought and said," it commits to examining all that has been thought and said (although in practice most effort has been focused on popular culture). Although this means that there is no privileged place in cultural studies for the literary text, it does not mean—nor should it—that cultural studies is uninterested in literary or other forms of high culture (see Gripsrud; Storey, "Expecting").

To put it simply, culture is how we live nature, including our own biology; it is the shared meanings we make and encounter in our everyday lives. Culture is not something embodied in particular "texts" (i.e., any commodity, object, or event that can be made to signify); it is the practices and processes of making meanings with and from the "texts" we encounter in our everyday lives. Thus, cultures are made from the production, circulation, and consumption of meanings. Yet to see culture as the practices and processes of making shared meanings does not mean that cultural studies believes that cultures are harmonious, organic wholes. On the contrary, cultural studies maintains that the "texts" from which cultures are made are "multi-accentual" (Volosinov). That is, they can be made to mean in many different ways.

How cultural studies thinks of the relations between culture and power is informed most often by the work of ANTONIO GRAMSCI and MICHEL FOUCAULT. Though cultural studies has been influenced by and in turn influenced FEMINIST THEORY AND CRITICISM, poststructuralism, POSTCOLONIAL STUDIES, PSYCHO-ANALYTIC THEORY AND CRITICISM, POSTMODERNISM, and QUEER THEORY AND CRITICISM, the work of Gramsci and Foucault remains fundamental to cultural studies as it is practiced in the United Kingdom. The introduction of Gramsci's concept of "hegemony" produced a rethinking of the politics of popular culture: popular culture was now seen as a key site for the production and reproduction of hegemony. Capitalist industrial societies are divided unequally in terms of, for example, ethnicity, gender, generation, sexuality, and social class. Cultural studies argues that popular culture is one of the principal sites where these divisions are established and contested; that is, popular culture is an arena of struggle and negotiation between the interests of dominant and of subordinate groups. The introduction of hegemony into British cultural studies also produced a rethinking of the concept of popular culture itself (Hall, "Cultural Studies"; Storey, "Expecting"). This rethinking involved bringing into active relationship two previously dominant but antagonistic ways of thinking about popular culture. The first tradition (e.g., the FRANKFURT SCHOOL, STRUCTURALISM, some versions of poststructuralism, political economy) viewed popular culture as a culture imposed by the capitalist culture industries, a culture provided for profit and ideological manipulation. This is popular culture as "structure." The second tradition (e.g., some versions of culturalism, social history, and "history from below") saw popular culture as a culture spontaneously emerging from below, an "authentic" folk, working class, or subculture. This is popular culture as "agency." From the perspective of the cultural studies appropriation of hegemony, however, popular culture is neither an "authentic" folk, working class, or subculture nor a culture imposed by the capitalist culture industries but a "compromise equilibrium" (Gramsci) between the two; a contradictory mix of forces from both "below" and "above"; both commercial and authentic, marked by both resistance and incorporation, structure and agency.

As a result of this approach, cultural studies concerns itself with the study of the consumption of popular culture for two reasons. The first is theoretical. To know how "texts" are *made to mean* requires a consideration of consumption. This view carries us beyond an interest in the meaning of a "text" (i.e., meaning as something essential, inscribed, and guaranteed) to a focus on the range of meanings that a "text" makes possible (i.e., its social meanings, how it is appropriated and used in the consumption practices of everyday life). The second reason why British cultural studies is concerned with consumption is political. Cultural studies has always rejected the pessimistic elitism that haunts so much work in cultural theory and analysis (e.g., Leavisism, the Frankfurt School, most versions of structuralism, economistic versions of Marxism, political economy), which always seem to want to suggest that agency is overwhelmed by structure, that consumption is a mere shadow of production, and that audience negotiations are fictions, merely illusory moves in a game of economic power. Although cultural studies recognizes that the capitalist culture industries are a major site of ideological production, cultural studies rejects the view that to consume these productions is to become the hopeless victim of false consciousness (whether capitalist, imperialist, patriarchal, or heterosexual).

This is not to say that consumption is always empowering and resistant. To deny the passivity of consumption is not to deny that sometimes consumption is passive. But it is to deny that the cultures of everyday life are little more than degraded landscapes of commercial and ideological manipulation imposed from above in order to make profit and secure social control. Cultural studies insists that to decide on these matters requires vigilance and attention to the details of the active relations between production and consumption. These are not matters that can be decided once and for all, outside the contextual contingencies of history and politics. Nor can they be read off from the moment of production, which would locate meaning, pleasure, ideological effect, incorporation, and resistance in the means of production itself. These are only aspects of the contexts for consumption as "production in use," and it is ultimately in "production in use" that questions of meaning, pleasure, ideological effect, incorporation, or resistance can be (contextually and contingently) decided. A consumer, situated in a specific social context, always confronts a "text" in its material existence as a result of particular conditions of production. But in the same way, a "text," situated in a specific social context, is confronted by a consumer who appropriates it as culture and "produces in use" the range of possible meanings the "text" can be made to bear; these cannot just be read off from the materiality of a "text" or from the means or relations of its production (Du Gay et al.; Hall, "Encoding"; Morley).

Whereas the appropriation of Gramsci usually leads to a focus on the relations between production and consumption, the deployment of Foucault tends to generate work on representation, especially on the productive nature of representation. Cultural studies takes a constructionist approach to representation (Hall, "Work"). Because things do not signify by themselves, representation (through processes of description, conceptualization, and substitution) constructs the meaning of what is represented. The world certainly exists outside representation, but it is only in representations that the world can be made meaningful. Representation is therefore a practice through which we make reality meaningful and through which we share and contest meanings of ourselves, of each other, and of the world. From a Foucauldian perspective (as developed in British cultural studies), representation always takes place in a discourse, which organizes what can and cannot be said about a particular "text." Meaning is made in discourses, where power produces knowledge and knowledge produces power, including the production of the "subject positions" from which meanings can be made and actions carried out. The power entangled in representation, therefore, is not a negative force; it is productive: "We must cease once and for all to describe the effects of power in negative terms: it 'excludes,' it 'represses,' it 'censors,' it 'abstracts,' it 'masks,' it 'conceals.' In fact, power produces; it produces reality; it produces domains of objects and rituals of truth" (Foucault, *Discipline* 194). This is why representation is a key concept in cultural studies' focus on the relations between culture and power.

British cultural studies got its institutional start with the opening of the Centre for Contemporary Cultural Studies (CCCS) at the University of Birmingham in 1964 (see Green). Although other universities introduced postgraduate programs in cultural studies, it was not until the 1980s that cultural studies became available at Birmingham and elsewhere (most notably at the Open University) as an undergraduate program of study. Although the Department of Sociology and Cultural Studies, which replaced the CCCS in 1992, was closed in 2002, the future of cultural studies in Britain still seems fairly buoyant, with thirty universities in Britain now offering degree programs that include "cultural studies" in their title. The future development of cultural studies in the United Kingdom will depend to a large extent on the context in which it is taught, that is, whether it operates as a "discipline" in its own right or as an important component of, for example, communication studies, cultural geography, cultural history, English studies, media studies, or sociology. Whatever its future may be, the work of Gramsci and Foucault (and the introduction, development, and elaboration of this work within cultural studies by Stuart Hall) will continue to play a significant role in the research and publication of work in the United Kingdom that describes itself as cultural studies.

JOHN STOREY

Matthew Arnold, "Culture and Anarchy" (1869); Paul Du Gay et al., *Doing Cultural Studies: The Story of the Sony Walkman* (1997); Michel Foucault, *The Archaeology of Knowledge* (1972), *Discipline and Punish* (1979), *Power/Knowledge* (1980); Antonio Gramsci, *Selections from Prison Notebooks* (1971); Michael Green, "The Centre for Contemporary Cultural Studies" (Storey, *What Is Cultural Studies?*); Jostein Gripsrud, " 'High Culture' Revisited" (Storey, *Cultural Theory*); Stuart Hall, "Cultural Studies: Two Paradigms" (Storey, *What Is Cultural Studies?*), "Encoding and Decoding," *Culture, Media, Language* (ed. Stuart Hall et al., 1980), "Notes on Deconstructing 'The Popular'" (Storey, *Cultural Theory*), "On Postmodernism and Articulation," *Stuart Hall: Critical Dialogues in Cultural Studies* (ed. David Morley and Kuan-Hsing Chen, 1996), "The Rediscovery of Ideology: The Return of the Repressed," *Culture, Society, and the Media* (ed. Michael Gurevitch et al., 1982), "The Work of Representation," *Representation: Cultural Representations and Signifying Practices* (ed. Stuart Hall, 1997); Richard Hoggart, *The Uses of Literacy* (1990); F. R. Leavis, "Mass Civilisation and Minority Culture" (Storey, *Cultural Theory*); Daniel Miller, *Material Culture and Mass Consumption* (1987); David Morley, *The "Nationwide" Audience* (1980); John Storey, *Cultural Consumption and Everyday Life* (1999), "Expecting Rain: Opera as Popular Culture?" *High-Pop* (ed. Jim Collins, 2001); John Storey, ed., *Cultural Theory and Popular Culture: A Reader* (1998, 2nd ed., 2001); John Storey, ed., *What Is Cultural Studies? A Reader*; E. P. Thompson, *The Making of the English Working Class* (1963); V. N. Volosinov, *Marxism and the Philosophy of Language* (1973); Raymond Williams, "The Analysis of Culture" (Storey, *Cultural Theory*), *Culture and Society* (1959).

2. United States

In the United States academic interest in cultural studies first flowered during the mid-1980s and 1990s, primarily among university intellectuals and critics on the left. In addition to the establishment of pioneering programs, new journals appeared, including *Cultural Critique*, *Differences*, *Public Culture*, and *Social Text*. The editors of *Cultural Critique* (founded in 1985 at the University of Minnesota), for example, declared their wide-ranging objects of study to be "received values, institutions, practices, and discourses in terms of their economic, political, social, and aesthetic genealogies, constitutions, and effects" (5). In its North American setting, cultural studies sometimes aspired to be a new discipline but served instead as an unstable meeting point for various combinations of critics and specialists in interdisciplinary MARXIST THEORY AND CRITICISM, FEMINIST THEORY AND CRITICISM, literary and media studies, POSTMODERNISM, anthropological theory and criticism, SEMIOTICS, POSTCOLONIAL STUDIES, rhetoric, RACE AND ETHNICITY, visual culture, body and GENDER, and the sociology and history of culture and science.

Among the objects of study commonly examined in programs of cultural studies are such wildly diverse "discourses" as advertising, art, architecture, movies, fashion, popular literary genres (thrillers, romances, westerns, science fiction), photography, music, magazines, youth subcultures, urban folklore, cartoons, theory movements, theater, radio, women's literature, television, and working-class literature. Instead of focusing on aesthetic masterpieces of canonized high literature, advocates of cultural studies characteristically advance the claims of "low," popular, and mass cultures. Potentially, the whole spectrum of cultural objects, practices, and texts constituting society provide materials for cultural studies. In this context literature is framed as a communal practice or document with social, historical, and political roots and ramifications; it is not treated as an autonomous aesthetic icon separable from its conditions of production, distribution, and consumption.

The modes of inquiry employed in cultural studies include not only established survey techniques, ethnographic observation, textual explications, and researches into sociohistorical backgrounds but also, and especially, institutional analysis and ideology critique. For scholars of cultural studies institutional analysis entails a conception of institutions as productive agencies that both constitute and disseminate knowledge and belief by means of systematic practices and conventions affecting cultural discourses. Whereas institutional analysis is focused on the material means and methods employed by institutions that participate in the circulation of cultural objects and texts, ideology critique is given over to examining the ideas, feelings, beliefs, and representations embodied in and promulgated by the artifacts and practices of a culture. Because the objects, texts, and institutions of a culture create and convey ideology, the use of ideology critique is fundamental to the work of cultural studies.

Characteristic of academic cultural studies across English-speaking universities is a leftist political orientation rooted variously in Marxist, non-Marxist, and post-Marxist intellectual traditions all critical of the aestheticism, formalism, antihistoricism, and apoliticism common among the dominant postwar methods of literary criticism. Cultural studies seeks to analyze and assess the social roots, the institutional relays, and the ideological ramifications of communal events, organizations, and artifacts, privileging methodologically the cultural circuits of production, distribution, and consumption. It predisposes analysts to intervene actively in arenas of cultural struggle, to be committed public intellectuals and political activists. The conservative role of the traditional intellectual as morally engaged yet disinterested connoisseur and custodian of culture is widely regarded as suspect and unworthy by proponents of cultural studies. As a result, conservative cultural critics, especially American neoconservative intellectuals, regularly attack cultural studies, as seen, for instance, in the pages of the journal *New Criterion* or at the conferences of the National Association of Scholars.

In the late 1980s the work of John Fiske, a British critic educated at Cambridge University who joined the faculty of the Department of Communication Arts at the

University of Wisconsin–Madison in 1988, substantially contributed to the codification and popularity of cultural studies in the United States, particularly among media critics. In such widely read works as his *Television Culture* (1987), *Reading the Popular* (1989), and *Understanding Popular Culture* (1989) Fiske focuses on how ordinary people take pleasure in making their own meanings out of mass-produced cultural commodities. Indebted to Gramsci, as well as to MICHEL DE CERTEAU, PIERRE BOURDIEU, and the general French poststructuralist line of thinking in cultural studies, Fiske rejects the long-standing idea of the passive consumer, articulated most famously by the Frankfurt School theorists Max Horkheimer and THEODOR W. ADORNO in their *Dialectic of Enlightenment* (1944). Instead, he traces a process in which consumers actively resist commercial culture and transform it into popular culture. This view was attacked on the grounds that Fiske celebrates consumption-as-pleasure at the expense of ideology critique, not to mention organized politics.

The late 1980s witnessed a growing internationalization of cultural studies, signified most notably by the launching in January 1987 of the journal *Cultural Studies* under the guidance of an international editorial collective with the explicit goal of fostering "developments in the area worldwide, putting academics, researchers, students and practitioners in different countries and from diverse intellectual traditions in touch with each other and each other's work." From this point on, cultural studies increasingly diffused itself by diversifying into multiple branches and modes around the globe as well as within national academic systems. By the turn of the millennium U.S. cultural studies, for instance, had taken the definitive form of a conglomeration of loosely affiliated subspecialties, including most prominently media studies; gender, sexuality, and body studies; science and technology studies; the study of identity and MULTICULTURALISM; urban and community studies; political economy, culture, and GLOBALIZATION studies; and the study of popular culture, commodification, and consumerism.

This wide range of interests associated with cultural studies was famously first manifest in the United States at the 1990 conference "Cultural Studies Now and in the Future," a major international event at the University of Illinois at Urbana-Champaign that contributed to both the popularization and the institutionalization of cultural studies. According to Lawrence Grossberg, Cary Nelson, and Paula Treichler, the organizers of the conference and the editors of the published proceedings, titled *Cultural Studies* (1992), the forty papers could be seen as representing sixteen overlapping areas of interest within the field: the history of cultural studies itself, gender and sexuality, nationhood and national identity, colonialism and postcolonialism, race and ethnicity, popular culture and its audiences, identity politics, pedagogy, the politics of aesthetics, culture and its institutions, ethnography and cultural studies, the politics of disciplinarity, discourse and textuality, the rereading of history, global culture in a postmodern age, and lastly science, culture, and the ecosystem (17–22). This broad array of topics and subfields quickly led to the widespread belief that cultural studies was anything that an intellectual happened to be investigating. Against this vexing impression, Cary Nelson, in a perhaps futile gesture of affiliation with Birmingham cultural studies titled "Always Already Cultural Studies" (1991), laid down fourteen criteria for the new discipline in the United States, including most insistently that American cultural studies must position itself within the existing context of the field, most especially its "engagement with Marxism, from Raymond Williams to Stuart Hall." In Nelson's view, "To treat that history as irrelevant, as many Americans do, is to abandon cultural studies for a fake practice that merely borrows its name" (32). Not insignificantly, a number of related scholars working in subspecialties such as, for instance, postcolonial studies, media analysis, and ethnic studies have disavowed any connection with cultural studies and its traditions, seeking their own autonomy and identity.

During the course of the 1990s certain leading critics helped to shape the field of cultural studies in the United States. In the area of SCIENCE STUDIES, an especially productive subfield, Andrew Ross figured prominently. In his *Strange Weather: Culture, Science, and Technology in the Age of Limits* (1991), for instance, Ross calls on cultural critics to examine the ways that science and technology contour the political parameters of popular culture. The underlying idea here is that technology and science are "social artifacts" subject to critique. Significantly, Ross pioneered the institutionalization of cultural studies in the 1990s when he took over the graduate program in American studies at New York University, which under his direction became arguably the leading U.S. program in cultural studies. In the mid-1990s Ross became embroiled in a high-profile controversy now known as the "Sokal affair" when *Social Text*, coedited by him, accepted an essay by the New York University physicist Alan Sokal that purported to be a critique of modern scientific method. Making radical claims about science, the article was a hoax intended to discredit the journal and cultural studies, showing that the journal would accept dubious scholarship as long as it expressed postmodern ideas. After the essay was published, Sokal went public with the news. Thus began a heated but productive controversy—sometimes referred to as the "science wars"—in which the authority of both science and cultural studies was challenged.

Another prominent figure in science studies is the American biologist DONNA HARAWAY, who innovatively links science and technology with feminism, socialism, and the study of postmodern culture. Her most celebrated publication, "A Cyborg Manifesto: Science, Technology, and Socialist-Feminism in the Late Twentieth Century" (1991), explores the interconnections between the human body and technology, promoting the concept of the cyborg, defined as a "cybernetic organism, a hybrid of machine and organism, a creature of social reality as well as a creature of fiction" (149). For Haraway, the cyborg is an ideal-typical form of human subjectivity that has arisen in the high-tech culture of the postmodern world. Crossing traditional boundaries and borders, it marks the breakdown of such classical distinctions as mind and body, self and other, animal and human, organism and machine, public and private, and nature and culture, all first carefully distinguished for the modern world by earlier Enlightenment philosophy and science. Such breakdowns constitute a destabilization of subjectivity, calling into question both "human essence" and its related identity politics and most reigning master narratives, such as the eventual triumph of human reason or spirit. These implosions prompt the recognition of the constructed nature of subjectivity and the proliferation of innumerable differences among beings. They also prompt continuous critique of what Haraway calls the "informatics of domination," that is, the disciplinary, panoptic postindustrial society of global capitalism with all its inequalities. In a world of multiple constructed subjectivities and perspectives, Haraway's cyberfeminism points out that today progressive politics should arise through networking, coalitions, and affinity rather than through totalizing formulations of identity based on exclusions and marginalizations.

By the early twenty-first century academic cultural studies in the United States had evolved into a highly disaggregated field composed of several dozen relatively autonomous subfields, whose numbers seemed ready to increase. At the same time there were only a few actual departments of cultural studies, a belated national organization (initiated in 2003), no universally read journals, and no institutional clearinghouse or recognized center, institute, or summer school. The most disorganized of university "disciplines"—much more so than women's studies or race and ethnicity studies—"cultural studies" had become an accepted term of convenience for all kinds of historical or popular-culture-based inquiries, very often disconnected from the British line of cultural studies, from French poststructuralism, from Frankfurt School theory, and from Anglo-American traditions of cultural criticism deriving from writers from Swift to Williams and Ralph Waldo Emerson to Susan Sontag to Noam Chomsky. With the passage of time, each subfield produced its own distinct problems, major texts, and leading figures. Still, disorganization aside, an inner corps of scholars staffing major programs, leading journals, and flagship university-press series in cultural studies gradually developed a loose set of defining key concepts and problems, main texts and figures, and interwoven traditions. Such traditions invariably included Western Marxism; the new social movements of the 1960s and 1970s (especially civil rights, feminism, Third World liberation, and gay rights); Birmingham cultural studies and French poststructuralism; and contemporary psychoanalysis. In addition, common enemies remained essentially what they had been during the closing years of the cold war period, namely aestheticism, great traditionalism, formalism, antihistoricism, and neoconservatism. Cultural studies in the United States during the coming years promises an increasing specialization of subfields, a growing discipline-wide preoccupation with globalization, an ongoing attenuation of leftist politics and activism, and a continuing uncertain relationship with the university.

VINCENT B. LEITCH AND MITCHELL R. LEWIS

Louis Althusser, "Idéologie et appareils idéologiques d'état," *La pensée* 151 (1970) ("Ideology and Ideological State Apparatuses," *Lenin and Philosophy and Other Essays*, ed. and trans. Ben Brewster, 1971); Houston A. Baker Jr., Manthia Diawara, and Ruth H. Lindeborg, eds., *Black British Cultural Studies: A Reader* (1996); Anne Balsamo, "Feminism and Cultural Studies," *Journal of the Midwest Modern Language Association* 24 (1996), *Technologies of the Gendered Body: Reading Cyborg Women* (1996); Roland Barthes, *Mythologies* (1957, *Mythologies*, trans. Annette Lavers, 1972); Janet Batsleer et al., *Rewriting English: Cultural Politics of Gender and Class* (1985); Susan Bordo, *Unbearable Weight: Feminism, Western Culture, and the Body* (1993); Pierre Bourdieu, *La distinction: Critique sociale du jugement* (1979, *Distinction: A Social Critique of the Judgement of Taste*, trans. Richard Nice, 1986); Centre for Contemporary Cultural Studies, *On Ideology* (1978); Michel de Certeau, *L'invention du quotidien, vol.1: Arts de faire* (1980, *The Practice of Everyday Life*, trans. Steven Rendall, 1984); John Clarke, Chas Critcher, and Richard Johnson, eds., *Working Class Culture: Studies in History and Theory* (1979); Ioan Davies, *Cultural Studies and Beyond: Fragments of Empire* (1995); Simon During, *The Cultural Studies Reader* (1993, 2nd ed., 1999); John Fiske, *Media Matters: Race and Gender in U.S. Politics* (1994, rev. ed., 1996), *Reading the Popular* (1989), *Television Culture* (1987), *Understanding Popular Culture* (1989); Michel Foucault, *Histoire de la sexualité* (1976, *The History of Sexuality*, vol. 1., trans. Robert Hurley, 1978), *Surveiller et punir* (1975, *Discipline and Punish*, trans. Alan Sheridan, 1979); John Frow and Meaghan Morris, eds., *Australian Cultural Studies: A Reader* (1993); Paul Gilroy, *The Black Atlantic: Modernity and Double Consciousness* (1993), *There Ain't No Black in the Union Jack: The Cultural Politics of Race and Nation* (1987, rpt., with foreword by Houston A. Baker Jr., 1991); Henry Giroux, *Border Crossings: Cultural Workers and the Politics of Education* (1992), *Impure Acts: The Practical Politics of Cultural Studies* (2000); Antonio Gramsci, *Selections from the Prison Notebooks* (ed. and trans. Quintin Hoare and Geoffrey Nowell Smith, 1971); Lawrence Grossberg, *Bringing It All Back Home: Essays on Cultural Studies* (1997), *Dancing in Spite of Myself: Essays on Popular Culture* (1997); Lawrence Grossberg, Cary Nelson, and Paula Treichler, eds., *Cultural Studies* (1992); Stuart Hall and Tony Jefferson, eds., *Resistance through Rituals: Youth Subcultures in Postwar Britain* (1976); Stuart Hall, "Cultural Studies: Two Paradigms," *Culture, Ideology, and Social Process* (ed. Tony Bennett et al., 1981), Stuart Hall, Dorothy Hobson, Andrew Lowe, and Paul Willis, eds., *Culture, Media, Language: Working Papers in Cultural Studies, 1972–79* (1980); Donna Haraway, *Simians, Cyborgs, and Women: The Reinvention of Nature* (1991); John Hartley and Roberta E. Pearson, *American Cultural Studies: A Reader* (2000); Dick Hebdige, *Cut 'n' Mix: Culture, Identity, and Caribbean Music* (1987), *Hiding in the Light: On Images and Things* (1988), *Subculture: The Meaning of Style* (1979); Richard Hoggart, *The Uses of Literacy: Aspects of Working-Class Life* (1957); Max Horkheimer and Theodor W. Adorno, *Dialektik der Aufklärung* (1944, *Dialectic of Enlightenment*, ed. Gunzelin Schmid Noerr, trans. Edmund Jephcott, 2002); Richard Johnson, "What Is Cultural Studies Anyway?" *Social Text* 16 (1986–1987); Ernesto Laclau and Chantal Mouffe, *Hegemony and Socialist Strategy: Towards a Radical Democratic Politics* (trans. Winston Moore and Paul Cammack, 1985, 2nd ed., 2001); Lingua Franca, ed., *Sokal Hoax: The Sham That Shook the Academy* (2000); Toby Miller, ed., *A Companion to Cultural Studies* (2001); Laura Mulvey, "Visual Pleasure and Narrative Pleasure," *Screen* 16 (1975); Cary Nelson, "Always Already Cultural Studies: Two Conferences and a Manifesto," *Journal of the Midwest Modern Language Association* 24 (1991); Cary Nelson and Dilip Parameshwar Gaonkar, eds., *Disciplinarity and Dissent in Cultural Studies* (1996); Constance Penley, ed., *Feminism and Film Theory* (1988); Donna Przybylowicz and Abdul R. JanMohamed, "Prospectus," *Cultural Critique* 1 (1985); Janice Radway, *A Feeling for Books: The Book-of-the-Month Club, Literary Taste, and Middle-Class Desire* (1997), *Reading the Romance: Women, Patriarchy, and Popular Literature* (1984, 2nd ed., 1991); Andrew Ross, *Strange Weather: Culture, Science, and Technology in the Ages of Limits* (1991); Andrew Ross, ed., *Science Wars* (1996); Edward Said, *Culture and Imperialism* (1994), *Orientalism* (1978); John Storey, ed., *What Is Cultural Studies? A Reader* (1996); E. P. Thompson, *The Making of the English Working Class* (1963); Graeme Turner, *British Cultural Studies: An Introduction* (1990, 3rd ed., 2003); Gauri Viswanathan, *Masks of Conquest: Literary Study and British Rule in India* (1989); Catherine A. Warren and Mary Douglas Vavrus, eds., *American Cultural Studies* (2002); Raymond Williams, *Culture and Society, 1780–1950*

(1958); Women's Studies Group, Centre for Contemporary Cultural Studies, *Women Take Issue: Aspects of Women's Subordination* (1979).

3. Australia

The incorporation of Australian cultural studies into university programs in film, media, and communications studies was initially more comprehensive than in the United Kingdom and has been less implicated in debates on literary theory than cultural studies in either the United Kingdom or the United States. Further, notwithstanding the convenience of the national label, Australian cultural studies is not a theoretically homogeneous project. Indeed, it developed through a process of relatively promiscuous "indigenization": the appropriation of overseas theoretical models that were tested against, and if necessary modified in response to, local political and cultural conditions (Frow and Morris; Turner, "It works for me" and *Nation*).

The expansion of Australian cultural studies through the 1980s benefited from a number of unique institutional and academic enabling conditions. During the 1970s and 1980s both popular and academic interest in the analysis of Australian culture, literature, histories, and identities mounted, resulting in the emergence of the field of Australian studies and in the political renovation of Australian literary studies. Initially a nationalist and eventually a postcolonial project, the new paradigm of Australian literary studies focused more on cultural than aesthetic issues. Similar interests were also implicated in the development of a nationally focused tradition of media and film studies, itself given particular relevance by revived government investment in local film and, later, television production.

At this time, a new sector of institutions (the colleges of advanced education, similar to the polytechnics in the United Kingdom) and a new group of interdisciplinary universities was established in Australia. These provided the circumstances for the establishment of the interdisciplinary programs demanded by the growing student population generated by the abolition of university fees in the early 1970s. Among the most significant beneficiaries of these changes were the new interdisciplinary areas of media studies, communication studies, Australian studies, film studies, and ultimately cultural studies. Key appointments from the United Kingdom, especially John Tulloch, John Fiske, Tony Bennett, and John Hartley, contributed significantly to course planning and to the development of both national and international publication opportunities for Australian writers.

Partly as a result of the influence of these British academics, the local market for academic publishing within the broad fields of Australian cultural, literary, media, and film studies expanded. This increased exposure led eventually to significant international interest in the work of Australian cultural studies writers such as Meaghan Morris, Ian Hunter, John Frow, Stuart Cunningham, and Ross Gibson. This work, importantly, moved across the disciplinary boundaries between literary theory, film and media studies, and the incipient tradition of Australian cultural studies. At this time, Frow, Hunter, Bennett, and Morris, for example, all spoke from (and contributed to) a European Marxian tradition of literary theory even when dealing with Australian subject matter. In a separate development that also exerted a significant influence on the international field from the mid-1980s well into the late 1990s, Australian cultural studies academics engaged with government policy-making processes related to the cultural and media industries in collaboration with a series of state and federal administrations. This highly specific mode of involvement was theorized through the work of Michel Foucault and claimed as the new field of cultural policy studies (Bennett, *Culture*; Cunningham; Hunter).

While it would be wrong to see Australian cultural studies as a nationalist development, "nation" has been a consistent if often bitterly contested term within it. The focus of Australian cultural studies has been resolutely local, partly because of the political nature of its objectives but also partly because of the specificity of so many cultural debates. Australia's geographical isolation and its relatively short history as a settler society makes it a special case in, for instance, arguments about globalization and about the construction and maintenance of national cultural identities. Perhaps as a result of this isolation and short history, the interrogation of the political function of the nation's narratives and histories occurred relatively late in Australia. The disciplines of history and literature were both slow to take up the benefits of structuralist and poststructuralist theory. As a result, although history and literary studies had been interested in the production of "the national character," they did not have the theoretical tools that might enable them to develop that interest. Starting in the 1980s, however, as perspectives from poststructuralism and NARRATOLOGY became more widely known, literary scholars (and later, historians) began to accept the notion that the national character might be approached as the highly contingent product of cultural invention, of narrative, or in terms of a Barthesian notion of mythology. At this time the first theoretical attempts to provide an account of Australian literature as a cultural product (Hodge and Mishra; Schaffer; Turner, *National*; White) appear, in which there is a clear cross-fertilization between Australian literary studies, historical studies, and cultural studies.

Where British cultural studies of this period tended to "ex-nominate" the nation, those following their lead in Australia were vigorously and explicitly concerned with the meanings attached to the national culture, to the patterns of inclusion and exclusion enforced through these meanings and to the interests they served. If 1980s British cultural studies regarded "the national culture" as something that was overwhelmingly in the capture of the conservative side of cultural politics and therefore hardly worth bothering about, Australian cultural studies saw it as worth contesting. As a result, Australian cultural studies focused on how "Australia" was or had been represented in all kinds of texts and media, as well as on the consequences and effects of these representations. The focus for such work included the representation of indigenous Australians and of the non-Anglo-Saxon ethnicities gathered under the rubric of multiculturalism. The gradual imbrication of Australian cultural studies into international debates helped expand these kinds of focus in the latter half of the 1990s, making it a less nationalist and more politically diverse field of inquiry.

The British influence on Australian cultural studies, while only one of many contributing streams, has nevertheless been significant. The theorizing of ideology by the Centre for Contemporary Cultural Studies at the University of Birmingham in England and, a little later, its version of Gramscian hegemony was, and to some extent remains, extremely influential. Initially, Stuart Hall's encoding and decoding version of textual analysis, with its privileging of Saussurean and Barthesian semiotics, was a fundamental analytic tool (Fiske, Hodge, and Turner). Other traditions, however, that did not originate in Birmingham have been no less influential or powerful. A local tradition of film and media analysis, for instance, developed in close parallel with the government-funded revival of the Australian film industry in the 1970s. This tradition was initially dominated, again, by a nationalist or at least anti-imperialist politics aimed at defending the production of local cinema for local audiences. The key methodological orientation at first was political economy, but this eventually gave way to a concern with the connection between film and national culture, the cultural politics of the film text (see O'Regan). In a parallel development over the 1980s that shared some of its impetus with work in literary and cultural theory, there was a theoretically sophisticated body of work impressed by Metzian semiotics and Lacanian appropriations of SIGMUND FREUD (see JACQUES LACAN).

In the 1980s, poststructuralist, narratological, and psychoanalytic methods of textual analysis—first in relation to film and then in relation to literary texts—were added to the disciplinary mix. In Sydney during the 1980s, many literary critics and scholars did not want to be aligned with the term "cultural studies." Such critics and scholars were more interested in European literary theory and Continental philosophy than in the pragmatic applications of the Birmingham school. For some—those working at the University of Technology, Sydney, for instance—JEAN BAUDRILLARD and JACQUES DERRIDA were far more influential than Louis Althusser, Antonio Gramsci, or Hall. At Griffith University from the late 1980s on, Foucault's work, in particular his notion of governmentality, was pivotal to the work of Tony Bennett and Ian Hunter, and it provided the theoretical underpinnings for the mutation of cultural studies into cultural policy studies.

The work of the Key Centre for Cultural and Media Policy Studies at Griffith University, under the leadership first of Tony Bennett and later of Tom O'Regan, is of crucial importance for Australian cultural studies. Cultural policy studies represented an intervention into cultural studies that set out to replace a traditionally oppositional politics with a more pragmatic and collaborative relation with government. Cultural policy studies was highly contentious within Australia since the various traditions in the Australian academy remained intact and intent on pursuing their long-standing concerns and since it offered itself not as an augmentation but as a replacement for cultural studies. However, cultural policy studies has generated a great deal of important and useful argument and research that has been widely used and discussed outside Australia and that has been integrated into accounts of cultural policy studies generated elsewhere (McGuigan).

Australian cultural studies from the mid-1990s onward has looked increasingly to a transnational cultural studies while nonetheless speaking from its Australian location. That said, the concerns and subjects of Australian cultural studies remain overwhelmingly local, while its theoretical approaches and alignments remain highly diverse. That diversity is indicated by a characteristic pragmatism that encourages skepticism about the usefulness of any single approach and, often, even about the label "cultural studies" itself.

GRAEME TURNER

See also MULTICULTURALISM.

Ien Ang and Jon Stratton, "Asianising Australia: Notes towards a Critical Transnationalism in Cultural Studies," *Cultural Studies* 10 (1996); Tony Bennett, *Culture: A Reformer's Science* (1998), "Putting Policy into Cultural Studies" (Grossberg, Nelson, and Treichler); Stuart Cunningham, *Framing Culture: Criticism and Policy in Australia* (1992); Susan Dermody and Elizabeth Jacka, *The Screening of Australia* (2 vols., 1987–1988); John Fiske, Robert Hodge, and Graeme Turner, *Myths of Oz: Reading Australian Popular Culture* (1987); John Frow, *Cultural Studies and Cultural Value* (1995); John Frow and Meaghan Morris, eds., *Australian Cultural Studies: A Reader* (1993); Ross Gibson, *South of the West: Postcolonialism and the Narrative Construction of Australia* (1992); Lawrence Grossberg, Cary Nelson, and Paula Treichler, eds., *Cultural Studies* (1992); Robert Hodge and Vijay Mishra, *The Dark Side of the Dream: Australian Literature and the Postcolonial Mind* (1991); Ian Hunter, *Culture and Government* (1988); Jim McGuigan, *Culture and the Public Sphere* (1996); Meaghan Morris, "On the Beach" (Grossberg, Nelson, and Treichler), *The Pirate's Fiancée: Feminism, Reading, Postmodernism* (1988), *Too Soon Too Late: History in Popular Culture* (1998); Tom O'Regan, *Australian National Cinema* (1996); Kay Schaffer, *Women and the Bush: Forces of Desire in the Australian Cultural Tradition* (1988); Graeme Turner, " 'It works for me': British Cultural studies, Australian Cultural Studies, Australian Film" (Grossberg, Nelson, and Treichler), *National Fictions: Literature, Film, and the Construction of Australian Narrative* (1986); Graeme Turner, ed., *Nation, Culture, Text: Australian Cultural and Media Studies* (1993); Richard White, *Inventing Australia* (1981).

4. Canada

To be able to experience and understand the consequences of a difference virtually no one else registers is both a necessity and a virtue of the situation of Canadian cultural studies. North American culture, politics, economy, and society are not assimilable to that of the United States, and yet proximity, dependence and domination by that imperial behemoth overdetermines all cultural-political debates regarding social justice, substantive political equality, national identity, and popular cultural production in Canada. As Marshall McLuhan once put it, Canada has thus a "hidden ground"

("Counter-Environment" 73), for this superpower and the singularity of the Canadian situation is precisely what makes the characteristic concerns and debates in Canadian cultural studies useful and instructive to the rest of the world, which also has to negotiate such relations of power, whether in a regional or global context. Canada's difference from the United States is no sooner grasped than it dissolves into a multiplicity of differences and contested and conflicting collective identities: Québécois, First Peoples, métis, and Newfoundlanders; regional and rural identifications; racialized ascriptions of immigrant and visible minority status; class consciousness; and, finally, the cultural political traditions of an activist public sector that even the Washington Consensus was unable to fully extirpate.

Anglophone Canadian cultural studies has closely monitored and quickly appropriated developments and debates in British, American, Australian and inter-Asian cultural studies. Nonetheless, insofar as local sites and subjectivities emerge from singular historical passages and are not mere examples that can be used to fill in the blanks of canonical formulae of theories without date or place, engagement and intervention in local sites and situations requires that these transnational discourses be reverse-engineered through some strategy of localization. To this end, the work of a disparate group of scholars writing in the immediate postwar decades preceding the transatlantic crossings of British cultural studies and French poststructuralism has continued to play an important role as a kind of geopositional system through which debates in transnational cultural studies have been locally mapped. The work of Harold Innis, George Grant, Marshall McLuhan, NORTHROP FRYE, Fernand Dumont, Howard Cardinal, and Anthony Wilden remain relevant because their scholarship explores in wide-ranging ways Canada's collective passage between subordination to the British Empire and a new kind of domination under the American cold war global system. The works of these writers serve as a set of threshold texts for Canadian cultural studies scholars because this historical problematic of Canada's passage between empires continues to impose itself on cultural studies in Canadian situations, ever more so now as the American-led global world economy and geopolitical space sinks into deeper crises, and local and distant events once more bear the possibility of uncharted passages. Without constituting anything like a school or movement, these writers respond in divergent ways to Canada's economic and political subordination to and cultural intimacy with the United States following the end of the old British Dominion of Canada.

In relation to the mid-twentieth century liberal optimism at the height of the postwar boom that progress had been reinstated under American leadership in the wake of the disasters of the first half of the century, Frye's work, for example, echoes and articulates the countercultural liberal despair of a broad formation of Canadian literary and cultural positions for which progress had turned out to be merely the inexorable progress of alienation. This pathos urgently animates Frye's theorization of a mythic deep structure underlying the historical institution of literature. Conceiving myth to be a collective resource of narrative archetypes linked to the "great code" of the Bible itself, Frye theorizes culture as a practice of transcendence in order to argue for the imagination as a therapy for alienation: "Literature is conscious mythology: as society develops, its mythical stories become structural principles of story-telling, its mythical concepts, sun-gods and the like, become habits of metaphorical thought" ("Conclusion" 836). Frye's theory of deep structural myth enables him to plot a story of progress as a story of reconciliation through his history of the development of Canada's national culture from wilderness garrison to its affirmative and triumphal arrival as a postnational (but nonetheless geopolitical) culture of the modern and developed West.

George Grant, Frye's contemporary, rejected such sublimated strategies for affirming postwar American globalism. In a seminal essay in his *Technology and Empire* (1969), "Canadian Fate and Imperialism," Grant writes that "our fate today becomes most evident in the light of Vietnam." Though Canadians tend to remember this as a U.S. war, not theirs, Grant remains important for contemporary Canadian cultural studies precisely for his insight that "as the U.S. becomes daily more of our own, so does the Vietnam war" (74), especially so since Grant understood that there would yet be many more Vietnams. For many Canadians, he observes, Vietnam presents a profound existential crisis in which there erupts an "open conflict" between "our love of the good" and "our love of our own." Canadian complicity with American barbarism in Vietnam brought considerable profits to Canadian mining and manufacture in supplying the U.S. war machine. Postwar economic growth resulting from Canadian membership in the "Western industrial empire" is itself historically rooted in a deeper consent to anglophone hegemony. "To most Canadians," Grant observes, "as public beings, the central cause of motion in their souls is the belief in progress through technique, and that faith is identified with the power and leadership of the English-speaking empire in the world" (64). Grant traces the historical roots of postwar American hegemony to both a historic Whig victory in the anglosphere and to the decisive Calvinist moment of colonialism and merchant capital during which human domination of nature made great strides around the world and turned inward. This diagnosis, made at a time when the influence of what we have come to call neoliberalism was at its lowest ebb, presciently grasped that any global extension of liberal democracy would cost the common classes of the world further colonization by modern techno-military biopower. Democracy would therefore always be undermined by the deepening of American imperialist hegemony, as the establishment of instruments of imperial-corporate governance such as the International Monetary Fund and World Bank demonstrate. Social democracy, Grant thought, however radical, would for the rest of the world be transformed into mere American "democracy" (as in Iraq and Afghanistan today), as the aspiration for American consumer lifestyles and for progress through technique cannot be pursued without exploiting whoever happens to be more desperate around us. In this early critique of liberal governmentality, Grant argues that there is a fundamental connection between the historical project of liberalism and the Marines bursting through somebody's front door.

Unlike Grant, however, Dumont and Cardinal could find in the histories they investigated various passages to futures worth struggling for, even if the immediate prospects seemed grim. For both Dumont and Cardinal, the collective projects of decolonization and nationalism kept open a future in thought, culture, and politics that Grant did not think was possible. Dumont writes on a wide range of subjects, including theology, economics, literature, culture, education and sociology. Throughout this voluminous corpus, the complex and singular situation of Québec's history as an enclave in anglophone North America is a recurrent preoccupation. Dumont theorizes the Quiet Revolution as a cultural revolution in which the tasks of economic and political revolution (some new kind of socialism in an independent Québec) is yet to be achieved. In order to invent an "original model for economic and cultural development" in which culture and economy are no longer mutually alienated, Dumont posits the need for a language of politics in which "this time more closely than before, the past will be mingled with the imperatives of the future" (*Vigil* 195–99). For Dumont, this means constructing an interpretation of the history of the peoples of Québec that connected it to the histories of other peoples. In this regard, "our cultural problem," Dumont argues, "has then become openly what it has always been implicitly, a problem of communication, in the sense however it no longer applies to reception difficulties but more to those of emission."

Howard Cardinal also turns back to the past in order to reclaim a future in the *Unjust Society* (1969), a book that profoundly altered Canadian perceptions of the relations between aboriginal peoples and the crown. The immediate context of Cardinal's intervention is the Indian policy proposed in 1969 by the new government of Pierre Elliott Trudeau (1968–1979) that would have extinguished the rights of aboriginal peoples as enshrined in various historical treaties made between different First Nations and the British Crown or the Government of Canada. The policy would also have abolished the Department of Indian Affairs and transferred governmental responsibility for aboriginal peoples to the provinces. Cardinal argues in reply that this policy would not only constitute the ultimate betrayal of the treaties in a history of innumerable betrayals but also result in the final cultural extermination of aboriginal people, an objective long pursued by the Canadian government's assimilationist policies, which *The Unjust Society* authoritatively details. Crucially, Cardinal raised the alarm that the extinction of treaty rights would result in a handover of natural resources (to which aboriginal peoples have treaty-based claims) to multinational corporations. Cardinal's book moreover establishes three principles that have been decisive for aboriginal struggles for self-government as well as alterglobalization social movements in Canada. *The Unjust Society* establishes the principle that the spirit and intent of the treaties must be the grounds on which nation-to-nation negotiations proceed. Furthermore, a crucial aspect of the treaties is their recognition of collective rights, a principle now enshrined in the Canadian Charter of Rights. Thirdly, the principle of self-government itself ought to be recognized as the legitimate content of the reform to be negotiated between Canada and the First Nations. The issues raised and explored in this book have been crucially important in defining the agendas and debates over aboriginal self-government ever since. But they have had a broader cultural-political resonance as well. Cultural studies scholars Daniel Francis, Terry Goldie, and Gail Guthrie Valaskasis, and many writers and visual artists (Joane Cardinal-Schubert, Jane Ash Poitras, Kent Monkman) have demonstrated the ubiquity and libidinal power of an archive of the "imaginary Indian" to Canadian self-representation. The electrifying exchange of valences achieved by Cardinal's book, in which the history of imperial and then racist domination is retrieved as a heroic account of First Nations' collective agency and political innovation while staring historical oblivion in the eye, has ever since fed a growing current of pathbreaking cultural-political thought in the work of Taiaiake Alfred, John Borrows, Patrick Macklem and the aboriginal feminisms of Lee Maracle, Jeanette Armstrong, and Patricia Monture in which the legacy of the treaties and the utopianism of self-government serve as a vital ethical and political imaginary that now energizes the alter-globalization movement's visions of "postnational democracies against the state." Along these lines, cultural historian Anthony Hall's magnum opus *The American Empire and the Fourth World* (2003) retraces the long overlooked influence of aboriginal ideas of egalitarian self-government on French Enlightenment republicanism through the fur trade social networks and political alliances of New France.

The equally distinctive tradition of Canadian communication theory inaugurated by Harold Innis, Marshall McLuhan, Dallas Smythe, and Anthony Wilden comprise another set of threshold texts through which Canadian scholars localize transnational cultural studies. Harold Innis's theory of the bias of communication, still a singular breakthrough in cultural theory today, may perhaps be best grasped as a dialectical ultimate step not yet to be taken in current standard accounts of the crisis of representation. A commonplace of cultural theory asserts that what we call space and time are better understood as chronotopical representations that effect discursive mediations of experiences (rather than as what Immanuel Kant and the Enlightenment called transcendental a priori forms of experience). The bias of communication theory goes one step further and argues that it is not merely the case that representation mediates our experiences but that this mediation itself is mediated by a given communication system's bias toward either temporal or spatial capacities that depend on the sociohistorical conditions of its deployment. Moreover, Innis's communication theory anticipates both the widely discussed spatial turn of postmodern societies of the spectacle and the broad lines of Benedict Anderson's arguments about the role of print capitalism in the emergence of nationalism (see NATIONAL LITERATURE). Innis's diagnosis of our unsustainable and self-destructive "present-mindedness" that owes to the overwhelming space bias of the corporate-governmental world information order leads him to urge his readers to attend to the latent and liminal temporal capacities of our media in order to mount a cultural counterstrategy of resistance.

Marshall McLuhan's far more widely known media theory develops another dimension of Innis's work that, under the concept of communication, draws attention to relationships between different media practices and forms, thereby forestalling the reification of media processes and effects (especially those of the new "cool" media of his era—television, video, digital media) into all-too-familiar discrete shapes resembling the "hot" auratic objects the humanities have traditionally studied. In McLuhan, this becomes a full-blown media ecology, a field theory of media environments, and is ultimately formalized in the remarkable dialectical figure of the hermeneutic tetrad. The tetrad, mapping out the social and historical force field through which any given media operates, enables critical attention to return to the specificities of a given media technology in order to probe the embodied, techno-mediated sensory and proprioceptive systems that the given technology under study extends, retrieves, obsolesces, and repurposes. McLuhan argues that Canadian society and culture was historically positioned to work as a counterenvironment to the world environment projected by the postmodern United States. Scholars, artists, and content providers have followed the trajectories of the speculative probes of McLuhan's media ecology and Innis's communication theory in order to think through the possibilities of local, alternative and critical cultural production in a situation where the means of spectacular mass cultural production, bunkered in the world system of states, cannot be directly revolutionized. (See the writings of Charles Acland, Richard Cavell, Gary Genosko, Robert Hackett, Susan Lord, Janine Marchessault, Kim Sawchuk, Roger Simon, and Will Straw.)

Anthony Wilden extends this relational and ecological approach to rethinking the conventional binary oppositions of cultural studies such as popular/high culture, high culture / mass culture, mass culture / popular culture, popular culture / ethnicity, and ethnos/nature by crafting an original critical bricolage of the ecological thought of Gregory Bateson, cybernetic theory, Lacanian psychoanalysis, and New Left Marxism. The result is a distinct and different approach to the handling of binary oppositions, especially imaginary, ideological oppositions, which Wilden argues are the result of an operation he calls the "symmetrization of dependent hierarchies." All historical understanding and ecological adaptations are mediated by communicative codes, yet, as Wilden's work repeatedly and systematically demonstrates, the symbolic does not transcend the history of environments. Wilden's communication theory sets out to patiently untangle the double binds that follow from this. Among the fruits of these efforts are Wilden's semiotic grammar of competition and cooperation and his theory of strategic envelopment, which provide very suggestive concepts for thinking through the contradictions and cultural politics of the creative economy.

This group of threshold texts establishes a problematic that contemporary Canadian cultural studies continues to negotiate in a wide range of ways. One aspect of this problematic stems from the need to develop historically erudite critiques in a situation of unremitting "present-mindedness" (Innis) in which the stories of the past have turned out to be ideologies. A major current of contemporary cultural studies research thus confronts the colonial, patriarchal, and racist histories of state and nation formation as well as class domination and the ideological resolution of class and gender contradictions through multiculturalist nationalism (as in the work of Constance Backhouse, Himani Bannerji, Dionne Brand, Jenny Burman, Diana Brydon, Richard Day, Len Findlay, Frances Henry, Smaro Kamboureli, Stephen Slemon, Dorothy Smith, and Sunera Thobani). Yet having to confront such histories with and through the "fragments of empire," as Ioan Davies argues, has resulted in a thoroughgoing skepticism in Canadian cultural studies regarding linear or developmental narratives of transition or change in an era when transnational cultural theory has wanted to prefix a post to all its big ideas. Another aspect of this problematic is constituted out of persistent everyday reminders that the concept of culture with which scholars operate can never be identical with itself in Canada (if it ever can be anywhere else either). Not only is the idea of culture fatally fragmented between serving as an analogue for ethnicity and an euphemism for race, on one hand, and standing for a school or reformatory for subjectivity on the other, but because of economies of scale, Canadian mass culture cannot ever really amount to mass culture. An irrepressible nonidentity imposes itself here, too: Canadian mass culture turns out to be popular culture (as in popular music, popular literatures, radio, and television) and yet Canadian popular culture turns out to be made up of complex relationships (of national allegory, of the double screen, of the border, etc.) to American mass culture (as in fashion, design, sports, animation, gaming, internet communication, technoculture). As Jody Berland observes, "cultural studies can never be singly about culture because that is a misinterpretation of what culture is" (319). For this reason, many contemporary scholars, drawing on the pathbreaking work of Innis, McLuhan, Smythe and Wilden, have strategically focused their critical energies on diagramming various cultural technologies of space in order to register both the nonlinear temporality of local history and the historical situation of cultural identifications and locations (as in the work of Ian Angus, Robert Babe, Maurice Charland, Nick Dyer-Witheford, Arthur Kroker, and Rob Shields).

SOURAYAN MOOKERJEA

Charles R. Acland, *Residual Media* (2007), *Screen Traffic* (2003); Taiaiake Alfred, *Peace, Power, Righteousness: An Indigenous Manifesto* (2009); Ian Angus, *A Border Within: National Identity, Cultural Plurality, and Wilderness* (1997); Robert E. Babe, *Culture of Ecology: Reconciling Economics and Environment* (2006); Constance Backhouse, *Colour-Coded: A Legal History of Racism in Canada, 1900–1950* (1999); Himani Bannerji, *The Dark Side of the Nation: Essays on Multiculturalism, Nationalism and Gender* (2000); Jody Berland, *North of Empire: Essays on the Cultural Technologies of Space* (2009); John Borrows, *Recovering*

Canada: The Resurgence of Indigenous Law (2002); Dionne Brand, A Map to the Door of No Return: Notes to Belonging (2001); Diana Brydon and Helen Tiffin, Decolonising Fictions (1993); Jenny Burman, Transnational Yearnings: Tourism, Migration, and the Diasporic City (2010); Howard Cardinal, The Unjust Society (1969); Richard Cavell, McLuhan in Space (2002); Ioan Davies, Cultural Studies and Beyond: Fragments of Empire (1995); Richard J. F. Day, Multiculturalism and the History of Canadian Diversity (2000); Fernand Dumont, The Vigil of Québec (1974); Northrop Frye, "Conclusion," Literary History of Canada (ed. Carl F. Klinck, 1965); Northrop Frye et al., City of the End of Things (2009); Gary Genosko, McLuhan and Baudrillard (1999); Barbara Godard and Smaro Kamboureli, Canadian Literature at the Crossroads of Language and Culture: Selected Essays by Barbara Godard, 1987–2005 (2008); George Parkin Grant, Lament for a Nation: The Defeat of Canadian Nationalism (1965), Technology and Empire (1969); Harold A. Innis, The Bias of Communication (1951), The Cod Fisheries: The History of an International Economy (1940), The Fur Trade in Canada (1930); Arthur Kroker, Technology and the Canadian Mind: Innis, McLuhan, Grant (1984); Marshall McLuhan, Understanding Media (1964); Sourayan Mookerjea, Imre Szeman, and Gail Faurschou, eds., Canadian Cultural Studies: A Reader (2009); Patricia Monture-Angus, Journeying Forward: Dreaming First Nations' Independence (1999); Sherene Razack, Malinda Sharon Smith, and Sunera Thobani, eds., States of Race: Critical Race Feminism for the 21st Century (2010); Kim Sawchuk, Barbara A. Crow, and Michael Longford, eds., The Wireless Spectrum: The Politics, Practices, and Poetics of Mobile Media (2010); Rob Shields, Places on the Margin: Alternatives Geographies of Modernity (1991); Roger I. Simon, The Touch of the Past: Remembrance, Learning, and Ethics (2005); Roger I. Simon, Sharon Rosenberg, and Claudia Eppert, eds., Between Hope and Despair: Pedagogy and the Remembrance of Historical Trauma (2000); Stephen Slemon and Helen Tiffin, ed., After Europe: Critical Theory and Post-Colonial Writing (1989); Dorothy E. Smith, Institutional Ethnography: A Sociology for People (2005); Sunera Thobani, Exalted Subjects: Studies in the Making of Race and Nation in Canada (2007); Gail Guthrie Valaskakis, Indian Country: Essays on Contemporary Native Culture (2005); Anthony Wilden, The Imaginary Canadian (1980), System and Structure: Essays in Communication and Exchange (1980).

de Man, Paul

Paul de Man (1919–1983) was born in Antwerp, Belgium and died in New Haven, Connecticut. He strongly influenced the emergence of literary "theory," first through his teaching at Cornell (1960–1966), Johns Hopkins (1967–1970), and Yale (1970–1983) and then, beginning in the 1970s, through his writings, which came to be associated with DECONSTRUCTION but might best be characterized as "rhetorical reading." De Man's work focuses on reading as it arises from the rhetorical character of any text: its possibility of having a figural as well as a literal meaning. Like JACQUES DERRIDA's, de Man's work brings to the fore questions of language; he writes that "the advent of theory . . . occurs with the introduction of linguistic terminology in the metalanguage about literature," when historical and aesthetic considerations give place to linguistic ones (*Resistance* 8). Rhetorical reading, for de Man, is a practice of reading attentive to the tension between a text's figures and its "grammar," between a text's statements and its process, or, most broadly, to "a non-convergence of 'meaning' with the devices that produce 'meaning'" (*Allegories* 7; *Resistance* 66).

De Man's work is poststructuralist in the sense that it refutes the idea that texts can be reduced to their code, structure, or "grammar"; it departs from the philosophical tradition within which literature is subsumed under the category of the aesthetic, grasped as the phenomenalization or sensible presentation of a meaning. For de Man, literature or texts undo claims of authority, claims based on assumptions of the continuity of form with meaning and the possibility of totalizing a structure. As a critique of these assumptions and others that his later writings call "the aesthetic ideology," de Man's work premises that "one could approach the problems of ideology and by extension the problems of politics only on the basis of critical-linguistic analysis, which had to be done in its own terms" (*Resistance* 121).

In 1987 it was discovered that de Man's earliest writings include 180 book reviews and short articles on cultural topics for newspapers in Brussels that had been taken over by collaborators after the German invasion of Belgium in the early 1940s. One of these articles, "Les Juifs dans la littérature actuelle" (*Wartime Journalism* 45), uses the language of antisemitism and, not surprisingly, its discovery provoked considerable debate—"the de Man affair"—primarily about the relation of de Man's youthful journalism to his mature work. Some of these articles, at the same time, praise writers disapproved of by the Nazis (such as French surrealist poets) and also contain statements about literature's direct expression of transcendent truths and other critical pronouncements that de Man would criticize as "aesthetic ideology" in his later writings.

A distinctive feature of de Man's essays from 1953 through 1983 is the status they accord to literature or the literary as the undoer of ideological mystifications. Ideology is "the confusion of linguistic with natural reality, of reference with phenomenalism" (*Resistance* 11); literature, as we acknowledge when we speak of "fiction," assumes the divergence between sign and meaning. In de Man's first book, *Blindness and Insight*, "literature" appears as a kind of language "privileged" in the sense that it is not blind to its own statement: literature is "any text that implicitly or explicitly signifies its own rhetorical mode and prefigures its own misunderstanding" (136). In *Allegories of Reading*, emphasis shifts from the text's cognition of its rhetorical mode to a noncognitive dimension of the text. Implicit in the literary or rhetorical dimension of language is the impossibility of deciding on purely linguistic grounds between a literal and a figurative meaning of a text. Literary texts posit realities rather than reveal given ones. Thus literature has the critical power of disclosing the unreliability of linguistic artifacts that are passed off by the dominant ideology as truthful representations of the world (Klein). A text does *not* have the power of closing off its performance or reading, of existing as self-knowledge or self-reflection. For it begins in a linguistic positing, which cannot be derived and which does not signify, although this positing is the presupposition for any communicable meaning (Frey 132).

This nonsemantic dimension of discourse is stressed as the materiality of language, or "inscription," in de Man's late essays in *The Resistance to Theory*. "Everyday" and "literary" language are finally inseparable because the representational function of both—the function of cognition—derives from the illegitimate power without authority of a *figure*, the figure whereby the materiality of language gets confused with and conferred on meanings and ultimately on things. Rhetorical reading does not deny the referential function of language (as is sometimes supposed); rather, it challenges the "authority" of that linguistic function "as a model for natural or phenomenal cognition" (11). Reading that is responsive to language's positing its realities rather than mirroring phenomenal givens is "a powerful and indispensable tool in the unmasking of ideological aberrations," de Man argues, even as "the linguistics of literariness is . . . a determining factor in accounting for their occurrence" (11).

An earlier phase in de Man's work, in which the main categories of criticism are consciousness, intentionality, and temporality, can be distinguished from a later one, in which the major categories are linguistic and rhetorical: symbol, allegory, irony, metaphor, metonymy, prosopopoeia, and catachresis. An influential transitional work is the 1969 essay "The Rhetoric of Temporality," where, reexamining the supposed shift from allegorical to symbolic diction in late eighteenth-century poetry, de Man challenges the assumed superiority of symbol to allegory on the grounds that allegory locates the subject in a world in which "time is the originary constitutive category," preventing its illusory self-coincidence or identification with a natural world (*Blindness* 207). *Allegories of Reading* (1979) uses the same term, "allegory," to describe the second- or third-order narratives about the conditions of signification that follow from the impossibility of closing off the reading of a text in a deconstruction of that text's figures. The second half of this book, on the *Social Contract* and other works of Rousseau, uses linguistic categories and the analysis of speech acts to analyze the structure of political institutions, such as property, the national state, and statutory law.

Throughout his work, de Man raises questions of history, including questions of texts' impingement on historical events. De Man's own chief contribution to literary history is the revaluation of early Romanticism as the decisive, not yet superseded moment of the modern period. Essays written between 1956 and 1983 gathered in *The Rhetoric of Romanticism* read English, German, and French Romantic and late Romantic literature; complementary to them are rhetorical readings of texts of Immanuel Kant, Friedrich Schiller, and G. W. F. Hegel gathered in *Aesthetic Ideology*, focused on the concept of the sublime and on the category of the aesthetic. Close consideration of a literary text staging the Schillerian notions of "aesthetic education" and the "aesthetic state" (Kleist's "On the Marionette Theater") leads de Man to diagnose and indict, as a fundamental strategy of the aesthetic ideology he links with the totalitarian state, "aesthetic formalization": the aesthetification, as a satisfying, recognizable *form*, of the arbitrary, contradictory processes of language. His counterproposal is a reading process in which the formal and referential aspects of language are continually in conflict and at stake.

CYNTHIA CHASE

Paul de Man, *Aesthetic Ideology* (ed. Andrzej Warminski, 1996), *Allegories of Reading: Figural Language in Rousseau, Nietzsche, Rilke, and Proust* (1979), *Blindness and Insight: Essays in the Rhetoric of Contemporary Criticism* (1971, 2nd ed., 1983), *Critical Writings, 1953–1978* (ed. Lindsay Waters, 1989), *The Resistance to Theory* (1986), *The Rhetoric of Romanticism* (1984), *Romanticism and Contemporary Criticism: The Gauss Seminars and Other Papers* (ed. E. S. Burt, Kevin Newmark, and Andrzej Warminski, 1992), *Wartime Journalism, 1939–1943* (ed. Werner Hamacher, Neil Hertz, and Tom Keenan, 1988); Hans Jost Frey, "Undecidability," *Yale French Studies* 69 (1985); Richard Klein, "De Man's Resistances" (Hamacher, Hertz, and Keenan).

Deconstruction

1. Derrida, de Man, and the Yale Critics

"Deconstruction" is the name given to a radical and wide-ranging development in the human sciences, especially philosophy and literary criticism, initiated by the French philosopher JACQUES DERRIDA in a series of highly influential books published in the late 1960s and early 1970s, including *Of Grammatology, Writing and Difference, Speech and Phenomena, Margins of Philosophy*, and *Dissemination*. "Deconstruction," Derrida's coinage, has subsequently become synonymous with a particular method of textual analysis and philosophical argument involving the close reading of works of literature, philosophy, psychoanalysis, linguistics, and anthropology to reveal logical or rhetorical incompatibilities between the explicit and implicit planes of discourse in a text and to demonstrate by means of a range of critical techniques how these incompatibilities are disguised and assimilated by the text. In one of its typical analytical procedures, a deconstructive reading focuses on binary oppositions within a text, first, to show how those oppositions are structured hierarchically, second, to overturn that hierarchy temporarily, as if to make the text say the opposite of what it appeared to say initially, and third, to displace and reassert both terms of the opposition within a nonhierarchical relationship of "difference."

Both historically and methodologically, deconstruction as a form of critical reading is related to the advent of poststructuralism. In addition to influences from Friedrich Nietzsche and MARTIN HEIDEGGER, several of its key concepts are derived from the structural linguistics of FERDINAND DE SAUSSURE's *Course in General Linguistics* (1916), which inaugurated STRUCTURALISM by postulating the arbitrary nature of the linguistic sign, by proposing that the sign can be divided into *signifier* (the spoken or written word) and *signified* (the mental concept), by positing the notion of linguistic value as a function of "difference" or noncoincidence rather than of correspondence or nomenclature, and by adumbrating SEMIOTICS or semiology, the study of signs and their mechanisms of signification. By grounding his theory in the arbitrary nature of the sign, Saussure affirmed that there is no intrinsic, organic, or "motivated" reason for signifying a particular concept by means of a particular word; the meaning of a word is arbitrary but agreed upon by social convention.

The concept of difference is crucial to Derrida, who uses it to "deconstruct" Western philosophy, which he argues is founded on a theory of "presence," in which metaphysical notions such as truth, being, and reality are determined in their relation to an ontological center, essence, origin (*archè*), or end (*telos*) that represses absence and difference for the sake of metaphysical stability. The best-kept secret of Western metaphysics is thus the historical repression of difference through a philosophical vocabulary that favors presence in the form of voice, consciousness, and subjectivity. Derrida calls this philosophy "logocentrism" or "phonocentrism" be-

cause in his view it is based on a belief in a *logos* or *phonè*, a self-present word constituted not by difference but by presence (*Writing and Difference* 278–82). Logocentrism
for Derrida represents Western culture's sentimental desire for a natural or Adamic
language whose authority is guaranteed by a divine, transcendental signified. On the
surface, language seems unwilling to face up to its human arbitrariness, yet on closer
inspection it also appears to call attention to its differential structure: language at
once posits and retracts its own desire for presence.

One of Derrida's clearest examples of a deconstructive reading can be found in
his account of the relation between speech and writing in Saussure's *Course* (*Of Grammatology* 27–73). Whereas Saussure, as a "phonocentric" linguist, favors speech as
the proper object of linguistic investigation rather than writing, which he takes to be
a secondary representation or even disguise of speech, he is forced to acknowledge
the dangerous, usurping power of writing over speech (*Course* 24–31). Derrida approaches this problem, first, by confirming historically the priority of voice over the
letter: speech is immediate, self-present, and authentic in that it is uttered by a speaker
who hears and understands himself or herself in the moment of speaking; by contrast, writing is the copy of speech and is therefore derivative, marginal, and delayed.
But having outlined a speech/writing hierarchy in this way, Derrida shows how Saussure's text inverts the hierarchy, giving priority to writing over speech. The inversion of the hierarchy constitutes one half of a deconstruction; Derrida completes the
procedure by showing how in *Saussure's own terms* both speech and writing are subsumed into a larger linguistic field in which all language, spoken and written, is
constituted by difference rather than hierarchy.

The privileging of speech and the repression of writing represent for Derrida a
fundamental aspect of the logocentric history of Western culture. In order to deconstruct this hierarchical tradition of presence, Derrida elaborates Saussure's notion of
linguistic difference by introducing the idea of *différance*, spelled with an *a* (*Speech*
129–60). (In French there is no phonetic difference between *différence* and *différance*; the
difference, seen and not heard, thus reveals in writing something speech does not
have.) *Différance* retains its Saussurean structuralist connotation of noncoincidence—as
well as its meanings of deferring in time / differing in space—but Derrida expands
the concept to include the whole field of signs. This field he names *écriture*, or "writing," not in the literal sense of graphic script but in the figural sense of writing as any
system inhabited by différance. The study of writing, which he calls "grammatology,"
is the science of différance itself, involving the analysis of the play of terms within a
closed semiotic system in which each term acquires value only through its opposition
to the other terms. "Play," another name for différance, is Derrida's word for the interpenetration of terms—that is, how each sign simultaneously confers and derives
meaning with respect to other signs, so that any given sign is tacitly implied in another as a "trace" or an effect of linguistic interdependence (*Speech* 154–58; *Writing
and Difference* 292).

Critics of deconstruction have tended to address two polarized issues. The first issue, in a sense superficial, is Derrida's prose style, a challenging, allusive, witty, even literary style—it has been compared to the style of James Joyce, and Derrida himself has written on Joyce—that some readers feel is "mere wordplay," ingenious in its puns and other tropes but also obfuscating and resistant to comprehension. Derrida's prose may dazzle, critics say; however, it does not enlighten but rather indulges in jargon, rhetorical games, and overly subtle metaphysical conceits. Against such a criticism it is possible to argue that Derrida's style, difficulties of English translation notwithstanding, is a deliberate and strategic expression of his theory: there is nothing "mere" or trivial about wordplay; on the contrary, "play" is what constitutes words themselves, what gives them linguistic value in their very difference.

The second issue is much deeper than surface style. If language, metaphysics, and consciousness really are structured by difference, then there can be no solid foundation, no fixed point of reference, no authority or certainty, either ontological or interpretive. Everything can be "put in question," that is, viewed as arbitrary, free-floating elements in a closed system of "writing," with the result that previously settled assumptions of stability and coherence, both in words and in things, become radically shaken, even, as a number of critics have claimed, to the point of nihilism. Again, it is possible to counter this charge, as some of Derrida's followers have done, by showing that deconstruction seeks not to destroy meaning but to expose the production of meaning as an arbitrary effect of writing. The exposure of this arbitrariness is most apparent at those points where a text's explicit statement is incompatible with its implicit principles of logic or rhetoric.

Despite these and other resistances to deconstruction, Derrida's impact on critical thought has been significant and extensive. As part of a general poststructuralist tendency to move language to the forefront of discussion—that is, to rethink both word and world from the point of view of textuality—deconstruction has had a vital influence in multidisciplinary studies involving feminism, theology, psychoanalysis, Marxism, anthropology, and linguistics. As a method of literary criticism, however, deconstruction first became identified largely with the work of certain critics at Yale University—Geoffrey H. Hartman, J. Hillis Miller, and PAUL DE MAN—though these critics have responded to Derrida in markedly different ways.

Hartman's engagement with deconstruction can be seen most obviously in terms of style, though Hartman would quickly remind readers that the question of style is also the question of method. In its own method, Hartman's style operates largely on the level of the signifier in a punning, associative manner that incorporates both learned allusion and verbal cliché, always calling attention to questions of language and forcing the reader to recognize that texts are also intertexts. In this way Hartman attempts to reclaim for interpretation a sense of literary history—classical, Romantic, and modern.

J. Hillis Miller enters deconstruction through language itself, the "groundless ground" of words that offers an illusion of presence and reference only then to swallow them up in an abyss of difference. Miller repeatedly uses the concept of an abyss structure, or mise en abyme, to suggest the possibility of infinite play in language, the endless substitution of one sign for another (*Deconstruction and Criticism* 232). The expression mise en abyme, taken from heraldry via André Gide and used strategically by Derrida, denotes the repetition in miniature of a whole within itself, as in the example of a painting within a painting. Miller sees such a theory as part of a "tradition of difference" working within and against a "tradition of presence" ("Tradition and Difference"). Every presence in language, Miller argues, can be deconstructed and exposed as difference, shown to be based on a baseless fabric of words, not a real metaphysical ground. Whether the key to the abyss in a text is a semantic ambiguity, a double-faced etymology, or a tropological deviance, it is in any event a linguistic problem, a question of language as such. The critic's function is to face that problem, not to attempt to solve or neutralize it but to recognize the abyss as an inherent feature of an arbitrary and differential system of language. In this sense, deconstruction for Miller is not a method of analysis that a critic "applies" to a text. It is something that the text has already done to itself. Every text is always already deconstructed. What the critic does, then, is repeat the text in his or her analysis, that is, repeat its rhetorical operations, its linguistic maneuvers, its very difference.

While Miller is often regarded as the spokesperson for Yale deconstruction in that he has attempted in his writing, in conferences, and in panel discussions and interviews to explain deconstruction and defend it against charges of hermeneutical anarchy and nihilism, Paul de Man, by contrast, is a deconstructor who makes no apology for either his method or its startling results. De Man's interest is in the operation of rhetorical figures, and his essays often focus on a single trope—metaphor, prosopopoeia, apostrophe, or metonymy—as a means of opening up a text to its "allegory of reading." De Man's method of textual analysis resembles Derrida's in its recurrent effort to uncover hierarchical oppositions within texts and to reveal the linguistic and philosophical grounds on which those hierarchies are built. Such a method, called a "critique," seeks to make explicit what is implicit, assumed, repressed, or contradicted in a text. Thus de Man is less concerned to explicate theme than to show how rhetoric is "thematized," that is, how the literal or narrative level of a text may repeat its figural substructure. Stylistically, however, de Man is far from Derrida: puns, multilingual resonances, and other rhetorical flourishes do not play a significant role in de Man's prose, which by contrast is sedate and analytical.

In the initial stages of deconstruction, from 1966 through the early 1980s, the Yale critics exerted the chief influence on the development of deconstructive criticism. Since then, however, deconstruction has not been confined to any one school or group of critics, though many of today's leading deconstructors do trace their critical affiliations back to the Yale school, as former students or otherwise. Not un-expectedly (nor unproblematically), this second phase of deconstruction can be described as *applied* deconstruction, or "deconstruction and *x*"—deconstruction and feminism, deconstruction and psychoanalysis, deconstruction and Marxism, and so on. In each case the insights and techniques of deconstructive reading are transferred to another field of the human sciences, sometimes with very fruitful results. The best-known second-generation deconstructor is undoubtedly Barbara Johnson, whose books *The Critical Difference: Essays in the Contemporary Rhetoric of Reading* (1980) and *A World of Difference* (1987), along with her translations of Derrida, quickly became regarded as classics of deconstructive criticism. Deeply influenced by de Man's teaching, Johnson brilliantly adapts his mode of dismantling texts through close readings of their rhetorical operations. Johnson takes deconstruction, and theory generally, out of the realm of critical abstraction and uses it to address political concerns: feminist literature, African American writing, and polemics and patriarchy in criticism. For Johnson, deconstruction is not just a technique of reading literary texts but an attitude toward a whole field of signs, an entire world composed of textual, sexual, and racial difference. Johnson's later work thus may be viewed as the second stage of deconstruction, as its applied rather than purely theoretical mode, or simply as what Johnson calls the "consequences of theory."

Attempts to discuss deconstruction in connection with MARXIST THEORY AND CRITICISM and NEW HISTORICISM have been made by critics such as Marjorie Levinson, Andrew Parker ("Between Dialectics and Deconstruction" [1985]), Michael Ryan (*Marxism and Deconstruction* [1982]), and GAYATRI CHAKRAVORTY SPIVAK ("Speculation on Reading Marx" [1987]). The marriage has not been particularly fruitful; not surprisingly, deconstruction and Marxism have been seen as oxymoronic bedfellows, and critics inevitably tend to privilege one methodology over the other. While Ryan in "Political Criticism" argues that deconstruction "put[s] the very possibility of a totalistic [i.e., Marxist] reading into question" (204), many critics have tried to find common ground. Levinson, for example, envisions a "deconstructive materialism" that would employ shared aspects of Marxism and deconstruction (10), yet her readings clearly privilege materialism over deconstruction. Spivak has brought her knowledge of deconstruction (she translated Derrida's *De la grammatologie* into English) to bear on feminist and cultural studies, particularly issues in colonialism and phallocentrism ("Displacement and the Discourse of Woman" [1983] and "Poststructuralism, Marginality, Postcoloniality, and Value" [1990]). As her essays demonstrate, deconstruction and Marxism can intersect profitably, though not entirely rigorously, in the analysis of hierarchies, oppositions, and power structures, about which the two methodologies may yet have something to teach each other. A genuine dialogue between them remains to be achieved, however. The same must be said for the engagement of deconstruction and New Historicism: insofar as the ground of history, as constructed by new historicists, carries with it, as Derrida would say, "the theme of a final repression of difference" (*Speech* 141), the engagement remains unproductive. Parker suggests that rather than taking sides on Marx versus Derrida, or on history versus difference, critics need to maintain the differences "both to discourage the premature assimilation of the one to the other as well as to mitigate the increasing hostility displayed by advocates of each 'opposing' mode" (72).

On the interface between PSYCHOANALYTIC THEORY AND CRITICISM and deconstruction, critics such as Shoshana Felman and Stephen W. Melville, reading Derrida's work "as in large measure an extension of psychoanalysis into the history of philosophy" (Melville 84), have with the help of JACQUES LACAN mounted poststructuralist psychoanalytic readings of both literary and nonliterary texts. Felman's work exhibits a brilliant combination of psychoanalysis and deconstruction in its insistent "interpretation of difference" and its Lacanian-Derridean "analysis of the signifier as opposed to an analysis of the signified" (43, 44). Much of Derrida's work has been an explicit dialogue with SIGMUND FREUD (and some of it a mute dialogue with Lacan); his essay "Freud and the Scene of Writing" (*Writing and Difference* 196–231) and his book *The Post Card* amply show the possibilities of a deconstructive psychoanalysis.

By the 1990s, deconstructive criticism was literally and figurally all over the map. While early fears that deconstruction would destroy the academy by questioning Western values proved to be unfounded, there is no denying that deconstruction underwent considerable changes in focus and application over its relatively brief development. The turning outward by some deconstructors from literary matters to political issues and current events can be construed, in the context of late twentieth-century attacks on theory, as an attempt to make deconstruction "relevant," to demonstrate the practical or social benefits of deconstruction as part of a larger defense of theory. Deconstruction has forced critics to reexamine their philosophical assumptions and to rethink their own language. Deconstructive criticism has brought an intellectual rigor to the reading of texts not just by questioning previous readings but by questioning reading itself. As the initiator of deconstruction, Derrida began a project that, in taking language, arbitrary and differential, as its medium and focus, continues to engage a striking array of topics, from philosophy to psychoanalysis to contemporary architecture, that have implications for virtually all aspects of human activity— culture, discourse, science. After more than three decades of productive theory and practice, deconstruction remains one of the most significant developments in the critical thought of the last forty years.

J. DOUGLAS KNEALE

See also JACQUES DERRIDA, FRENCH THEORY AND CRITICISM: 1945 AND AFTER, and SPEECH ACTS.

Harold Bloom et al., *Deconstruction and Criticism* (1979); Paul de Man, *Allegories of Reading: Figural Language in Rousseau, Nietzsche, Rilke, and Proust* (1979), *Blindness and Insight: Essays in the Rhetoric of Contemporary Criticism* (1971, 2nd ed., 1983); Jacques Derrida, *Acts of Literature* (ed. Derek Attridge, 1992), *La carte postale: De Socrate à Freud et au-delà* (1980, *The Post Card: From Socrates to Freud and Beyond*, trans. Alan Bass, 1987), *De la grammatologie* (1967, *Of Grammatology*, trans. Gayatri Chakravorty Spivak, 1976), *A Derrida Reader: Between the Blinds* (ed. Peggy Kamuf, 1991), *La dissémination* (1972, *Dissemination*, trans. Barbara Johnson, 1981), *L'écriture et la différence* (1967, *Writing and Difference*, trans. Alan Bass, 1978), *Marges de la philosophie* (1972, *Margins of Philosophy*, trans. Alan Bass, 1982), *Positions* (1972, *Positions*, trans. Alan Bass, 1981), *La voix et le phénomène: Introduction au problème du signe dans la phénoménologie* (1967, *Speech and Phenomena, and Other Essays on Husserl's Theory of Signs*, trans. David B. Allison, 1973); Shoshana Felman, *Jacques Lacan and the Adventure of Insight: Psychoanalysis in Contemporary Culture* (1987); Geoffrey H. Hartman, *Criticism in the Wilderness: The Study of Literature Today* (1980), *Saving the Text: Literature/Derrida/Philosophy* (1981), *Wordsworth's Poetry, 1787–1814* (1964); J. Hillis Miller, "The Critic as Host" (Bloom et al.), *The Linguistic Moment: From Wordsworth to Stevens* (1985); Marjorie Levinson, *Wordsworth's Great Period Poems: Four Essays* (1986); Stephen W. Melville, *Philosophy beside Itself: On Deconstruction and Modernism* (1986); Andrew Parker, " 'Taking Sides' (On History): Derrida Re-Marx," *diacritics* 11 (1981); Michael Ryan, "Political Criticism," *Contemporary Literary Theory* (ed. G. Douglas Atkins and Laura Morrow, 1989).

2. The 1980s and After

Beginning in the 1980s, deconstruction became more varied and diverse than ever. Its history has been marked by polemics as well as by a renewed sense of urgency and possibility. Indeed, the word "deconstruction" itself has entered into the idiom of our age. As Herman Rapaport puts it, "It seems that everyone now wants to deconstruct something, whether an administrative structure, an economic plan, an educational procedure, or, as in the case of Woody Allen's *Deconstructing Harry*, a neurotic movie character" (1). In a more scholarly vein, the already impressive (both in terms of its quality and its quantity) scholarly work on deconstruction, and JACQUES DERRIDA in particular, speaks to a growing sense of its importance.

Yet while such dissemination, as Derrida might term it, of the word "deconstruction" would seem to bespeak a certain popularity, it has hardly signaled clarity or consensus as to what deconstruction "is," what it "does," and what it might still do. Indeed, a good deal of writing on the subject, and especially on Derrida, has been concerned precisely with the question of the possibility or impossibility of any such definition. Along these lines, Rodolphe Gasché's highly influential *Tain of the Mirror: Derrida and the Philosophy of Reflection* (1986) has been central to debates on deconstruction for its attempt to locate Derrida's work in the tradition of Western philosophy and thus to claim for him his rightful place as a philosopher. At stake in such arguments is deconstruction's claim to the title—and thus the prestige and dignity—of philosophy, as well as questions over its effectiveness. Thus, Richard Rorty argues that works such as *The Post Card* and *Glas* mark a turn in Derrida's career at which he becomes a "private writer . . . a writer without public mission" and that there is no "public (pedagogic or political) use to be made" of these later writings and, presumably, other deconstructive texts characterized by a similar "playfulness" (123).

It bears noting in this context that the French book series Derrida codirected, in which many of his own works appeared, is entitled "La philosophie en effet." As the title suggests, one of the stated goals of the series is to explore philosophy in *effect*, in *fact*, or, as a slightly more idiomatic translation might put it, in *action*, to explore the effects philosophy (and, for Derrida, the effects that deconstruction) can in fact bring about, the difference they can make. The extent of Derrida's political engagements, not to mention that of his pedagogy, which he came to not despite but *through* the work of deconstruction, was considerable, and his writing on contemporary pressing social and political issues is likewise significant (see, e.g., *Negotiations*). Contrary to assertions of the type made by Rorty, then, one of Derrida's principal arguments on pedagogy and politics is that any attempt to confine philosophy to institutions such as schools or universities suggests that it poses a threat to all those who would limit it and to any socioeconomic or political system that must orient all education toward profitability and efficiency. Derrida's own deconstruction of such attempts at containment not only exposes them but in effect demonstrates the very real effects deconstruction can have.

Debates over deconstruction's potential political investments and repercussions give a glimpse of what has perhaps been most troubling to its critics, that is, what they often perceive to be its overly narrow concern with language and its questioning of conventional notions of history and the subject. Deconstruction has been accused of neglecting or even eliding history and politics (although it has been argued that such criticism arises from a failure to read the texts of Derrida, Paul de Man, and others); it is, some of its critics argue, politically irresponsible, even dangerous. Arguments of this type were given added fuel by two "events" in particular: the discovery of journalistic articles written by de Man during World War II and renewed controversy over Martin Heidegger's political engagements during his tenure as rector at the University of Freiburg.

In 1987 it was discovered that de Man, who alongside Derrida has been widely held to be the guiding force behind deconstruction, particularly in North America, had written numerous articles for newspapers in his native Belgium. Many of the articles were written for the French and Flemish newspapers *Le Soir* and *Het Vlaamsche Land* during the German occupation of Belgium. (German authorities appropriated the name and facilities of *Le Soir*, and publication of *Het Vlaamsche Land* began in 1941 using equipment appropriated by the occupation authorities [see de Man, *Wartime*, vii].) This alone was enough for some of de Man's critics to call his reputation, and his critical work, into question; what is worse, one of the articles, although problematical and self-contradictory, is held even by de Man supporters to be antisemitic, providing critics who saw deconstruction as dangerously ahistorical with grounds to condemn it outright. Furthering the cause of such attacks was renewed debate on Heidegger's thought, so seminal for both Derrida and the early de Man, and its relation to his politics, particularly in the wake of the publication of Victor Farias's *Heidegger and Nazism* (1987).

There were many serious attempts to come to terms with the issues raised by "the de Man affair" and its aftermath, including the collection of all of de Man's known journalism in the volume *Wartime Journalism* (1988) and a lengthy volume devoted to assessing those writings and their relation to his critical work and to deconstruction in general, *Responses: On Paul de Man's Wartime Journalism* (1989). Moreover, key figures in deconstruction took up questions of the politics of both thinkers directly in important works, most notably Derrida in *Memoires for Paul de Man* (1986) and *Of the Spirit: Heidegger and the Question* (1987) and Philippe Lacoue-Labarthe in *Heidegger, Art, and Politics: The Fiction of the Political* (1987). Nonetheless, accusations and condemnations followed that dealt deconstruction a blow—at least to its public image—that it perhaps only began to overcome in the late 1990s.

This is not to say, however, that deconstruction died in the 1990s, as some at the time suggested, or that it has since stopped producing varied and important texts. To the contrary, in addition to Derrida, some of the most noteworthy writers in the tradition of deconstruction continued to explore the questions that occupied it in new ways and in different styles. In what is at least apparently recognizable as a now "traditional" form of deconstructive writing, Carol Jacobs and Werner Hamacher, for example, produced books and articles that attracted critical attention of their own: Jacobs's *Telling Time: Lévi-Strauss, Ford, Lessing, Benjamin, de Man, Wordsworth, Rilke* (1993) and *In the Language of Walter Benjamin* (1999) and Hamacher's *Premises: Essays on Philosophy and Literature from Kant to Celan* (1996) and *Pleroma—Reading in Hegel* (1998). It became more and more apparent that deconstruction had long been concerned with problems of history and politics, as well as with its own responsibilities, which were perhaps felt even more acutely in light of controversy around de Man in particular and in the wake of it. Indeed, already in such seminal essays as "Shelley Disfigured" (1979) de Man himself takes up the question of history, and others can be read as having gone on to work out the implications of his thinking. In this vein, Kevin Newmark's *Beyond Symbolism: Textual History and the Future of Reading* (1991) explores the French symbolist tradition as a privileged moment for thinking the relation of the symbol to literary history (symbolism), while E. S. Burt's *Poetry's Appeal: Nineteenth-Century French Lyric and the Political Space* (1999) is concerned to show how lyric poetry, despite its apparent remove from the mundane concerns of the world, in fact inscribes itself in politics and politics in itself, and David Ferris's *Theory and the Evasion of History* (1993) performs the closest of close readings to theorize the intersection of language and history.

Theory's purported evasion of history, or rather the resistance to theory that purportedly evades history, is precisely what concerns de Man in much of his late writing. These essays take up questions of politics and ideology more directly than did his previous work and in so doing offer an alternative account for the seeming fall from grace of deconstruction. In a now oft-quoted article, de Man claims that the "resistance to theory" does not come from outside theory but actually arises from within, as theory's resistance to itself; the resistance to theory is a "resistance to the use of language about language" and therefore "a resistance to language itself or to the possibility that language contains factors or functions that cannot be reduced to intuition" (*Resistance* 12–13).

If other works that have similarly explored questions of politics, including those of Derrida, have not been read as having a political use, it is no doubt because these works question the very term "use." What is more, it is not always easy to appropriate the language of deconstruction for discussions about politics, history, and culture in their most self-evident or customary terms. To choose just one example, Philippe Lacoue-Labarthe's deconstruction of the notion of mimesis (in *Typography: Mimesis, Philosophy, Politics* [1989]) as straightforward reproduction of reality would call into question any discourse of the political as a simple rendering of a given situation. Nonetheless, Lacoue-Labarthe has emerged, along with his sometimes coauthor JEAN-LUC NANCY, as a leading thinker on the political. Nancy, whose work has been widely translated into English and whose influence spread throughout North American academia in the 1990s, emerged as one of the most influential thinkers in deconstruction itself, as is witnessed by Derrida's monumental work devoted to him, *On Touching, Jean-Luc Nancy* (2000).

Perhaps the most widely read of Nancy's works is *The Inoperative Community* (1986), which begins with an invocation of the experience of a dissolution and dislocation of community and the questions raised by the "end" of communism. The consideration of community that follows, however, does not immediately explore the sociopolitical, socioeconomic, technological, or cultural roots of this situation, as might, for instance, certain strains of cultural studies. Rather, Nancy explores the very "logic" of community and the ontological conditions that make anything like society possible in the first place. Nancy argues that the absolute or totalizing logic of metaphysics necessarily articulates the subject with and in terms of community. Community is not preceded by an independent and autonomous subject that enters into relation with other subjects to form a social and perhaps community bond; on the contrary, the subject can now only ever be thought of as a *relation*, the relation to the Other that allows it to emerge as a subject in the first place. By challenging the possibility of autonomy, Nancy discloses how metaphysics necessarily deconstructs (although this is not a term he uses) its own terms, undermining the absoluteness of the absolute, or the totality of totality.

Although deconstruction certainly cannot be subsumed under CULTURAL STUDIES, it has intervened in the study of culture in the broadest sense, and some of its critics have addressed topics as diverse as video and technology more generally, politics and its rhetoric, AIDS, the media, and trauma, to name only a few. Avital Ronell's *Crack Wars: Literature, Addiction, Mania* (1992) and her essays (in *Finitude's Score: Essays for the End of the Millennium* [1999]) on the rhetoric of the Gulf War, on the video of the Rodney King beating and subsequent trial, on AIDS, and on a variety of other subjects together constitute an impressive deconstruction of the metaphysical terms that still ground much discourse on questions of culture. Cathy Caruth's work on trauma would certainly fall into this category and is remarkable also for the way in which it enacts the very trauma it describes. In *Unclaimed Experience: Trauma, Narrative, and History* (1996), Caruth defines trauma as "an overwhelming experience of sudden or catastrophic events in which the response to the event occurs in the often delayed, uncontrolled repetitive appearance of hallucinations and other intrusive phenomena" (11). Trauma thus emerges as an experience in which one does not coincide with one's own experience but rather (re)lives it, repeatedly and uncontrollably, as an intrusion upon the self.

One might say that with work on topics that are, broadly speaking, cultural and political, deconstruction entered a new phase. Still, one of the remarkable characteristics of the contemporary history of deconstruction is that even on such questions as politics and culture, institutions and archives, cosmopolitanism and globalization, ethics and the death sentence, as well as more recognizable questions of philosophy, literature, and the human sciences, it is Derrida who remained the leading figure in deconstruction and who continued to undertake its most probing and extensive questioning up until and even after the time of his death in 2004 with the publication of numerous posthumous works. Derrida's later works range from an extended reading of (the haunting of) Marx (*Specters of Marx* [1993]) to an important consideration of ethics through a reading of EMMANUEL LEVINAS (*Adieu to Emmanuel Levinas* [1997]), from work on psychoanalysis (*Resistances to Psychoanalysis* [1996]) to readings of Blanchot (*Demeure: Fiction and Testimony* [1996]), from a consideration of how the political has been constructed around the opposition of friends and enemies (*Politics of Friendship* [1994]) to questions of hospitality and refuge (*On Hospitality* [1997]; *On Cosmopolitism and Forgiveness* [1997]), from the question of language in a postcolonial context (*Monolingualism of the Other; or, The Prosthesis of the Origin* [1996]) to work on (occasional and other) political, institutional, and ethical questions (for instance, in *Negotiations, Without Alibi*, and *Who's Afraid of Philosophy?*, all published in 2002). And this list could be added to considerably. Over the last two decades of the twentieth century, Derrida repeatedly articulated these issues anew and in different contexts whose stakes became more evident than ever, and he developed masterful accounts of particular political or cultural problems at the same time that he elaborated a theory of the political itself.

If over the past decade Derrida's work has become even more broadly accepted in much theory and criticism, if not always in philosophy, it is not simply because he addressed such contemporary problems in culture and politics. It may be because the work of deconstruction began to be felt and done more widely than it might have seemed. Indeed, it may well be that as deconstruction passed through the high point of its popularity, and that as those who are prone to such gestures seized on more recent currents in criticism and theory, it became less a question of deconstruction *and*, that is, of an articulation between deconstruction and other approaches, and more a question of deconstruction *of*. For while the *and* might seek a point of conjunction, the deconstruction *of*, say, feminism or postcolonialism, and so on, attempts to elaborate a deconstructive reading of the problematics *of* postcolonialism or feminism, those facing them and those they themselves pose. A critic such as HOMI K. BHABHA (*The Location of Culture*, [1994]), then, has sought to formulate a theoretical approach to the questions of postcolonialism in which deconstruction is not simply subsumed within, or reconciled with, other approaches but questions their presuppositions, their "grounds," just as it deconstructs the metaphysical, ontological, hierarchizing, and other thought these fields confront. Similarly, Derrida and Drucilla Cornell are among those who have undertaken a deconstruction of the law and thus question the terms and indeed the possibility of anything like justice (see Cornell, Michael Rosenfeld, and David G. Carlson's edited volume *Deconstruction and the Possibility of Justice* [1992]).

One might wish that deconstruction presented easier options than this, clearer choices, that it intervened at least to the extent that it provided a solid ground of knowledge, that one might know exactly what is to be done, that one might do it. But to put this in terms of Thomas Keenan's observations on the role of the media in conflicts, this could be precisely the "ethico-political difficulty and opportunity" deconstruction allows us to face: the very difficulty of the articulation between "knowledge and action" ("Publicity" 107, 106), the recognition that knowledge does not necessarily or inevitably lead to action (efficacious or not) and that action does not necessarily follow on or imply knowledge, that it might in fact circumvent it. While much contemporary deconstruction has been concerned to explore a deconstruction *en effet*, in effect, in fact, "at work," and thus to explore the articulations between knowledge and action—or as it is more commonly and more problematically put, theory and praxis— it does so by exploring their very relation, which is also to say their difference, or *différance*, as Derrida might have it. At the same time, then, deconstruction resists any facile empiricism, as it does the facility of a passage between these two, or between language and intuition, as de Man might put it. As counterintuitive and paradoxical as this might seem, as far removed from the realm of intuition and action, this might be deconstruction's most accurate rendering of and, at the same time, intervention in history, deconstruction's becoming, again and always, contemporary.

JAN PLUG

Cathy Caruth, *Unclaimed Experience: Trauma, Narrative, and History* (1996); Paul de Man, *Aesthetic Ideology* (ed. Ardrzej Warminski, 1996), *The Resistance to Theory* (1986), *Romanticism and Contemporary Criticism: The Gauss Seminar and Other Papers* (ed. E. S. Burt, Kevin Newmark, and Andrzej Warminski,

1993), *Wartime Journalism, 1939–1943* (ed. Werner Hamacher, Neil Hertz, and Thomas Keenan, 1988); Jacques Derrida, *Adieu à Emmanuel Lévinas* (1997, *Adieu to Emmanuel Levinas*, trans. Pascale-Anne Brault and Michael B. Naas, 1999), *Cosmopolites de tous les pays, encore un effort!* (1997, *On Cosmopolitanism and Forgiveness*, trans. Mark Dooley and Michael Hughes, 2001), *De l'esprit: Heidegger et la question* (1987, *Of Spirit: Heidegger and the Question*, trans. Geoffrey Bennington and Rachel Bowlby, 1989), *De l'hospitalité* (1997, *Of Hospitality*, trans. Rachel Bowlby, 2000), *Demeure: Maurice Blanchot* (1996, *Demeure: Fiction and Testimony*, trans. Elizabeth Rottenberg, 2000), *Du droit à la philosophie* (1991, *Who's Afraid of Philosophy? Right to Philosophy 1*, trans. Jan Plug, 2002), *Memoires for Paul de Man* (1986, trans. Cecile Lindsay et al., *Mémoires for Paul de Man*, 1988), *Monolinguisme de l'autre; ou, La prothèse d'origine* (1996, *Monolingualism of the Other; or, The Prosthesis of the Origin*, trans. Patrick Mensah, 1998), *Negotiations: Interviews and Interventions, 1975–2001* (ed. and trans. Elizabeth Rottenberg, 2002), *Politiques de l'amitié* (1994, *Politics of Friendship*, trans. George Collins, 1997), *Résistances de la psychanalyse* (1996, *Resistances to Psychoanalysis*, trans. Peggy Kamuf, Pascale-Anne Brault, and Michael B. Naas, 1998), *Spectres de Marx: L'état de la dette, le travail du deuil et la nouvelle Internationale* (1993, *Specters of Marx: The State of the Debt, the Work of Mourning, and the New International*, trans. Peggy Kamuf, 1994), *Without Alibi* (ed. and trans. Peggy Kamuf, 2002); Thomas Keenan, *Fables of Responsibility: Aberrations and Predicaments in Ethics and Politics* (1997), "Publicity and Indifference (Sarajevo on Television)" *PMLA* 117 (2002); Jean-Luc Nancy, *La communauté désoeuvrée* (1986, *The Inoperative Community*, ed. Peter Connor, trans. Peter Connor et al., 1991); Herman Rapaport, *The Theory Mess: Deconstruction in Eclipse* (2001); Avital Ronell, *Crack Wars: Literature, Addiction, Mania* (1992), *Finitude's Score: Essays for a New Millennium* (1999), *The Telephone Book: Technology, Schizophrenia, Electronic Speech* (1989); Richard Rorty, *Contingency, Irony, Solidarity* (1989).

Deleuze, Gilles, and Félix Guattari

The collaboration between Gilles Deleuze (1925–1995) and Félix Guattari (1930–1992) is surely one of the more sparkling in the history of critical theory and resulted in some of the most intellectually exciting work of the twentieth century. When he first met Guattari, Deleuze had recently published *Difference and Repetition* (1968) and *Logic of Sense* (1969), two books that were every bit the equal of JACQUES DERRIDA's early landmark texts, *Of Grammatology* (1967) and *Writing and Difference* (1967). Indeed, it was these two works that moved MICHEL FOUCAULT to pronounce in 1970 that perhaps one day the twentieth century would be known as Deleuzian.

Deleuze had already gained widespread attention, prior to his work with Guattari, with a sequence of short but incisive monographs on Baruch Spinoza, David Hume, Immanuel Kant, Friedrich Nietzsche, Henri Bergson, Marcel Proust, and Leopold von Sacher-Masoch. Deleuze stated that the presiding aim of his work was to overturn Platonism, the most pernicious species of which was to be found in the work of G. W. F. Hegel. Before he met Deleuze, Guattari had also enjoyed notoriety for his public campaigning for alternatives to psychiatry. With his colleague Jean Oury he cofounded a private "anti-psychiatry" clinic at La Borde in 1953. It was Guattari's presiding goal to overturn the hegemony of psychoanalysis, particularly its Freudian and Lacanian forms (see *Molecular Revolution* [1977]) in psychotherapy.

The philosophical coordinates of Deleuze and Guattari's collaborative work can already be detected in Deleuze's *Difference and Repetition* and *The Logic of Sense*. Aside from being the key that unlocks *Anti-Oedipus* (1972) and *A Thousand Plateaus* (1980), one finds in Deleuze and Guattari's two volumes of *Capitalism and Schizophrenia* the first development of the concept of "virtuality," perhaps Deleuze's most important contribution to philosophy. Indeed, it would not be going too far to claim that the majority of Deleuze's concepts, and subsequently Guattari's, refer to the virtual domain. Nowhere is this truer than in the case of the "body without organs," which is the body in its virtual form, which for Deleuze means the very condition of possibility for the actual body. (The body without organs is connected to the actual world and/or other body without organs via something Deleuze and Guattari call "desiring-machines.") It is not an imaginary or a symbolic body, much less a real body that has somehow been deprived of its viscera, but the image the body has of itself. "Image" is used here in the special sense Deleuze gives it in his discussion of the "image of thought" (in *Difference and Repetition*) and should not be confused with psychotherapy's body image. Like PIERRE BOURDIEU's "habitus," the body without organs is both always already there and constantly being rebuilt: we act according to its dictates but must continuously shore it up with increasingly complex and concrete affirmations.

While it is premature to speak of a Deleuzian branch of literary and critical theory, one can speak of is a Deleuzian complication and intensification of the literary and critical field. In general, four particular elements in Deleuze and Guattari's work have been especially influential for literary criticism: (1) their reconceptualization of desire as an affirmative force that, in contrast to its psychoanalytic conception, does not have to "lack to be" (as JACQUES LACAN puts it) but is able to function on its own and for-itself; (2) their development of schizophrenia as an articulation of the process of thought itself (although it is something of a misprision of their work, their discussion of schizophrenia has in some sectors become emblematic of POSTMODERNISM); (3) their elaboration of the entirely new critical domain of becoming, which should not be compared to or confused with its apparent (Hegelian) cognate in ontology; and (4) the notion of the rhizome, which perhaps because it is their most thinly theorized concept has proven incredibly suggestive, particularly in the arts, where it has spawned a form of creativity comparable to the surrealist uptake of SIGMUND FREUD in what they called "automatic writing." Known as philosophers of desire, Deleuze and Guattari themselves say they are proudest of the fact their work short-circuited the connection between Freud and Marx established by the FRANKFURT SCHOOL and reaffirmed by the Althusserians (Louis Althusser, ÉTIENNE BALIBAR, Pierre Macherey, and more recently SLAVOJ ŽIŽEK). This short-circuiting of the connection between Marx and Freud should not be taken to mean that Deleuze and Guattari reject both Marx and Freud, as several commentators have assumed. On the contrary, it clears the way for a conscientious rereading of both, not in order to return to Freud or Marx à la Lacan and Althusser, but rather with a view to extracting those concepts that retain pertinence. The one concept that stands out in this respect is desire: it is the obvious point of convergence between Marx and Freud and for this reason demands careful handling. For Deleuze and Guattari, desire is a kind of intransitive life force that is under constant pressure from all sectors of society to become a desire for something, which is the only form in which it can be regulated. This formula, they argue in *Anti-Oedipus*, is the point of the incest prohibition: it deceives us into thinking we secretly desire the very thing it prohibits and thereby persuades us to renounce desire. Because we assume that a thing would not be prohibited if it were not already desired, we accept that a prohibition is evidence enough of the existence of a desire. In effect, we are made to feel guilty for a desire we can only assume we had because our knowledge of it is simultaneous with our knowledge of the prohibition itself. Since we harbor this loathsome desire without even knowing it, we must suspect ourselves of harboring any number of other equally loathsome desires. What the Oedipus complex teaches us is precisely that we cannot trust ourselves to desire appropriately. For this reason we concede the need for desire to be regulated and accept pleasure as its commuted substitute. Pleasure is precisely the realization of a desire for something, and in that sense it is for Deleuze and Guattari a deformation of desire itself.

Their commitment to desire has been criticized as apolitical, but this is mistaken. For Deleuze and Guattari the liberation of desire is the only genuine basis for politics, since politics in all its forms has always been a matter of enchaining desire. It was as a process for freeing desire from the imperative to be a desire for something that Deleuze and Guattari began using the notion (not the clinical reality) of schizophrenia. For them, schizophrenia is an example of what they call a deterritorialized and deterritorializing mode of thought, by which they mean a mode of thought that is somehow radically "in between" the usual dialectical coordinates of identity and nonidentity, not as a "third term" but rather as the inherent potential of both. The clear boundary lines identity likes to draw can at times give rise to wild tangents or a certain fuzziness or smudging that is not yet the erasure of the line altogether but is nevertheless a profound transformation of it. By the same token, the absence of lines characterizing nonidentity must logically harbor the implicit desire to materialize an identity or else it would not be a structural opposite. This ineradicable potential to change and mutate from within, found equally in identity and nonidentity, is what Deleuze and Guattari call deterritorialization, the purest example of schizophrenia. The frequent accusation that they romanticize schizophrenia overlooks their strident caution that one can indeed go too far in one's deterritorializations and that just a little identity is always needed to keep things steady. In this respect, when it comes to change, they are rather more "gradualist" than their more radical exponents would have them be.

In order to better theorize the process of schizophrenia, Deleuze and Guattari repurpose the notion of becoming. Becoming does not have a subject, nor is it something that happens to a subject; indeed, it cannot be said to happen at all since becoming belongs entirely to the realm of the virtual, not the actual (but is no less real despite this). Perhaps its best cognate is something on the order of what JUDITH BUTLER has theorized using the work of Foucault and J. L. Austin as the domain of the performative (see SPEECH ACTS), an incorporeal dimension whose effects are entirely real and finally bodily. Gender, for instance, both constitutes us and is constituted by us: if we did not act out its demands, it would have no substance, yet without it we should not be compelled to act at all. This, for Deleuze and Guattari, is the realm of becoming, a place where the set of performatives that constitute the framework of our daily lives can in fact be apprehended, engaged, and possibly even altered. So when Deleuze and Guattari say, provocatively, that we must all become-woman, what they mean is that we must all learn to come to grips with this dimension of our existence.

In order to theorize this process more fully, Deleuze and Guattari were compelled to abandon a linear model of connectivity. In its place they conceive a model, which they term the "rhizome," in contrast to the "tree," that is able to think connectivity in multiple terms, both spatially and temporally. The rhizome's defining characteristic is that a connection can *and must* be made from any and all points. Their final collaborative work, *Qu'est-ce que la philosophie?* (1991), treats the rhizome as its matrix and stipulates that the key problem of philosophy today is the lines of convergence and divergence of the different strands of thought—art, philosophy, and science. In this sense, it is best read as a clarification and a refinement of their previous books.

IAN BUCHANAN

See also FRENCH THEORY AND CRITICISM: 1945 AND AFTER and PSYCHOANALYTIC THEORY AND CRITICISM: 3. THE POST-LACANIANS.

Gilles Deleuze, Critique et clinique (1993, Essays Critical and Clinical, trans. Daniel Smith and Michael Greco, 1997), Différance et repetition (1968, Difference and Repetition, trans. Paul Patton, 1994), Logique du sens (1969, Logic of Sense, trans. Mark Lester and Charles Stivale, 1990), Nietzsche et la philosophie (1962, Nietzsche and Philosophy, trans. Hugh Tomlinson, 1983), Proust et les signes (1964, Proust and Signs, trans. Richard Howard, 1972); Gilles Deleuze and Félix Guattari, Anti-Oedipe, vol. 1 of Capitalisme et schizophrénie (1972, Anti-Oedipus, trans. Robert Hurley, Mark Seem, and Helen R. Lane, 1977), Kafka: Pour une littérature mineur (1975, Kafka: Toward a Minor Literature, trans. Dana Polan, 1986), Mille Plateaux, vol. 2 of Capitalisme et schizophrénie (1980, A Thousand Plateaus: Capitalism and Schizophrenia, trans. Brian Massumi, 1987), Qu'est-ce que la philosophie? (1991, What Is Philosophy?, trans. Hugh Tomlinson and Graeme Burchell, 1994); Félix Guattari, The Guattari Reader (ed. Gary Genosko, 1996), La révolution moléculaire (1977, Molecular Revolution, trans. Rosemary Sheed, 1984).

Derrida, Jacques

The difficulty of introducing a major contemporary philosopher such as Jacques Derrida (1930–2004) in a reference work presenting issues of literary criticism is double, and this danger has already been systematically addressed in the writings of the philosopher himself. First, there is the danger of oversimplifying, of pigeonholing, of reducing, of imposing artificial boundaries, when facing a movement of thought that constantly evolves so as deliberately to defeat and baffle preordained categories. Then, there is the risk of being merely mimetic, of repeating strategies and gestures that have been identified with an author's signature that tend to be singular, unrepeatable, yet endowed with universal validity. However, the possibility of bypassing such an initial aporia exists, and it consists in considering the fundamentally affirmative nature of Derrida's writing rather than in stressing the "playful," "antifoundational," or "nihilistic" element of his textual practices (as was often the case in the first decade of their American and British reception). In short, it is crucial to resist two current reductions or distortions of Derrida's thought identifying it either with philosophical skepticism or with a more sophisticated version of New Criticism.

This affirmative aspect is confirmed by the final works published during Derrida's lifetime, where he engages strenuously with new problematics and fields such as legal discourse, European politics, racism, architecture, technology, ghosts, computers, dance, concepts of nationalism, justice, religion, fundamentalism, mourning, globalization, all the while stressing ethics, "messianicity," and a keener sense of hospitality to others and the Other. This entailed moving some distance from misconceptions brought about by an early enthusiastic adoption of deconstructive tenets in North American universities. This phenomenon dates from the 1970s, and this very modish enthusiasm was soon followed by disappointment if not outright rejection when it looked as if the "De Man affair" had revealed the hidden underpinnings of deconstruction. From the beginning, though, Derrida objected to the interpretations of DECONSTRUCTION (a term he accepted as his own coining and invention) that see it as a purely destructive notion of criticism, deploying an almost nihilistic critique of all institutions, hierarchies, and values (this is Richard Rorty's interpretation, for instance). Derrida repeats in numerous places that "deconstruction is not negative" and points out that the term's first goal had been to translate MARTIN HEIDEGGER's notions of *Abbau* and *Untergang*, concepts that are not negative either. Deconstruction is "not destructive, not having the purpose of dissolving, distracting or subtracting elements in order to reveal an internal essence. It asks questions about the essence, about the presence, indeed about this interior/exterior, phenomenon/appearance schema" (Mortley 96–97). Even if these remarks beg the question of what deconstruction is or does, they point to a gesture that hesitates between the assertive and the interrogative. And they show that Derrida's concepts, exploited as they are by literary critics, should be seen less as tools than as landmarks in a philo-sophical meditation on the essence of literature. Therefore, there cannot be anything such as a "Derridean criticism," nor should one be on the lookout for a positive notion of "grammatology" if by "grammatology" one understands a new "science of writing" meant to replace the ancient metaphysical "logocentrism." Indeed, we need to under-stand why no "grammatology" is possible as a science and why it is such an impos-sibility that nevertheless releases incalculable critical energies.

A second commonplace current among exegetes of "deconstruction" is the blur-ring of philosophy and literature. Indeed, one can note that Derrida's earliest theo-retical project, dating from the late 1950s, consisted in an investigation of "the ideal-ity of the literary object." In Edmund Husserl's "Origin of Geometry" (1939), Derrida found a similar approach to another type of ideality, the ideality of science. Just as Husserl studies the conditions of possibility of ideal objects and situates them within language, Derrida came to meditate on the conditions of possibility of literature. Derrida's major "family"—it is rather a matter of "style" in the development of philo-sophical argumentation—remains that of phenomenology, starting with Husserl and Heidegger, Jean-Paul Sartre, and Maurice Merleau-Ponty, although caught up within psychology and the trivialization of Heideggerianism dubbed as existentialism so that it ties up more closely with thinkers and writers as closely associated and as cre-ative as MAURICE BLANCHOT and EMMANUEL LEVINAS. Rather than to the major exponents of the movement, with whom Derrida kept discussing crucial concepts, such as JACQUES LACAN, Claude Lévi-Strauss, ROLAND BARTHES, and MICHEL FOUCAULT, one should merely point to the writings of the linguist who inspired them all, FERDINAND DE SAUSSURE.

Most structuralists took their cue from Saussure's system, endorsing his ideas about the prevalence of synchrony over diachrony, the arbitrary nature of the link between signifier and signified, the conception of language as a system made up of differential tokens. Derrida uses this theory of the sign to criticize Husserl and then Heidegger, while bringing the phenomenological inquiry to bear on the foundations (or lack of foundation) of structuralist scientism, thus forcing two very different tra-ditions to grind ceaselessly against each other. Or perhaps, by a bold structural ho-mology, one might say that Derrida takes up Heidegger's critique of linguistic theo-ries that would attempt to bypass a certain type of hermeneutics, showing how they remain trapped up in instrumental approaches, thus betraying their complicity with a very ancient metaphysical system, but changes the ground of Heideggerian founda-tional criticism.

Thus Derrida demonstrates how Husserl meets considerable difficulties as soon as he tries to ground the tradition necessary to the preservation of mathematical truths in a concept of consciousness defined by an intentionality of meaning, ulti-mately identical to the capacity of "hearing oneself speak," and points at the same time to Saussure's strange overrating of speech phenomena and parallel dismissing of writing, seen as a mere tool bringing confusions. Both commonsense evidence and a tradition dating back to Plato tend to pin consciousness down to a form of vocalization of the self. Against this alleged evidence, Derrida stresses writing, not as a tool or concept but as a limit experience or an experience of the limits of the living self, and this recognition of writing implies the disquieting fact that an author can leave a trace that can survive without his or her presence.

Writing implies in itself the capacity of an endless repetition deprived of any fixed standard of authorization, therefore an ambivalent knot of death and survival. Writing is a trace that cannot be present here and there without having already divided itself, since it always refers back to another being, to another trace. The fold between Being and beings exploited by Heideggerian hermeneutics is thus reinscribed as the operation of an "original trace," with the added difference that it rules out any belief in an absolute, pristine origin.

The complex strategies of reading elaborated by Derrida in fact take a lot of time to unfold and take up a lot of space: they deliberately resist summary and often entail a complete and varying scenography. One may note the constant shifting back and forth between philosophers, poets, and novelists. It is not only that one would find in literature what remains lacking in philosophy, the awareness of the opacity of signs, the deeper insight into the metaphorical nature of language being too often obscured by the philosophical wish to hit on absolute truths. Indeed, the first two magazines with which Derrida associated himself at the beginning of his "public" career, *Critique* and *Tel Quel*, had been dominated by personalities who refused a strict dichotomy between literary and philosophical endeavors, GEORGES BATAILLE and Philippe Sollers. Varied and multiple as they are, Derrida's literary authors all fall under three rough headings: the Romantics (in a vague sense), where Rousseau, Percy Bysshe Shelley, and Charles Baudelaire figure prominently; the postsymbolists, with Paul Valéry and Stéphane Mallarmé; and the "moderns," among whom one could distinguish a purely Jewish tradition with Franz Kafka, Edmond Jabès, and Paul Celan, and an avant-gardist mode, with James Joyce, Antonin Artaud, Bataille, Sollers, Francis Ponge, and Jean Genet (the last ten names would in fact make up the entire *Tel Quel*ian canon), with a special mention for Blanchot because of the proximity of his own status as author of novels, narratives, and literary essays.

One could roughly oppose a first moment in Derrida's strategies when he aims at showing how a text always subverts or exceeds the author's intended meaning thanks to a complex functioning of metaphors, tensions, or distortions between layers of sense owing to an unperceived linguistic instability typical of textuality in general and a second moment when the notions of "undecidability" and "incalculability" run counter to the economic metaphors still implied by the first approach. The first moment would be distinguished by the notion that there is "nothing outside the text"— "pas de hors-texte"—(*Grammatology* 58), which is often misunderstood, and the second by a stress on critical gestures themselves, with an ethical or political questioning

of boundaries and global economies of meaning. The first moment stresses a continuously plural language—"one must speak several languages and produce several
texts at once" (*Margins* 135); the second points to the endless autobiographical task of
unveiling and confession implied by any writing (*Circumfession*).

But throughout this progression in the constitution of a general aesthetics of
paradoxes and transgression of accepted limits, Derrida sticks to a few critical tenets. One is that no hermeneutics of literature is possible. A crucial confrontation
with Hans-Georg Gadamer reveals that there has been no compromise with current
versions of post-Heideggerian hermeneutics. One could compare the various readings of Celan and Mallarmé by Gadamer and Derrida so as to list everything that
opposes them. Gadamer concludes a reading of Mallarmé's *Salut* with the statement
that "both dimensions of meaning can be carried out as the same melodious gesture
of language and in the same unity of discourse" (*Dialogue* 45–46), a position that
could hardly be further from Derrida's constant contention that no single "plane of
discourse" can be established, that the metaphors always clash violently and dangerously in a poem, and, fundamentally, that any writer attempts to achieve the impossible by leaving the trace of an absolute singularity. In this sense, one could speak of
an approach very close to the radical psychoanalysis invented by Nicolas Abraham
and Maria Torok, an approach that is not so far even from certain of Lacan's formulas
("to love means to give what one hasn't got") even as it staunchly opposes the neo-
Hegelianism of Lacan's system (see *Resistances*).

The central questions of these poetics become indissociable from the new philosophical problematics of Derrida's ethical turn. What is an event? Under which conditions is it possible? Why has it become "impossible" to remain an event? What is a
signature? What is a name in a text? How can the title be distinguished from the
name of the author and from the content of the text? What is a "corpus"? These problems still imply the strategy of "double b(l)inds" and "vicious performatives" invented in order to destroy John Searle's hasty reappropriation of Austinian theories
of SPEECH ACTS, while hesitating between broad recontextualizations (within large
institutions defining areas of supposed competence) and extremely precise issues
posed by untranslatable idioms. Yet as soon as one "translates" a proper name, the
gesture may trigger off a violent style of punning, as when, in "Limited Inc a b c . . ."
(1977), Searle's name is deftly turned into the French abbreviation "Sarl" ("société à
responsabilité limitée" [*Limited Inc* 36]).

The wish to come closer to an untranslatable idiom implies a more writerly or
autobiographical style; indeed, after *Glas*, a very baroque piece of writing that proves
that "doing things with words" is possible, Derrida often includes anthropological
or psychoanalytical motifs such as incorporation, introjection, fetishism, mourning,
eating, and sexual difference, broaching at times religious themes such as baptism,
the Eucharist, circumcision, alliance, and negative theology, without abandoning a
strong political commitment, taking sides on very contemporary issues (Derrida was

arrested in Prague in 1981 on trumped-up charges because of his active support for dissident intellectuals), such as the end of Communist regimes in Eastern Europe, the foundation of the American constitution, the Gulf War, Nelson Mandela, the concept of a new European community, and so on. These multiple activities, involving countless texts on painting, architecture, and drawing as well, finally place Derrida in the already long line before him of French *engagé* intellectuals exemplified by Sartre or Foucault, never loath to plan a state reform of philosophy teaching or to launch a new teaching institution such as the Collège de Philosophie in Paris.

In view of this committed stance, can we speak with Christopher Norris (Gasché is more reserved; see 157–58) of Derrida as a neo-Kantian, propounding a more sophisticated and updated version of transcendental criticism? To be sure, in various interviews Derrida insists that deconstruction continues a dialogue with post-Kantian critique. Criticism supposes, after Immanuel Kant, Karl Marx and Friedrich Engels, and the whole Enlightenment, a judgment between two terms in a situation of crisis. If it refuses alternatives set by binary logics or dialectics, deconstruction does not attempt a "criticism of criticism" but aims at thinking the same process from another side, linked to the genealogy of judgment, of will, of consciousness: the decidability of truth criteria cannot be reached by a blindness to the aporias of undecidability. Deconstruction therefore strives to let appear the affirmative (not positive) movement presupposed by any criticism. This has consequences for politics—the politics of a different Europe to be thought anew in *The Other Heading* (1991)—as well as for the intelligence of an intellectual heritage dominated by German philosophy and its mystique of the *Geist*.

In a series of twists and turns on what was taken for deconstruction's negative debunking, Derrida seems to recant even his antiphonological stance when answering the question "What is poetry?" by saying that poetry can best be evoked by a desire to "learn by heart." This is no falling back into naïve immediacy, however. To learn by heart is the only chance of an "embodiment" of letters in a subject: "Eat, drink, swallow my letter, carry it, keep it in you, like the law of a writing transformed into your body: *writing as such*"—this would be the lesson or "fable" conveyed by any poem that *gives* itself entirely, in the familiar Mallarméan gesture of legacy (Ferraris 240). This poetical and subjective text about poetry is rather typical of Derrida's later mode of confessional writing: he writes about his own desire to incorporate letters thanks to poems that have relinquished their Heideggerian pretensions, their claim to let language (or truth) speak. This is a pure passivity—there is no pathos of creation—that is deprived of either quotations or title, and yet that bears witness to the "passion of the singular mark," a "signature rehearsing its own disappearance." Derrida concludes wistfully, however, that such an account finally rules out any question in the form of "What is ——?," for as soon as this is asked, not only does metaphysics hold sway again but the form of the question heralds in itself the birth of prose.

A similar note is sounded by Derrida when he reviews the history of his institutional success in American universities during a conference on the fate of "French theory" in America. In a revealing survey, Derrida regrets that deconstruction has turned into an easily repeatable formulaic discourse, in short "organized bodies of rules, of procedures and techniques, in a word, *methods*, know-how applicable in a recurrent fashion." He ironically describes what such methods would be reduced to: "Among the examples of these procedural or formalizing formulae that I had proposed . . . there was the reversal of a hierarchy. After having reversed a binary opposition, whatever it may be—speech/writing, man/woman, spirit/matter, signifier/signified, signified/signifier, master/slave, and so on—and having liberated the subjugated and submissive term, one then proceeded to the generalization of this latter in new traits, producing a different concept, for example another concept of writing such as trace, *différance*, gramme, text, and so on" ("Deconstructions: The Im-possible" 19). Rarely has one seen the "inventor" of a critical discourse assess so self-critically what has been too often systematized into easy vanishing tricks. Here, Derrida is not so much eager to pastiche his disciples and engage in contorted self-parody as to evaluate the validity of the problematic: the problematic keeps being deconstructive only if it resists an all-too-"possible" drift inherent in its methodology. In order to let the chance of a future open, Derrida wants to gamble on the "impossible," for, even after having traversed all the paradoxes, aporias, and double binds, his concepts keep their relevance if they lead to the event that will exceeding any program, a radical novelty incommensurable with methodological protocols.

This led to a new turn in Derrida's evolution. Taking its cue from Marx's dramatization of what can be called a "hauntology" (an ontology always already undermined by the specter of ethical issues), *Specters of Marx* signals a focus on the ethical and the political under the global heading of the ghostly. Less a late reconciliation with Marxism than an assertion that Marx's concern with social justice had always been at the heart of deconstruction, this text initiates a confrontation with what are the most insistent themes in Derrida's last writings: death and mourning, justice and ethics, religion and a paradoxical messianism. This "turn to ethics" is not a "return to religion" but more likely a consequence of the autobiographical movement that had come to the fore with *Circumfessions* in 1991. There, to counterpoint Bennington's skillful exposition of his philosophical system (which could have announced an unwholesome closure), Derrida wants to surprise his readers not only by exhibiting his body, namely own circumcision, but by calling himself a "little black and very Arab Jew" so as to multiply parallels with Augustine, a saint and one of the church's founding fathers. Derrida complicates the question of religion, suggesting a deep but unstable fraternity among Jewish and Muslim positions in so far as they both refuse the historical necessity of what seems to be the "fate" of our modern world, a globalized post-Christianity that has spread its "globalatinization" through the domination of American English, techno-sciences, and a vague "pagano-Christian" continuum

(*Acts of Religion* 51). This is how Derrida finally makes a truce with Levinas, and instead of stressing as he did in 1964 with "Violence and Metaphysics" that no "Jewish" thinking of alterity could overcome or forget its own inscription in the Greek language of philosophical discourse in which we are born and breathe, he relentlessly calls for a renewed concept of justice, and hope for "messianicity" without messianism or the Messiah (56).

JEAN-MICHEL RABATÉ

Jacques Derrida, *Acts of Literature* (ed. Derek Attridge, 1992), *Acts of Religion* (ed. Gil Anidjar, 2002), *L'autre cap suivi de La democratie ajournée* (1991, *The Other Heading: Reflections on Today's Europe*, trans. Pascale-Anne Brault and Michael B. Naas, 1992), *Circonfession: Cinquante-neuf périodes et periphrases* (1991, *Circumfession: Fifty-nine Periods and Periphrases*, trans. Geoffrey Bennington, in *Jacques Derrida*, 1993), *Cosmopolites de tous les pays, encore un effort!* (1997, *On Cosmopolitanism and Forgiveness*, trans. Mark Dooley and Michael Hughes, 2001), "Deconstructions: The Im-possible," *French Theory in America* (ed. Sylvère Lotringer and Sande Cohen, 2001), *De l'esprit: Heidegger et la question* (1987, *Of Spirit: Heidegger and the Question*, trans. Geoffrey Bennington and Rachel Bowlby, 1989), *De la grammatologie* (1967, *Of Grammatology*, trans. Gayatri Chakravorty Spivak, 1976), *La dissémination* (1972, *Dissemination*, trans. Barbara Johnson, 1981), *Donner le temps* (1991, *Given Time: Counterfeit Money*, trans. Peggy Kamuf, 1992), *L'écriture et la différence* (1967, *Writing and Difference*, trans. Alan Bass, 1978), "Fors: The Anglish Words of Nicolas Abraham and Maria Torok" (trans. Barbara Johnson, foreword to *The Wolf Man's Magic Word: A Cryptonymy*, by Nicolas Abraham and Maria Torok, 1986), *Glas* (1974, *Glas*, trans. John Leavey and Richard Rand, 1986), *Limited Inc* (trans. Samuel Weber, Jeffrey Mehlman, and Alan Bass, 1988), *Marges de la philosophie* (1972, *Margins of Philosophy*, trans. Alan Bass, 1982), *Politiques de l'amitié* (1994, *Politics of Friendship*, trans. George Collins, 1998), *Parages* (1986, *Parages*, trans. John P. Leavey and Tom Conley, 2010), *Résistances de la psychanalyse* (1996, *Resistances of Psychoanalysis*, trans. Peggy Kamuf, Pascale-Anne Brault, and Michael B. Naas, 1998), "Shibboleth," *Midrash and Literature* (ed. Geoffrey H. Hartman and Sanford Budick, trans. Joshua Wilner, 1986), *Spectres de Marx: L'état de la dette, le travail du deuil et la nouvelle Internationale* (1993, *Specters of Marx: The State of the Debt, the Work of Mourning, and the New International*, trans. Peggy Kamuf, 1993), "Ulysses Gramophone: Hear say yes in Joyce," *Acts of Literature* (ed. Derek Attridge, 1992), *La vérité en peinture* (1978, *The Truth in Painting*, trans. Geoffrey Bennington and Ian McLeod, 1987), *The Work of Mourning* (ed. and trans. Pascale-Anne Brault and Michael B. Naas, 2001); Jacques Derrida and Hans-Georg Gadamer, *Dialogue and Deconstruction: The Gadamer-Derrida Encounter* (ed. Diane P. Michelfelder and Richard E. Palmer, 1989); Maurizio Ferraris, *Postille a Derrida: Con due scritti di Jacques Derrida* (1987); Rodolphe Gasché, *The Tain of the Mirror: Derrida and the Philosophy of Reflection* (1986); Raoul Mortley, *French Philosophers in Conversation: Levinas, Schneider, Serres, Irigaray, Le Doeuff, Derrida* (1991).

Discourse

1. Discourse Analysis

For some years, discourse analysis was constituted less by an explicit theory than by a practical and empirical approach for supporting research and fieldwork on relatively little-recorded languages and cultures. One domain that attracted notice in wider humanistic circles was the cross-cultural study of stories and narratives. Subsequent major concerns included the discourse of schooling and education and, with a sociological turn, the organization of conversation.

These practical and empirical emphases were somewhat at variance with the "theoretical linguistics" postulating a dichotomy between language and discourse (*langue* versus *parole* for FERDINAND DE SAUSSURE, or "competence" versus "performance" for Noam Chomsky). The project of abstracting "language" away from its cultural and social contexts as a human phenomenon seemed attractive on theoretical grounds, especially for an emergent science like linguistics, but this project was unrealistic. The rising pressure to resituate language in these contexts accounts for the lively interest in discourse analysis, which has always acknowledged the unity of language as both structure and event, knowledge and action, system and process, potential and actual (Firth, Halliday, Pike).

In the 1970s, a range of trends converged in discourse analysis: text linguistics on the European continent; functional or systemic linguistics in Czechoslovakia, Britain, and Australia; cognitive linguistics, ethnography of communication, and ethnomethodology in the United States; STRUCTURALISM, poststructuralism, DECONSTRUCTION, and feminism in France (see FEMINIST THEORY AND CRITICISM: 3. POSTSTRUCTURALIST FEMINISMS); and SEMIOTICS (or semiology) and cognitive science, which are arenas of convergence themselves. Contemplating discourse from multiple viewpoints—linguistic, philosophical, cognitive, psychological, social, anthropological, literary, historical, political, ideological—makes us dauntingly aware of how multifarious and complex discourse transactions can be, but they are very successful in social practice.

To describe the systematic and intersubjective organization that underwrites this success, theories and models have been developed on numerous fronts: for the local syntactic cohesions and the global semantic coherence of discourse; the interactive performance of discourse actions or SPEECH ACTS; the plans, goals, and strategies of discourse participants; the interface of meaning or significance with culture, ideology, personality, gender, attitude, and emotion; the roles and relations of power or solidarity among participants or institutions in discourse; and so forth.

The concept "discourse" has been commensurately expanded. Besides being the standard designation for a recorded sequence of utterances or of "texts," "discourse" may designate elaborate complexes up to the entire practice of communication within a society and its institutions, as in MICHEL FOUCAULT's *The Archaeology of Knowledge* (1969) and *Language, Counter-Memory, Practice* (1977). Such is the diversity that one can find two "introductions" to discourse analysis with no overlap at all (Coulthard, Macdonnell).

Still, discourse analysis does manifest some general and consistent principles, which might be formulated as follows:

1. *A "discourse" is not merely a linguistic unit, but a unit of human action, interaction, communication, and cognition.* The deeply entrenched tendency to identify the "discourse" with its recorded (usually written) language trace must be resisted.

2. *The source of data should be naturally occurring discourses rather than isolated brief examples invented by investigators.* We must discard the expedient academic notion of "context-free" words or sentences. We should inquire how we may be changing the significance of such items by disregarding, for example, constraints or mystifying institutional commitments.

3. *Discourse analysis should balance analytic with synthetic viewpoints.* The traditional methods of discovering "linguistic units" and "constituents" by segmenting discourse should be more evenly correlated with methods that focus on how discourses arise from processes of selection and combination.

4. *A discourse is not a static, idealized, or totalized unity of words and significances but a dynamic field of interests, engagements, tensions, conflicts, and contradictions.* This field in turn reflects the organization of society and its institutions and their inherent roles and power structures.

5. *A discourse or discourse domain should not be isolated from others but explored in mutual relevance.* The nature and problems of a domain such as "technical language" do not inhere in its outward features, such as special terms, tables of formulas. We must inquire how it functions within the general or special acquisition of knowledge through discourse.

6. *Discourse analysis should systemically reflect on its own procedures.* Each project must be selective and focused and should declare and justify its motives in terms of epistemological interests. The discourse of science itself should be examined, as should that of specific fields such as anthropology.

7. *Discourse analysis obliges the investigator to engage and reengage with discourse.* The ideal separation of subject from object, or investigator from data, is not feasible here. We can ask, for example, how the discourse being analyzed correlates with the discourse of the analysis.

8. *Discourse analysis is rich and expansive rather than formalized and reductive.* Discourse cannot be rationally analyzed by a fixed algorithm or converted into a configuration of formal symbols. Instead, our analysis should explore discourse in any direction and to any degree appropriate for grasping its status within social practices.

9. *To master its issues and problems, discourse analysis must adopt an encompassing interdisciplinary perspective.* We need to fill in the content of interdisciplinary programs

with a substantive array of results. Hence, discourse analysis should not be one more battleground for warring "paradigms" (in Thomas S. Kuhn's sense) but a domain for cooperation and integration among alternative paradigms.

10. *Discourse analysis should interact with institutions and groups both inside and outside the academy to pursue urgent issues and problems.* We should periodically take stock of and adapt our methods to pressing issues.

11. *The highest goals of discourse analysis are to support the freedom of access to knowledge through discourse and to help reveal and rebalance communicative power structures.* Following the lead of "critical linguistics" (Fowler et al.), "critical discourse analysis" has now widely acknowledged this thesis (Fairclough). Special attention has been devoted to geopolitical problems such as public policy, colonialism, racism, and sexism, which, though restricted by laws and statutes, persist at deeper levels in discourse, not merely through lexical choices but through background assumptions, hierarchical structuring, rights of turn taking, and so on.

12. *The demanding tasks facing us call for an explicit, coherent research plan.* With a global expansion of discourse study under way, larger projects seem feasible, provided that scholars can interact over long distances and shorter intervals.

The future of discourse analysis will depend to no small degree on whether principles like these can be fully implemented and suitable frameworks and resources provided for research. The prospects seem especially favorable for interaction between discourse analysis and literary studies, a field in which the conception of discourse is now widely recognized as a foundational problem. The principles just enumerated readily invoke some promising trends:

1. The traditional focus on the literary text as language has been complemented by a concern for literary action, interaction, communication, and cognition, though often (inspired by French scholars like Foucault) more from a philosophical than from a sociological or psychological orientation.

2. Groundwork has been supplied by literary journals with an empirical outlook, such as *Poetics* and *Empirical Studies in the Arts*, in formulating and understanding the ways in which literary texts, unlike isolated sentences, occur naturally under specific conditions and conventions.

3. The balance has been improved between the analytic tactics of "close reading" or "text exegesis" and synthetic models of literary "production" and "reception" (Jauss; RECEPTION THEORY).

4. The traditional harmonizing or "totalizing" tendencies of literary criticism have been offset by widening probes of literary discourse as a field of interests, engagements, and conflicts, including the estrangement from the putative "real world" of the reader (Iser; READER-RESPONSE CRITICISM).

5. Scholars have manifested a renewed willingness to resituate literature—long isolated as a privileged preserve set above all other discourse or even in opposition to

it—among the plurality of social and ideological discourses of its own time and ours (Fowler; White; FREDRIC JAMESON).

6. The enterprise of reflecting on procedures is at the very heart of the prestigious "literary theory" movement (Beaugrande, *Critical Discourse*), though the theorizing is sometimes obscure about its methods and goals.

7. The fastidious reaching for ultimate, tidy closure of the "meaning" of the literary work has yielded to an open-ended readiness to engage and reengage the work (Miller), and the individual work has been redefined as an "intertextual weaving" of other discourses (Hartman).

8. The brief "structuralist" turn to some strict "scientism" based on formal linguistic methods has swerved toward the wide-ranging "poststructuralist" revision (both trends documented by Harari).

9. The value of an encompassing interdisciplinary perspective on literature is no longer seriously contested, and joint projects have become commonplace.

10. Shifts of focus outside the academy are still regrettably rare, but some hopeful signs can be seen.

11. The freedom of access to the unique experiences literature affords is still not a firmly established goal, owing to the elitist stance of many literary scholars. However, discourse analysis has shown the processing of quite ordinary discourse to be enormously sophisticated and has refuted the image of the naïveté of nonelite readers.

12. The paradigm of discourse analysis, as well as those of text linguistics and general linguistics, has been radically renewed by access to very large corpora of authentic data, which reveal regularities more general than the discourse but more specific than the language (Beaugrande).

The challenges facing discourse analysis in the coming years are obviously immense, but the trends afford some firm grounds for optimism.

ROBERT DE BEAUGRANDE

See also LINGUISTICS AND LANGUAGE and SPEECH ACTS.

See also bibliography for MICHEL FOUCAULT.

Robert de Beaugrande, *Critical Discourse: A Survey of Contemporary Literary Theorists* (1988), *A New Introduction to the Study of Text and Discourse* (2004), *Text, Discourse, and Process* (1980), *Text Production* (1984); Malcolm Coulthard, *An Introduction to Discourse Analysis* (1985); John Rupert Firth, *Papers in Linguistics, 1934–1951* (1957); Norman Fairclough, *Critical Discourse Analysis* (1996); Roger Fowler, *Literature as Social Discourse* (1981); Roger Fowler et al., *Language and Control* (1979); Michael Halliday, *Introduction to Functional Grammar* (1985); Josué V. Harari, ed., *Structuralists and Structuralism: A Selected Bibliography of French Contemporary Thought* (1971), *Textual Strategies: Perspectives in Post-Structuralist Criticism* (1979); Geoffrey H. Hartman, *Saving the Text: Literature, Derrida, Philosophy* (1981); Wolfgang Iser, *Der Akt des Lesens: Theorie ästhetischer Wirkung* (1976, *The Act of Reading: A Theory of Aesthetic Response*, trans. Wolfgang Iser, 1978), *Der implizite Leser: Kommunikationsformen des Romans von Bunyan* bis Beckett (1972, *The Implied Reader: Patterns of Communication in Prose Fiction from Bunyan to Beckett*, trans. Wolfgang Iser, 1974); Fredric Jameson, *The Political Unconscious: Narrative as a Socially Symbolic Act* (1981); Hans Robert Jauss, *Ästhetische Erfahrung und literarische Hermeneutik* (1982, *Aesthetic Experience and Literary Hermeneutics*, trans. Michael Shaw, 1982), *Toward an Aesthetic of Reception* (trans. Timothy Bahti, 1982); Thomas S. Kuhn, *The Structure of Scientific Revolutions* (1962, 2nd ed., 1970); Robert Longacre, *An Anatomy of Speech Notions* (1976), *Grammar of Discourse* (1983); Diane Macdonnell, *Theories of Discourse* (1986); J. Hillis Miller, "Deconstructing the Deconstructors," *Theory Now and Then* (1991); Kenneth Lee Pike, *Language in Relation to a Unified Theory of the Structure of Human Behavior* (1967); Hayden White, *Metahistory: The Historical Imagination in Nineteenth-Century Europe* (1973), *Tropics of Discourse: Essays in Cultural Criticism* (1978).

2. Discourse Theory

Discourse theorists take discourse, rather than language, as their domain because they find language as it is constituted by modern linguistics to be oriented too much toward abstract system and too little toward use and social function. The standard definition of "language" in linguistics, a set of units and the rules for combining them to make well-formed sentences, treats language as invariant over domains, occasions, speakers, and purposes. Discourse, for discourse theory, is not sets of formally identified structures but a type of social action. Discourse theory criticizes theories of speech acts for their focus on the acts of individual agents speaking without social determination or constraint.

Discourse theory also distinguishes itself sharply from philosophical concerns with the truth of statements and the validity of arguments, substituting a concern for conditions under which one can be judged to have made a serious, sound, true, important, authoritative statement. This program is clearly sketched by Michel Foucault in *The Archaelogy of Knowledge* and very concisely in "The Discourse of Language" (1970), a lecture appended to the English translation of *Archaelogy*. Foucault speaks of "rules" of discourse, but the conditions under which one can make serious, authoritative statements include material and social institutions and practices. A theory of discourse therefore implies a theory of society, most particularly of power, legitimacy, and authority. Moreover, since society can largely be viewed as the sum of discourses, discourse theory, particularly in its French varieties, often merges into praxis, undermining the commonsense ("Anglo-Saxon") distinction between talking and doing. Similarly, discourse sidesteps the traditional oppositions of thoughts and words, intentions and expressions, and has provided the key concept for a reformulation of psychology as "discursive psychology" by Rom Harré and others.

Broadly construed, discourse theory draws insights and support from three intellectual traditions. First, the tradition of hermeneutics as transmitted by Hans-Georg Gadamer, Jürgen Habermas, and Thomas S. Kuhn emphasizes that every discourse takes place within a shared horizon of preunderstanding (or "lifeworld") that cannot be fully or explicitly formulated. No discourse can be completely self-grounded, and the ability to function as a participant arises from initiation and experience. Relevant concepts here include the notions of discourse community and "culture" (in one sense). Habermas argues that argumentation oriented toward reaching understanding, with its implicit commitment to assent to the force of best reasons, is the inner telos of human language and can provide an ideal of undistorted (not coercive or manipulative) communication.

A second major source is ethnography and social theory that is concerned with offering and validating accounts of cultural practices, including the writings of Clifford Geertz, Erving Goffman, and others supporting the program of symbolic interaction or social construction. These approaches typically seek to "make strange" or denaturalize or make visible rules and practices underlying various institutions and transactions. Like hermeneutics, they sense discourse's rootedness in particular social forms and practices and tend to foreground the analyst's uncertain status as an outsider and the potential artificiality of accounts of insider understanding. In *Outline of a Theory of Practice* (1972), PIERRE BOURDIEU emphasizes that practical knowledge and action are rooted in a "habitus" that resists theorizing or systematization in terms of abstract, "underlying" principles, including those of economic interest. Though Bourdieu is perhaps best known as a social theorist and researcher, one of his research sites is French academic discourse (*Reproduction in Education, Society, and Culture* [1970]; *Homo Academicus* [1984]).

Third, Marxists such as Louis Althusser, Michel Pêcheux, Ernesto Laclau and Chantal Mouffe, and Fredric Jameson emphasize discourse as a mode of power, which in late capitalist societies means the enactment and legitimation of inequality. These writers have stimulated new interest in V. N. Voloshinov's *Marxism and the Philosophy of Language* (1929) and the more general view of discourse as embodying the conflicting values and stances of different groups found in MIKHAIL BAKHTIN's "Discourse in the Novel" (written in 1934–1935). Discourse as a mode of concealing and perpetuating inequality and of regulating behavior is a theme also of such non-Marxist advocates of resistance to discursive regulation as Foucault and feminists focusing on the silencing and marginalizing effects of hegemonic discourses. Since theorizing itself is an activity not untinged by hegemonic aspirations, feminists such as HÉLÈNE CIXOUS adopt the devices of myth, contradiction, and hyperbole and could be said to refuse to do theory at all. Most of these theorists make use of and develop Althusser's notion of discourses as creating subject positions for those who engage in them (e.g., social agency discourse creates roles of interviewer and applicant), with associated restrictions on what can be said and by whom.

In addition, most of the very large amount of work on language in institutional settings—medical, legal, educational, media—explores the intertwining of discourse and historical-material fact, either through the shaping and maintaining of the "client" (pupil) role or through the management and manipulation of mass audiences.

So much of discourse theory is oriented toward unmasking, debunking, and raising our consciousness about the ways discourses serve power that one sympathizes with Foucault's suggestion that it reflects intellectuals' uneasiness, embarrassment, or fear of power, which has as much a creative, positive aspect as it does an exclusionary, silencing one. That observation, made late in his life, remains to be fully assimilated into discourse theory.

GEORGE L. DILLON

See also FEMINIST THEORY AND CRITICISM and LINGUISTICS AND LANGUAGE.

See also bibliographies for MIKHAIL BAKHTIN, PIERRE BOURDIEU, HÉLÈNE CIXOUS, MICHEL FOUCAULT, and FREDRIC JAMESON.

Louis Althusser, *Lenin and Philosophy and Other Essays* (trans. Ben Brewster, 1971); Hans-Georg Gadamer, *Wahrheit und Methode: Grundzüge einer philosophischen Hermeneutik* (1960, 5th ed., *Gesammelte Werke*, vol. 1, ed. J. C. B. Mohr, 1986, *Truth and Method*, ed. and trans. Garrett Burden and John Cumming, 1975, 2nd ed., trans. rev. Joel Weinsheimer and Donald G. Marshall, 1989); Jürgen Habermas, *Theorie des kommunikativen Handelns*, vol. 1, *Handlungsrationalität und gesellschaftliche Rationalisierung* (1981, *The Theory of Communicative Action*, vol. 1, *Reason and the Rationalization of Society*, trans. Thomas McCarthy, 1983); Rom Harré et al., eds., *Rethinking Psychology* (1995); Ernesto Laclau and Chantal Mouffe, *Hegemony and Socialist Strategies* (1985); Michel Pêcheux, *Les verites de la Palice* (1975, *Language, Semantics, and Ideology*, trans. Harbans Nagpal, 1982); Valentin N. Voloshinov, *Marksizm i filosofiia iazyka* (1929, *Marxism and the Philosophy of Language*, trans. Ladislav Matejka and Irwin R. Titunik, 1973).

Eagleton, Terry

Terry Eagleton was born in Salford, in northwest England, in 1943. At Cambridge University, mentored by Dominican priest and theologian Herbert McCabe and drama professor RAYMOND WILLIAMS, Eagleton merged leftist Catholic theology and radical socialist politics into what is sometimes referred to as his early Marxist-Catholic phase (*The New Left Church* [1966], *From Culture to Revolution* [1968], *The Body as Language* [1970]), though both currents of thought remain in his more mature work.

Eagleton's dialogue with Williams nourished the preoccupation with the meaning and value of culture that persists from his early writings in the 1960s to *The Idea of Culture* (2000). His first full-length work of literary criticism, *Shakespeare and Society* (1967), seeks to extend the kind of cultural analysis that Williams (to whom it was dedicated) had developed in *Culture and Society* (1958), connecting the needs and interests of the present with those of an earlier epoch and breaking down unhelpful distinctions between "the individual" and "society." *Exiles and Émigrés* (1970) shows Eagleton confidently extending the idea of "the knowable community" that Williams had explored in *The English Novel from Dickens to Lawrence* (1970). Both Williams and Eagleton register dissatisfaction with GEORG LUKÁCS's fervent commitment to social realism and his belief that literature can effectively register the totality of a particular social epoch.

Exiles and Émigrés looks at the problems of achieving a comprehensive vision of any community or society, especially when the vantage point is that of an outsider or exile, as in prominent works of modernist literature by Joseph Conrad, Henry James, T. S. Eliot, James Joyce, and W. B. Yeats. The book breaks fundamentally with Lukács's ardent social realism (and antipathy to modernism), and its spirited approach to questions of Englishness, expatriation, and national identity have given it a broader and lasting relevance for literary theory and criticism. Eagleton's shrewd attempt to connect the modernist writings of the early twentieth century with European colonial politics anticipates the much later emergence of a more explicit postcolonial theorizing in literary criticism.

Throughout the 1970s Eagleton grappled with the politics of literature and with ways of locating and identifying historical shifts and tendencies in fictional texts. In *Myths of Power: A Marxist Study of the Brontës* he applies the structuralist methodology of the Romanian Marxist Lucien Goldmann, whose focus on the worldview or mental structure of a particular social group or class suggested one way of establishing a correspondence between the historical structures of society and the aesthetic structures of the text. Stridently exposing the deficiencies of ahistorical, mystificatory readings of *Wuthering Heights*, it firmly positions the novel within the power struggles of the landed gentry and the industrial bourgeoisie in nineteenth-century England.

Eagleton made his most formidable and decisive intervention in critical theory in 1976 with the publication of *Criticism and Ideology* and *Marxism and Literary Criticism*. In *Criticism and Ideology*, he breaks with the idealist epistemology and political gradualism of his mentor Williams, pointing toward a new Marxist theory of literary production based on a semiotic approach to language and a materialist conception of history. If Louis Althusser and Pierre Macherey offer convenient models for understanding ideology's nature and function, ANTONIO GRAMSCI provides the theory of hegemony through which Eagleton seeks to understand the role of culture in establishing and maintaining class power and dominance. The book remains a valuable account of the relations between literature and the ideological formations in which it is produced. Its most valuable and engaging sections are those that offer a critique of the social and aesthetic organicism with which writers seek to conceal or resolve historical conflict. The smaller, more accessible *Marxism and Literary Criticism* provides a basic student introduction to Marxist literary theory, but it shares with *Criticism and Ideology* a deep and abiding interest in the relations between text and ideology, problems of aesthetic value, and questions of literary form.

The 1980s were perhaps Eagleton's most politically optimistic and revolutionary years. *Walter Benjamin; or, Towards a Revolutionary Criticism* (1981) attempts to put WALTER BENJAMIN's insights to new political ends. Eagleton candidly addresses the problems facing a revolutionary criticism at a time when socialism was itself undergoing transformation on a global scale. The book turns explicitly from questions of textuality to questions of cultural production and cultural practice, and the influence of Bertolt Brecht and MIKHAIL BAKHTIN is clearly evident in Eagleton's musing on the political uses of theater and comedy. This alliterative trio—Benjamin, Brecht, and Bakhtin—continue to inform much of Eagleton's subsequent work, including his fiction and drama. The book also contains a formidable attack on JACQUES DERRIDA, rejecting a fashionably skeptical, depoliticized deconstruction in favor of the more revolutionary deconstructive mode, of which Benjamin's writings are the nascent type.

The Rape of Clarissa (1982) also reveals the excitement of deconstruction and its potentially destabilizing effects while remaining at odds with its patently unhistorical methods. The book draws liberally on poststructuralist theories of textuality but supplements these with feminist and psychoanalytic perspectives on sexuality and Marxist ideas of history. *William Shakespeare* (1986) purports, like *The Rape of Clarissa*, to be an exercise in political SEMIOTICS, delighting in drawing attention to unruly and disruptive textual practices while insisting on the text's material nature and the intricate interrelations of language, desire, law, money, and the body.

Eagleton's newfound eclecticism, encouraged in part by Benjamin's willingness to grasp whatever theoretical materials suited his purposes, is evident in the stimulating 1986 selection of essays published under the Benjaminesque title *Against the Grain*. For many readers, however, Eagleton's most significant work from the 1980s is *Literary Theory: An Introduction* (1983), his most popular and commercially successful work. Written with impressive panache and devastating wit, the book offers a provocative and staunchly independent line of inquiry. In keeping with his deeply divided response to deconstruction, Eagleton is both an enthusiastic advocate of theory and its harshest critic. *Literary Theory* is thus very far from an anodyne survey of theory, nor does it show any diminution of Eagleton's Marxist convictions. Underpinning the book is an investigation into the rise of English studies as an academic discipline and the social function of literary criticism. A companion volume, *The Function of Criticism* (1984), looks at critical practice's history since the Enlightenment and argues that criticism has had significance only when it has freely engaged not just with literature but with the epoch's broad cultural and political life.

Undeterred by fashionable postmodern skepticism, Eagleton held firmly to Marxist critical theory's central tenets, including the concept of ideology, which he sought to clarify and refine in *Ideology: An Introduction* and *Ideology* (1991). The fall of the Berlin Wall and the dismantlement of the Soviet Union seemed only to strengthen his convictions, and his undiminished political commitment is evident in *Marx*, one of his shortest but most inspiring works of the 1990s. His major project during these difficult years, *The Ideology of the Aesthetic* (1990), traces the complex relationships between aesthetics, ideology, and political society from Immanuel Kant to THEODOR W. ADORNO. The book contests the idea that the aesthetic is a neutral, disinterested concept, showing how it gives ideological coherence to the needs of modern class society. If the aesthetic serves to soften and sublimate the crude operations of class power, it can also at times serve as a powerful critique of class society by revealing alternative modes of thinking and feeling. *The Ideology of the Aesthetic* reveals an increasing impatience with some of the more extreme varieties of postmodernist theory, as does *The Illusions of Postmodernism* (1996), Eagleton's sharpest attack on contemporary criticism's evasions and irresponsibilities. The book deplores the ethical relativism of much postmodern theory, as well as its seeming disregard for justice, equality, and human rights.

Eagleton's dismay with contemporary cultural politics found some relief in his warm embrace of Ireland. Three books—*Heathcliff and the Great Hunger* (1995), *Crazy John and the Bishop* (1997), and *Scholars and Rebels in Nineteenth-Century Ireland* (1999)—bring together contemporary cultural theory and Irish social history, probing the deficiencies and exposing the blind spots that have hindered both recent postcolonial theorizing and conventional empiricist accounts of the Irish past. Eagleton ranges ambitiously across the field of major and minor Irish writers, provocatively intervening in current debates on Irish historiography and historical revisionism. He also offers a comic guide to the land of saints and scholars in *The Truth about the Irish* (1999). Likewise, *The Gatekeeper* (2002), a candid, hilarious, and moving memoir exploring Eagleton's Irish roots and his painful journey to academic success in Cambridge and Oxford, goes a long way toward explaining the mind and heart of one of our time's most impressive and distinguished critics.

STEPHEN REGAN

See also ETHICS and MARXIST THEORY AND CRITICISM: 2. STRUCTURALIST MARXISM.

Terry Eagleton, *After Theory* (2003), *Against the Grain* (1986), *The Body as Language* (1970), *Crazy John and the Bishop* (1997), *The Crisis of Contemporary Culture* (1993), *Criticism and Ideology* (1976), *The English Novel: An Introduction* (2005), *Exiles and Émigrés* (1970), *Figures of Dissent: Critical Essays on Fish, Spivak, Žižek, and Others* (2003), *From Culture to Revolution* (1968), *The Function of Criticism* (1984), *The Gatekeeper* (2002), *Heathcliff and the Great Hunger* (1995), *Holy Terror* (2005), *How to Read a Poem* (2007), *The Idea of Culture* (2000), *Ideology* (1994), *Ideology: An Introduction* (1991), *The Ideology of the Aesthetic* (1990), *The Illusions of Postmodernism* (1996), *Literary Theory: An Introduction* (1983, 2nd ed., 1996, anniversary ed., 2008), *Marx* (1997); *Marxism and Literary Criticism* (1976), *The Meaning of Life* (2007), *Myths of Power: A Marxist Study of the Brontës* (1975, 2nd ed., 1988), *Nationalism, Irony, and Commitment* (1988), *The New Left Church* (1966), *On Evil* (2010), *The Rape of Clarissa* (1982); *Reason, Faith, and Revolution: Reflections on the God Debate* (2009), *Saint Oscar* (1989), *Saint Oscar and Other Plays* (1997), *Saints and Scholars* (1987), *Scholars and Rebels in Nineteenth-Century Ireland* (1999), *Shakespeare and Society* (1967), *The Significance of Theory* (1990), *Sweet Violence: The Idea of the Tragic* (2002), *Trouble with Strangers: A Study of Ethics* (2009), *The Truth about the Irish* (1999), *Walter Benjamin; or, Towards a Revolutionary Criticism* (1981), *William Shakespeare* (1986); Terry Eagleton, ed., *Raymond Williams: Critical Perspectives* (1989); Terry Eagleton and Matthew Beaumont, *The Task of the Critic: Terry Eagleton in Dialogue* (2009); Terry Eagleton and Drew Milne, *Conservations with Terry Eagleton* (2008); Terry Eagleton and Drew Milne, eds., *Marxist Literary Theory* (1995).

Ecocriticism

In the introduction to her (and Harold Fromm's) influential collection, *The Ecocriticism Reader: Landmarks in Literary Ecology* (1995), Cheryll Glotfelty succinctly defines "ecocriticism" as "the study of the relationship between literature and the physical environment [taking] an earth-centered approach to literary studies" (xviii). Glotfelty insists on defining the term in part to help establish ecocriticism as a legitimate branch of literary studies even as she acknowledges both an earlier (and perhaps original) coinage by William H. Rueckert that integrates the science of ecology and literature, as well as the choice of other critics in the field to use other terms. Ultimately, the appeal of ecocriticism for literary studies as framed by Glotfelty's definition is its openness. Indeed, Scott Slovic has felt confident enough to assert that "there is not a single literary work anywhere that utterly defies ecocritical interpretation" ("Forum"). Presumably, this opens the field up to infinite possibilities.

However, Glotfelty's succinct definition and Slovic's invitation mask the activist practice central to this area of literary studies. Glotfelty identifies her own work for social and political change on environmental issues as the impetus behind her formal push for the greening of literary studies through publication and academic association. This emphasis on activism necessitates a broader definition of ecocriticism. Perhaps Lawrence Buell gets closer in his groundbreaking 1995 study, *The Environmental Imagination: Thoreau, Nature Writing, and the Formation of American Culture*, in which he promotes ecocriticism as a multiform inquiry into "the relationship between literature and environment conducted in a spirit of commitment to environmental praxis" (430).

If environmental activism is central to ecocriticism, how to practice it is less established. Several major approaches, some more "in the world" than others, have emerged. Environmental justice aligns itself with the international social justice movement in order to address issues of environmental discrimination, such as, for example, the disproportionate exposure of people of color to hazardous environmental conditions. The introduction of the concepts "environmental racism" and "environmental classicism" have forced a discussion of diversity issues within ecocriticism. Many ecocritics participate directly in the environmental justice movement, and their work focuses on literary texts and nonliterary texts that efface and evade environmental responsibility and/or document and reflect on the destruction of the environment and the uprooting and marginalizing of humans and other animals who have a historical and holistic relationship to specific bioregions. Through the promotion and canonization of literary texts by writers of color on land-use issues and other aspects of environment, views of the environment based on racial and cultural differences broaden and challenge dominant views of the natural world.

The term "nature writing," then, is redefined to acknowledge nature as always already politically inscribed. In her *Borderlands/La Frontera: The New Mestiza* (1987), for example, Gloria Anzaldúa describes the cultural meaning of the U.S.-Mexican border from an earth-centered, transnational perspective that pinpoints environmental and human degradation based on white, Western principles and abstractions, such as the boundaries that divide nation-states. Environmental justice also locates inequality in the gender, class, and racial barriers that limit access to wilderness areas. As a result, classic literary works, nature writing, and natural histories can be reread as reflections of privilege. Even as writers revel in natural wonders and connect their relationships in nature to psychological wholeness and well-being, their aristocratic and middle-class advantage goes undeclared. As a result of this critical scrutiny, the environmental justice movement increasingly promotes the interrogation of the role of privilege in shaping environmental ideologies and argues for expanding the landscape of study to include considerations of urban nature where the poor, the elderly, the disabled, and other marginalized groups tend to live.

The attention of literary critics to what Cynthia Deitering calls "toxic consciousness" or a late twentieth-century proliferation of postnatural novels dealing with apocalyptic themes, as in Don DeLillo's *White Noise* (1985) and in novels set against toxic backdrops, such as Margaret Atwood's *The Handmaid's Tale* (1985), acknowledges how fiction documents environmental crises. Yet the form's tendency to favor human over nonhuman activities through the relegation of nature to the role of "setting" may not, for example, meet Lawrence Buell's first "requirement" of an ecocentric text, that the "non human environment is present not merely as a framing device but as a presence" (7–8). Creating that presence foregrounds the assumed connection between the well-being of the natural world and the writer's practice. This large subset of ecocriticism includes nature writing, ecocomposition, environmental life writing, and ecopoetry. British and American nature-writing classics, such as Gilbert White's *Natural History of Selbourne* (1789), Henry David Thoreau's *Walden* (1854), and Aldo Leopold's *Sand County Almanac* (1948) become subject to critical analysis and are used in the classroom as aids to composition. Of particular interest are works such as Edward Abbey's *Desert Solitaire* (1968), which according to Don Scheese "transcend natural history's purpose of merely naming and classifying natural phenomena" and go "beyond simple nature writing to become criti[cal] of society" (Glotfelty and Fromm 304). This focus on "ecocomposition" foregrounds the role of pedagogy in developing ecosensitive human relationships in nature. In the classroom, ecocritics encourage introspection through the development of writing practices and strategies such as cataloging and journal writing as ways for students to better understand their own relationship to nature. Environmental "life writing" specifically foregrounds issues of autobiography and environment through the study of appropriate texts and the creation of autobiographical works. This category includes both traditional autobiographies in nature writing and complex, experimental works such as Terry Tempest Williams's *Refuge: An Unnatural History of Family and Place* (1991).

An emphasis on recovery has also helped to counter accusations of a post-Thoreau American studies bias in environmental literary studies. Recovery has meant that critics interested in pre-1800 writers and/or noncanonical and marginalized writers have become integral to the growth of the discipline. Among the key works here is Leo Marx's *Machine in the Garden* (1964), which explores the idea of progress as an inherent good—especially in its attachment to technology—and the implications of this paradigm for nature. Ecocritics working in British literature, particularly pre-1800 literature, cite the important influence of RAYMOND WILLIAMS's *The Country and the City* (1973), especially in its sophisticated mapping of literary texts to highlight the relationship between land use and ideology and its focus on the relationships of laboring people to nature.

Ecocritics also acknowledge the groundbreaking work of Joseph Meeker, who early on, in *The Comedy of Survival: Studies in Literary Ecology* (1972), identified "the intimate and causal relationship between human culture and environmental crisis" (xx). In his examination of literary genres, Meeker exposes tragedy as a Western invention that internalizes the affirmation of human mastery over nature. In opposition to this tragic ethic and its environmental implications, Meeker casts comedy as an optimistic partner in its depiction of "the loss of equilibrium and its recovery" (25). Meeker employs Joseph Wood Krutch's "tragic fallacy" to assert that tragic values are in decline owing to the erosion of basic cultural assumptions such as the transcendent moral order, human supremacy over nature, and the importance of the individual (52). This supports Meeker's view that the comic mode is fundamentally connected to human survival and that literature as a result is inextricably knitted to ecology. Extensions of Meeker's work on genre include Dominic Head's argument that the novel is too closely implicated in the ascendancy of industrialized capitalism to be of much assistance in the establishment of an activist ecocritical practice.

This view of generic inadequacy, coupled with Lawrence Buell's promotion of nature writing as a genre potentially or inherently more ecocentric than fiction, throws the fledgling practice of ecocriticism into a conundrum. If ecocriticism uses formalism as a critical approach to identify and champion the work of writers with an explicitly ecocentric practice, the movement risks slipping into a prescriptive mode that perhaps addresses ecocriticism's activist imperative but constricts inquiry and may even be seen to sanction a particular orientation of writers to and in nature. This perception is bolstered by an emerging list of authors given the ecocritical "seal of approval." Practitioners of ecocomposition struggle with the apparent contradictions between the uncommitted, "how-to" aspects of teaching composition and learning to write and the clear activist position underlying the "eco" prefix. The discipline seems to be managing this challenge through an appeal to pluralism and the compromise of acknowledging multiple ecocriticisms. This tack speaks once again to the prerogative of any emerging field to be pluralistic even as it reflects the contentious fear that compromise and openness may undermine the activist goals underlying and necessitating its establishment in the first place.

The movement from a potentially prescriptive ecopoetry to a descriptive ecopoetics does not allay this concern. While ecopoetry identifies and unpacks nature's presence in literary texts, ecopoetics connects a close analysis of forms, language, and the writer's relationship in nature to theory. This more philosophical orientation—for example, Michael Branch's "ecosophy"—attempts to locate ecocriticism within and in relation to poststructural theory. In this way, ecosophy distinguishes itself by its refusal to be contained in language. The critique of anthropomorphism at the center of ecosophy encompasses a holism that necessarily diminishes humans' conceptions of their own central place. However, this has created fundamental difficulties for the definition of ecocriticism. For one thing, poststructuralism appears to have little to offer ecocriticism because of its emphasis on textuality. Though textual practice can reveal underlying ideologies, in and of itself it appears not to have an inherent connection to environmental activism. And ecocriticism's contribution to poststructuralist discourse appears limited. As Dominic Head points out, ecocriticism's commitment to decentering human agency underpins a grand narrative of saving the planet, a position that poststructuralism would unequivocally reject. In addition, it inadequately addresses the issue of how nonhuman nature can contribute to any "discussion" beyond or outside of textuality. For Head, ecocriticism's effectiveness as part of literary studies "necessitates a compromise on ecocritical values" (38).

Certainly, the associations between ecocriticism and theory do not end here. Other attempts have been made to join theory and practice in ecofeminism. Here two inherently activist practices are interwoven, helped by explicit connections and a central concern with oppression. Specifically, ecofeminism focuses on the connections between the domination of women and the domination of nature. Ynestra King teases out some of the inherent feminist critiques and contradictions of ecofeminism by locating it along a feminist continuum between rational feminism, which would reject any link between woman and nature as a dangerous acknowledgment of biological determinism, and radical feminism, which would argue that women are more natural than men. Critiques of rationalism as a male construct deeply implicated in both the oppression of women and the enslavement of nature to utilitarian ends constitute much of the insightful work of the Australian ecofeminist Val Plumwood and in Carolyn Merchant's *Death of Nature: Women, Ecology and the Scientific Revolution* (1990), which shows that metaphors of nature are historically connected to the twin exploitations of women and nature. Another group of ecofeminists, including Carol J. Adams and ecocentric women writers such as Ursula K. LeGuin, focus on the blurred boundaries between woman and animal. At the level of textuality, unpacking sexist and speciesist language and advocating for the creation of alternative ecofeminist languages has been the project of writers such as Susan Griffin.

As with ecofeminism, the success or failure of ecocriticism, the necessity or impossibility of this literary discipline, is the subject of an ongoing exchange and exploration. Addressing activism remains a general concern for ecocriticism. Other activist disciplines within literary studies have remained viable despite discomfort and resistance. Like institutionalized racism and sexism, discourses harmful to the environment can be identified through sustained, sophisticated critical work. There is certainly more opportunity for expanded ecocritical study focused on new areas such as postcolonialism. Indeed, supporting a plurality of literary-critical practices may constitute a kind of environmental activism whose results can accumulate incrementally. By its very openness, the current definition addresses at some level the attacks on the discipline from those who fear a strident environmentalist polemic. The continuing debates suggest that for now at the very least the relationship between literature and the environment is worthy of concentrated and serious critical consideration.

ANNE MILNE

Stacy Alaimo, Undomesticated Ground: Recasting Nature as Feminist Space (2000); Ian Angus, A Border Within: National Identity, Cultural Plurality, and Wilderness (2007); Gloria Anzaldúa, Borderlands/La Frontera: The New Mestiza (1987); Karla Armbruster and Kathleen R. Wallace, eds., Beyond Nature Writing: Expanding the Boundaries of Ecocriticism (2001); Jonathan Bate, "Poetry and Biodiversity" (Kerridge et al.); Michael Branch, "Ecocriticism: The Nature of Nature in Literary Theory and Practice," Weber Studies 11 (1994); Lawrence Buell, The Environmental Imagination: Thoreau, Nature Writing, and the Formation of American Culture (1995), The Future of Environmental Criticism: Environmental Crisis and the Literary Imagination (2005); Robert D. Bullard, Dumping in Dixie: Race, Class, and Environmental Quality (3rd ed., 2000); Cynthia Deitering, "The Postnatural Novel: Toxic Consciousness in Fiction of the 1980s" (Glotfelty and Fromm); "Forum on Literatures of the Environment," PMLA 114 (1999); Barbara Gates and Ann B. Shteir, eds., Natural Eloquence: Women Reinscribe Science (1997); Cheryl Glotfelty and Harold Fromm, eds., The Ecocriticism Reader: Landmarks in Literary Ecology (1995); Susan Griffin, Women and Nature: The Roaring Inside Her (1978); Dominic Head, "The (Im)possibility of Ecocriticism," Writing the Environment: Ecocriticism and Literature (Kerridge et al.); Richard Kerridge et al., eds., Writing the Environment: Ecocriticism and Literature (1998); Ynestra King, "Feminism and the Revolt of Nature," Heresies 4 (1981); Annette Kolodny, The Lay of the Land: Metaphor as Experience in American Life and Letters (1975); Leo Marx, The Machine in the Garden: Technology and the Pastoral Ideal in America (1964); David Mazel, "American Literary Environmentalism as Domestic Orientalism" (Glotfelty and Fromm); Joseph Meeker, The Comedy of Survival: Literary Ecology and a Play Ethic (1972, 3rd ed., 1997); Carolyn Merchant, The Death of Nature: Women, Ecology and the Scientific Revolution (1980); Patrick D. Murphy, Literature of Nature: An International Sourcebook (1998); Val Plumwood, Feminism and the Mastery of Nature (1991); Diana M. A. Relke, Greenwor(l)ds: Ecocritical Readings of Canadian Women's Poetry (1999); Raymond Williams, The Country and the City (1973); Terry Tempest Williams, Refuge: An Unnatural History of Family and Place (1991).

Ethics

There are at least two ways of defining ethical criticism. In its largest sense, the term designates an ethical mode of inquiry into the interpretation of literary texts of which, historically, moral criticism has been the dominant branch. However, the term has also recently taken on new and specific meanings, particularly as *contrasted* with moral criticism. Until the 1970s at least, the dominant, postwar English tradition of literary criticism—particularly of fiction—was ethical in the sense that it was a moral one. In this respect, F. R. Leavis is the most eminent twentieth-century representative of the dominantly British moral tradition as embodied in the work of a host of critics, from his contemporaries (Q. D. Leavis, L. C. Knights, D. W. Harding) to later figures, in some quite obviously (David Holbrook, Ian Robinson, Ian McKillop), in others in a more ambivalent or conflicted form (John Bayley, Frank Kermode, Donald Davie, Christopher Ricks, Martin Dodsworth). A particular valuation of judgment was crucial to Leavis's work. In *The Great Tradition*, for instance, Leavis asserts the superior value of what he calls the "pre-eminent few" great novelists, whose work is "distinguished by a vital capacity for experience, a kind of reverent openness before life, and a marked moral intensity." The greatest writers also tend to be great moral judges. Correspondingly, so are the greatest critics. Underlying Leavis's project is the assumption that literary criticism must "enter overtly into questions of emotional hygiene and moral value" and (more generally) "spiritual health." The moral value of a literary text will partly depend on the value of the moral judgments within it, of the moral intelligence at work.

While Leavis was significant chiefly for British culture, he had a certain amount of influence in the United States (Marius Bewley, the Kenyon critics). In postwar American criticism, the moral strain was similarly pronounced, if less dominant and often inflected rather differently. Lionel Trilling was the most eminent figure, but, in the long run, Wayne C. Booth has been the more representative. Ostensibly, Booth's *The Rhetoric of Fiction* (1961) is an early example of the pseudoscientific, taxonomic manual of narrative theory that would become increasingly common with the impact of structuralism on the theory of the novel. Yet Booth's modes of analysis goes hand in hand with a tenacious moral insistence. For Booth, the rhetoric of fiction cannot but be a moral matter, since what it involves is the manipulation of the reader for good or for ill. Like Leavis's, Booth's moralism is insistently judicial: the work of the great moral realists of the English tradition were cardinal points of reference. By contrast, Booth tends either to make modernist writers look like nineteenth-century realists or to disparage their work.

The Anglo-American critical tradition of which Leavis and Booth are notable instances flourished on the basis of seldom-questioned assumptions. Firstly, for the most part, moral critics maintained a curiously naïve faith in the mimetic principle.

However sophisticated the discourse in question, at least two generations of critics tended to talk about characters in novels as though they were people. Secondly, moral critics were universalists: both author and critic were deemed to know what was good (or evil) for all. Thirdly, as a superior judge, the critic would serve as mentor to the reader, who lacked the critic's knowledge and whose powers of discrimination needed "guidance," to quote Booth. The relationship between critic and author was hierophantic, and the relationship between critic and student or reader paternalistic. Of course, both relationships were reflections of institutional structures that were historically and culturally determined and determinate. In Britain they were conditioned by the reassertion of patriarchal formations and official religion and by the comparatively rigid relations between classes that persisted even alongside the emergence of a liberal state system of higher education. In the United States, unsurprisingly, moral criticism was most significant in the period running from 1945 through the McCarthy years and from the Cuban missile crisis to the beginning of the Vietnam War.

However, the politicization of academic and intellectual life that was to a large extent the result of student unrest in the late 1960s spelled seeming decline for the moral tradition of criticism. New and politically more sophisticated conceptions of representation invaded English studies from continental Europe, chiefly as a consequence of the emergence of structuralism in Paris. And the increasing prestige of Marxist criticism promoted various forms of Ideologiekritik. Ahistorical as it so often was, and wary of the very concept of ideology, moral criticism was not likely to resist demystification successfully. Most importantly of all, the universalism whose validity moral criticism had presupposed came under increasing pressure. Feminists and, later, black and Asian critics, queer and postcolonial theorists, postmodernists and many others insisted on the specificity of particular histories, discourses, and subject positions.

Yet one of the most remarkable things about such "oppositional" criticism has been how far, under its political and historical astuteness, the assumptions of the old moral criticism are repeatedly detectable. The paradigmatic figure here is TERRY EAGLETON, a "left moralist" whose roots were in Leavisism. For all Eagleton's proclaimed interest in dialectics, he exhibits a profoundly eschatological impulse to separate saints from sinners. The kind of modification of traditional moralism that is perceptible in Eagleton's work was widespread in English and American criticism of the 1980s and, to some extent, persisted into the 1990s. Indeed, one principal manoeuver in the literary criticism of the period was the separation of moralizing structures from grand narratives and the surreptitious transferal of those structures to micronarratives instead.

The moral concerns of feminist criticism, for example, have been hardly less significant than those of Leavis and Eagleton. On one level, the power of feminist theory has arguably resided in the moral conviction from which it springs and that informs its critique of the history and morality of patriarchy. There are plenty of examples of a straightforward feminist moralism: Sandra Gilbert and Susan Gubar's classic *The Madwoman in the Attic* (1979), for example, sets out to provide not just an account of the female literary tradition in the nineteenth century but an elaborated theory of women's literary creativity. Gilbert and Gubar conceive of this creativity as a moral struggle with the masculine will to domination. Mary Daly's *Gyn/Ecology* (1979) develops an unrelentingly ferocious moral attack on patriarchal morality, thus simultaneously affirming its radical difference from and reversing into identity with its antagonist. Most notably, perhaps, Elaine Showalter has always been at heart an American moralist. In *A Literature of Their Own* (1977), she promotes what she calls "gynocritics" (a criticism focusing on the themes, genres, and forms of literature by women). "Gynocritics" now looks like an exercise in critical fortress building, gathering the good, just, and right into a moral stockade.

Anglo-American critical traditions, then, have been insistently moral, not least when implicitly laying claim to a different rationale. But this moral tradition should be precisely distinguished from what might be called the new ethical criticism. The emergence of this criticism may be dated to two particular texts: J. Hillis Miller's deconstructive *The Ethics of Reading* (1987) and Barbara Herrnstein Smith's pragmatist *Contingencies of Value* (1988). In all its varied forms, moralism almost invariably produces an assured, assertive hermeneutics. At some level, however subtle and discreet, the moral critic is confident that he or she self-evidently possesses the right kind of knowledge about how to act and be. The moral critic also assumes that any truth or truths in question are unproblematically available to language. Moral criticism commonly proceeds on the assumption that morality and representation are inseparable—that literary texts cannot have ethical dimensions outside their mimetic projects.

Miller and Smith stand at the beginning of a criticism that puts such certainties into question. Smith mounts an assault on concepts of absolute moral value. She argues that systems of moral value can have no given or objective significance, that they are always both constructed and situated. Since they always involve questions of power rather than truth, or truth as power, they are always open to dispute. Smith proposes a form of evaluative criticism that would precisely and carefully refrain from objectivism and be scrupulously conscious of its own contingency or partiality. Hillis Miller's book is the first to argue for the vital relevance specifically of a deconstructive ethics to literary criticism. For Miller, the ethics of reading is indissociable precisely from the final inaccessibility of the truth of the text. Reading involves a response to an ethical imperative. But that imperative stems rather from the law of language itself, which insists that texts are boundlessly interpretable, that no readings can embrace their secrets.

Taken together, whatever their differences, Smith's and Miller's books represent the inception of the dominant trend in ethical criticism from the 1990s through the beginning of the twenty-first century. In *Getting It Right* (1992) Geoffrey Galt Harpham makes explicit an argument already implicit in Smith's and Miller's work. Humanists had sometimes claimed that literary theory was indifferent to ethical questions. But there is in fact a close relationship between theory and ethics. However, the ethics of and in theory is one of "august reticence" or "principled irresolution," a fidelity to the "strictly undecidable" which "suffers determination by morality." Harpham also adds in "Ethics" (1995) and *Shadows of Ethics* (1999) that ethics should not be thought of as a refined form of dithering and that morality "realizes ethics." But ethics also operates a kind of play within morality, holding it open, hoping to restrain it from violence, and subjecting it to a "kind of auto-deconstruction." The new ethical criticism thus appeared to differ from the older moral criticism in working not from a grounding in particular values, but from a concept of the groundlessness of value itself. Of course, the groundlessness of value swiftly turns into a value. In contrast to Harpham, one of the earliest contributions to the new ethical criticism also issued it with a powerful and important caution. Steven Connor's *Theory and Cultural Value* (1992) starts out from Smith and Miller. But Connor shows that both Smith's and Miller's books are dependent on absolutizing habits of ethical thought. Connor argues that this must invariably happen: concepts of the relativity of ethical value will necessarily imply absolutes, if only because they promote relativity to the status of an absolute. But equally, statements of absolute value endlessly prompt disagreement and debate and are thereby ceaselessly relativized.

For Connor, criticism must thus attempt to think absolute and relative value together. The task is difficult if not forbidding, and it is probably because of this that Connor's skeptical book now seems to stand a little to one side of the mainstream of ethical criticism in the 1990s. The more central text has doubtless been Simon Critchley's *The Ethics of Deconstruction*. Like Miller, Critchley vigorously disputes the view that DECONSTRUCTION in general and the work of JACQUES DERRIDA in particular espouse nihilistic textual free play and are therefore indifferent to ethical questions. But Critchley argues that Miller's conception of ethics is "explicitly and narrowly textual." Deconstruction can and indeed should be conceived of as an ethical demand, as long as the ethics in question are understood in the particular and radical sense provided by the work of EMMANUEL LEVINAS. In placing Levinas at the center of a critical ethics, Critchley inaugurated what was to become the most important strand in ethical criticism since the early 1990s.

Adam Zachary Newton's *Narrative Ethics* (1994), for example, shifts the ethics of the criticism of fiction precisely in a postfoundational and, in large part, Levinasian direction. Unlike Critchley, however, Newton seeks to maintain a distinction between ethics and deconstruction. Robert Eaglestone's *Ethical Criticism* (1997) offers a more rigorous, provocative and much more wide-ranging account both of Levinas's ethical thought and its relevance to literary criticism. Eaglestone argues that Levinas's philosophical engagement with language offers a new and different way of attending both "to the ethical in the textual" and "the responsibility of reading." It is precisely in their moments of what Levinas calls "saying," interrupting the designated world of what Levinas calls "the said," that literary texts become ethical. Levinas's thought cannot be converted into a critical methodology. But Eaglestone maintains that it provides a frame in which theory can be understood as properly ethical. For theory opens up the saying in criticism, "making discussions that appear to be closed open." In *Altered Reading: Levinas and Literature* (1999), Jill Robbins produces a still more austere view of the bearing of Levinas's philosophy on literature. Robbins insists that for Levinas ethics and literature or literary criticism are incommensurable. Levinas is concerned to emphasize what he takes to be the irresponsibility of art, even its monstrosity, as both a parasite on and a caricature of life. However, Robbins pays particular attention to Levinas's more affirmative accounts of particular writers. Here, at least, if within strict limits, Levinas is able to envisage a movement toward the convergence of the ethical experience of alterity and the kind of experience of alterity available from literature.

Others wondered, however, whether Levinas was either quite as consistent a thinker or as immune to question as Eaglestone and Robbins appeared to imply. Might not some literature be read as radicalizing Levinas's ethics? Might certain strands in his thought not be turned against his suspicion of art, making a Levinasian criticism possible? Thus in *Postmodernity, Ethics and the Novel* (1999), Andrew Gibson turns to Levinas for "a sophisticated, many-sided, non-foundational ethics" relevant to the criticism of fiction but also with an awareness of how frequently the philosopher of alterity has been taken to task for obtuseness to the very other by whom he claims to set such store. Each chapter in Gibson's book stages a confrontation between Levinas and "his other," another theorist or other theorists (postcolonial, feminist, queer, Lyotardian-postmodern). Gibson thus seeks to challenge, ask questions of, extend or complicate the boundaries of the Levinasian project by allowing a different kind of theory to cut across it. At the same time, he uses Levinas to bring out the ethical implications of a contemporary problematic of narration and representation produced by theory itself.

Throughout the 1990s, then, Levinas seemed progressively more central to conceptions of the ethics of criticism. Theorists like Zygmunt Bauman (in *Postmodern Ethics* [1993]) and Edith Wyschogrod (in "Towards a Postmodern Ethics" [1996]) argued that postmodernity was urging the need for an ethics commensurate with a new set of philosophical questions. Levinas's ethics seemed to answer that need. Firstly, it does not proceed on the basis of or in the hope of establishing a secular, objective, universal morality on securely rational foundations. Secondly, it does not give primacy to cognition. In Levinas's by now famous phrase, the ethical relation is the first relation. It does not consist in a resort to categories, principles, or codes assumed to be knowable prior to the ethical relation, prior to the immediate encounter with an exteriority. Thirdly, Levinas's ethics is nonontological. To think ethically is to think "otherwise than being." The ethical relation does not presume an exteriority comprehensible in terms of hypostasized essences. Fourthly, the ethical relation is always both immediate and singular, a question of responsiveness and responsibility to what is at hand. Finally, the ethical relation is radically across what Levinas calls the naïve, arbitrary, spontaneous dogmatism of the self that insists on reducing exteriority to the terms of cognition.

It is therefore not surprising that a more differentiated range of specific and focused forms of ethical criticism began to appear. In the United Kingdom, the "Literature and Ethics" conference at the University of Aberystwyth in 1996 led to the publication of two important collections of essays: *Critical Ethics: Texts, Theory and Responsibility* (1999), edited by Dominic Rainsford and Tim Woods, and *The Ethics in Literature* (1999), which they edited together with Andrew Hadfield. Some of the authors of the most groundbreaking studies returned to the issues, sometimes from a slightly different perspective: Steven Connor, for example, in "After Cultural Value: Ecology, Ethics, Aesthetics" (1996), and Robert Eaglestone in "Flaws: James, Nussbaum, Miller, Levinas" (1999). Ethical criticism became increasingly important in the study of specific authors and specific fields of literature, as in the case of Stefan Herbrechter's *Lawrence Durrell: Postmodernism and the Ethics of Alterity* (1999), Colin Davis's *Ethical Issues in Twentieth-Century French Fiction* (2000), and Marian Eide's *Ethical Joyce* (2002). It has been in large measure in its more recent forms that ethical criticism has migrated to what was, in a certain respect, its original source, continental Europe. Christina Kotte's *Ethical Dimensions in British Historiographic Metafiction* (2001), for example, seeks to forge an arresting connection between the new ethical criticism and the postmodern critique of history.

Critchley puts Levinas and deconstruction together at the center of ethical criticism. By and large, however, those who have followed in his wake have tended to concentrate on Levinas at the expense of deconstruction. Eaglestone argues that Levinas's understanding of language does not simply encourage the "acute concentration on the actual language of literary texts" that is characteristic of deconstructive "graphireading" but also brings it together with a more traditional ethical commitment to a world beyond language. Gibson claims allegiance with the thinkers "promoting a deconstructive ethics" but the "confrontations" he stages between theorists seemed to owe less to Derrida than to JEAN-FRANÇOIS LYOTARD.

Not everyone interested in ethical criticism, however, fought quite so shy of deconstruction. In *Posts: Re Addressing the Ethical* (1996), for example, Dawne McCance explores both the possibilities and the problems opened up by a deconstructive ethics. But the most important work produced in 1990s on the relationship between deconstruction and ethics came out of feminism. Drucilla Cornell is principally a legal theorist. But in works like *Beyond Accommodation* (1991) and *Philosophy of the Limit* (1992), her deconstructive and ethical concern with law overflows into literature. Rather like Harpham, Cornell associates ethics with the undetermined. She distinguishes it from morality, which she associates with deontology: the determination of the undetermined as duties, obligations, systems, rules, norms, "a right way to behave." Ethics is the excess that cannot be known positively within any given system of morality. Cornell justifies a writing committed to the "elaboration of the suffering of women as unique to women" while noting that the feminine is precisely denied "the specificity of a 'nature' or a 'being' within the masculine symbolic." She thus argues that an adequate feminist ethics would challenge established modes of writing, for these had evolved under and therefore been contaminated by patriarchy. Cornell insistently refers to the imperative of guarding "the unerasable moment of utopianism." Whether associated with deconstruction, ethical feminism, or literature by women, for Cornell, ethics is a response to that imperative.

What is most remarkable about Cornell's case is partly the fact that it makes ethics inseparable from "the full disruptive power of the imagination." For Cornell, however, the power in question is one of speculation and adumbration, a power to break up the given—to entertain, even to conjure possibility. It is not to be confused with the moral power of the imagination as understood by humanism, a power of "profound comprehension" of what is already there. Yet the 1990s also saw the appearance of a criticism that precisely reasserted the humanist conception of the relationship between the imagination and morality, in, for example, the emergence of what Daniel Schwarz refers to as "neohumanism." Predictably, neohumanism cast theory as inimical to ethics. Thus in *Literary and Moral Understanding* (1992), Frank Palmer unashamedly asserts a pre-Leavisite faith in the idea "that fictional characters are to be regarded as human beings" in the teeth of the linguistic emphases of structuralism and deconstruction. In *Agents and Lives* (1993), S. L. Goldberg sweeps theory aside as irrelevant in its "abstraction" to human concerns. Similarly, in *Ethics, Evil, and Fiction* (1997), Colin McGinn defended the "moral thinking" that "lives and breathes on the page" in novels against "the relativism and formalism that afflict so much of contemporary literary studies."

David Parker and a resurgent Wayne Booth engage more knowledgeably with the opposition and thereby produce more interesting cases. In *The Company We Keep* (1988), Booth argues that ethical criticism has suffered "theoretical ostracism." But theory is unable to promote stable values and standards. Booth argues for a conception of ethics that is both pluralist and pragmatist. Ethical value is generated "through acts of continuing conversation, in which judgments about literary texts are tested by and against other judgements." In *Ethics, Theory and the Novel* (1994), Parker claims that the "neo-Nietzschean" challenge of theory had made reading literature merely a straying in a moral wilderness. Parker maintains that there is no retreat from what theory has taught us and rejects any nostalgic relapse into "essentialist or universalist" notions of "conscience," "human nature," or moral value. Yet he construes novels in terms of the moral "systems" supposedly latent in them and interprets fictional characters in terms of the moral qualities they represent. Not surprisingly, he concentrates on literary texts favored by the Leavisite tradition.

The humanist revival, however, was not only stimulated by the fact that literary criticism appeared to be returning to ethical concerns. By one of those strange, anachronistic twists that are sometimes the result of contemporary interdisciplinarity, moral philosophy was also increasingly attributing major ethical significance to literature and even to literary criticism. In *Situating the Self* (1992), for example, Seyla Benhabib argues for a reconstruction rather than any further postmodern dismantling of the moral and political universalism that she takes to be a legacy of modernity. She presents a case for an interactive as opposed to a legislative universalism, one shorn of metaphysical illusion and born of negotiation between historical and cultural contingencies. Three philosophers, however, were particularly important for Booth, Parker, and other neohumanists: Alasdair MacIntyre, Richard Rorty, and Martha Nussbaum. In his historical study of moral theory in *After Virtue* (1981) MacIntyre attributes particular significance to the work of Jane Austen. Austen turned away from the emptily competing, modern catalogs of the virtues, uniting Christian and Aristotelian themes in a determinate social context and restoring a teleological perspective. She thereby became "the last great effective imaginative voice" of an ancient tradition.

Rorty and Nussbaum similarly promote what they take to be the ethical power of fiction, even as they remain opposed to the ethical power of modern philosophy. In *Contingency, Irony, and Solidarity* (1989) and one or two of the essays in his *Philosophical Papers* (1991), Rorty argues from his American pragmatist position that specific, limited, and finite moral practices were of greater ethical importance than universal principles. Literature provides "a safer medium than theory" for this recognition. For "novels are usually about people—things which, unlike general ideas and final vocabularies, are quite evidently time-bound" (*Contingency* 107). By contrast, philosophical and theoretical books always look "like descriptions of eternal relations between eternal objects" (*Contingency* 107). The novelist presents us with individuality and diversity alike without any attempt to reduce either to the terms of a totality. The novel thereby becomes the expression of an ethics of free, democratic pluralism. For Nussbaum, too, in *The Fragility of Goodness* (1986) and *Love's Knowledge* (1990), literature is a primary vehicle for ethics in what she deems to be a postphilosophical age. There are "certain truths about human life" that "can only be fittingly and accurately stated in the language and forms characteristic of the narrative artist." Philosophy lacks a capacity for focus on the concrete, always tending to sacrifice it to "systematic considerations." By contrast, literature admits the priority of the particular over the general and captures the ethical importance of contingency and the passions, laying open to view "the complexity, the sheer difficulty of human deliberation."

But whatever their importance for philosophy, Rorty's and Nussbaum's arguments have carried only limited conviction with literary critics. Rorty and Nussbaum turn away from contemporary theory and toward Leavis, T. S. Eliot, Edmund Wilson, Trilling, and Kermode. Though they are aware of poststructuralism, their ethics of fiction are prestructuralist. They ignore all the various problematizations of narrative and narrative form, for instance, that at the time had been current in the theory of the novel for more than three decades. MacIntyre manages to read Austen as a paradigmatic Aristotelian partly by ignoring how far an Aristotelian aesthetics had been subjected to radical question. That the moral philosopher's sense of narrative theory was almost invariably pre-Barthesian was unlikely to make his or her arguments seem very convincing to partisans of post-Barthesian criticism (see ROLAND BARTHES).

Yet if the neohumanists made little headway against a post-theoretical ethical criticism, it was nonetheless clear that, in the opening years of the twenty-first century, the moment of that criticism was waning. There are historical, political, and cultural reasons for this. In the 1980s, the reactionary turn in American and European politics had helped generate a fiercely "oppositional" theory. But the failure of radical politics in the 1980s and the disappearance of the left from political institutions in the 1990s seemed to call for a theory and criticism that conceived of political possibilities according to different time frames. Some of the most brilliant new ethical critics were principally concerned with ethical as a modified version of political work. This is preeminently the case with Cornell, and, above all, Thomas Docherty. In *After Theory* (1990) and *Alterities* (1995), Docherty presents postmodern literature as turning characters and readers alike into "endlessly displaced and 'differing' " figures. To read postmodern characterization involves replacing a philosophy of identity with one of alterity, discovering "what it means—without yet *representing* what it means— to speak always from the political disposition of the Other."

By the end of the 1990s, ethics had become a buzzword in the larger culture. Multinationals claimed to be concerned with ethics. Governments instituted "ethical" foreign policies. British American Tobacco funded the study of "corporate ethics" at the University of Nottingham. Paying lip service to an adulterated version of an ethics of respect for difference looked more and more smoothly compatible with the new forms of social democracy. Yet the social democrats and their supporters were scarcely less enthusiastic for neoliberal economics than the reactionaries of the 1980s had been. The result, at least among intellectuals, was an increasingly skeptical attitude toward social democratic politics. Thus the past few years have seen a search for new inspirations. JACQUES RANCIÈRE's work on literature—as in *Mallarmé* (1996), *Mute Speech* (1998), and *The Flesh of Words* (1998)—has begun to look important. Rancière argues for a concept of the "suspensive" existence of literary worlds. Literature works precisely to separate language from the mirage of incarnation. Yet if it never embodies anything, it always anticipates embodiment. Literature becomes the ethical paradigm of ideas that have yet to find fulfillment.

The philosophy and, above all, the ethics of ALAIN BADIOU (as in Ethics [1998]) have also attracted attention. Badiou's is a philosophy of truth or, rather, truths. But truths (including artistic truths) are both singular and rare. A truth is determined by an event, understood as a break with a given situation that makes possible the seemingly impossible. It is inseparable from the subjects it convokes and who declare and uphold it. Ethics is a question not just of openness to the event but of staying faithful to it, what Badiou calls fidelity—the determination to see the world from the point of view of the event that has come to supplement it, to change it or make it new. Truths "make holes" in established knowledge and pit their subjects against doxa, savoir, the realm of opinion. Thus in "Demanding Approval: On the Ethics of Alain Badiou" (2000), Simon Critchley argues for Badiou's concept of "affirmative ethical courage" as the subject's response to a demand made by an event that breaks with an established order. Badiou has also produced various accounts of Samuel Beckett's work, and Critchley's essay pursues some of their ethical implications and the ethical problems they raise. Andrew Gibson does the same in "Badiou and Beckett" (2002) and "Badiou, Beckett, Watt, and the Event" (2002). In "Poem, Theorem" (2001), Stephen Clucas considers the ethical significance of Badiou's concern with the relationship between philosophy and poetry.

GIORGIO AGAMBEN has also begun to exert an influence on ethical criticism. Like Badiou, Agamben effectively asserts that the very foundations of ethics must be recast. This is imperative for the world after Auschwitz. What Homo Sacer (1998) calls the "bloody mystification of the new planetary order" remains deeply implicated in the biopolitics of the camps. What is principally at stake, here, is jurisdiction over "bare life," man not as bios but as zoē, stripped of all political and civil status, "he who can be killed but not sacrificed" and who is distinct from both the citizenry and "the people." Agamben's argument is that ethics will remain at an impasse until we learn to contemplate the curious structure of inclusion and exclusion that determines our attitude to "bare life." He himself seeks to think it both in relation to the camps and through a series of analogies. The effort to do so is what motivates his (heavily Foucauldian) preoccupation, for example, with language as what speaks man. Man is the creature that has no voice, cannot seize hold of the faculty of language. In entering language, he occupies the "vacant place" of the subject position. Subjectification is therefore also desubjectification. In a series of often brief but brilliant meditations on such writers as Paul Celan, Fernando Pessoa, Franz Kafka, Arthur Rimbaud, and John Keats, Agamben has increasingly reflected on the degree to which the literary realm may be identified with the shadowy, ambivalent zone of "bare life." Like Rancière, Badiou, and others, Agamben points us in a very different direction to the postmodern ethics of difference now swiftly installing itself in every "advanced" democratic assembly. Indeed, for Agamben, we may be just at the beginning of ethics.

ANDREW GIBSON

Giorgio Agamben, La comunità che viene (1990, The Coming Community, trans. Michael Hardt, 1993), Homo Sacer: Il potere sovrano e la nuda vita (1995, Homo Sacer: Sovereign Power and Bare Life, trans. Daniel Heller-Roazen, 1998), Idea della prosa (1985, Idea of Prose, trans. Michael Sullivan and Sam Whitsitt, 1985), Infanzia e storia: Distruzione dell'esperienza e origine della storia (1978, Infancy and History: Essays on the Destruction of Experience, trans. Liz Heron, 1993), Il linguaggio e la morte: Un seminario sul luogo della negatività (1982, Language and Death: The Place of Negativity, trans. Karen Pinkus with Michael Hardt, 1991), Quel che resta di Auschwitz: L'archivio e il testimone (1998, Remnants of Auschwitz: The Witness and the Archive, trans. Daniel Heller-Roazen, 1999); Derek Attridge, "Innovation, Literature, Ethics: Relating to the Other," PMLA 114 (1999); Alain Badiou, Beckett: L'increvable désir (1995, On Beckett, ed. and trans. Nina Power and Alberto Toscano and Bruno Bosteels, 2003), L'éthique (1998, Ethics: An Essay on the Understanding of Evil, trans. Peter Hallward, 2002); Zygmunt Bauman, Postmodern Ethics (1993); Seyla Benhabib, Situating the Self (1992); Wayne Booth, The Company We Keep (1988), The Rhetoric of Fiction (1961); Stephen Clucas, "Poem, Theorem," Parallax 7 (2001); Steven Connor, "After Cultural Value: Ecology, Ethics, Aesthetics," Ethics and Aesthetics: The Moral Turn of Postmodernism (ed. Alfred Hornung and Gerhard Hoffmann, 1996), Theory and Cultural Value (1992); Henry Corbin, En Islam Iranien: aspects spirituels et philosophiques (1971–1972), Histoire de la philosophie islamique (1964, History of Islamic Philosophy, trans. Liadain Sherrard, 1993); Drucilla Cornell, Beyond Accommodation (1991), Philosophy of the Limit (1992); Simon Critchley, "Demanding Approval: On the Ethics of Alain Badiou," Radical Philosophy 100 (2000), The Ethics of Deconstruction: Levinas and Derrida (1999); Mary Daly, Gyn/Ecology (1979); Colin Davis, Ethical Issues in Twentieth-Century French Fiction (2000); Thomas Docherty, After Theory (1990), Alterities (1995); Robert Eaglestone, Ethical Criticism: Reading After Levinas (1997), "Flaws: James, Nussbaum, Miller, Levinas," Critical Ethics: Text, Theory and Responsibility (ed. Dominic Rainsford and Tim Woods, 1999); Marian Eide, Ethical Joyce (2002); Andrew Gibson, "Badiou and Beckett," Beckett and Philosophy (ed. Richard Lane, 2002), "Badiou, Beckett, Watt, and the Event," Journal of Beckett Studies 10 (2002), Postmodernity, Ethics and the Novel (1999); Sandra Gilbert and Susan Gubar, The Madwoman in the Attic (1979); S. L. Goldberg, Agents and Lives (1993); Andrew Hadfield, Dominic Rainsford and Tim Woods, eds., The Ethics in Literature (1999); Peter Hallward, Subject to Truth (2003); Geoffrey Galt Harpham, "Ethics," Critical Terms for Literary Study (ed. Frank Lentricchia and Thomas McLaughlin, 1995), Getting it Right: Language, Literature, and Ethics (1992), Shadows of Ethics (1999); Stefan Herbrechter, Lawrence Durrell: Postmodernism and the Ethics of Alterity (1999); Christian Jambet, La logique des orientaux (1983); Christina Kotte, Ethical Dimensions in British Historiographic Metafiction (2001); F. R. Leavis, The Great Tradition (1954); Dawne McCance, Posts: Re Addressing the Ethical (1996); Colin McGinn, Ethics, Evil, and Fiction (1997); Alasdair MacIntyre, After Virtue (1981); J. Hillis Miller, The Ethics of Reading (1987); Adam Zachary Newton, Narrative Ethics (1994); Martha Nussbaum, The Fragility of Goodness (1986), Love's Knowledge (1990); Frank Palmer, Literary and Moral Understanding (1992); David Parker, Ethics, Theory and the Novel (1994); Dominic Rainsford and Tim Woods, eds., Critical Ethics: Texts, Theory and Responsibility (1999); Jacques Rancière, La chair des mots: Politiques de lécriture (1998, The Flesh of Words: The Politics of Writing, trans. Charlotte Mandell, 2004), Mallarmé (1996), La parole muette (1998, Mute Speech, trans. James Swenson, 2011); Jill Robbins, Altered Reading: Levinas and Literature (1999); Richard Rorty, Contingency, Irony, and Solidarity (1989), Philosophical Papers (1991); Elaine Showalter, A Literature of Their Own (1977); Barbara Herrnstein Smith, Contingencies of Value (1988); Edith Wyschogrod, "Towards a Postmodern Ethics: Corporeality and Alterity," Ethics and Aesthetics: The Moral Turn of Postmodernism (ed. Alfred Hornung and Gerhard Hoffmann, 1996).

Fanon, Frantz

Frantz Fanon (1925–1961) was born on the Caribbean island of Martinique. He went to medical school in France and specialized in psychiatry. He served in Algeria as a practicing psychiatrist in the French colonial administration of North Africa. The Algerian revolutionary war of independence, one of the bitterest anticolonial wars of the twentieth century, broke out during the period of Fanon's service there, allowing Fanon to observe the colonial system at the point of its most violent and neurotic contradictions. He resigned from the colonial administrative and medical service and went over to the Algerian revolutionaries, becoming one of their most eloquent and effective spokespersons. His writings offer penetrating analyses of colonialism, fervent advocacy of revolt, and apocalyptic visions of the reconstitution of humans and society.

Given this focus, it is not surprising that some of Fanon's books, especially *Black Skin, White Masks* (1952), *A Dying Colonialism* (1959), and *The Wretched of the Earth* (1961) became primers and manifestoes for Third World national liberation movements and were embraced by militants and activists of racial, ethnic, and national minorities in the "First World" in North America and Europe; these included the black struggles in the United States in the 1960s, the autonomist struggles in Puerto Rico and Québec, and the struggles of Northern Ireland.

His writings have also been of great interest for critics and theorists of the new national literatures of Africa, parts of Asia, and the Caribbean, as well as for cultural critics of oppositional movements of women and minorities in North America and Europe. Fanon's theory of the stages in the evolution of the literature of all colonized peoples has been widely applied, often rather schematically. According to this theory, the first "derivative" or "imitative" stage in the emergence of the "national literatures" of the colonized world is a stage of apprenticeship to the traditions and models of the colonizing countries. The second stage is characterized by the rejection of the authority and dominance of the colonizers' paradigms and traditions and, simultaneously, nostalgia for the indigenous, autochthonous traditions of the colonized. The third and final stage in this process is a "fighting" stage that produces a genuinely revolutionary literature, a people's literature that forges new forms and themes closer to the movement to end colonial rule and the attempt to construct a genuinely democratic and egalitarian postcolonial culture. Fanon's work also prefigures current theoretical obsessions with issues such as subject formation, otherness, and alterity; identity politics; and the centrality of psychoanalytic and linguistic paradigms for literary and CULTURAL STUDIES.

Although Fanon entered twentieth-century intellectual history as patron and prophet of Third World national liberation movements and one of the major theorists of decolonization, he started writing as an *evolué*, as indeed a French patriot who, despite his brilliant, penetrating critique of the colonial system, nonetheless saw himself as a Frenchman, an *assimilé* into French culture and the intellectual legacy of Western civilization. With his education, professional training, and intellectual gifts, Fanon belonged to the small circle of "black Frenchmen" who rose to this level of assimilation into French culture and civilization and began to powerfully assail the system from within. Three particular inscriptions of Fanon's analysis of race, culture, and colonialism are pertinent to this point. First, he shifts the analysis of colonialism away from the political and economic factors emphasized by other theorists of decolonization and toward an emphasis on psychoanalytic and phenomenological factors. This enables him to plumb the depths of subjectivity in the construction of the colonizer and the colonized as *racialized* subjects and to thereby indicate the differential paths of the neuroses generated by colonial domination: inferiorization and delusions on the part of the colonized, phobias and anxieties on the part of the colonizer. Second, Fanon insists that the psychoanalytic categories, though crucial, are not enough to explicate the colonial system, that racism is not a mere psychic aberration or mental quirk but is part of a total structure that involves economic exploitation, political disenfranchisement, and cultural imposition through vast signifying systems: language, novels, films, folklore and ethnology, scientific discourses, media, and popular culture. And third, Hegelian PHENOMENOLOGY weighs heavily, for the transcendence and liberation he envisaged embraces both the colonizer and the colonized in an appropriately *deracinated* French culture and civilization. Fanon wanted, in his own words, to break with both "the great white error" and the "great black mirage."

The central tension of Fanon's work lies in the fact that his revolutionary fervor and partisan identifications do not always sit well with the unbounded, irrepressible energy of his intellect. First, though he ultimately casts his lot with the colonized, with "the wretched of the earth," this solidarity with the disenfranchised and inferiorized of the colonial order is tempered by a rigorously dialectical, nonvoluntaristic keenness to historical and social processes. Second, though Fanon's work, no doubt influenced by his psychiatric training, is imbued with an acute awareness of the play of neurotic, irrational drives and the preponderant role of fantasy in culture and society, he is an ultrarationalist who believes in the power of logic and persuasion. And third, while Fanon worked for a disciplined revolutionary movement and became a spokesperson for its set objectives and program, his mode of radical, innovative cultural analysis ranges across disparate disciplines and domains: from psychiatry, psychoanalysis, and philosophy to economic theory, literature, and popular culture and from linguistic, aesthetic, and ethical investigations to the uncovering of the play of sexuality, the affects of the body, and the dispositions of the psyche.

Since the mid-1980s, scholars have continued to use Fanon's work in interrogations of the dialectic, modernity, history, revolution, diaspora, Western science, embodiment, subjectivity, rationality, and language. Increasingly, Fanon has informed theorists of feminism, gender, sexuality, and visual art. As exemplified by the work of Lewis Gordon, Fanon has also been made use of in new critiques of Western modernity. The debate over Fanon's significance and applicability has also intensified with his appropriation by varied philosophical and political thinkers. Those who privilege the Fanon of Black Skin, White Masks over that of The Wretched of the Earth often favor psychoanalytic and linguistic analyses, whereas those who privilege the latter book stress the material implications of his radical politics.

HOMI K. BHABHA is generally credited with the renewed attention to Black Skin, White Masks within psychoanalytic, poststructuralist, and discourse theories. Others, however, like Ato Sekyi-Otu, who underscores his own African perspective, seek to engage the more material Fanon and challenge his appropriation by critics like Bhabha. For example, Sekyi-Otu claims that "postmodernist commitment result[s] in the evisceration of Fanon's texts: they excise the critical normative, yes, revolutionary humanist vision which informs his account of the colonial condition and its aftermath" (3). Fanon's ideas have been similarly contested by feminist theorists, who trace his problematic formulation of gender and colonial identities yet have also worked at recovering his usefulness for contemporary feminist theory (Sharpley-Whiting). Other thinkers, like Nigel Gibson, working with the definition of context as "movement, conflict, and tension" (32), warn against decontextualizing Fanon, a sentiment also advocated by Anthony C. Alessandrini and Sekyi-Otu; indeed, Sekyi-Otu encourages reading Fanon's entire corpus as "one dramatic dialectical narrative" (3). Because of the range and complexity of Fanon's work, his relevance for cultural studies, especially in contested social and political spaces, continues to flourish.

ZUBEDA JALALZAI AND BIODUN JEYIFO

See also POSTCOLONIAL STUDIES.

Frantz Fanon, L'an V de la révolution algérienne (1959, A Dying Colonialism, trans. Haakon Chevalier, 1965), Les damnés de la terre (1961, The Wretched of the Earth, trans. Constance Farrington, 1963), Peau noire, masques blancs (1952, Black Skin, White Masks, trans. Charles Lan Markmann, 1967), Pour la révolution africaine (1964, Toward the African Revolution, trans. Haakon Chevalier, 1967); Nigel Gibson, Rethinking Fanon: The Continuing Dialogue (1999); Ato Sekyi-Otu, Fanon's Dialectic of Experience (1996); Tracy Denean Sharpley-Whiting, Frantz Fanon: Conflicts and Feminisms (1998).

Feminist Theory and Criticism

1. From Movement Critique to Discourse Analysis

Feminist literary theory, criticism, and scholarship form one strand of the knowledge produced in the field of feminist studies, which investigates gender, race, ethnicity, nationality, class, and sexuality as categories that organize social and symbolic systems. In the United States, there are over six hundred women's studies programs and over seventy-five campus-based research centers, scores of professional associations, and hundreds of feminist journals and presses.

In 1963, two years after President John F. Kennedy established the President's Commission on the Status of Women, a pair of books ignited public discussion of "the woman question." The commission's report, *American Women*, edited by Margaret Mead and Frances Balgley Kaplan, painstakingly documented women's inequality in education, employment, and public life, and Betty Friedan's best-selling *Feminine Mystique* exposed the ideology of domesticity that made middle- and upper-class women economically and emotionally dependent on men. In 1966, twenty-eight women founded the National Organization for Women (NOW) and elected Friedan as president. NOW grew from a thousand members in 1967 to thirty-thousand members and nearly four hundred chapters in 1973. It attracted primarily white middle-class women but developed a sweeping social agenda. Women in the late 1960s analyzed systemic oppression that would guide four complementary types of activism: sponsoring political education to recruit members and train organizers; building an infrastructure of alternative organizations to network activists locally and nationally; working the channels of negotiation, lobbying, and litigation to change public policies; and orchestrating events to pressure elites. Precipitating the formation of second-wave feminism was the sexual politics that occurred in the very same arenas where women were acquiring social-change skills.

Early in 1969, the Modern Language Association of America (MLA) established the Commission on the Status of Women in the Profession (CSWP), the first such body in any academic association. During the 1969–1970 academic year, MLA women formed the Women's Caucus for the Modern Languages to continue exerting pressure on the association, and instructors taught the first experimental courses on women at a dozen universities. In early 1971 the CSWP and feminists at the University of Pittsburgh cosponsored the first national conference on feminist education.

During 1969 consciousness-raising (CR) groups were started in some forty cities, and in 1973 alone about one hundred thousand women belonged to CR groups, making it the largest women's political-education initiative in U.S. history. Women were "applying to women and to ourselves as women's liberation organizers the practice a number of us had learned as organizers in the civil rights movement in the South in the early 1960s" (Sarachild, "Consciousness" 145). By sharing intimate details of their lives they forged affective bonds, by aggregating and analyzing experiential data they limned the features of group oppression, and by expressing anger they catalyzed action. CR methods showed women that personal problems had social causes and therefore political solutions; CR groups served as the matrix for generating knowledge and power. Academic feminists brought CR groups to campuses and CR methods into the disciplines, where they were used to produce new knowledges. Carolyn Heilbrun and Catharine Stimpson depicted themselves as "textual archeologists" trying "to dig up fragments of attitudes about sexuality, sex roles, their genesis, and their justifying ideologies" in order to piece together the patterns of literary sexism (62).

Second-wave feminists introduced a whole lexicon of concepts that most women had not previously encountered, exhuming "misogyny" and "patriarchy" from the English literary tradition, analogizing "male supremacy" and "sexism" from the discourse of race, and borrowing women's "alienation" and "oppression" from Marxist theory. These concepts were fleshed out by analyses that circulated in movement publications: manifestos issued by liberation groups, newsletters mailed to NOW members, periodicals edited by collectives, and anthologies produced by the New York Radical Women (see also Crow). Yet the publishers and universities that were supposed to carry feminism to wider audiences soon reformulated movement critique as scholarly criticism.

In 1970 American commercial presses began to publish hybrid books that wove movement and academic discourses into a wide-ranging indictment of sex-class oppression. Anthologies—including Robin Morgan's *Sisterhood Is Powerful* (1970) and Vivian Gornick and Barbara K. Moran's *Woman in Sexist Society* (1971)—paint a composite picture of women's oppression. *Woman in Sexist Society* contains movement papers, scholarly articles, and creative pieces written by thirty-five contributors and divided into issue-focused sections. Among the landmark essays in *Woman in Sexist Society* written by academic women are Elaine Showalter's "Women Writers and the Double Critical Standard," Linda Nochlin's "Why Are There No Great Women Artists?," and Naomi Weisstein's "Psychology Constructs the Female," each one examining the institutional production of gender ideology and its subjects.

The other format was the monograph, whose lineage could be traced from Mary Wollstonecraft's *Vindication of the Rights of Woman* (1792) through SIMONE DE BEAUVOIR's *Second Sex* (1949) to Kate Millett's *Sexual Politics* (1970) and Germaine Greer's *Female Eunuch* (1970). *Sexual Politics* looks like a work of academic criticism because it contains chapters devoted to a hypothesis, a history, and exegeses of literary texts topped off by endnotes and a bibliography. But it does not read like such a work because it hybridizes radical feminism's theory of sex-class domination with Beauvoir's learned tour of the disciplines. Millett defines sexual politics as the "arrangements whereby one group of persons is controlled by another" (23) and then proceeds to show how a host of arrangements—physical, economic, social, psychological, and ideological—maintain the system of oppression.

Reviewers praised *Woman in Sexist Society* but made *Sexual Politics* the butt of unprecedented hostility. Reviewers decried Millett's tone as angry, belligerent, and vanguardist, with *Time* magazine dubbing her "the Mao Tse-tung of Women's Liberation" in its 31 August 1970 cover story (16). *Sexual Politics* disempowered the reviewers, who were incapable of neutralizing its arguments and therefore deterring buyers and readers. Within months of publication *Sexual Politics* had sold fifteen thousand copies and gone into a fourth printing, an astounding market penetration for the time.

Second-wave discourse soldered affect and analysis to action. Also, the analytic process was tessellation from bits. Experience by experience, insight by insight, and issue by issue, feminists developed a critique of the system of women's oppression in the United States. Third, "women as an oppressed sex-class" was not simply a conceptual product but a movement-building process. Later feminists criticized it as a flawed totalizing concept, but social-movement theory casts it as necessary because without conjoining statements in political analysis and linking women in political action there could have been no movement. Finally, commercially published hybrid books had no impact on academic canons and curriculums. Feminists had to navigate the preliminaries of earning doctoral degrees, securing faculty positions, and performing the expected research and teaching before they could produce criticism and theory that would have an impact in academic arenas.

A widely read series of curricular materials, five volumes published by KNOW Press and five by the Feminist Press, sparked the development of feminist studies, the institutionalization of which proceeded at an astounding pace. After the first few courses taught in 1969–1970 the number multiplied so quickly that only approximate counts from the next few years survive: 103 courses and 4 programs in December 1970, 600 courses and 17 programs in December 1971, and 4,500 courses and 75–110 programs in the 1972–1973 academic year. It is hard to imagine that those teaching these courses had virtually no status or resources. Most were adjunct instructors or assistant professors who jeopardized their tenuous standing to engage topics that mainstream faculty regarded as unworthy of attention. They did not have a single name for this venture—variously calling it "female," "women's," or "feminist" studies—or an exacting description to persuade colleagues that it might become a distinctive, let alone distinguished, academic field. They lacked local conveniences, such as library collections and course designators, as well as national conferences and publications. Nevertheless, these teachers began reclaiming women's lives and criticizing received knowledges, assigning texts that took a synoptic approach to women's oppression, such as Virginia Woolf's *A Room of One's Own* (1929), Eleanor Flexner's *Century of Struggle* (1975), Aileen Kraditor's *Up from the Pedestal* (1970), William O'Neill's *Everyone Was Brave* (1969), Mary Ellmann's *Thinking about Women* (1968), Leo Kanowitz's *Women and the Law* (1969), Shulamith Firestone's *Dialectic of Sex* (1970), as well as Millett's book and the two anthologies. By reading them alongside emerging feminist scholarship, teachers were forming the field's intellectual core with a tension between cross-sector social problems and intradisciplinary analysis.

Feminists in literary studies, too, began with the projects of reclamation and critique. They searched libraries and archives for books on female lives and letters. In British history and culture, for instance, they rediscovered in books written from the 1890s to the 1950s the sacred revelations and domestic manuals of medieval women; the learning and literature of Renaissance ladies; the spread of female literacy; the political treatises of eighteenth-century women; the popular and high cultures of nineteenth-century women; and the activities of suffragists, birth-control advocates, union organizers, and educators in Britain and the United States. The next steps involved compiling bibliographies, producing editions of out-of-print and never-published female-authored texts, and writing articles and books, in each case combining reevaluation of female-authored texts with criticism of societal and literary sexism. Scholarship and criticism provided empirical grounding for books that theorized a swath of the literary territory, such as the feminine, feminist, and female traditions in Elaine Showalter's *A Literature of Their Own* (1977) and phallic authorship in Sandra M. Gilbert and Susan Gubar's *Madwoman in the Attic* (1979).

The other project was exposing the forms of sexism that had made it possible to construct the discipline's androcentric criteria and canons. Katharine M. Rogers traces literary misogyny through the ages. Mary Ellmann investigates commonplace gender stereotypes that infuse modern literary criticism, exemplified by Anthony Burgess's statement that he could "gain no pleasure" from a "serious reading" of Jane Austen's prose because it "lacks a strong male thrust, an almost pedantic allusiveness, and a brutal intellectual content" (23).

"Images of women," the most popular approach to literary sexism, was subsequently disparaged as naïve representationalism. But most feminists read the images as manifestations of gendered conventions that in turn buttressed ruling-class interests. The goal of such criticism, Lillian Robinson and Lise Vogel argue in "Modernism and History" (1971), is "less to demonstrate that literature does convey ideas than to show that those ideas have a class origin and class function," namely, the function of perpetuating the naturalized order (298). Progress toward that goal was not straightforward, as a 1971 feminist issue of *College English* shows. In one essay, Annis Pratt summarizes the four main tasks of feminist criticism: rediscovering women's works, analyzing texts' formal aspects, understanding what literature reveals about women and men in their socioeconomic contexts, and describing "the psychomythological development of the female individual in literature" (877). But in another essay, Lillian Robinson retorts that Pratt is merely reiterating the bourgeois modes of biographical, formal, sociological, and archetypal criticism, modes that require critics to acknowledge that a virulently chauvinistic text is beautifully crafted or that a "historically useful" feminist text is "artistically flawed" (888).

Feminist literary critics began to analyze the paradigms that mainstream practitioners used to select, interpret, and evaluate texts. Interpretationism, an open method of drawing on ideas and methods from other discourses such as history, sociology, psychology, and myth, allowed sex stereotypes to seep into and steep critical practices. Heilbrun and Stimpson report that they had been trained to read "all works in the light of the conventions of the male critic" (65). New Criticism, in contrast, precluded critics from referring a text to anything outside of the text, such as the author's life, the social context, or the themes recapitulated from other discourses, or from introducing their own viewpoints, feelings, and judgments. New Criticism's cultural program of aestheticizing literature and esotericizing knowledge was seen as fitting into the larger system of distributive injustice.

By 1972 four powerful forces were driving specialization within feminist studies. First, universities were structured by departmentalized disciplines, and as a result, feminist studies was slow to realize its interdisciplinary objectives. Second, universities heightened their faculty publishing requirements just as commercial presses were starting to be acquired by media conglomerates and university presses were publishing little feminist work. Third, needing venues that could bestow legitimacy on the new field, feminists launched the first scholarly periodicals, featuring historical scholarship in *Feminist Studies*, literary scholarship in *Women's Studies*, eighteenth- and nineteenth-century studies in the *Mary Wollstonecraft Newsletter* (later retitled *Women and Literature*), bibliographical data in *Women's Studies Abstracts*, and program resources in the *Women's Studies Newsletter*. In 1975, the interdisciplinary *Signs* presented itself as the most rigorous journal. Its methods of quality control and its adoption of conventional formats (the article, the review essay, the citation apparatus) produced scholarship and criticism for academic readers. Finally, each axis in a cross-hatched grid of disciplines, social identities, and political ideologies generated its own specialisms and also mutated new specialisms wherever it crossed the others.

No sooner did feminists gain toeholds in higher education than the system's structure began to organize their knowledge-producing practices. As feminist studies attracted more scholars, they generated more knowledges that grew more particularized by political ideology, social identity, and disciplinary specialism. Movement feminists had cast social change as a practical objective to be achieved through collective analysis and action, and academic feminists had recast it as the subject matter of academic research. By the late 1970s the "social problems" academic feminists addressed were being fabricated at the sites where esoteric theories collided, abstract categories ruptured, and arcane knowledges avalanched.

In 1971 Lillian Robinson had a premonition of what would come to pass: "I am not terribly interested in whether feminism becomes a respectable part of academic criticism; I am very much concerned that feminist critics become a useful part of the women's movement. . . . In our struggle for liberation, Karl Marx's note about philosophers may apply to critics as well: that up to now they have only interpreted the world and the real point is to change it" (*College English* 889). Her cautionary words appeared at a pivotal moment when the focus of feminism was shifting from oppositional struggle to female culture, from political activism to intellectual inquiry, from integrative categories to differential ones. The institutionalization that made it possible for academic-feminist scholarship, criticism, and theory to flourish from 1973 on also disciplined an insurgent political project.

ELLEN MESSER-DAVIDOW

See also bibliography for SIMONE DE BEAUVOIR.

College English 32 (1971, special feminist issue); Barbara A. Crow, ed., *Radical Feminism: A Documentary Reader* (2000); Mary Ellmann, *Thinking about Women* (1968); Betty Friedan, *The Feminine Mystique* (1963); Vivian Gornick and Barbara K. Moran, eds., *Woman in Sexist Society: Studies in Power and Powerlessness* (1971); Germaine Greer, *The Female Eunuch* (1971); Carolyn Heilbrun and Catharine Stimpson, "Theories of Feminist Criticism: A Dialogue," *Feminist Literary Criticism: Explorations in Theory* (ed. Josephine Donovan, 1975); Margaret Mead and Frances Balgley Kaplan, eds., *American Women: The Report of the President's Commission on the Status of Women* (1965); Kate Millett, *Sexual Politics* (1970); Robin Morgan, ed., *Sisterhood Is Powerful: An Anthology of Writing from the Women's Liberation Movement* (1970); Lillian Robinson and Lise Vogel, "Modernism and History" *Images of Women in Fiction: Feminist Perspectives* (ed. Susan Koppelman Cornillon, 1972, rev. ed., 1973); Katharine M. Rogers, *The Troublesome Helpmate: A History of Misogyny in Literature* (1966); Kathie Sarachild, "Consciousness-Raising: A Radical Weapon," *Feminist Revolution: An Abridged Edition with Additional Writings* (ed. Kathie Sarachild, 1976).

2. Anglo-American Feminisms

Women's experience as encountered in female fictional characters, the reactions of women readers, and the careers, techniques, and topics of women writers was the focus of the most accessible second-wave feminist criticism in the United States and Britain starting in the mid-1970s. A goal became the detection and further cultivation of a women's tradition in literature. Originally opposed to theory as male-inflected, scholars who were engaged in these projects gradually acknowledged and cultivated it. By the early 1990s, institutions that had been slow to start women's studies programs were recruiting feminist scholars at the top level. Feminists Florence Howe and Catharine R. Stimpson had been elected to the presidency of the Modern Language Association of America, Phyllis Franklin had become executive director, and Women's Studies in Language and Literature had developed into the third-largest division in the organization and a major force in its programming.

The process of recovering neglected work by women writers was greatly assisted by feminist reprinting houses, such as the Feminist Press in the United States and Virago Press and the Women's Press in Britain. Feminist periodicals such as *Signs*, *Feminist Studies*, *Women's Studies Quarterly*, *Women and Literature*, and *Chrysalis* provided a forum for feminist theoretical discussion. Founded in 1975, *Signs* set out to publish "the new scholarship about women" (Stimpson et al. v) and has also published land-mark French feminist work in translation. Signs declared itself interdisciplinary, and theoretical borrowing from history, sociology, and psychology has remained crucial to literary study.

Virginia Woolf offered the most important literary-critical model to feminists interested in recovering the experience of women writers. Now a standard text, A Room of One's Own gives an account of the frustrations that a fictional female re-searcher must go through to arrive at a theory of women and fiction. Woolf imagines historical woman writers in their social contexts and searches out the sources of the bitterness she reads in their works. The importance of female experience is marked in Arlyn Diamond and Lee R. Edwards's significantly titled collection The Authority of Experience (1977), an early example of the importance of anthologies and collec-tions to the development of feminist theory (see also collections edited by Abel, Hirsch, and Langland; Benstock [Private]; Cooper, Munich, and Squier; Friedman and Fuchs; Gilbert and Gubar [Shakespeare's]; and Scott, as well as theoretical collec-tions incorporating diverse practices edited by Benstock [Feminist], Miller, and two by Showalter).

Judith Fetterley's The Resisting Reader (1978) considers the work of male writers from Washington Irving to Norman Mailer and discusses the loss and mental confu-sion of the "immasculated" woman reader, forced to identify against herself with male characters, whose essential experience is betrayal by the female, and forced to see women characters scapegoated and killed off in the typical scenarios. Against this politics of male empowerment, Fetterley offers the female reader the power of naming what is real in terms of her own experience. Fetterley's representation of American literature as a "masculine wilderness" and of America as a female to be discovered and conquered resonates with Annette Kolodny's The Lay of the Land (1975) and with the ecofeminism of Susan Griffin.

Marginal development of a female countercanon posed a challenge to the cen-tral literary canon and contributed to a questioning of canonicity itself. Nina Baym's Women's Fiction (1978), for example, introduces an alternate tradition of trivialized women writers. Feminists also tested the adequacy of periodization based exclusively on male literary production and introduced gender as a factor in genre. Annette Kolodny introduces the concept of a coded language of a female subculture in "A Map for Rereading," its title a reaction to the narrow literary culture defined in Harold Bloom's A Map of Misreading.

Elaine Showalter gave the name "gynocritics" to those critics wishing "to con-struct a female framework for the analysis of women's literature, to develop new mod-els based on the study of female experience" ("Toward" 131) and in a series of essays became increasingly willing to talk about various schools of feminist theory. Femi-nist freedom from male theory was a goal for her, but its accomplishment remains problematical in critiques of gynocritics' practices. Toril Moi places Showalter in a humanist tradition, the empirical methods and close textual analysis of gynocritics linking it to the male practice of New Criticism, though its construction of female social history certainly mitigates this. Kolodny has advocated a "playful pluralism" for feminist theory and practice ("Dancing"), a model that sparked objections from GAYATRI CHAKRAVORTY SPIVAK, whose juxtaposition of feminism with Marxism, psychoanalysis, DECONSTRUCTION, and, later, subaltern studies discloses numerous perils. Further discussion by Judith Kegan Gardner offers a political model of several schools of feminist criticism: liberal, socialist, and radical. The radical views of lesbians and black critics had been neglected in the pluralist concept and indeed in much of the 1970s feminist criticism. Standpoint epistemology emerged as a means of discussing racial and ethnic differences among women. Barbara Smith's *Home Girls* (1983) and Gloria Anzaldúa's *Making Face, Making Soul/Haciendo Caras* (1990) are important women-of-color collections of this period.

By the late 1970s major female-centered studies had begun to appear. In *Literary Women* (1976) Ellen Moers expresses the intention not to impose doctrine on women writers—an attitude that resembles Showalter's in its distrust of theory. She presents a practical, living history of women writers from the eighteenth century through the twentieth, attempting to shape it with their concerns and language. In her book's second half she sets out to familiarize readers with literary feminism, a heroic structure for the female "voice" in literature that she calls "heroinism." Her categories of heroinism incorporate characters in roles of loving, performing, and educating. Her discussion of female erotic landscape emerges from an introduction of SIGMUND FREUD's sexual dream symbols, assessing male bias that goes back to the naming of female anatomy (vagina = scabbard). This introduction of metaphors of the female body finds a response in French feminist theory, with LUCE IRIGARAY's "two lips" of the female body and HÉLÈNE CIXOUS's concept of writing in mother's milk.

Showalter's landmark work, *A Literature of Their Own*, constructs a history of British women novelists' literary subculture in three phases: "feminine" (1840–1880), "feminist" (1880–1920), and "female" (continuing since 1920, with a new phase beginning in 1960). Showalter's dates overlap, and multiple phases can be seen in a single writer. Critical of the practice of selecting only great figures for analysis, in an appendix she lists 213 women writers with "sociological" data, writers who provide diversity and generational links. She also avoids concepts of female imagination, preferring to look at the ways "the self-awareness of the woman writer has translated itself into a literary form in a specific place and time-span" and to trace this self-awareness within the tradition (12). The concept of androgyny, explored from the Greeks to Bloomsbury in male as well as female authors by Carolyn Heilbrun in 1973, comes under attack as an escapist "flight" in Showalter's controversial handling of Woolf (263–97). The phase of the female novelists since 1960 operates in Freudian and Marxist contexts and for the first time accepts anger and sexuality as "sources of female creative power" (35).

Sandra Gilbert and Susan Gubar theorize the position of woman and the literary imagination in the nineteenth century (The Madwoman in the Attic) and the twentieth (No Man's Land [1987–1994]) and offer a large selection of women authors who conform to their paradigms in their edition of The Norton Anthology of Literature by Women (1985). Their approach includes historical references to the material, social, and gendered conditions of authors' lives; to literary canons and archives; and to popular movements and artifacts—typical strengths of American feminist theory. Like Showalter and Moers, they detect historical stages of a female literary tradition, but they ground these in male comparisons and frequently make their points through metaphors and puns, as in their titles.

In The War of the Words, volume 1 of No Man's Land, which offers numerous studies of male authors, the battle is manifested in tropes of erotic dueling, the advent of the "no-man" to replace the virile man, and plots of males defeating alarming forms of female sexuality through a theology of the phallus, mutilations, rapes, and campaigns against the mothers of "castrated" sons. Gilbert and Gubar's collection of stereotypes and misogynistic plot types that progress through the decades is reminiscent of Kate Millett's Sexual Politics. Women writers express belligerence less directly and render characters who are victorious through duplicity, subterfuge, or luck. Volumes 2 and 3, Sexchanges and Letters from the Front, sustain the model of sex war refined into the consideration of ways: "The sexes battle because sex roles change, but when the sexes battle, sex itself (that is eroticism) changes" (2:xi). Major changes include the rebellion against the feminization of the American woman, powerful roles assumed by women in World War I, varied lesbian arrangements, and transvestism.

Gilbert and Gubar also implicate fantasies in theory, The War of the Words focusing on linguistic fantasies, and Sexchanges on fantasy identifications. The feminist linguistic fantasy grants an intuitive primacy in language acquisition to the mother rather than to the father, a more powerful position than the male-associated symbolic language and social contract of JULIA KRISTEVA's post-Lacanian analysis (see JACQUES LACAN). Proceeding from Woolf's remarks on women's language, Gilbert and Gubar suggest that women fantasize a revision—not of women's language but of women's relation to language. Increasingly, women writers find enabling fantasies and roles—Sappho as a predecessor, Aphrodite as an erotic authority, and transvestism as metaphor. In the same sexchanges, men express loss and failure. The interest in the turn to the twentieth century, also embraced by Showalter in the introduction of her expanded Literature of One's Own, is increasingly discussed in terms of the gender of modernity, (see Rita Felski's 1995 study). Transnational geographies have been mapped, for example, by Susan Stanford Friedman (1998). Third-wave feminists assess their relationship to second-wave feminism, to which works by Moers, Showalter, and Gilbert and Gubar are now assigned.

BONNIE KIME SCOTT

Elizabeth Abel, Marianne Hirsch, and Elizabeth Langland, eds., *The Voyage In: Fictions of Female Development* (1983); Gloria Anzaldúa, ed., *Making Face, Making Soul/Haciendo Caras* (1990); Nina Baym, *Women's Fiction: A Guide to Novels By and About Women in America, 1820–1870* (1978); Shari Benstock, ed., *Feminist Issues in Literary Scholarship* (1987), *The Private Self: Theory and Practice of Women's Autobiographical Writings* (1988); Helen M. Cooper, Adrienne Auslander Munich, and Susan Merrill Squier, eds., *Arms and the Woman: War, Gender, and Literary Representation* (1987); Arlyn Diamond and Lee R. Edwards, eds., *The Authority of Experience* (1977); Rita Felski, *The Gender of Modernity* (1995); Judith Fetterley, *The Resisting Reader: A Feminist Approach to American Fiction* (1978); Ellen G. Friedman and Miriam Fuchs, eds., *Breaking the Sequence: Women's Experimental Fiction* (1989); Susan Stanford Friedman, *Mappings: Feminism and the Cultural Geographies of Encounter* (1998); Judith Kegan Gardner et al., "An Interchange on Feminist Criticism: On 'Dancing through the Minefield,'" *Feminist Studies* 8 (1982); Sandra M. Gilbert and Susan Gubar, *The Madwoman in the Attic: The Woman Writer and the Nineteenth-Century Literary Imagination* (1979), *No Man's Land: The Place of the Woman Writer in the Twentieth Century* (3 vols., 1987–1994); Sandra M. Gilbert and Susan Gubar, eds., *The Norton Anthology of Literature by Women: The Tradition in English* (1985, 2nd ed., 1996, 3rd ed., 2007), *Shakespeare's Sisters: Feminist Essays in Women Poets* (1979); Susan Griffin, *Woman and Nature: The Roaring Inside Her* (1978); Carolyn Heilbrun, *Toward a Recognition of Androgyny* (1973); Annette Kolodny, "Dancing through the Minefield: Some Observations on the Theory, Practice, and Politics of Feminist Literary Criticism," *Feminist Studies* 6 (1980), *The Lay of the Land: Metaphor as Experience and History in American Life and Letters* (1975), "A Map for Rereading; or, Gender and the Interpretation of Literary Texts" (Showalter, New); Nancy K. Miller, ed., *The Poetics of Gender* (1986); Ellen Moers, *Literary Women: The Great Writers* (1976); Toril Moi, *Sexual/Textual Politics: Feminist Literary Theory* (1985, 2nd ed., 2002); Bonnie Kime Scott, ed., *The Gender of Modernism* (1990); Elaine Showalter, *A Literature of Their Own: British Women Novelists from Brontë to Lessing* (1977, rev. ed., 1999), "Toward a Feminist Poetics" (Showalter, New); Elaine Showalter, ed., *The New Feminist Criticism: Essays on Women, Literature, and Theory* (1985), *Speaking of Gender* (1989); Barbara Smith, ed., *Home Girls: A Black Feminist Anthology* (1983, rev. ed., 2000); Catharine R. Stimpson, Joan N. Burstyn, Domna C. Stanton, Sandra M. Whisler, editorial, *Signs* 1 (1975).

3. Poststructuralist Feminisms

"The question of gender is a question of language." Barbara Johnson's succinct formulation (*World* 37) does much to characterize the approach of feminists who draw on the discourses of poststructuralism. This work starts from the premise that gender difference dwells in language rather than in the referent, that there is nothing "natural" about gender itself. These feminists are not suggesting a retreat into a world made only of words. Rather, language intervenes so that "materiality" is not a self-evident category; indeed language itself is understood as radically marked by the materiality of gender. The understanding of writing and the body as sites where the material and the linguistic intersect requires the interrogation of woman as a category of gender or sex.

CONTESTING PATRIARCHAL DISCOURSE. Questioning the political and ethical grounds of language, poststructuralist feminists share a common opponent in patriarchal discourse, a feature that emerges in their readings of literature, philosophy, history, and psychoanalysis. If, as Hélène Cixous suggests, "it has become rather urgent to question this solidarity between logocentrism and phallocentrism—bringing to light the fate dealt to woman," how one might go about such questioning is a point of dispute (*Newly* 65).

According to Luce Irigaray, we cannot simply step outside of phallogocentrism to suddenly write and think in ways completely free of the rules of patriarchy, for language and discourse are themselves inscribed with those rules. Instead, we have to work like a virus from within patriarchal discourses to infect and radically change them. Not surprisingly, the discourses of philosophy and psychoanalysis have become prime "hosts" for Irigaray. She hopes to expose ways in which patriarchal discourses are politically determined and to disrupt altogether the power structures they hold in place. Similar political interventions have been made by Catherine Clément in *Opera, or the Undoing of Woman* (1979) and *The Newly Born Woman* (coauthored with Cixous [1975]), her consideration of the sorceress and the hysteric; by Michèle Le Doeuff in "Women and Philosophy," which interrogates the role of lack and the place of knowledge acquisition in Western philosophy; by Barbara Johnson in her readings of literature and deconstruction; by Julia Kristeva in her numerous works on linguistics, psychoanalysis, and literature; and by Gayatri Chakravorty Spivak in her analyses of the relationship between philosophy, Marxism, deconstruction, and subaltern studies (*In Other Worlds* [1987]).

Some poststructuralist feminists, however, have preferred to develop an alternative to patriarchal discourse in place of the strategy of subversive rewriting. Monique Wittig attempts to create completely new, nonphallogocentric discourses in her fictional works *Les Guérillères*, *The Opoponax*, and *The Lesbian Body*. Wittig proposes a structural change in language that will destroy the categories of gender and sex. Frequently this change takes the form of experimentation with pronouns and nouns, which she calls the "lesbianization of language" ("One" 53).

Cixous also engages in a political project designed to create an alternative, nonphallogocentric discourse. Like Wittig, she turns to fiction, but she relies heavily on psychoanalysis and Derridean deconstruction, which are anathema to Wittig. Also, Cixous develops "feminine writing" (*écriture féminine*), envisaged in terms of bisexuality rather than Wittig's "lesbianization." For Cixous, the space of feminine writing cannot be theorized or defined, enclosed, or encoded. It is also the province of metaphor, not limited to written words and possibly taking the form of "writing by the voice," a harmonic *écriture féminine* metaphorized as writing in mother's milk or the uterus (*Illa* 208, *Newly*). Although her metaphors here are maternal, biologically the province of women, for Cixous neither biological women nor men need be condemned to the space of phallogocentrism, feminine writing being a bisexual political act.

Cixous's practice of *écriture féminine* has its detractors. Wittig sees complicity with heterosexual, bourgeois capitalism. Hélène Wenzel argues that it "perpetuates and recreates long-held stereotypes and myths about woman as natural, sexual, biological, and corporal by celebrating essences" (272).

WRITING (AND) THE BODY. At stake in this feminist attention to language is the relationship between the twin materialities of writing and the body. Cixous's work specifically stresses the importance of the connection, exhorting women to write through their bodies in order to make "the huge resources of the unconscious" burst out (Newly 94–97). Irigaray turns to the female body to develop an account of woman's pleasure that does not privilege sight, arguing that all accounts of bodily pleasure have traditionally been dominated by the scopophilic drive of male pleasure described by psychoanalysis. Irigaray argues that "woman takes more pleasure from touching than from looking" (26); woman's pleasure is fluid, tactile, and, what is most important, plural: "Woman has sex organs more or less everywhere" (28).

Irigaray's political move away from vision is not, however, borne out in work by other psychoanalytically informed feminists. In Alice Doesn't (1984) Teresa de Lauretis attempts to reclaim visual pleasure for the female spectator, and in The Acoustic Mirror (1988) Kaja Silverman stresses the subversive quality of women's voice. More harshly, Wittig criticizes Cixous and Irigaray for fetishizing the body and not seeing the body as only part of the total subject, and for Ann Rosalind Jones "the French feminists make of the female body too unproblematically pleasurable and totalized an entity" (254).

The poststructuralist feminists' engagement with writing and the body has crucially led to a revalorization of the mother or, more precisely, of the maternal body. This "valorization of the maternal . . . marks a decisive break with the existentialism of The Second Sex, wherein Simone de Beauvoir stressed the oppressiveness of motherhood" (Stanton 160). For Cixous, Irigaray, and Johnson, the mother is an important affirmative figure, while Kristeva worries about the absolute rejection or acceptance of motherhood. Susan Suleiman generally questions the psychoanalytic framework tout court as adequate for the analysis of mother's writing.

SEX AND GENDER. The meanings of "gender" and "sexual difference" have been extensively debated. Joan Scott usefully explains that gender denotes "a rejection of the biological determinism implicit in the use of such terms as 'sex' and 'sexual difference'" (28). De Lauretis prefers to privilege the term "gender," which for her is not only a "classificatory term" in grammar but also "a representation of a relation" that is an ongoing social "construction" (Technologies 3–5). Wittig calls for the destruction of gender and sex altogether. Within language women are marked by gender, and within society they are marked by sex. As a way of eluding this patriarchal economy of heterosexual exchange, Wittig appeals to a lesbianization of language.

Cixous takes a still different approach, concentrating on the way sexual difference "becomes most clearly perceived at the level of jouissance, inasmuch as a woman's instinctual economy cannot be identified by a man or referred to the masculine economy" (Newly 82), and in turn the best way to engage with these different economies is through recourse to a theory of bisexuality. Kristeva maintains, however, that bisexuality, no matter what qualifications accompany the term, always privileges "the totality of one of the sexes and thus [effaces] difference" (209). Despite such objections, Cixous insists that bisexuality is a notion meant to call attention to the multiplicity of possible sites for desire and pleasure (Newly, "Laugh"); it "doesn't annul differences but stirs them up, pursues them, increases their number" ("Laugh" 254). In this respect, Cixous's position lines up with JACQUES DERRIDA's belief in the possibility of "the multiplicity of sexually marked voices" (76).

In the most complex analysis of the distinction between gender and sex, JUDITH BUTLER contends that "gender is not to culture as sex is to nature" (7). Rather, gender as a discursive element gives rise to a belief in a prediscursive, natural sex. Sex is retrospectively produced through our understanding of gender, so that in a sense gender comes before sex (7). Butler argues that "it becomes impossible to separate out 'gender' from the political and cultural intersections in which it is invariably produced and maintained" (xiii, 3) and that gender "proves to be performative" (25).

The question of woman. Poststructuralist feminists have formulated significantly different answers to the question "What is woman?" Kristeva contends that there is no such thing as "woman" (Marks 137). As a way to keep open as many subject positions as possible, she favors "a concept of femininity which would take as many forms as there are women" (Moi, French 114).

Drucilla Cornell argues, too, that there is no essential woman, no possibility of sharing experience based on a common female nature: "woman 'is' only in language, which means that her 'reality' can never be separated from the metaphors and fictions in which she is presented" (18). For Butler, even the plural form "women" is always incomplete and permanently a contested site of meaning: "It would be wrong to assume in advance that there is a category of 'women' that simply needs to be filled in with various components of race, class, age, ethnicity, and sexuality in order to become complete" (15).

By contrast, for Wittig "woman" is "the equivalent of slave" and only has meaning in heterosexual systems of thought and economics, in which women are defined in terms of their reproductive function ("Mark" 70). This leads Wittig to conclude that "lesbians are not women" but rather are the undivided "I" of the total subject ("Straight" 110). Irigaray takes a similarly skeptical view, arguing that "woman" is man's creation, a masquerade of femininity: "In our social order, women are 'products' used and exchanged by men. Their status is that of merchandise, 'commodities'" (84). Instead of creating a theory of woman, Irigaray wants "to secure a place for the feminine within sexual difference" where "the feminine cannot signify itself in any proper meaning, proper name, or concept, not even that of woman" (156). Thus, her refusal to answer the question "What is woman?" can be understood as a refusal to reproduce the phallogocentric system, which keeps in place oppressive language and systems of representation.

POLITICS AND ETHICS. No difference among the poststructuralist feminists has been more divisive than the division between the political argument about the oppression of women in society and the *psychoanalytic* argument about the role of gender difference in the psychic construction of the individual. This split reached perhaps its most controversial moment in the French group Psychanalyse et Politique (Psych et Po), under the leadership of the psychoanalyst Antoinette Fouque, who in their defense of psychoanalysis derided feminism for its interest in obtaining power for women within the terms of the patriarchy. After the late 1970s, however, there was an increasing interest in bringing together political and psychoanalytic discourses. For Jacqueline Rose, for instance, deconstruction can serve as a hinge between the political and psychoanalytical positions in order to produce a feminist ethics.

Cixous claims that "for me, there is only ethics" ("Exchange" 138), and Irigaray argues for a needed revolution in thought and ethics (Moi, *French* 128). Ethics importantly allows us to think the social and the psychic, the questions of the political and of the subject, beside each other. "It is only if we see the inevitable intertwinement of justice, politics, and utopian possibility in feminism, that we can understand the promise and the necessity for the affirmation of the feminine, even if as a transition, as a threshold" (Cornell 20). The ethical intervenes for deconstructive feminism as the condition of thought outside the determinations of patriarchal discourse (for which ethics would only be moral philosophy). The ethical is invoked, much like *écriture féminine*, as the site of an exploratory thought for which neither the self nor the field of the political is a fixed entity—what happens once the personal is the political, and the political is personal.

DIANE ELAM

See also JUDITH BUTLER, HÉLÈNE CIXOUS, ETHICS, LUCE IRIGARAY, JULIA KRISTEVA, and PSYCHOANALYTIC THEORY AND CRITICISM: 3. THE POST-LACANIANS.

See also bibliographies for HÉLÈNE CIXOUS, LUCE IRIGARAY, JULIA KRISTEVA, and GAYATRI CHAKRAVORTY SPIVAK.

Judith Butler, *Gender Trouble* (1990); Hélène Cixous, "An Exchange with Hélène Cixous," *Hélène Cixous: Writing the Feminine* (ed. Verena Andermatt Conley, 1984), *Illa* (1980), "Le rire de la Méduse" (1975, "The Laugh of the Medusa," trans. Keith Cohen and Paula Cohen, *Signs* 1 [1976]); Hélène Cixous and Catherine Clément, *La jeune née* (1975, *The Newly Born Woman*, trans. Betsy Wing, 1986); Catherine Clément, *L'opéra; ou, La défaite des femmes* (1979, *Opera; or, The Undoing of Women*, trans. Betsy Wing, 1988); Drucilla Cornell, *Beyond Accommodation: Ethical Feminism, Deconstruction, and the Law* (1991); Teresa de Lauretis, *Alice Doesn't: Feminism, Semiotics, Cinema* (1984), *Technologies of Gender: Essays on Theory, Film, and Fiction* (1987); Luce Irigaray, *Ce sexe qui n'en est pas un* (1977, *This Sex Which Is Not One*, trans. Catherine Porter with Carolyn Burke, 1985); Jacques Derrida and Christie V. McDonald, "Choreographies," *diacritics* 12 (1982); Barbara Johnson, *The Critical Difference* (1980), *A World of Difference* (1987); Ann Rosalind Jones, "Writing the Body: Toward an Understanding of 'l'Écriture Féminine,'" *Feminist Studies* 7 (1981); Julia Kristeva, *Kristeva Reader* (ed. Toril Moi, 1986); Michèle Le Doeuff, "Cheveux longs, idées courtes," *L'imaginaire philosophique* (1980, "Women and Philosophy," trans. Debbie Pope, Moi, *French*); Elaine Marks and Isabelle de Courtivron, eds., *New French Feminisms:*

An Anthology (1980); Nancy K. Miller, ed., *The Poetics of Gender* (1986); Toril Moi, ed., *French Feminist Thought: A Reader* (1987); Jacqueline Rose, *Sexuality in the Field of Vision* (1986); Joan Wallach Scott, *Gender and the Politics of History* (1988); Kaja Silverman, *The Acoustic Mirror: The Female Voice in Psychoanalysis and Cinema* (1988); Domna C. Stanton, "Difference on Trial: A Critique of the Maternal Metaphor in Cixous, Irigaray, and Kristeva" (Miller); Susan Rubin Suleiman, "On Maternal Splitting: A Propos of Mary Gordon's *Men and Angels*," *Signs* 14 (1988); Hélène Vivienne Wenzel, "The Text as Body/Politics: An Appreciation of Monique Wittig's Writings in Context," *Feminist Studies* 7 (1981); Monique Wittig, *Le corps lesbien* (1973, *The Lesbian Body*, trans. David LeVay, 1975), *Les guérillères* (1969, *Les Guérillères*, trans. David LeVay, 1971), "The Mark of Gender" (Miller), "One Is Not Born a Woman," *Feminist Issues* 1 (1981), *L'opoponax* (1969, *The Opoponax*, trans. Helen Weaver, 1976), "The Straight Mind," *Feminist Issues* 1 (1980).

4. Materialist Feminisms

Although feminists and socialists have engaged in continuous conversations since the nineteenth century, those crosscurrents within literary theory that might be designated "materialist feminisms" have their origins in the late 1960s with various attempts to synthesize feminist politics with Marxist analyses. Early work on this projected alliance directed itself to the problem of bringing feminist questions of gender and sexuality into some form of strategic dialogue with class analysis. The materialist feminist problematic has extended to questions of race, nationality or ethnicity, lesbianism and sexuality, cultural identity, including religion, and the very definition of power.

The term "materialist feminisms" proves contentious since there has been little general consensus as to whether women's interests can, or indeed should, be addressed in terms of traditional socialist and Marxist formulas. UK feminist Juliet Mitchell analyzes the position of women in terms of relations of production and private property and also of psychoanalytically based theories of sexuality and gender in her groundbreaking "Women: The Longest Revolution" (1966) (expanded to book length in *Woman's Estate* [1971]). Michèle Barrett, another UK feminist, insists in her highly influential *Women's Oppression Today* (1980) that feminists will necessarily engage directly with and transform Marxist class analysis. In their editorial to the final issue of the important UK journal m/f Parveen Adams and Elizabeth Cowie state that they sought "to problematise the notion of sexual difference itself" through a fundamental critique of psychoanalytic categories (3). In the United States, however, diverse feminists identify themselves as "socialist feminists," distinguishing their work from that of radical and liberal feminists, who contend that women's oppression will end with the achievement of women's power, or women's equality, within existing capitalist societies, positions strangely like the traditional Marxist view that women's oppression would end once women entered into production.

The foundations of these critical positions lie in political theory, psychoanalysis, and sociology rather than in traditional literary concerns with questions of canon, form, genre, author, and oeuvre. Materialist feminist literary critics focus instead on key problems in language, history, ideology, determination, subjectivity, and agency from the basic perspective of a critique of the gendered character of class and race relations under international capitalism.

Mitchell focuses on questions concerning the family and child rearing by means of a feminist critique of psychoanalytic theories of sexual development largely based on a literary-critical examination of texts within the Freudian and Marxist canons. Her project, developed further in *Psychoanalysis and Feminism* and *Women: The Longest Revolution* (1974), involves inflecting feminist politics with insights from Marxism and psychoanalysis. With Jacqueline Rose (in their edition of Jacques Lacan's *Feminine Sexuality* [1985]), she has continued the engagement between the psychoanalytic theories of Lacan and materialist feminist thinking in Britain.

For a sociologist of knowledge like Barrett, literary questions are not central, but her treatment of ideology in *Women's Oppression Today* has been highly influential among feminist literary theorists. The political urgencies of women's liberation bear directly on the need for a feminist analysis of "culture," and here Marxism and feminism engage questions important to literary theory, in particular questions of aesthetics, subjectivity, and ideology. In "Feminism and the Definition of Cultural Politics" (1982), Barrett addresses three issues of direct importance to materialist feminist literary theory: (1) the indeterminacy of artistic and literary meaning, (2) the relationship between women's art and feminist art, and (3) the problem of judging aesthetic value and pleasure. Barrett regards literary texts, art objects, and dramatic performances as marked by inner contradictions that cannot easily be adjudicated by reference to the artist's life or intentions. Barrett is reluctant to abandon female experience entirely, but she does argue that feminist political interests are not necessarily served by the recovery of women's past artistic achievements or even by self-proclaimed feminist artworks like Judy Chicago's *The Dinner Party* (1979). Arguing that feminists to their peril ignore the dual question of aesthetic value and pleasure, Barrett finds the traditional assumption that value judgments can and should be made a highly suspicious assumption for feminist politics, since such judgments about "value" invariably tend to reinforce the values of the dominant classes as apparently natural and universal.

Barrett's materialist aesthetics seeks to democratize the relation between the producer and the consumer of art. Skills, though socially defined, are not innate but acquired and therefore improvable, while the imaginative rendering of social life in works of art and literature is typically foreclosed in much feminist criticism by an undue emphasis on the work's content as unmediated representation. Politics comes first for Barrett, since literature and art help constitute social life but do not determine it.

For other critics, the study of literary texts is of primary importance to the development and enunciation of a feminist politics firmly committed to socialism. In

Patriarchal Precedents (1983) Rosalind Coward critically historicizes from a feminist perspective the various disciplines within which sexual relations have traditionally been studied. Catherine Belsey's *Critical Practice* (1980) argues that "the recurrent suppression of the role of language" in traditional literary criticism is an ideological move by which the " 'correct' reading" of a text installs the reader as "transcendent subject addressed by an autonomous and authoritative author" (55). In *The Subject of Tragedy* (1991) Belsey brings together Lacanian and Althusserian theories of the subject, arguing that the emergence of liberal ideologies during the capitalist era has required the "interpellation" of women as, in part, willing subjects of their own oppression in relation to a normative and universal male self. Toril Moi's *Sexual/Textual Politics* (1985) challenges the humanist presuppositions informing the influential feminist literary criticism of Elaine Showalter, Sandra Gilbert and Susan Gubar, Annette Kolodny, and Myra Jehlen. Celebrating women writers and readers reinscribes the unitary self and thereby begs the political questions of agency and resistance.

Cora Kaplan writes that her experience in the UK Marxist-Feminist Literary Collective enabled her to overcome her fear of "theory," an antipathy that persists among the U.S. feminist literary critics Moi examines. Not all U.S. feminist critics, however, share this fear. Gayle Rubin's much-cited essay "The Traffic in Women" (1975) remains a useful reading of Karl Marx and Friedrich Engels, Claude Lévi-Strauss, and Lacan in the interests of rethinking the sex-gender system within social relations. Pioneering articles by Ann Rosalind Jones and Biddy Martin ("Feminism, Criticism, and Foucault" [1982]) brought French feminism and Foucauldian theory to bear upon feminist criticism in the United States, while Judith Newton's *Women, Power, and Subversion* (1981) raised questions concerning the class character of gender ideology for literary historians. Written with Deborah Rosenfelt, Newton's 1985 introduction to *Feminist Criticism and Social Change* enthusiastically proclaims the emergence of "materialist feminist criticism" in a collection that reprints important studies by, among others, Barrett, Belsey, Jones, and the editors. In challenging the increasing institutional influence of liberal feminism in the later 1980s, the theoretical perspective of the introduction privileges literature over politics, thereby reversing the emphasis of many of its contributors.

Some of the most important U.S. contributions have come from socialists and feminists working directly with the interrelated literary problems of sexuality, racial difference, the politics of language, and postcoloniality, questions barely addressed by UK materialist feminists. The autobiographical essays by Elly Bulkin, Minnie Bruce Pratt, and Barbara Smith in *Yours in Struggle* (1984) and literary studies by Biddy Martin ("Lesbian Identity and Autobiographical Difference(s)" [1988]) and other lesbian feminists have fundamentally challenged the heterosexist biases and presuppositions of both capitalist ideology and socialist critique. DONNA HARAWAY's influential "Manifesto for Cyborgs" (1991) explores how recent developments in the technologies of the body destabilize not only gender categories but also the unity of self and body, with a view to constructing a socialist-feminist mythology of the future. Her *Primate Visions* (1989) analyzes the interconnections of gender and racial ideologies within the history of primatology as a representative twentieth-century science.

In several books, bell hooks (Gloria Watkins) documents how the history of class and race blindness among U.S. feminists continues to affect the work of feminist scholars and cultural critics. Valerie Smith analyzes the institutional pressures toward commodification that specifically affect African American feminist critics. From the perspective of Jacques Derrida-inspired deconstruction, the essays in Gayatri Chakravorty Spivak's *In Other Worlds* and the interviews in *The Post-Colonial Critic* (1990) emphasize the complicities and dangerous instabilities of "class," "gender," and "race" among the analytic languages that are needed to negotiate a global politics that will destabilize the continuing logic of capitalism in the contemporary postcolonial era. Also working from a poststructuralist problematic, Hortense Spillers argues that African American women writers, and women generally, are betrayed by liberal feminist literary critics who rely on master narratives that reinscribe legitimacy crises based on patriarchal and imperialist myths of Oedipal anxiety. Barbara Harlow examines literary texts from West Asia, Africa, and South and Central America from a race-conscious materialist feminist perspective. Not all race-sensitive U.S. feminist critics in the 1990s were sympathetic to recent theoretical developments, however; Barbara Christian raised her influential voice against "theory," by which she means poststructuralism.

Materialist feminist critics in the United Kingdom and the United States have contributed significantly to film theory, semiotics, and the study of popular culture, though work in these fields has often developed independently of socialist politics and outside of traditional Marxist analytical categories. Important materialist feminist essays in theory, film studies, semiotics, and popular culture can be found in the UK journals *Feminist Review*, *I&C* (formerly *Ideology and Consciousness*), *LTP*, *m/f*, *New Left Review*, *Oxford Literary Review*, *Red Letters*, and *Screen* and the U.S. journals *Camera Obscura*, *Cultural Critique*, *enclitic*, *Feminist Issues*, *Feminist Studies*, *Genders*, *Jump Cut*, *Signs*, and *Socialist Review*.

While feminist theorists such as Teresa de Lauretis, Annette Kuhn, Tania Modleski, Meaghan Morris, and Kaja Silverman are critical of the unitary self of liberal feminism and insist on the materiality of signifying practices (such as film and mass fiction) in the ideological construction of gender, their concern with gender and subjectivity all but abandons the basic materialist questions of history, class, and the economic that variously remain crucial in Mitchell, Barrett, Coward, Belsey, Kaplan, Haraway, Martin, Spivak, Spillers, and others. It may be that the attempts of the 1970s and early 1980s to bring feminism into dialogue with Marxism are over, doomed from the start. But the many important questions raised by Barrett's exploration of the aesthetic, ideological, and class bases of women's oppression, Belsey's

and Kaplan's analyses of the historical constructions of female subjectivity in literary texts by and about women, Martin's and Katie King's theoretical examinations of
lesbianism and sexuality, Spivak's materialist-deconstructionist readings of the
global texts of postcoloniality via *Capital*, Spillers's critique of Judeo-Christian, Oedipal, imperialist historiography, and Haraway's excavations of the ideology of what
we so often mistake for "nature" or scientific "truth" continue to generate new problems demanding the attention of feminists engaged in the construction of a leftist
theory and practice of literary criticism.

DONNA LANDRY AND GERALD MACLEAN

See also AFRICAN AMERICAN THEORY AND CRITICISM, GENDER, and MARXIST
THEORY AND CRITICISM.

See also bibliographies for DONNA HARAWAY and GAYATRI CHAKRAVORTY
SPIVAK.

Parveen Adams and Elizabeth Cowie, "The Last Issue between Us," *m/f* 11/12 (1986); Michèle
Barrett, "Feminism and the Definition of Cultural Politics," *Feminism, Culture, and Politics* (ed. Rosalind Brunt and Caroline Rowan, 1982), *Women's Oppression Today: Problems in Marxist Feminist Analysis*
(1980, rev. ed., *Women's Oppression Today: The Marxist/Feminist Encounter*, 1988); Catherine Belsey, *Critical
Practice* (1980), *The Subject of Tragedy* (1987); Elly Bulkin, Minnie Bruce Pratt, and Barbara Smith, *Yours
in Struggle: Three Feminist Perspectives on Anti-Semitism and Racism* (1984); Barbara Christian, "The Race
for Theory," *Gender and Theory* (ed. Linda Kauffman, 1989); Rosalind Coward, *Patriarchal Precedents*
(1983); Barbara Harlow, *Resistance Literature* (1987); bell hooks, *Ain't I a Woman: Black Women and Feminism* (1981), *Feminist Theory: From Margin to Center* (1984), *Yearning: Race, Gender, and Cultural Politics*
(1990); Ann Rosalind Jones, "Writing the Body: Toward an Understanding of l'Écriture Féminine,"
Feminist Studies 7 (1981); Cora Kaplan, *Sea Changes: Culture and Feminism* (1986); Katie King, "Audre
Lorde's Lacquered Layerings: The Lesbian Bar as a Site of Literary Production," *Cultural Studies* 2
(1988); Biddy Martin, "Feminism, Criticism, and Foucault," *New German Critique* 27 (1982), "Lesbian
Identity and Autobiographical Difference(s)," *Life/Lines: Theorizing Women's Autobiography* (ed. Bella
Brodzki and Celeste Schenck, 1988); Juliet Mitchell, *Psychoanalysis and Feminism* (1974), *Woman's Estate* (1971), "Women: The Longest Revolution," *New Left Review* 40 (1966), *Women: The Longest Revolution* (1984); Toril Moi, *Sexual/Textual Politics: Feminist Literary Theory* (1985, 2nd ed., 2002); Judith Newton, *Women, Power, and Subversion: Social Strategies in Women's Fiction, 1780–1860* (1981); Judith Newton
and Deborah Rosenfelt, eds., *Feminist Criticism and Social Change: Sex, Class, and Race in Literature and
Culture* (1985); Gayle Rubin, "The Traffic in Women: Notes on the 'Political Economy' of Sex," *Toward an Anthropology of Women* (ed. Rayna R. Reiter, 1975); Hortense J. Spillers, "A Hateful Passion, A
Lost Love," *Feminist Studies* 9 (1983), "Mama's Baby, Papa's Maybe: An American Grammar Book,"
diacritics 17 (1987).

5. 1990 and After

Since the late 1960s debates within feminism have been marked by radically different
and often incompatible approaches to gender that have shaped feminist analyses of
literature and culture. This continues to be the case. Issues raised by liberal, radical,

and materialist feminisms remain on the agenda, while postmodern feminists argue for the usefulness of poststructuralist theory for feminist analysis and politics. Postcolonial and Third World feminists seek to understand the implications for women of colonialism, imperialism, and GLOBALIZATION, and feminists of color raise the issue of RACE AND ETHNICITY within First World locations. Queer feminists look at issues of sexuality and explore the dynamics of gender performativity (see QUEER THEORY AND CRITICISM: 3. QUEER THEORY and GENDER). Some writers argue that we have entered a postfeminist phase.

In feminist literary and cultural studies much contemporary debate in the West continues to center on the political usefulness and explanatory power of what has come to be termed "postmodern feminism." Postmodern theory is, however, a site of both influence and contention. For many of its critics, the critique of fixed ideas of truth and of general "grand theories" signifies the loss of the foundations necessary for political action. A further controversial aspect is postmodern feminism's use of decentered theories of power that draw on MICHEL FOUCAULT. Major disagreements have emerged between historical/cultural views that come out of Foucauldian paradigms and those that argue that this elides important psychoanalytic and psychic processes. Postcolonial feminists argue that postmodern critiques of essentialism often lead to a dismissal of "localized questions of experience, identity, culture and history" (Alexander and Mohanty xvii).

Poststructuralist critiques of liberalism (universalizing, liberal feminist ideas of the rights of women as human beings, demands for women's access to literary institutions and for their work to be evaluated without reference to the gender of the author in question), Marxism (importance of ideology and the centrality of class struggle to cultural analysis and social change), and radical feminism (women's emancipation requires the removal of global patriarchal power structures and seeks, among other things, to analyze representations of patriarchal power in literary texts) see these approaches as based on too simple models of power. They insist on the partiality of metanarratives and their truth claims, which will always be historically and culturally located. Poststructuralist feminists attempt to rethink the foundations of politics and of literary and cultural analysis. Diane Elam, for example, calls for a feminism based on an "ethical activism" and a "groundless solidarity" rather than identity politics (109).

Many critics of postmodern discourse see this view of theory as leading to pluralism, relativism, and ultimately individualist politics and argue that, to avoid relativism, feminists need a shared category "woman" and a general theory of oppression and liberation. In the various forms of identity politics that developed after 1970 the category "woman" was dispersed into specific groups (e.g., lesbians, black women, or working-class women), and work in literary and cultural studies reflected this move. Attention turned to images of women and literary production by women from the different groups. Individual and group identity was privileged as the basis for both political action and cultural production.

Poststructuralist critiques of identity question the sovereignty of the rational, intentional subject and argue for subjectivity as an unstable and plural discursive construct, seeing literature, like other forms of cultural practice, as an influential site for the discursive construction of subjectivity. Many feminist writers, arguing that deconstructive approaches to subjectivity do not allow for agency, reject this position. Women of color in particular have emphasized the importance of experience and identity as "the primary organizing principles they theorize and mobilize" (Moya 127). While some versions of poststructuralism fail to address the question of lived subjectivity or agency, in many feminist appropriations of Foucault, Jacques Derrida, GILLES DELEUZE, Luce Irigaray, and Julia Kristeva, agency is seen as discursively produced in the social interactions between culturally constituted, contradictory subjects. Like gender, subjectivity and agency are assumed not to exist prior to their constitution in the discursive practices in which individuals assume subjectivity. For feminists who draw on the work of Foucault, discursive practice is always material, shaping bodies as much as giving meaning to the world. Writing of postmodern theories of subjectivity in the context of race, bell hooks points out that while problematic, "the critique of essentialism encouraged by postmodern thought is useful for African-Americans concerned with reformulating outmoded notions of identity" (*Yearning* 28). The construction of notions of the self and agency have become key focuses of postmodern feminist literary criticism.

An answer to the charge of politically disabling relativism is partial—recognizing the incomplete and interested nature of both theory and practice—and located in theory and practice. Pluralism does not have to be negative. It can allow for the representation of many competing and sometimes conflicting voices, histories, and interests, the identification of which becomes an important aspect of literary analysis. Yet pluralism, in societies governed by class, racism, sexism, heterosexism, and the legacy of colonialism, is always structured by relations of power, which any adequate feminism must recognize and address.

Debates in feminism in the 1990s and after have focused in particular on the materiality of the body, on gender as performance, and on the separate (but related) widespread move from women's studies into queer theory and gender studies. Each of these areas has influenced and been influenced by feminist theory and criticism. The 1990s saw extensive debate on the body as a cultural construct. Elizabeth Grosz, for example, is critical of what she identifies as the tendency to analyze the representation of bodies without due attention to their materiality. She attempts to disrupt the binary oppositions that define the body—inside/outside, subject/object, active/passive, fantasy/reality, surface/depth—using the image of the body as a hinge or threshold, located between psychic interiority and sociopolitical exteriority (*Volatile* 189). "The body must be reconceived, not in opposition to culture but as its preeminent object" (*Space* 32).

In literary and cultural studies the body has become an important object of critical analysis. Judith Butler has developed influential theories of gender as performance. Drawing on Foucauldian theory, psychoanalysis, and speech act theory, her
work is framed by a critique of what she terms the "heterosexual matrix," that is, the
assumption that heterosexuality is the norm. Both poststructuralist feminist theory
and queer theory question the naturalness of heterosexuality, suggesting that the
relations posited between sex, gender, and desire are political and not natural or
causal and that, indeed, all norms are social constructs. Butler wishes to consider
how "gendered regulatory schemas" produce "a domain of unthinkable, abject, un-
liveable bodies" (xi).

In Butler's theory of performativity, gendered subjectivity is acquired through
the individual's repeated performance of discourses of gender. The body is an effect
of power; embodied subjectivity is discursively produced, and there is no sex outside
of culture. From this position feminist literary and cultural criticism read texts as
part of specific discursive fields that contribute to the reproduction of existing power
relations, including hegemonic discourses of gender, sexuality, and gendered modes
of subjectivity. Literary texts can, however, also subvert existing discourses of gender
and sexuality and social relations, as in the case, for example, of postmodern feminist writers.

Some of the most hostile critiques of this type of poststructuralist feminism
have come from radical feminists. The radical lesbian feminist Sheila Jeffreys interprets much recent postmodern feminism as part of a "return to gender" exemplified
in the work of Butler and Diana Fuss, arguing that this approach marks a dangerous
depoliticization of feminism in which gender becomes a question of play rather than
of politics. A true lesbian feminist perspective would contest both patriarchy and
heterosexism and celebrate lesbian literary production as an engagement with and
affirmation of lesbian subjectivity, identity, and history.

This reading of postmodern feminism and queer theory emphasizes the dangers of postmodern approaches to difference that obscure the hierarchical relations
of power that produce it. Similar arguments are made about the shift from women's
studies to gender studies, which is seen as abandoning the full force of feminism's
critique of patriarchy and signaling a liberal depoliticization of the radical project
of women's studies. In literary studies this would mean a shift away from a concern
with the mechanisms of patriarchy to analyses of gender that often lose sight of
oppression.

In very different contexts, similar issues are being raised by postcolonial and
Third World feminists, whose issues have their own specificity and political and
social location and cannot be reduced to Western feminist concerns. Decolonization of theory as well as political practice is a key concern. One important focus of
debate is the question of universalism versus cultural specificity, particularly as it

relates to women and human rights. Much Third World criticism has focused on Western feminism's Eurocentric tendency to assume that its standards and practices are the best and to measure the needs of women in non-Western societies simply according to Western norms. Indeed, Third World feminist critiques of Western feminism argue that Western feminists tend to view Third World women as victims of forms of patriarchy based on less rational and enlightened cultural norms. Chandra Mohanty's influential essay "Under Western Eyes" shows this strategy producing an undifferentiated Third World subject who is a passive victim of patriarchy and tradition, placed outside of history and without agency. Feminist postcolonial literary and cultural studies seeks to draw attention to the ways in which Western literature, including writing by women, valorizes particular discourses of whiteness. This implies a detailed knowledge of context and history that does not impose outside meanings and judgments on non-Western literary production but is attentive to the voices of Third World writers and critics.

Postcolonial feminism has placed the legacies of colonialism at the center of the contemporary feminist agenda, including feminist literary and cultural studies. The legacy for both Third World and Western feminisms is often focused on Eurocentrism, including the "colonial gaze" and the question of who speaks for whom. These issues are privileged in feminist postcolonial rereadings of literary texts, as in Gayatri Chakravorty Spivak's "Three Women's Texts" (1985) and Critique of Postcolonial Reason (1999). For Uma Narayan, history tends to be absent in colonial modes of representation and the Third World is represented as static and timeless; attending to the detailed specificity of particular practices works against the colonialist tendency to represent the Third World as lacking internal differences and complexity. There is, she suggests, a double standard in the work of many Western feminists who represent Western societies as complex and changing and the Third World as uniform and outside of history.

Postcolonial writers have questioned the possibility of speaking for others in ways that do not do violence to them (Spivak). It is, however, equally important not to deny Third World writers and critics access to narratives of emancipation simply because their origin is Western and they have been used in the past to justify colonialism. Important here, for example, is the strategic reappropriation of discourses of human rights by oppressed groups. In different contexts, such discourses will always already be overlaid with local differences and reappropriated for political purposes under different material and ideological conditions.

Many critics of postmodern theory argue that feminism necessarily stands on Enlightenment ground with women as its constituency. All narratives are necessarily partial, founded on selection and exclusion, and invoking Western feminist theories as general theories of historical progress often leads to a denial of the specificity of black and Third World women's interests. But postcolonial feminist advocates of poststructuralist theory argue that its questioning of universals and the possibility of objectivity and its focus on the very criteria by which claims to knowledge are legitimized provide for theorizations that can avoid generalizing from the experiences of Western, white, heterosexual, middle-class women. In its questioning of essences and its relativizing of truth claims, postmodern theory can be used to create a space for political perspectives and interests that have hitherto been marginalized. It also helps guard against creating alternative generalizing theories.

The question of difference continues to be a major focus of debate. As early as the 1970s, black feminists formulated powerful critiques of white feminism's marginalization of questions of race. Audre Lorde argues that "ignoring the differences of race between women and the implications of those differences presents the most serious threat to the mobilization of women's joint power" (117). The marginalization of writing by women of color within the academies is still a problem. White women have begun to theorize whiteness and its role in the perpetuation of racism and ethnocentrism. Barbara Smith argues that white women need to work on racism for their own sake, not as a favor to black and Third World women (26).

Recent feminist debate offers possibilities for thinking difference differently. Much of this work is indebted to women of color in both the developing world and the West. It also draws on the political mobilization of poststructuralist theory's insights. While the struggle for equal rights remains an important dimension of feminist politics, it is no longer necessary to link rights to sameness. Instead, feminists imagine a world in which difference is celebrated and enjoyed free from the hierarchical structures of class, racial, sexual, and gender power. Literary and cultural studies are important areas in which this site of (re)imagining becomes possible. Yet to move toward such a world continues to require the articulation of marginalized voices and the self-affirmation of oppressed groups, as well as the recognition by white, Western, heterosexual, middle-class women of their structural privileges. This recognition and acceptance of difference has profound implications for the future of literary and cultural studies, demanding a much more inclusive approach to what is widely read, analyzed and acclaimed.

CHRIS WEEDON

See also bibliographies for JUDITH BUTLER and GAYATRI CHAKRAVORTY SPIVAK.

M. Jacqui Alexander and Chandra Talpade Mohanty, eds., *Feminist Genealogies, Colonial Legacies, Democratic Futures* (1997); Gloria Anzaldúa, ed., *Making Face, Making Soul/Haciendo Caras: Creative and Critical Perspectives by Feminists of Color* (1990); Diane Bell and Renate Klein, eds., *Radically Speaking: Feminism Reclaimed* (1996); Diane Elam, *Feminism and Deconstruction* (1994); Elizabeth Grosz, *Space, Time, and Perversion* (1995), *Volatile Bodies: Towards a Corporeal Feminism* (1994); Clare Hemmings, *Why Stories Matter: The Political Grammar of Feminist Theory* (2011); bell hooks, *Yearning: Race, Gender, and Cultural Politics* (1991); Sheila Jeffreys, "Return to Gender: Post-modernism and Lesbianandgay Theory" (Bell and Klein); Audre Lorde, "Age, Race, Class, and Sex: Women Redefining Difference,"

Sister Outsider (1984); Angela McRobbie, *The Aftermath of Feminism: Gender, Culture and Social Change* (2009); Chandra Talpade Mohanty, "Under Western Eyes: Feminist Scholarship and Colonial Discourse," *Feminist Review* 30 (1988); Paula M. L. Moya, "Postmodernism, 'Realism,' and the Politics of Identity" (Alexander and Mohanty); Uma Narayan, *Dislocating Cultures: Identities, Traditions, and Third World Feminism* (1997); Barbara Smith, "Racism and Women's Studies" (Anzaldúa); Gayatri Chakravorty Spivak, "Can the Subaltern Speak?" *Colonial Discourse and Post-colonial Theory* (ed. Patrick Williams and Laura Chrisman, 1993).

Fish, Stanley

Stanley Fish (b. 1938), one of the best-known contemporary American literary theorists, is a controversial figure, widely imitated yet widely criticized. There is less disagreement over his writing's clarity and power. After a first book on John Skelton with few theoretical implications, Fish quickly attained prominence as a literary theorist with his second book, *Surprised by Sin: The Reader in "Paradise Lost"* (1967), which argues that the reader reenacts and experiences the fall and ultimate redemption of humanity as he or she reads. This approach to Milton's poem conflicted with a central principle of New Criticism, the affective fallacy, which argued that the meaning of a work of literature should not be confused with its effect on a reader.

Fish went on to argue that what had at first seemed a peculiarity of Milton's work was characteristic of all literature. READER-RESPONSE CRITICISM argues that reading is a temporal phenomenon and that writers depend upon this in several significant ways. Texts are constructed with dilemmas, changes in direction, and false starts, and meaning is in our experience of these phenomena, not simply some final, spatialized, or thematized resolution of them. The meaning of a literary work is the work a reader does while reading it.

Fish's work moved first in a text-centered, then in a reader-centered direction. The former is most fully represented by his third book, *Self-Consuming Artifacts* (1972), which argues that various seventeenth-century works of English prose begin by adumbrating a proposition or view of the world that they end by rejecting. The texts seem to be designed to be that way, making the multiplicity of the reader's experience—now seen to be controlled by the text—more apparent than real. But the range of actual response to any work of literature seems too multifarious to be designed.

Fish subsequently decided that the reader's response he had purported to describe in *Surprised by Sin* and *Self-Consuming Artifacts* was really a response he had been prescribing. But this is true of all theories: they create meaning by prescribing in advance what will count as meaningful in a text. Readers—not texts—make meanings, and they do so by virtue of the theories or beliefs about meaning and about texts that they hold to be true. This new formulation, the theory of interpretive communities, replaces the individual reader of reader-response criticism with a community of readers sharing a set of interpretive strategies in common.

Fish collected his theoretical essays of the 1970s in his fifth book, *Is There a Text in This Class? The Authority of Interpretive Communities* (1980) (his fourth book, *The Living Temple* [1978], was on George Herbert). These essays, beginning with "Literature in the Reader" but tracing his shift away from reader-response criticism toward the theory of interpretive communities (see "Interpreting the Variorum"), consolidated his position as one of the most influential and cited theorists of his time, influential despite or perhaps because of his refusal to settle on a fixed position or stance. The dynamic quality Fish once ascribed to reading was by now a property of his work on reading and interpretation. *Is There a Text in This Class?* is a wide-ranging collection, with essays on topics as diverse as stylistics and the application of theories of SPEECH ACTS to William Shakespeare's *Coriolanus.* The most sustained section, a group of four lectures that gave the book its title, offers an extended exposition of interpretive communities. No, there is no text if by that one means an unchanging entity with a fixed meaning; yes, there is a text because every interpretive community fixes and defines the meaning of the text it reads and, in a sense, writes.

The subsequent geometry of Fish's career is more complex and more difficult to render as a coherent narrative. Fish's subsequent theoretical books—*Doing What Comes Naturally* (1989), *There's No Such Thing as Free Speech, and It's a Good Thing, Too* (1994), and *The Trouble with Principle* (1999)—collect independent essays, mostly published initially in article form, in which there are overlapping themes but not a single over-arching argument or design. Also, Fish took on increasing and multiple commitments to institutions outside of literary theory: in the early 1980s he became a professor of law at Duke University as well as professor of English, reflecting his increasing inter-est in legal as well as literary theory; he then became chair of the English department at Duke and director of the Duke University Press before becoming dean at the Uni-versity of Illinois at Chicago. In 2005 he became a professor of humanities and pro-fessor of law at Florida International University.

Fish's later work dramatically extends his earlier positions in a variety of direc-tions. Fish comes to see the idea that nothing makes an interpretation true except for the specific context in which it is made—the central theme of *Is There a Text in This Class?*—as valid beyond questions of literary interpretation. He developed his position on literary interpretation into a philosophical position, best known as "antifoundationalism." As Fish does this, above all in *Doing What Comes Naturally,* he becomes more explicit about his intellectual debts and allies, including some of the familiar pantheon of French poststructuralist or postmodernist thinkers—especially JACQUES DERRIDA—but Fish's approach has been equally influenced by a number of Anglo-American or analytic philosophers, including J. L. Austin. Anti-foundationalism's central claim that truth is relative to a situation, a community, or a context has been criticized as viciously self-contradictory on the grounds that it does not claim to be true only contextually, leaving antifoundationalism as the only truth claim not governed by its own premises. Fish's foray into formal philosophical theorizing is probably the weakest part of his work, and Fish may agree, given his tendency after *Doing What Comes Naturally* to avoid general philosophical claims.

Fish has shown originality and a great deal of panache in his attempt to apply general antifoundationalism in specific contexts and local situations. Key here is his work in legal theory and public policy, begun in *Doing What Comes Naturally* but domi-nant in *There's No Such Thing as Free Speech* and *The Trouble with Principle.* Most of the work that falls under the LAW AND LITERATURE rubric remains firmly grounded on one side or the other, borrowing at most some concepts from legal studies to apply to literary studies, or vice versa, but Fish uniquely works in and contributes to both disciplines at once. His position in legal studies remains much more unorthodox than his position in literary studies; nonetheless he publishes in law journals and works within the framework of the discipline. His argument is that most of what the legal profession and American society take as self-evident, freestanding, and universally valid principles are nothing of the kind but are instead true only within a given community, valid only in a particular setting, and often fair or just only to the community in that setting. This includes such fundamental principles as free speech or even the notion of principle itself. We do not see this because we are so enmeshed in our context or situation that we fail to recognize our own enmeshedness.

Fish's work in this direction has a wonderful gadfly effect, forcing anyone who instinctively disagrees to try to articulate much better counterarguments. But Fish is taking aim at the central principles of liberalism and of the dominant culture of the legal profession, at least the academic legal profession. His work has not had the effect he would like it to have in this respect, mostly because of the question of where the revelation that what one has taken as a universal truth is generated by one's particular situation leaves one. For Fish, it leaves everything unchanged, since theory has no consequences, and he has argued at length—especially in *Professional Correctness* (1995)—against NEW HISTORICISM and other critics who argue that critical self-consciousness about the situation one is in changes that situation. This "theory hope" suggests that its faith in rising above one's situation because of the critical awareness produced by antifoundationalism ignores the central tenet of antifoundationalism. To adopt a theoretical perspective is to be in a different situation, not to have risen above situations.

Surprised by Sin, Fish's entry onto the theoretical scene, was the most important book on Milton for a generation, and he came full circle several decades later with a massive book on Milton, *How Milton Works* (2001). Curiously, this book seems to have been written by an author who has paid virtually no attention to the theory wars over the thirty-five years since *Surprised by Sin*. Its account is textualist, not contextualist, in many respects frankly intentionalist: this is the right way to read Milton, and it accords with how Milton would have wanted to be read. The book is a testimony to Milton's enduring presence in Fish's imagination; Milton is the real influence on Fish's practice as a controversialist. The Milton of the controversialist prose was deeply partisan, never on the fence, more interested in correcting and attacking his near friends than his outright enemies, a great hater, someone about whom no one was indifferent. No one manages to be indifferent about Stanley Fish either.

REED WAY DASENBROCK

See also LAW AND LITERATURE and READER-RESPONSE CRITICISM.

Stanley Fish, *Doing What Comes Naturally: Change, Rhetoric, and the Practice of Theory in Literary and Legal Studies* (1989), *The Fugitive in Flight: Faith, Liberalism, and Law in a Classic TV Show* (2010), *How Milton Works* (2001), *How to Write a Sentence, and How to Read One* (2011), *Is There a Text in This Class? The Authority of Interpretive Communities* (1980), *John Skelton's Poetry* (1965), *The Living Temple: George Herbert and Catechizing* (1978), *Professional Correctness: Literary Studies and Political Change* (1995), *Self-Consuming Artifacts: The Experience of Seventeenth-Century Literature* (1972), *Surprised by Sin: The Reader in "Paradise Lost"* (1967, 2nd ed., 1971), *There's No Such Thing as Free Speech, and It's a Good Thing, Too* (1994), *The Trouble with Principle* (1999); H. Aram Veeser, ed., *The Stanley Fish Reader* (1999).

Foucault, Michel

Michel Foucault (1926–1984) took licences in both philosophy and psychology and spent several years observing in hospitals and writing about mental illness. In the mid-1950s he went abroad to teach first in Sweden, then in Poland, where he wrote his first major work, *Madness and Civilization* (1961). In 1970 he was awarded a chair in the history of systems of thought at the prestigious Collège de France, a post he held until his death. Although briefly associated with the French Communist Party in the 1940s, Foucault did not actively participate in politics until after the events of May 1968. In the 1950s and early 1960s his work was associated with an emerging critique of psychology and medical practice in general that came to be known as the antipsychiatry movement. With R. D. Laing in England and eventually Félix Guattari in France as the most prominent members (see GILLES DELEUZE AND FÉLIX GUATTARI), antipsychiatry exposed hidden levels of domination in the practices and discourse of what appeared to be a humane science.

Beginning in the mid-1960s Foucault's interests turned to STRUCTURALISM, a then-new intellectual trend that opposed "philosophies of consciousness" such as existentialism, PHENOMENOLOGY, humanist forms of Marxism, and psychoanalysis. Foucault's *The Order of Things* (1966) and *The Archaeology of Knowledge* (1969) reflect structuralism's tendency to reject the author's or subject's vantage point in favor of that of the text's or object's.

The political upheaval of May 1968 had a profound impact on French intellectuals. Structuralists rethought their rejection of the subject; Marxists and socialists in general no longer based their critique on the unique suffering of the working class nor limited its scope to capitalism as a mode of production. Foucault's work reflected this change in intellectual mood: *Discipline and Punish* (1975) argues the imbrication of power with discourse and uncovers a new dimension of domination in modern society, "technologies of power." Volume 1 of *The History of Sexuality* (1976) rejects the Freudo-Marxist analysis of repressed libido in favor of a focus on the normalizing effects of discourses on sex. During these years Foucault participated in political movements concerned with the reform of prisons and gay liberation.

The promised further volumes of *The History of Sexuality* did not appear until 1984, in the urgent months after Foucault discovered that he was seriously ill. From 1976 to 1984 his thinking underwent still another change. Without abandoning the political and epistemologically radical stance of the concept of discourse/practice, he became concerned with the way subjects constitute themselves through these discourse/practices. In volumes 2 and 3 his emphasis shifts from the theme of sex to that of the constitution of the self in the "truth" of discourse. When he died, Foucault left behind manuscripts for volume 4 of *The History of Sexuality*, which was to cover the confessional of the medieval period.

Foucault's writing has had a remarkable reception in the humanities, especially from literary theorists. During the 1970s and 1980s his books were read as part of French "poststructuralism"—writers connected more by their rejection of certain features of structuralism than by any positive commonality—and his impact has been second only to that of JACQUES DERRIDA and DECONSTRUCTION.

The implications of Foucault's theoretical work for literary criticism vary considerably depending on which period of his writings the critic considers primary. Attention to *Madness and Civilization* leads to a reading of texts for silences and exclusions; *The Order of Things* suggests a search for *épistèmes*—unconscious, regulating structures that limit what can be written in any epoch; *Discipline and Punish* encourages a more political reading that stresses the power effects of discourse; *The History of Sexuality*, volumes 2 and 3, sensitizes the critic to the textual problematic of self-constitution. Since the late 1980s, Foucauldian readings in literature and culture have proliferated widely, becoming mixed with deconstruction, CULTURAL STUDIES, queer studies (see QUEER THEORY AND CRITICISM), FEMINIST THEORY AND CRITICISM, POSTCOLONIAL STUDIES and other interdisciplinary tendencies.

In general, Foucault's major theoretical tendency is to regard the literary text as part of a larger framework of texts, institutions, and practices. EDWARD W. SAID's *Orientalism* and STEPHEN GREENBLATT's *Renaissance Self-Fashioning* are stunning examples of this kind of reading. Foucault's texts urge the critic to complicate the interpretation, to reject the turn to the author's intention as the court of last resort, to look in the text for articulated hierarchies of value and meaning, above all to trace filiations of inter- and extratextuality, to draw connections between the given text and others, between the text and the intellectual and material context. Foucauldian readings are sensitive to the text's political impact and the political unconscious behind the text that informs its statements and shaping its lines of enunciation.

Foucault is a reluctant theorist, unwilling to elaborate univocal concepts. The concept, a sign that is "adequate" to the object ("reality"), presupposes a transparency to language that allows words to represent things, to stand in their place, without introducing distortion. The concept also empowers the rational subject as one who stands above and outside the representation. In place of the concept Foucault has offered two methodological innovations: archaeology and genealogy.

Archaeology is a synchronic analysis of what Foucault calls the statements or enunciations in any discourse. Every discourse contains "rules of formation" that limit and shape what may be said and are not at the disposal of the author, coming into play as the text is composed, out of phase with the writer's consciousness. Archaeological analysis elaborates the figure of the *épistème* (from *The Order of Things*). A sort of structuralist analysis, it uncovers complexities within texts.

Genealogy, a diachronic method, attempts to reconstruct the origins and development of discourses by showing their rootedness in a field of forces. Genealogy is a Nietzschean effort to develop a critical method undermining all absolute grounds, demonstrating the origins of things only in relation and in contest with other things. It disallows pure beginnings, historical formations denying their historicity by naturalizing themselves, absolutizing themselves, grounding themselves in some transcendent principle. From the vantage point of those who hold to absolute principles, genealogy appears as nihilist, relativist, amoral. Hubert Dreyfus and Paul Rabinow, in *Michel Foucault: Beyond Structuralism and Hermeneutics* (1982), argue more convincingly that together with archaeology, genealogy constitutes "an analytic of finitude," one that undercuts metaphysical pretensions, overblown notions of reason's ability to ground discourse, but not ethical action in the term's best sense.

The archaeological-genealogical method is most suited to an exploration of the interplay between discourse and practice. As an interpretive strategy it is far less purely textual than SEMIOTICS or deconstruction. Foucault rejects the haven of the text, literary or otherwise, on the grounds that the disciplines that have developed over the past two centuries around such texts are themselves part of the problem in need of analysis. Phenomena like language are not neutral tools or containers serving the pursuit of truth without interference. A major issue for interpretation is precisely the way disciplines constitute "rules of formation" for the regulation of discourse. The first "move" in the disciplines of literary criticism has been to disavow or obscure the discipline's role as context of discourse. In this sense New Criticism and deconstruction constitute a continuous line of development: from a disciplinary strategy of formalism and aestheticism to a movement of subversion of hierarchies. In both, though, the traditional apparatus of textuality is affirmed in practice and the limits to what is done under the rubric "literary criticism" are reinforced.

Foucault's impact on literary criticism often takes the shape of a renewed form of Marxist criticism, perhaps along lines developed by the practitioners of NEW HISTORICISM who, like Foucault, are averse to systematizing theory. Even though Foucault has been read in North America primarily as a theorist, his hostility to theory leads to several difficulties for those attempting to practice his strategies of reading. First, his texts betray a continual shifting of the author's position. Only in his late essays (such as "What Is Enlightenment?," delivered as a lecture at Berkeley in the fall of 1983) does he affirm the writer's need to take responsibility for the act of writing by constituting him- or herself through writing in critical antagonism to the present. Second, Foucault's later works lead in the direction of a critique of the way discourse constitutes the self in "truth" but fail to provide the criterion by which to distinguish the discursive effects of Foucault's own texts from that of those texts that confirm structures of domination. Finally, Foucault is unable adequately to justify his choice of topics, such as sex, prisons, and so forth. In "What Is Enlightenment?" he weakly contends that topics receive the "generality" of import from their historical repetition. The writer's choice of topic is thereby divorced from his or her "responsibility" to take a critical stance toward the present, to strive for reflexivity by situating one's own project firmly in the context of the present conjuncture.

Since the 1990s scholars have increasingly paid attention to another side of Foucault's work. Best seen in relation to the notion of disciplinary power in *Discipline and Punish*, the idea of "governmentality" is for Foucault a form of power developed in modern society in contrast to "sovereignty." In sovereignty, the king had the ability to deny acts to others, a negative form of power. In modern society the state added another kind of power, one that controlled populations in the manner of a priest with his flock. The state actively sought to regulate the people's life, welfare, health, and general condition. Governmentality, or biopower, extended the reach of the state in a productive if highly dangerous manner. The reach of Foucault's influence clearly continues and even takes on new directions as scholars discover features of his writing that previously had been little noticed.

MARK POSTER

See also CULTURAL STUDIES, DISCOURSE: 2. DISCOURSE THEORY, and FRENCH THEORY AND CRITICISM: 1945 AND AFTER.

Michel Foucault, *L'archéologie du savoir* (1969, *The Archaeology of Knowledge and the Discourse on Language*, trans. A. M. Sheridan-Smith, 1972), *Ceci n'est pas une pipe* (1973, *This Is Not a Pipe*, ed. and trans. James Harkness, 1983), *Essential Works of Michel Foucault* (ed. Paul Rabinow, 3 vols., 1977–1979), *Folie et déraison: Histoire de la folie* (1961, *Madness and Civilization: A History of Insanity in the Age of Reason*, trans. Richard Howard, 1965), *Foucault Live: Interviews, 1966–1984* (ed. Sylvère Lotringer, 1989), *The Foucault Reader* (ed. Paul Rabinow, 1984), *Histoire de la sexualité*, vol. 1, *La volonté de savoir* (1976, *The History of Sexuality*, vol. 1, *An Introduction*, trans. Robert Hurley, 1978), vol. 2, *L'usage des plaisirs* (1984, vol. 2, *The Use of Pleasure*, trans. Robert Hurley, 1986), vol. 3, *Le souci de soi* (1984, vol. 3, *The Care of the Self*, trans. Robert Hurley, 1986), *"Il faut défendre de societé": Cours au Collège de France, 1975–1976* (1997, *Society Must Be Defended: Lectures at the Collège de France, 1975–1976*, trans. David Macey, 2003), *Language, Counter-Memory, Practice* (ed. Donald Bouchard, trans. Bouchard and Sherry Simon, 1977), *Les mots et les choses* (1966, *The Order of Things: An Archaeology of the Human Sciences*, 1970), *Naissance de la biopolitique: Cours au Collège de France, 1978–1979* (2004, *The Birth of Biopolitics: Lectures at the Collège de France, 1978–1979*, trans. Graham Burchell, 2010), *Naissance de la clinique: Une archéologie du regard médical* (1963, *The Birth of the Clinic: An Archaeology of Medical Perception*, trans. A. M. Sheridan-Smith, 1973), *Politics, Philosophy, and Culture: Interviews and Other Writings, 1977–1984* (ed. Lawrence Kritzman, 1989), *Power/Knowledge: Selected Interviews and Other Writings, 1972–1977* (ed. Colin Gordon, 1980), *Résumé des cours, 1970–1982* (1989), *Raymond Roussel* (1963, *Death and the Labyrinth: The World of Raymond Roussel*, trans. Charles Ruas, 1986), *Sécurité, territoire, population: Cours au Collège de France, 1977–78* (2004, *Security, Territory, Population: Lectures at the Collège de France, 1977–78*, trans. Graham Burchell, 2009), *Surveiller et punir: Naissance de la prison* (1975, *Discipline and Punish: The Birth of the Prison*, trans. Alan Sheridan, 1977); Michel Foucault, ed., *Herculine Barbin dite Alexina B.* (1978, *Herculine Barbin: Being the Recently Discovered Memoirs of a Nineteenth-Century French Hermaphrodite*, trans. Richard McDougall, 1980), *Moi, Pierre Rivière, ayant égorgé ma mère, ma soeur et mon frère . . . : Un cas de parricide au XIXe siècle* (1973, *I, Pierre Rivière, Having Slaughtered My Mother, My Sister, and My Brother . . . : A Case of Parricide in the Nineteenth Century*, trans. Frank Jellinek, 1975).

Frankfurt School

The name Frankfurt School generally denotes a diverse body of neo-Marxian social theory, produced by the Institut für Sozialforschung (Institute for Social Research). The institute was founded on 3 February 1923, at the University of Frankfurt, and continues to the present day. More specifically, the name refers to a smaller group of scholars in exile after 1933 and their "critical theory" of society. This independent institute was conceived by Felix J. Weil, Max Horkheimer, and Friedrich Pollock, and endowed initially by Weil's father, a grain merchant. Early members included Horkheimer, Pollock, Leo Lowenthal, Carl Grünberg (its first director), and others. The institute's research was grounded in nondogmatic Marxian thought. It took as its object, in Grünberg's words, "social existence in its never-ending, constantly renewed transformations" with a special focus on subjective life in consumer capitalism (Wiggershaus 26).

Horkheimer became director of the institute in 1931 and remained its guiding force into the 1950s. THEODOR W. ADORNO was attached in the late 1920s, joining officially only in 1938 and becoming codirector in 1955. Herbert Marcuse joined in 1932. Erich Fromm, among many others, was affiliated in the 1930s but had severed his ties by the end of the decade. WALTER BENJAMIN, though linked more closely to individuals such as Adorno than to the institute itself, depended on its funding in the late 1930s. The Institute for Social Research fled Germany with Hitler's rise to power in 1933 and worked for a time from offices in Geneva, London, and Paris.

In 1936 the institute found a new home at Columbia University in New York, where it also had links to Paul Lazarsfeld's Radio Research Project at Princeton. Horkheimer and Adorno moved to Los Angeles in the 1940s. Its investigations of prejudice in the 1940s (cosponsored by the American Jewish Committee) resulted in a series of publications under the heading Studies in Prejudice. The institute returned to Frankfurt in 1950, though many of its members resigned and accepted positions in American universities. A "second generation" of Frankfurt School theory began to develop in the 1960s, with Jürgen Habermas as the leading figure. Some intellectual historians consider a third generation to have emerged in the wake of Habermas's retirement in 1994, centering on Axel Honneth and his concept of the politics of recognition.

Economically and politically, the Frankfurt School's beginnings were rooted in the troubles of Germany's Weimar years. Most of its early members were the assimilated sons of middle- and upper-middle-class Jewish families, and for many the economic conflicts of postwar German society inspired a commitment to revolutionary politics. Their form of Marxism, however, did not depend for its validity on the imminent collapse of obviously damaged capitalist relations. The rigidity of the Communists and the splintering of more radical opposition led the institute to remain unaffiliated with any particular party or faction. This distance from practical politics has been a contentious issue throughout the institute's history, notably during the exile years of the 1930s and the student uprisings of the 1960s. Individually, the institute's members have taken varying approaches to praxis, however. Adorno was never very interested in political activism, and his skepticism only deepened with time. Marcuse's early political involvement would survive dormant periods and surface again in the 1960s. Several early members belonged to the Communist Party. None of the members accepted conventional academic positions during their membership, and throughout its history the Frankfurt School has remained a research-oriented enterprise independent of overt political affiliations and critical of Soviet Communism. In the 1970s and 1980s one of Habermas's goals was to realign Frankfurt School theory in a more practical though decidedly reformist relation to political life. Subsequent work associated with the institute has often addressed issues of human rights, law, and the politics of identity and emotion.

Made up largely of secular German-Jewish intellectuals, the Frankfurt School eventually found itself at a turning point in European history. Early sponsors of the institute hoped to encourage research into the origins of antisemitism, but only in 1939 did the institute begin to address such questions directly; they became central to research done in the following two decades. Especially for Horkheimer and Adorno, antisemitism would come to exemplify basic flaws in Enlightenment humanism's faith in progressive reason and secular culture. In *Dialectic of Enlightenment* (1947) they consider it the primary symptom of a philistine's return to barbarism, and it was in this historical context that Adorno famously commented on the impossibility of a simply restorative poetry being written after Auschwitz.

After 1933 the production of "critical theory" was the Frankfurt School's cohesive project. Broadly, critical theory can be understood as a sustained reflection on the dialectical relation between reason and freedom. Following GEORG LUKÁCS, critical theory rejected Immanuel Kant's distinction between formal and substantive reason (between reason as means and reason as necessarily embodying certain ends) because such a distinction in fact promoted the "instrumental" character of thought. Likewise, the theory would treat G. W. F. Hegel (as well as Karl Marx) dialectically, attempting to reveal and account for the discrepancies between Hegel's formal methods (the recognition and sublation of determinant contradiction) and his substantive claims (the necessary unfolding of reason in history toward freedom). Characteristic of the approach was attention to the socially grounded irrationality at work in any system of reason.

In many ways the struggle was with the Enlightenment itself. Critical theory wished to preserve the notion that reason served radical human emancipation while rejecting all claims of any preestablished harmony between formal (instrumental) rationality and liberation. Right theory did not necessarily lead to right practice. As a historically grounded project, critical theory presented only the vaguest notions of what "substantive" reason and "true" freedom would be, nor did it explain how to achieve them objectively. The theory abandoned the more overt totalizations of Hegel and Soviet Communism as inadequate and stultifying. For a critical theory attuned to the falsely disenchanted worlds of capitalism and communism alike, Hegel's dictum "The true is the whole" meant mass deception. "The whole is the false," Adorno's response, bluntly summarized a perspective that had been present in much of critical theory all along (Minima Moralia 50). Such a perspective demanded a renewed concern for individual existence, a concern blocked by both totalitarian communism and administered capitalism. This desire to preserve theoretical reflection equally from bureaucratic destruction and from the chimera of commodified "individualism" would be especially central to Adorno's aesthetics, musical theory, and literary criticism. On these grounds, too, Adorno's philosophy has repeatedly been claimed as an anticipation of poststructuralist critiques of totality and, by FREDRIC JAMESON in Late Marxism (1990), as a pessimistic dialectic uniquely suitable to the condition of postmodernity.

Five motifs run through critical theory—but these motifs develop dynamically and never achieve structural stability. First, Marxian social science is reinterpreted in light of the growing discrepancies between dialectical materialism as theory and as practice. This means the rejection of any reductive totalization of history, of more mechanical relations of reflection between cultural superstructure and economic base, and of the proletariat as the necessary subject-object of historical progress (see especially the early Horkheimer and Pollock). Early empirical research led institute members to consider class struggle in the context of monopolization and rationalization. Such a perspective also resulted in arguments, such as those between Pollock and Franz Neumann in the 1940s, over the specific relation of capitalism to Nazism. In response to more orthodox views, Horkheimer and others propose a dialectical social theory whose changing categories would be responsive to present historical conditions but that (especially in its early forms) would still depend on nonrelativized axioms aimed at the reconciliation of social contradiction (see, e.g., Horkheimer's "On the Problem of Truth" [1935]).

Second, critical theory critiques the value-free claims and instrumental vision of positivist and pragmatist sociology. That is, it argues that social research must be "critical" and engaged, since the claims of scientific neutrality and practical expediency blindly serve to justify adaptation to existing conditions (see, e.g., Horkheimer's "Traditional and Critical Theory" [1937]). While members of the institute accommodated empirical methods of data collection during the institute's time in America in the 1940s, a deeply rooted skepticism toward positivist sociology remained. In the 1980s and 1990s Habermas attempted to reestablish ties between the "critical" and "positivist" sociological traditions.

Third, through attempts to bridge the gap between SIGMUND FREUD and Marx, critical theory addresses the social and psychological grounds of modern authoritarianism. It investigates the relation between the structure and the stability of social groupings such as the family, the formation of prejudice, and fascist proclivities (Adorno et al.'s, *Authoritarian Personality* [1950], and the institute's *Studien über Autorität und Familie* [1936]). Such research attempts to evaluate, through the use of quantified scales, the psychic structure of tendencies such as ethnocentrism, antisemitism, and political-economic ideology. Also, Fromm and Marcuse use Freudian psychology to provide an alternative view of social hegemony, one related to but quite distinct from that found in Lukács and ANTONIO GRAMSCI. Fromm's identification of a link between the merely formal (Kantian) aspect of bourgeois tolerance and the adaptive purposes of orthodox psychoanalysis prefigures Marcuse's later elaboration of a specifically "repressive" tolerance in late capitalist societies (see Marcuse, "Repressive Tolerance"). For Marcuse, as for Horkheimer and Adorno, modern mass-communication systems play a large role in falsifying the public's experience of its own desires and dominating it by deceptively appearing to desublimate libidinal energy that ultimately ties it more tightly to centralized power.

Fourth, Enlightenment rationality is itself reevaluated. This motif derives from Lukács's early work on reification and from Freud's theories of the necessity of psychic repression in the development of human culture. In the 1940s Adorno and Horkheimer raised the possibility, already expressed by Friedrich Nietzsche, that Enlightened thought implicitly contained an ascetic drive toward domination: reason by turns liberated humanity by giving it the ability to demystify and control a mythicized natural world and subjugated humanity in the newly mystified imperative to dominate nature (including human nature) at all costs (Horkheimer and Adorno, *Dialectic*). Thus, reason for the Frankfurt School is a damaged tool for a damaged world, and its members (especially Adorno in *Minima Moralia*) experiment with a self-consciously rational critique of rationality, a critique that draws on the fragmentary and imagistic qualities of the aesthetic. In Adorno's late work the philosophical drive toward the identity of concept and reality itself represents an instrumental danger to be dialectically negated (*Negative*).

Finally, the Frankfurt School developed a distinctive approach to aesthetics, perhaps the most salient aspect of its intellectual project for the field of literary criticism. While for many Frankfurt School members the aesthetic was peripheral to larger aims, for Adorno, Benjamin, Lowenthal, and Marcuse it is central. For Adorno, the aesthetic represents perhaps the last remaining "refuge for mimetic behavior" (*Aesthetic* 79), that is, for the preservation of reason on other than instrumental grounds. Viewed through Kant and Marx, art holds out a *promesse de bonheur* abandoned and resented by alienated bourgeois society. His early musical studies with Alban Berg further motivated Adorno's support for modernist aesthetics: "The modernity of art lies in its mimetic relation to a petrified and alienated reality. This, and not the denial of that mute reality, is what makes art speak" (31). Thus, any interpretation that focuses solely on the ideological content of a work of art is doomed to be inadequate, as indeed is a more mechanical historical account of the work's static relationship to a situation. The utopian promise of the work of art is embodied, rather, in its formal appeal to the possibility of an autonomy and coherence that is necessarily impossible if the work fully replicates the divisive, conflict-ridden society in which it is produced. To know art as dialectically related to its social world, then, one must balance "transcendent" (ideological) criticism with an "immanent" (formal) critique of those contradictions internal to the work itself (see "Cultural Criticism and Society," in Prisms). The contradictions of the work displace and reorganize those of the world in which it was produced, as well as offering glimmers of dimensions currently blockaded by the dominated character of social life.

Adorno's sense of a dialectic between ideological and formal properties has greatly influenced contemporary Marxian literary and cultural criticism (as in Jameson's interpretation of narrative). Texts such as Prisms (1977) and Notes to Literature (1957) reveal Adorno's rigorously antisystematic, discipline-crossing, and constantly self-reflexive method of reading, one that reappears in the criticism of figures such as Susan Sontag and EDWARD W. SAID. His writings have also had a direct impact on debates over mass culture and POSTMODERNISM. Adorno and Horkheimer elaborate a notion of the "culture industry" in modern capitalism. Extending Lukács's theory of reification as rationalization, they focus on the organization of culture, entertainment, and leisure as instruments of social hegemony, complicating and reorganizing earlier forms of patronage and aesthetic semiautonomy (Adorno, "The Culture Industry: Enlightenment as Mass Deception," in Horkheimer and Adorno). In this project their work anticipates motifs in Louis Althusser, MICHEL FOUCAULT, and JEAN BAUDRILLARD and reveals a new interest in processes of consumption as well as of production. The "culture industry" thesis has also become central to debates in CULTURAL STUDIES.

While Adorno's aesthetics have influenced methods of reading, Benjamin's have provided luminous suggestions for rethinking the material conditions of production and reception (see "The Author as Producer," in Reflections). His attention to urban space, technological reproduction, cinema, and Bertolt Brecht's epic theater reclaim the work of art from requirements that it emanate a sacred aesthetic "aura"; for Benjamin, an aesthetic effect, when transferred to politics, only serves fascist goals in modern society (see Illuminations). On the other hand, Benjamin is no ultramodernist. His investigations into nostalgia, collecting, and Paris in the nineteenth century often display a messianic quality in his thought. Benjamin's essays on Nikolai Leskov, Charles Baudelaire, and Franz Kafka have influenced contemporary reassessments of the novel and of modernism, and his essays on translation and on history (in Illuminations) have had a wide currency within postmodernism. Following PAUL DE MAN, some have also claimed that his early work on the Trauerspiel and allegory anticipate certain ideas in deconstructive criticism. The English translation and publication of his *Arcades Project* (left incomplete at his death in 1940) has also trig-gered renewed interest in the Frankfurt School's analysis of the utopian qualities of everyday life.

Lowenthal did perhaps the most to develop a practical and scholarly sociology of literature. His interest in popular culture looks forward to later trends in sociologi-cal and historicist criticism (*Literature, Popular Culture and Society* [1961]). Like Adorno, he attempts to relate formal technique to social relations. In essays on Fyodor Dosto-evsky, Henrik Ibsen, and Knut Hamsun from the 1930s, he examines ideological ten-dencies in literature and in its popular and critical reception. (*Literature and the Image of Man* [1957] contains versions of some of these essays.) Like Benjamin, Lowenthal ex-periments with a mode of criticism that stresses the need to investigate the popular consumption of the work of art, a mode that would be further developed decades later by, among others, reader-response critics.

Habermas's work represents both a continuation of and a reaction against previ-ous "critical theory." In his early work he returns to the fundamental relation of rea-son to freedom in the philosophical tradition he inherited, where Nietzsche becomes a pivotal and largely destructive force (*Knowledge*). Habermas would later reprove the import of Nietzschean thought into critical theory in the late 1930s (*Philosophical*). His interests expanded for a time toward systems theory and a more Weberian un-derstanding of social rationalization. Not only is modernized social organization necessary in efficiently promoting the material quality of life but it actually resists totalitarian control. The danger lies in the extension of managerial values to a non-institutionalized lifeworld. In his later work Habermas elaborates a theory of "com-municative action" that rejects the "philosophy of consciousness" presupposed by earlier critical theory in favor of the implicit formal constraints on consciousness assumed by intersubjective communication (*Theory*). Throughout his career Haber-mas has promoted and defended modernity, in stark contrast to many of his prede-cessors. This position also distinguishes his work from the approaches to the post-modern taken by the next generation (e.g., Honneth).

With its depth and range, the Frankfurt School represents an influential experi-ment in collaborative and interdisciplinary theory and research concerning modern Western society. The institute never articulated a concrete plan for political action, nor does it present a positive utopian vision. Instead, exemplary in their complex and transnational solidarity with one another and the future, the members of the Frankfurt School propose that the project of thinking itself might prefigure a more full-blown social ethics. Their open-ended synthesis of main themes in Continental philosophy with materialist accounts of a fragmented and scarred world has pro-vided several strong foundations for theory as an independent multidiscipline. The first generation of the Frankfurt School essentially defined the problem of intellectu-als exiled in a massified culture; the second renewed rationalist grounds for postwar legal and social reconstruction; and a new generation, equipped with republications and translations of major texts by Adorno and Benjamin, is poised to revive critical and dialectical analysis of the social structures of suffering in the global situation.

VINCENT P. PECORA AND CAREN IRR

See also THEODOR W. ADORNO, WALTER BENJAMIN, SIGMUND FREUD, and MARXIST THEORY AND CRITICISM.

See also bibliographies for THEODOR W. ADORNO and WALTER BENJAMIN.

Theodor Adorno, Ästhetische Theorie (1970, Aesthetic Theory, trans. Robert Hullot-Kentor, 1997), Minima Moralia: Reflexionen aus dem beschädigten Leben (1950, Minima Moralia: Reflections from Damaged Life, trans. Edmund Jephcott, 1978); Theodor W. Adorno with Else Frenkel-Brunswik, Daniel J. Levinson, and R. Nevitt Sanford, The Authoritarian Personality (1950); Andrew Arato and Eike Gebhardt, eds., The Essential Frankfurt School Reader (1978); Jürgen Habermas, Erkenntnis und Interesse (1968, Knowledge and Human Interests, trans. Jeremy J. Shapiro, 1972), Der philosophische Diskurs der Moderne (1985, The Philosophical Discourse of Modernity, trans. Frederick Lawrence, 1987), Theorie des kommunikativen Handelns (2 vols., 1981, The Theory of Communicative Action, trans. Thomas McCarthy, 1983–1987); Axel Honneth, Kampf um Anerkennung: Zur moralischen Grammatik sozialer Konflikte (1992, The Struggle for Recognition: The Moral Grammar of Social Conflicts, trans. Joel Anderson, 1995); Max Horkheimer, Kritische Theorie (ed. Alfred Schmidt, 2 vols., 1968, Critical Theory, trans. Matthew J. O'Connell et al., 1972), "Traditionelle und kritische Theorie" (1937, "Traditional and Critical Theory," Horkheimer, Critical Theory), "Zum Problem der Wahrheit" (1935, "On the Problem of Truth," Arato); Max Horkheimer and Theodor W. Adorno, Dialektik der Aufklärung: Philosophische Fragmente (1947, Dialectic of Enlightenment, trans. John Cumming, 1972); Institute for Social Research, Studien über Autorität und Familie (1936), Leo Lowenthal, Literature and the Image of Man (1957), Literature, Popular Culture, and Society (1961); Herbert Marcuse, "Repressive Tolerance" (Marcuse et al., Critique); Herbert Marcuse with Robert P. Wolff and Barrington Moore Jr., A Critique of Pure Tolerance (1965); Rolf Wiggershaus, The Frankfurt School: Its History, Theories, and Political Significance (1994).

French Theory and Criticism: 1945 and After

Since contemporary French theory traverses many fields, one should not be surprised that it eludes synthesis. It, however, commonly draws on G. W. F. Hegel, Karl Marx and Friedrich Engels, Friedrich Nietzsche, Edmund Husserl, SIGMUND FREUD, FERDINAND DE SAUSSURE, MARTIN HEIDEGGER, Claude Lévi-Strauss, and Jean-Paul Sartre as basic reference points. Those who have recognized the important contributions of French theory have themselves mapped out new fields of critical inquiry based on the works of writers such as MICHEL FOUCAULT, JACQUES DERRIDA, LUCE IRIGARAY, JACQUES LACAN, JEAN BAUDRILLARD, and JULIA KRISTEVA. Although it appears to have emerged full-blown in the 1960s, a longer view shows that it reflected a profound rediscovery of intellectual currents that predated World War II as well as their reworking by a very young generation of intellectuals who were using structuralist approaches.

To a large extent, theorists such as GEORGES BATAILLE and Lacan had already forged these links prior to the 1960s. However, the younger generation had taken such analyses further by applying them to a number of fields and projects that argued for a more profound paradigm shift in intellectual history than had been previously thought plausible. Whereas Bataille, MAURICE BLANCHOT, Lacan, Lévi-Strauss, Roman Jakobson, and Alain Robbe-Grillet had gone a long way toward demystifying the Cartesian notion of the subject by means of anthropological, phenomenological, psychoanalytic, linguistic, and even existential analyses, the younger generation of theorists during the 1960s radically redefined entire historical periods and institutional histories. What makes this period especially exciting is the fact that most of the younger intellectuals produced brilliant analyses without having a well-defined sense of where they were headed as a group. Although in retrospect we can talk about STRUCTURALISM or poststructuralism, during the 1960s almost every major book or essay had the effect of opening up ways of thinking that had been unimaginable in the 1950s.

Given time, of course, we have become familiar with many antecedents. For example, Lacan's publication of the *Écrits* in 1966 was largely an object lesson in intellectual history, given that most of the essays were developed in the decade prior to what some have called the new learning. Yet, even the *Écrits* had the force of yet another pathbreaking text. Lévi-Strauss's *The Savage Mind* (1966) and *Mythologies* (1964–1971) had a very similar impact, as did translation and republication of many essays by Jakobson and the discovery of the work of MIKHAIL BAKHTIN. Developed in the years prior to the 1960s, then, the theories of these writers were read as if a lost continent of thought had suddenly been rediscovered.

Literary analysis, which had been important for figures such as Bataille, Blanchot, Lacan, Jakobson, and Lévi-Strauss, played a major role in the development of French thought in the 1960s, as can be seen in the journal *Tel Quel*, begun in the first year of the decade under the direction of a young novelist, Philippe Sollers. In many respects, *Tel Quel* could be considered the single most important French periodical of the second half of the twentieth century, since under its auspices contemporary French theory as we know it was brought into being. *Tel Quel* staged the intellectual context within which the writings of Foucault, Derrida, ROLAND BARTHES, Lacan, Kristeva, Sollers, and Gilles Deleuze could be understood as a highly diversified intellectual movement that overturned Sartrean existentialism (see GILLES DELEUZE AND FÉLIX GUATTARI).

An important and often overlooked prelude to this displacement is the conflict between Sartrean *littérature engagée* and the *nouveaux romanciers*, whose major proponents in the 1950s were the novelist Robbe-Grillet and the literary critic Barthes. While Sartre in "Why Write?" (1947) argues that a literary work affirms or negates various relations with the world, Robbe-Grillet claims that the logic of writing cannot be reduced to the reliable judgment of a real or implied author or to the real conditions of the world. In "Authors and Writers" (1960), Barthes argues that language should not be reduced to a vehicle or instrument for the "writer," who is a "transitive" individual for whom writing is merely communication. In a sentence indebted to the thinking of Robbe-Grillet, Barthes notes that

> by identifying himself with language, the author loses all claim to truth, for language is precisely that structure whose very goal (at least historically, since the Sophists), once it is no longer rigorously transitive, is to neutralize the true and the false. But what he obviously gains is the power to disturb the world, to afford it the dizzying spectacle of praxis without sanction. This is why it is absurd to ask an author for "commitment." (146).

Such literary theorizing also had direct antecedents in Blanchot's wartime criticism and fiction, which deemphasized the subject as an active agent, even though there were strong suggestions of willed negativity. In "The Silence of Mallarmé," Stéphane Mallarmé is praised as follows:

> One could say that Mallarmé, by an extraordinary effort of asceticism, opened an abyss in himself where his awareness, instead of losing itself, survives and grasps its solitude in a desperate clarity. Having detached himself utterly and ceaselessly from all that appears, he is like the hero of emptiness, and the night that he touches reduces him to an indefinite refusal to be no matter what—which is the very designation even of spirit. (101)

"The Silence of Mallarmé" is reminiscent of Sartrean negation ("le Néant" is explicitly mentioned). Yet in Blanchot the subject simply disappears and utterly disavows itself of the presence with which it might make any sort of claim, a disappearance Sartre could have viewed as existentially counteractive. Mallarmé simply subtracts himself from the world.

Mention of Blanchot is crucial in considering not only the history of a French avant-garde debate with *littérature engagée* that preceded the 1950s but a political division as well, since, unlike Sartre, Blanchot inclined to the right before World War II. In fact, critics such as Jeffrey Mehlman have pointed out that the intellectual movement associated with *Tel Quel* thinking had numerous affinities with French intellectuals who had not unambiguously sided against fascism. However, *Tel Quel* had taken pains to advance itself as a leftist theoretical movement by exploring the possibilities of a structuralist Marxism, which it sought to apply to linguistic and psychoanalytic theory (see MARXIST THEORY AND CRITICISM: 2. STRUCTURALIST MARXISM). One was left to puzzle, then, the extent to which the leftist slant was used to repatriate a number of intellectuals who before the 1960s were relatively isolated, obscure, and, in some people's eyes, politically objectionable.

Such a collapsing of difference was also reflected in the hybridization of disciplines such as linguistics, psychoanalysis, literary criticism, history, social theory, anthropology, and philosophy. And here once more common cause was the result, as fairly incompatible figures such as Saussure and Freud or Marx and Heidegger were being revised in order to achieve theoretical linkage. Overall, such violations of difference were viewed as liberating insofar as they produced sensationalistic theoretical advances that would become fundamental for a future generation of French humanists.

It is often forgotten that Foucault was himself an excellent literary critic whose early book *Raymond Roussel* (1963) discusses discursive multilevels, false bottoms, embedding, mistaken conjunctions, antitextualities, metagrams, self-generated sentences, cryptograms, reversed images, coincidences, fragmented spaces, and seriality. In short, *Raymond Roussel* can be read both as a commentary on the practices of the *noveau roman* written before its advent in the 1950s and as a prototypical text anticipating studies such as *The Archaeology of Knowledge* (1969). Already in *Birth of the Clinic* (1963) Foucault looks at eighteenth-century medicine in a way quite reminiscent of the Roussel book in that he defines medical knowledge according to the "regularities" and "mappings" of discourse and how they create orders that do not, in fact, coincide. What in Roussel is viewed as the development of a writing whose "surface" negates space and time is now discovered in the medical writing of the eighteenth century.

The Order of Things (1966) similarly applies literary-critical paradigms borrowed from structuralism. Although Foucault's heterogeneous descriptions of the Middle Ages and the Renaissance do not withstand close archival scrutiny, they succeed in demonstrating how discursive and cultural practices determine and are determined by shifting assumptions about signification that are not always in phase when one looks at culture synchronically. That this view, so important today for American NEW HISTORICISM, is traceable back to the study of an avant-garde writer such as Roussel suggests the extent to which Foucault transgresses disciplinary differences.

The application of literary-critical practices to social or historical phenomena is also evident in the work of Barthes, whose *Mythologies* (1957) combines acute aesthetic sensibilities with an ability to improvise with semiological categories derived from linguistics. In *Roland Barthes: The Professor of Desire* (1983), Steven Ungar notes that "instead of concentrating on the objective forms of [popular myths], Barthes analyzes how they are produced, circulated, and exchanged—in other words, how myths manipulate the processes of meaning in order to create what purport to reflect collective conceptions of reality and 'human nature'" (21). Here, Barthes's mode of analysis depends largely on a talent for grasping inferences and details in a way characteristic of literary and art critics. Barthes demonstrates, for example, how cultural events are secondary or even tertiary modeling systems whose deep structure could be explained through linguistic and semiotic categories.

Indeed, by the latter half of the 1960s a common question for many *Tel Quel* intellectuals was how to think of language as a mode of production within Freudian, Marxist, and Saussurean contexts. Jean-Joseph Goux, who went furthest in terms of linking economy to linguistics, attempted to develop his work primarily in relation to Marxist thought. And for those who have wondered about the road not taken by Derrida in the late 1960s, when Marxism awaited him with open arms, Goux's "Marx and the Inscription of Work" of 1968 provides a rare glimpse of how Derrida's *Of Grammatology* was viewed by his Marxist contemporaries. Goux argues that the concrete labor of producing signs needs to be seen in terms of Derridean "traces" accompanying a system of meaning in which the difference between production (writing) and circulation (exchange, value, meaning) is effaced in bourgeois culture (201).

Kristeva's "Semiotics: A Critical Science and/or a Critique of Science" (1968) makes a similar case; however, Kristeva is more sensitive to matters of literary contexts. She, too, writes that one ought to "adopt the term writing when it concerns a text seen as a production, in order to distinguish it from concepts of 'literature' from 'speech'" (86). According to Kristeva, the literature of writers such as James Joyce, Mallarmé, Roussel, and the comte de Lautréamont is not reducible to representation and can only be considered in terms of its practices of productivity. Like Goux, Kristeva argues that

> the semiology of production will therefore accentuate the *alterity* of its object in its relation with the representable and representative) object of exchange examined by the exact sciences. At the same time, it will accentuate the upheaval of (exact) scientific terminology by shifting it towards that other sense of work that exists prior to value and which can only be glimpsed today. (86)

Often overlooked is that by this time Kristeva, only in her mid-twenties, already exerted considerable influence on her immediate circle. Jean-Louis Houdebine, for example, was a Marxist critic whose conception of language and textuality was almost entirely indebted to Kristeva's intertextual understanding of SEMIOTICS. And Goux also appears to have been influenced by her. However, in Goux, and already to some extent in Kristeva herself, the influence of Derrida's notions of écriture and "trace" were quite perceptible in the wake of the simultaneous publication in 1967 of Derrida's *Of Grammatology, Writing and Difference,* and *Speech and Phenomena.*

Clearly, the *Tel Quel* group, of which Derrida was a part, saw *Of Grammatology* as a preface to a major work on Marx and Lenin. Unlike Derrida, however, *Tel Quel* critics such as Kristeva did not see the philosophical implications of their approach in a very broad historical sense. For their sights were too narrowly trained on, first, developing formal semiotic methods of analysis and, second, reinventing Marxism-Leninism. Because Derrida was not too interested in either venture, he could engage intellectual history in a broader manner even while he attacked the very people the *Tel Quel* critics held in high esteem, particularly Saussure and Lévi-Strauss. If *Of Grammatology* is an assault on the metaphysics of eighteenth-century language theory, it is just as much a disassembling of the rationales for trusting the semiotic adventure.

In fact, *Tel Quel's* interest in semiotics extended back to a general interest in Russian formalism, which Kristeva and others were hoping to merge with semio-linguistic approaches pioneered by Jakobson, Louis Hjelmslev, Noam Chomsky, Lévi-Strauss, and Émile Benveniste. However, within the *Tel Quel* group there were also theorists who, like Barthes, were conversant in semiotics while at the same time able to subordinate that study to structural analyses. Jean Ricardou, for example, was a formalist critic whose main interest was the *nouveau roman.* His work of the period focuses largely on literary devices or strategies that were the stock in trade of novelists such as Robbe-Grillet, Michel Butor, and Claude Simon.

Tzvetan Todorov's readings of Henry James in *Poetics of Prose* (1971) were, like Anglo-America readings, concerned with metatextuality. Todorov's earlier writings also develop Kristeva's notion of the intertext by considering the code formed by means of an identification of predicates. In medieval romance the following schema is typical: the sun illuminates; Christ illuminates; the sun therefore signifies Christ. Narrative descriptions in which terms such as "sun" occur can thus be linked to prefabricated religious intertexts. Todorov's assertion that emphasis on predication deemphasized agency mirrors the general slant of structuralist poetics away from subject-centered analyses.

Gérard Genette, also closely affiliated with *Tel Quel,* published a number of essays under the title *Figures* (1966–1972) that similarly focused on literary language as a complex interrelation of multiple signifying processes that constitute rather than merely imitate the referent. One of Genette's major accomplishments is overturning the mimesis-diegesis hierarchy in which showing is considered superior to telling. The overturning of this distinction has some resonances with the overturning of the distinction between voice and writing in Derrida's *Of Grammatology.* But Genette's aim is not to utterly scrap all narrative theory but rather to reformulate it and provide us with a more reliable analytical vocabulary.

Whereas Kristeva's semiotic analyses are beyond the competency of most language and literature professors, Genette's methods and terminology are accessible and user-friendly. Whereas Barthes proliferated numerous semiological approaches, Genette has attempted to build a systematic approach to considering narrative. In general, Genette and other structuralist critics (Claude Bremond, Michael Riffaterre, Philippe Hamon, Laurent Jenny, Paul Zumthor) make plausible the Russian formalist assumption that we should not read by way of reference to what Riffaterre has called a mimetic fallacy, according to which words transparently reflect a priori referents. Hence, notions such as character, point of view, or setting should be considered not as things but as artificially constituted verbal structures.

May 1968 marked an important moment in French history as students and workers unified in a strike against the government. For many intellectuals, this time resembled the Paris Commune, roughly a century earlier. In 1968, however, the Communist Party was less revolutionary than the nonparty Left, which encouraged free self-expression. Tel Quel, for example, maintained that the invention of new practices of writing (semiotics, grammatology) would change the modes of signifying production, thereby triggering a social revolution through the transformation of the French language. Certain followers of Jacques Lacan connected the liberation and transformation of language to the conviction that the unconscious is structured like a language, seeking to allow the unconscious to be heard and to have its effect on authoritarian, bourgeois forms of expression.

While contemporary French feminism did not originate in the events of May 1968, this historic moment contributed to the public's awareness that the time had come for social revolution and that reconsidering the status of women was integral to this process. Importantly, 1968 witnessed the formation of Psychanalyse et Politique (Psych et Po), which founded the feminist publishing house Éditions des Femmes. With the support of this press, feminist writers began exploring écriture féminine. Such writing refers specifically to a mode of semiotic production, in the Kristevean sense, that is inseparable from the impact of unconscious processes on somatic conditions particular to the female gender. From a theoretical standpoint, écriture féminine emphasizes the possibility that gender introduces yet another set of questions pertaining to "difference" that must be considered alongside the Derridean critique of semiotic binarism ("Différance"). (See FEMINIST THEORY AND CRITICISM: 3. POSTSTRUCTURALIST FEMINISMS).

The group supporting Tel Quel had been important in this development, but owing to its diversity and the emergence of autonomous thinkers from within its ranks, it began to split apart by 1970. In 1968, the radical leftist critic Jean Pierre Faye formed the Change group and criticized Tel Quel for its overly linguistic orientation and sympathy for right-wing ideologies (i.e., Derrida's Heideggerianism). The enthusiasm of

May 1968 affected many Tel Quel contributors, encouraging more political and revolutionary theories and impelling the group toward Leninism and, via Philippe Sollers and Julia Kristeva, Maoism. By June 1971, Tel Quel had made a decided commitment to Maoist thought, marked by Maria Antonietta Macciocchi's Daily Life in Revolutionary China (1971) and underscored in 1974 by Kristeva's About Chinese Women.

By 1970, Derrida had left Tel Quel, departing through his famous interviews with Kristeva, Jean-Louis Houdebine, Guy Scarpetta, and Henri Ronse. The interviews address Derrida's rejection of Tel Quel's materialist interpretation of grammatology, his closeness to Heideggerian thinking, and his rejection of Lacan. Arguing against the Tel Quel group, Derrida indicates that he was politically much more conservative than had been generally assumed. During the 1970s, Derrida became closely associated with a group of sympathetic colleagues whose most prominent figures included JEAN-LUC NANCY, Philippe Lacoue-Labarthe, Sarah Kofman, and JEAN-FRANÇOIS LYOTARD.

Meanwhile, although never strictly affiliated with Tel Quel, Lacan became an important theoretical presence for the group, with Sollers's writings increasingly reflecting Lacanian thought and Kristeva participating in his seminars. Broadly speaking, Lacan's career falls into roughly four phases: a relatively conservative French psychiatric phase flirting with psychoanalysis and surrealism before World War II; a renegade phase in the 1950s, when he brought Husserlian, Hegelian, Saussurean, Heideggerian, Jakobsonian, and Lévi-Straussian thought to bear on Freud; an Olympian phase in the 1960s and early 1970s, when he had successfully founded his own École Freudienne and began to develop mathematical and logical models built on his earlier teachings; and a somewhat diminished phase in the late 1970s, when he drifted into maddening inscrutability and turned the reins over to his son-in-law, Jacques-Alain Miller. Essentially, Lacan is an existential psychologist who radicalizes Jean-Paul Sartre's disassembly of Cartesianism by transferring Sartre's central insights into contexts that Sartre was unable to negotiate, particularly structuralist linguistics and anthropology. Furthermore, Lacan grounds such intellectual acrobatics in Freudian psychology and clinical experiences.

Lacan's idea that the unconscious is structured like a language appealed to the Tel Quel critics because it opened the way for a materialist interpretation embraced by feminists of the Psych et Po group. His semio-linguistic analyses not only "decenter" the Cartesian subject but also address modes of linguistic production, paying attention to gender difference. His argument that the "phallus" is just a signifier whose meaning is divided between two incommensurable sexualities allows for an anthropological understanding of gender that escapes patriarchal essentialism. Yet even as Lacan deconstituted phallogocentrism, feminists criticized the misogyny of many of his comments. Furthermore, despite his historically progressive stands as regards homosexuality, his psychoanalysis nevertheless presupposes a nuclear triadic relation between father, mother, and child. What he called the "Law of the Father" is always operative, even in female homosexuality.

In 1974, Luce Irigaray, a linguist and Lacanian psychoanalyst, published a break-away study entitled *Speculum of the Other Woman* (1974), in which she turned against Freud the father and, by implication, Lacan. Like the surrealists of the 1920s, Irigaray embraces hysteria not as a malady but as another way of thinking systematically suppressed by Western society in a manner that carries the traces of hysteria's irrationality within itself. In *Tel Quel*'s terms, the semiotic is effaced in the symbolic, although its traces can be detected in the very place of its repression. Linking hysteria and the feminine, Irigaray analyzes its semiotic trace-work in the writings of influential male thinkers: Plato, Aristotle, René Descartes, Freud. As *Speculum* argues, it is this trace- or out-work in male discourse that constitutes woman as Other. Irigaray considers woman not as a reified Other but rather as an arche-trace that is unrepresentable and unrealized. Although Irigaray's work seeks to depart from Lacanianism, her thesis still confirms Lacan's saying that "for man woman is a symptom." In *This Sex Which Is Not One* (1977) Irigaray argues that, physiologically, woman's body has consequences for expression that impact on a phallocentric discourse. This thesis champions an *écriture feminine* in which woman's writing is necessarily a writing of the body, an argument that stems from Lacan's topological models in which psychology is configured geometrically in terms of "bodies." Whereas Lacan avoids literalizing these topological spaces in terms of male and female physiology, Irigaray argues for a materialization of gender that reintroduces the essentialist and empirical assumptions avoided by Lacan.

HÉLÈNE CIXOUS, a literary critic, writer of fiction, and dramatist, shares Irigaray's sense that Freudian psychoanalysis is yet another institution sanctioning violence against women. Cixous's dramatization of the Dora case is a terrible indictment of Freud. In 1975, she collaborated with Catherine Clément to write *The Newly Born Woman*. In that work, Clément, one of Lacan's most devoted seminarians and perhaps his clearest expositor, contributes an essay on sorcery and hysteria that raises the question of abjection and the female body in order to speak about repression, transgression, and revolution. In particular, hysteria and witchcraft are seen in historical terms as linked to the feminine, exposing the unrepresentable, dredging up abjection, and heightening castration anxiety. Clément attacks the Lacanian belief that woman, as hysteric, presents her mystery to an other because she believes that this will lead to a meaningful relationship, when, in fact, she is obviating the very object through which a proper (sexual) relationship can be established. The hysteric or witch, Clément believes, "returns the repressed" in such a way that we have to think entirely outside of these Lacanian parameters. In "Sorties," Cixous strategically overturns prejudicial oppositions in order to create a systemic revaluation of hierarchical structures. Influenced by Derrida's "Plato's Pharmacy" (1968), she views the distinction between logos and writing as akin to distinctions between male and female, master and slave, son and father. Whereas Clément reveals the historical condition of woman as viewed by patriarchy, Cixous writes from the side of the Other. In doing so, she considers a body that is not definable in masculine terms, since it is not logocentric but rather typified by polymorphous intensities that do not necessarily converge.

Whereas feminists explored the surrealist notion of hysteria as a theoretical model for contemporary feminism, Gilles Deleuze and Félix Guattari rediscovered a surrealist passion for more general psychotic experience. In *Anti-Oedipus* (1972), they reinvent schizophrenia as a new cultural paradigm. This thinking develops a libidinal notion of capitalist economy whose logic is made up of "flows" that deterritorialize and reterritorialize not only geographical but psychical boundaries. *Anti-Oedipus* argues that capitalist production relies on "antiproduction," or the violent undoing of codes, lack amid overabundance, and increased illiteracy amid increases in knowledge. In *A Thousand Plateaus* (1980), the second volume of *Capitalism and Schizophrenia*, Deleuze and Guattari define the notion of deterritorialization in terms of rhizomes, molecules, nomads, stratoanalyses, black holes, and particle physics. Central to the notion of a "thousand plateaus" are all the possible assemblages formed in both the organic and inorganic spheres and how they defy Western categories of thought inherited from the ancient Greeks.

Guattari, whose work is less well known than Deleuze's, has written a number of independent studies that focus on molecularization. In *Molecular Revolution* (1977) and *The Machinic Unconscious* (1979), he developed the biological, geological, and cosmic analogies crucial to *A Thousand Plateaus*. Guattari's antipsychiatric bias led him to see schizophrenia as a model for explaining phenomena on a more or less global order.

Deleuze, one of the most prolific among the French theorists, published his first book, *Empiricism and Subjectivity*, in 1953 and continued to explore radical subjectivities for the rest of his life. He published two books on Friedrich Nietzsche, two on Baruch Spinoza, and two on Henri Bergson, as well as book-length studies of Immanuel Kant, Gottfried Wilhelm Leibniz, and Marcel Proust. Additionally, in the late 1960s, he published what are perhaps his two most outstanding volumes, *Logic of Sense* (1969) and *Difference and Repetition* (1968). *Logic of Sense* introduces concepts, such as the body without organs, the disorganization and reorganization of libidinal zones, the traversal of surfaces, pathological models of replication, the dismantling of Oedipus, and modes of antiproduction—all of major significance to the capitalism-and-schizophrenia project, but also the central concerns of his very significant contribution to film studies, *The Movement-Image* (1983) and *The Time-Image* (1985). Deleuze's writings on cinema interrogate what is marginal to the image and what has fallen into its background. He argues that cinema studies has erred in assuming a presence of the image as perceptual event, a presence that effaces the fading or dissolution of the image according to a logic of time that plays havoc with a metaphysical or presenced understanding of film as a totalized unity that can be categorically split up into thinglike appearances.

Another major thinker of this period who uses scientific analogies is Michel Serres, one of the most lyrical and erudite of all contemporary French critics. Serres became known for analyzing the aberrant or catastrophic nature of complex systems of referenceless exchange. He was not a Marxist but a communications or information theorist. Having a rare grasp of many fields, Serres published five books on communications theory and culture under the general title *Hermès* (1968–1980) and a number of other books on topics such as Jules Verne, Émile Zola, Vittore Carpaccio, and the cybernetic notion of parasitism. He argues that communication is determined by chance and is not, strictly speaking, a reversible process. Meaning is controlled by the unpredictable interruption of nonmeaning, parasitic intrusions that ultimately become nodal points for new signifying systems. *The Parasite* (1980) is perhaps Serres's most ambitious study and marks the limit where formality and randomness become undecidable and open onto a "fuzzy logic." The parasite demonstrates how scientific models allow us to transcend a binary logic of communication in order to consider literature in terms of fuzzy sets where a stochastic fraying of differences overcomes dialectic.

While Serres implicitly relates to the scientific interests of Deleuze and Guattari, Jean Baudrillard shares their economic interests. Unlike Deleuze and Guattari, however, Baudrillard is more closely tied to figures such as Roland Barthes, Michel Foucault, Jean-Joseph Goux, and even Lacan. Like his *Tel Quel* contemporaries, Baudrillard sought to fuse Marxism with Ferdinand de Saussure and Freud. *The System of Objects* (1968) suggests that bourgeois objects are part of a symbolic economy with linguistic features and that consumption is linked to the performance of this language. In *The Mirror of Production* (1973) Baudrillard notes that in First World countries the chief economic modes of production have shifted from fabricating material goods to producing symbolic codes of exchange. Following Deleuze and Lyotard, Baudrillard argues in *Symbolic Exchange and Death* (1976) that the symbolic orders of capitalist production have no absolute anchorage point or reference and that their value fluctuates erratically as they are hastily exchanged throughout society. These symbolic orders are predicated not on reality but on hyperreal or imaginary constructions. He predicts that eventually the processes of symbolic exchange will collapse into their absent center of reference.

In *Simulacra and Simulations* (1981) Baudrillard argues that we live in a simulation society and that our consciousness is formed by performing processes of symbolic exchange that are always on the verge of crashing. Between 1987 and 2000, he published four volumes of *Cool Memories*, a commentary on postmodern culture in America, and in 1990 came *The Transparency of Evil*. In *Transparency*, Baudrillard argues that Westerners live in a state of radical agnosticism in which everything tends toward complete "indifference," the only appropriate attitude in a world where beliefs no longer refer to universally held truths. Unlike Foucault and Althusser, Baudrillard is very indebted to Lacanian psychoanalysis and to a Deleuzian notion of simulation.

An important part of Baudrillard's work, however, has been a moralistic disapproval of mass culture. Whereas Deleuze and Guattari celebrate the rhizome, Baudrillard is suspicious of a postmodern condition that produces a collective surface composed of simulations feigning difference.

As the 1970s waned, many of the intellectuals associated with *Tel Quel* during the 1960s had achieved great distinction as major thinkers. By the late 1970s, Derrida's major work was translated into English, though long before that he had had a strong influence on critical theorists in England and America. Foucault's numerous interviews and his *Archaeology of Knowledge, Discipline and Punish* (1975), and *The History of Sexuality* (1976–1984) also had especial impact in Anglo-American universities. Because Foucault's work often centered on victims it invited a recuperation of the social subject in the English and American tradition, thereby producing movements such as New Historicism. Kristeva's *Revolution in Poetic Language* (1974), *Polylogue* (1977), and *Powers of Horror* (1983) mark a decisive shift from semio-Marxism to post-Lacanian psychoanalytical analyses. As a practicing analyst, she advanced a pathbreaking notion of abjection, later followed by a study on depression (*Black Sun: Depression and Melancholia* [1987]). Anglo-American feminists, wary of Kristeva's allegiance to Lacan, have studied these texts with intensity since the early 1980s. Baudrillard and Deleuze, for their part, had to wait for recognition abroad, which grew out of interest in POSTMODERNISM.

Importantly, since the late 1970s there has been very little interest outside of French departments in the younger generations of French intellectuals who have moved away from what one might call the *Tel Quelism* of the 1960s, what some in France have called *la pensée soixante-huit*. Toward the close of the 1970s, for example, the *nouveaux philosophes*, such as André Glucksmann (*The Master Thinkers* [1977]) and Bernard-Henri Lévy (*Barbarism with a Human Face* [1977]), received little recognition abroad, despite their anticipation of the breakup of the Soviet Union and the liberal Left's lurch to an intolerant politics. During this time, a number of young French philosophers, registering considerable annoyance with *la pensée soixante-huit*, turned to pragmatism. Analytic philosophy rather than existential phenomenology also became privileged.

Clément Rosset's work of the 1970s on the "real" moved away from the structuralists' notion that reality is a "language effect." For Rosset, the real is composed of singular objects pointing to nothing other than "aspects of the real." In *The Unique Object* (1979), Rosset explains that the singular object's uniqueness precedes its becoming unusual, strange, or *l'idiot*. The object is not unique because it is unusual; it is unusual insofar as it is unique. Rosset maintains that the singularity or uniqueness of an object distances it from any discourse that would put it into a categorical (i.e., imaginary) relationship with any other object. For Rosset, the uniqueness of all things possesses a latent "absurdity." In *The Philosopher and Sorcery* (1985) Rosset argues that thinkers such as Bataille, Derrida, and Lacan have appealed to an exorcism of the real by invoking that which is always "other" or "elsewhere." Rosset argues that the notions of "evil" in Bataille, of the "arche-trace" in Derrida, and of "lack" in Lacan are part of a philosophical magic trick that grounds the spectral in a kind of backhanded positivism.

Like Rosset, Jacques Bouveresse has been highly critical of the so-called *pensée soixante-huit*. In *The Autophagic Philosopher* (1984), Bouveresse draws on figures such as Manfred Frank, Peter Sloterdijk, Peter Geach, Karl Popper, and Richard Rorty in order to question what *real* philosophers are supposed to undertake as philosophical research. The thinkers of 1968, Bouveresse argues, catapulted philosophy into a postphilosophical moment where "revolutionary phraseologies" have been subject to automatization thanks to STRUCTURALISM's bracketing of the cogito. Citing Manfred Frank's *The Subject and the Text* (1980), Bouveresse agrees with the Heidelberg school that the "subject"'s being difficult to locate (as in, presumably, the works of Foucault) does not mean that individuals have not worked collectively to achieve some aim. Structuralism, according to Bouveresse, conveniently dispatches the individual into the dustbin of intellectual history so that it can develop poetic styles of writing that cumulatively build up responses to diverse questions that are not specifically philosophical at all. Bouveresse also attacks the "corporatist mentality" of academics for whom philosophy is merely a careerist enterprise. Bouveresse seeks a less self-aggrandizing role for philosophers and a return to more restricted and "properly" philosophical, that is, rationalist, topics of inquiry.

Although close to Rosset and Bouveresse in some respects, Vincent Descombes has not been overtly hostile to the thinkers who rose to prominence during the 1960s. In *The Unconscious against Itself* (1977), Descombes explores what is not said or given in the disjunction of enunciation and the enunciated. Following Lacanian theory, Descombes argues that the unconscious is the unsaid that accompanies every enunciation, an unsaid not necessarily known to the speaker but detectable nonetheless. In *Objects of All Sorts* (1983), Descombes touches on a number of issues close to Rosset and turns toward analytical philosophy, particularly to Ludwig Wittgenstein. Philosophical grammar, Descombes cautions, is not reducible to linguistics or to any other universal grammar. In studying the "object," Descombes explores various grammatical implications that are raised in a number of different disciplinary contexts, such as linguistics, ontology, and literature. In part, his study seeks to show the logical and grammatical incongruity of defining the object as one traverses various fields of inquiry. In his work on Proust (*Proust: Philosophy of the Novel* [1987]), he argues against those who read *Remembrance of Things Past* as a *récit pur*, seeing it rather as an interweaving of various rhetorical constructions. Proust's text, in other words, resembles the "object" discussed in *Objects of All Sorts*.

While those moving away from poststructuralism have been concerned with objects, grammatical relationships, the real, and rationality, intellectuals affiliated with deconstruction have considered these questions in relation to the postmodern and the sublime. These intellectuals abandoned Hegel for Kant, a striking move within the context of French intellectual history. While Derrida enacts this shift in *The Truth in Painting* (1978), Lyotard, who has published a number of studies on Kant, stands as the movement's pivotal figure. A prolific and difficult critic whose *Discourse, Figure* (1971) and *Libidinal Economy* (1974) reveal strong *Tel Quelist* concerns, his texts of the 1980s have been extremely influential.

Lyotard's complex argument spans the various trajectories of all his later publications. A useful means of organizing the major ideas is to begin with his premise in *The Postmodern Condition* (1979), where he argues that we have entered a period in which there are no master narratives. Lyotard notes that even in Kant a master narrative cannot be produced and that the faculties, far from being actual mental structures, are merely names that organize an archipelago of phrase regimes that obey the logic of the "differend" (*The Differend* [1983]). With Kant, however, the differend bears on the notion of the sublime and its relationship to what Kant calls enthusiasm. The differend is that unstable site of language wherein something cannot be put into phrases. In Kant, the term "enthusiasm" is deconstructed at the moment that it is called on to mark incompatible phrase regimes, one in which enthusiasm manifests itself as the pleasure of making rational sense out of something and another in which enthusiasm represents that negativity associated with the sublime.

The larger context for this discussion concerns Lyotard's notion of the inhuman: the dismantling of a universal subject in the name of whom societies seek liberty, freedom, and justice for all. In *The Differend*, the name Auschwitz stands for a postmodern condition in which the universal subject has been subject to the differend, the suspension of liberty, freedom, and justice for certain people. Lyotard suggests that thinkers such as Jürgen Habermas have misunderstood the role of reason and the public sphere in the Enlightenment. Moreover, Lyotard argues that the "postmodern condition" is itself not a determinate historical break but a differend that traverses a number of historical contexts.

During the 1990s, Derrida continued to publish numerous books, many of them monograph-essays like *Archive Fever* (1995) (on the Freud archives), *Monolinguism of the Other* (1996) (on language in relation to the foreign), and *Demeure* (1998) (on Maurice Blanchot). He also published larger works like *Specters of Marx* (1993) (on historical revenance) and *The Politics of Friendship* (1994) (on the concept of the friend). In general, much of this work addresses Blanchot's idea of the "unavowable community" and is in correspondence with the work of EMMANUAL LEVINAS and Nancy.

Meanwhile, the world of Lacanian psychoanalysis fell into disunity following Lacan's death in 1980, a process that Lacan himself precipitated by dissolving his school. The most dominant group to emerge was led by Jacques-Alain Miller (Lacan's son-in-law). Other French Lacanians who rose to prominence in the 1990s include Colette Soler, Eric Laurent, Charles Mehlman, Philippe Julien, and Gérard Pommier. Nevertheless, the star who emerged among Lacan's former seminarians in the late

1990s, André Green, isn't part of the Lacanian world at all. Arguably the most respected and important psychoanalytic theorist today, Green is also affiliated with more orthodox Freudian analysts and has come to see Lacan's contributions as important but not of such significance that they should displace more orthodox understandings of the fundamentals of psychoanalysis.

A figure of interest to those who follow Jacques-Alain Miller is the philosopher ALAIN BADIOU, whose many books include Theory of the Subject (1985), Must One Think the Political? (1985), Manifesto for Philosophy (1989), Deleuze (1997), Saint Paul (1997), and Handbook of Inaesthetics (1998). His Manifesto argues for "the events of the matheme, the poem, thinking on love and inventive politics that prescribe the return of philosophy" (79). The matheme addresses "indiscernible multiplicity" (80) by defining this multiplicity in the absence of naming it as a thing in itself. Hence Badiou is concerned with what lies beyond language, but not the matheme, which is an algorithm irreducible to language.

At the end of the 1990s, Dominique Lecourt published his very polemical The Mediocracy: French Philosophy Since the Mid-1970s. Lecourt dismisses the so-called nouveau philosophes, André Glucksmann and Bernard-Henri Lévy, as part of the generation that gained prominence in the late 1970s as pretty-boy media stars of the intelligentsia. Lecourt criticizes their rejection of Marxism for some form of libertarian humanism suited to the sorts of marketing practices with which they have been associated. Some ten years after the revolution associated with May 1968, of which Tel Quel seemed so much a part, a younger generation of intellectuals had gained the public's attention. Unlike Foucault, Sollers, Kristeva, and Deleuze, they represented a return to traditional Enlightenment concerns. Glucksmann's The Master Thinkers questions paradoxes of power and calls Tel Quel's decentering, if not annihilation, of the subject into question. Alain Finkielkraut, whose work became known in the 1980s, has written a number of short books considering the Holocaust in historical and cultural retrospect. He argues that the kind of thinking advanced by intellectuals of 1968 contributes to a worldview in which historical revision is more likely to occur, because it relativizes our understanding of reality and undermines public consensus about the past. In the 1990s, Finkielkraut opposed the philosophical underpinnings of what Anglo-Americans call CULTURAL STUDIES. In Defeat of the Mind (1987), he sees the interest in "cultural identity" as a replay of the Nazi understanding of Volksgeist: political romanticism. He views culturalist conceptions of diversity and plurality as anti-Enlightenment insofar as a focus on "difference" undermines social agreement and hence its acceptance of historical reality. Similarly, Luc Ferry's Homo Aestheticus (1990) returns to questions of existential humanism by asking what representation of the self could have any meaning in the wake of deconstruction. Like Glucksmann and Finkielkraut, Ferry is also concerned with matters of individual liberty, human subjectivity, and political power. Ideologically, such thinkers wrestle with Bernard-Henri Lévy's Barbarism with a Human Face, which demonstrates that the

Enlightenment merely disguised barbarism rather than eradicated it. For such thinkers, attacks on meaning, the subject, and truth only set the stage for barbarous conflict.

Lastly, it should be noted that during the 1980s and 1990s, Kristeva and Derrida began to respond to the sorts of humanist issues raised by the *nouveau philosophes*. Derrida's ethical turn by way of Levinas and his increasing interest in the vicissitudes of rhetorical performatives that generate paradoxes of position and power, and Kristeva's critiques of the postmodern subject as narcissistic and lacking stable boundaries, are quite different reactions to the sorts of concerns introduced by the *nouveau philosophes* in the late 1970s. In the late 1990s, Kristeva and Derrida converged on the work of Hannah Arendt, Kristeva in her biography *Hannah Arendt* (1999), and Derrida in his essay "History of the Lie" (1996). Looking back at the 1980s and 1990s, Lecourt observes that even former young radicals of *Tel Quel* appear to have turned into the respectable moralizing humanitarians they once decried. At the very least, this would mean that French thought has remained in dialogue with Enlightenment questions and that these issues remain crucial for Western Europeans.

HERMAN RAPAPORT

See also bibliographies for JEAN BAUDRILLARD and GILLES DELEUZE AND FÉLIX GUATTARI.

Georges Bataille, *Oeuvres complètes* (12 vols., 1970–1988); Jean-Louis Baudry, *Les Images* (1963), *Personnes* (1967); Walter Benjamin, *Das Passagen-Werk* (ed. Rolf Tiedemann, 1982, *The Arcades Project*, ed. Rolf Tiedemann, trans. Howard Eilman and Kevin McLaughlin, 1999); Maurice Blanchot, "Le Silence de Mallarmé," *Faux pas* (1943, "The Silence of Mallarmé," *Faux Pas*, trans. Charlotte Mandell, 2001); Pierre Bourdieu, *La distinction: Critique sociale de jugement* (1979, *Distinction: A Social Critique of the Judgement of Taste*, trans. Richard Nice, 1984); Jacques Bouveresse, *Le philosophie chez les autophages* (1984); Joan Brandt, *Geopoetics* (1997); Claude Bremond, *Logique du récit* (1973); Roger Caillois, "La hiérarchie des êtres," *Les Volontaires* 5 (1939); Jean-Francois Courtine et al., *Du Sublime* (1988, *Of the Sublime*, trans. Jeffrey Librett, 1993); Michel Deguy, *Oui dire* (1966); Jacques Derrida, "Histoire du mensonge: Prolégomènes," *Euresis* 1–2 (1996, "History of the Lie," *Futures: Of Jacques Derrida*, ed. Richard Rand, 2001); Vincent Descombes, *Grammaire d'objets en tous genres* (1983, *Objects of All Sorts: A Philosophical Grammar*, trans. Lorna Scott-Fox and Jeremy Harding, 1986), *L'inconscient malgré lui* (1977), *Le même et l'autre* (1979, *Modern French Philosophy*, trans. Lorna Scott-Fox and Jeremy Harding, 1980), *Proust: Philosophie du roman* (1987, *Proust: Philosophy of the Novel*, trans. Catherine Chance, 1992); Marguerite Duras, *L'amour* (1971), *India Song* (1973, *India Song*, trans. Barbara Bray, 1976), *Le ravissement de Lol V. Stein* (1964, *The Ravishing of Lol Stein*, trans. Richard Seaver, 1966), *Le vice-consul* (1965, *The Vice-Consul*, trans. Eileen Ellenbogen, 1968); Luc Ferry, *Homo aestheticus: L'invention du gout à l'âge démocratique* (1990, *Homo Aestheticus: The Invention of Taste in the Democractic Age*, trans. Robert Loaiza, 1993); Luc Ferry and Alain Renaut, *La pensée 68: Essai sur l'anti-humanisme contemporain* (1985, *French Philosophy of the Sixties: An Essay on Antihumanism*, trans. Mary Schnackenberg Cattani, 1990); Alain Finkielkraut, *La défait de la pensée* (1987, *The Defeat of the Mind*, trans. Judith Friedlander, 1995), *Le Juif imaginaire* (1980, *The Imaginary Jew*, trans. Kevin O'Neill and David Suchoff, 1994); Michel Foucault et al., *Théorie d'ensemble* (1968); Manfred Frank, *Das Sagbare und das Unsagbare: Studien zur neuesten französischen Hermeneutik und Texttheorie* (1980, *The Subject and the Text: Essays on Literary Theory* and Philosophy, ed. Andrew Bowen, trans. Helen Atkins, 1997); Mike Gann, Baudrillard: Critical and Fatal Theory (1991), Baudrillard's Bestiary: Baudrillard and Culture (1991); Gérard Genette, Figures (3 vols., 1966–1972, Figures of Literary Discourse, trans. Alan Sheridan, 1982); André Glucksmann, Les maîtres penseurs (1977, The Master Thinkers, trans. Brian Pearce, 1980); Jean-Joseph Goux, "Marx et l'inscription du travail" (Foucault et al.); André Green, Les chaînes d'Éros (1997, Chains of Eros, trans. Luke Thurston, 2000), Un oeil en trop (1969, The Tragic Effect, trans. Alan Sheridan, 1979), On Private Madness (1996); Michel Haar, Le chant de la terre (1985, The Song of the Earth, trans. Reginald Lily, 1993); Dominique Janicaud, L'ombre de cette pensée (1990, The Shadow of That Thought, trans. Michael Gendre, 1996); Philippe Hamon, Texte et idéologie (1984); Roman Jakobson, Questions de poétique (1973); Laurent Jenny, La terreur et les signes (1982); Tony Judt, Past Imperfect: French Intellectuals, 1945–1956 (1992); Philippe Julien, Le retour à Freud de Jacques Lacan (1986, Jacque Lacan's Return to Freud, trans. Devra Beck Simiu, 1994); Julia Kristeva, L'avenir d'une révolte (1998, Intimate Revolt; and The Future of Revolt, trans. Jeanine Herman, 2002), Contre la dépression nationale (1998, Revolt, She Said, trans. Brian O'Keeffe, 2002), Crisis of the European Subject (trans. Susan Fairfield, 2000), Etrangers à nous-mêmes (1988, Strangers to Ourselves, trans. Leon Roudiez, 1991), Le genie feminin, vol. 1, Hannah Arendt (1999, Hannah Arendt, trans. Ross Guberman, 2001), "La sémiologie: Science Critique et/ou Critique de Science" (1968, "Semiotics: A Critical Science and/or a Critique of Science," trans. Seán Hand, The Kristeva Reader, ed. Toril Moi, 1986), Sens et non-sens de la révolte (1996, The Sense and Non-Sense of Revolt, 2000); Philippe Lacoue-Labarthe, Le sujet de la philosophie (1979, The Subject of Philosophy, ed. Thomas Trezise, trans. Thomas Tresize et al., 1993); Dominique Lecourt, Le piètres penseurs (1999, The Mediocracy: French Philosophy Since the Mid-1970s, trans. Gregory Elliott, 2001); Emmanuel Levinas, "Tout autrement," L'Arc 54 (1973, "Wholly Otherwise," trans. Simon Critchley, Re-reading Levinas, ed. Robert Bernasconi and Simon Critchley, 1991); Bernard-Henri Levy, La barbarie à visage humain (1977, Barbarism with a Human Face, trans. George Holoch, 1979); Maria Antonietta Macciocchi, Della China (1971, Daily Life in Revolutionary China, 1972); David Macey, Lacan in Contexts (1988); Jean Luc Marion, Réduction et donation (1989, Reduction and Givenness, trans. Thomas Carlson, 1998); Danielle Marx-Scouras, The Cultural Politics of Tel Quel (1996); Jeffrey Mehlman, Legacies: Of Anti-Semitism in France (1983); Jean-Luc Nancy, La remarque spéculative (1973, The Speculative Remark, trans. Céline Suprenant, 2001); Gérard Pommier, Le dénouement d'une analyse (1987); Jean Ricardou, Problèmes du nouveau roman (1967); Michael Riffaterre, Semiotics of Poetry (1978); Alain Robbe-Grillet, Pour un nouveau roman (1963, For a New Novel: Essays on Fiction, trans. Richard Howard, 1965); Clément Rosset, L'objet singulier (1979), Le philosophe et les sortilèges (1985); Elizabeth Roudinesco, Le bataille de cent ans, vol. 2, 1925–1985 (Jacques Lacan & Co., trans Jeffrey Mehlman, 1990); Jean-Paul Sartre, Qu'est-ce que la littérature? (1946, What Is Literature? trans. Bernard Frechtman, 1949, "What Is Literature?" and Other Essays, trans. Bernard Frechtman, 1988); Michel Serres, Esthétiques sur Carpaccio (1975), Feux et signaux de brume: Zola (1975), Hermès I: La communication (1968), Hermès II: L'interférence (1972), Hermès III: La traduction (1974), Hermès IV: La distribution (1977), Hermès V: Le passage du nord-ouest (1980), Hermes: Literature, Science, Philosophy (ed. Josué V. Harari and David F. Bell, 1982), Jouvences sur Jules Verne (1974), Le parasite (1980, The Parasite, trans. Lawrence R. Schehr, 1982); Philippe Sollers, Logiques (1968), Paradis (1981); Tzvetan Todorov, Poétique de la prose (1971, Poetics of Prose, trans. Richard Howard, 1977); Sherry Turkle, Psychoanalytic Politics: Jacques Lacan and Freud's French Revolution (1978, 2nd ed., 1992); Steven Ungar, Roland Barthes: The Professor of Desire (1983); Monique Wittig, Le corps lesbien (1973, The Lesbian Body, trans. David LeVay, 1975), Les guérillères (1969, Les Guérillères, trans. David LeVay, 1971); Paul Zumthor, Introduction à la poésie orale (1983, Oral Poetry: An Introduction, trans. Kathryn Murphy-Judy, 1990).

Freud, Sigmund

Sigmund Freud (1856–1939) was not a literary theorist. His belief in his work's objective and scientific validity was unshakable, but its impact and significance have obviously extended far beyond the narrowly scientific field. No consideration of his place in contemporary cultural thinking can ignore the fact that his theories—such as those of infantile sexuality—changed forever humanity's confidence in its mastery and control of the self.

Freud was not in any way a deliberate or conscious aesthetic theorist, but he left his mark on both literature and critical theory through his general psychoanalytic framework and also his specific turning to art to show that the range of applicability of psychoanalysis extended beyond dreams and neurosis to even the highest cultural achievements. Freud had always been interested in literature. In his "Contribution to a Questionnaire on Reading" (1906) he lists the works of Copernicus and Charles Darwin under the heading "most significant books," but he also ranks the poems and plays of Homer, Sophocles, Johann Wolfgang von Goethe, and William Shakespeare under "most magnificent works" (9:245–47). These are also among the works that provide him with his best illustrations of psychoanalytic theories.

Freud is generous in attributing to the artist the role of precursor of psychoanalysis in his or her insights into the unconscious, be it in prefiguring the significance of dreams, fetishism, repression, childhood eroticism, parapraxes, the object choice in love, the uncanny, the role of eros, daydreams, or almost anything else. Artists' sensitive perception of the hidden indicates that in their knowledge of the human mind "they are far in advance of us everyday people, for they draw upon sources which we have not yet opened up for science" (9:8). That "not yet" is both interesting and significant. In *The Childhood of Art* Sarah Kofman shows how Freud's reading of Wilhelm Jensen's *Gradiva* develops from admiration for the author's insights to astonishment that he could possibly have prefigured Freud's own findings. In other words, Freud elevates Jensen's work to the status of a case study while undercutting his achievement by pointing out that *Gradiva* only describes and does not explain: that task is left to psychoanalysis.

Whatever Freud's own ambivalence about the relation of literature and literary criticism to psychoanalysis, Freudian literary critics have explored the concerns and processes of interpretation the two share: meaning and hermeneutical method, symbolism and stylistic deviation, discourse and narrative. In addition, at least five areas of what we might call Freud's "implied" aesthetic are of special interest to literary theory. The first and most central is the primacy of the unconscious to theories of creativity and culture. There are obvious implications of such a view for the second and third areas, theories of reception (aesthetic pleasure) and theories of interpretation. The fourth area is the relationship between the artist and the work, the psyche

and the productions of its sublimation processes. And the final area is a methodological one, for Freud's comments both on art and on psychoanalysis in general
suggest a number of possible literary-critical models for applied psychoanalysis.

Whether we believe that in writing on art Freud wants only to verify his interpretation of neurotic symptoms, dreams, jokes, and parapraxes or, on the contrary, that
his ambition is actually to create an entire theory of culture, Freud sees in all cultural
and psychic phenomena the same source: the unconscious. This means that the
same principles (repression and the economy of psychic expenditure) operate and the
same mechanisms (condensation, displacement, symbolization, etc.) are brought into
play. Freud did not discover the unconscious, but he posits the unconscious mind's
general psychic structural principles and contents. He argues that despite individual
variants, the unconscious has universal laws.

Since the unconscious is essentially and radically asocial, it can instigate the
creation of cultural phenomena only by sublimation, that is, only when the sexual
aim of the libido is turned into a cultural one via the mediation of the ego. For Freud,
this displaced libido is actually more than just animal instinct, and its sublimation is
a complex process of repression and transformation of these unconscious drives into
something more acceptable to society. Sublimation, in other words, has the power to
transform individual unconscious fantasy into universal art—a kind of legalized fantasy, halfway between a wish-frustrating reality and a wish-fulfilling world of imagination: "Art is a conventionally accepted reality in which, thanks to artistic illusion,
symbols and substitutes are able to provoke real emotions" (13:188). Freud sees art as
a path linking fantasy and reality (16:375–77). But this makes art into a kind of alternative to neurosis rather than the unrepressed, unconscious sexual drives; the artist
"can transform his phantasies into artistic creations instead of into symptoms"
(11:50) and by this linking path of art regain contact with reality. Art is social and
public; neurosis is asocial and private. For Freud, the artist, always seen as male, is "in
rudiments an introvert, not far removed from neurosis" (16:376), a man who is oppressed by excessively powerful instinctual needs for honor, power, wealth, fame, and
the love of women but lacks the means of achieving satisfaction. This was where sublimation comes into play: fantasy, the substitute satisfaction of all people, becomes
the reserve, the psychic realm free from the reality principle.

This central Freudian tenet, as expressed in the 1916–1917 Introductory Lectures in
Psycho-Analysis, was first expounded in 1908 in an important paper entitled "Creative
Writers and Day-Dreaming." For Freud, the artist is one who can eliminate the
overly personal (and therefore repellent) from his daydreams and thereby let others
enjoy them too. He is able to hide the "origin from proscribed sources" of the daydreams and also possesses "the mysterious power of shaping some particular material until it has become a faithful image of his phantasy" (16:376). Therefore, others
can derive consolation from their own unconscious depths, which had been inaccessible until this pleasure yield lifted the repression. So the artist manages to

achieve *through* fantasy what he had wished for *in* fantasy: the fruits of success (see also 13:187).

In suggesting non-rational origins for art, Freud is in a sense only reworking a version of the old tradition of the divinely inspired poet. But the artist, in Freud's view, is also like a daydreamer because he can objectify the subjective into a public, socially acceptable form—art—instead of turning it into private neurotic symptoms. This analogy allows Freud to suggest that fantasies called art can therefore be interpreted by means of the methods of dream analysis. Freud had made an early and very strong commitment to the value of such analysis. "The interpretation of dreams," he emphasizes, "is the royal road to a knowledge of the unconscious activities of the mind" (5:608). Writers, Freud duly notes, have always granted dreams great significance. His study of the dreams in Jensen's *Gradiva* corroborated his own clinical findings about the structures, mechanisms, and interpretations of dreams, but this did not surprise Freud in the least.

Works of art support Freud's theories, but the artist's fantasy involves more than daydreaming or hallucinatory wish fulfillment and its reworking into a shareable form. Here Freud turns to children's fantasies in play for an additional analogy, for play involves control and mastery as much as fantasy. The hero of every story, the one who controls, is an embodiment of the ego, the part of the psyche whose role it is to master both reality and the unconscious. Daydreams, writes Freud in summary, "are the raw material of poetic production. . . . The hero of the day-dreams is always the subject himself, either directly or by an obvious identification with someone else" (15:99).

Many questions can be raised at this point regarding Freud's choice of analogue for art and artistic creation. Since dreams have no aesthetic value per se for Freud, where does the aesthetic value in art lie? Form is seen only as a disguise or as a bribe of forepleasure. Even though dreams (and daydreams) and art can fulfill the same functions for the psyche—both acting as safety valves—and share similar latent structures and mechanisms, as the laws of the unconscious are said to be universal ones, daydreams and dreams are private and relatively formless on the surface, whereas art is social and formal. The main, obvious objection is that the use of dreams as a model for art reduces art to a psychological framework for something else. Part of the history of psychoanalytic literary criticism seems to suggest that the dream model has led only to facile, if attractive, formulations of the creative process. The ego psychologists most radically questioned the adequacy of the concept of sublimation. Later, psychologists working directly with artists questioned even the primacy of the unconscious in creativity. The nonlogical primary processes of the unconscious, they argued, do not resemble the conscious elaboration that results in works of art. In other words, art resembles, if anything, the patient's *narration* of his or her dream, not the dream itself, as Émile Benveniste also argues from a linguistic point of view in *Problems in General Linguistics* (1966–1974). The repressed elements of the unconscious may exert influence, but alone they cannot account for novelty, aesthetic form, artistic conventions, or, given their discontinuity, the humanist assertion of the essential organic unity of both art and the subject. This is where poststructuralists such as JACQUES DERRIDA have been able to play with Freud's model and thereby challenge such assertions.

Condensation, displacement, symbolization, which mediate between preconscious censorship and unconscious desire, obviously resemble the processes of metonymy, metaphor, and symbol in poetry, but the actual equation of the two does not necessarily logically follow. Like works of art, those dreams, slips of the tongue and pen, jokes, and neurotic symptoms are all overdetermined, capable of being interpreted in more than one way. Freud attributes this overdetermination to an element of dreamwork that he calls "secondary revision." This is still not conscious aesthetic elaboration, for meanings are hidden and not intended for communication, but, unlike parapraxes and neurotic symptoms, jokes surely share with works of art the desire to communicate precisely their overdetermined ambiguities. For Freud, however, jokework is like dreamwork (8:54), both providing analogies for art. Freud argues that the overt, conscious order of art arises logically but from unconscious premises. The "much abused privilege of conscious activity" seems to serve only to conceal what is truly important: "We are probably inclined greatly to over-estimate the conscious character of intellectual and artistic production" (5:613). The deep unconscious structures that art shares with myth and religion as well as with dreams is what interests Freud. The manifest individuality of the work is less significant than its latent universality.

Freud's theory of the unconscious as the root of artistic creativity has certain implications not only for the production of art but also for the theory of its reception. Given the belief in psychic universality, the pleasure the viewer or reader derives from art must be directly linked to that of its creator. As early as *The Interpretation of Dreams* (1900) Freud had seen the universality of safely released repression as the key to the continuing impact of works such as *Oedipus Rex* and *Hamlet*. Artists' disguised and objectified presentation of their unconscious fantasies in the form of art produces a yield of pleasure so great that repression is lifted and the audience can "derive consolation and alleviation" (16:376). To study creativity is automatically to study reception.

Freud claims that nothing is arbitrary in art—or in any other manifestations of unconscious psychic processes. His determinism is clear as he assigns meaning to all verbal ambiguities and seeming incongruities (in jokes, dreams, parapraxes, or works of art), determinism with obvious implications for interpreting art as well as for responding to it. If we accept a manifest-latent structure for all the productions of the unconscious, the task of the analyst, literary or psychological, is to divine secret and concealed meanings by paying attention to the small, seemingly unimportant detail, which is then assumed to have significance (13:222, 229). Freud's interpretation of

Michelangelo's *Moses*, for instance, centers on the attitude of the statue's right hand and the position of the Tables of the Law. Most traditional interpretations see Moses's pose as representing the inception of action, but for Freud the statue represents the remains of a completed action. That Moses does not break the tablets can be attributed to Michelangelo's inner motives in his relations with Julius II, whose tomb this statue was to adorn. But as several generations of commentators have asked since then, by what criteria are we to judge the validity of Freud's interpretation?

The same question has been posed regarding Freud's dream interpretations. Freud is a wily defender of his own views: contradictions are often shown to be apparent, not real, and negatives are claimed to conceal positives. In dream analysis Freud uses a mixture of free association and symbol decoding (5:360). Dream symbols don't have a fixed, known meaning, but dreams use existing symbols to escape censorship and allow the repressed to be represented. And some symbols seem to have universal meanings, he argues. In addition, most dream symbols seemed to represent people, parts of the body, or activities invested with erotic interest. But given Freud's theories of repressed infantile desire, they could hardly do otherwise. The circularity of Freud's hermeneutical theory has not gone unnoticed.

Believing in these symbols' universality, Freud feels justified in applying the laws of the unconscious, which he learned from the dreams of living patients, to the creative works of dead artists. In *Leonardo da Vinci and a Memory of His Childhood* (1910) he goes beyond an interpretation of a particular work to investigate and pronounce on the psyche of the artist himself. In his writings on Goethe and Fyodor Dostoevsky, he works more in the opposite direction, interpreting works in the light of psychological details gleaned from the lives of the writers. In both cases, the artist is cast in the role of the analysand and the critic in that of the analyst. Yet Freud had earlier also credited the artist with the insights of the analyst himself. This ambivalence in Freud's characterization of the role of the artist raises the last major aspect of Freud's "implied" aesthetic. Aside from the dreamwork concept, at least three possible investigative models implied in Freud's writings theoretically could prove useful to literary theory and criticism: the model of the analytic situation, the image of archaeology that Freud loved so dearly, and the technique of superimposition of examples to yield common factors.

In the first case, if the character is seen as manifesting the symptoms of a real neurotic person, the artist is credited with prefiguring Freud's own clinical findings. The author is a protoanalyst and the character his patient. This shows Freud's deeper ambivalence about the value of art: art could be a theoretical model that could be used to validate psychoanalysis and give it credibility with the public at large, and yet it could also be reduced to little more than an illustration (rather than a confirmation) of Freud's version of psychic truth. Lady Macbeth could thus become only another example of one of "those wrecked by success," a character type Freud said he met constantly in his clinical practice (14:318–24). Henrik Ibsen's *Rosmersholm* could be reduced to "the greatest work of art of the class that treats of this common phantasy in girls" (331).

Freud, however, also suggests that the psychoanalyst's task is like the archaeologist's rather than the artist's, though the object of study is more complex. In both cases fragments have to be discovered and pieced together. A seemingly insignificant detail—the position of Moses's right hand—might provide the key to reconstituting the work of art's whole form and its probable context. In dream analysis this reconstruction of latent meaning is the product of a series of successive decodings and unravelings—a model that has been used by many psychoanalytic theorists since. But any such reconstitution can only be hypothetical, and the evidence for this might lie, for example, in the many very different psychoanalytic readings offered since Freud of such texts as *Hamlet* and *Oedipus Rex*.

The third and final theoretical model is not so much a model as a method, one we now call intertextual in the sense that it involves superimposing various manifest versions of a literary (or mythic) structure in such a way that the latent common denominators show through. Freud uses this method in "The Theme of the Three Caskets," as does the French critic Charles Mauron as the basis for his theory of *psychocritique*.

Although no complete and coherent aesthetic system can be derived from Freud's writings, these five aspects of his theory and practice suggest that at the very least Freud gave to literary theory a new vocabulary with which to discuss the functioning of the psyche and perhaps the imagination and that this addition opened up potential new significance for literary symbolism and also for our concept of literature at large.

Starting in the 1970s, a renewed interest in Freud came from rereadings of his psychoanalytic and aesthetic theories in terms of structural linguistics and poststructural thought (JACQUES LACAN) and feminism (LUCE IRIGARAY). For many feminist theorists, the Freudian unconscious is seen as a repository of the structural relations of patriarchy. Yet even given the fact that Freud was a man socialized into nineteenth-century ideas about women, he not only had female disciples but his work has also been examined by such feminist literary theorists as Juliet Mitchell in *Psychoanalysis and Feminism* (1974) and Teresa de Lauretis in *Alice Doesn't* (1984) to see what could be salvaged. In a related move, Hortense Spillers has argued in " 'All the Things You Could Be by Now If Sigmund Freud's Wife Was Your Mother': Race and Psychoanalysis" (1996) that psychoanalysis could help race theory with its gaps.

Race, gender, and sexuality studies are not the only ones to confront or explore the possibilities of Freudian psychoanalysis today (see GENDER and RACE AND ETHNICITY). Through the work of SLAVOJ ŽIŽEK and others, popular culture has come under the scrutiny of a more philosophized and postmodernized version of Freudian and Lacanian psychoanalysis. Postcolonial theory too has borrowed from both Lacan and Freud. But perhaps the most influential of revisitings of Freud for literary purposes has been in the area of trauma theory. Freud's "Mourning and

Melancholia" (14:239–58) and other works have offered critics a new means of access to literary texts from all periods and places.

That there are today almost as many kinds of Freudian-inspired literary theory as there are Freudian-inspired literary theorists certainly points to a potentially disabling pluralism that highlights fundamental ambiguities and a radical subjectivity in Freud's own work. But it also bears witness to that work's fecundity and its continuing interest for aesthetic theory.

LINDA HUTCHEON

See also PSYCHOANALYTIC THEORY AND CRITICISM.

Sigmund Freud, *The Standard Edition of the Complete Psychological Works of Sigmund Freud* (ed. James Strachey, trans. Strachey et al., 24 vols., 1953–1974).

Frye, Northrop

Northrop Frye (1912–1991) was born in Sherbrooke, Québec, and received his early education in Moncton, New Brunswick. He studied English and philosophy and then, after studying theology, was ordained a minister in the United Church of Canada in 1936. After a short period of pastoral work in Saskatchewan, he proceeded on a scholarship to Merton College, Oxford, to study English. He returned to Canada in 1939 and was appointed to the Department of English in Victoria College, where he subsequently served as chair, then as principal, and finally in 1978 as chancellor of the college. In 1967 he became the first University Professor of the University of Toronto, a position he held until his death.

Frye was influenced by the structures in the works of Sir James Frazer and Oswald Spengler, though he was repelled by many of their concepts, and when he began to publish, he showed encyclopedic interests, writing as frequently on music, the visual arts, and political matters as on literary topics. In 1983 he agreed with an interlocutor that his theory probably differs little from William Blake's "because I've learned everything I know from Blake" ("Survival" 32). In *The Great Code* (1982) he states that from Blake, medieval exegetes, and "certain forms of Reformed commentary" (xvii) he learned how to read the Bible typologically and adapt the medieval fourfold interpretation of the Bible to poetic texts, so that his debts to Blake and the Bible are one (xiv).

In clarifying Blake's poetry Frye was intent on helping readers to recover "a lost art of reading poetry" (*Fearful* 11) that depends on counterpointing narratives and metaphors. Blake shows "that all poetry is allegorical" (9) and that adroitness in analogical reading develops the reader's ability to understand polysemous meaning, as medieval and Renaissance audiences did. Any literary work can be read first in terms of its linear units of narrative, then for its spatial structure of imagery (in this way narrative and metaphor interpenetrate to create the rhythm of the work), then in relation to those structures in other works of the same genre, and so on to the structures of the literary universe itself. Frye calls such recurrent units the archetypes of literature. As Tzvetan Todorov argues in *Literature and Its Theorists* (1984), for Frye "every text is a palimpsest" (91) and "all textuality is intertextuality" (96).

Frye reads Blake's poetry as organized on the biblical myth, or narrative, of creation, fall, redemption, and apocalypse and juxtaposes that temporal narrative with the spatial paradigm of Blake's images on four levels: a redeemed apocalyptic world, a level of unfallen nature accessible to the mind, a fallen world of time and space, and a demonic world of isolation. This model of interpenetrating narrative and imagery (Aristotle's *mythos* and *dianoia*) becomes the center for the structure of all Frye's subsequent work. The hero's quest down through the levels of the fourfold world and back up becomes the radical narrative that Frye explores thoroughly in his works on romance, most schematically in *The Secular Scripture* (1976). He modulates Blake's seven stages of Albion in *The Four Zoas* into Giambattista Vico's four stages—stories of gods, aristocratic heroes, and the people, followed by a *ricorso* through chaos back to the beginning—to arrive at the five stages of the development of modes in Western literature in the first essay of *Anatomy of Criticism* (1957): myth, romance, high mimetic, low mimetic, irony. In action within these modes the hero in myth is divine, different in kind and degree from human beings and their world; in romance, different in his degree of power to act but not in kind; in high mimetic, superior to human beings but not to their environment; in low mimetic, only equal to others; in irony, inferior to others in the power to act. This circle of narrative modes has revolved throughout Western literary history and is in the process of wheeling back to myth, already evident in Blake and confirmed by writers like James Joyce and W. B. Yeats.

In such works as *A Study of English Romanticism* (1968) and *The Critical Path* (1971) Frye finds Blake's patterns in other Romantic poets, through whose works a mythology, or cluster of narratives, shifts the focus from the traditionally objective God and nature to constructs of the human creative imagination that are the organizing forms of the culture and civilization in which we live.

Caterina Nella Cotrupi, in *Northrop Frye and the Poetics of Process* (2000), places both Vico and Frye in the critical tradition descending from Longinus on account of their concern with feeling and the poetics of process rather than in the Aristotelian approach centering on logic and the poetics of product. The pivotal age for the modern world is the Romantic period because its poets stopped projecting their own creative powers outward and began recalling those powers into the human imagination. The narrative quest in literature since the Romantic period has been an internal one, and its metaphors embody the psychological problems of the creative imagination. Frye repeatedly acknowledges the influence of Oscar Wilde's criticism on these conceptions of the artist as creator.

After *Fearful Symmetry* Frye extended his study of myth to literature as a whole. He published preliminary articles that were later collected in *Fables of Identity* (1963); the full argument appeared in *Anatomy of Criticism*. In *Anatomy* Frye argues that criticism, like any science, should be developed descriptively and that value judgments should not be the basis of the structure of poetics. Many critics have described *Anatomy* as revolutionary because Frye rejects the subordination of literary criticism to any other conceptual framework. He also breaks the newly ascendant New Critics' isolation of individual works from each other and ends their denigration of Romantic theories of poetry and the imagination while incorporating into his treatment of rhetorical criticism their emphasis on close reading of the figural structures of texts. It has been argued that this revolution made possible such later ones as STRUCTURALISM and DECONSTRUCTION, as well as the renewed interest in PHENOMENOLOGY and hermeneutics. Frye aims in *Anatomy* to bring together as many possible critical approaches and methods as he can.

In his discussion of the four forms of continuous prose fiction, Frye defines the genre that gives its title to *Anatomy* as the one that "relies on the free play of intellectual fancy . . . present[ing] us with a vision of the world in terms of a single intellectual pattern" (310). The vision in this instance is from the perspective of the total structure of criticism. If the first essay is temporal, the second is spatial in its patterning of the symbol (for Frye, the basic literary unit) on the medieval four levels of interpretation. The first level is split between the descriptive sign, which moves centrifugally outward to other areas of discourse, and the symbol as motif, which moves centripetally into the language of literature. Then the symbol is treated as image, which includes formal or rhetorical analyses; treated generically in terms of its place as archetype; and finally, on the anagogic level, revealed as a microcosm of the literary universe itself. In the third essay, Frye explores the variations of the pregeneric mythoi of comedy, romance, tragedy, and irony or satire on a wheel of the parallel seasons beginning with spring; these mythoi lie behind all narratives. In the fourth essay, he writes on genre both in poetry and in prose. In what he terms a "tentative conclusion" he widens the reference of his anatomy to all verbal structures, to a verbal universe beyond the literary one.

Many critics have been uneasy with what they have taken to be the static nature of the paradigms Frye elaborates and their isolation from the world of becoming. Yet Frye strives to energize his model with such words as "counterpoints," "resonates," "drive," and "desire"; he conceives this model to be both diachronic and synchronous at the same time: "The *mythos* is the *dianoia* in movement; the *dianoia* is the *mythos* in stasis" (83). Only individual, mentally awakened readers can hold these tensions in the energy of their imaginations. Frye resists a social resolution in a synthesis of the contending opposites: "Antithesis or tension of opposites is the only form in which [the ideal society] can exist" (*Critical* 168). A fitting emblem of Frye's model and of the interpenetration that energizes it—one that Frye himself used—is the gyroscope, seemingly static when revolving most rapidly. Todorov uses the similar metaphor of the Viconian spiral to describe Frye's method; Frye himself repeatedly used Jerome Bruner's spiral curriculum to characterize his own circling back to restate earlier positions and to develop them further.

Indeed, Bruner's theory is important in Frye's working out of his own thoughts on the social function of literary criticism, particularly in *The Critical Path*. Criticism can awaken students to successive levels of awareness of the mythology that lies behind the ideology in which their society indoctrinates them. A society must have myths of concern, but above all a myth of freedom is needed if its citizens are to perceive these myths as archetypes, not stereotypes. Education, then, is the source of social freedom, and the universities are the dynamo of education because they allow students, through the discipline of study, to become free in their imaginations and hence citizens in their later work of creating human culture and defending against the anarchy of undisciplined minds. Matthew Arnold's influence, especially his concept of the four powers—the power of conduct, of beauty, of truth, and of social life and manners—may be discerned here. From the 1960s on, Frye used public lectures and the media to extend education in mythology to a wider audience; he campaigned relentlessly to demystify criticism and to bring it to the largest possible number of people, as in the lectures in The Educated Imagination (1963) and in the collections The Bush Garden (1971), Divisions on a Ground (1982), and Mythologizing Canada (1997).

After Frye's death, the novelist Margaret Atwood was quoted as saying that his greatest influence on Canadian writers had been in his treating writing as a serious occupation. In his conclusion to the revised edition of Literary History of Canada, published in 1976, he celebrates what he calls the new professionalism of Canadian poets. His first conclusion (1965) is largely dedicated to defining Canadian culture by contrasting it to the American. Whereas Americans have proceeded deductively from the eighteenth-century a priori ideas of their revolution, Canadians, whose loyalist forebears rejected that revolution, have moved inductively and expediently through their subsequent experience. That experience has been of nineteenth-century sophisticated ideas being thought out in the setting of the vast emptiness of an often terrifying and primitive nature. Frye argues that the result has been that Canadians have been forced to ask not "Who am I?" but "Where is here?" and to develop technology in transportation and communication to provide a vocabulary and grammar in which to answer that question. Frye argues that the early Canadian preoccupation with formulating, asserting, and defending social and moral values created a garrison mentality in the literary mind that operated on the level of the conceptual rather than the poetic and thus revealed its origin in history rather than in myth. Consequently, he sees the coming to maturity of Canadian poets and novelists as a result of their moving back from history and argument to the more primitive metaphorical mode of thinking. "Literature is conscious mythology" becomes a refrain in this essay, as he insists that a mature literature presents an autonomous world of the imagination that gives readers a place from which to see their actual world. Recovering this power to think metaphorically opens the gates of the garrison mentality and frees writers and readers alike from conformist assertions. Only then does writing cease to be a rhetorical contest and become what he calls it in his second conclusion, an expression of play, which is for Frye the highest form of the serious. Ever the optimist, Frye found in the Canadian literature of the preceding few decades a steadily increasing playfulness.

Frye returns to his beginning in The Great Code (1982), as he counterpoints once more his theories of narrative, language and metaphor, typology, and polysemous interpretation in a detailed study of the Bible. The form of The Great Code is itself an emblem of Frye's criticism. The two testaments are reflected in the binary structure of the book, "The Order of Words" and "The Order of Types." The first part moves through chapters on language, myth, metaphor, and typology; the second part explores the same topics in reverse order. The result is a structure of double mirrors reflecting each other rather than any "outside." So in narrative the types in one testament become the antitypes in the second, the continuity of the myth of the whole Bible being U-shaped. The quest of descent and ascent is the pattern of romance that Frye so frequently discusses, and yet again the reader becomes the hero of that romance in search of identity. And, typically for Frye, the quest ends in the mode of comedy, the mode of freedom, renewal, and joy.

In a companion book, *Words with Power* (1990), Frye parallels the way in which the Bible "is held together by an inner core of mythical and metaphorical structure" (102) with the way in which Western literature is constructed and calls *The Great Code* a successor to *Anatomy of Criticism* and "to a considerable extent a summing up and restatement of my critical views" (xii). Frye continues to find the coherence of criticism and of literature in the mythology at the center of every society. For Western societies, the first and fullest expression of that mythology is the Bible. In every verbal utterance Frye postulates five linguistic modes, though differing in degree and developing in history. The descriptive mode of science is the latest, preceded by the conceptual mode of history and philosophy, the rhetorical mode of ideology, and the imaginative mode of the poetic. Beyond the imaginative is a fifth linguistic mode, which Frye calls the "kerygmatic" and for which he suggests "prophetic" and "metaliterary" as synonyms.

This book's title is adapted from Luke's description of the reception of Jesus's parabolic preaching at Capernaum: "His word was with power" (4:32). Such power is of the imaginative mode, which does not address auditors/readers directly nor compel their belief but presents them with hypothetical poetic models. These models embody their primary concerns, their desires for food and drink, sex, property, and freedom of movement; they are condensations of myth and metaphor in an autonomous poetic world (148). Movement outward to other linguistic modes involves displacement. First, the pure metaphor becomes metonymic in the rhetorical mode, made to stand for secondary concerns such as patriotism or religious belief in a social environment. Rhetoric, used in the poetic mode to ornament, becomes a means of persuasion to compel belief in some ideology; for Frye, "an ideology is applied mythology" (23). Mythos is displaced further and is more fully subordinated to the authority of logic in the conceptual mode, in which a dialectic forces the separation of subject and object. History and philosophy are the expressions in argument and logic of this dialectic. Now it is the structures of logic that compel belief, though Frye argues that behind them may still be discerned myth and metaphor. The last linguistic mode to strengthen the dominance of logos is the descriptive, which scientists use to compel belief in facts, though genuine scientists recognize that science is a structure made by the human creative imagination.

Frye consistently defines his work as a criticism of metaphor, as opposed to the criticism of concept practiced by historians of ideas, Marxists, structuralists, and followers of JACQUES DERRIDA. These other critics have their function in exploring the displacements of the poetic into the other three linguistic modes, but they are also inadequate because they accept the subordination of myth to logic, of the unity of myth and metaphor to the dialectic of subject and object in history, philosophy, and science. This subordination dates from Plato and Aristotle, and Frye finds it still dominant in Western culture (33). The Romantics attempted to reverse this relationship and to exalt myth over logic once again; Frye endeavors to extend their enterprise in order to help readers perceive behind all verbal structures those myths and metaphors that may be found in their pure state as "two aspects of one identity" (71) only in literature. In responding to this pure model with heightened consciousness, readers may experience an epiphany going beyond the imaginative to the kerygmatic mode and the experience of the Longinian sublime. For Frye, only when readers dehistoricize experience can they escape the cycles of history and "become what they see" (84), transforming the poetic model into a model to live by, an existential metaphor, for "literature is a technique of meditation, in the widest and most flexible sense" (96).

Frye's influence was sweeping in the decade following the publication of *Anatomy*, and it has remained strong. Other critical schools have developed, and Frye himself was aware that some of their proponents had argued that his influence was over. Frye will, however, continue to be useful to readers who focus on the literary structure itself, and Frye always strove to reach readers rather than other critics. Entirely fittingly, his last publication was *The Double Vision* (1991), which reworks public lectures that were designed to present "a shorter and more accessible version of the longer books, *The Great Code* and *Words with Power*" (xvii).

RICHARD STINGLE

Northrop Frye, *Anatomy of Criticism: Four Essays* (1957), *The Bush Garden: Essays on the Canadian Imagination* (1971), *The Collected Works* (gen. ed. Alvin A. Lee, 28 vols. to date, 1996–), conclusion, *Literary History of Canada* (ed. Carl F. Klinck, 1965, 2nd ed., vol. 3, 1976), *The Critical Path: An Essay on the Social Context of Literary Criticism* (1971), *Divisions on a Ground: Essays on Canadian Culture* (1982), *The Double Vision: Language and Meaning in Religion* (1991), *The Educated Imagination* (1963), *Fables of Identity: Studies in Poetic Mythology* (1963), *Fearful Symmetry: A Study of William Blake* (1947), *The Great Code: The Bible and Literature* (1982), *Mythologizing Canada: Essays in the Canadian Imagination* (ed. Branko Gorjup, 1997), *Rereading Frye: The Published and Unpublished Works* (ed. David Boyd and Imre Salusinkszy, 1999), *The Secular Scripture: A Study of the Structure of Romance* (1976), *A Study of English Romanticism* (1968), "The Survival of Eros in Poetry," *Romanticism and Contemporary Criticism* (ed. Morris Eaves and Michael Fischer, 1986), *Words with Power: Being a Second Study of the Bible and Literature* (1990); Caterina Nella Cotrupi, *Northrop Frye and the Poetics of Process* (2000); Tzvetan Todorov, *Critique de la critique* (1984, *Literature and Its Theorists: A Personal View of Twentieth-Century Criticism*, trans. Catherine Porter, 1987).

Gates, Henry Louis, Jr.

Henry Louis Gates Jr. (b. 1950), scholar, critic, editor, and high profile articulator of African American history and culture, is one of the most prominent intellectuals of our time. Gates directs the W. E. B. Du Bois Institute for African and African American Research at Harvard University, where he is the Alphonse Fletcher University Professor. Born in Piedmont, West Virginia, Gates attended a local community college for a year, originally intending to study medicine, before entering Yale University, where he studied history. Graduating summa cum laude in 1973, he went to Cambridge University on a Mellon Fellowship; there he met the Nigerian writer and future Nobel laureate Wole Soyinka, who became his friend and mentor and inspired the young Gates's subsequent intellectual trajectory by encouraging him to switch to the study of literature.

If Gates's experience at Yale was transformational, his Cambridge sojourn was pivotal. It was there that, in his own words, he "embarked upon a mission for all black people, especially for . . . the intellectuals who collect, preserve, and analyze the most sublime artifacts of the black imagination" (*Figures in Black* xvi–xvii). He conceived an audacious plan to put on Du Bois's mantle and produce an Encyclopedia Africana (Du Bois's original idea), which not only came to fruition as *Encarta Africana* (1999) but indeed has been eclipsed by the truly encyclopedic scope of Gates's subsequent enterprises.

In 1981, by then an assistant professor at Yale, Gates became one of the first recipients of the MacArthur Foundation's "genius" grants. Among Gates's earliest and most fruitful endeavors was the Black Periodical Literature Project. He later edited the forty-volume Schomburg Library of Nineteenth-Century Black Women Writers. Indeed it is crucial to emphasize that Gates was instrumental in helping to restore black women writers to their rightful place in the tradition, both by recuperating their presence in the past and by articulating their power in the present.

In editing *The Norton Anthology of African American Literature* (1996), Gates took a major step in defining a new canon that could stand shoulder to shoulder with the canons already established by the Norton anthologies of English and American literature. His edited volume *Black Literature and Literary Theory* (1984) explores the application of contemporary literary theory to the reading of black literature. But his own subsequent critical work took a more dramatic course. His first major book, *Figures in Black: Words, Signs, and the "Racial" Self* (1987), a series of close readings of significant African American texts, is an endeavor to establish a context for the development and application of a critical theory grounded in a black tradition. It is the initial volume in a trilogy, the second volume of which, The Signifying Monkey: A Theory of Afro-American Literary Criticism (1988), is his most iconic work.

In The Signifying Monkey, Gates seeks a foundation for a black hermeneutics in the complex operation of what he terms "Signifyin(g)"—defined in Figures in Black as "the trope of revision, of repetition and difference" (xxxi) and distinguished from the ordinary term "signifying" by virtue of the fact that it is "not so much a process of generating meaning per se as it is a stance that declares both a willingness and a de-monstrable ability to be (in the role of) the signifier, the one who is in command of words" (Fox 847)—which Gates explores through the figures of the Yoruba divinity Eshu-Elegbara and the African American folkloric character the Signifying Monkey. Gates also analyzes at length the trope of the "talking book" and its importance with regard to the literature of the slave, that body of materials constituting the ur-texts of the black literary tradition, which, Gates persuasively argues, is double-voiced. The "talking book" gives voice to the other—not simply a speaking but a talking through, "talking back." This testimony of "representation and reversal" (Signifying Monkey 128)—the strategy of slave literature—also could be seen as the strategy of black/Africana studies. The book remains one of the most important and influential texts in the canon of African American criticism.

Gates's project in The Signifying Monkey received extraordinary praise; on the other hand, it also was excessively derided (see D. G. Myers, "Signifying Nothing," New Criterion [February 1990]). Much of the negative criticism came from those for whom theory itself is philosophically suspect, an abstraction that distracts from the social-revolutionary thrust of what they believe African American studies ought to be. One can readily imagine the response of "ordinary" African Americans, let alone black power advocates, to Gates's assertion that "Blackness exists, but only as a func-tion of its signifiers" (Figures 275). Gates has been accused of being more ivory tower than "street" and of being more accommodationist than militant.

Although Gates did not inaugurate it, he has come to exemplify the role of the academic superstar, which—whatever its value within the university system—gave him the intellectual and personal capital to extend his ambitions well beyond the academy into the public and corporate spheres. He has made stellar use of the media as well as technology (the internet, DNA testing, etc.) to advance his historical/cultural initiatives. Among numerous other ventures, he is editor in chief of the on-line Oxford African American Studies Center and the online African American news magazine The Root, and is cofounder of AfricanDNA, which enables individuals to explore their genealogies through genetic testing.

Gates's admirable refusal to shrink from the complexities and the demystifying, if sometimes bitter, truths of history and culture has drawn fire from those with more essentialized agendas. His PBS television series "The Wonders of the African World" (1999), for example, enriching as it was, nonetheless incited heated contro-versy because of its discussion of the role of Africans in the slave trade, a subject

Gates returned to in an op-ed piece in the *New York Times* in 2010 ("Ending"). He was vigorously assailed for supposedly easing the burden of guilt for slavery borne by white people, when in fact he was examining exercises of power and material gain that went beyond color alone.

It is unfortunate that Gates is now probably most recognizable in the public's consciousness as a result of the publicity surrounding his arrest in 2009 for breaking into his own home in Cambridge, Massachusetts. In the aftermath, Sergeant James Crowley, the arresting officer, gave Gates the handcuffs he used in the encounter, and Gates has indicated that he plans to give these handcuffs to the new Smithsonian National Museum of African American History and Culture—a "signifying" act (in both senses of the term) that, interestingly, echoes an incident in Ralph Ellison's masterpiece *Invisible Man*.

That this incident occurred when, for the first time in American history, there was a black chief executive, raised serious questions about the extent to which—if at all—we have achieved a post-racial society. It also was ironic, given the fact that Gates was one of those most insistent on bracketing the word "race" as a way of emphasizing its fictiveness (see, for example, his introduction to *"Race," Writing, and Difference*). This regrettable but instructive episode produced a national teaching moment in which we could plainly see that, its socially constructed nature notwithstanding, "race" still retains the power to produce unwelcome consequences.

If Gates had done nothing more than write his academic books and steer Harvard's Black Studies program from a state of caretakership to preeminence, he would have established himself as a significance force in the field. As it is, he has gone far beyond this academic dimension to become an important public figure who has done more than any other individual to bring the black experience—its personalities, its history, its cultural genius—to a level of awareness more commensurate with the depth and breadth of its role in the United States and the world.

ROBERT ELLIOT FOX

See also AFRICAN AMERICAN THEORY AND CRITICISM: 2. 1977 TO 1990, NATIVE THEORY AND CRITICISM: 1. UNITED STATES, and RACE AND ETHNICITY.

Henry Louis Gates Jr., *Africana: An Encyclopedia of the African and African American Experience* (1999), *America Behind the Color Line: Dialogues with African Americans* (2004), *Black Literature and Literary Theory* (1984), *Colored People: A Memoir* (1994), "Ending the Slavery Blame-Game," *New York Times* (23 April 2010), *Faces of America: How 12 Extraordinary People Discovered Their Pasts* (2010), *Figures in Black: Words, Signs, and the "Racial" Self* (1987), *Finding Oprah's Roots, Finding Your Own* (2007), *In Search of Our Roots: How 19 Extraordinary African Americans Reclaimed Their Past* (2009), *Loose Canons: Notes on the Culture Wars* (1992), *The Signifying Monkey: A Theory of Afro-American Literary Criticism* (1988), *Thirteen Ways of Looking at a Black Man* (1997), *Tradition and the Black Atlantic: Critical Theory in the African Diaspora* (2010), *The Trials of Phillis Wheatley: America's First Poet and Her Encounters with the Founding Fathers* (2003), *Wonders of the African World* (1999); Henry Louis Gates Jr., ed., *African-American Women Writers, 1910–1940*, 10 vols. (1996); *The Dictionary of Global Culture* (1997); *In the House of Osugbo: Critical Essays* on *Wole Soyinka* (1988); *Reading Black, Reading Feminist: A Critical Anthology* (1990), *The Schomburg Library of Nineteenth Century Black Women's Writings*, 40 vols. (2002); Henry Louis Gates Jr. and Anthony Appiah, eds., *Identities* (1996); Henry Louis Gates Jr., Maria Dietrich, and Carl Pedersen, eds., *Black Imagination and the Middle Passage* (1999); Henry Louis Gates Jr. and Gene Andrew Garrett, eds., *The New Negro: Readings on Race, Representation, and African American Culture, 1892–1938* (2007); Henry Louis Gates Jr. and Evelyn Brooks Higginbotham, eds., *African American Lives* (2004), *African American National Biography*, 8 vols. (2008); Henry Louis Gates Jr. and Nellie Y. McKay, eds., *The Norton Anthology of African American Literature* (1997, 2nd ed., 2003); Henry Louis Gates Jr. and Hollis Robbins, *In Search of Hannah Crafts* (2004); Henry Louis Gates Jr. and Cornel West, *The Future of the Race* (1996); Robert Elliot Fox, review of *Figures in Black*, *Black American Literature Forum* 22 (1988).

Gender

If, as many critics have argued, feminism has been the single most influential cultural theory of the twentieth century, it is because it has made gender an integral component of humanities and social science discourses. A product of the confluence of feminism and poststructuralism, gender studies focuses on the historical, social, and psychological systems within which sexual identity becomes meaningful. Fundamental to gender criticism is the premise that sex (male/female), gender (masculine/feminine), and sexuality (heterosexual/homosexual) are distinct. These divisions have theoretical as well as political implications, since, as gender theorists argue, the essentialist tendency to equate gender and sexuality with anatomy can mask the ideological function of the male/female binary: namely the reproduction or naturalization of a patriarchal system that defines male heterosexuality as the norm. Separating gender from biology thus helps make possible the radical reimagining of traditional gender roles that is necessary for the interrogation of patriarchal structures.

The origins of contemporary theorizing about gender can be traced back to early feminist critiques of the "natural" distinctions between the sexes. In *A Vindication of the Rights of Woman* (1792), one of the first extended cultural analyses of gender and power, Mary Wollstonecraft illustrates the dangers, for both sexes, of limiting the education and responsibilities of women. An equally foundational work for the study of gender is existential feminist philosopher SIMONE DE BEAUVOIR's *The Second Sex* (1949). Beauvoir's famous maxim "One is not born, but rather becomes a woman" (267) calls attention to the ideological role of social, legal, and economic forces in the production and reproduction of gender. In her encyclopedic analysis of philosophy, psychoanalysis, and literature, Beauvoir powerfully illustrates that throughout Western history the "feminine" has been constructed as "Other" in opposition to masculine norms. Beauvoir's work opened gender to scrutiny, revealing how mythic cultural structures deny liberty to women and men alike (720). While Wollstonecraft's and Beauvoir's texts have inspired a range of feminist thought (see FEMINIST THEORY AND CRITICISM) that has in turn been influential in the formation of gender studies, these two works represent particularly crucial steps in the analysis and critique of pervasive patriarchal ideologies. This is due, in part, to the way that both authors establish the essential connection between individual values and broad social structures. The assertion of this connection—"the personal is political"—would become the celebrated slogan of "second-wave" 1960s feminism, which decisively moved the "private" issue of gender into the public realm.

The 1960s and 1970s saw a shift from feminist activism in the social/political field to a critical cultural analysis of gender that was often conducted within the academy (also a "public" realm that had excluded women) and particularly U.S. literary studies departments. Feminist critiques of the representation of women in canonical male authored texts and the "rediscovery" of marginalized female authors were important steps in historicizing—and gendering—the aesthetic and epistemological categories that had been the bedrock of academic literary study. These "second-wave" feminists (see FEMINIST THEORY AND CRITICISM: 2. ANGLO-AMERICAN FEMINISMS) illustrate that gender is both a product and a producer of art and narrative and that literary texts (and literary criticism) have helped define what it means to be male and female in the world.

PSYCHOANALYSIS AND POSTSTRUCTURALISM. Gender as it has been studied and understood over the last hundred years is necessarily indebted to the psychoanalytic work of SIGMUND FREUD and particularly to his arguments concerning the psychosexual acquisition of identity. Freud's formulation of the Oedipal and castration complexes have been criticized for resting on apparently "stable," coherent notions of the gendered body, as well as on a normative—father/penis-centered—heterosexuality (see, for example, Chodorow, Lauretis, Queer, Mitchell, Mulvey, Rose). However, in his stress on the polymorphous nature of the infant's desire and the central but generally problematic status of sexuality in the process of psychological development, Freud's theories do present a significant challenge to biological determinism that has proven highly productive for gender theorists.

Contemporary analysis of gender reflects the influence of French feminist theorists like HÉLÈNE CIXOUS, LUCE IRIGARAY, and JULIA KRISTEVA, who responded to and participated in rereadings of Freud. Gender, for these poststructuralist theorists, becomes firmly situated as a category of language. This discursive positioning cannot be understood without reference to the work of JACQUES LACAN, MICHEL FOUCAULT, and JACQUES DERRIDA. In his "return to Freud," Lacan reformulates the basic tenets of psychoanalytic theory (and specifically Freud's stress on the division and instability of identity) in light of the way that language constructs subjects. Lacan's setting of Freud's theories of the unconscious and sexuality in a Saussurean linguistic framework powerfully sutures gender, language, and subjectivity. Working out of a philosophical tradition but also influenced by FERDINAND DE SAUSSURE and Freud, Derridean DECONSTRUCTION has also been crucial for contemporary gender theories. In the deconstruction of binary oppositions that is a foundational aspect of Derrida's work, "woman" is given a unique position, as the "side" from which one begins to dismantle European phallogocentric structures. Derrida's privileging of femininity, however, is only meant to be a preliminary gesture. In the second deconstructive "stage," sexual opposition would be replaced by sexual difference: "opposition is two, opposition is man/woman. Difference on the other hand, can be an indefinite number of sexes" ("Women in the Beehive" 198). Finally, Foucault's work, especially in Discipline and Punish (1975) and The History of Sexuality (1976–1984), has been pivotal for understanding structures of pleasure and power, as well as the ways that sexuality is produced discursively within specific social/historical contexts.

Despite the obstacles that these theories present to imagining alternatives to patriarchy, gender critics have utilized the antiessentialism of such positions to challenge conventional notions of gender. In different ways, Cixous, Irigaray, and Kristeva each focus on the disruption of patriarchal structures through the celebration of "the feminine." Irigaray, for example, envisions a way that order can be modified by women: rather than "repeating/interpreting the way in which the feminine finds itself defined as lack, deficiency, or as imitation," women "should signify that with respect to this logic a disruptive excess is possible on the feminine side" (This Sex 78). These methods, however, as has been pointed out by other feminist critics (see, for example, Toril Moi in Sexual/Textual Politics), are risky, potentially functioning merely to reproduce an essentialist, binary logic.

One of the most influential poststructuralist theorists of gender is JUDITH BUTLER. While the term "performative" was coined earlier by J. L. Austin (see SPEECH ACTS), it is Butler who, in her groundbreaking work Gender Trouble (1990), shifts the term's linguistic focus (on how certain utterances actually "bring into being" that which they declare) to the realm of gender and power. Butler points out that gender itself relies on principles of performance ("persistent impersonation" [viii]), as well as parody. Thus, gender is always unstable and must continually be inspected, repaired, and regulated vis-à-vis compulsory heterosexuality. Most challengingly, Butler's performativity takes a step beyond a metaphysics of substance, abolishing the so-called authenticity of the doer behind the deed: "There is no gender identity behind the expressions of gender; that identity is performatively constituted by the very 'expressions' that are said to be its results" (25). In her 1997 work The Psychic Life of Power, Butler examines the formation of the identifications "man" and "woman" and argues that these socially pervasive categories are "achieved" only through the foreclosure of identifications that exist as the "outside" of cultural intelligibility (i.e., homosexuality) (168–70). Rather than accepting this melancholic foreclosure as the inevitable result of ego formation, Butler insists that the "outside" of discourse is always historically determined and political and thus contingent.

GENDER AND QUEER THEORY. Butler's work is integral to queer theory, a far-reaching methodology that engages with gender and sexuality in all of their ambiguity, paradox, and contradiction (see QUEER THEORY AND CRITICISM). Heavily influenced by psychoanalysis and poststructuralism, queer theory developed out of the identity-based gay and lesbian criticism movements of the 1970s and 1980s. Queer theory rejects any notion of stable identity and instead pursues the spectacular, though often vigorously concealed/disavowed, contradictions of desire. This is basically a deconstructive practice but one also informed by feminist and historicist methodologies, especially the genealogical mode presented in Foucault's The History of Sexuality. In this way, queer theory is characteristically interested in how gender identities, and disruptions of identity codes, relate to questions of history and power. The use of the term "queer" as an identifier for either sexual identity underlies this theoretical mode; yet, this term is still debated in the academy. One criticism leveled at queer theory is its very amorphousness (see Norton), as its referentless status risks rendering it meaningless or reducing it to a co-optable tag that can be redeployed by dominant culture to connote abject otherness.

TRANSGENDER STUDIES. As feminist theorist Patricia Duncker writes, "Queer also means to 'fuck with gender' " (57), and perhaps the most radical "queering" of gender and identity occurs in transgender studies. Contemporary artist and theorist Sandy Stone has said that "the transsexual currently occupies a position which is nowhere, which is outside the binary oppositions of gendered discourse." ("Posttranssexual Manifesto" 295). Transgender theorists (Kate Bornstein, Pat Califia, Leslie Feinberg, Dave King, Susan Stryker) are therefore concerned with the multiplicities and identity dynamisms (performative-subversive possibilities) indicated in the "trans." Consequently, "transgender" may refer to cross-dressers, transsexuals, transvestites, and those whose performance(s) of gender(s) (including the performing of a nonmarked gender) trouble identities and sex conventions. As transgender studies distrusts restrictive binaries, it is also necessarily interested in the cultural force of gender-inscribed bodies, revealing most powerfully how culturally/psychically crucial the "marked" body (the knowable referent) is for dominant culture.

CYBERGENDER. In the 1990s and beginning of the twenty-first century, cybergender theory has radically deepened the denaturalization of sexual identity by positing the body as a highly unstable site of cultural, sexual, racial, ethnic, and techno-biological meaning. Cybergender studies draws from and informs other postmodern theories (JEAN BAUDRILLARD's simulacra, FREDRIC JAMESON's critique of the logic of late capitalism, queer studies' fascination with gender "incoherence"), understanding the subject as a node in a vast network of information and technology and thus collapsing traditional oppositions between nature and culture. To this end, and perhaps most prominently, the work of DONNA HARAWAY has pioneered the analysis of cyborgs—a term that Haraway argues describes all contemporary human subjects. She writes, "We are all chimeras, theorized and fabricated hybrids of machine and organism; in short, we are cyborgs. The cyborg is our ontology; it gives us our politics" ("A Manifesto" 191). The theoretical force of the " cyborg" for gender studies lies in its ability to utterly demolish essentialist sexual binaries. Thus, for cybergender theorists, if what is "natural" is also necessarily "machined" or constructed, the reconstruction of gender (and its attendant social laws) must be possible.

MASCULINITY STUDIES. An essential aspect of gender studies, masculinity studies documents both the vicissitudes and implications of masculinities within a heteropatriarchal system. While early feminist inquiry sought to analyze and address the place of women in patriarchal culture, it also revealed that no gender designation (including "male/man") is ever politically neutral. Thus, masculinity studies was born, in part, out of a context of growing "male feminism" that became especially preoccupied with men "writing the feminine" and then later with how the concept of

"masculinity" itself relates to patriarchy. This development was somewhat controversial; some feminists argued that that this "male feminism" was potentially exploitative because it allowed male academics to recenter their own discourse and experience through the appropriation of feminist discourse and political strategies
(what Elaine Showalter in 1987 called "critical cross-dressing"). (For examples of
both "male feminism" and its feminist critics, see Jardine and Smith, Morgan, and
Digby.) Masculinity studies, however, grew to establish itself as a legitimate pro-
feminist mode of gender inquiry—dedicated to challenging the privileged "obvious-
ness" of the masculine signifier within patriarchal capitalism. Responsible for this
growth is not only the early sociological work on masculinity (Deborah David and
Robert Brannon; Joseph H. Pleck) but also the work of later theorists (Harry Brod;
Robert W. Connell; Stephen M. Whitehead and Frank J. Barrett), especially as they
began to investigate strategies for subverting patriarchal domination.

In literary studies, an important early work was Peter Schwenger's *Phallic Critiques: Masculinity and Twentieth Century Literature* (1984), which proposes an "écriture
masculine" as a language of the male body. Robert Bly's *Iron John* (1990) is a significant mytho-anthropological work that propounds a male-specific critique of patriarchy. Bly describes contemporary American men as suffering a lack of paternal guidance. His text can be seen as inaugurating a host of popular masculinities (texts and
movements) that sought to therapeutically broach the subject of men's pain. These
so-called mythopoetic movements have been popularly caricatured as kinds of glori-
fied boy-scout camps for disaffected white males, and, more seriously, have been
critiqued as at least *potentially* both antifeminist and homophobic (see Kimmel).

Queer literary criticism, and particularly the work of EVE KOSOFSKY SEDGWICK,
has been instrumental in increasing the attention paid to masculinity in the field of
gender studies. In *Between Men* (1985), for example, Sedgwick deconstructs literary
and visual texts, charts a "continuum" of male desire that moves from the homosocial to the homoerotic, and uncovers the importance of homophobia within conventional patriarchy. Gay-male-focused critical works (such as Paul Hammond's *Love between Men in English Literature*, Edmund White's *The Burning Library*, and Tim Edwards's
Erotics and Politics: Gay Male Sexuality, Masculinity, and Feminism) have also been vitally
important to masculinity studies as they work to theorize the place of masculine desire in antipatriarchal politics.

RACE AND GENDER. In the 1970s and 1980s, African American feminist critics
pointed out the differences between racism as it is experienced by black men and
black women. This debate played itself out with some bitterness in the realm of literature, with the woman-centered fiction of Toni Morrison, Alice Walker, and Gloria
Naylor being castigated by male African American writers and critics for its alleged
denigration of the black man. The canonical works of African American fiction—for
example the novels of Richard Wright and Ralph Ellison, which emphasized the struggles of black men in racist environments—were, however, just as harshly criticized by

female writers and critics for their masculinist bias (see AFRICAN AMERICAN THE-
ORY AND CRITICISM). Ultimately, as bell hooks writes, "Since all forms of oppression are linked in our society because they are supported by similar institutions and
social structures, one system cannot be eradicated while the others remain intact"
(*Feminist Theory* 37). Gender theory has thus been profoundly affected both by the
recognition that all forms of social and psychological domination are intercon-
nected and the understanding that definitions of masculinity and femininity are always racialized (as recent theorists have argued, this includes "white" masculinity
and femininity, which are inevitably defined in opposition to nonwhite "others"; see
Dyer, Morrison, Frankenberg, and Pfeil, and on whiteness as constructed vis-à-vis
Native Americans, see Faery).

Colonial and postcolonial theorists have also demonstrated the connections
between race and gender through their analysis of the ways that imperialism is implicated in the production of sexual difference. One of the earliest and most influential explorations of colonialism and gender is FRANTZ FANON's 1952 *Black Skin,
White Masks*. Focusing primarily on the struggles of the Afro-Caribbean male, Fanon
demonstrates that colonialism functions as an all-encompassing structure that en-
gineers and subjugates colonized peoples culturally, psychologically, and sexually.
Challenging the discourse of academic discussion of the so-called Third World—
and specifically white feminist analyses of Third World women—critics such as
GAYATRI CHAKRAVORTY SPIVAK, Chandra Talpade Mohanty, Avtar Brah, Uma Narayan, and Trinh T. Minh-Ha have been instrumental in calling for a de-ethnocentrizing
of "man" and "woman," terms that have typically signified (within scholarly discourse) the white, middle-class European.

Studies of race and gender have also been undertaken from a masculinity studies perspective (see Carby, Blount and Cunningham, and Ouzgane and Coleman), as
well as with an attention to sexuality (see Hawley and also Somerville, which explores how the notion of the "queer" existed as a sign of both racial and sexual marginality in early twentieth-century).

GENDER AND MATERIALISM. The strategic synthesis of Marxist criticism and gender
studies has proven to have far-reaching implications for contemporary theories of
subjectivity and cultural history. Materialist feminist criticism (see Barrett, Hen-
nessey and Ingraham, Kaplan, and Moi) suggests that formations of gender and
sexuality are indisputably inflected by political, social, and economic structures.
Materialist analyses of gender have drawn attention to how gender has been historically constructed around designations of public (male) and private (female) liberal-
capitalist categories. Carole Pateman, for example, in "Critiques of the Public/Private
Dichotomy" (1987), illustrates how these categories encourage the subordination
and finally commodification of the female body. RAYMOND WILLIAMS, in his seminal 1961 essay "Advertising: The Magic System," shows that the modern marketing
machine of capitalism sells products to consumers but also peddles magical "fetishes"

of gender identity (for example, the consumption of beer validates a male fantasy of macho masculinity [335]).

Materialist gender inquiry also focuses on issues of GLOBALIZATION, and specifically the interrelation of First and Third World economies. Of primary importance here is the work of Spivak, who draws on the fields of psychoanalysis, deconstruction, feminism, and Marxism to consider the material conditions of the "subaltern" subject (see also McClintock, Shohat, and Mufti, Kelly, and Ria).

GENDER AND FILM THEORY. Film theory has most notably impacted gender studies at the level of viewership and identity. Building on formalist writings on film, early 1970s film theorists (for example, Jean-Louis Baudry and Christian Metz) began to understand film within its ideological (capitalist) context. Most importantly for gender studies, this Marxist-informed mode of inquiry also utilized Lacanian psychoanalytic theory in order to interrogate the reception of filmic images. This was significant precisely because it proposed not only a compelling narrative of ideological production but also suggested that gender identity is deeply implicated in that process/production. The nature of sexual differentiation, in particular, was interrogated in film studies by feminist and poststructuralist theorists. Laura Mulvey's groundbreaking 1975 essay "Visual Pleasure in Narrative Cinema" utilizes a Freudian-Lacanian framework to investigate how desire itself becomes gendered in the visual field (specifically the classic Hollywood film). She suggests that "in a world ordered by sexual imbalance, pleasure in looking has been split between active/male and passive/female" (19). While her essay has been criticized (even by Mulvey herself) for reproducing binary definitions of gender and for ignoring the place of the female viewer, her call to disrupt/destroy the pleasurable patriarchal patterns of viewing inaugurated a productive and ongoing analysis of the ways gender is (re)produced in visual narratives. This analysis has included further investigations of the feminine in film (see, for example, Silverman, *Acoustic*, Rose, and Lauretis, *Alice*, *Technologies*), as well as studies of masculinity (see Neale, Bingham, Lehman, and Cohan), the queer in film (see Hanson, Doty), and race and gender in film (see hooks, *Reel*, and Willis).

As with most poststructuralist theories, the decentered, performative, discursive "subject" of gender studies has been viewed as compromising the possibility of solidarity between members of oppressed groups that is necessary for political action (see, for example, Bell and Klein). Feminists have been wary of gender studies' inclusion of men, and critical of its embracing of white- and male-dominated "inaccessible" poststructuralist theories. Despite these ongoing debates, gender theorists and their critics share a belief that traditional conceptions of masculinity and femininity need to be understood and challenged.

MARLO EDWARDS

Henry Abelove, Michele Aina Barele, David M. Halperin, eds., *The Lesbian and Gay Studies Reader* (1993); M. Jacqui Alexander and Chandra Talpade Mohanty, eds., *Feminist Genealogies, Colonial Legacies,*

Democratic Futures (1996); Michèle Barrett, Women's Oppression Today: Problems in Marxist Feminist Analysis (1980, rev. ed., Women's Oppression Today: The Marxist/Feminist Encounter, 1988); Jean Baudrillard, Simulacres et simulation (1981, Simulacra and Simulations, trans. Paul Foss, Paul Patton, and Philip Beitchmen, 1983); Simone de Beauvoir, Le deuxième sexe (1949, The Second Sex, trans. H. M. Parshley, 1953); Diane Bell and Renate Klein, eds., Radically Speaking (1996); Dennis Bingham, Acting Male: Masculinities in the Films of James Stewart, Jack Nicholson, and Clint Eastwood (1994); Marcellus Blount and George P. Cunningham, Representing Black Men (1996); Robert Bly, Iron John (1990); Joseph Allen Boone and Michael Cadden, eds., Engendering Men: The Question of Male Feminist Criticism (1990); Kate Bornstein, Gender Outlaw (1995); Avtar Brah, Cartographies of Diaspora: Contesting Identities (1996); Rose M. Brewer, "Theorizing Race, Class, and Gender," Materialist Feminisms (Hennessy and Ingraham); Harry Brod and Michael Kaufman, eds., Theorizing Masculinities (1994); Judith Butler, Bodies that Matter (1993), Gender Trouble (1990), The Psychic Life of Power (1997); Pat Califia, Sex Changes: The Politics of Transgenderism (1997); Hazel Carby, Race Men (1998); Lynn Cherny and Elizabeth Reba Weise, eds., Wired Women: Gender and New Realities in Cyberspace (1996); Nancy Chodorow, The Reproduction of Mothering: Psychoanalysis and the Sociology of Gender (1978); Hélène Cixous, "Le rire de la Méduse" (1975, "The Laugh of the Medusa," trans. Keith Cohen and Paula Cohen, Signs 1 [1976]); Steven Cohan, ed., et al., Screening the Male: Exploring Masculinities in Hollywood Cinema (1993); Robert W. Connell, Gender and Power (1987), Masculinities (1995), The Men and the Boys (2001); Deborah David and Robert Brannon, eds., The Forty-Nine Percent Majority: The Male Sex Role (1976); Teresa de Lauretis, Alice Doesn't: Feminism, Semiotics, Cinema (1984), Queer Theory: Lesbian and Gay Sexualities (1990), Technologies of Gender: Essays on Theory, Film, and Fiction (1987); Jacques Derrida, "Women in the Beehive: A Seminar with Jacques Derrida" (Jardine and Smith); Tom Digby, ed., Men Doing Feminism (1998); Alexander Doty, Flaming Classics: Queering the Film Canon (2000); Patricia Duncker, "Postgender: Jurassic Feminism Meets Queer Politics," Post-theory: New Directions in Criticism (ed. Martin McQuillan et al., 1999); Richard Dyer, White (1997); Tim Edwards, Erotics and Politics: Gay Male Sexuality, Masculinity, and Feminism (1994); Julia Epstein and Kristina Straub, eds., Bodyguards: The Cultural Politics of Gender Ambiguity (1991); Rebecca Blevins Faery, Cartographies of Desire: Captivity, Race, and Sex in the Shaping of an American Nation (1999); Frantz Fanon, Black Skin, White Masks (1952); Leslie Feinberg, Transgender Warriors (1997); Mary Flanagan and Austin Booth, eds., Reload: Rethinking Women and Cyberculture (2002); Jane Flax, Thinking Fragments (1990); Michel Foucault, Histoire de la sexualité, vol. 1, La volonté de savoir (1976, The History of Sexuality, vol. 1, An Introduction, trans. Robert Hurley, 1978), vol. 2, L'usage des plaisirs (1984, vol. 2, The Use of Pleasure, trans. Robert Hurley, 1986), vol. 3, Le souci de soi (1984, vol. 3, The Care of the Self, trans. Robert Hurley, 1986), Surveiller et punir: Naissance de la prison (1975, Discipline and Punish: The Birth of the Prison, trans. Alan Sheridan, 1977); Ruth Frankenberg, White Women, Race Matters: The Social Construction of Whiteness (1993); Nancy Fraser, Unruly Practices: Power, Discourse, and Gender in Contemporary Social Theory (1989); Betty Friedan, The Feminine Mystique (1963); Marjorie Garber, Vested Interests: Cross-Dressing and Cultural Anxiety (1992); Eileen Green and Alison Adam, eds., Virtual Gender: Technology, Consumption and Identity Matters (2001); Sandra M. Gilbert and Susan Gubar, The Madwoman in the Attic: The Woman Writer and the Nineteenth-Century Literary Imagination (1979), No Man's Land: The Place of the Woman Writer in the Twentieth Century (3 vols., 1987–1994); Elizabeth Grosz, Volatile Bodies: Toward A Corporeal Feminism (1994); Paul Hammond, Love Between Men in English Literature (1996); Ellis Hanson, ed., Out Takes: Essays on Queer Theory and Film (1999); Donna J. Haraway, "A Manifesto for Cyborgs: Science, Technology, and Socialist Feminism in the 1980s" (Nicholson); John C. Hawley, Postcolonial, Queer (2001); Katherine Hayles, How We Became Posthuman: Virtual Bodies in Cybernetics, Literature, and Informatics (1999); Carolyn Heilbrun, Toward a Recognition of Androgyny (1973); Rosemary Hennessy and Chrys Ingraham, eds., Materialist Feminisms (1997); Leslie Heywood and Jennifer Drake, eds., Third Wave Agenda: Being Feminist, Doing Feminism (1997); bell hooks, Feminist Theory: From Margin to Center (1984), Reel to Real: Race, Sex, and Class at the Movies (1996); Luce Irigaray, Ce sexe qui n'en est pas un (1977, This Sex Which is Not One, trans. Catherine Porter with Carolyn Burke, 1985); Fredric Jameson, Postmodernism; or, The

Cultural Logic of Late Capitalism (1991); Alice A. Jardine and Hester Eisenstein, eds., The Future of Difference (1980); Alice Jardine and Paul Smith, eds., Men in Feminism (1987); Barbara Johnson, A World of Difference (1987); Cora Kaplan, Sea Changes: Culture and Feminism (1986); Rita Mae Kelly, Gender, Globalization, and Democratization (2001); Michael Kimmel, ed., The Politics of Manhood (1995); Dave King, The Transvestite and the Transsexual: Public Categories and Private Identities (1993); Julia Kristeva, La révolution du langage poétique: L'avant-garde à la fin du XIXe siècle, Lautréamont et Mallarmé (1974, Revolution in Poetic Language, trans. Margaret Waller, 1984); Annette Kuhn and AnnMarie Wolpe, eds., Feminism and Materialism: Women and Modes of Production (1978); Jacques Lacan, "Le stade du miroir comme formateur de la fonction du je" (1949, "The Mirror Stage as a Formative of the Function of the I," Écrits, trans. Alan Sheridan, 1982); Peter Lehman, ed., Masculinity: Bodies, Movies, Culture (2001); Brian D. Loader, ed., Cyberspace Divide: Equality, Agency and Policy in the Information Society (1998); Nina Lykke and Rosi Braidotti, eds., Between Monsters, Goddesses, and Cyborgs: Feminist Confrontations with Science, Medicine, and Cyberspace (1996); Larry McCaffery, ed., Storming the Reality Studio (1991); Anne McClintock, Imperial Leather: Race, Gender, and Sexuality in the Colonial Conquest (1995); Anne McClintock, Ella Shohat, and Aamir Mufti, eds., Dangerous Liaisons: Gender, Nation, and Postcolonial Perspectives (1997); Michael A. Messner, Politics of Masculinities: Men in Movements (1997); Hazel Mew, Frail Vessels (1969); Nancy K. Miller, ed., The Poetics of Gender (1986); Kate Millett, Sexual Politics (1970); Juliet Mitchell, Psychoanalysis and Feminism (1974), Woman's Estate (1971), "Women: The Longest Revolution," New Left Review 40 (1966), Women: The Longest Revolution (1984); Tania Modleski, Loving with a Vengeance: Mass-Produced Fantasies for Women (1982); Chandra Talpade Mohanty, "Under Western Eyes: Feminist Scholarship and Colonial Discourse," Third World Women and The Politics of Feminism (ed. Chandra Talpade Mohanty et al., 1991); Toril Moi, Sexual/Textual Politics: Feminist Literary Theory (1985); Thaïs E. Morgan, Men Writing the Feminine (1994); Toni Morrison, Playing in the Dark: Whiteness and the Literary Imagination (1992); Laura Mulvey, "Visual Pleasure and Narrative Cinema" (1975); Uma Narayan and Sandra Harding, eds., Decentering the Center: Philosophy for a Multicultural, Postcolonial, and Feminist World (2000); Linda J. Nicholson, ed., Feminism/Postmodernism (1990); Steve Neale, "Masculinity as Spectacle: Reflections on Men in Mainstream Cinema," Screen 6 (1983); Rictor Norton, The Myth of the Modern Homosexual: Queer History and the Search for Cultural Unity (1997); Mary Ann O'Farrell and Lynne Vallone, eds., Virtual Gender: Fantasies of Subjectivity and Embodiment (1999); Lahoucine Ouzgane and Daniel Coleman, Postcolonial Masculinities, Jouvert 2 (1998); Carole Pateman, "Feminist Critiques of the Public/Private Dichotomy," Feminism and Equality (ed. Anne Phillips, 1987); Fred Pfeil, White Guys: Essays in Postmodern Domination (1995); Joseph H. Pleck, The Myth of Masculinity (1981); Shirin Ria, Gender and the Political Economy of Development (2001); Adrienne Rich, On Lies, Secrets, and Silence: Selected Prose, 1966–1978 (1979); Katherine M. Rogers, The Troublesome Helpmate (1966); Jacqueline Rose, Sexuality in the Field of Vision (1986); Peter Schwenger, Phallic Critiques: Masculinity and Twentieth Century Literature (1984); Joan Wallach Scott, Gender and the Politics of History (1988); Eve Kosofsky Sedgwick, Between Men: English Literature and Male Homosocial Desire (1985); Elaine Showalter, "Critical Cross-Dressing: Male Feminists and the Woman of the Year" (Jardine and Smith), A Literature of Their Own (1977), Speaking of Gender (1989); Kaja Silverman, The Acoustic Mirror: The Female Voice in Psychoanalysis and Cinema (1988), Male Subjectivity at the Margins (1992); Siobhan B. Somerville, Queering the Color Line: Race and the Invention of Homosexuality in American Culture (2000); Gayatri Chakravorty Spivak, A Critique of Postcolonial Reason: Toward a History of the Vanishing Present (1999), In Other Worlds: Essays in Cultural Politics (1987); Sandy Stone (Allucquere Rosanne), "A Posttranssexual Manifesto" (Epstein and Straub), The War of Desire and Technology at the Close of the Mechanical Age (1996); Susan Stryker, ed., The Transgender Issue (1998); Calvin Thomas, ed., Straight with a Twist: Queer Theory and Subject of Homosexuality; Trinh T. Minh-ha, When the Moon Waxes Red: Representation and Cultural Politics (1991), Woman, Native, Other (1989); Edmund White, The Burning Library (1994); Stephen M. Whitehead and Frank J. Barrett, eds., Masculinities Reader (2001); Raymond Williams, "Advertising: the Magic System" (1980); Sharon Willis, High Contrast: Race and Gender in Contemporary Hollywood Film (1997), "The Mark of Gender" (Miller), "One Is Not Born a Woman," Feminist Issues 1 (1981); Mary Wollstonecraft, A Vindication of the Rights of Woman (1792).

Gilroy, Paul

Paul Gilroy (b. 1956) earned his PhD from the Centre for Contemporary Cultural Studies at Birmingham University where he worked under the guidance of STUART HALL and was part of a collective that produced *The Empire Strikes Back: Race and Racism in 70s Britain* (1982). While at Birmingham, Gilroy was not sure if he was destined for academic work and contemplated a career as a musician. During this time he also coauthored studies of policing and racial harassment for the General London Council while working there between 1982 and 1985. He has written numerous sleeve notes for records and catalog texts for art exhibits. Gilroy has taught at numerous universities, including Yale, where he served as chair of the African American Studies Department and was the Charlotte Marian Saden Professor of Sociology and African American Studies, and the London School of Economics, where in 2005 he became the first Anthony Giddens Professor of Social Theory.

Gilroy's dissertation, "Racism, Class and the Contemporary Politics of 'Race' and 'Nation'" (1986), was quickly published as a book titled *"There Ain't No Black in the Union Jack": The Cultural Politics of Race and Nation* (1987). *"There Ain't No Black,"* like all of Gilroy's subsequent works, advances the argument that "race" is a logically insufficient and ethically irredeemable category for structuring identity and human relationality. Gilroy persistently writes the word "race" in quotation marks to emphasize that the concept is a social-discursive construct rather than a natural quality of human existence. He reiterates his core thesis in *Small Acts: Thoughts on the Politics of Black Cultures* (1993), *The Black Atlantic: Modernity and Double Consciousness* (1993), *Against Race: Imagining Political Culture Beyond the Color Line* (2000), and *Postcolonial Melancholia* (2004), and *Darker Than Blue: On the Moral Economies of Black Atlantic Culture* (2010). His attention to "race" and public culture is unwavering, but he avoids redundancy by addressing an abundance of topics, including social policy, postcolonial theory, literature, musical production and performance, colonial histories, continental philosophy, genetic science, celebrity culture, and contemporary multiculturalism. Though Gilroy has consistently held academic posts in sociology departments, his work, like that of the FRANKFURT SCHOOL scholars who heavily influence his thinking, problematizes academic culture by resisting easy categorization.

Gilroy's sustained critique of "race" often takes black political culture and art as its object of analysis. Taking his cue from the work of THEODOR W. ADORNO— particularly in his attention to the ideological effects of popular music—Gilroy's writing clarifies the relationship between ethics and aesthetics, a relationship that often escapes rigorous scrutiny in public culture. This effort requires that he create wildly broad research parameters. He discusses the contradictions lived by contemporary hip-hop artist-cum-actor Ice Cube and the satirical value of Sacha Baron Cohen's character "Ali G" as seriously as he analyzes the impact of *négritude* ideologues

Aimé Césaire and Léopold Sédar Senghor, postcolonial theorist FRANTZ FANON, or writer-theorist Edouard Glissant. (See AFRICAN AMERICAN THEORY AND CRITICISM and POSTCOLONIAL STUDIES: 1. ORIGINS TO THE 1980S.)

Although Gilroy focuses on black culture, his analysis of any singular political movement, social act, or text can never be divorced from his overarching project of critiquing "race" itself. Gilroy exposes the racialized knowledge-building enterprises, political structures, and capitalist economic practices that have constituted Western modernity. His writing consistently addresses the systemic violence to which black people have been subject and strives to ignite the utopic potential that he sees as immanent in artistic production. Gilroy is critical of black popular and political cultures only insofar as their participants reproduce the strategies and conceptual categories that have, historically, served as bulwarks for white privilege. These include an ethnic-absolutist faith in the nation, the displacement of history by nostalgic mythologies of kinship and pure origins, and an aversion to uncomfortable self-reflexive scrutiny. In his calculations, any of these habits result in untenable claims to cultural authenticity and unethical beliefs in racial essentialism regardless of who is practicing them.

Gilroy argues against ethnic absolutism in all of his texts, but this position is most commonly associated with *The Black Atlantic*. Here, he claims that the experience of blackness in the Western world constitutes the protomodern human condition. Modeled after EDWARD W. SAID's *Orientalism* (1978) and building on W. E. B. Du Bois's notion of double consciousness, the text posits that this condition was caused by black people's insider/outsider position in the narrative of progress that defined the modern age. (See AFRICAN AMERICAN THEORY AND CRITICISM: 1. HARLEM RENAISSANCE TO THE BLACK ARTS MOVEMENT and RACE AND ETHNICITY.) Under dehumanizing conditions, black bodies were included in narratives of progress only as perverse ciphers for a primitive, premodern state against which white civility defined itself. The places assigned to black people in narratives of cultural evolution—"from racial slavery to Jim Crow citizenship, from southern shack to metropolitan tenement block" (172)—created feelings of fragmentation, anxiety, and alienation that were only belatedly diagnosed by the European avant-garde as the defining condition of the period.

Crucially, for Gilroy, this situation is not particular to African Americans but is a much more complex transatlantic, diasporic phenomenon. To lay the foundation for this argument, Gilroy arranges a dialectic between the authoritative voices of European modernity such as Immanuel Kant and Friedrich Nietzsche and early- to mid-twentieth-century pan-Africanist scholars such as Martin Delaney and Du Bois. Gilroy resolves this dialectical tension by proposing to study "the black Atlantic" as a distinct and unified object of analysis in its own right, a diasporic entity that exceeds "that narrowness of vision that is content with the merely national" (4). Gilroy credits Du Bois's *The Souls of Black Folk* (1903) as the first articulation of "a diasporic, global perspective on the politics of racism" in his claim that promising hopes for an anti-racist future can emerge from the antiphonic "connective culture" of the transatlantic diaspora (121, 82).

Gilroy's decision to deploy the diaspora concept is, in part, a reflection of his historical sensibility: "diaspora" allows him to adamantly disavow practices of communal solidarity that are bound by theories of racial essentialism. The concept also enables him to commemorate the multiple and uneven trajectories along which black people were violently displaced throughout Europe, North America, and the Caribbean, as well as to address the more recent cosmopolitan forms of travel that have enabled philosophical, literary, and musical production.

Gilroy's use of the diaspora concept is not restricted to The Black Atlantic, where he expresses his preference for "routes," as exemplified by the transnational evolution of reggae and hip-hop, over its homonym "roots," or narratives of origins and racial-ethnic authenticity (19, 33). His simple, memorable articulation of this distinction in The Black Atlantic has ensured that the text is cited in virtually every critical lexicon entry for "diaspora."

The convenience of the routes/roots pairing, however, belies the deeper value of Gilroy's work, which recognizes the contributions of black artists and thinkers to modernity. Viewed in this way, "the black Atlantic" signifies not as a defensive reaction to or diseased symptom of the modern age but as a lively and historically verifiable "counterculture of modernity." This concept, borrowed from Zygmunt Bauman, calls into question conventional accounts of intellectual evolution in the Western world and makes space for future antiracist efforts.

Gilroy's antiracist focus is asserted most bluntly in the title of his fourth book, Against Race. In this text he urges readers "to demand liberation not from white supremacy alone, however urgently that is required, but from all racializing and raciological thought, from racialized seeing, racialized thinking, and racialized thinking about thinking" (40). Published on the eve of the millennium, the introductory and concluding sections of Against Race convey his utopic impulse through futurist language that stands in a marked contrast to his earlier critiques of class, social policy, and modernist aesthetics. In Against Race he adopts what he describes as a "postracial" stance in the context of the world's "DNA revolution" (42, 15).

Gilroy's futurist renunciation of race is grounded in the present by his ongoing critique of modernity, ethnic absolutism, and nation. In Against Race, a text modeled after Hannah Arendt's Origins of Totalitarianism (1951), he mobilizes this critique through an analysis of fascism. He argues that authoritarianism is increasingly the political-cultural norm rather than a historical aberration that was safely contained in mid-twentieth-century Europe. He continues to challenge not only what people think about race and nation but how people think about race and nation by drawing unlikely connections between various manifestations of fascism. His postracial perspective allows him to perceive the continuities between "white supremacists and black nationalists, Klansmen, Nazis, neo-Nazis and ethnic absolutists, Zionists and anti-Semites" in such a way that they appear to "encounter each other as potential allies rather than sworn foes" (219). Again following the lead of Frankfurt school scholars, his account becomes even more provocative when he compares these extremist groups to the corporations that define the terms of global consumer culture.

In *Against Race* Gilroy theorizes that the shift from an era of epidermal biopolitics to an era of genomic nanopolitics presents us with an opportunity to stop using science as an instrument for racist social domination. He distances himself from the term GLOBALIZATION by describing this utopic philosophy with the term "planetary humanism" (2, 356). In *Postcolonial Melancholia*, however, he strips this idea of its futurist rhetoric in the course of offering a defense of spontaneous, vernacular multiculturalism in Britain under the rubric of "planetary conviviality" (xv). Appearing in the post-9/11 context, this published series of lectures avoids all futurist jargon as it discusses the failure of mid-twentieth-century liberal human rights discourses to prevent contemporary forms of imprisonment, degradation, and torture that are carried out by global-imperial powers in the twenty-first century. As in earlier projects, Gilroy seeks moral courage in vernacular articulations of cosmopolitan community—for instance, in the work of human rights activists of the International Solidarity Movement.

In 2010, Gilroy published *Darker Than Blue: On The Moral Economies of Black Atlantic Culture*, a text that grew from material originally delivered at Harvard University in 2006. This book seeks to radically reinvigorate African American studies by suggesting that the field's attention to "freedom" as a central mobilizing paradigm be put to rest. The core of this impetus is Gilroy's strenuous admonishment that the "world-historic culture of freedom" that was "the slaves' gift to the world" (5) was never truly allowed to flourish but continues to be flattened, exploited, and exported, robbed of its universal transformative potential both by market forces—which substitute an infinite succession of illusory consumer freedoms for genuine political and social freedom—and by the contemporary diplomatic rhetoric of the United States, in which that country's complex history of slavery is channeled into a modern-day war cry of evolved moral authority on matters of freedom, citizenship, multiculturalism, diversity, and security. Gilroy's new philosophical reflections on political morality are buoyed by familiar themes: a marked distaste for nationalism and essentialist approaches to identity; disgust for the culture of conspicuous consumption and the signs of class ascendancy that are valorized by the hip-hop elite; and an equal measure of reverence for thinkers Fanon and Du Bois and musicians Bob Marley and Jimi Hendrix, all for their ability to organize feeling and to synchronize consciousness around the "not yet" through transformative encounters with ideas and music that pronounce—and in so doing, he argues, have the potential to produce—a better, truly deracialized world.

As Gilroy increasingly considers "the human," it seems that perhaps his greatest omission is a direct and sustained analysis of how feeling works. In *Small Acts* he identifies the "inner dialectics" of diasporic identification; in *The Black Atlantic* he repeatedly hints at the importance of a certain "structure of feeling"; in *Postcolonial Melancholia* he briefly invokes a formulaic theory of mass anxiety and shame; and in *Darker Than Blue* he urges readers "to reframe the internality of racial identity without presupposing either essence or interiority" (146). Gilroy never offers a sustained theorization of feeling itself, however, despite the fact that he always attends extensively to the affect that others produce and is himself heavily invested in producing affect as a definitive rhetorical effect of his writing style. After all, in *The Black Atlantic* he writes that he "prefer[s] to see [*The Souls of Black Folk's*] combination of tones and modes of interpellating the reader as a deliberate experiment produced from the realisation that none of these different registers of address could, by itself, convey the intensity of feeling that Du Bois believed the writing of black history and the exploration of racialised experience demanded" (115). Perhaps the same is true of Gilroy's own indomitable critical aesthetic.

JOHN CORR

See also MULTICULTURALISM, POSTCOLONIAL STUDIES: 2. 1990 AND AFTER, RACE AND ETHNICITY, and EDWARD W. SAID.

Paul Gilroy, *Against Race: Imagining Political Culture Beyond the Color Line* (2000), *The Black Atlantic: Modernity and Double Consciousness* (1993), *Darker Than Blue: On the Moral Economies of Black Atlantic Culture* (2010), "Paul Gilroy—In Conversation," *darkmatter* (7 May 2007), *Postcolonial Melancholia* (2004), *Small Acts: Thoughts on the Politics of Black Cultures* (1993), "*There Ain't No Black in the Union Jack*": The Cultural Politics of Race and Nation (1987); Paul Gilroy and Iain Chambers, *Hendrix, hip-hop e l'interruzione del pensiero* (1995), Centre for Contemporary Cultural Studies, *The Empire Strikes Back: Race and Racism in 70s Britain* (1982).

Globalization

Though literature has long been a globalized cultural form, only recently has there been a concerted attempt to understand what globalization means for literary theory and criticism. By its nature, globalization insists on the supposedly unique character of the present moment (the 1990s and the first decade of the twenty-first century) in a way that renders past relations and theories moribund and inadequate. In considering the significance of globalization for literary theory and criticism, there is a real danger of reinforcing and rearticulating globalization's presentism. Equally, however, the concept of globalization has the potential to refocus literary theory and criticism on historical gaps and lost connective opportunities, most insistently in the still relatively limited intersection of Western theory with its non-Western counterparts.

Attempts to connect globalization and literary studies have run into the blizzard of contradictory meanings, relationships, and discourses that have swirled around the concept of globalization since it came into existence in the early 1990s. Globalization discourses became prominent only after the end of the Soviet bloc in 1989, originating in part to explain the characteristics of the "new world order" announced by U.S. president George H. W. Bush at the conclusion of the cold war. Globalization has thus been taken as a periodizing term, a description of contemporary geopolitics, and an ideological project or agenda. Most generally, "globalization" is the name given to the social, economic, political, and cultural processes that, taken together, have produced the characteristic conditions of contemporary (late twentieth-/early twenty-first-century) existence. In particular it refers to the ways previously distant parts of the world have become connected in a historically unprecedented manner, such that developments in one part of the world are now able to rapidly produce effects on geographically distant localities. This in turn has made it possible to begin to imagine the world as a single, global space linked by a wide array of technological, economic, social, and cultural forces that are able to cross and crisscross the imagined boundaries of cultures or nations with relative ease.

Globalization has been used to refer both to this larger, historical process and to the effects produced separately in a variety of conceptual registers, as in discussions of contemporary finance capitalism and the scale of corporatization and privatization (economic), the erosion of the nation-state system and the rise of transnational organizations and corporations (political), the threat posed by global culture to local cultures and traditions (culture), the deleterious impact of human activity on the natural world (ecological), and the communications revolution introduced by new technologies like the Internet (communications). In the West, these changes have resulted in the shattering of the fragile post–World War II accommodation between labor and capital through the elimination or rollback of the (always already modest) programs of the welfare state. In much of the rest of the world, the shift of capitalism from Fordist to post-Fordist regimes of flexible production and accumulation has led to the transformation of imperialist economic relationships into even more powerful and debilitating neoimperialist ones, stifling the sovereign ambitions of postcolonial states almost immediately following their independence. One of the most misleading and yet the most common narrative of globalization is one that substitutes economic cause for effect. Never has it been clearer that the state is the executive committee of the ruling class than in the oft-repeated claims of Western governments that globalization (treated as an abstract, invisible, and irresistible force) has made it impossible to rein in the excesses of mobile capital and that the only course of action is to go along for the ride, whatever consequences this might have for the majority of citizens.

Literary theory has been impacted both implicitly and explicitly by these global economic transformations and their public policy outcomes. Thinkers such as FREDRIC JAMESON and PIERRE BOURDIEU (Acts of Resistance [1998]) have speculated on the cultural dimensions of contemporary conservative or "neoliberal" ideology, drawing attention to how the logic of the market has all but obliterated the public sphere and broken down the semiautonomy of different elements of society (e.g., the cultural and the economic). In the wake of fiscal attacks on the humanities and the reorganization of the professoriate into a flexible work force of contract labor there has been renewed attention to the material conditions that underlie the institutions of literary theory and criticism. In addition, an examination and critique of the effects of global economics and politics has played an important role in work produced within politically engaged modes of theory, such as Marxism and POSTCOLONIAL STUDIES, especially in terms of the material and discursive perpetuation of economic and cultural imperialism. Contemporary feminist theories, too, have had to address the political and social consequences of the worsening situation of women worldwide.

It should be stressed, however, that these points of connection between literary theory and globalization remain at an early stage of development. Literary-theoretical responses to globalization only came at the end of the 1990s, whereas in the social sciences treatments of globalization started to appear at the beginning of that decade. There are several reasons for this lag: postcolonial criticism had already been addressing many of the issues and concerns that seemed to be contained within discussions of globalization (e.g., cultural imperialism, global shifts in political power, etc.), and the existence of other global cultural discourses (e.g., world systems theory, dependency theory, theories of the "global" conditions of literary and cultural production) seemed to interfere with the quick generation of connective tissue between the literary-theoretical and the global. Insofar as there have been attempts to make this connection, they have taken the form of a variety of sophisticated ways of extending or moving beyond existing literary discourses toward a more global frame of analysis that includes not only an acknowledgment of the complex intercultural dynamics of the literary but also the ways in which these have always been suspended in a network of global forces. These attempts include ambitious works such as Emily Apter's Continental Drift (1999), Timothy Brennan's At Home in the World (1997), Pascale Casanova's The World Republic of Letters (1999), and Peter Hitchcock's Transnational Trilogies and Tetralogies (2010), all of which both interrogate globalization theory and its impact on literary theory (and vice versa) and offer a theory of literature in a global frame. Notable here as well is FRANCO MORETTI's Modern Epic: The World System from Goethe to García Márquez (1996), which offers a theory of the "modern epic" as a globe-hopping genre that includes works from Herman Melville's Moby-Dick to Gabriel García Márquez's One Hundred Years of Solitude.

Globalization has introduced new theories of culture, especially of the ways culture circulates and the processes through which it produces effects. There has, for example, been an insistence on the need to understand culture in terms of "networks," "flows," and "routes" or through its mode of transmission rather than through its relationship to concrete spaces and places. For the most part, however, globalization names a set of complex problems and questions for literary and CULTURAL STUDIES rather than any new theory or group of theories. These problems and questions are only beginning to be articulated and relate to at least five major issues in literary studies that have already been subjects of concerted analysis in other contexts and for other reasons: (1) the object of literary studies; (2) the framework or context of analysis of this object; (3) the future of the institution of literary studies; (4) the relationship between art, literature, and consumer culture; and (5) the politics of the aesthetic.

Object of analysis. Over the past several decades, traditional ideas about the character of the literary object have undergone intensive theoretical probing and questioning. These questions supplement the deconstructive fragmentation and splintering of the unity of literary texts by interrogating the political, social, and cultural role and function of literary texts in present historical circumstances. The emphasis within globalization discourses on telecommunications, popular culture, and consumer culture has led many scholars to shift away from literary studies and traditional forms of humanistic research toward those forms that reflect contemporary mass experience. The deemphasis on the literary also reasserts the need expressed in cultural studies to deal with cultural phenomena that interpellate and affect greater numbers of people than do contemporary fiction, drama, and poetry. Likewise, the tools of literary theory have been increasingly directed toward a new use, the analysis of those policy documents and international agreements that performatively and discursively construct the global present (Harlow and Carter). There has been increased attention, for instance, to the investigation of contemporary regimes of intellectual property and their related aesthetic and cultural significance. The wholesale questioning of the (Western) literary object in the context of globalization is not limited to analyses dealing with contemporary literature. Indeed, one of the most interesting outcomes of discussions and debates over globalization has been the extension of these arguments concerning the appropriate object of study to the whole of the Western canon. For instance, the widespread circulation in globalization of discourses concerning cultural hybridity and transmigration has led to an exploration of these themes in the whole history of English and American literatures (e.g., Kaplan and Pease) and to increased attention by literary critics to popular culture and the circulation of cultural objects other than literature in periods prior to the development of mass culture.

Framework of analysis. Though there has been growing attention to the complex origins and contexts of literary fields, literary studies have nevertheless continued to be organized institutionally and intellectually around the study of discrete national literatures and national literary histories. The analytic limitations of this approach, as well its problematical debt to a parochial nationalism, have been articulated and rearticulated with increasing frequency over the past several decades. Continuing to assert a national basis for literary studies captures the importance of discourses of nationalism to the construction of literature and literary criticism. What it disallows or disables, however, are forms of analysis that cut across the literary text in different ways, not simply acknowledging multiple, extranational influences (literary or otherwise) on national texts but rethinking the literary text in a fundamental way that does away with the geographical frame entirely.

Globalization has pushed literary theorists and critics to attempt to fundamentally rethink the spaces of culture that have undergirded literary analysis since the late eighteenth century. Most successful in this respect so far have been various forms of postcolonial studies, especially those that emphasize cultural and literary relations produced in in-between or liminal spaces, and discussions of literary regionalism or of alternative modernities, which interrupt the idea that modernity has "flowed" from one definite space to another. Marxism and other internationalist or antinationalist cultural discourses have also offered models for a new frame in which to understand the production and circulation of literary texts. Finally, there has been a critical reinvigoration of the discourse of "world literature," as exemplified in David Damrosch's *What Is World Literature?* (2003), as well as in GAYATRI CHAKRAVORTY SPIVAK'S call for a reconstituted comparative literary studies in *Death of a Discipline* (2003).

The institution of literary studies. Over the past two decades the contemporary neoliberal agenda has also led to a concerted attack on literary studies and the humanities more generally. Due in part to the waning of the importance of nation-state to the operations of global capitalism, there is now less of a need for a social institution geared toward the production of a national narrative or a discourse mediating the relationship between the populace and the state: the replacement of the "citizen" with the "consumer" is just one sign that such a mediating discourse is now to be found within the operations of capital itself. As a result, it is not surprising that it has become increasingly hard to justify and explain the value of the humanities, whether in the neoliberal vocabulary of economic efficiency (i.e., the "output" of a humanities education) or in terms that do not simply invoke forms of "bad" humanism, trumpet its essential criticality, or reimagine an Arnoldian vision of the humanities for a new gilded age. Though it is unlikely that literary studies will survive unchanged, this can also be seen as potentially opening up the possibility of new forms of analysis and critique that capitalize on a whole range of post–World War II challenges to humanism.

Art, literature, and consumer culture. With respect to culture, globalization continues to be most commonly understood as the worldwide spread of American-style mass and/or consumer culture. This vision of globalization comes with a "ready-to-hand" politics that tends to simplify complex processes and histories: powerful, dominant cultures overwhelm weaker, smaller, more vulnerable ones, threatening difference and polysemy with a form of negative universalism whose sole aim is to create a single, planetary culture defined by shopping and cultural consumption— the "McWorld" envisioned by Benjamin Barber as our planetary future. Though this ready-to-hand discourse about globalization is frequently employed, the vision of culture that it articulates has itself been powerfully challenged from within literary theory and criticism. Without wishing to deny the importance of relations of power, and highly unequal ones at that, the process by which cultures interact and come into contact with one another mitigates against the easy equation of the popularity of U.S. cinema abroad with the imposition of U.S. values—whatever those might be in a society as internally complex as the United States. The tendency to fall back on theories generally disavowed in other theoretical registers suggests that literary and cultural critics still face a significant challenge in producing a sophisticated theory concerning the relationship between consumer culture and literature or the literary. More sophisticated and open analyses of the complex dynamics of popular culture in a global frame can be found, for instance, in Naomi Klein's widely read analysis of branding in *No Logo* (2000) and in Thomas Frank's challenge to theories of the corporate appropriation of supposedly genuinely "popular" culture in *The Conquest of Cool* (1997). Strangely, however, it is in this area, where perhaps the most has been written on globalization from a cultural perspective, that there has been the least insight into contemporary culture and the place of the literary within it.

The politics of aesthetic form. The contemporary politics of the aesthetic continues to draw energy from its modernist definition, that of a cultural intervention into the social via shock and transgression. Without ever being explicitly stated, it is the criterion that informs the choice of exemplary literary models in most theoretical essays; DECONSTRUCTION, for instance, has been constructed on the back of the monuments of high modernism, as has (perhaps more problematically) much of Western Marxist literary theory. Globalization has presented a challenge to this connection between aesthetics and politics. The global phantasmagoria of visual images, blending high art and pop culture to a degree and extent adumbrated in postmodern discourses, has made it apparent that "aesthetic experience is now everywhere and saturates social and daily life in general" (Jameson 100). The ubiquity of the aesthetic, the generalization of its shocks and transgressions into the cultural landscape at large, necessitates a wholesale rethinking of the presumed politics of the aesthetic. Globalization suggests that the "society of the spectacle" is indeed a global phenomenon: there are no longer spaces "outside" of the spectacle that can be recuperated for the purposes of aesthetic renewal, the function, for instance, that African art and literature performed at different moments in the history of Western modernism (Brown).

It is not just the formal, social, or cultural function of cultural objects that needs to be rethought. Increasingly, globalization has prompted a reexamination of modernism itself. For example, Malcolm Bull has argued that the opposition commonly drawn between modernism and both classicism (which precedes it) and commodity culture (which follows) is mistaken. Modernism is seen as a slim moment of aesthetic and political possibility between two epochs that block effective resistance to capitalism; this is why modernist aesthetics continue to be the site at which the conjunction of aesthetics and politics is theorized. Bull suggests, however, that the opposition between modernism and capitalism is overstated. Modernism is not a gap in the seamless and inexorable development of a commodity culture on its way to becoming global. "Modernists were not partisans resisting the present and pressing on eternity, they were negotiating the equally tricky but rather more mundane path between the two cultures of capitalism[.] . . . [W]orking between two antithetical cultures meant that resistance to the one almost always involved some degree of complicity with the other" (97).

Far from signaling the end of literature or the end of theory, globalization has forced literary theory to address in substantive ways criticisms of those problems and limits that have led to feelings of "crisis" in contemporary theory. Spivak's attempt in *Death of a Discipline* to reinvigorate comparative literature and area studies alike by placing them into radical dialogue with one another is but one example of an attempt to think past this sense of crisis in a highly sophisticated way that avoids easy returns to literary humanism or uncritical universalisms. However, discussions of the institutions of literary theory in the context of globalization must remain vigilant against their (perhaps unavoidable) complicity with neoliberal discourses of globalization. As Masao Miyoshi and Arif Dirlik have pointed out, the academic fascination with globalization has in some cases reinforced the belief in both its empirical reality and its historical inevitability. While the internationalization of the theory conference circuit has led to an ever-increasing realization of the contexts in which Western literary theory arose, as well as to greater cultural and intellectual interchange among scholars, it has also led to globalization discourses' being written largely from the perspective of what Zygmunt Bauman describes as the mobile class of "tourists" rather than the increasingly immobile "vagabonds" that make up most of the world's population.

Though it is important to remain wary of the limits (and inevitable contamination) of the theoretical enterprise as practiced in the Western university, it is equally important to stress that the spreading global awareness of the enormous challenges facing humanity has generated an ever-expanding articulation of and struggle for a "globalization against globalization," a *genuine* globalization (as opposed to a rhetorical screen for capitalism) that strives to produce a world characterized by real social justice. The "movement of movements" that makes up the (misnamed) anti-globalization struggles that came to prominence in the protests against the World Trade Organization in Seattle in 1999 has found its rallying cry in the slogan popularized by the World Social Forum: "Another world is possible." Contemporary literary theory and the humanities more generally no doubt still have a role to play in helping to bring this world into existence.

IMRE SZEMAN

Arjun Appadurai, *Modernity at Large: Cultural Dimensions of Globalization* (1996); Emily S. Apter, *Continental Drift: From National Characters to Virtual Subjects* (1999); Daniel Archibugi, ed., *Debating Cosmopolitics* (2003); Benjamin Barber, *Jihad vs. McWorld: How Globalism and Tribalism Are Re-Shaping the World* (1996); Zygmunt Bauman, *Globalization: The Human Consequences* (1998); Nicholas Brown, *Utopian Generations: The Political Horizon of Twentieth-Century Literature* (2005); Frederick Buell, *National Culture and the New Global System* (1994); Malcolm Bull, "Between the Cultures of Capital," *New Left Review* 11 (2001); Pascale Casanova, *La republique mondiale des lettres* (1999, *The World Republic of Letters*, trans. M. B. DeBevoise, 2004); Manuel Castells, *The Rise of Network Society* (1996, 2nd ed., 2000); Jean Comaroff and John Comaroff, eds., *Millennial Capitalism and the Culture of Neoliberalism* (2001); Arif Dirlik, "Globalization as the End and the Beginning of History," *Rethinking Marxism* 12 (2000); Néstor Garcia Canclini, *Culturas híbridas: Estrategias para entrar y salir de la modernidad* (1992, *Hybrid Cultures: Strategies for Entering and Leaving Modernity*, trans. Christopher L. Chiappari and Silvia L. López, 1995); Anthony Giddens, *Runaway World: How Globalization Is Reshaping Our Lives* (2000); Simon Gikandi, "Globalization and the Claims of Postcoloniality," *South Atlantic Quarterly* 100 (2001); Giles Gunn, ed., "Globalizing Literary Studies," special issue, *PMLA* 116 (2001); Suman Gupta, *Globalization and Literature* (2008); Michael Hardt and Antonio Negri, *Empire* (2000); Barbara Harlow and Mia Carter, eds., *Archives of Empire* (2 vols., 2003); Paul Hirst and Graeme Thompson, *Globalization in Question* (1999); Fredric Jameson, *The Cultural Turn: Selected Writings on the Postmodern, 1983–1998* (1998); Amy Kaplan and Donald E. Pease, eds., *Cultures of United States Imperialism* (1993); David Leiwei Li, ed., *Globalization and the Humanities*, special issue, *Comparative Literature* 53.4 (2001); Masao Miyoshi, "Ivory Tower in Escrow," *boundary 2* 27 (2000); Susie O'Brien and Imre Szeman, eds., "Anglophone Literatures and Global Culture," special issue, *South Atlantic Quarterly* 100 (2001); Imre Szeman, *Zones of Instability: Literature, Postcolonialism, and the Nation* (2003); John Tomlinson, *Globalization and Culture* (1998); Malcolm Waters, *Globalization* (2001).

Gramsci, Antonio

For over half a century the works of Antonio Gramsci (1891–1937) have circulated internationally. Diverse critics have been influenced by his distinctive analysis of culture and its relation to politics. He identified with the south of Italy, where he was born and where he lived until 1911, when he left southern Sardinia to study literature, linguistics, and philosophy at the University of Turin. He became active there in the Socialist Party, organizing factory workers and publishing articles on politics and critical reviews of drama in newspapers and journals. In 1921 he broke with the socialists and was instrumental in founding the Partito Communista d'Italia, traveling to Moscow in 1922 as the party's representative to the International's executive council. There he was elected a deputy to the Italian parliament, but upon his return to Italy and despite his parliamentary immunity, he was arrested by the fascist regime for political activities and imprisoned first in Rome and then in Turi. Afflicted with physical ailments since childhood, prison exacerbated his ill health. In 1933, suffering from arteriosclerosis and pulmonary pneumonia, he was transferred to a prison clinic at Formia and finally to a clinic in Rome, where, after several years, he died.

Between 1929 and 1935, primarily while in Turi di Bari, Gramsci outlined an ambitious plan of study that entailed a multifaceted analysis of how ruling classes were able historically and philosophically to gain power over subaltern groups through coercion and consent. Under the watchful eyes of the prison censors, he committed his ideas to paper, culminating in thirty-three notebooks addressing a wide range of topics, such as the cultural and political role of intellectuals, the "Southern question," the political importance of Machiavelli, popular literature, common sense and folklore, subaltern groups, education, the study of philosophy, the philosophy of Benedetto Croce, linguistics, grammar, literary criticism, journalism, and observations on Americanism and Fordism.

Gramsci's sister-in-law, Tatjana Schucht, smuggled the *Prison Notebooks* (1948–1950) out of Italy following his death, yet they did not arrive in Moscow until almost a year later. At roughly the same time, Palmiro Togliatti, like Gramsci a charter member of the Italian Communist Party, received copies to read while in exile in Spain. Owing to the massive editorial enterprise required to prepare Gramsci's writings for publication, the works written during his incarceration did not begin to appear until the late 1940s and early 1950s. The notebooks, more than his other writings, have been the source of Gramsci's intellectual legacy. However, Gramsci's comments in the notebooks indicate that they were not intended for publication in their fragmentary form. They rather constituted provisional and incomplete observations on the various issues he undertook to discuss that he hoped later to order and expand.

From Gramsci's point of view, culture does not function as a mere reflection of the economic base, nor is it envisioned as a totally separate entity. While Gramsci rejects both standard Marxist reflection theory and such post-Marxist theories of parallel realms (in which each sociocultural category would have its own internal relations of base to superstructure) as those advanced by Louis Althusser and Ernesto Laclau, he never abandons the Marxian infrastructure-superstructure schema. Rather, he recasts the underlying notion of reflection, in which the vital economic base generates its masked and/or obfuscating reflective superstructure, by changing the nature of the relationship from one of *reflection* to one of *reciprocity*. This theoretical conception of mutually reciprocal forces gives culture its power.

In his characterization of the possibilities for new hegemonic formations Gramsci's focus on intellectuals and education is pivotal. In the notebooks he made the following general observations offering an unconventional conception of the role and nature of intellectuals: "Although one can speak of intellectuals, one cannot speak of non-intellectuals, because non-intellectuals do not exist. . . . There is no human activity from which every form of intellectual participation can be excluded." Gramsci's notes on intellectuals are set in the context of creating "a new stratum of intellectuals," "organic-collective" intellectuals who become "the foundation of a new and integral conception of the world" (SPN 9; *Quaderni* 1516). Since history is created, not divinely ordained, the role of intellectuals as cultural and political critics is integral to Gramsci's thought.

Gramsci's work demonstrates his penchant for adopting other thinkers' critical categories and terminology and his reworking of these prior concepts to his own ends. His interest in cultural history also encompasses the history of folklore, as the cultural expression of Italy's subaltern classes; he may be seen as the modern father of the sociology of literature and culture in Italy. This combination of popular and historical studies is also evident in his examination of the phenomenon of "national-popular" literature, which he finds signally lacking in modern Italy. His writings on common sense as folklore are connected to his conception of traces of the past in the present and of the role of literature as a cultural and political force. Gramsci, in sympathetic fashion, identified folklore with the philosophy of the people as a form of common sense that functions for survival but also as an obstacle to new forms of thought and action.

Gramsci's objective, it would seem, is not to eradicate common sense but to transform it to "good sense" or critical thought, that is, the effort to "order in a systematic, coherent, and critical fashion one's own intuitions of the life and of the world" (SPN 187; *Quaderni* 1379). His conception of common sense bears relation to GILLES DELEUZE's and Henri Bergson's examinations of habituation as a sensorimotor response to the world. Attachment to the past is not in itself pernicious. What is pernicious in hegemonic historiography is its uncritical investment in formulaic sanctified versions of the past. The modes of forgetting and of rewriting the past endemic to common sense have pragmatic value in safeguarding conditions of survival in the present. Common sense is affectively invested in unexamined habits and beliefs, the sedimented layers of different experiences and forms of knowledge. "Experience" with its penchant for crisis, catastrophe, and salvation holds these contradictory elements together.

Gramsci's analysis of state and of its connection to civil society is germane to his conception of culture. Conventionally, civil society is equated with the "private sphere" and with personal "freedom," religious institutions, the family, and other cultural affiliations, whereas the state is usually identified with governmental power. Gramsci does not posit a simple binary distinction between civil society and the state and explored the amalgamation of civil society into the state.

Literature enters most directly into the Gramscian framework of the politics of culture as social expression, at once individual and communal. Criticism too can be seen to join in this struggle either explicitly or implicitly, through idealist evasion (as in the writings of Croce) or through attempted sociocultural engagement (as in the work of one of the often acknowledged models for Gramsci's own critical practice, Francesco De Sanctis). In the more advanced countries of the West, in which social revolutions will most likely come from a gradual and thoroughgoing "war of position" rather than from a violent and immediate "war of movement," culture in general and literature in particular can come to play a key role both in countering existing hegemonies and in establishing new ones.

At times in the notebooks Gramsci's analysis of individual authors and their works is detailed and specific. More commonly, however, Gramsci's discussion of literature in the notebooks functions to support a broader characterization of literary expression as a form of voluntary praxis. The forces of hegemony are in various ways the historical object of fictional representation, but with greater or lesser degrees of awareness in individual works. Gramsci repeatedly castigates those writers who in attempting to represent the truth of everyday life only manage to reproduce their own cultural prejudices, which is to say, most often those of the church and the dominant bourgeoisie. The futurists are treated with an acerbity bordering on disdain primarily for their immaturity and their distinctly non-"national-popular" character. However, Dante Alighieri is the object of extended admiring discussion in Gramsci's treatment of canto 10 of the *Inferno*. There are also, dispersed here and there, commentaries on the other arts (the "collective" nature of architecture, the immediate force of music) and on the future of Italian literature, which, to fulfill its potential, must set its roots in what Gramsci terms the rich "humus" of popular culture (*SPN* 102; *Quaderni* 1882). Of all Gramsci's comments on art, perhaps the most fascinatingly suggestive, given the period in which he wrote, are contained in those few passages in which he links the immediate and collective effects of music and oratory with, first, the theater as melodrama and, second, the cinema as, at least *in potentia*, the genuine *romanzo popolare*, or popular novel, of the West's cultural future (*SPN* 380, 101, 361–62; *Quaderni* 1677, 1821, 2122, 2195).

Following Gramsci's lead, literary and cinema critics and filmmakers from 1950 to the present have focused on the political dimensions of culture. In studying and accounting for the decisive and slippery role of language (literary and cinematic) in the formation and deformation of the subaltern, Gramsci stresses the importance of creating an oppositional culture to displace dominant political and social formations. The creation of a new collective subject is achieved only through an effort on both cultural and political fronts, and in his pre-prison writings, as well as in the *Prison Notebooks*, Gramsci provides examples of their interconnectedness through his analysis of a wide array of cultural forms—theater, opera, detective novels, Catholic popular novels, and to some slight degree the cinema.

Gramsci was aware that in Italy there was in fact no popular culture but a dependency on foreign literary models of both canonical and popular character. In Italy the cleavage between north and south was a factor in the fragmentation of the nation and thus in the fragmentation of social and regional classes; hence the creation of a popular culture was important to Gramsci as a major form in creating conditions conducive to transforming the subaltern, those exploited and dispossessed, into the dominant class. While allusions to cinema in his writings are sparser than those relating to literature, Gramsci recognized that cinema vies with and even surpasses popular literary, operatic, and dramatic forms. Under the rubrics "operatic" and "melodramatic" Gramsci subsumed the uses of language, oratory, lecture, the theatricality of the law courts, and even "sound films." In his analysis of various cultural forms, Gramsci is attentive to the "role of gestures, tone of voice . . . ; gesture in the broad sense, which scans and articulates the wave of feeling and passion" (SCW 123; Quaderni 2194–95). However, cultural artifacts—the novel, drama, poetry, opera, painting, and cinema, and so on—are not contained in a progressive or regressive category: "It is a serious error to adopt a 'single' progressive strategy according to which new gain accumulates and becomes the premise of further gains. Not only are the strategies multiple, but even in the most 'progressive' ones there are regressive moments" (SCW 101; Quaderni 1821).

The force, range, and complexity of Gramsci's writings on culture and politics remain as powerful and as pressing today as ever in the past and have been highly significant not only for Italian critics, writers, and filmmakers but for English and American theorists, among them TERRY EAGLETON, STUART HALL, Stanley Aronowitz, FREDRIC JAMESON, and EDWARD W. SAID.

MARCIA LANDY AND GREGORY LUCENTE

See also CULTURAL STUDIES and MARXIST THEORY AND CRITICISM.

Antonio Gramsci, *Further Selections from the Prison Notebooks* (ed. and trans. Derek Boothman, 1995), *Letteratura e vita nazionale* (Quaderni del carcere, ed. Felice Platone, vol. 5, 1950), *Letters from Prison* (ed. and trans. Lynne Lawner, 1973), *Letters from Prison: Antonio Gramsci* (ed. Frank Rosengarten and

Raymond Rosenthal, 1994), *Quaderni del carcere* (ed. Valentino Gerratana, 4 vols., 1975, *Prison Note-books*, ed. and trans. Joseph A. Buttigieg, 3 vols., 1991–2007), *Selections from Cultural Writings* [SCW] (ed. David Forgacs and Geoffrey Nowell-Smith, trans. William Boelhower, 1985), *Selections from the Political Writings: 1910–1920* (ed. Quintin Hoare, trans. John Mathews, 1977), *Selections from the Political Writings: 1921–1926* (ed. and trans. Quintin Hoare, 1978), *Selections from the Prison Notebooks of Antonio Gramsci* [SPN] (ed. and trans. Quintin Hoare and Geoffrey Nowell-Smith, 1971).

Greenblatt, Stephen

Stephen Greenblatt (b. 1943) is an American scholar of early modern English literature who is best known for his work as a theorist and practitioner of NEW HISTORI-
CISM. He was educated at Yale University and Pembroke College, Cambridge, before
going on to teach at the University of California, Berkeley, and then at Harvard University, where he became the John Cogan University Professor of the Humanities in 2000.

After publishing *Three Modern Satirists: Waugh, Orwell, and Huxley* (1965) in a series
designated for the publication of undergraduate theses, Greenblatt studied under
RAYMOND WILLIAMS at Cambridge, an opportunity that informed his subsequent
scholarship by providing it with a sense of political and historical sensitivity. More
specifically, he began to ask questions about the relationship between literary texts
and the cultures in which they are produced that characterize New Historicism and
are familiar to MARXIST THEORY AND CRITICISM. After publishing *Sir Walter
Ralegh: The Renaissance Man and His Roles* (1973), his PhD thesis, these questions were
crystallized in an informal, interdisciplinary reading group whose members subsequently edited the journal *Representations*.

None of the group's wide reading in modern theory ever translated for Greenblatt
into a set of orthodox or strict methodological presumptions that would guide his
work. Rather, the loose theoretical network has allowed him to incorporate vastly different intellectual traditions into his writing. From the American social anthropologist Clifford Geertz Greenblatt borrowed "thick description," a rhetorical and intellectual gesture that situates acts in a semiotically ordered "imaginative universe" and
discerns their "meanings" (*Practicing* 27); from his idiosyncratic reading of MICHEL
FOUCAULT he derived a vision of the subject as wholly a discursive effect, as the concluding chapter of his influential *Renaissance Self-Fashioning* (1980) makes evident.

Greenblatt provided the name "New Historicism" in 1982 in the introduction to
a special issue of *Genre*, entitled "The Forms of Power and the Power of Forms in the
Renaissance." Though New Historicism is methodologically heterogeneous, these
Genre essays reflect a resistance to both formalism and a presumably "older" form of
historicism. Countering formalism, typical of postwar scholarship in America, they
argue that literary texts are always and only meaningful within a variety of discourses
that constitute a given culture. They also argue that these literary texts produce effects within their cultural sites of production and circulation and thus enable a degree
of social agency within a limited field of ideological "negotiation." This vision of literature and its place in a wider cultural world marks a divergence from "old" historicism, which largely tended to homogenize the ideological worlds it discussed and to
understand literary texts as mirror-like reflections of this homogenous world.

Because New Historicism relies on a specific understanding of the relationship
between texts and contexts, Greenblatt has theorized this relationship at length,

most explicitly in his essay "Culture" and in "Towards a Poetics of Culture" (*Learning to Curse*). Characterizing New Historicism as a project that attempts to understand and make visible "the poetics of culture," Greenblatt is "opposed on principle to the rigid distinction between that which is within a text and that which lies outside" it ("Culture" 227). Contrary to typically Marxist and postmodern visions of literary production—literary texts as either the effect of social forces or the product of wholly autonomous belletrism—Greenblatt claims that the interrelationship between literary texts and the cultures in which they operate is essentially and necessarily fluid: literature reflects and is partially determined by the world in which it circulates, but it also informs that world because "social discourse is already charged with aesthetic energies" (*Learning* 157). A "poetics of culture" seeks to "develop terms" that make visible the ways that such "material is transferred from one discursive sphere to another" (*Learning* 157).

The fluidity of the relationship between literature and culture provides the producers of literary texts a degree of agency but also restricts that agency and forecloses the possibility of radical ideological or political intervention. Greenblatt frames such questions of agency in "Invisible Bullets," a widely influential discussion of "subversion" and "containment" that has provoked a significant amount of criticism, particularly from predominantly English cultural materialist literary scholars. Literary texts' apparent ideological and social subversions, Greenblatt claims, are always and only apparent because the wider cultural world and its amorphous systems of influence preemptively determine and delimit the terms by which writers might be subversive. Such a vision of the relationship between subversion and containment speaks clearly the influence of Foucault's discussion of power's productivity in the first volume of *The History of Sexuality* (1976).

Greenblatt imagines culture as broadly heterogeneous rather than violently orthodox. This imagined cultural heterogeneity significantly informs his often-emulated use of the anecdote. After rejecting the sort of totalizing visions of early modern culture that might, for instance, engender an "Elizabethan world picture," Greenblatt argues that the anecdote best serves to stage this imagined cultural heterogeneity by providing a fragmentary, dislocated "touch of the real" ("Touch"). These anecdotes create a sense of cultural discordancy and complexity by refusing to be incorporated into a broader narrative. Historically responsible literary scholarship can begin from them because they provide access to an aspect of a given culture with which a given literary text might be concerned, thus enabling conversation between text and context in a way that refuses to read the literary text as an aesthetic articulation of a hypostatized, fixed, and totalizing culture.

Many of Greenblatt's critics refer explicitly to his use of the anecdote when they challenge the visions of culture and history on which he and other New Historicists rely. Walter Cohen argues, for instance, that Greenblatt's use of the anecdote, at least in practice, speaks to a fantasy of "arbitrary connectedness" according to which "any social practice has at least a potential connection to any theatrical practice" 34). The anecdote may attempt to demonstrate cultural fragmentation and heterogeneity, but its juxtaposition of text and context ultimately proves too limited for dealing with literary texts that are variously overdetermined and informed simultaneously by a diversity of contexts in which they are imbricated. Carolyn Porter, in "Are We Being Historical Yet?" (1990), insists that the anecdote functions as a synecdoche for a homogenous culture and thus replaces one totalizing form of historical criticism with another. For Joel Fineman, in "The History of the Anecdote: Fiction and Fiction" (1989), to become an anecdote a piece of historical matter must already be imagined within a context that determines its meaning *as* an anecdote. Rather than providing a potentially disruptive "touch of the real," that is, the anecdote (as anecdote) serves only to reinforce the broader historical vision in which it already operates as a historically meaningful fragment.

Apart from his New Historical scholarship, Greenblatt serves as the editor of the *Norton Shakespeare* and as the general editor, with M. H. Abrams, of the *Norton Anthology of English Literature*, a popular anthology that has expanded under his supervision to include significantly more writers from marginalized groups. Greenblatt has also published a bestselling biography of Shakespeare, *Will in the World* (2004), and with Charles Mee he has written a play called *Cardenio* (2008). Both *Will in the World* and *Cardenio* have proven somewhat controversial among Shakespeare scholars, the former because Greenblatt implies Shakespeare's crypto-Catholicism and the latter because he claims that his play is based on a "lost" Shakespeare play by the same name—a play that most contemporary Shakespeareans identify as Thomas Middleton's *The Second Maiden's Tragedy*.

ANDREW GRIFFIN

See also NEW HISTORICISM.

Stephen Greenblatt, "Culture," *Critical Terms for Literary Study* (ed. Frank Lentricchia and Thomas McLaughlin, 1990, 2nd ed., 1995), *The Greenblatt Reader* (ed. Michael Payne, 2005), *Hamlet In Purgatory* (2001), *Learning to Curse: Essays in Early Modern Culture* (1990), *Marvelous Possessions: The Wonder of the New World* (1991), *Renaissance Self-Fashioning: From More to Shakespeare* (1980), *Shakespearean Negotiations: The Circulation of Social Energy in Renaissance England* (1988), *Sir Walter Ralegh: The Renaissance Man and His Roles* (1973), *Three Modern Satirists: Waugh, Orwell, and Huxley* (1965), "A Touch of the Real," *Representations* 59 (1997), *Will in the World: How Shakespeare Became Shakespeare* (2004); Stephen Greenblatt, ed., *The Power of Forms in the English Renaissance* (1982); Walter Cohen, "Political Criticism of Shakespeare," *Shakespeare Reproduced: The Text in History and Theory* (ed. Jean E. Howard and Marion F. O'Connor, 1987); Catharine Gallagher and Stephen Greenblatt, *Practicing New Historicism* (2000).

Hall, Stuart

Stuart Hall (b. 1932) is one of the most important theorists of culture in the twentieth century and the early years of the twenty-first. As an intellectual who works at the conjuncture of culture, politics, and ideology, he has demonstrated theoretical innovation, as well as philosophical breadth, depth, and adaptability. Hall has shown himself able to borrow astutely from other thinkers and contexts, and his work has proved translatable into different locales.

Born in Kingston, Jamaica, in 1932, Hall left the West Indies for England in 1951 to pursue a BA in English at Oxford University's Merton College. He completed his BA in 1954 and stayed on at Oxford to pursue a doctorate in English. His proposed thesis was a study of the American novelist Henry James, an artist whose work negotiates, much as does Hall's own, the demands of two cultures. After the momentous events of 1956—the Suez Crisis, Soviet Secretary-General Nikita Khrushchev's denunciation of his predecessor Joseph Stalin, and the Soviet invasion of Hungary—Hall became deeply immersed in the politics of the New Left and of the various British leftist formations that succeeded it. One of the founding members of the (first) New Left, together with RAYMOND WILLIAMS, E. P. Thompson, and Richard Hoggart, Hall became the first editor of the movement's journal, the *New Left Review*. Although his tenure as editor was brief, the issues the *New Left Review* addressed—from left-wing politics to literature to nascent debates about the study and status of popular culture—would be central to Hall's later work.

Hall's intellectual persona and his oeuvre are synonymous with the advent and development of CULTURAL STUDIES, broadly conceived as the study of working-class, popular, marginal, and subaltern cultures, all of which are marked, to varying degrees, by their proclivity for resistance to the dominant culture. Building upon the critical ethos of its foundational texts, Thompson's *Making of the English Working Class* (1963), Williams's *Culture and Society* (1958), and Hoggart's autobiographical *Uses of Literacy* (1957), cultural studies articulated the New Left's commitment to rethinking the Left's position on working-class and other popular cultural practices. Hall's contributions to cultural studies have been wide, from his theorization of jazz as a cultural practice (in *The Popular Arts*) to the deployment of ANTONIO GRAMSCI's notion of hegemony, to his commitment to contextualism (understanding the particularities of the historical conjuncture and both the possibilities and the limitations of theory within that moment), to his concept of articulation (and "double articulation"), from his mapping of the significance of identity politics and single-issue social movements to his critique (borrowing from Gramsci) of Thatcherism as an "authoritarian populism."

Once installed at the Centre for Contemporary Cultural Studies (CCCS) at the University of Birmingham, Hall served for five years as Hoggart's assistant director before taking charge in 1969. In his ten years as director Hall contributed significantly to the theoretical transformation of cultural studies. He moved it away from its literary approach based on *Scrutiny* (the journal edited by F. R. Leavis) to a more sociological, philosophical, ideological, and culturally Marxist form of criticism. Especially crucial to the CCCS project was SEMIOTICS (influenced by the writings of ROLAND BARTHES and, to a lesser extent, those of the French structuralists—and poststructuralists—such as JACQUES LACAN and MICHEL FOUCAULT; see STRUCTURALISM) and the work of thinkers such as Louis Althusser and Gramsci, all of which was becoming important at that moment in the theorization of literary studies. Under Hall's leadership, a retooled humanistic Gramsci produced a Marxist cultural studies that saw Birmingham scholars addressing issues such as working-class and youth cultures, as well as subcultures. This mode of scholarship is inaugurated in *Resistance through Rituals: Youth Cultures in Post-War Britain* (1975), a collection of essays Hall coedited with Tony Jefferson that investigates the "structural and cultural origins of British youth cultures" (5) and includes essays by key figures in the first generation of CCCS thinkers trained in the "Birmingham tradition." Among the essays are Paul Willis's "The Cultural Meaning of Drug Abuse," Dick Hebdige's "The Meaning of Mod," and Angela McRobbie and Jenny Garber's "Girls and Subcultures."

In rethinking culture, the most important and lasting aspect of the Birmingham phase for Hall was his use of Gramsci's writings. It was through Gramsci's *Prison Notebooks*, published in Italian between 1948 and 1950 and translated into English in the early years of Hall's CCCS directorship, that he achieved a different understanding of how cultural struggles could transform the prevailing leftist conception of politics largely indifferent to the political import of popular practices. Equally important, Gramsci's ideas about "traditional" and "organic" intellectuals offered CCCS a model for understanding the Birmingham venture as a politically engaged intellectual project. Hall and his colleagues offered in place of the usual Marxist "pieties" a "Marxism without guarantees," a left-wing politics prepared to struggle with itself, to argue seriously over its modes of opposition, and to reflect continuously upon the society it wanted to construct. Hall argued for a radical politics insistently attentive to the conjunctures of the moment—to a self-conscious Marxism rather than a mode of leftist thought that believed in an inexorable historical victory for the working class and its allies.

Sharply critical as Hall was of the Labour Left, he was still deeply committed to constructing a mode of ideological opposition that could be useful to the party. Hall's Gramscian paradigm drew inspiration from the new struggles around issues of identity, race, gender, sexual orientation, and ethnicity (see GENDER and RACE AND ETHNICITY). In the forefront of theorizing the "new social movements" and endorsing grassroots, non- or loosely institutional political structures such as the

Greater London Council, Rock Against Racism, and other cultural movements, Hall articulated more incisively than other political thinkers how Thatcherism created the need for a more appropriate, affiliative, creative series of oppositional alliances that could contest authoritarian populism. Recently arrived and settled black constituencies, gays, lesbians, environmentalists, women's groups, and civic and cultural groupings (around music, art, sport) organized themselves into discrete and sometimes overlapping political constituencies that conducted their campaigns against local authorities and occasionally against the state itself.

Hall's involvement in identity politics represented more than a major ideological break with the (predominantly white) British Left. It marked the fruition of a process that he had begun at CCCS in the 1978 collective volume Policing the Crisis: Mugging, the State, and Law and Order. The last major endeavor of his tenure at Birmingham before he left in 1979 to work at the Open University, Policing the Crisis is a sustained engagement with the issues of black immigration and race. Girded by Hall's initial rethinking of hegemony and anticipating his critique of Thatcherism, this book announces Hall's entry into the politics of immigration in the metropolis. Hall cowrote Policing the Crisis in order both to combat the British state's disproportionately harsh sentences handed down to three immigrant youths who had committed a "mugging" against an elderly white resident of Handsworth, an inner-city Birmingham community, and to challenge the prevailing, increasingly criminal media image of the black community. Although Hall had been politically involved in the protests that grew out of the 1958 murder of the West Indian immigrant Kelso Cochrane (which led to the Notting Hill riots), his opposition had never found articulation in his writing. Policing the Crisis represents an intervention into that discourse, deploying a Gramscian cultural studies to explicate the conjuncture between British ideology and the racial politics of im/migration. Through this fledgling, nascent conception of the role of identity in the formation (and maintenance) of the racially constituted state, of how identity locates, enfranchises, or disenfranchises various (racial, gendered, sexually oriented) constituencies, Hall converts his New Left ideology into a political tool for a new campaign against the British state's racist proclivities.

Even the single text that includes mainly his own writing (apart from a cowritten essay), The Hard Road to Renewal: Thatcherism and the Crisis of the Left (1988), was conceived collectively. As a collection of essays, The Hard Road to Renewal is "predicated on the end of conventional wisdom that there is a simple, irreversible correspondence between the economic and the political, or that classes, constituted as homogenous entities at the economic or 'mode of production' level, are transported in their already unified form onto the 'theatre' of political and ideological struggle" (4). This collection of essays, many of which originally appeared in the journals Marxism Today and New Socialist, constitutes Hall's most sustained criticism of the British Left—the Labour Party, the trade unions, and orthodox Marxism. The Hard Road to Renewal (the title is itself a Gramscian phrase) marks Hall's response to the repeated electoral failure of the Labour Party (its inability to both understand and defeat Thatcherism), the declining influence of the trade unions, and the disarticulation of the British Left in general. This is Hall's renovation of Marxism, his reimagining of how the socialist project might be revitalized and retooled for the new demands and challenges presented by Thatcherism. Hall conceived Thatcherism as "authoritarian populism," a mode of political consent achieved by reorganizing traditional blocs into a new hegemony that complicated existing Left notions of class identity and allegiances in part by appealing to neoimperialist notions of nationalism and patriotism.

Collaboration is the salient feature of Hall's intellectual and political modus operandi—in his multiple theorizations of politics and culture, his work with the New Left, his ideological interventions, his academic endeavors at CCCS, and his tenure at the Open University as a professor of sociology, a position from which he retired in 1997. CCCS especially valued the collective project, both with faculty and students. It is the mode adopted by its alumni in the communally produced The Empire Strikes Back (1982), a volume of essays on race in postimperial Britain that includes the work of Hazel Carby, Pratibha Parmar, and Paul Gilroy.

Hall's influence manifests itself disparately and discretely—in a wide range of texts, in journals, in collections of essays edited both by him and by others, and now, in the last decade or so, in interviews and in collections of critical writing on him. There is thus no singular or "major" Hall text but rather a substantive corpus stretching over more than four decades. His work addresses a panoply of issues, has consistently shown itself conscious of its historical conjuncture, and is intellectually mobile and always self-reflexive: prepared to rethink itself, to anticipate how political events might not only unfold but also impact—and be influenced by—that key conjuncture among culture, ideology, literary criticism, and economics, a conjuncture whose intersections and political effects he has been instrumental in articulating and theorizing.

GRANT FARRED

See also CULTURAL STUDIES and MULTICULTURALISM.

Stuart Hall, "The Emergence of Cultural Studies and the Crisis of the Humanities," October 53 (1990), The Hard Road to Renewal: Thatcherism and the Crisis of the Left (1988); Stuart Hall, Chas Critcher, Tony Jefferson, John Clarke, and Brian Roberts, Policing the Crisis: Mugging, the State, and Law and Order (1978); Stuart Hall and James Donald, eds., Politics and Ideology: A Reader (1986); Stuart Hall and Paul du Gay, Questions of Cultural Identity (1998); Stuart Hall and Bram Gieben, eds., Formations of Modernity (1992); Stuart Hall, David Held, and Tony McGrew, eds., Modernity and Its Futures (1992); Stuart Hall, Dorothy Hobson, Andrew Lowe, and Paul Willis, Culture, Media, Language: Working Papers in Cultural Studies, 1972–79 (1980); Stuart Hall and Martin Jacques, eds., New Times: The Changing Face of Politics in the 1990s (1990); Stuart Hall and Tony Jefferson, eds., Resistance through Rituals: Youth Subcultures in Post-War Britain (1976); Stuart Hall, Gregor McClennan, and David Held, eds., State and Society in Contemporary Britain: A Critical Introduction (1984); Stuart Hall and Paddy Whannel, The Popular Arts: A Critical Guide to the Mass Media (1964).

Haraway, Donna

Donna Haraway (b. 1944) teaches feminist theory and SCIENCE STUDIES in the History of Consciousness and Women's Studies programs at the University of California, Santa Cruz. After studying the philosophies of evolution in Paris in 1966, she completed her doctoral dissertation in biology at Yale University in 1972.

Haraway's multiple engagements in the discourse of science, technology, and feminist epistemology focus on the negotiation of the binary between nature and culture. Her work is central to feminist debates regarding the sex-gender divide in the encounter between modernist and postmodernist notions of the body. She questions the foundational status of the category "woman" as it has been produced through and by feminist interrogations. Haraway illustrates how human subjects are intimately produced through and by the environments they inhabit—technological, literary, cultural, political, economic, and social. Each of her major contributions to feminist theoretical inquiry has been situated in the spatial, temporal, and material oscillations of transnational global capitalist accumulation.

In the groundbreaking *Primate Visions: Gender, Race, and Nature in the World of Modern Science* (1989), Haraway works to uncover the construction of nature: "Nature is only the raw material of culture, appropriated, preserved, enslaved, exalted, or otherwise made flexible for disposal by culture in the logic of capitalist colonialism" (13). Haraway focuses on the centrality of primatology in American science cultures after World War II, which she uses to illustrate the remaking of the social order in emergent industrial economies and decolonized states. Through her materialist critique of science writing she reveals how the taxonomic system of biology is reflected in political orderings and describes this negotiating of boundaries and articulating of differences as a social practice. Haraway points to the systems of race and sex that are productive of and produced through the orientalist nature of primatology, demonstrating that the system of "simian orientalism" established through colonial practices remains embedded within the discourse of Western primatology.

As a socialist feminist, Haraway's techno-scientific project of writing cannot be separated from an implicitly political engagement with a "phallogocentric and authoritarian" (Olson 45) production of knowledge. Though complementary to Sandra Harding's notion of a "standpoint epistemology," Haraway's project differs in its use of a deconstructive critique of foundational concepts and its commitment to what she understands as the "materiality of language" (58). Haraway understands her own method as materialist because language and systems of signification are posited as thinking and acting processes that cannot be understood outside of their materiality (45). Her materialist critique of the philosophy of science argues for the need to understand the narrative forms of scientific knowledge and shows how literary criticism can be applied to scientific knowledge as a way of demonstrating how "facts" and "objective knowledge" depend on the semiotic structure in and through which that knowledge is produced. "We are not simply born into some sort of 'natural' order"; rather "organisms emerge from a discursive process" (*Simians* 199).

Similarly, Haraway chronicles the construction and introduction of the term "gender identity" to explain how biological and cultural predispositions combine to create functionalist identities. She argues that the functionalist identity "woman" was accepted into the American academy in a way that permitted an understanding of female sexuality (and thus of women as well) as passive subjects/objects to be known and controlled by knowledge. Haraway suggests that it is important to produce forms of narrative legitimacy for a whole array of (supposedly) noncoherent genders. "The task is to 'disqualify' the analytic categories, like sex or nature that lead to univocity. This move would expose the illusion of an interior organizing gender core and produce a field of race and gender difference open to resignification" (135).

In her seminal article "Manifesto for Cyborgs: Science, Technology, and Socialist Feminism in the 1980s" (1985), Haraway tries to fuse three projects: feminism, socialism, and materialism. However, she explains this fusion as one in which the totalizing aspects of these projects are left out, thus proposing a new type of theoretical amalgamation through the use of an "image of the cyborg" (149). The cyborg is defined as "a cybernetic organism, a hybrid of machine and organism, a creature of social reality as well as a creature of fiction" (149). This incorporative project is developed further in her book *Modest_Witness@Second_Millennium.FemaleMan©_Meets_Onco Mouse™* (1997). In this study of technoscience and culture, Haraway traverses the boundaries between capital, nature, and culture. She points to the need to recognize the constant breakdown of distinctions between animal, human, and machine that occurs in the increasingly ambiguous gap—especially in our own age—that always exists between the natural and the artificial. In this sense, Haraway's cyborg myth is firmly grounded in the need to dispense with antiquated and/or empty modes of signification. The cyborg figure is necessarily partial, hybrid, and at odds with any ontological foundations. The cyborg is "a configurational move in a politicized narrative," a situatedness that necessitates the examination of the many faces and forms of contemporary domination.

DAVINA BHANDAR

See also CULTURAL STUDIES: 2. UNITED STATES, FEMINIST THEORY AND CRITICISM: 4. MATERIALIST FEMINISMS, and GENDER.

Donna Haraway, *The Companion Species Manifesto: Dogs, People, and Significant Otherness* (2003), *Crystals, Fabrics, and Fields: Metaphors of Organicism in Twentieth-Century Developmental Biology* (1976), "Ecce Homo, Ain't (Ar'n't) I a Woman, and Inappropriate/d Others: The Human in a Post-Humanist Landscape," *Feminists Theorize the Political* (ed. Judith Butler and Joan W. Scott, 1992), "A Game of Cat's Cradle: Science Studies, Feminist Theory, Cultural Studies," *Configurations: A Journal of Literature and Science* 1 (1994), *The Haraway Reader* (2003), *How Like a Leaf: An Interview with Thyrza Nichols*

Goodeve (1999), "Manifesto for Cyborgs: Science, Technology, and Socialist Feminism in the 1980s," Socialist Review 80 (1985, revised as "A Cyborg Manifesto: Science, Technology, and Socialist-Feminism in the Late Twentieth Century," Simians, Cyborgs, and Women), Modest_Witness@Second_Millennium.FemaleMan©_Meets_OncoMouse™ (1997), Primate Visions: Gender, Race, and Nature in the World of Modern Science (1989), "The Promises of Monsters: A Regenerative Politics for Inappropriate/d Others," Cultural Studies (ed. Larry Grossberg, Cary Nelson, and Paula Treichler, 1992), Simians, Cyborgs, and Women: The Reinvention of Nature (1991), "Situated Knowledge: The Science Question in Feminism as a Site of Discourse on the Privilege of Partial Perspective," Feminist Studies 14 (1988), "When Man™ Is on the Menu," Incorporations (ed. Jonathan Crary and Sanford Kwinter, 1992), When Species Meet (2008); Donna Haraway and David Harvey, "Nature, Politics, and Possibilities: A Debate and Discussion with David Harvey and Donna Haraway," Environment and Planning D: Society and Space 13 (1995).

Heidegger, Martin

The early philosophical career of Martin Heidegger (1889–1976), culminating in the publication of Being and Time (1927), is dominated by Gottfried Wilhelm Leibniz's old question "Why is there something rather than nothing?" Heidegger's idea is that the philosophical tradition has lost the sense of this question. Being, like nothing, is an empty category. There are no conditions in which it makes sense to speak of it. The history of philosophy, or of ontology or metaphysics, is, Heidegger likes to say, the history of the "forgetfulness of being."

There is also a sense, however, in which Being is not forgotten at all but is rather always already understood, and this understanding is what characterizes our relationship with the world around us, our being-in-the-world. It is this fundamental, pretheoretical understanding that Heidegger tries to clarify in Being and Time by means of a phenomenological analysis of our everydayness. Heidegger's idea is that our relationship with the world is not one of knowing. The world is not made of objects present before us or before our conceptual gaze. We belong to the world; we are in it and involved with it. We are not spectators at a passing show. Rather, things surround us—they are what Heidegger calls "ready-at-hand"—and our relation to them is one of practical familiarity, or knowing what they are for, rather than one of theoretical interest, or knowing what they are as such. Philosophy quarrels over the existence of the world, but what matters to us is not the existence of the world but our ontological involvement with it.

Heidegger's word for us in Being and Time is Dasein, "being-there," which does not mean we ourselves but rather where we find ourselves. Against the subjectivist tradition of picturing an individual as an ego or self, a thinking subject or transcendental unity of apperception, a mind or a consciousness, Heidegger characterizes us in terms of our historicality and belongingness, our situatedness, our finitude or temporality. We are historicized beings. Transcendence, seeing the world from God's point of view, is closed to us. We can never conceptualize or objectify ourselves or see ourselves either from the outside or from the inside out; rather, we encounter ourselves in our temporality in a strange way.

Most commentators think that the question of being remained dominant for Heidegger until the end of his life, but after Being and Time his reflections on philosophical subjects came to be mediated extensively by questions of language, technology, poetry, and thinking itself, while becoming increasingly fragmented and obscure. Never a systematic thinker, Heidegger moved further and further away from the propositional style of philosophical discourse, so that many do not regard his later writings as having anything to do with philosophy at all. Frequently his writings are free commentaries on poetic texts and pre-Socratic thinkers. Crucial to his turn away from rigorous philosophy was his study of Friedrich Nietzsche during the

1930s and his increasing absorption in the poetry of Friedrich Hölderlin. The meaning of this turn is complicated further by his affinity with fascism, which saw him involved with the Nazis during the most critical period of his philosophical development. In light of this involvement, many commentators see Heidegger as aestheticizing philosophy, shrouding it in a mysticism that isolates it from historical and cultural reality. Others see Heidegger as a primary influence in the postmodern critique of rationality, particularly in his characterization of a technocratic culture so dominated by ideologies of totalization and control that the freedom of what is wayward and singular, strange or different, is no longer thinkable (see POST-MODERNISM). It is not clear that these two interpretations of Heidegger are entirely opposed to one another; nor is it clear that they exclude other readings. Heidegger's thinking is always shifting, heterogeneous, open ended, and resistant to final interpretation.

Of all Heidegger's ideas, the most important for criticism and theory is his reformulation and critique of the Romantic idea that art is foundational for human culture. Ontological rather than formal and aesthetic, Heidegger argues in "The Origin of the Work of Art" (written 1933–1934) that the work of the work of art, its truth, is to open up a world, a human dwelling place. The work is no longer reducible to a product of subjective expression or the object of aesthetic contemplation. It is less an object than an event that sets us free from what is merely timeless and fixed, inserts us into history, situates us together in an ongoing world. The task of art is to set up a world, but the work does not belong to the world it establishes. The work belongs to the earth, which constitutes something like the absolute horizon of the world, the limit that determines the world's historicality and finitude. Heidegger emphasizes the density and strangeness of the work of art, its refusal of every effort we make to grasp it conceptually and to reduce it to its essence. The work opens a clearing in the density of the forest; it lightens a place within the darkness of what withholds itself. But it belongs to density and darkness; the work opens the world but proves uncontainable within it, hence the ontological peculiarity of the work of art, which is always excessive with respect to human history and culture.

In "The End of Philosophy and the Task of Thinking" (1972) Heidegger says that the history of philosophy has come to an end, not in the sense that philosophy is now over and done with but in the sense that it can no longer undergo any internal changes and still remain philosophy. In our present age systematic rationality has become dominant and can be displaced only at the cost of philosophy itself. But systematic rationality, Heidegger says, is not thinking. The question of thinking remains open. In his later writings Heidegger is interested in what thinking can learn from that which philosophy excludes as foreign to its nature; above all, this amounts to asking what thinking can learn from poetry (Dichten). Heidegger works through this question in writings collected in On the Way to Language (1959). Systematic philosophy seeks to bring language and all that language brings into the open under the rule of logic and the construction of concepts. With poetry it is far otherwise. In an essay entitled "The Word" (1957) Heidegger says that "the poet renounces having words under his control" (On the Way 147). Poetry is the letting go of language; poetry is release (Gelassenheit).

The speaking of language is an event (Ereignis) that Heidegger calls the worlding of the world. This is no longer understood as a process of world making over which the poet presides. It is rather a movement of the concealment and disclosure of things into which poetry lets itself go. Perhaps in a dialogue of poetry and thinking we can learn what it would be for thinking to let itself go in similar fashion. Certainly it would mean the abandonment of philosophy as the practice of conceptual reasoning and the reduction to logical form. What would it be for thinking to expose itself to poetry? Heidegger's answer to this question is perhaps not very different from Plato's. But unlike Plato, Heidegger imagines the thinker staying with, instead of banishing, the poet, as if it were only in the nearness of poetry, in the freedom of its company, that thinking could occur. Thinking in this case would resemble listening more than it would reasoning, responsiveness more than assertiveness. Although it seems to be generally accepted that Heidegger's philosophy is an important part of the conceptual background of our current intellectual situation, the bulk of his writings remain largely unstudied except among specialists in Continental philosophy, and for many literary critics and theorists, he often remains more interesting for his involvement with National Socialism than for his writings on poetry and language.

GERALD L. BRUNS

Martin Heidegger, Basic Writings (ed. David Farrell Krell, 1977), Erläuterungen zu Hölderlins Dichtung (1951, Elucidations of Hölderlin's Poetry, trans. Keith Hoella, 2000), "Heimkunft/An die Verwandten" (1943, "Remembrance of the Poet," trans. Douglas Scott, Existence and Being, 1949), "Hölderlin und das Wesen der Dichtung" (1936, "Hölderlin and the Essence of Poetry," trans. Douglas Scott, Existence and Being, 1949), Hölderlins Hymne "Der Ister" (1942, Hölderlin's Hymn "The Ister," trans. William McNeill and Julia Davis, 1996), Holzwege (1950, Off the Beaten Track, ed. and trans. Julian Young and Kenneth Haynes, 2002), Nietzsche (1961, 4 vols., Nietzsche, trans. David Farrell Krell, 1979), Poetry, Language, Thought (trans. Albert Hofstadter, 1971), The Question Concerning Technology and Other Essays (trans. William Lovitt, 1977), Sein und Zeit (1927, Being and Time, trans. John Macquarrie and Edward Robinson, 1962), Unterwegs zur Sprache (1959, On the Way to Language, trans. Peter D. Hertz, 1971), Was heisst Denken? (1961, What Is Called Thinking? trans. J. Glenn Gray, 1968), Zur Sache des Denkens (1969, On Time and Being, trans. Joan Stambaugh, 1972).

Irigaray, Luce

Psychoanalyst, linguist, and philosopher, Luce Irigaray (b. 1932) is concerned, particularly in *Speculum of the Other Woman* (1974) and *This Sex Which Is Not One* (1977), with exposing how Western discourse has effaced woman as the specular image of man. By contrast, Irigaray carefully eschews enclosing her own ideas as "theory" to avoid an essentialism that will support patriarchalism. Accordingly, *Speculum*, which caused her expulsion from psychoanalytic and academic circles, "has no beginning or end . . . [and] confounds the linearity of an outline, the teleology of discourse, within which there is no possible place for the 'feminine,' except the traditional place of the repressed, the censured" (*This Sex* 68).

This major text of the 1970s takes its title from the curved mirror of feminine self-examination (a mirror folded back on itself) as opposed to the flat mirror, which privileges the relation of man to other men and excludes the feminine. The book "begins" with a DECONSTRUCTION of SIGMUND FREUD's lecture "Femininity" and "ends" with Plato, traversing history backward and ending at the beginning with a decentering of male discourse in Western philosophy and a transformation of Plato's cave into the mother's womb. The substituting of the curved for the flat mirror challenges psychoanalysis's attempt to despoil woman of "all valid, valuable images of her sex/organs, her body" (*Speculum* 55), condemning her to psychosis or hysteria for lack "of a valid signifier for her 'first' desire and for her sex/organs" (55). Irigaray's strategy for exposing woman's effacement within Western discourse, then, is a form of critical mimesis in which she cites and inverts influential texts, thereby warping the specular image of man and enabling a reading of those texts based on what they exclude and depend on: woman.

Irigaray returns to Freud repeatedly to reiterate the fact of psychoanalysis's blindness to female sexuality. Haunted by Freud as it elaborates important themes in *Speculum*, *This Sex* presents all the difficulties of breaking with tradition and yet enacts some of the disruptions it considers necessary to create the interstices in which woman's voice can be heard. In this way, writing itself becomes a means through which she is able to suggest an approach to reading literary texts, as a critique of the underlying masculine economy of texts—that is, as a critique of the male underpinning of the very idea of texts. To this end, as a reader Irigaray explores textual representations of female "fluid" mechanics—images and metaphors of plurality, polysemy, malleability, and dynamism—and of male "solid" mechanics—images and representations of unity, monologism, intractability, and fixity. These coordinates in many ways mark off her interests as a reader of texts. The title *This Sex Which Is Not One* summarizes Irigaray's thesis that a woman's sex is not one within the psychoanalytic framework, which only valorizes the masculine, and is not *one* in Irigaray's book either, where it is multiple.

And as psychoanalysis fails to investigate its own historical determinants, so any attempt to explore female sexuality cannot inscribe itself within Western discourse, simply reflecting it as if a flat mirror, but must operate radically to reinterpret Western discourse, a reinterpretation as critique that concerns not only science and political economy but particularly language. The masculine dimension of culture has maintained mastery over discourse by producing "a syntax of . . . discursive logic" that is "always . . . a means of masculine self-affection, or masculine self-production or re-production, or self-generation or self-representation, . . . whereas the 'other' syntax, the one that would make feminine 'self-affection' possible, is [always] lacking, repressed, censured" (This Sex 132). Speculum, with its defiance of chronology and closure, and "When Our Lips Speak Together," the last section in This Sex, emphasizing plurality, proximity, and difference perceived as resemblance to another woman rather than to a masculine standard, strive to make feminine self-affection possible.

Irigaray calls attention to psychoanalysis's effacement of the uterus, the vulva, the lips, the breasts, the unmentionable menstrual blood, and capitalizes on the plurality of female genitals to construct her idea of woman's syntax, therein fashioning her own version of Freud's notorious dictum "anatomy is destiny" to indicate that women have "sex organs more or less everywhere." Female sexuality is always in excess, everywhere at once, and a language that writes the body defies closure and resists interpretive mastery. In a culture that numbers everything by units—"the *one* of form, of the individual, of the (male) sexual organ, of the proper name, of the proper meaning"—she is an enigma, for "she is neither one nor two"; "she has no 'proper' name, and her sexual organ, which is not *one* organ, is counted as *none*" (This Sex 26).

Given the role played by hysteria in the development of psychoanalysis and the interest expressed by feminists in Freud's hysterics, Irigaray necessarily must address the presumed coincidence of the discourse of woman and the hysteric, a coincidence that JULIA KRISTEVA accepts as a given and HÉLÈNE CIXOUS tends to glorify but that Irigaray casts as the failure to speak. The hysteric is caught between silence and mimicry, repressed desire and a language that belongs to the father. The hysteric's ludic mimicry is not free, as Cixous would have it, but controlled and subject to repressive interpretation. It is necessary, then, to find a continuity between "that speech of desire—which at present can only be identified in the forms of symptoms and pathology—and a language, including a verbal language" (137), while granting that the hysteric may be the victim of a patriarchal maneuver to erase origin.

Irigaray believes that theory and practice are never separate, that they intersect in the field of analysis. Here, too, she shows her interest in deconstructing hierarchical relations such as those Cixous relies on. Arguing that male sexuality is scopophilic and questioning the privileging of the merely visible and of the "proper meaning," she is convinced of the need to strip the analyst of the screen of "benevolent neutrality" behind which he protects himself. While the analytic scene advocated by Freud and JACQUES LACAN involves a silent analyst and an analysand whose speech is ultimately silenced, Irigaray's analysis proposes a dialogue where difference is allowed to emerge and where a restaging of transferences runs parallel to the restaging of differences that she advocates for all of Western discourse. The analyst must no longer interpret the analysand but must attempt "a restaging [of] *both* transferences" (*This Sex* 148).

While Irigaray's earlier texts rely on a deconstructive analysis that criticizes monosexual discourse, her later works elaborate a set of conditions that must be present in order for intersubjective articulations to occur between the sexes. The recognition and affirmation of sexual difference is a necessary starting point if such intersubjective relations are to transpire, and Irigaray reiterates the significance of visible cultural and linguistic sexual difference in *Je, Tous, Nous* (1990) when she asserts that "women's exploitation is based on sexual difference; its solution will come only through sexual difference" (12). In other words, the task of ensuring that the feminine does not become repressed within discourse depends on a sustained recognition of difference within culture and discourse.

Irigaray refers to the practice of locating a female point of origin in a divine figure as a necessary starting point for female subjecthood in a number of works—*An Ethics of Sexual Difference* (1984), *Sexes and Genealogies* (1987), *Je, Tous, Nous*, and *Thinking the Difference* (1989). In *Sexes and Genealogies*, Irigaray states that in order "to posit a gender God is necessary" (61). God, gendered in Judeo-Christian traditions as male, secures, through a masculine identification with an infinite being, the conditions of a continual "becoming" for the masculine subject. The significance of female genealogies, then, is that it emphasizes another point of origin other than God the Father so that women are not subjected to subordination or alienation within the symbolic order. In this regard, the recognition of a female genealogy provides access to the mother-daughter relationship necessary for female subjecthood rather than subordinating that relationship to the father-son model.

The recognition of difference at the level of the cultural symbolic extends to linguistic practices as well. In works such as *I Love to You* (1992), Irigaray outlines certain trajectories for modifying language practices so that sexual difference is not suppressed. In *I Love to You*, Irigaray examines the lack of "sexuated" language within speech practices. Studying the effects of linguistic practices, Irigaray identifies the predominant use of the masculine pronoun in place of the feminine pronoun as an erasure of sexual difference and a reinforcement of the masculine as universal subject (69). Within this same text, Irigaray also identifies the need for a transformation in linguistic exchange between subjects so that communication practices reflect a respect for the "irreducibility" of the other to the one. For Irigaray, this is best expressed by a transformation in the phrase, "I love you" to "I love to you" (110). The "to" acts as an interlocutor and a barrier that, in securing two separate and different subjects, also ensures a point of passage from which mutual exchanges and communication can flow. If the symbolic order represents the censure and suffocation of sexual difference for Irigaray, then love can represent a resurrection of life through difference.

Generally speaking, Irigaray's work has had an impact on literary theory and criticism by opening up new intellectual possibilities for critically interrogating discourse and by emphasizing the ethical dimensions of sexual difference. Her influence can be seen in the writing of subsequent theorists, including JUDITH BUTLER, Drucilla Cornell, Naomi Schor, Elizabeth Grosz, and others. From *Speculum of the Other Woman* and throughout the work that followed it, Irigaray brings to bear the spirit of a playful critique that seems to give credit to precursor discourses to an incredible degree, especially, the Greeks, Freud, and Lacan, while generating insights and opening new sites for feminist investigation.

SHARLA HUTCHISON, CHIARA BRIGANTI,
AND ROBERT CON DAVIS-UNDIANO

Luce Irigaray, *Amante marine de Friedrich Nietzsche* (1979, *Marine Lover of Friedrich Nietzsche*, 1991), *Ce sexe qui n'en est pas un* (1977, *This Sex Which Is Not One*, trans. Catherine Porter with Carolyn Burke, 1985), "Le corps-à-corps avec la mere" (1981, "Body against Body: In Relation to the Mother," in *Sexes and Genealogies*, trans. Gillian C. Gill, 1993), *La democrazia comincia a due* (1994, *Democracy Begins between Two*, trans. Kirsteen Anderson, 2001), *Entre Orient et Occident* (1999, *Between East and West: From Singularity to Community*, trans. Stephen Pluháček, 2002), "Et l'une ne bouge pas sans l'autre" (1979, "And One Doesn't Stir without the Other," *Signs* 7 [1981]), *Ethique de la différence sexuelle* (1984, *An Ethics of Sexual Difference* trans. Gillian C. Gill and Carolyn Burke, 1993), *J'aime à toi: Esquisse d'une félicité dans l'histoire* (1992, *I Love to You: Sketch of a Possible Felicity in History*, trans. Alison Martin, 1996), *Je, tu, nous: Pour une culture de la différance* (1990, *Je, Tous Nous: Toward a Culture of Difference*, trans. Alison Martin, 1993), *L'oubli de l'air chez Martin Heidegger* (1983, *The Forgetting of Air in Martin Heidegger*, trans. Mary Beth Mader, 1999), *Parler n'est jamais neuter* (1985, *To Speak is Never Neutral*, trans. Gail M. Schwab, 2001), *Passions elémentaires* (1982, *Elemental Passions*, trans. Judith Still and Joanne Collie, 1992), *Sexes et parentés*, (1987, *Sexes and Genealogies*, trans. Gillian C. Gill, 1993), *Speculum de l'autre femme* (1974, *Speculum of the Other Woman*, trans. Gillian C. Gill, 1985), *The Way of Love*, (trans. Heidi Bostic and Stephen Pluháček, 2002), *Why Different? A Culture of Two Subjects* (trans. Camille Collins, 1999).

Jameson, Fredric

Fredric Jameson (b. 1934) is generally considered to be the foremost Marxist literary critic writing in English. He has published a wide range of works analyzing literary and cultural texts and developing his own neo-Marxist theoretical position, as well as a large number of texts criticizing alternate theoretical positions. A prolific writer, he has assimilated an astonishing number of theoretical discourses into his project and has intervened in many contemporary debates while analyzing a diversity of cultural texts, ranging from the novel to video, from architecture to POSTMODERNISM.

In his first book Jameson analyzed the literary theory and production of Jean-Paul Sartre. Written as a doctoral dissertation at Yale University, *Sartre: The Origins of a Style* (1961) was influenced by Jameson's teacher Erich Auerbach and by the stylistics associated with Leo Spitzer, focusing on Sartre's style, narrative structures, values, and vision of the world. The book is devoid of the Marxian categories and political readings characteristic of Jameson's later work but read in the context of the stifling conformism and banal business society of the 1950s, Jameson's subject matter (Sartre) and his intricate literary-theoretical writing style (already the notorious Jamesonian sentences appear full blown) can be seen as revealing an attempt to create himself as a critical intellectual against the literary establishment and the dominant modes of literary criticism.

Jameson's first three major books and most of his early articles involve the effort to develop a literary criticism that cuts against the dominant formalist and conservative models of New Criticism and the academic Anglo-American establishment. *Marxism and Form* (1971) can be read as an introduction to the new versions of Hegelian Marxism that began to appear in Europe and the United States in the late 1960s and early 1970s. Yet even as Jameson presents some of the basic positions of THEODOR W. ADORNO, WALTER BENJAMIN, Herbert Marcuse, Ernst Bloch, GEORG LUKÁCS, and Sartre, one finds his own concepts and positions emerging from the analyses. In particular, he makes clear his attraction both to Lukácsian literary theory and to his version of Hegelian Marxism, an allegiance that Jameson sustains in his later works.

Lukács's work on realism and on the historical novel have strongly influenced Jameson's way of seeing and situating literature. While Jameson has never accepted Lukács's polemics against modernism, he has appropriated key Lukácsian categories, such as reification, to describe the fate of culture in contemporary capitalism. The Hegelian markers of Jameson's work include the contextualizing of cultural texts in history, the broad historical periodizing, and the use of Hegelian categories. Dialectical criticism involves the attempt to synthesize competing positions and methods into a more comprehensive theory, as Jameson does in *The Prison-House of Language* (1972), where he incorporates elements of French STRUCTURALISM and SEMIOTICS, as well as Russian formalism, into his theory. In *The Political Unconscious* (1981) he draws on a wide range of theories, applying them to concrete readings that relate texts to their historical and cultural context, that analyze the "political unconscious" of the texts, and that depict both ideological and utopian moments of texts. Dialectical criticism for Jameson also involves thinking that reflexively analyzes categories and methods while carrying out concrete analyses and inquiries.

During the 1970s Jameson published a series of theoretical inquiries and many more diverse cultural studies. One begins to encounter the characteristic range of interests and depth of penetration in his studies of science fiction, film, magical narratives, painting, and both realist and modernist literature. One also encounters articles concerning Marxist cultural politics, imperialism, Palestinian liberation, Marxist teaching methods, and the revitalization of the Left. Many of the key essays have been collected in *The Ideologies of Theory* (1988); they provide the laboratory for the theoretical project worked out in *The Political Unconscious* and *Fables of Aggression* (1979). These texts, along with his essays collected in *Postmodernism* (1991), should be read together as inseparable parts of a multilevel theory of the interconnections between the history of literary form, modes of subjectivity, and stages of capitalism.

Jameson's theoretical synthesis is presented most systematically in *The Political Unconscious*. As it traverses through the field of culture and experience, the text offers an articulation of Jameson's literary method, a systematic inventory of the history of literary forms, and a hidden history of the forms and modes of subjectivity itself. Jameson boldly attempts to establish Marxist literary criticism as the most all-inclusive and comprehensive theoretical framework as he incorporates a disparate set of competing approaches into his model. He provides an overview of the history of the development of literary form and concludes by proposing a theory of the "double hermeneutic" of ideology and utopia—which critiques ideology while preserving utopian moments—as the basis for a rejuvenated Marxist method of literary criticism.

Jameson employs a Lukács-inspired historical narrative to tell how cultural texts contain a "political unconscious," buried narratives and social experiences, that requires sophisticated literary hermeneutics in order to be deciphered. One particular narrative of *The Political Unconscious* concerns, in Jameson's striking phrase, "the construction of the bourgeois subject in emergent capitalism and its schizophrenic disintegration in our own time" (9). Key stages in the odyssey of disintegrating bourgeois subjectivity are articulated in George Gissing, Joseph Conrad, and Wyndham Lewis, a story that will find its culmination in Jameson's account of postmodernism.

Indeed, Jameson's studies on postmodernism are a logical consequence of his theoretical project. He presented his first analysis of the defining features of postmodern culture in "Postmodernism and Consumer Society," a 1982 lecture that was subsequently published in Hal Foster's collection *The Anti-Aesthetic* (1983). Eventually, he synthesized and elaborated his emerging analysis in "Postmodernism; or, the Cultural Logic of Late Capitalism" (1984), which more systematically interprets postmodernism as a new "cultural dominant" (*Postmodernism* 1ff).

Within his analysis, Jameson situates postmodern culture in the framework of a theory of stages of society—based on a neo-Marxian model of stages of capitalist development—and argues that postmodernism is part of a new stage of capitalism. Every theory of postmodernism, he claims, contains an implicit periodization of history and "an implicitly or explicitly political stance on the nature of multinational capitalism today" (3). Following Ernest Mandel's periodization in his book *Late Capitalism* (1975), Jameson claims that "there have been three fundamental moments in capitalism, each one marking a dialectical expansion over the previous stage. These are market capitalism, the monopoly stage or the stage of imperialism, and our own (wrongly called postindustrial, but what might better be termed) multinational capital" (35). To these forms of society correspond the cultural forms realism, modernism, and postmodernism.

The important essay "The Existence of Italy" (in *Signatures of the Visible* [1990]) further develops this problematic, as do the conclusion to *Postmodernism* and the studies in *The Cultural Turn* (1998). Jameson emerges as a synthetic and eclectic Marxist cultural theorist who attempts to preserve and develop Marxist theory while analyzing the politics and utopian moments of a stunning diversity of cultural texts. His work goes beyond literary analysis, taking up popular culture, architecture, theory, and other texts and thus can be seen as part of the movement toward cultural studies as a replacement for canonical literary studies.

In his articles or books from the early 1970s through the late 1980s one finds strong similarities in concerns, style, and politics. Indeed, one gets the feeling in reading *The Ideologies of Theory* that all the essays therein could have been written yesterday or in the very recent past. Yet, as Jameson notes in the introduction to these essays, there is a fundamental shift of emphasis in his works that he describes as

> a shift from the vertical to the horizontal: from an interest in the multiple dimensions and levels of a text to the multiple interweavings of an only fitfully readable (or writable) narrative; from problems of interpretation to problems of historiography; from the attempt to talk about the sentence to the (equally impossible) attempt to talk about modes of production (1:xxix).

In other words, Jameson's focus has shifted from a vertical emphasis on the many dimensions of a text—its ideological, psychoanalytic, formal, mythic-symbolical levels—which requires a sophisticated and multivalent practice of reading, to a horizontal emphasis on the ways texts are inserted into historical sequences and on how history enters and helps constitute texts. Yet this shift in emphasis also points to

continuities in Jameson's work, for since the late 1960s he has privileged the historical dimension of texts and political readings, moving critical discourse from the
ivory tower of academia and the "prison-house of language" to the vicissitudes and
contingencies of that field for which the term "history" serves as marker.

DOUGLAS KELLNER

See also GLOBALIZATION, MARXIST THEORY AND CRITICISM: 2. STRUCTURALIST
MARXISM, MARXIST THEORY AND CRITICISM: 3. 1989 AND AFTER, and
POSTMODERNISM.

Fredric Jameson, *Archaeologies of the Future* (2005), *Brecht and Method* (2000), *The Cultural Turn: Selected Writings on the Postmodern, 1983–1998* (1998), *Fables of Aggression: Wyndham Lewis, the Modernist as Fascist* (1979), *The Geopolitical Aesthetic: Cinema and Space in the World System* (1992), *The Hegel Variations: On the "Phenomenology of Spirit"* (2010), *The Ideologies of Theory: Essays, 1971–1986*, vol. 1, *Situations of Theory*, vol. 2, *Syntax of History* (1988), *Jameson on Jameson: Conversations on Cultural Marxism* (2007), *Late Marxism: Adorno; or, The Persistence of the Dialectic* (1990), *Marxism and Form: Twentieth-Century Dialectical Theories of Literature* (1971), *The Modernist Papers* (2007), *The Political Unconscious: Narrative as a Socially Symbolic Act* (1981), "Postmodernism, or the Cultural Logic of Late Capitalism," *New Left Review* 146 (1984), *Postmodernism, or, the Cultural Logic of Late Capitalism* (1991), *The Prison-House of Language: A Critical Account of Structuralism and Russian Formalism* (1972), *Representing "Capital": A Reading of Volume One* (2011), *Sartre: The Origins of a Style* (1961), *Signatures of the Visible* (1990), *A Singular Modernity* (2002), *Valences of the Dialectic* (2009).

Kristeva, Julia

Julia Kristeva (b. 1941) is director of the department of Science of Texts and Documents at the University of Paris VII, where she teaches in the Department of Literature and Humanities. In her early writing, she is concerned to bring the speaking body back into PHENOMENOLOGY and linguistics. In order to counteract what she sees as the necrophilia of phenomenology and structural linguistics, which study a dead or silent body, Kristeva develops a new science that she calls "semanalysis." She describes semanalysis as a combination of semiology (or SEMIOTICS) from FERDINAND DE SAUSSURE, and psychoanalysis from SIGMUND FREUD. Unlike traditional linguistics, semanalysis addresses an element that is heterogeneous to language, the unconscious. The introduction of the unconscious into the science of signs, however, challenges the very possibility of science, meaning and reason.

With semanalysis, Kristeva attempts to bring the speaking body, complete with drives, back into language. She argues that the logic of signification is already present in the material body. In *Revolution in Poetic Language* (1974) she suggests that negation and identification, the two primary logical operations of language, are already operating within the body prior to the onset of signification: expelling waste from the body prefigures negation and incorporating food into the body prefigures identification. The second way in which Kristeva brings the speaking body back to language is by maintaining that bodily drives make their way into language. One of Kristeva's major contributions to literary theory is her distinction between two heterogeneous elements in signification: the semiotic and the symbolic. Within Kristeva's writings "semiotic" ("le sémiotique") becomes a technical term that she distinguishes from "semiotics" ("la sémiotique"). The semiotic elements within the signifying process are the drives as they discharge within language. This drive discharge is associated with rhythm and tone. The semiotic has meaning but does not refer to anything. The symbolic, on the other hand, is the element of language that allows for referential meaning. The symbolic is associated with syntax or grammar and with the ability to take a position or make a judgment that syntax engenders.

In her two volumes of *Powers and Limits of Psychoanalysis* (1996, 1997), Kristeva revisits the theme of revolution that is so prominent in her earlier work. In *Revolution in Poetic Language* Kristeva identifies the possibility of revolution in language—a revolution she deems *analogous* to social revolution—with (maternal) semiotic forces in avant-garde literature. In *Powers of Horror* (1980) this semiotic force of drives is not only associated with the maternal but more particularly with the abject or revolting aspects of the maternal. Here, the revolting becomes revolutionary through the return of the repressed (maternal) within (paternal) symbolic systems. More than a decade later, in *The Sense and Non-Sense of Revolt* (1996), Kristeva asks if revolt is possible today. In this first volume of the *Powers and Limits of Psychoanalysis*, she claims that within postindustrial and post-Communist democracies we are confronted with a new political and social economy governed by the spectacle within which it becomes increasingly difficult to think of the possibility of revolt. The two main reasons are that within media culture, the status of power and the status of the individual have changed. Kristeva argues that in contemporary culture there is a power vacuum that results in the inability to locate the agent or agency of power and authority or to assign responsibility. In addition to the power vacuum, she identifies the impossibility of revolt with the changing status of the individual. The human being as a person with rights is becoming nothing more than an ensemble of organs that can be bought and sold or otherwise exchanged, what she calls the "patrimonial individual." Not only is there no one or nothing to revolt against; there is also no one to revolt.

Without the possibility of revolt, there are both unhappy social consequences and unhappy psychic consequences. Kristeva suggests that entering the social order requires assimilating the authority of that order through a revolt by which the individual makes meaning his or her own. Revolt, then, is not a transgression against law or order but a displacement of its authority within the psychic economy of the individual. Psychoanalysis and literature become the primary domains of this revolutionary displacement. This displacement gives the individual a sense of inclusion in meaning making and the social that support creative activities and the sublimation of drives. Without this displacement and the resulting feeling of inclusion, the individual cannot have meaningful experiences but only traumatic ones because meaningful experience requires some assimilation into the social order.

Kristeva defines trauma as what is unrepresentable as a result of the inability to assimilate the meaning of the traumatic experience into the social; trauma is what is meaningless or unknown within the social order. In *New Maladies of the Soul* (1993), Kristeva describes how contemporary culture is losing its soul and with it the ability to create meaning and to feel fulfilled. She describes a "modern man" who is "losing his soul" and becoming merely "a body that acts." Kristeva describes a modern man for whom the collapse of time and space has collapsed the psyche, a modern man who has a suffering body but no soul. In *Tales of Love* (1983), she calls modern man "an exile, deprived of his psychic space, an extraterrestrial with a prehistory bearing, wanting for love." With drugs and the media, the psyche or soul has become two dimensional, worn on the skin of a body that suffers from their thinness. The body suffers and the modern Narcissus turns to more drugs and more images to ease the pain. But, drugs only regulate the oscillation between pain and relief, and media images reflect false selves that ultimately only exacerbate our feelings of out-of-placeness. Neither can compensate for what Kristeva calls the *erosion of the loving father*. In *Tales of Love*, Kristeva attempts to curb this erosion with her notion of an *imaginary father*, which she proposes as the counterbalance to the abject mother, a notion that she develops in *Powers of Horror* and *Black Sun* (1987).

In the trilogy, *Feminine Genius* (1999–2002), Kristeva presents two types of feminine genius—a monumental sort and an everyday sort—by analyzing the work of Hannah Arendt, Melanie Klein, and Colette. She describes her project as "one way to call attention to the singularity of every woman" (1:xiv). She argues that the genius of extraordinary women like Hannah Arendt, Melanie Klein, and Colette help all women to see what is extraordinary in their own ordinary lives.

KELLY OLIVER

Julia Kristeva, *Au commencement était l'amour: Psychanalyse et foi* (1985, *In the Beginning Was Love: Psychoanalysis and Faith*, trans. Arthur Goldhammer, 1987), *The Crisis of the European Subject* (trans. Susan Fairfield, 2000), *Étrangers à nous-memes* (1989, *Strangers to Ourselves*, trans. Leon Roudiez, 1991), *Le génie féminin*, vol. 1, *Hannah Arendt* (1999, *Feminine Genius*, vol. 1, *Hannah Arendt*, trans. Ross Guberman, 2001), *Le génie féminin*, vol. 2, *Melanie Klein* (2000, *Feminine Genius*, vol. 2, *Melanie Klein*, trans. Ross Guberman, 2001), *Le génie féminin*, vol. 3, *Colette* (2002, *Feminine Genius*, vol. 3, *Colette*, trans. Jane Marie Todd, 2004), *Histoires d'amour* (1983, *Tales of Love*, trans. Leon Roudiez, 1987), *The Kristeva Reader* (ed. Toril Moi, 1986), *Le langage, cet inconnu: Une Initiation à la linguistique* (1981, *Language, the Unknown: An Initiation into Linguistics*, trans. Anne M. Menke, 1989), *Lettre ouverte à Harlem Désir* (1990, *Nations without Nationalism*, trans. Leon Roudiez, 1993), *Les nouvelles maladies de l'âme* (1993, *New Maladies of the Soul*, trans. Ross Guberman, 1995), *Polylogue* (1977, partial trans., *Desire in Language: A Semiotic Approach to Literature and Art*, trans. Thomas Gora, Alice Jardine, and Leon Roudiez, 1980), *The Portable Kristeva* (2nd ed., ed. Kelly Oliver, 2002), *Pouvoirs de l'horreur* (1980, *Powers of Horror*, trans. Leon Roudiez, 1982), *La révolte intime*, (1997, *Intimate Revolt*, trans. Jeanine Herman, 2002), *La révolution du langage poétique: L'avant-garde à la fin du XIXe siècle, Lautréamont et Mallarmé* (1974, *Revolution in Poetic Language*, trans. Margaret Waller, 1984), *Les samouraïs* (1990, *The Samurai: A Novel*, trans. Barbara Bray, 1992), *Séméiotiké: Recherches pour une sémanalyse* (1969), *Sens et non-sens de la révolte* (1996, *The Sense and Non-Sense of Revolt*, trans. Jeanine Herman, 2000), *Soleil noir: Dépression et mélancolie* (1987, *Black Sun: Depression and Melancholia*, trans. Leon Roudiez, 1989).

Lacan, Jacques

Jacques Marie Émile Lacan (1901–1981) trained as a medical doctor specializing in psychiatry. He was inspired by phenomenological and psychoanalytic reformulations of psychiatric practice that began to criticize the constitutional model of mental disorders' causation. Surrealist considerations of hysteria and paranoia that interrogated the socially disruptive signifying economies of delirious subjects' discourses also shaped his early views. His doctoral thesis turned book, *Paranoid Psychosis and Its Relation to Personality* (1932), grounded itself on Karl Jaspers's phenomenological theory, which Lacan would later reject, that posited subjectivity as "personality." Lacan's thesis failed to appreciate the full consequences of the decisive break with the organicist view of psychopathology's etiology that SIGMUND FREUD had already made in his own work, but it nonetheless argued that the clinical treatment of paranoia requires a weakening of the resistances the subject's ego enforces. The beginnings of the properly Freudian orientation of Lacan's teaching are visible here as is a glimpse of what Lacan would come more rigorously to qualify as the imaginary status of the subject's ego identifications.

Over the next fifty years extensive clinical practice along with speculative theoretical argument distinguished what Lacan described as his "return to Freud." His massive impact on a wide variety of fields is at least partially due to the range of insights in his close readings of the Freudian texts from work in the theoretical and experimental sciences, philosophy and literature, linguistics and anthropology, logic and mathematics. Readings of specific literary texts form key elements of his seminars and writings, but Lacan's importance for literary theory and criticism derives primarily from his more general speculations on language, the subject, sexual difference, ethics, and the unconscious. When he died he was one of the world's most prominent and controversial intellectual figures. His theories also had a decisive impact on psychoanalytic clinical practice in many parts of the world, including Latin America and southwestern Europe. A growing interest in Lacan's work in the North American clinical community arose in the 1990s, due in part to the impact of Lacanian intellectuals writing in English in the theoretical humanities, including SLAVOJ ŽIŽEK and the members of his Slovenian school.

Lacan's career divides into four stages. From 1926 to 1953 his work evolved from the phenomenological model predominant in French psychiatry toward both an increasingly vociferous attack against the valorization of the ego in post-Freudianism and an utterly original interrogation of the effects of the subject's unconscious on its negotiation of language's signifying system. Beginning in the 1930s he wrote several articles that considered the importance of the "mirror stage" to the child's acquisition of motor and language skills during the first two years of life. Drawing on experimental work and on early texts by Claude Lévi-Strauss on the logic of symbolic systems, Lacan developed Freud's notion of narcissistic identification by showing not only how a young child can react to another's bodily injury as if it were his or her own but also how such forms of identification remain forever anticipated and incomplete. The failure of a perfectly integrated bodily mastery is one factor that leads to the subject's acquisition of a symbolic function predicated on a fundamental ontological lack. The acquisition of language allows the subject to evoke for itself an endless metonymical series of substitutive symbolic objects through which it attempts to compensate for its lack of being.

Ego psychologists recommended strengthening the ego's defenses as a means of buffering the subject's individuation, but for Lacan the mirror stage inaugurates a fundamentally frustrating relation in which perfect bodily wholeness may only be apprehended in the other with whom the subject identifies. This imaginary other becomes a threatening rival who tends to provoke a jealous and aggressive hostility. Lacan's insistence on the *méconnaissance* (misrecognition) underlying the ego's identifications presented a radical challenge to ego psychology's qualification of the ego as a source of psychic stability.

In the 1950s (his career's second stage) Lacan joined the new Société Française de Psychanalyse, and at the group's first meeting in Rome in 1953 he presented "The Function and Field of Speech and Language in Psychoanalysis" (Écrits 30–113). Informally known as the "Rome Discourse," this influential paper gained notoriety as the society's manifesto. Lacan argues that the neo-Freudians, following Anna Freud's analyses of the ego's resistances, fail to account for the primacy of speech and language in Freud's theoretical and clinical work. Rejecting efforts to illuminate psychoanalytic concepts through biology and neurology, Lacan turns instead to structuralist linguistics and anthropology to underscore how symbolic relations preexist the advent of the human subject and determine its place in the social world (see LINGUISTICS AND LANGUAGE and STRUCTURALISM). Lacan was careful even at this early stage to distinguish what he boldly characterizes as the subject's truth from both a factually accurate reconstruction of its experiential history and an exhaustive evocation of its cultural conditions. Provocatively, he asserts that the subject's truth is fictional, in that it refers to the unconscious mythology through which the subject explains its separation from its organic origin and mortal destiny. He reasserts what he views as a Freudian analysis's ultimate aim: to have the subject experience anew through transference the gap left open by the transition from nature to culture, a gap that manifests itself in the subject's speech through the repetition of key "signifiers" that emblematize its circumscription by language. On the basis of this emphasis on the signifier in unconscious life, he began to argue in favor of formalizing psychoanalytic conceptuality. Lacan thus sought to facilitate analytic theory's transmissibility between generations and to recognize the rightful place of the discipline and practice of psychoanalysis in the history of modern science.

Lacan's clinical practice tended to feature short sessions of variable length, some as brief as fifteen minutes. According to him, this technique provides the analyst with a greater capacity to "punctuate" the analysand's discourse and thereby to intensify the frustrating effects of the transference. The session's unpredictable end forces the patient to deal with the analyst as truly other to his or her discourse, not simply as a reflection of the patient's own fantasy world. In this way the analyst must abstain from playing the role of an ideal ego or imaginary other despite the patient's efforts to address the analyst as such. By resisting this demand the analyst forces the subject to recognize the difference between the "I" who speaks and the idealized ego the subject projects onto the analyst in consequence of its narcissistic desire for omnipotence. Because the subject's sense of self also depends on the way it represents the world and its place in it—what Lacan calls the "reality" of the subject's experience—the analyst's abstention also marks the boundary between the symbolic order of the subject's speech and what resists symbolization. Lacan calls this remainder the "Real" to distinguish it from the reality represented through the subject's discourse. Together, the terms "symbolic," "imaginary," and "Real" indicate three "elementary registers" of human experience that Lacan claims to have distinguished for the first time in psychoanalytic theory.

In a third stage, in 1964 at Louis Althusser's invitation Lacan and his followers moved his seminar to the prestigious École Normale Supérieure. Lacan's seminars started featuring a broader scope and addressed a more diverse audience, including a generation of Althusserian Marxists, than the analysts, physicians, psychiatrists, and Catholic priests who had attended the seminars in the 1950s. By the time his selected essays appeared as Écrits (1966), the seminars were drawing huge crowds and Lacan had become the object of an intense if often bemused scrutiny by the popular media, as well as, slowly but surely, by analytic communities outside France.

Lacan's fourth and final stage began in 1969 when the new, "experimental" faculty of the University of Paris at Vincennes founded a Department of Psychoanalysis. Lacan hoped that the integration of psychoanalysis within the university would broaden the impact of Freudianism on the traditional academic disciplines and further advance his quest to have psychoanalysis recognized as a legitimate modern science grounded in a solid, formalized conceptuality. Additionally, however, Lacan considered the presence of analytic thought within the university a subversion of the institutionalization of knowledge. In the 1969–1970 seminar, he identifies the university's discourse as one of four possible forms of the social bond, along with the discourses of the master, the hysteric, and the analyst. In its pursuit of systematic knowledge, Lacan suggests, the university effectively represses the scandal of Freud's discovery of the unconscious, which necessarily frustrates all ambitions to illuminate perfectly the forms of knowledge.

Lacan's three main points of reference—the registers of the imaginary, symbolic, and real—remain constant in his seminars. The first two official seminars engage psychoanalytic technique and the imaginary constitution of the ego. Extending the insights developed in his work on the mirror stage, Lacan provides an extensive commentary on an optical experiment in which a virtual image of a vase of flowers appears in consequence of a series of reflections off two mirror surfaces. In the experimental apparatus the flowers are suspended upside down beneath the vase, and the "corrected" virtual image becomes visible only when the subject is placed within a definite conical space before the mirrors. Lacan's commentary points out not only that the ego—represented by the image of the vase of flowers—is properly virtual and thus an effect of misrecognition but also that the restricted space from which the image is visible suggests how the subject must find a position for itself within the symbolic in order to acquire the fragile motor coordination the alienated ego identification manages to provide.

Lacan's third seminar, an extensive reading of Freud's consideration of Daniel Schreber's memoirs, shows how the failure of this symbolic introjection impedes the subject's individuation, causing vulnerability to auditory hallucinations. According to Lacan, these symptoms are imaginary manifestations of the symbolic function that the psychotic lacks because of "foreclosure" of the name of the father—the name that represents dependence on a system of symbolic relations bearing no direct relation to the signified, to the realm of meaning. The subject's alienated ego identification facilitates the acquisition of speech, the very medium that permits overcoming in part the effects of frustration to which the libidinal investment in the ego structure gives rise.

Lacan's introduction of structuralist linguistic paradigms into psychoanalytic theory through figures such as FERDINAND DE SAUSSURE, Émile Benveniste, and Roman Jakobson allowed him to conceptualize the unconscious, not as the realm of repressed libidinal fantasy, to which we have no direct access, but as the "logic of the signifier," which prevents us from expressing conscious, unambiguous intentions in speech. The unconscious, "structured like a language," allows desire to speak through us, in spite of our efforts to communicate our own meanings. Even sexuality is determined by the subject's relation to the signifier rather than by some innate biophysiological or genetic predisposition. Whereas for Freud the Oedipus complex refers to the static, nuclear kinship structure characteristic of European modernity, Lacan takes it to designate that moment when the subject faces the option of accepting or rejecting the signifier in the place of the imaginary or real other. Though Lacan considers the symbolic function to be associated with the nonorganic, mediated status of paternity, the Freudian Oedipus is just one, historically contingent socio-symbolic system into which a subject may be born. Additionally, no concrete subject may perfectly embody the symbolic function of separation and interdiction that the paternal agency is supposed to uphold. Freud identifies the signifier of interdiction with the penis. With his concept of the phallus Lacan chooses instead to emphasize the properly symbolic function of this agency. The phallic function is not perfectly reducible to the biological organ men possess. Lacan seeks to underline in this manner that sexuality is not biologically determined but instead constructed through one's relation to the symbolic order.

Having explored in his first seminars the agency of the imaginary registers in the experience of the speaking subject, Lacan began to place greater emphasis on those concepts he associated with the Real: the drive, *jouissance*, and *objet petit a* (object small *a*). Lacan defined this object as the cause of the subject's desire and evoked it with a memorable phrase from William Shakespeare's *The Merchant of Venice* as the "pound of flesh" the subject must sacrifice in order to gain entry into the order of symbols. Partial, decorporealized, formless, and capable of incarnating itself in the form of the breast, the gaze, the voice, or the turd, *objet petit a* represents for the subject the point of inscrutability in the Other, a kernel of *jouissance* that simultaneously fascinates and disgusts us, forever tempting us with the illusion that more can be known about the Other, that we can ascertain once and for all what the other wants from us. By "the desire of man is the desire of the Other," Lacan means that desire is both *for the Other* and experienced *as the Other's desire with respect to the subject*. Our desire results from our uncertainty about what is wanted of us and from the frustration of our attempts to interpret, to ascribe, definitive meaning to, the Other's desire. First introduced in the "Rome Discourse," Lacan associates the Other with a number of concepts: desire, the symbolic father, the locus of language, the unconscious. *Objet petit a*, on the other hand, functions as the Other's limit, or the point of its externality to itself. In this sense it is *dissimulated* in the Other. The object thereby acquires a quality for which Jacques-Alain Miller coined the neologism "extimate," suggesting the paradoxical, uncanny externalized intimacy that disturbs the subject by hinting that its essence exists "out there"—in the object that may never be symbolized, domesticated, or bound within the reassuring terms of consciousness.

Lacan's concept of *jouissance* discloses the intricate interdependence between sexuality and the symbolic order that subjects the biological body to a traversal by the signifier. Because the body is necessarily mediated by language, and the libidinal drive remains in excess of the limits of representation, *jouissance* tends to manifest itself symptomatically in the body as a kind of surplus meaning that resists symbolic mediation. In consequence, the subject tends to apprehend *jouissance* only in the Other's body and therefore as something beyond its grasp, of which it has been deprived. Because *jouissance* for the subject is marked by such a lack, sexual relations between two subjects are always structured in relation to a missing third element— the phallus—that disallows the formation of a harmonious, complementary relationship. Thus Lacan makes the notorious claim in his seminar *Encore* that "there is no such thing as a sexual relationship" (57), this lack between the sexes—or between any two subjects of either biological sex—distinguishing human sexuality from the instinctual satisfaction presumably at work in the animal realm. In his later career Lacan attempts to shed light on Freud's unclear theories of femininity and sexual difference by introducing his concept of "sexuation," claiming that every neurotic subject experiences symbolic castration in one of only two possible ways. He qualifies the modes of sexuation as "masculine" and "feminine" but makes clear that a subject's sexuation need not correspond to its anatomical sex because sexuation exposes a fundamental impasse or contradiction characteristic of human sexuality that results from the properly structural lack of adequation of the symbolic order with respect to the Real.

Lacan's formalization of sexual difference in his "formulas of sexuation," presented through an idiosyncratic usage of mathematical symbols derived from symbolic logic and set theory, attempts to distill Freud's efforts to distinguish the girl's experience of castration from the boy's. In the first logical moment of masculine sexuation, an exception to the phallic function—Lacan's term for the interdiction of castration—is posited, which is then followed by a contradictory assertion of the function's universality. Though abstracted beyond immediate recognition, the Freudian primal father, who lives in the masculine subject's fantasy as the exception that proves the universal rule of castration, can be discerned here. In the first logical moment of feminine castration, in contrast, there are no exceptions to the phallic function. But the notion follows that "not-all" elements of the feminine subject, elements Lacan represents with the symbol designating the negation of the universal quantifier, are subject to the rule of castration. This is the background to his controversial assertion that women are "pas-toute." Though numerous feminists, including LUCE IRIGARAY, have attacked this claim as a rationalization for what they see as women's secondary status within a patriarchal socio-symbolic order, others have argued that the assertion simply implies that women, or more precisely feminine subjects, do not subject themselves to categorization. Whereas masculine subjects routinely abstract themselves in such a way that they constitute a whole paradoxically unified by the exception embodied by the primal father fantasy (a masculine subject can be "just one of the guys"), feminine subjects feature an irreducible element of singularity, one resistant to counting, that renders each of them a world unto herself. The implications of Lacan's suggestive and oft-misunderstood theory of sexual difference for feminism and the theory of sexuality have yet to be fully elaborated. Clearly, however, sex emerges as an impasse resulting from the impossibility of representing sexual difference symbolically and therefore of establishing sexual identities. The Anglo-American ideology of "gender" upholds the idea that masculinity and femininity are socially preestablished meanings that may never be fully embodied, but sex in the Lacanian view refers instead to the impossibility of sexual meanings themselves, of the frustration of every attempt to define sexual difference in positive terms, and therefore of the unforgiving resistance with which sexuality necessarily thwarts the ambitions of our conscious intentions.

By the end of his career Lacan's efforts to ensure the transmissibility of psychoanalytic conceptuality through formalization had led him to investigate the mathematical fields of topology and the Borromean knot. Declaring that " mathematization alone reaches a real [atteint à un réel]" (On Feminine Sexuality 131) Lacan explores the intricate intersections connecting his three registers through a proliferating series of knots and even more complicated topological figures such as the Klein bottle and the torsus. During this late period he turned with increasing interest not only to mathematics but also to analytic philosophy, in particular to the work of Gottlob Frege and Ludwig Wittgenstein. Faced with what often seemed a bewildering array of topological figures, knots, and mathemes, even many of Lacan's most devout followers complained that his arguments had grown arcane, opaque, and increasingly irrelevant to clinical practice's everyday concerns. His late teaching split his followers into those who would pursue the mathematization of psychoanalysis as the royal road to scientific rigor and objectivity and those who, like JULIA KRISTEVA, argued that Lacan's formalism began effectively to marginalize both the poetic, affect-laden, "semiotic" dimensions of language and the progress of clinical technique. The eccentric difficulty of his last seminars and the baroque elusiveness of his écrits have given rise to an often bewildering array of organizations dedicated to the study of his work. These qualities of Lacan's life of teaching guarantee that his legacy for cultural theory and clinical practice will remain hotly contested.

MICHAEL P. CLARK AND JAMES PENNEY

See also FEMINIST THEORY AND CRITICISM: 4. MATERIALIST FEMINISMS, GENDER, and PSYCHOANALYTIC THEORY AND CRITICISM: 3. THE POST-LACANIANS.

Jacques Lacan, Autres écrits (ed. Jacques-Alain Miller, 2001), De la psychose paranoïaque dans ses rapports avec la personnalité (1932), Écrits (1966, Écrits: A Selection, trans. Alan Sheridan, 1977, Écrits: The First Complete Edition in English, trans. Bruce Fink, 2006), Feminine Sexuality: Jacques Lacan and the École freudienne (ed. Juliet Mitchell and Jacqueline Rose, trans. Jacqueline Rose, 1982), The Language of the Self: The Function of Language in Psychoanalysis (ed. and trans. Anthony Wilden, 1968, rpt., Jacques Lacan, Speech, and Language in Psychoanalysis, 1984), My Teaching (trans. David Macey, 2009), Les quatre concepts fondamentaux de la psychanalyse (1964, The Four Fundamental Concepts of Psychoanalysis, trans. Alan Sheridan, 1977), Le séminaire de Jacques Lacan (ed. Jacques-Alain Miller, 11 vols. to date, 1975– , trans. various, 7 vols. to date, 1988–), Le séminaire XX: Encore, 1972–1973 (ed. Jacques-Alain Miller, 1975, On Feminine Sexuality: The Limits of Love and Knowledge, 1972–1973, trans. Bruce Fink, 1999), Télévision (ed. Jacques-Alain Miller, 1974, Television, ed. Joan Copjec, trans. Denis Hollier, Rosalind Krauss, and Annette Michelson, 1990).

Law and Literature

Both law and literature are ancient fields of learning and practice, long preceding the modern organization of the academic profession into disciplines identified with distinctive research paradigms. More than academic fields, law and literature are also social practices, constituting their own objects of scholarly reflection. And one characteristic feature of such evolving, self-reflective traditions of social practice is constant contest over the purposes and limits of the practice itself.

The appeal of juxtaposing such indeterminate practices as law and literature is the hope of winning a contest over the direction of one of these practices by linking it with or contrasting it to the other. The indeterminacy of this other practice makes it a blank screen on which one can freely project aspirations and fears for one's own practice. And that is also the danger of the juxtaposition. The comparison is almost doomed to yield reductive or exploitative characterizations of both. "Law" will be stupidly rigid and morally insensitive; "literature" will indulge the senses and the imagination at the expense of prudence and truth.

The contemporary law and literature movement originated in American law schools in the 1970s and 1980s as part of an explosion of interdisciplinary legal scholarship, but it has older roots in America's peculiarly juridical public culture. In *Law and Letters in American Culture* (1984), Robert Ferguson documents an intimate connection between the legal and literary professions in antebellum America. Lawyers became Ciceronian orators and statesmen, taking leading roles in electoral politics but also in projects for civic and cultural betterment, including editing and writing of all kinds. As Brook Thomas has demonstrated in *Cross-Examinations of Law and Literature* (1987), much nineteenth-century American fiction is permeated by their authors' interest in the role of legal relations and legal processes in forming the social worlds and social identities of their characters.

Interpretation was a central intellectual concern in postrevolutionary American public life. Participants in public life saw themselves as interpreters and conservers of an authoritative tradition, chiefly embodied in a canonical artifact, the Constitution. Whig lawyers developed a vision of the American state as an edifice of legal institutions and constitutional structures, yet they acknowledged popular pressures for reform embodied in Jacksonian populism. Their answer to these pressures for change was a vision of the statesman as a creative and adaptive interpreter of institutions. Francis Lieber's extraordinary 1839 treatise *Legal and Political Hermeneutics* is a sophisticated work of critical theory, emphasizing that textual interpretation is always a social practice, conditioned by institutional purposes and processes. The Whig ideal of dynamic constitutional interpretation achieved lasting influence in American culture through its greatest exponent, Abraham Lincoln.

After the Civil War, the professionalization of political and intellectual life separated the enterprises of law and literature. Nevertheless, a few judges continued to think of themselves as literary stylists, using rhetorical art to persuade and lead. Some of the legal realists, most notably Lon Fuller, paid attention to literary theory and philosophy of language. Finally, the controversy in the 1950s and 1960s over school desegregation prompted two eloquent constitutional theorists, Alexander Bickel and Charles Black, to revive the idea of constitutional interpretation as a kind of rhetorical statesmanship, requiring creativity and aesthetic judgment. Ronald Dworkin began to write elegant essays on legal interpretation and judicial discretion for the *New York Review of Books*. As the judicial innovations of the Warren Court came under increasing political attack in the 1970s, liberal constitutional scholars responded with an explosion of theoretical justifications for the creative constitutional interpretation.

These intellectual developments coincided with important changes in the sociology of the legal academy in the seventies. As declining professional opportunities forced aspiring scholars out of the humanities and social sciences, many found their way onto rapidly growing law faculties, where they sparked a vigorous debate about the relative merits of different disciplines as models for legal scholarship. Law and economics was the most visibly successful new interdisciplinary enterprise, but literature promised to provide access to a world of value and meaning transcending cost-benefit analysis. In 1973 James B. White published *The Legal Imagination*, an innovative textbook using literary materials and methods to draw attention to the ethics and aesthetics of lawyers' rhetorical strategies.

Many of the new scholars, inspired by the social movements of the 1960s and 1970s, saw themselves as leftists. They arrived toting the theoretical baggage of neo-Marxist ideology critique, STRUCTURALISM, and poststructuralism. The critical legal studies movement, which began to coalesce in the late 1970s, produced many structuralist and poststructuralist analyses of legal discourse and reasoning. A number of "crits" mounted poststructuralist arguments that the constitutional text could not constrain interpretation. Since theories of justice and judicial role were only additional indeterminate texts, these theories could not constrain interpretation either. Several critical legal scholars, including Drucilla Cornell and Jack Balkin, were especially influenced by JACQUES DERRIDA.

Many of these ideas and developments were brought together in important conferences in the early 1980s. Sanford Levinson opened one at the University of Texas with the influential essay "Law as Literature" (in Levinson and Mailloux), which likened judicial interpretation of legal texts to the creative, but anarchic, practice of literary interpretation described by the literary theorists STANLEY FISH and Harold Bloom and the philosophers Richard Rorty and Friedrich Nietzsche. Dworkin offered a conception of adjudication as a literary art but one constrained by an aesthetic responsibility to maintain integrity with the past. Fish joined the debate, arguing in

Doing What Comes Naturally (1989) that the interpretive constraint Dworkin sought and the interpretive freedom Levinson feared were both impossible. The judge produced the meaning of the law, but he was only "free" to produce a meaning that made sense to a professional like himself.

Other writers have emphasized the common character of law and imaginative literature as narrative or figurative discourse. White examines law as a rhetoric, a language of appeal, persuasion, and justification. Drawing on the Aristotelian methods of Chicago critics Wayne Booth and R. S. Crane, he treats each text as an example of some language adapted for use in a particular community. He trains his readers to treat every text as a moral and political document, the constitution of a community. When he reads imaginative literature, he tends to look for self-conscious reflection on the constitution of relationships and community by language. Thus, he offers literature to lawyers as a source of wisdom about the moral and political implications of language.

Lawyers must be concerned with the moral dimensions of language because they are modern rhetoricians. If classical rhetoric presupposed consensus about civic values and virtues, modern rhetoric presupposes the subjectivity of value and strives to constitute consensus values. For White, law stands for the reconstitutive function that rhetoric must perform in all societies. In his best-known work, *When Words Lose Their Meaning* (1984), he argues that the need to constitute authority is a constant in all societies, whether traditional or modern, heroic or democratic. Historical changes constantly erode authority and occasion the need for new languages of value and virtue.

Richard Weisberg has also argued that literature is a source of moral insight into legal language. In *The Failure of the Word* (1984) he presents the formality of legal discourse as a resource for moral evasion distinctive to modern bureaucratic and commercial society, arguing that modern fictional characters often employ a recognizably legalistic rhetoric of complaint and engage in obsessive self-justification and contrasting the alienated and deceitful discourse of legalism with what he regards as the authentic voice of justice. In his later *Poethics* (1992) Weisberg equates aesthetic and ethical virtue, arguing that the truly well-written judicial opinion cannot be unjust as it forthrightly articulates its decisive principles and their implications for the concrete experience of flesh-and-blood human beings.

Other authors have also identified justice with a literary sensibility and an empathetic language of characterization and phenomenological description. In *Love's Knowledge* (1990), Martha Nussbaum reasons that our most salient moral obligations and our most compelling interests arise from love relationships and other sorts of interpersonal commitments. In *Poetic Justice* (1995) Nussbaum extends a claim for the literary nature of moral reasoning to legal argument and judgment. The art of judging requires an articulate appreciation for law's consequences within the unfolding drama of human lives. Robin West argues similarly for the importance of a certain kind of literary sensibility in the exercise of moral and legal judgment. Both the critique and the reform of law require a vivid phenomenological imagination, since, for example, appreciating suffering and oppression requires an understanding of the way the ever-present threat of violation constructs the experience and identity of victims. In the essays collected in *Narrative, Authority, and Law* (1993) she uses literary criticism as a method for apprehending and evaluating jurisprudence of any kind.

West's most wickedly dialectical reading of legal theory as narrative is her extended comparison of Franz Kafka with the legal economist Richard Posner. For West, Kafka and Posner are both tragic ironists, portraying the subjects of modern society in a seemingly inalterable state of social isolation. West's critique provoked Posner's well known but poorly received diatribe against the law and literature movement, *Law and Literature: A Misunderstood Relation* (1988), in which he argues that great literature had to be about universal themes rather than anything as culturally specific as law, politics, or social justice.

Law and literature scholarship began to move in a more historicist direction toward the close of the 1980s. NEW HISTORICISM in literary studies was an important influence. Walter Benn Michaels's *The Gold Standard and the Logic of Naturalism* (1987) draws connections between new legal forms of commerce and property and new modes of representing the self in fiction in America at the turn of the twentieth century. Howard Horwitz applies a similar strategy to the middle decades of the nineteenth century in *By the Law of Nature: Form and Value in Nineteenth Century America* (1991). Brook Thomas studies the historical context of realist literature in *American Literary Realism and the Failed Promise of Contract* (1997). A number of critics have explored the legal and economic context of authorship in the eighteenth and nineteenth centuries, notably Catherine Gallagher, Mark Rose, and Martha Woodmansee.

Several legal scholars were also influenced by New Historicist methods. In *Bloodtaking and Peacemaking* William Ian Miller uses revenge sagas to reconstruct the legal, cultural, and even economic world of medieval Iceland. Janet Halley has written a series of articles on the ways in which the legal regulation of sexual conduct constructs sexual identity and thereby indirectly shapes both sexual behavior and political self-expression. She also has addressed the legal regulation of religious worship and association in seventeenth-century England. Guyora Binder discusses war-crimes trials as contests over the authority to represent oneself against the perpetrators and reads patterns of slave accommodation and resistance to slavery as evidence of the political and legal thought of the slaves. Robert Weisberg (not to be confused with Richard) considers changing narratives of commercial investment and characterizations of merchant capital in the emergent law of bankruptcy.

This historicist turn gained momentum after the founding of the *Yale Journal of Law and Humanities*. In the new journal's first article, Robert Weisberg criticizes much of the first-generation law-and-literature scholarship for its reductive portrayals of both fields and for its limited assimilation of literary theory. He calls for a more complete interdisciplinary integration of the two fields in "cultural studies" of law. Such studies began to appear increasingly over the next decade, especially in the pages of the new journal. Binder and Robert Weisberg would explicate the new cultural criticism of law and compare it with rival approaches in their book Literary Criticisms of Law (2000). Other proponents of a CULTURAL STUDIES approach to law include Rosemary Coombe and Paul Kahn.

While the law-and-literature movement originated in the United States, it has gained increasing visibility in Europe. A number of European philosophers have been concerned with literary aspects of legal thought. Hans-Georg Gadamer explores legal interpretation as one model for a tradition-bound hermeneutics of cultural artifacts in Truth and Method (1960), and Chaim Perelman examines legal argumentation as a model of pragmatic rhetoric. Derrida's influence among leftists in the American legal academy eventually enmeshed him in American jurisprudential debates. His "Force of Law" lectures repudiate any notion that the DECONSTRUCTION of institutional authority could underwrite a revolutionary or populist radicalism. He argues that such a politics depends on the fallacious idea that law can be refounded on the basis of a radically new source of authority and claims that such a messianic aspiration involves too great a risk of totalitarianism. A 2001 German conference on law as literature suggested that the law-and-literature movement had finally begun to transcend its fixation on the figure of the common law judge and was now ready for export to other legal cultures.

Nevertheless, the liveliest European community of law and literature scholars has been in the United Kingdom. Peter Goodrich contributes historically informed and rigorous analyses of the rhetoric and SEMIOTICS of law in his early works Reading the Law (1986), Legal Discourse (1987), and Languages of Law (1990), and Bernard Jackson has applies structuralist analysis in Semiotics and Legal Theory (1997) and Law, Fact, and Narrative Coherence (1988). Costas Douzinas has preferred poststructuralist analyses and has drawn attention to aesthetic and ethical dimensions of law in his coauthored books Postmodern Jurisprudence (1991) and Justice Miscarried (1994). Other important British contributions include Ian Ward's Law and Literature: Possibilities and Perspectives (1996) and Michael Freeman and Andrew Lewis's massive anthology Law and Literature (1999).

GUYORA BINDER

See also bibliography for STANLEY FISH.

Guyora Binder and Robert Weisberg, Literary Criticisms of Law (2000); Jacques Derrida, "Force of Law: The Mystical Foundation of Authority," Cardozo Law Review 11 (1990, trans. Mary Quaintance); Costas Douzinas and Ronnie Warrington, Justice Miscarried: Ethics, Aesthetics, and the Law (1994); Costas Douzinas, Ronnie Warrington, and Shaun McVeigh, Postmodern Jurisprudence: The Law of the Text in the Texts of Law (1991); Ronald Dworkin, Law's Empire (1986); Robert Ferguson, Law and Letters in American Culture (1984); Michael Freeman and Andrew Lewis, eds., Law and Literature

(1999); Hans-Georg Gadamer, *Wahrheit und Methode: Grundzüge einer philosophischen Hermeneutik* (1960, 5th ed., *Gesammelte Werke*, vol. 1, ed. J. C. B. Mohr, 1986, *Truth and Method*, trans. Garrett Barden and John Cumming, 1975, 2nd rev. ed., trans. rev. Joel Weinsheimer and Donald G. Marshall, 1989); Peter Goodrich, *Languages of Law: From Logics of Memory to Nomadic Masks* (1990), *Legal Discourse: Studies in Linguistics, Rhetoric, and Legal Analysis* (1987), *Reading the Law* (1986); Harold Horwitz, *By the Law of Nature: Form and Value in Nineteenth Century America* (1991); Bernard Jackson, *Law, Fact, and Narrative Coherence* (1988), *Semiotics and Legal Theory* (1997); Sanford Levinson and Stephen Mailloux, eds., *Interpreting Law and Literature: A Hermeneutic Reader* (1988); Francis Lieber, *Legal and Political Hermeneutics* (1839); Walter Benn Michaels, *The Gold Standard and the Logic of Naturalism: American Literature at the Turn of the Century* (1987); William Ian Miller, *Bloodtaking and Peacemaking: Feud, Law, and Society in Saga Iceland* (1990); Martha C. Nussbaum, *Love's Knowledge: Essays on Philosophy and Literature* (1990), *Poetic Justice: The Literary Imagination and Public Life* (1995); Chaim Perelman, *The Idea of Justice and the Problem of Argument* (1963); Richard Posner, *Law and Literature: A Misunderstood Relation* (1988); Brook Thomas, *American Literary Realism and the Failed Promise of Contract* (1997), *Cross-Examinations of Law and Literature* (1987); Ian Ward, *Law and Literature: Possibilities and Perspectives* (1996); Richard Weisberg, *The Failure of the Word: The Protagonist as Lawyer in Modern Fiction* (1984), *Poethics and Other Strategies of Law and Literature* (1992); Robert Weisberg, "The Law-Literature Enterprise," *Yale Journal of Law and Humanities* 1 (1988); Robin West, *Narrative, Authority, and Law* (1993); James Boyd White, *The Legal Imagination* (1973), *When Words Lose Their Meaning* (1984).

Levinas, Emmanuel

Emmanuel Levinas (1906–1995) is notable for taking up several major philosophical traditions of the twentieth century whose mutual relevance has not otherwise been explored—Husserlian PHENOMENOLOGY, modern philosophies of Jewish existence, and the philosophy of dialogue advanced by Martin Buber—and for leaving a lasting impact on these currents of thinking and their reception. In addition, Levinas's role as an interlocutor of JACQUES DERRIDA and his central importance for the latter's "ethico-political" writings make his work an indispensable point of reference for students of contemporary philosophy and theory.

Levinas was born and grew up in Kaunas, Lithuania, in a Jewish family influenced by Enlightenment traditions. In 1923 he began studying philosophy at the university in Strasbourg, France, and his studies were supplemented by a stay in Freiburg, Germany (1928–1929), where he was introduced to the teaching of Edmund Husserl and his disciple, MARTIN HEIDEGGER. Levinas soon took on a key role in the earliest French reception of Husserl's phenomenology with his 1930 dissertation, *The Theory of Intuition in Husserl's Phenomenology*, and the first French edition of Husserl's *Cartesian Meditations* (1931), which he translated with Gabrielle Peiffer. Having completed his doctorate, Levinas moved to Paris, where he began teaching at the École Normale Israélite Orientale (ENIO), which trains teachers for the network of French-language schools for Jews throughout the Mediterranean region run by the Alliance Israélite Universelle. He continued writing about philosophy (notably *On Escape* [1935]) and contemporary political issues and stayed active in philosophical circles. Levinas published his first major work, *Totality and Infinity*, in 1961 and subsequently began a university career, which he pursued alongside his ongoing role at the ENIO. From 1961 to 1984 he taught philosophy at the University of Poitiers, the University of Paris X (Nanterre), and the University of Paris IV (Sorbonne). Levinas's philosophical work of the 1960s and early 1970s culminated in his second major work, *Otherwise Than Being; or, Beyond Essence* (1974).

Levinas's central project is to reorient philosophy around the principle of "ethics as first philosophy" (see ETHICS). In his critique of traditional Western philosophy, Levinas introduces a notion of ethics that differs radically from what had previously been understood by that term. If we take Immanuel Kant's conception of morality as representative of the modern philosophical tradition—that in order for my action to be good I must be able to affirm it as universally desirable and that human beings have the capacity to act ethically in accordance with this principle (Kant's "categorical imperative")—then the contrast with Levinas's analyses becomes apparent. For Levinas, the possibility of acting ethically is rooted in a condition of passivity, in which I am compelled to respond to a command from an absolute, transcendent Other (*autrui*), with whom I find myself in a "face-to-face" relation. This condition of responsibility in the face-to-face is something that Levinas regards as prior to any act of cognition, to any conscious act of which I could be the author. Responsibility is thus conceived not as something that I willingly, consciously, or actively engage in by making sovereign decisions based on knowledge I might have or principles I am able to apply but as a condition in which I find myself responding to an unconditional demand made on me.

This new elaboration of ethics as first philosophy goes hand in hand with a critique of Western philosophy as a philosophy of "totality"—a critique that takes as an important cue from Franz Rosenzweig's project of elaborating a philosophical system that effected a complete break with the Hegelian philosophical system. For Levinas, however, who wrote from a distinctly postwar and post-Holocaust vantage point, the project of breaking with totalization and a thinking of "the same" in favor of a thinking of "alterity" is aimed also at addressing the legacy of political-historical totalitarianisms and at demonstrating the shortcomings of the philosophy of Heidegger. Although Levinas was always explicit in denouncing Heidegger's involvement with National Socialism, he also regarded *Being and Time* (1927) as having "completely altered the course and character of European philosophy," such that "one cannot seriously philosophize today without traversing the Heideggerian path in some form or other" ("Dialogue" 51). However, Heidegger ultimately comes to represent in Levinas's writings an ontological view of human existence that misses the dimension of the ethical and of alterity. For Levinas, as for Rosenzweig, Jewish sources, and in particular the Hebrew Bible, are a prime inspiration from which an ethical critique of Western, or "Greek," thought can be effected. But Levinas shares Heidegger's sense of the difficulty of effecting a critique of metaphysics without recourse to the "Greek"—to philosophical language and concepts—and regards such an enterprise as itself still a work of philosophy.

Derrida was perhaps the earliest contemporary to publicly recognize Levinas's growing body of writings as that of a major thinker. Derrida's 1963 study "Violence and Metaphysics," a systematic introduction to a wide range of philosophical and Jewish writings published by Levinas up to that time, also represents an important stage in his own philosophical development. This long essay reveals powerful affinities between the two thinkers, reflecting on their shared intellectual heritage—both Derrida and Levinas had taken Husserl and Heidegger as their philosophical starting point—as well as engaging critically the Hebrew-Greek opposition that appeared to be operative in Levinas's works. Levinas later jokingly described the essay as an "assassination under anesthesia" ("assassinat sous narcose") (David 113), but many have read it as a touchstone of a lasting and transformative intellectual exchange in both directions, one that is especially visible in Derrida's sustained engagement with Levinasian articulations of the ethical.

Though the category of the aesthetic receives a mixed, not always consistent treatment in Levinas's writings, it remains highly relevant to his accounts of the ethical—and not only because of the many literary references found in his works. For one thing, just as Martin Buber characterizes the I-Thou relation in terms of language, so Levinas characterizes the ethical relation in terms of language, namely, language not as a neutral conveyor of meaning ("le Dit") but as the fact of saying, or address ("le Dire"), an idea that brings his philosophy into conversation with twentieth-century theories of language and art. Contemporary literary theorists have thus drawn on Levinas's writings as a resource for thinking about an ethics of literature and have even seen in his work the potential for an aesthetic theory or poetics. In this connection, Levinas's lifelong friendship with the critic and novelist MAURICE BLANCHOT is especially important, both for the essays Levinas devotes to Blanchot's literary and critical works (see *Proper Names* [1975–1976]) and for the presence of Levinasian themes in works by Blanchot, such as *The Writing of the Disaster* (1980).

DANA HOLLANDER

See also ETHICS.

Emmanuel Levinas, À l'heure des nations (1988, In the Time of the Nations, trans. Michael B. Smith, 1994), L'au-delà du verset: Lectures et discours talmudiques (1982, Beyond the Verse: Talmudic Readings and Lectures, trans. Gary D. Mole, 1994), Autrement qu'être; ou, Au-delà de l'essence (1974, Otherwise Than Being; or, Beyond Essence, trans. Alphonso Lingis, 1981), Basic Philosophical Writings (ed. Adriaan Peperzak, Simon Critchley, and Robert Bernasconi, 1996), Collected Philosophical Papers (trans. Alphonso Lingis, 1987), De Dieu qui vient à l'idée (1982, Of God Who Comes To Mind, trans. Bettina Bergo, 1998), De l'évasion (1935, On Escape, trans. Bettina Bergo, 2003), De l'existence à l'existant (1947, Existence and Existents, trans. Alphonso Lingis, 1978), En découvrant l'existence avec Husserl et Heidegger (1949, 2nd ed., 1967, partial trans., Discovering Existence with Husserl, ed. and trans. Richard A. Cohen and Michael B. Smith, 1998), "Dialogue," Dialogues with Contemporary Continental Thinkers (by Richard Kearney, 1984; also in Face to Face with Levinas, ed. Richard A. Cohen, 1986), Difficile liberté (1963, 2nd ed., 1976, Difficult Freedom: Essays on Judaism, trans. Seán Hand, 1990), Du sacré au saint: Cinq nouvelles lectures talmudiques (1977, partial trans., Nine Talmudic Readings, trans. Annette Aronowicz, 1990), Ethique et infini: Dialogues avec Philippe Nemo (1982, Ethics and Infinity: Conversations with Philippe Nemo, trans. Richard A. Cohen, 1985), Hors sujet (1987, Outside the Subject, trans. Michael B. Smith, 1993), Is It Righteous to Be? Interviews with Emmanuel Levinas (ed. Jill Robbins, 2001), Noms propres/Sur Maurice Blanchot (1975–1976, Proper Names, trans. Michael B. Smith, 1996), Nouvelles lectures talmudiques (1996, New Talmudic Readings, trans. Richard A. Cohen, 1999), Quatre lectures talmudiques (1968, partial trans., Nine Talmudic Readings, trans. Annette Aronowicz, 1990), Le temps et l'autre (1947, Time and the Other, trans. Richard A. Cohen, 1987), Totalité et infini (1961, Totality and Infinity, trans. Alphonso Lingis, 1979); Alain David, "Corpus," Rue Descartes 48 (2005).

Linguistics and Language

Contemporary linguistics, which comprises various studies of language structure and use, grew out of the methods of comparative philology. These historical language studies of the nineteenth century had mapped out relationships between languages by locating the evolutionary principles governing the sound systems of Indo-European languages (see Robins). But many scholars associate modern linguistic study with synchronic linguistics, inaugurated early in the twentieth century by FERDINAND DE SAUSSURE, himself a comparative philologist who strove to distinguish more clearly than his contemporaries between diachronic and synchronic explanatory concerns. Saussure's work marks the start of synchronic, nonevolutionary studies of language; besides language history, linguistic study now investigates present-time linguistic facts, principles governing the phonology (sound structure), morphology (grammatical inflection and word formation), syntax, and semantics of natural languages. And the field also extends to interdisciplinary studies of language acquisition and use, including psycholinguistics (accounts of language learning and processing); pragmatics and discourse analysis (studies inspired by linguistic philosophy of SPEECH ACTS), speech genres, and text structure; sociolinguistics (analyses of the social dimensions of language variation); and ethnographies of speech communities. What follows is an overview of recent linguistics and linguistic philosophy, largely as presented by its practitioners in paradigm texts, focusing on the terms and models most important to literature and literary theory.

SAUSSUREAN LINGUISTICS. Saussure's impact on both linguistics and literary study cannot be overstated. From within a discipline conceived as historical and philological, in lectures from 1906 to 1911 Saussure argued that scholars had confused those linguistic facts relevant from the point of view of speakers at any particular moment in time with those of exclusively historical interest (81–83, 90–98). A historically developing sound change, for example, could fail to impact existing linguistic distinctions; on the other hand, speakers could invest a new form with new significance, exploiting the expressive possibilities of the altered or introduced element. Further, the material form of a language could stabilize while distinctions expressed with those forms nevertheless altered, resulting in, from the speakers' perspective, a different language system (83–87). In distinguishing diachronic from synchronic facts, the linguist clarifies the kind of linguistic change at issue and at the same time identifies present-time structural relationships (79–100).

Saussure had been addressing a largely text-focused field, but the distinction between synchronic and diachronic linguistic facts implies a mentalist conception of language, involving a distinction between form itself and its (synchronic) signifying function. Language in this account resides not in sounds or written symbols but in speakers' knowledge of the rules and elements of the language. To cite another of

Saussure's binary oppositions, there is a distinction to be made between *langue*, speakers' shared knowledge of the language, and *parole*, acts of speaking. *Langue* is social, rule-governed, and potential; *parole* is individual, idiosyncratic, and actual (9–15, 19). Acts of *parole* express *langue* and are impossible without it; *parole*, on the other hand, gives life to *langue* and, through the idiosyncratic and accidental variations of everyday speech events, effects changes in it (19, 98).

If language is essentially form, not substance, then its elements or signs must derive significance relationally, within the context of *langue*, the language system as a whole. Signs themselves consist of a signifier, carved out of an otherwise undifferentiated stream of sound and an arbitrarily associated signified, delimited in an otherwise amorphous conceptual space (65–70, 102–5, 107–19). The signifier, material now assigned a representational function, achieves its significance within the system through an interplay of identity and difference. That is, an identity of acoustically varied utterances of the sound "p" are necessary to its stable signifying function. At the same time, "p" as a discrete unit is perceptually available as such only in its conventional contrast to closely related sounds (like "b") (108–11). These principles apply as well to signifieds or concepts. In Saussure's example, the value of "sheep" (opposed in English to "mutton") differs from (uncontrasted) *mouton* in French (115–16; see also 79–81, 87–89). In Saussure's famous formulation, "In language there are only differences without positive terms" (120). Principles of identity and difference finally structure signs within the larger system. Identity defines associative relationships—like elements, exchangeable categories (e.g., classes of verb inflections); difference defines syntagmatic or linear structure—the ordering of different associative classes (verb stems before inflections) (122–31).

European STRUCTURALISM, developed from elements of Saussurean linguistics, has most broadly impacted literary studies in the United States. Structuralist critics found many Saussurean terms suggestive, especially "system" (a literary text or corpus is a rule-governed system); *langue* and *parole* (a text, genre, or interpretive norm constitutes *langue*, and actualized instances make up *parole*); "sign" (art is a sign, its material a signifier, its signified shared and abstract); and "syntagmatic" versus "paradigmatic" axes of language (analogously the structural dimensions of narrative) (see Culler, Henkel). Additionally, Saussure's account has figured in poststructuralism and DECONSTRUCTION in the general conception of art as sign, here with an emphasis on the contingency and artificiality of the signifier, and in a negative and differential account of meaning (Derrida, *Of Grammatology* 52–53).

PRAGUE SCHOOL STRUCTURALISM. Saussure's immediate intellectual descendants were members of the Prague school, active from 1926 to 1939 and comprising both linguists and literary critics. Prague school linguists made many contributions to linguistics—for example, in phonology (Nikolai Trubetzkoy and Roman Jakobson [see overview in Robins]), morphology, (Jakobson with Pomorska; Robin Lakoff 23, 35–37), and syntactic theory lacking in Saussure's account.

The Prague school adopted a "functionalist" approach to language study and modified, reoriented, or criticized some of Saussure's ideas. Language, for them, is not a system, but, as Jakobson asserts, a "system of systems" ("Sign" 30). Moreover, Jakobson elaborates a structuralism SEMIOTICS that goes beyond arbitrary signification (here the "symbol"), featuring partially motivated, nonarbitrary signifiers (the "index" and "icon," which bear a causal or visual relation to a signified) (see "Quest"). Similarly, Mukařovský's metaphorized "sign" applies not just to language but to literature and other cultural practices as well (Aesthetic).

GENERATIVE GRAMMAR. Frustrated with certain forms of American linguistics, Noam Chomsky argued, first in 1957, against a restricted view of scientific practice. Linguistics should not deal with a corpus of collected sentences but of all possible sentences, those sentences native speakers deem grammatical (Syntactic 13, 15, 48; Aspects 15–16). "Competence"—that is, speakers' linguistic knowledge—is distinct from "performance," actual data or utterance acts (Aspects 4). Like Saussure, Chomsky thus locates interest in the shared linguistic norms of an idealized ("homogeneous") speech community, but "competence" is complete ("internalized") in every speaker (Aspects 3, 8) and thus less general than langue.

In a paradigm shift known as transformational-generative grammar, Chomsky modeled syntactic analysis on logic and mathematics, his explanatory goal being to formulate rules that describe and predict ("generate") sentences speakers find grammatical, excluding those they would not (Syntactic 13–14). Additionally, the grammar models crucial aspects of linguistic competence—the ability to produce new sentences, an infinite variety of sentences, and infinitely long sentences from finite means (Aspects 15–16).

Transformational-generative linguistics has made important inroads in language study, including semantics ("deep structure"), language processing, and language acquisition. While such directions may not relate to literary projects, Chomsky's earlier theory proved so suggestive to the reader-oriented critics of the 1970s and 1980s that certain generative metaphors persist in current critical vocabulary. Just as Chomsky focuses not on sentences but on the linguistic knowledge that makes production of sentences possible, critics argued, so should we now outline the rules of "literary competence," the knowledge by which readers "generate" or make sense of literary texts (Culler 48, 114, 117–18, 121–22; Fish 44–45, 48). Such an approach shifts critical interest from texts to readers; yet interpretive chaos does not ensue, for reading practices are rule governed, shared and understood within an "interpretive community" (Culler 113–22; Fish 292, 338–55).

SPEECH ACT THEORY. Speech act theory contrasts significantly with structuralism and transformational grammar; it is a species of ordinary philosophy in the analytic tradition, so called because it focuses on problems of reference, truth value, and meaning from the perspective of ordinary utterances. But since the 1970s, speech act accounts have had considerable impact on both linguistics and literary criticism—in linguistics, in studies of sentence-level semantics and discourse structure; in literary studies, in accounts of fictional and public language.

The term "speech act theory" itself is particularly associated with the work of J. L. Austin, John Searle, and H. Paul Grice. Their shared, basic insight derives from the disjunction in ordinary discourse between what is said and what is meant. That is, sentences do not mean the sum of their word meanings, and sentence meaning is itself problematic since a sentence has different meanings in different conversational contexts. Thus arises a distinction between locutions (involving syntactic form, basic sense, and reference) and illocutions, or utterance acts (Austin 94–108). In Austin's example, the locution "Bull!" constitutes different illocutions, depending on the whether it is uttered as a description or a warning (55–62); conversely, different locutions may encode identical illocutions (e.g., the invitation "Come!" and "We hope to see you") (Searle, *Speech* 22–26). If meaning does not reside in form, then in communicating interlocutors must rely on conventionally signaled speaker intentions, on conventions governing speech practices, and on shared extralinguistic knowledge of the world and conversational context.

The intentions at issue are narrowly linguistic; unconscious intentions are at play, but by definition they cannot constitute the stable and publicly shared signifying practice that is the theory's focus (Henkel 156–63). Speakers strategize speech actions, and hearers ponder speakers' motives. Nevertheless, the event itself, a hearer's "illocutionary uptake" or recognition of the promise as such, is often not at issue (Austin 117). The conscious and unconscious intentions and effects that attend illocutionary acts are to be distinguished from specifically linguistic intent. Illocutionary acts—assertions and promises—are predictable, convention bound; on the other hand, "perlocutionary acts"—effects of belief, suspicion, gratitude—are unpredictable and nonlinguistic (Austin 121–22; Searle, *Speech* 46–50).

Thus, Austin and Searle focus on both illocutionary conventions and embedding institutions. Austin's central example, the "performative" utterance "I do" of the marriage ceremony, is of interest because it cannot meaningfully be termed true or false, unlike descriptions or assertions ("constatives"); instead, saying "I do" is doing rather than describing or asserting something (1–11). Yet even if such utterance acts cannot be false, they can nevertheless go wrong. As Austin considers such possible "infelicities" for the performative "I do," he outlines institutional conditions necessary for its success (12–38). In this case, authorized (unmarried) persons must participate, the ceremony must be complete, and the speaker must not be obviously insincere. Austin finally subsumes all utterance acts to the performative, including descriptions and assertions, for similar conventions finally bear on less obviously institutionalized constatives (133–47).

In Searle's account, such conventions, obliquely invoked, explain not just infelicitous but also indirect speech acts (from which derives the conversational logic of "Can you help me?" that is related to a norm such as "speakers request actions hearers can accomplish" ["Indirect"].) In Grice's scheme, a general conversational logic applies: hearers understand what speakers imply by calculating the distance between what was said and expectations of conversational relevance and economy. Thus, an apparent irrelevance prompts hearers to work out an implied but related proposition.

Speech act theory figures largely in pragmatic accounts of politeness, irony, indirection, and implication (see Sperber and Wilson) and in analyses of language institutions and social class (Bourdieu 66–89, 105–26). In literary criticism, the theory has suggested accounts of literary reference; of fictive indirection and implication, especially in drama (see Petrey); of genre conventions and institutionalized interpretative norms (Culler, Fish); of literary language as playful, performative (Derrida "Limited"; Felman); and of utterance acts as forms of institutional action (Butler, *Bodies* 1–23, *Excitable*).

SOCIOLINGUISTICS. Sociolinguistic study focuses on language variation and use. Its impetus was William Labov's work, beginning in the 1960s. Labov aimed, first, to expand the domain of mainstream linguistics beyond "homogeneous speech communities" and, second, to improve on existing variation research, which had focused on regional, rural, and mostly lexical speech differences. Labov proposed instead to apply both social science methodology and generativist linguistics to the diversity of urban speech.

In a now classic study, Labov investigates New York department store clerks' use of postvocalic [r], a phonetic variant said to be linguistically unpredictable, sometimes occurring, sometimes not ("Social"). Labov suggests that such variants are in fact not random but socially constrained; noting that r-pronunciation represents a new prestige norm for the city, he further hypothesizes its association with status, with careful speaking styles, and with younger, presumably innovating, speakers. A larger, related study reveals that low social status delays speakers' exposure to prestige norms, complicating generalizations about age, and the "linguistic insecurity" of mid-status speakers prompted hypercorrect speech in formal styles, complicating assumptions about class (52–54, 57–65). Scholars in women's studies have naturally remained conversant with sociolinguistic work on language and gender. Other critics refer to sociolinguistic studies on topics that, for example, relate spoken genres to literary narratives or modes of criticism (Gates, Pratt) or compare linguistic variation to literary representation (Fisher Fishkin).

COGNITIVE LINGUISTICS. While generative grammar offers a theory of language that is founded on a set of specifically linguistic universal principles, cognitive linguists theorize that such universals derive instead from general *cognitive* processes. Historically, this approach to language emerges from the arguments of generative semantics, and in fact George Lakoff, associated with this earlier challenge to generative grammar, authored its founding text, *Women, Fire, and Dangerous Things* (1987). Since work in cognitive linguistics attends to the linguistic effects of (immediate) speech contexts, to the semantics of apparent sentence paraphrases, alternate syntactic forms, and to culturally general patterns of metaphor, it is obviously suggestive for literary analysis (see overview in Lee). Of interest to critics are Eve Sweetser's pragmatics of polysemy, ambiguity, and lexical change and Elizabeth Traugott and Richard Dasher's recent discourse-grounded historical semantics; Ellen Spolsky metaphorically extends basic precepts of cognitive linguistics to literary interpretation.

Other, future connections between studies of language and literature are difficult to predict. But public controversies suggest an important shared educational role on issues at once literary and linguistic—on the expressive and literary value of nonmainstream dialects and multiple codes; on problems of promoting written standard language; and on issues of language education.

JACQUELINE HENKEL

See also FERDINAND DE SAUSSURE and SPEECH ACTS.

J. L. Austin, *How to Do Things with Words* (ed. J. O. Urmson and Marina Sbisà, 1962, 2nd ed., 1975); Pierre Bourdieu, *Ce que parler veut dire: L'économie des échanges linguistiques* (1982, partial trans., *Language and Symbolic Power*, ed. John B. Thompson, trans. Gino Raymond and Matthew Adamson, 1991); Penelope Brown and Stephen Levinson, "Universals in Language Use: Politeness Phenomena," *Questions and Politeness* (ed. Esther Goody, 1978); Judith Butler, *Bodies That Matter: On the Discursive Limits of "Sex"* (1993), *Excitable Speech: A Politics of the Performative* (1977); Jennifer Coates, *Women, Men, and Language* (1986, 2nd ed., 1993); Noam Chomsky, *Aspects of the Theory of Syntax* (1965), *Knowledge of Language: Its Nature, Origin, and Use* (1986), "New Horizons in the Study of Language," *New Horizons in the Study of Language and Mind* (2000), *Syntactic Structures* (1957); Noam Chomsky and Morris Halle, *The Sound Pattern of English* (1968); Jonathan Culler, *Structuralist Poetics: Structuralism, Linguistics, and the Study of Literature* (1975); Jacques Derrida, *De la grammatologie* (1967, *Of Grammatology*, trans. Gayatri Chakravorty Spivak, 1976), "Limited Inc. abc . . ." *Glyph* 2 (1977) ("Limited Inc. abc . . . ," trans. Samuel Weber, 1977); Shoshana Felman, *Le scandale du corps parlant: Don Juan avec Austin; ou, La séduction en deux langues* (1980, *The Literary Speech Act: Don Juan with J. L. Austin; or, Seduction in Two Languages*, trans. Catherine Porter, 1983, rpt., *The Scandal of the Speaking Body: Don Juan with J. L. Austin, or Seduction in Two Languages*, 2003); Stanley Fish, *Is There a Text in This Class? The Authority of Interpretive Communities* (1980); Shelley Fisher Fishkin, *Was Huck Black? Mark Twain and African-American Voices* (1993); F. W. Galan, *Historic Structures: The Prague School Project, 1928–1946* (1985); H. Paul Grice, "Logic and Conversation," *Syntax and Semantics*, vol. 3, *Speech Acts* (ed. Peter Cole and Jerry Morgan, 1975); M. A. K. Halliday, "Language Structure and Language Function," *New Horizons in Linguistics* (ed. John Lyons, 1970); Jacqueline Henkel, *The Language of Criticism: Linguistic Models and Literary Theory* (1996); Roman Jakobson, "Closing Statement: Linguistics and Poetics," *Style and Language* (ed. Thomas Sebeok, 1960), *Language in Literature* (ed. Krystyna Pomorska and Stephen Rudy, 1987), "Quest for the Essence of Language" (1965), *Readings in Russian Poetics: Formalist and Structuralist Views* (ed. Ladislav Matejka and Krystyna Pomorska, 1971), "Zeichen und System der Sprache," *Selected Writings* (1962, "Sign and System: A Reassessment of Saussure's Doctrine" (1962, trans. Benjamin Hrushovski, *Verbal Art, Verbal Sign, Verbal Time*, ed. Krystyna Pomorska and Stephen Rudy, 1985); Roman Jakobson with Krystyna Pomorska, "The Concept of Mark," *Dialogues* (trans. Christian Huber, 1983); William Labov, "The Social Stratification of (r) in New York City Department Stores," *Sociolinguistic Patterns* (1972); George Lakoff, *Women, Fire, and Dangerous Things: What Categories Reveal about the Mind* (1987); Robin Lakoff, *Language and Woman's Place* (1975);

David Lee, *Cognitive Linguistics: An Introduction* (2001); Jan Mukařovský, *Estetická funkce, norma a hodnota jako sociální fakty* (1936, *Aesthetic Function, Norm, and Value as Social Facts*, trans. Mark E. Suino, 1970), "O jazyce básnickám," *Kapitoly z české poetíky* 1 (1940) ("On Poetic Language," *Word and Verbal Art*, ed. and trans. John Burbank and Peter Steiner, 1977); Frederick Newmeyer, *Linguistic Theory in America: The First Quarter Century of Transformational Generative Grammar* (1st ed., 1980, 2nd ed., *Linguistic Theory in America*, 1986); Sandy Petrey, *Speech Acts and Literary Theory* (1990); Mary Louise Pratt, *Toward a Speech Act Theory of Literary Discourse* (1977); R. H. Robins, *Short History of Linguistics* (1967, 4th ed., 1997); Ferdinand de Saussure, *Cours de linguistique générale* (ed. Charles Bally and Albert Sechehaye, 1916, *Course in General Linguistics*, trans. Wade Baskin, 1959); John Searle, "Indirect Speech Acts," *Expression and Meaning: Studies in the Theory of Speech Acts* (1979), *Speech Acts: An Essay in the Philosophy of Language* (1969); Dan Sperber and Deirdre Wilson, *Relevance: Communication and Cognition* (1986, 2nd ed., 1995); Ellen Spolsky, *Gaps in Nature: Literary Interpretation and the Modular Mind* (1993); Jurij Striedter, *Texte der russischen Formalisten* and *Die Struktur der literarischen Entwicklung* (1969, partial trans., *Literary Structure, Evolution, and Value: Russian Formalism and Czech Structuralism Reconsidered*, trans. Matthew Gurewitsch, 1989); Eve E. Sweetser, *From Etymology to Pragmatics: Metaphorical and Cultural Aspects of Semantic Structure* (1990); Tzvetan Todorov, *Mikhaïl Bakhtine: Le principe dialogique* (1981, *Mikhail Bakhtin: The Dialogical Principle*, trans. Wlad Godzich, 1984); Elizabeth Closs Traugott and Richard B. Dasher, *Regularity in Semantic Change* (2002); Yuri Tynianov and Roman Jakobson, "Problemy izucheniia literatury i iazyka," *Novyi Lef* 12 (1928) ("Problems in the Study of Language and Literature," trans. Herbert Eagle, *Verbal Art, Verbal Sign, Verbal Time*, ed. Krystyna Pomorska and Stephen Rudy, 1985); Ronald Wardhaugh, *An Introduction to Sociolinguistics* (1986, 4th ed., 2001).

Lukács, Georg

Georg Lukács (1885–1971) was a politically committed thinker with a lifelong talent for aligning himself with small, oppositional, and inevitably doomed political factions. By contrast, his aesthetic, critical, political, and philosophical writings have had a marked and often decisive effect on Western Marxist and post-Marxist critical theory. The FRANKFURT SCHOOL, genetic STRUCTURALISM, and more indirectly, poststructuralism and cultural materialism are all in his debt.

From 1909 to 1917 he studied in Berlin and Heidelberg, where his work was influenced by George Simmel, Heinrich Rickert, Wilhelm Dilthey, Emil Lask, Erwin Szabo, Georges Sorel, Max Weber, G. W. F. Hegel, and Karl Marx and Friedrich Engels. In these years, Lukács wrote (in German) his best-known pre-Marxist works, *Soul and Form* (1911) and *The Theory of the Novel* (1916), as well as the posthumously published *Heidelberg Aesthetics*, and he laid the foundations for his *Literatursoziologie*. In *History of the Development of Modern Drama* (1911) and in *Theory of the Novel* he considers literary form as an expression of a worldview or ideology that grows out of economic and cultural relations or out of the writer's experience of them and tries to show why different literary forms develop in different periods of social development. In *Heidelberg Aesthetics* he is concerned with the way literary form acts as "the bearer of adequate communication" between writer and public while at the same time permitting "normative misunderstandings" in the reception of works.

In 1918 Lukács joined the Hungarian Soviet as minister of culture and education and almost immediately became deputy leader of the party's "left Communist opposition," later known as the Landler faction. In exile in Vienna during the 1920s, he drafted the controversial Blum Theses, which argued for Soviet-based democracy in the party, and wrote *History and Class Consciousness* (1923), which assumes that the proletarian revolution is "on the agenda of world history" and uses the standpoint of the proletariat for a far-reaching critique of the reification of bourgeois society and of positivist science. *History and Class Consciousness* elaborates the Hegelian dimension of Marxism and makes alienation and reification central categories of analysis and insists that by puncturing the false consciousness of the proletariat and raising critical consciousness, theory can produce revolutionary practice and become a material force capable of transforming society.

During the 1930s and the war years, most of which he spent in Russia, Lukács worked for the Popular Front against fascism and intervened in a heated debate in the Communist Party about the form and function of proletarian literature. Against the Proletkult line (which became party orthodoxy), which held that literature is a class product and an instrument in the hands of the dominant class that must be used for the organization and education of the masses, Lukács argued (with Trotsky and the Russian Association of Proletarian Writers) that literature provides critical understanding of underlying social and historical processes by revealing hidden causalities and inherent contradictions. Attacking the crude tendentiousness, the stereotyped characters, and the "reportage" he thought socialist realism shared with naturalism, Lukács urged proletarian writers to learn from bourgeois realists such as Walter Scott, Honoré de Balzac, Leo Tolstoy, and Thomas Mann how to portray society critically by showing typical characters wrestling with social conflicts during historical periods of transition. Lukács's most frequently anthologized pieces are those in which he advocates critical realism and attacks socialist realism, naturalism, modernism, and stream-of-consciousness techniques in Studies in European Realism (a volume comprised of essays written in the 1930s and published in 1950), The Historical Novel (1937), Essays on Realism (1948), Realism in Our Time (1958), and Solzhenitsyn (1964).

Lukács was widely criticized for submitting to Stalinism. At the same time, careful examination of such writings as The Young Hegel (written in 1938 but published in 1948), Goethe and His Age (1947), and The Destruction of Reason (written between 1946 and 1949 and published in 1954), which Lukács described as "theoretical masquerades," shows that during the period of Stalinism he was practicing veiled writing and painfully reexamining his Marxist premises. His defense of Marxism after the war in his polemic with Jean-Paul Sartre, Existentialism or Marxism (1948), suggests that he had decided to remain faithful to Marxism because he saw it as the only alternative to fascism and to ideological and historical nihilism and because he could still justify Marxist theoretical work to himself with the hope that, as he wrote in The Young Hegel, "once the realm of ideas has been revolutionized, reality cannot hold out" (506).

Lukács returned to Hungary in 1945 in the wake of the Red Army as a member of the Hungarian Academy of Sciences and professor of aesthetics and philosophy at Budapest University. With Imre Nagy and the Petofi circle, Lukács opposed the country's Stalinization and organized the Hungarian Revolution of 1956, during which he served as Nagy's minister of culture and as a member of the party's central committee. After the suppression of the Hungarian Revolution, Lukács was deported to Romania and expelled from the Communist Party, only to be reinstated before his death. During these years Lukács worked on a vast, systematic Marxist aesthetic, The Peculiarity of Aesthetics (1963), and—with labor as a central category—on a multivolume Marxist ontology, The Ontology of Social Being (1971). These works, neither of which he managed to complete, have been almost entirely ignored in the West.

Despite continuities, Lukács's writings are not all of a piece. In some of his pre-Marxist works and in History and Class Consciousness, Lukács uses Simmel's notion of abstract sociological form to establish correspondences between the "economic forms of society," its "cultural forms," its "forms of expression," and its literary forms and to show that the same worldview or ideology manifests itself in different ways in all strata of social life. This homological approach was adopted by some members of the Frankfurt School and by genetic structuralism, and it was used to some effect by Marxist critics such as TERRY EAGLETON and FREDRIC JAMESON in the 1970s. In the same works, Lukács argues that the objectification of all aspects of production, its alienation from producers, the reification of social relations, the quantification and depersonalization of culture, and the rational calculation practiced by bureaucracy subject individuals in capitalist society to systems of relation that seem to operate according to their own laws, independent of anyone's will or control. He also criticizes positivist social and natural science for "uncritically" accepting "the nature of the object" as a given and for reflecting "the manner in which data immediately present themselves" (History 7) and thus for accepting the status quo and acting as an apologist for capitalist society. Elaborated by members of the Frankfurt School into an analysis of advanced capitalism and a critique of instrumental reason and later translated into a theory of language, this view of society as an impersonal, reified system operating independently of individuals and subjecting them to its constraints has dominated poststructuralism and post-Marxism.

Although often identified with the Marxist theory of reflection, Lukács never subscribed to that theory as it is generally understood. He believed that knowledge of objective reality is possible but only if it goes beyond the reflection of immediate reality (which for him characterizes positivist science and descriptive naturalist literature). Lukács emphasized the active role of the subject both in constructing knowledge of the real world and in transforming objective circumstances. He argued that theory has a radical, transformative role to play in society and history. And after the failure of the Hungarian Revolution, he argued that creative intellectual work was the only form of work that could enable workers to overcome their alienation from themselves, from their world, and from other people.

Bertolt Brecht, with whom Lukács had several confrontations, criticized the "utopian and idealistic element" in his work. Methodologically, this utopian and idealistic element manifests itself in Lukács's emphasis on totality and in his insistence that realist literature constructs a coherent nonalienated human world by relating everything back to man and by creating meaningful connections between people and things and between interiority and exteriority. But Lukács is not completely simpleminded about his ideal of wholeness. He argues, much as Pierre Macherey and ÉTIENNE BALIBAR do, that realist fictions measure the real against an ideal that is "always and never there in reality" in such a way as to show the limits and deficiencies of extant ideologies and modes of being. And he looks to literary and theoretical demonstrations suggesting that all aspects of the social totality interrelate to mend what he perceived to be the principal evils of society in his time: fragmentation, alienation, overspecialization, and anomie.

Pervasive as Lukács's influence has been on Western Marxism and contemporary theory, the collapse of Soviet Communism, together with the discrediting by poststructuralism of grand master narratives and the increasing marginalization by GLOBALIZATION and POSTCOLONIAL STUDIES of the nation-state as the exclusive sociohistorical context for literature, has made it difficult for critics seeking to "re-habilitate" Lukács to show where he has renewed relevance to the present. The most promising work in this direction has been done by SLAVOJ ŽIŽEK, who reads Lukács "against the grain." On the whole, the focus of scholarly attention has shifted to exploration of the historical, political, social, and intellectual contexts of Lukács's thought and to his influence on—and/or personal relations with—important con-temporaries. Since these include Leo Popper, Arnold Hauser, Emil Lask, Max Weber, Karl Jaspers, Ernst Bloch, Martin Buber, Maurice Merleau-Ponty, MIKHAIL BAKHTIN, and members of the Frankfurt School, this is a vein of research that may well change our perception of Lukács and his still significant and influential generation of Cen-tral European theorists.

EVE TAVOR BANNET

See also MARXIST THEORY AND CRITICISM.

Georg Lukács, A Defence of History and Class Consciousness: Tailism and the Dialectic (trans. Esther Leslie, 2000), Demokratisierung heute und morgen (1985, The Process of Democratization, trans. Susanne Bernhardt and Norman Levine, 1991), Deutsche Realisten des 19. Jahrhunderts (1951, German Realists in the Nineteenth Century, trans. Jeremy Gaines and Paul Keast, 1992), Essays uber Realismus (1948, Essays on Realism, ed. Rodney Livingstone, trans. David Fernbach, 1981), Geschichte und Klassenbewusstsein: Studien uber Marsistische Dialektik (1923, History and Class Consciousness, trans. Rodney Livingstone, 1971), Gespraeche mit Georg Lukács (1967, Conversations with Lukács, ed. Theo Pinkus, trans. Hans Heinz Holz, Leo Kofler, and Wolfgang Abendroth, 1975), Goethe und seine Zeit (1947, Goethe and His Age, trans. Robert Anchor, 1968), Heidelberger Äesthetik (1916–1918) (ed. György Márkus and Frank Benseler, 1975), Der Junge Hegel (1948, The Young Hegel, trans. Rodney Livingstone, 1976), The Lukács Reader (ed. Arpad Kadarkay, 1995), Modern dráma fejlodésének története (1911), Political Writings, 1919–29: "The Question of Parliamentarianism" and Other Essays (ed. Rodney Livingstone, trans. Michael Mc-Colgan, 1972), Die Seele und die Formen (1911, Soul and Form, trans. Anna Bostock, 1974), Selected Corre-spondence, 1902–1920: Dialogues with Weber, Simmel, Buber, Manheim, and Others (ed. and trans. Judith Marcus and Zoltán Tar, 1986), Solzhenitsyn (1964, Solzhenitsyn, trans. William David Graf, 1970), Studies in European Realism (trans. Edith Bone, 1950), Die Theorie des Romans (1916, The Theory of the Novel, trans. Anna Bostock, 1971), A történelmi regeny (1937, Der historische Roman, 1955, The Historical Novel, trans. Hannah Mitchell and Stanley Mitchell, 1962), Wider den missverstandenen Realismus (1958, Realism in Our Time, trans. John Mander and Necke Mander, 1964), "Writer and Critic" and Other Essays (trans. Arthur D. Kahn, 1970), Die Zerstörung der Vernunft (1954, The Destruction of Reason, trans. Peter Palmer, 1981).

Lyotard, Jean-François

One of the most versatile of the poststructuralist French philosophers, Jean-François Lyotard (1925–1998) is most remembered as the "philosopher of the postmodern." Despite this title, Lyotard participated equally in a range of fields including political theory, ethics, aesthetics and art criticism, Judaic studies, theology, and literary theory. Lyotard's account of "the figural"—an affective countercurrent in discourse—is fundamental to an understanding of both avant-gardist experimentation within modern art and the ways in which artistic manifestations inflect thinking through a variety of media. Furthermore, Lyotard's interpretation of Kantian idealism contributed to the increasing significance and import of justice, judgment, rules, and rights in the late twentieth century, rendering an engagement with his work mandatory in ethical and legal philosophy.

Lyotard emerged as a major voice in philosophy with the publication of his doctoral study, *Discourse, Figure* (1971). Before that, his principal public activity had consisted in dissident Leftist political activism. In the early 1950s, the historian Pierre Souyri introduced Lyotard to the anti-Stalinist, anti–Communist Party group, Socialism or Barbarism. For the next decade, Lyotard lived as a militant intellectual, writing (under the pseudonym "François Laborde") scathing critiques of France's colonial regime in Algeria for the group's eponymous journal (see *Political Writings*). Although Lyotard would break altogether with collective action by the mid-1960s, the antiauthoritarian, anti-ideological grounds informing his earlier career define the mood and thrust of his subsequent written corpus.

Lyotard's interest and success in pedagogy is an often-neglected biographical influence that enlightens many seemingly obscure aspects of his work. Originally crafted for the amphitheater or seminar room, all of Lyotard's writings bear witness to his diverse oratorical style and subtle irony. A beloved educator, Lyotard taught at a variety of institutions, including La Flèche military school, the Sorbonne, and Nanterre (now University of Paris X). Following the May 1968 student-worker uprising, he was appointed to the "experimental" University of Vincennes, where he taught in close association with GILLES DELEUZE. He also served as the first president of the Collège International de Philosophie, founded in 1983. A visiting professor at many foreign universities, he held an active and permanent visiting professorship at Emory University at the time of his death.

In the years following 1970, Lyotard abandoned his former interest in the thought of Karl Marx and SIGMUND FREUD. The drift of his later work, however, was as much a renewed alliance with the unadulterated core of these thinkers' work as it was an attack *against* the uses and abuses to which he saw their work subjected. This nuanced position informed Lyotard's attempt to describe the thought and critique later known as "the postmodern." As Lyotard's struggle against capital evolved into a broader struggle against "system," so the Freudian notions of *Affekt* and *Nachträglichkeit* ("belatedness") remained steadfastly crucial to his reflection on aesthetic and ethical judgment.

During the 1980s, an initially obscure "report on knowledge" that the provincial government of Québec commissioned Lyotard to write thrust him into the center of the debates surrounding POSTMODERNISM. The broad celebrity of this report, published as *The Postmodern Condition* (1979), did not prevent the widespread misunderstanding of its claims and implications. Although the postmodern subject places under suspicion "grand narratives" promising universal emancipation, such as Christianity or Marxism, these are, according to Lyotard, far from doomed to immediate and wholesale collapse. Instead, under postmodern conditions, the ways that groups choose to live their lives tend to resist unification under any one dominant discursive model. The "little narratives" of the small groups and individuals who manage to coexist despite their differences subsume the "grand narratives" and their sometimes inhuman consequences. Furthermore, though characteristic of culture in the second half of the twentieth century, "postmodern," in Lyotard's use of the term, is not so much a chronological descriptor as a category for discussing "minoritary" or experimental thinking *concurrent with modernism* or even similar to the creativity of pre-Enlightenment times, nor is it a term that Lyotard himself wholeheartedly endorsed. In any case, the report's publication brought Lyotard worldwide attention and sparked a contentious debate, the participants of which included Jürgen Habermas, who defended the viability of consensual politics under what he termed the "unfinished project" of modernity, and FREDRIC JAMESON, who differed with Lyotard on the desirability of a postmodern, rather than Marxist, response to liberalism.

To think of Lyotard primarily as a "postmodernist," however, falsely emphasizes the ruptures in his career rather than the continuities and misrepresents his relation to the very notion of postmodernity. Lyotard was highly ambivalent about the appropriateness of the term "postmodern" for describing a state of affairs in which incredulity toward narratives of emancipation is the prevailing attitude. "Postmodernist" implies, further, an adherence to or an advocacy of the corresponding position: the "-ism." This view ignores Lyotard's visceral resistance to all group-driven rallying calls. Given that Lyotard exhibits a striking consistency of thought, one should not confuse the heterogeneity of his interests and discursive styles with the inclination to reduce philosophical positions to an encompassing relativism.

Lyotard's readings of Edmund Burke (*A Philosophical Enquiry into the Origin of Our Ideas of the Sublime and Beautiful* [1757]) and Immanuel Kant ("Analytic of the Sublime" in *Critique of Judgment* [1790]) led to another major path of his career, the extension and repositioning of the sublime as a key notion in the postmodern. The "delight" (Burke) or "negative pleasure" (Kant) that makes up the feeling of the sublime and its inflection of rational thought allowed Lyotard to bring his abiding reflection on affect, anamnesis, and infancy ("infans") to bear on judgment in relation to the presence and absence of criteria.

Although it has yet to produce the impact of *The Postmodern Condition*, *The Differend* (1983) is, from a philosophical perspective, Lyotard's most important work. The concepts developed throughout his entire oeuvre either lead to or emanate from this text. Throughout this massive and meticulous refutation of revisionist claims about the extent of the Shoah, Lyotard argues that, in order to be believable, a witness need not necessarily have actually *seen* that to which she bears witness. Judgment according to rules may well listen to such testimony, but it will not *hear* it because an intractable differend renders such understanding impossible. A complex interweaving of philosophical history from Protagoras to EMMANUEL LEVINAS, *The Differend* focuses in particular on Ludwig Wittgenstein's theory of language games, Aristotle's reflections on "now" (from which Lyotard develops his notion of "event"), and Lyotard's own prior research on the sublime. All of these elements are combined in order to "save the honor of thinking," the most noble purpose of which is to judge. Lyotard's wager is that freeing the criteria for judgment from predefined rules may enable the "critical guardian" ("le veilleur critique") to attend to the admissibility of such witnesses beyond reality as defined by law.

Lyotard's exploration of aspects of Judaism has been hailed as the most extensive of any non-Jewish twentieth-century thinker. The range of texts considering this subject include shorter pieces, such as "Jewish Oedipus" (1970) (a study of Shakespeare's *Hamlet*) and "Return upon the Return" (1988) (a reading of Joyce's *Ulysses*). Longer works on this subject include sustained passages of *The Differend*, where Lyotard's "infinite conversation" with Levinas helps him advance the notion of judgment without criteria, as well as *Heidegger and "the Jews"* (1988) and *The Hyphen* (1993), a commentary on Paul of Tarsus's caesarean of Christianity from Judaism.

In tandem with his philosophical work, Lyotard sustained a significant interest in painting. Including a vast array of books and essays on Marcel Duchamp, Albert Ayme, Pierre Skira, and numerous other artists, Lyotard's corpus tirelessly tests its philosophical claims against the work of art. By "work of art," Lyotard means both the object itself *and* the work that art performs collaboratively with the spectator, a concept based upon the Freudian dream-work.

Lyotard's engagement with literature is equally wide ranging. His analyses of Duchamp and Newman arguably deal as much with these painters' writing as they do with their contributions to visual art. What literary figures have demonstrated stylistically or asserted directly about the power of a phrase—whether it be Gertrude Stein (*The Differend*) or Pierre Klossowski (*Libidinal Economy* [1974])—is frequently the crucible from which Lyotard deploys his highly original thought. The problematic that Lyotard explores in his final works on André Malraux and Augustine, for example, could be characterized as philosophy's adoption of literary style in order to speak or write itself.

Many of Lyotard's readers were dismayed by his late publications on Malraux, a novelist whose subsequent espousal of Gaullism was never forgiven by the Left. Yet the works that most abidingly intrigue Lyotard are Malraux's writings on art. Lyotard shared with Malraux an almost mystical belief in art's capacity to protect a space in which innovative politics and ethics could still be invented. Employing widely disparate voices and discursive genres, Signed, Malraux (1996) and Soundproof Room (1998) significantly extend Lyotard's meditation on what remains intractable in the human. A similar examination of intractability can be found in The Confession of Augustine, Lyotard's last work, which was left unfinished but published posthumously in 1998.

ROBERT HARVEY

Jean-François Lyotard, Chambre soured: L'antiesthétique de Malraux (1998, Soundproof Room, trans. Robert Harvey, 2001), La condition postmoderne: Rapport sur le savoir (1979, The Postmodern Condition: A Report on Knowledge, trans. Geoff Bennington and Brian Massumi, 1984), La confession d'Augustin (1998, The Confession of Augustine, trans. Richard Beardsworth, 2000), Dérive à partir de Marx et Freud (1973, partial trans., Driftworks, trans. Roger McKeon, 1984; partial trans., Toward the Postmodern, ed. Robert Harvey and Mark S. Roberts, 1993), Des dispositifs pulsionnels (1973), Le différend (1983, The Differend: Phrases in Dispute, trans. Georges Van den Abbeele, 1988), Discours, figure (1971, Discourse, Figure, trans., Antony Hudek and Mary Lydon, 2011), Économie libidinale (1974, Libidinal Economy, trans. Iain Hamilton Grant, 1992), La guerre des Algériens (1989, partial trans., Political Writings, trans. Bill Readings with Kevin Paul Geiman, 1993), Heidegger et "les juifs" (1988, Heidegger and "the Jews," trans. Andreas Michel and Mark Roberts, 1990), L'inhumain: Causeries sur le temps (1988, The Inhuman: Reflections on Time, trans. Geoff Bennington and Rachel Bowlby, 1991), Instructions païennes (1977), Leçons sur l'analytique du sublime (1991, Lessons on the Analytic of the Sublime, trans. Elizabeth Rottenberg, 1994), Lectures d'enfance (1991, partial trans., Toward the Postmodern, ed. Robert Harvey and Mark S. Roberts, 1993), The Lyotard Reader (ed. Andrew Benjamin, 1989), Misère de la philosophie (2000), Moralités postmodernes (1993, Postmodern Fables, trans. Georges Van Den Abbeele, 1997), Le mur du Pacifique (1975, The Pacific Wall, trans. Bruce Boone, 1990), La phénoménologie (1954, Phenomenology, trans. Brian Beakley, 1991), Le postmoderne expliqué aux enfants (1986, The Postmodern Explained, ed. and trans. Julian Pefanis and Morgan Thomas, trans. Julian Pefanis et al., 1992), Que peindre? Adami Arakawa Buren (2 vols., 1987), Récits tremblants (1977), Rudiments païens: Genre dissertatif (1977), Signé Malraux (1996, Signed, Malraux, trans. Robert Harvey, 1999), Tombeau de l'intellectuel et autres papiers (1984), Toward the Postmodern (1993, ed. and trans. Robert Harvey and Mark S. Roberts), Les transformateurs Duchamp (1977, Duchamp's Trans/Formers, trans. Ian McLeod, 1990), Un trait d'union (1993, The Hyphen: Between Judaism and Christianity, trans. Michael Naas and Pascale-Anne Brault, 1999); Jean-François Lyotard et al., La faculté de juger (1985); Jean-François Lyotard with David Carroll, Peregrinations: Law, Form, Event (1988); Jean-François Lyotard and Thierry Chaput, Les immatériaux (1985); Jean-François Lyotard and Jean-Loup Thébaud, Au juste: Conversations (1979, Just Gaming, trans. Wlad Godzich, 1985); Eddie Yeghiayan, "Jean-François Lyotard: A Bibliography" (www.lib.uci.edu/about/publications/wellek/lyotard/).

Marxist Theory and Criticism

1. Classical Marxism

Karl Marx and Friedrich Engels produced no systematic theory of literature or art, nor has the subsequent history of Marxist aesthetics comprised the cumulative unfolding of a uniform perspective. Rather, Marxist literary and cultural theory has emerged as a series of responses to concrete political exigencies and achieves a dynamic and expansive coherence (rather than the static coherence of a finished system) through both a general overlap of political motivation and the persistent reworking of a core of predispositions about literature and art deriving from Marx and Engels themselves. These predispositions include:

1. The rejection, following G. W. F. Hegel, of the notion of "identity" and a consequent denial of the view that any object, including literature, can somehow exist independently. The aesthetic corollary of this is that literature can only be understood in the fullness of its relations with ideology, class, and economic infrastructure.

2. The view that the so-called objective world is actually a progressive construction out of collective human subjectivity. What passes as truth, then, is not eternal but institutionally created. Language itself, as Marx said in The German Ideology (1846), must be understood not as a self-sufficient system but as social practice (Marx-Engels Reader 158).

3. The understanding of art as a commodity, sharing with other commodities an entry into material relations of production. If, as Marx said, human beings produce themselves through labor, artistic production can be viewed as a branch of production in general.

4. A focus on the connections between class struggle as the inner dynamic of history and literature as the ideologically refracted site of such struggle. This has sometimes gone hand in hand with prescriptions for literature as an ideological ancillary to the aims and results of political revolution.

In the general introduction to the Grundrisse (completed in 1858, published in 1939), Marx acknowledges, in speaking of Greek art, that "it is well known that certain periods of their flowering are out of all proportion to the general development of society, hence also to the material foundation, the skeletal structure as it were, of its organization" (Marx-Engels Reader 245). What, then, is the connection between art and the material base into which its constituting relations extend? Given the inconclusive and sometimes ambiguous nature of Marx and Engels's scattered comments on art, the proposed solutions to such dilemmas have been as various as the political soils in which they were sown.

The first generation of Marxist intellectuals emphasized the highly mediated connection between economic conditions and artistic production. Franz Mehring (1846–1919), who wrote *Karl Marx: The Story of His Life* (1918), the first authoritative biography of Marx, and *The Lessing Legend* (1892–1893) applies Marxist categories to the analysis of major German literary figures, bringing these within the reach of working-class readers. Karl Kautsky (1854–1938), another German and a propagandist for the Social Democratic Party and founder in 1883 of the prestigious Marxist journal *Die neue Zeit*, argues in his *Foundations of Christianity* (1908) that religious ideas are tied to the levels of artistic and industrial maturity allowed by a particular economic substructure. Georgi Plekhanov (1856–1918), the "father of Russian Marxism" and a founder of the Russian Social Democratic Party, argues in *Fundamental Problems of Marxism* (1908), *Art and Social Life* (1912), and some shorter pieces, such as *The Role of the Individual in History* (1898), that gifted individuals appear in history only where social conditions facilitate their development: every talent that acts as a social force is the product of social relations. In *Art and Social Life*, Plekhanov notes that an "art for art's sake" tendency arises "where the artist is in disaccord with his social environment" (172).

Vladimir Ilyich Lenin (1870–1924) occupied a central role not only in the Russian Revolution of 1917 but also in the unfolding of Marxist aesthetics toward a more politically interventionist stance. Lenin's most controversial piece, "Party Organization and Party Literature" (1905), belongs to a politically volatile period, and it comes as no surprise that Lenin, at this juncture, insists that literature "must become *part* of the common cause of the proletariat, 'a cog and screw' of one single great Social-Democratic mechanism" (23). Lenin is well aware that art cannot be "subject to mechanical adjustment or leveling, to the rule of the majority over the minority" (24). But he is not prescribing partisanship (*partynost*) for all literature: only for literature that claims to be party literature. He grants that freedom "of speech and the press must be complete" (25). This echoes Marx's comment that the "first freedom of the press consists in not being a trade" (*On Freedom* 41).

Lenin's articles on Tolstoy (1908–1911) exemplify his aesthetic approach, especially his ability to explain the circumstances limiting the potential partisanship of great writers. According to Lenin, the contradictions in Tolstoy's works—for example, his "merciless criticism of capitalist exploitation," his denunciation of "poverty, degradation and misery among the working masses" as against his "crackpot preaching of . . . 'resist not evil' with violence," and his preaching of a reformed religion—mirror the contradictory conditions of the revolutionary peasantry (*Collected* 15:205). Tolstoy's misguided renunciation of politics reflects the "pent-up hatred, the ripened striving for a better lot, the desire to get rid of the past—and also the immature dreaming, the political inexperience, and the revolutionary flabbiness" characterizing the peasantry (15:208). For Lenin, the contradictions in Tolstoy can *only* be apprehended from the standpoint of the class that led the struggle for freedom during the revolution (16:325). This point helps to put into perspective some of Lenin's earlier comments on "party literature": not only is it impossible to write as an individual but, equally, "individual" acts of reading and interpreting are conducted within parameters dictated by class interests. At a deeper level Lenin's approach to aesthetic value, embracing as it does the totality of historical circumstances—including class, preceding literary traditions, and relation to political exigency—can be seen to derive from his acknowledgment, in his *Philosophical Notebooks*, of the dialectical character of Marxism, which insists on viewing any "individual" entity in its necessary historical connection with what is universal.

The other major protagonist in the Russian Revolution, Leon Trotsky (1879–1940), played a crucial role in debates on the role of art in Soviet Union and in proletariat culture more generally. His works include *Lenin* (1924), *History of the Russian Revolution* (1932), and *The Revolution Betrayed* (1937), as well as his renowned *Literature and Revolution* (1924). In *Literature and Revolution* (1924), Trotsky stresses that only in some domains can the party offer direct leadership; the "domain of art is not one in which the party is called upon to command. It can and must protect and help it, but it can only lead it indirectly" (Trotsky 56). He states quite clearly that what is needed is "a watchful revolutionary censorship, and a broad and flexible policy in the field of art" (58). What is important for Trotsky is that the limits of such censorship be defined very clearly: he is against "the liberal principle of *laissez faire* and *laissez passer*, even in the field of art" (58). Hence Trotsky cannot be accused of indifference to the ideological threats posed by reactionary literature and ideas, although in a 1938 manifesto, *Towards a Free Revolutionary Art*, drawn up in collaboration with André Breton, Trotsky urges a "complete freedom for art" (119) while acknowledging that all true art is revolutionary in nature. The latter position evolved in reaction to what Trotsky calls Stalin's "police patrol spirit" (115–21).

In *Literature and Revolution* Trotsky also urges that the party give "its confidence" to what he calls "literary fellow-travelers," those nonparty writers sympathetic to the revolution. Behind this lies Trotsky's insistence that the proletariat "cannot begin the construction of a new culture without . . . assimilating the . . . old cultures" (Trotsky 59). In the same work, Trotsky addresses whether proletarian culture is possible. To Trotsky, the question is "formless" because not only will the energy of the proletariat be consumed primarily in the acquisition of power but, as it succeeds, the proletariat "will be more and more dissolved into a socialist community and will free itself from its class characteristics and thus cease to be a proletariat. . . . The proletariat acquires power for the purpose of doing away forever with class culture and to make way for human culture" (42). Other aspects of Trotsky's approach to aesthetics are exemplified in his *Class and Art*, in which he suggests that art has "its own laws of development" and that there is no guarantee of an organic link between artistic creativity and class interests. Trotsky maintains that certain great writers, such as Dante, Shakespeare, and Goethe, appeal to us precisely because they transcend the limitations of their class outlook (Solomon 194–96).

The call to create a proletarian culture was the originating theme of Proletkult, a left-wing group of writers whose foremost ideologist was Alexander A. Bogdanov (1873–1928). This group, opposed by the Bolshevik leadership, insisted on art as a weapon in class struggle and rejected all bourgeois art. Also active in the debates of this period were the formalists and the futurists, notably the critic Osip Brik, whose term "social command" embodied the ideal of interventionist art, and the poet Vladimir Mayakovsky, who wrote an influential pamphlet titled How Are Verses Made? (1926). The formalists and futurists, as well as the radical constructivist El Lissitsky (1890–1941), found a common platform in the journal LEF (Russian acronym for the Left Front of Art). The formalists, focusing on artistic forms and techniques on the basis of linguistic studies, had arisen in prerevolutionary Russia but now saw their opposition to traditional art as a political gesture, allying them somewhat with the revolution. All these groups were attacked by the most prominent Soviet theoreticians, such as Trotsky, Nikolai Bukharin (1888–1937), Anatoly Lunacharsky (1875–1933), and Alexander Voronsky (1884–1943), who decried the attempt to break completely with the past and what they saw as a reductive denial of the social and cognitive aspects of art. Valentin N. Voloshinov later attempted to harmonize the two sides of the debate—formal linguistic and sociological analysis—by treating language itself as the supreme ideological phenomenon (see MIKHAIL BAKHTIN).

The Communist Party's attitude toward art in this period was epiphenomenal of its economic policy. A resolution of 1925 voiced the party's refusal to sanction any one literary faction. This reflected the New Economic Policy (NEP) of a limited free-market economy. The period of the first Five Year Plan (1928–1932) saw a more or less voluntary return to a more committed artistic posture, and during the second Five Year Plan (1932–1936) this commitment was crystallized in the formation of a writer's union. The first congress of this union in 1934, featuring speeches by Maxim Gorki and Bukharin, officially adopted socialist realism, as defined influentially by Andrei A. Zhdanov (1896–1948). Aptly dubbed "Stalin's cultural thug" by TERRY EAGLETON, it was Zhdanov whose proscriptive shadow thenceforward fell over Soviet cultural affairs. Although Bukharin's speech at the congress had attempted a synthesis of formalist and sociological attitudes, premised on his view that the word is a microcosm of history, Bukharin was eventually to fall from his position as leading theoretician of the party: his trial and execution, stemming from his political and economic differences with Stalin, were also symptomatic of the atmosphere in which formalism soon became a sin once more. Bukharin had called for socialist realism to portray reality not "as it is" but rather as it exists in socialistic imagination. Zhdanov defined socialist realism as the depiction of "reality in its revolutionary develop-ment." The "truthfulness . . . of the artistic portrayal," he went on to say, "should be combined with . . . ideological remolding" (12).

Socialist realism had a considerable impact outside the Soviet Union and re-ceived its most articulate and powerful theoretical expression in the work of the Hungarian philosopher GEORG LUKÁCS (1885–1971), whose notion of realism con-flicted with that of Bertolt Brecht (1898–1956). Their debate could be regarded as a collision between two personalities, or between a writer (Brecht) and a critic (Lukács), since their "definitions" of socialist realism overlap in crucial ways, a fact that is often ignored. According to Lukács, modern capitalist society is riven by con-tradictions, by chasms between universal and particular, intelligible and sensible, part and whole. The realist artist expresses a vision of the possible totality embracing these contradictions, a totality achieved by embodying what is "typical" about vari-ous historical movements. But Brecht, in his notebooks, also equates realism with the ability to capture the "typical" or "historically significant." Realists, says Brecht, identify the contradictions in human relationships, as well as their enabling condi-tions. Socialist realists, moreover, view reality from the viewpoint of the proletariat. Brecht adds that realist art battles false views of reality, thereby facilitating correct views (109). Contrasting dramatic theater (which follows Aristotle's guidelines) with his own "epic" theater, Brecht avers that the audience's capacity for action must be roused and that far from undergoing catharsis, the audience must be forced to make decisions, partly by its standard expectations being disappointed, a procedure Brecht called "the alienation effect" (91). The action on stage must also implicitly point to other, alternative versions of itself. Far from being sterile, the disputes between Lukács and Brecht display the multidimensional potential of any concept approached from Marxist viewpoints, as well as the inevitable grounding of those viewpoints in political circumstances.

M. A. R. HABIB

See also GEORG LUKÁCS.

Bertolt Brecht, Schriften zum Theater (1957, Brecht on Theatre: The Development of an Aesthetic, ed. and trans. John Willett, 1964); Vladimir I. Lenin, Collected Works (46 vols., 1960–1970, 1978), On Lit-erature and Art (1970), Selected Works (1971); Karl Marx, On Freedom of the Press and Censorship (1974, trans. Saul K. Padover), Selected Writings (ed. David McLellan, 1977); Karl Marx and Friedrich En-gels, Selected Correspondence, 1846–1895 (ed. and trans. Dona Torr, 1942), The Marx-Engels Reader (2nd ed., ed. Robert C. Tucker, 1978), On Literature and Art (1978); George V. Plekhanov, Art and Social Life (ed. Andrew Rothstein, 1970); Maynard Solomon, ed., Marxism and Art: Essays Classic and Contempo-rary (1973); Leon Trotsky, The Basic Writings of Trotsky (ed. Irving Howe, 1965), Leon Trotsky on Litera-ture and Art (ed. Paul N. Siegel, 1970); Andrei A. Zhdanov, Essays on Literature, Philosophy, and Music (1950, trans. Eleanor Fox, Stella Jackson, and Harold C. Feldt).

2. Structuralist Marxism

Karl Marx's mature writing from *Zur Kritik der politischen Okonomie* (1859) through the first edition of *Das Kapital* (1867) offers a materialist study of social and economic relations as systems and structures that follow scientific laws. In Marx's vocabulary, a distinction is drawn between the "forces" and "relations" of economic production, on the one hand, and class contradictions and human oppression, on the other. These distinct lines of inquiry between economic theory and the history of the human subject have never been completely resolved in Marxism. Different Marxist schools have placed emphasis either on the analysis of the determinate structures and relations of production or on the investigation of phenomenological states of consciousness and human action. In the period after World War II, primarily in France, the theoretical divisions within the Marxist tradition were reawakened with the emergence of STRUCTURALISM as a challenge to established practice in the social sciences of anthropology, psychology, and linguistics. In favoring structure over subject and synchronic over diachronic analysis, structuralism offered a theoretical means for Marxists like Louis Althusser, ÉTIENNE BALIBAR, and Pierre Macherey to counter the dominant Hegelian and existential philosophical practices of Alexander Kojève, Georg Lukács, and Jean-Paul Sartre.

The specific structuralist challenge within Marxism made its debut with Louis Althusser's two most important books: *For Marx* (1965) and *Reading Capital* (1965). Althusser was a professor of philosophy at the École Normale in Paris, where he worked alongside the most influential French structuralists of the 1960s. The thesis of *Reading Capital* was the assertion that Marx had anticipated and surpassed apparent contributions made within the structuralist paradigm by overcoming the humanistic concerns of his earlier writings, such as *The Economic and Philosophical Manuscripts of 1844* (1932) and *The German Ideology* (written in 1845–1846, published in full in 1932), in order to develop what was truly original and revolutionary about the scientific laws of production and their relation to cultural history. As a first principle Althusser set out to develop Marx's proposition in *Capital* that the noneconomic levels of a social formation are determined in relation to the mode of economic production. Combating the tendency toward mechanistic Marxism advanced in texts such as Nikolai I. Bukharin's *Historical Materialism* (1921), *Reading Capital* argues that the social totality had to be approached as a "structure in dominance." In this formulation, society is seen to be constituted by relatively autonomous and reciprocally determining levels. Economic (feudal, industrial, finance capital), political (empire, state, nongovernmental organization), and ideological (nationalism, androcentrism, multiculturalism) instances exist in historically specific combinations and hierarchies.

In proposing this decentered view of capitalist social formations, Althusser gave particular attention to ideology. Traditionally, Marxist theory had considered ideology in the negative sense as a form of "false consciousness" that functioned in the interests of the dominant classes to mystify the real operation of society and prevent subordinate classes from realizing their own true interests; however, the relative autonomy of social practices posited in For Marx and Reading Capital formulate ideology as a domain of consciousness inscribed in material practice and existing within specific institutions and rituals for the reproduction of capitalist social relations. In Althusser's work there is no lived space outside of ideology, and the reproduction of the conditions of production is realized through the process of interpellation. In Althusser's well-known essay "Ideology and Ideological State Apparatuses" (1970) interpellation is carried out by ideological state apparatuses—churches, universities, political parties, and trade unions—which ensure the existence of subjects capable of responding and submitting to the needs of a given mode of production and social order.

These founding works of structuralist Marxism set out to renew historical materialism as a science of social formations by offering a revolutionary analysis of the structured system of capitalist production and the constitution of social subjects. While influential in the work of political theorists like Ernesto Laclau, Nicos Poulantzas, and Eric Olin Wright, Althusser also made it possible to see cultural artifacts as the result of symbolic production and ideological conflict rather than the creative expression of a humanistically defined author. By shifting from the normative hermeneutics of reading literature to the problematic of literary production, structuralist Marxism offered Balibar, Macherey, and Terry Eagleton the basis for developing a radical and revisionary analysis of both the function and the status of cultural production. For Althusser, the concept of production contains the most revolutionary aspects of the entire Marxist theory. It defies analysis and understanding within the narrowly "classical" theories of economics, psychology, and epistemology that immediately preceded it and that it attempts to surpass completely. Classical writers, including empiricists such as John Locke, Adam Smith and David Ricardo, require a definition of human needs in order to analyze the value of economic commodities. To the extent that we are still held by these classical notions, Althusser would say we have failed to grasp the revolutionary philosophical and scientific significance of Marxism or that we treat it very narrowly as one economic doctrine centered upon the relations between capital, labor, and exchange value. Althusser argues that Marx's thought is marked by an "epistemological break," a shift away from the early influence of Hegelian historicism and classical political economy to what Althusser recognizes as a radically new "science" of historical materialism in Capital and Marx's later writing. By recognizing the forces and relations of production as class relations, the "mature" Marx introduced a new materialist reformulation of history as the productive power of labor to transform nature and society.

At a very sophisticated level of theoretical debate, Althusser distinguishes Marx's contribution to the concept of production from the tradition of Hegelianism on one side and from non-Marxist structuralism on the other. Hegelianism had already put forward the total mediation of the given world to the critical, ever-developing human subject. In fact, if production were synonymous with mediation, there would be nothing philosophically new in Marxism. Althusser's writings could be described in terms of Marx's own characterization of his relationship to G. W. F. Hegel as the inversion of dialectical idealism into dialectical materialism. But for Althusser, the difference between Hegel and Marx lies precisely in Marx's realization that the process of mediation could never be completed in the name of the human subject, that reality and subjectivity never reach a state of identity, as they are meant to in Hegelian logic. In Althusser's project "history is a process without a Subject or a Goal" (*Lenin and Philosophy* 99). The burden of Marxist analysis, therefore, becomes the effort to determine or specify with ever greater precision the nature of productive activity without ever being able to put it into the terminology of appearances or conscious reflections. In a manner that is nonreductive, Althusser asserts that art, theology, literature, and family life are determined according to their own relatively autonomous laws of production, which are not governed by or identical to the laws of production in the ordinary sense of goods and commodities (see Althusser, "Ideology"). The inevitable gap between the real base of production and its ideologically inflected apprehension brings Althusser into proximity with the discourse of the structuralists.

Althusser's primary contribution to literary theory and CULTURAL STUDIES has been to theorize a mode of critique sophisticated enough to engage with the production of knowledge as a form of human labor. Literature must be approached as a practice rather than an exercise in explicating the meanings contained within stable textual objects. In one of the earliest and most influential texts of structuralist Marxist literary criticism, *A Theory of Literary Production* (1966), Pierre Macherey opens by announcing that he will "pose a new question" within literary theory that will surpass conventional and limiting critical modes, which take as their object an always already finished product to be transmitted and consumed, asking, "What are the laws of literary production?" (12). One of the most important propositions that Macherey makes is that the raw material of literary production is ideology. This initial level of ideological practice on which literary production is constructed has been theorized by the structuralist Marxist linguist Michel Pêcheux. Rejecting the pregiven speaking subject as the object of linguistic analysis, Pêcheux's writing explores some of the specific ways in which language itself functions as an ideological practice. In *Language, Semantics, and Ideology: Stating the Obvious* (1976) Pêcheux explains the process of interpellation as one developed through the processes of self-identification and social identifications. It is against this everyday level of ideological practice that literary production must be approached.

In this case structure does not refer to form but to the material and cultural relations that constitute literature as a specific form of ideological practice. Structure is not in any way exterior to the meaning of the literary work; it is immanent in the work itself and cuts deeper into the culture than traditional literary terms such as "plot" or "genre," and it cannot be related to culture at large by the trope of structure as a mirror of reality. Pierre Macherey observes that Honoré de Balzac does not reflect the realities or experiences of Paris; rather, he fictionalizes Paris as a complex system of relations that derive their meaning from within the text and not from the exterior order. Eagleton puts this most clearly in his 1976 engagement with Althusser and Macherey's work, *Criticism and Ideology*. In his formula, literature can be understood as a form of ideology to the second power since literary discourse is the result of a labor of transformation performed upon everyday ideology: "History is 'present' in the text in the form of a double-absence. The text takes as its object, not the real, but certain significations by which the real lives itself—significations which are themselves the product of its partial abolition" (72). One of the conclusions both Eagleton and Macherey reach is that literary texts must be read in terms of their instability. But if Macherey originally stresses that literary practice "explores ideology" (*Theory* 132), Eagleton is quick to point out that this exploration is no guarantee that the text might not function to reproduce the conditions of production by positively reinforcing the structure of ideology.

FREDRIC JAMESON is probably the most important anglophone Marxist literary critic since World War II. His work can be seen as an engagement of POSTMODERN-ISM with the Marxist tradition. While his formative and ongoing work has been produced in the context of this movement from the structuralist to the poststructuralist paradigm, the influence of Althusserian and structuralist Marxist theory is particularly apparent in the foundational text *The Political Unconscious* (1981), where Jameson borrows the concepts of mediation and the social totality that Althusser offered in *Reading Capital*. Althusser's work offers a powerful rejection of mechanical causality (cause and effect) and expressive causality (essence expressed within all elements) as modes for understanding the interrelationship between specific instances and the relationship of different instances to the larger social totality. Althusser approaches the totality in terms of the relative autonomy of instances; such a move highlights contradiction and differentiation and concludes that the only plausible way to conceptualize the totality is as an "absent cause." Jameson, while accepting the structuralist Marxist critique, points out that even to conceptualize the totality as relatively autonomous instances assumes a priori that these elements take their meaning against the background of a larger identity. He argues that there would be no impetus to talk about the relative independence of art from politics and religion if one did not already assume them to be related at some fundamental level.

In *The Political Unconscious* the concepts of mechanical and expressive causality are not completely discarded. Instead, Jameson argues that these two practices of mediation can be made useful when applied to specific textual cases. He points out, for example, that the notion of mechanical causality is a productive tool for explaining how a shift in the nineteenth-century publishing industry, the move from the three-volume to the single-volume novel, determined the final form of George Gissing's fiction. Moving to a second register, Jameson asserts that the notion of expressive causality remains relevant because of its ability to facilitate an interpretation of the cultural logic that is materially inscribed into both the production and the consumption of a given social formation and constitutes its "collective thinking and . . . collective fantasies about history and reality" (34). Jameson skillfully develops a strategy that gives primacy to the notion of interpretation as ideological practice. Borrowing from Althusser's conception of the totality as an "absent cause," The Political Unconscious introduces a fundamental level of mediation linked to the mode of production. Here the totality becomes history itself, "the untranscendable horizon," which is understood in terms of its narrativization in the political consciousness (17). Jameson attempts to recuperate Althusser's work within a framework that is both postmodernist and Hegelian, and texts like The Political Unconscious and Postmodernism; or, The Cultural Logic of Late Capitalism (1991) rearticulate structuralist Marxism as a means of understanding the complex linkages and intersections between economic and cultural levels of production.

Francis Mulhern, reflecting on the introduction of Althusser's work into the field of literary studies, has observed that the reception and spread of Althusserian theory can best be characterized as an inflationary boom and ensuing rapid devaluation of the paradigm. This is not surprising given the political and social context framing the structuralist Marxist intervention. Althusser's and Macherey's projects began in the aftermath of Khrushchev's belated denunciation of Stalin and reached its most productive point in the years immediately following the uprisings of May 1968. For many intellectuals the theoretical advances of structuralist Marxism were inexorably linked to the political "crisis" of Continental Marxism. The historian E. P. Thompson was not alone in expressing alarm at the primacy given to social formations and the reduced role given to the individual as agent. Until very recently, the response to structuralist Marxism has been overdetermined by the trauma that marked the precipitous decline of the workers' movement during the 1970s and 1980s. However, with the posthumous collection and release of Althusser's unpublished work, there has been a certain willingness to reassess the legacy of structuralist Marxism. The list of contributions is impressive. Not only did structuralist Marxist work incorporate the work of JACQUES LACAN, Claude Lévi-Strauss and MICHEL FOUCAULT into the Marxist lexicon, but theorists like Althussser, Balibar, and Macherey provide a materialist critique that exposes the limiting modernist and humanist inheritances of Marxist theory. The materialist analysis of social formations and social subjectivities reinitiated by structural Marxism remains essential to the work of cultural critics like Jameson, JUDITH BUTLER, and Ernesto Laclau as they attempt to analyze the emerging structures, cultures, and identities of GLOBALIZATION.

JULIAN HOLLAND AND GARY WIHL

See also STRUCTURALISM.

Louis Althusser, "Idéologie et appareils idéologiques d'état," La pensée 151 (1970) ("Ideology and Ideological State Apparatuses," Lenin and Philosophy and Other Essays, ed. and trans. Ben Brewster, 1971), Pour Marx (1965, For Marx, trans. Ben Brewster, 1969); Louis Althusser and Étienne Balibar, Lire le "Capital" (1965, Reading "Capital," trans. Ben Brewster, 1970); Renée Balibar, Les français fictifs: Le rapport des styles littéraires au français national (1974); Renée Balibar and Dominique Laporte, Le français national: Politique et pratique de la langue nationale sous la révolution (1974); Terry Eagleton, Criticism and Ideology: A Study in Marxist Literary Theory (1976); Fredric Jameson, The Political Unconscious: Narrative as a Socially Symbolic Act (1981), The Prison-House of Language: A Critical Account of Structuralism and Russian Formalism (1972); Pierre Macherey, A quoi pense la littérature? (1990, The Object of Literature, trans. David Macey, 1995), Pour une théorie de la production littéraire, (1966, A Theory of Literary Production, trans. Geoffrey Wall, 1978); Pierre Macherey and Étienne Balibar, "Sur la littérature comme forme idéologique: Quelques hypothèses marxistes," Littérature 13 (1974) ("Literature as an Ideological Form: Some Marxist Propositions," trans. Ian McLeod, John Whitehead and Ann Wordsworth, Oxford Literary Review 3 [1978]); Francis Mulhern, "Message in a Bottle: Althusser in Literary Studies," Althusser: A Critical Reader (ed. Gregory Elliott, 1994); Michel Pêcheux, Les vérités de la palice: Linguistique, sémantique, philosophie (1976, Language, Semantics, and Ideology: Stating the Obvious, trans. Harbans Nagpal, 1982); Nicos Ar. Poulantzas, L'état, le pouvoir, le socialisme (1978, State, Power, Socialism, trans. Patrick Camiller, 1980); E. P. Thompson, "The Poverty of Theory; or, An Orrery of Errors," The Poverty of Theory and Other Essays (1978).

3. 1989 and After

The years since 1989 have provided a very different world for Marxist theory, and the waning of state-sponsored Marxism has made its theoretical correlative more rather than less prescient. The names for this new vitality are many, but the relationship between Marxist theory and literary criticism and the keywords "post-Marxism," "posthumanism," "postcolonialism," "postmodernism," "poststructuralism," "globalization," and "transnationalism" is agonistically symptomatic. If we cannot do justice here to the range of Marxist thinking this implies, we can at least register the valence that some theorists and critics have brought to these terms.

Fredric Jameson's Postmodernism; or, The Cultural Logic of Late Capitalism has been enormously influential not just in coming to terms with the somewhat amorphous behemoth nominated as postmodern but also in framing Marxist theory in a particular way. If Jameson's Political Unconscious affirmed a certain structuralist Althusserianism, then Postmodernism pushes this conceptual framework to a profound apotheosis, namely, that cultural logic itself inscribes in each object a properly dialectical totality of base and superstructure operative in classical Marxism. For Jameson, the cultural is not some mischievous displacement of the economic, as it was for the modernists: now it is the battlefield of commodification, its signs the very substance of capital, and Jameson's Marxism is concerned to reconstellate the ways in which we figure the world system, in all its abstractions. In this regard the notion of cognitive mapping is crucial. Drawn, as Jameson notes, from the architectural theorizing of

Kevin Lynch, in Jameson's work cognitive mapping is meant to address the peculiar difficulties of cognition in a postmodern world saturated by signification and commodification. If for poststructuralism there is no outside of such eternal schizophrenic presencing, for Jameson this collusion enables the possibility of reconceiving the totality by allowing one to coordinate its contradictions and political opportunities using a map imprinted on the mind by being-in-the-world itself. For discourse theorists any intimation of totality is immediately canceled by the wily excesses of the signifier and the conspicuous absence of an already dead subject to map. If this pushes Jameson's utopian instincts closer to idealism, it nevertheless draws attention to Jameson's contribution to another key characteristic in post-1989 Marxist thinking: the reemergence of space as a conceptual tool.

The reconceptualization of space is certainly symptomatic of a postmodern turn in Marxism, but one should be cautious about overloading the aura of postmodernism (whose logic demands precisely this kind of piling on). Ironically, there is no space here to do justice to the range of spatial thought in Marxism, but much of it naturally emerges out of materialist geography (David Harvey, Henri Lefebvre, Neil Smith, Edward Soja) and critiques of the urban landscape (Mike Davis's work on Los Angeles, for instance). In cultural criticism, many non-Marxist tropings on space have been influential (MAURICE BLANCHOT, MICHEL DE CERTEAU, Gaston Bachelard), but a concomitant trajectory in Marxist literary theory is relatively thin except, of course, in studies of postcolonialism and globalization.

Like Jameson, much of the work of GAYATRI CHAKRAVORTY SPIVAK after 1989 draws on theoretical frameworks elaborated in some detail earlier. Spivak's close reading of Marx stands out in a world of materialist cultural criticism where Marx is given little more than an obligatory nod. Spivak not only deconstructs (in the Derridean rather than the popular sense) the status of the referent in Marx's texts, the orientalist *différance* of the "asiatic mode of production," for instance, but signals in an elaborate and deeply committed manner what is living in Marx for literary theory and criticism. The pitfalls of any putatively Marxist subject position in global capitalism, including her own, are evoked simply by the title of her 1993 book, *Outside in the Teaching Machine*, but it is in her 1999 *Critique of Postcolonial Reason* that the full force of Spivak's reading of Marx for her postcolonial and feminist politics makes its most striking contribution. Rather than recapitulate a truth from Marx for "Third World," South, or "non-Western" constituencies, Spivak deploys a knowledge from within these subject positions to unthink the orientalism and Eurocentrism that a "Marx first" theoretical model can engender. Historically sensitive, Spivak tracks the movement in Marx's thinking, particularly after the failures of 1848, that urge the contextualization of her own project ("Marx keeps moving for a Marxist as the world moves" [67]). Spivak understands all too well that transnational or global capitalism has foregrounded the epistemological and political weight of postcolonial and diasporic studies. Multicultural and transnational literature is a symptom of this synergy, but it has intensified the need for a complex, materialist understanding of the global movements of people, capital, and trade that is fully cognizant of the hierarchies and inequalities of power that obtain. The four sections of her Critique on philosophy, literature, history, and culture touch crucially on some of the main trajectories of contemporary Marxist thinking: on the fateful collusion of neoliberalism and neocolonialism, on the genuflections of race in a global imaginary, on the rapid spread of capitalist apparatuses of speculation and financialization, and on a fluid and virulent international division of labor that leaves class analysis breathless as wealth flows ever more urgently to the "golden billion."

JACQUES DERRIDA's own contribution to Marxism, Specters of Marx (1993), also tells us something of what is lost and gained in some of the new configurations of Marxist critique. As an exegesis of a few of Marx's texts (and also Hamlet), Derrida's Specters is a tour de force, a brilliant evocation of what remains to return in Marxist theory itself. Begun as a two-part plenary address in 1993 that evolved into a book, Derrida's deconstructive reincarnation of Marxism has spawned much more than a subgenre on "spectrality." He has inspired a more rigorous conceptualization of postmodern Marxism or materialism evident in several important collections of Marxist theorizing, including Bernd Magnus and Stephen Cullenberg's Whither Marxism? (1995) and Antonio Callari and David F. Ruccio's Postmodern Materialism and the Future of Marxist Theory (1996), as well as in the pages of the influential journal Rethinking Marxism. Just as Spivak's tenacious reading of value and the value form provides Marxism with a new impetus, Derrida's philosophical articulation of "debt" and in particular the nature of the commodity allows us to understand in an illuminating way why Marx and Marxism must continue to haunt the present. His basic question is about Marxist methodology: does not Marx's own approach imply somewhat more than empiricism, humanism, and objectification? If it is not always clear what kind of politics might emerge from this approach, it is demonstrably the case that Marxism is not best served by eliding the ways in which Marx thinks outside representationality, especially if one seeks to elaborate a nonreductive and dynamic sense of a social relation as complex as class.

That said, one does not read Derrida for a Marxist exposition of class. Indeed, Derrida's Specters is indicative of a post-Marxist strain of theory in which class is often much diminished as a conceptual category. Rather than post-Marxism, this "development" can be viewed as metonymic Marxism, a Marxism in which the major terms have been transposed or substituted (one can see this in some of the work of Ernesto Laclau, SLAVOJ ŽIŽEK, and Judith Butler). There are good historical reasons for this terminological waywardness that have to do with the commodification of theory in academic life, an ineluctable mutability in Marxism itself, and the controversial efficacy of poststructuralist categories of identity and identity politics in postindustrial, consumer-based societies. Metonymy, then, does not simply mean missing the point. Think, for instance, of the way Žižek extols the centrality of jouis-

sance, or enjoyment, from Lacan, a libidinal symptom of the nonrepresentational that nonetheless appears throughout Žižek's writing. In *The Sublime Object of Ideology* (1989) the libidinal is posed as the Real's dirty secret, so that the core meaning of ideology is the way that it encourages desire to superadequate itself while rendering the "subject" maddeningly fettered by precisely this prospect of enjoyment. In truth, Žižek is a brilliant theorist of the Lacanian Thing, which he (ir)reverently uses as a tuning fork simultaneously on the popular and the political. No one should doubt the impress of the Thing on the daily circulation of desire, but the metonymy rests in its feverish substitution for the commodity. For all the psychic brio Marx attaches to the latter, it is not ultimately a category of the Real but the real, or else social transformation is but a good shrink away and anticapitalism awaits only a referral. Žižek's prolific work is much more than this, of course, since a good deal of his refreshing materialism issues forth from those concrete coordinates that led to 1989 and the eventual disappearance of Yugoslavia, allowing for very specific symptoms of enjoyment for a repressed intelligentsia. This is why, for Žižek at least, language is not a game or even simply a discourse.

The early work of Étienne Balibar was most closely associated with Louis Althusser and French STRUCTURALISM (which has, as it does for Žižek, a complex Lacanian connection). In the 1980s, however, his work increasingly questioned the conceptual categories associated with his own Althusserianism. The result was some quite stunning theoretical production, both in the *Race, Nation, Class: Ambiguous Identities* (1988) (a book he coauthored with Immanuel Wallerstein) and in his essay collection *Masses, Classes, Ideas* (1994). The former responds to a specific shortfall in "Western Marxism," an inability to elaborate the imbrication of race (and racism) in studies of the capitalist nation-state and world-systems theory. Just as feminism and queer theory have changed the way materialism can be thought (evident in some writers more than others), so the great wake of decolonization and diaspora have focused a rethinking of race and ethnicity in the articulation of economic systems. Balibar's move is crucial: instead of conceiving class as the founding principle that solidifies a properly bourgeois social order, he avers that one should critique the way the category actually *destroys* that very possibility. The texture of history thus becomes the nature of reactions within complex "noneconomic" social relations (8) to the ambivalent and ambiguous mechanisms of class that seek unity in the moment of compulsive social destruction. Such an approach points further to the ambiguities in Marxist categories themselves that are not detrimental and to a thorough materialist critique of the logic of capitalism today. In *Masses, Classes, Ideas* Balibar extends and deepens his approach in a series of cogent readings of Marx and other texts. "Rights of man" discourses, the status of the proletariat as a concept in Marx's writing, and the "vacillation" of ideology all point to a Marxism that is less sure of its categorical assertions yet is therefore more alive to the genuflections of economic and social formations. By repositioning Marx within his own history, Balibar is able to tease

out the shortcuts and dead ends in Marxist thought, especially in the telling difference between class formation and "proletarian" as a subject position. The assumption of "being" in the latter as a ground of class has been debilitating in the extreme
and quite clearly allowed state socialism to flourish in the name of the proletariat
rather than as a culmination of its historical struggle. Balibar is not out to dismiss the
institutional histories of Marxist politics; he is, however, concerned to understand
under what conditions or conceptual frameworks they might come to flounder.

Antonio Negri, like Balibar, takes seriously the need to rethink the methodological coordinates of Marxist analysis. His *Marx beyond Marx* (1979), for instance,
provides a salient reading of *Grundrisse* that builds on Negri's political work for the
autonomia movement in Italy (work that led to his imprisonment in a classic case of
guilt by association). The emphasis throughout is on what forms of practical politics
are available based on Marx's own elaboration of the constituent elements of political economy. A more controversial book is the work he cowrote with Michael Hardt
called *Empire* (2000), which tracks the historical movement from imperialism to what
they term "empire," which is "the political subject that effectively regulates these
global exchanges, the sovereign power that governs the world" (xi). Žižek has commented that *Empire* rewrites the *Communist Manifesto* for today, and since such a rewriting seems necessary, it is worth considering this claim. Marx and Engels's book
was crisis writing; it responded in a deeply provocative and practical fashion to a
history in the making, so much so that it became part of the very texture of that history. Hardt and Negri are also answering and interpreting a historical movement, the
economic and geopolitical development of globalization in the meaning of that term
at the end of the twentieth century and beginning of the twenty-first. In a speculative
way, *Empire* does indeed emulate its illustrious forebear, but that is both its strength
and its shortcoming. First, it is no longer clear in the postmodern, mediatized, and
fragmented world that Hardt and Negri describe that a "manifesto" of this kind has
any bearing on world historical change at a macro- or micrological level. Second,
Marx and Engels postulate an agency that is precipitate in the social structures they
invoke, but again it is not altogether obvious that the same could be said of Hardt and
Negri's prime agency of opposition to empire, the "multitude." Nevertheless, if the
immediate parallels do not work, the differences offer some valuable lessons for
Marxist theory. *Empire* is an extraordinarily ambitious work of synthesis that outlines
the enormous challenges facing Marxist theory in the new millennium. All the
symptoms we have tracked in other writers, questions of the decolonized and far
from uniformly industrialized forms of late capitalism, are brought into vivid focus
in *Empire*, and if nothing else, it will participate in burgeoning debates on precisely
these issues. But if Marxist theory after 1989 finds sustenance in the conditions of a
certain globalization as the grounds for anticapitalism or a new internationalism, in
general it remains hesitant about the ways in which globalization can be transformed. Almost all of the alibis of moribund Communist parties may have dis-

appeared, but new forms of political constituency and community have yet to assume a material force. As Marx and Engels remind us in the *Communist Manifesto*, we still have "a world to win."

PETER HITCHCOCK

See also GLOBALIZATION, FREDRIC JAMESON, GAYATRI CHAKRAVORTY SPIVAK, and SLAVOJ ŽIŽEK.

Aijaz Ahmad, *In Theory* (1993), "The Third World in Jameson's *Postmodernism or the Cultural Logic of Late Capitalism*," *Social Text* 31/32 (1992); Étienne Balibar, *Masses, Classes, Ideas* (trans. James Swenson, 1994); Étienne Balibar and Immanuel Wallerstein, *Race, nation, classe: Les identités ambiguës* (1988, *Race, Nation, Class: Ambiguous Identities*, trans. Chris Turner, 1991); Antonio Callari and David F. Ruccio, eds., *Postmodern Materialism and the Future of Marxist Theory* (1996); Jacques Derrida, *Spectres de Marx* (1993, *Specters of Marx*, trans. Peggy Kamuf, 1994); Michael Hardt and Antonio Negri, *Empire* (2000); Rosemary Hennessy, *Materialist Feminism and the Politics of Discourse* (1993); Peter Hitchcock, *Oscillate Wildly: Space, Body, and Spirit of Millennial Materialism* (1999); Fredric Jameson, *The Geopolitical Aesthetic: Cinema and Space in the World System* (1992), *Late Marxism: Adorno; or, The Persistence of the Dialectic* (1990), *The Political Unconscious: Narrative as a Socially Symbolic Act* (1981), "Postmodernism; or, The Cultural Logic of Late Capitalism," *New Left Review* 146 (1984), *Postmodernism; or, The Cultural Logic of Late Capitalism* (1991); Donna Landry and Gerald MacLean, *Materialist Feminisms* (1993); Bernd Magnus and Stephen Cullenberg, eds., *Whither Marxism? Global Crises in International Perspective* (1995); Karl Marx, "Der 18te Brumaire des Louis Napoleon," *Die Revolution* (1852) ("Eighteenth Brumaire of Louis Napoleon," *Surveys from Exile*, ed. and intro. David Fernbach, trans. Ben Fowkes et al., 1973), *Das Kapital*, vol. 1 (1867, *Capital*, vol. 1, trans. Ben Fowkes, 1976), *Grundrisse der Kritik der politischen Ökonomie* (1953, *Grundrisse: Foundations of the Critique of Political Economy*, trans. Martin Nicolaus, 1973), *Karl Marx: Early Writings* (trans. Rodney Livingstone and Gregor Benton, 1975); Toril Moi, *Sexual/Textual Politics* (1985); Toril Moi and Janice Radway, eds., "Materialist Feminism," special issue, *South Atlantic Quarterly* 93 (1994); Antonio Negri, *Marx oltre Marx* (1979, *Marx beyond Marx*, trans. Harry Cleaver, Michael Ryan, and Maurizio Viano, 1984); Gayatri Chakravorty Spivak, *A Critique of Postcolonial Reason* (1999), *In Other Worlds: Essays in Cultural Politics* (1987), *Outside in the Teaching Machine* (1993); Slavoj Žižek, *The Sublime Object of Ideology* (1989).

Modernist Theory and Criticism

Until the 1980s, the term "modernist" was most often used in literary studies to refer to a radical break with the literary forms of the past in the experimental, avant-garde style of writing prevalent between World Wars I and II. During the late 1980s and early 1990s, understandings of the term underwent a temporary reversal. The emergence of POSTMODERNISM as the preserve of emancipatory language practices and experimental negotiations between "high" and "low" culture (technology, popular culture) temporarily realigned modernism with Enlightenment rationality and the traditional "elitist" notion of aesthetics as necessarily divorced from cultural concerns. (Modernism is an international movement, erupting in different countries at different times, and one characteristic is its transgression of national and generic boundaries. Our main focus here, however, is on English-language modernism.) In the 1990s, the "return to the scene of the modern" in literary studies further redefined modernism. "Modernity" increasingly refers to a highly contradictory movement, often characterized by startling juxtapositions and incongruities, whose criticism and theory both affirmed traditional notions of "high" art and drew links between the modernist poetics of change and the culture at large.

Thus, T. S. Eliot's insistence in essays such as "Tradition and the Individual Talent" (1917) that the young poet need only assimilate the (all-male) canon of established authors contributed to public definitions of literary modernism that would exclude mass culture. Simultaneously, Eliot's essays on the music hall and its performers, including "Marie Lloyd" (1922), helped make popular culture a legitimate object of criticism and a subject for art. Similarly, prewar aesthetic manifestoes linked to movements such as imagism and vorticism, including Ezra Pound's "A Few Don'ts by an Imagiste" (1913) and Pound and Wyndham Lewis's 1914 manifesto published in the first number of their journal BLAST, urged writers to "make it new" and praised the aesthetic possibilities of urban, technological "steel" but also claimed to preserve the high cultural values of tradition. Consequently, the project of identifying a modernist criticism and theory is often vexed by contradictory definitions of the relation between art, society, tradition, and the individual within the profusion of manifestoes and essays seeking to characterize the modernist period.

One pervasive axiom of modernist theory that resulted in both reactionary and progressive interpretations of art, society, and the individual, importantly articulated by T. E. Hulme in "Romanticism and Classicism" (written in 1913–1914 and posthumously published in *Speculations* [1924]), is an acceptance of limits that are identified with classicism. Hulme argues that the classical poet "may jump, but he always returns back; he never flies away into the circumambient gas" (120). The classical style is carefully crafted, characterized by accurate description and a cheerful "dry hardness" (126). Hulme's preference is for the visual and the concrete over the general and abstract, for freshness of idiom, for the vital complexities that are "intensive" rather than extensive (139).

The note Hulme sounds resonates widely through the work of other modernist writers. Pound's dictum "make it new," Eliot's "objective correlative" ("Hamlet" [1919]), James Joyce's epiphanies, Virginia Woolf's moments of being, and the explosive power of the concrete image celebrated in imagism are all instances of a "classical" technique, a preference for the local and well defined over the infinite.

The classical style is characteristic of much, but not all, modernist writing (D. H. Lawrence's work being one well-known exception). However, the classical theory begins to bifurcate, producing political implications that are diametrically opposed, when the insistence on finitude is applied to the individual. Both groups of classical writers accepted the view that the individual is limited, but one group, which included Woolf, Joyce, H. D., and W. B. Yeats, began to develop a theory of supplemental "selves" that points toward a celebration of diversity as an antidote to individual limitation. In *Mrs. Dalloway* (1925) Woolf has Clarissa propose a theory that she is many things and many people. Yeats worked out an analogous idea in his theory of the antiself in "Per Amica Silentia Lunae" (1917), a notion that each individual is implicit in his or her opposite, which eventuated in the complex theory of interlocking personality types outlined in *A Vision* (1925). In the novel *The Sword Went Out to Sea*, written in 1946–1947 but not published until 2007, H. D. urges a process whereby "the ego or centre of our amorphous, scattered personality crystallizes out" to become "one of a million, or a single wax-cell of a honey-comb." In *Ulysses* (1922), Joyce also pursues the idea that the heterogeneous self is brought to the surface by multiple encounters with difference. As Stephen Dedalus argues, "Every life is many days, day after day. We walk through ourselves, meeting robbers, ghosts, giants, old men, young men, wives, widows, brothers-in-love, but always meeting ourselves" (9: 1044–46).

The same recognition of the humankind's limitation produced in other modernist writers an insistence on strict, authoritarian regulation of the individual, the germ of fascist tendencies for which the movement became notorious. Hulme again articulates the premises of this position: "Man is an extraordinarily fixed and limited animal whose nature is absolutely constant. It is only by tradition and organisation that anything decent can be got out of him" (116). He speaks of liberty and revolution as essentially negative things. Like Eliot, he appreciated religion for its power to control human depravity through traditional order.

The problem with controlling "human depravity" through institutional restrictions is that the controlling "order" tends to legislate sameness, so that some orders of existence are seen as preferable to—less depraved than—others. And this is where the seams of "classical" modernist theory split: not over the limited nature of humanity but over the value of difference. The split was a jagged one; some writers, such as Pound, could cultivate difference in their writing and denounce it in society (as he did in his infamous radio broadcasts of the 1930s). The varying premium

accorded to ethnic, social, religious, and sexual differences by writers who agreed on
the limited nature of the individual, however, explains how the offensive tirades of
Lewis and the brilliant feminism of Woolf, the antisemitic propaganda of Pound and
the Jewish hero of Joyce's Ulysses, could stem from the same "classical" root.

In a period that was to culminate in World War II, racism was an inevitably controversial issue. The related cause of feminism was also hotly debated during the period, since women had been granted suffrage only after World War I (1920 in the
United States, 1928 in Great Britain). In A Room of One's Own (1929), Woolf details
clearly and unpolemically the historical and material restrictions on women that denied them full participation in artistic and professional life. Her best illustration is
her invention of a wonderfully gifted sister for Shakespeare named Judith, his coun-
terpart in everything but freedom and opportunity. "Who shall measure the heat and
violence of the poet's heart when caught and tangled in a woman's body?" she asks
(48). Woolf's main argument is that women need space—a room of their own—and
economic freedom (a fixed income) for their hitherto pinched genius to flourish.

Finally, no discussion of modernist criticism and theory is complete without an
account of the collapse of plot and its replacement by intertextual allusion and the
"stream of consciousness." In "Ulysses, Order, and Myth" (1923), a much-cited review
of Ulysses, Eliot argues that developments in ethnology and psychology, along with
Sir James Frazer's The Golden Bough, had made it possible to replace the narrative
method with the "mythical method," which was first adumbrated by Yeats. The mythical method works not through narrative but through allusion to different mythical
narratives that, when fleshed out and juxtaposed, illuminate both the text in which
they appear and each other in surprising and often revisionary ways. Eliot chose to
highlight myth as the key to modernist stylistics, but actually myth was just one category of narrative accessed through allusion; one might say that all kinds of narratives were situated behind the page, identifiable only through "tags" in the text, and
that the interplay between these narratives produces a submerged commentary on it
that imitates the pressure of the cultural unconscious (in narrativized form) on any
individual performance. The stream-of-consciousness technique is yet another way
of drawing the reader's attention from conscious, deliberate, intentionalized discourse to the pressure of the unsaid on the said, of the repressed on the expressed.
The apparent randomness of associative thought prompts the reader to question the
submerged "logic" of connection, to listen for the unconscious poetry of repressed
desire. This attention to the unknown as the shadow of the known is reversed in
Joyce's Finnegans Wake (1939), in which the known is obscured by the highly organized distortions of language and history as processed by the unconscious mind and
the "mudmound" of the past (111). In light of this sensitivity to the muted voice of the
unconscious in the literature of the period, another great modernist theorist was, not
surprisingly, SIGMUND FREUD.

In fact, the opposing political tendencies of modernist writers bear a significant relationship to their different attitudes toward the unconscious. Bounded by the eruption of two world wars, the modernist period can be read as a historical enactment of the tension between Friedrich Nietzsche's Apollonian and Dionysian forces. The Dionysian power of the unconscious was making itself felt, and the writers who sought to contain or deny it through the Apollonian power of civic or religious authority were, like Pentheus in Euripides' *Bacchae*, torn apart. Others sought to express the creative potential of the unconscious, its capacity to unify without homogenization, to proliferate via division, and it is the writing of this group that is most animated by the zest of manifold contradictions.

VICKI MAHAFFEY AND CASSANDRA LAITY

T. S. Eliot, *Essays Ancient and Modern* (1936), *On Poetry and Poets* (1957), *Selected Essays* (1932, 3rd ed., 1950), *Selected Prose of T. S. Eliot* (ed. Frank Kermode, 1975), *To Criticize the Critic* (1965), *The Use of Poetry and the Use of Criticism* (1933); T. E. Hulme, *Speculations: Essays on Humanism and the Philosophy of Art* (ed. Herbert Read, 1924, 2nd ed., 1936); James Joyce, *Finnegans Wake* (1999), *Ulysses* (ed. Hans Walter Gabler, 1984); Lawrence I. Lipking and A. Walton Litz, eds., *Modern Literary Criticism, 1900–1970* (1972); Ezra Pound, *ABC of Reading* (1934), *Guide to Kulchur* (1938), *Literary Essays of Ezra Pound* (ed. T. S. Eliot, 1954), *Make It New: Essays* (1934), *Selected Prose, 1909–1965* (ed. William Cookson, 1973), *The Spirit of Romance* (1910); Ezra Pound and Wyndham Lewis, "Manifesto," *BLAST* 1 (1914); Virginia Woolf, *Collected Essays* (ed. Leonard Woolf, 4 vols., 1966–1967), *The Common Reader: First Series* (1925, ed. Andrew McNeillie, 1984), *The Essays of Virginia Woolf* (ed. Andrew McNeillie, 5 vols. to date, 1986–), *A Room of One's Own* (1929, rpt., 1981), *The Second Common Reader* (1932, ed. Andrew McNeillie, 1986), *Three Guineas* (1938); W. B. Yeats, *Essays and Introductions* (1961), *Mythologies* (1959), *A Vision* (1925, rev. ed., 1937).

Moretti, Franco

Franco Moretti (b. 1950) is professor of English and comparative literature at Stanford University, where he also directs the Center for the Study of the Novel. Since his first contribution to the discipline of literary history, *Signs Taken for Wonders: Essays in the Sociology of Literary Forms* (1983), Moretti has used an array of quantitative, evolutionary and geographical models to delineate the social, temporal and spatial dynamics of literary production. His primary focus on novelistic writing has generated a number of detailed histories that explore topics pertaining to novels and their formal trends and genres, but his work also exceeds this focus and explores related issues of the changing nature of readership, the implications of literature's commodification, and the expansion of literary markets beyond national boundaries.

Deemed a literary heretic by some of his fellow historians and literature scholars, Moretti refutes the widely held belief that knowledge about literature arises out of the ritualistic parsing of canonical texts. Implicitly, his works are antithetical to the practice of "close reading," which was proposed most influentially by the Anglo-American school of New Criticism. Moretti contends that a more representative knowledge of literature can be developed, but only to the extent that literary critics give up simply scrutinizing the details—characters, plots, the innumerable themes—of a minuscule number of venerated works. His methods are encapsulated in the concept of "distant reading," which stands in opposition to "close reading." In this way, his studies are a dramatic and well-conceived overturning of many contemporary methods by which novels are given their intelligibility, classified, and subsequently studied.

Moretti suggests that readers should examine literary forms within a larger field of cultural and economic conditions that cut across national and linguistic borders. He argues that it is a mistake to locate shifts in literary forms in the imagined dialogue between authors and their styles. For instance, the famous interpretation of the "rise of the novel" offered by Ian Watt is limited by its narrow, exclusively British sample of writers. Alternatively, Moretti presents a statistical analysis of "a multiple rise of the novel" (*Graphs, Maps, Trees*, 9), which occurred at different times in many regions of the world (i.e., Brazil, Denmark, Italy, India, Japan, Nigeria, Russia, Spain), and according to social and economic factors that differ from those found in Britain in the nineteenth century. Moretti's project implies that the orthodox historical, aesthetic and spatial norms that inform research and reading practices need to be critiqued and researched anew. Concerning the difference in scale of his project to the norm of contemporary literary research, he writes that "a field this large cannot be understood by stitching together separate bits of knowledge about individual cases, because it isn't a sum of individual cases: it's a collective system, that should be grasped as such, as a whole" (4).

Two studies of genre exhibit Moretti's desire to subject traditional forms of narration to unconventional criteria for their assessment. First, *The Way of the World: The Bildungsroman in European Culture* (1987) proposes that the bildungsroman was the primary medium of class socialization in the nineteenth century, with "the conflict between the ideal of *self-determination* and the equally imperious demands of *socialization*" (15) directing the narratives. He compares this form with other narratives of human maturation such as the fairy tale, and he differentiates formal modes within the genre itself. Moretti critiques the identification of the bildungsroman as a mirror of human development, conflict, and aspiration and reveals the values of *embourgeoisement* behind this form of narration, which shelters characters and readers from "the onslaught of events" (6) beyond the milieu of home and habit.

In *Modern Epic: The World System from Goethe to Marquez* (1995), Moretti argues that the formal breakthrough of the epic novel and its sustained reinvention through the contingencies and catastrophes of modernity is a symptom of the less visible historical continuity of European capitalist hegemony. Citing such modern epics as *Faust*, *The Ring*, *Ulysses* and *One Hundred Years of Solitude*, he explains how the epic novel arises from a desire to totalize a vision of the world by "rejecting the calm agnosticism of the novel: it rebels against the slow decline of the sacred, and seeks to restore lost transcendence" (35). In this way, epic narratives extol an unwavering faith in the ideals of progress, possibility, and human freedom while mystifying the ways in which these ideals are used to justify inequalities and violence within the field of historical events. In short, the modern epic or "world text" is reinvented by its authors, who choose to fulfill its formal demands, "to have faith once more in the story" (246), rather than admit that the epic has some connection to spurious contemporary beliefs.

In 1998 Moretti published *Atlas of the European Novel, 1800–1900*. Using approximately one hundred maps and diagrams, Moretti rethinks the relation between the novel form and the cartography of Western Europe. *Atlas* is unique for its reinterpretation of "the place-bound nature of literary forms" and "the semiotic domain around which a plot coalesces and self-organizes" (5). The theoretical wager of the work, and of his method on the whole, is expressed in the following remark:

> My object is an artificial one because a series is never found, but always constructed
> by what is repeatable and can turn discrete objects into a series. And this, of course,
> is what makes quantitative methods so repugnant to literary critics: the fear that they
> might suppress the uniqueness of texts . . . but as I don't believe in the epistemological
> cal value of the unique, its suppression doesn't really bother me. (143)

Atlas cites many literary critics who have attempted to determine the relation between novels and maps. However, Moretti distinguishes himself by constructing a theoretical knowledge of the preconditions for narration that makes maps *the* analytic tool of choice. Maps are not metaphors or "ornaments of discourse" but "analytic tools" that "dissect the text in an unusual way, bringing to light relations that would otherwise remain hidden" (3). Moretti emphasizes the relationship between space and aesthetic norms; how urbanization, anonymity and stratification in Paris and London affects fictional accounts of racial difference, youth, and fear; the experience of national and regional border spaces as depicted in novels; and the rise of "narrative markets," which becomes a key index of popularity for books in the nineteenth century. Moretti also maps the European diffusion of *Don Quixote*, *Buddenbrooks*, and the great nineteenth-century bestsellers as evidence of the first truly international instance of literature's commercial trade.

In the self-declared manifesto *Graphs, Maps, Trees: Abstract Models for Literary History* (2005), Moretti reiterates the virtues of quantitative history, geography, and evolutionary theory in "delineat[ing] a transformation in the study of literature" (2). Moretti seeks a system of analysis for the novel, one that addresses the entire spectrum of its forms. Mindful of prior attempts to build a single theory of novelistic writing, he adds that previous theories have not examined the novel in all of its possible deviations or drawn on what Margaret Cohen calls "the great unread": "All great theories of the novel have precisely reduced the novel to one basic form only (realism, the dialogic, romance, meta-novels); and if the reduction has given them their elegance and power, it has also erased nine-tenths of literary history. Too much" (30).

A way to analyze a large cross-section of novel forms in one study is to chart the way the novel evolves as a result of its gradual commodification. All novels regardless of aesthetic form gradually become commodities, yet the impact of this change on the novel form itself is unknown. Moretti's belief is that the demands from the market for "reliable products" and the loyalty of the consumer are as intrinsic to novel writing today as they were in the nineteenth century. Today the observation that cultural forms are also commercial products is common, but Moretti's desire to shape this historical data into a prospective historiographic model for future cooperative literary research is unparalleled.

Critical responses to Moretti's work have suggested it shows an "overcommittment to general laws, to global postulates operating at some remove from the phenomenal world of particular texts" (Dimock 90). The belief is that his work elides the particularity of what texts represent and how they represent them. Moretti believes that whatever is lost in the practice of "distant reading" is necessary for his models of analysis to develop separately from the regular order of literary authority. The attention Moretti pays to producing antithetical models for literary history certainly removes him from innumerable debates concerning, for example, reception theory, psychological studies of authors, and identity politics. However, Moretti's models simultaneously challenge the academic practice of literary study while examining the ordinary, assumed place of novels and narratives in daily life.

TIM KAPOSY

Franco Moretti, *Atlante del romanzo europeo, 1800–1900* (1997, *Atlas of the European Novel, 1800–1900*, 1998), "Conjectures on World Literature," *New Left Review* 1 (2000), *Graphs, Maps, Trees: Abstract Models for Literary History* (2005), *Opere mondo: Saggio sulla forma epica dal Faust a Cent'anni di solitudine* (1994, *Modern Epic: The World System from Goethe to Marquez*, trans. Quentin Hoare, 1995), "Planet Hollywood," *New Left Review* 9 (2001), *Signs Taken for Wonders: Essays in the Sociology of Literary Forms* (trans. Susan Fischer, David Forgacs, and David Miller, 1983), "The Slaughterhouse of Literature," *Modern Language Quarterly* 61 (2000), *The Way of the World: The Bildungsroman in European Culture* (trans. Albert Sbragia, 1987); Wai Chee Dimock, "Genre as World System: Epic and Novel on Four Continents," *Narrative* 14 (2006).

Multiculturalism

In the context of the United States, "multiculturalism" is often associated with a movement in the 1980s and 1990s that sought to disrupt the cultural homogeneity of the educational and literary "canon" by including the writings and viewpoints of minority and international authors. The struggle over the canon, which usually took place within universities, became a much broader ideological battle over inclusion and exclusion in the United States and was sometimes also called the "culture wars." Although U.S. writers often speak of multiculturalism in an unspecified manner as if it were universal, multiculturalism has a range of different meanings, as well as an unexpectedly complex history, which emerge when it is examined more broadly and from various geographical locations.

Multiculturalism is always intricately linked to the related concepts of culture, nationalism, cultural difference, ethnicity, identity, race, postcolonialism, and POSTMODERNISM, concepts that are highly contested in and of themselves. Further, ideologies and practices of multiculturalism indicate very specific and diverse ideas and processes in different contexts and must therefore always be examined within specific national and international contexts and histories and over time. STUART HALL distinguishes between ideas of "the multicultural" expressed by the adjective "multicultural" and those expressed by the noun "multiculturalism." The first addresses the social characteristics and problems of governance inherent in any society in which different cultural communities live together and attempt to build a common life while at the same time retaining something of their "original" identities. In contrast, "multiculturalism" is substantive, referring to "strategies and policies adopted to govern or manage the problems of diversity and multiplicity which multi-cultural societies throw up" ("Conclusion" 209). Thus, "the multicultural" is a site of debate and contest, and "multiculturalism" is a governing policy and managerial strategy.

Multiculturalism is implicitly opposed to monoculturalism, a hegemonic ideal for nation-states that has held sway for most of the twentieth century (Goldberg, *Multiculturalism* 3). The idea that a nation should possess a single shared culture is based on commonsense notions of personhood and nationhood that emerged during the Enlightenment. In this historically specific formulation of selfhood, possession of a differentiated, bounded, and defined identity comes to be an essential feature of "normal personhood" or normal nationhood, as constituted in a modern Western framework (Asad, "Multiculturalism" 12). In *Nations and Nationalism* (1983) Ernst Gellner argues that a unified and homogeneous culture was necessary for the development of industrial capitalism and that the state, or nation-state, provided it. As Benedict Anderson points out in his *Imagined Communities* (1983) nationalist ideals emerging from the nineteenth century assumed that geographical and cultural boundaries should be synonymous. As a result, it is axiomatic that a nation or group must have a differentiated and often singular culture and identity in order to be seen to exist, as well as to claim rights and powers.

Such modernist ideals of nation were and are embedded in cultural and immigration policies in many parts of the globe, many of which were and are also based on the ideal of racial homogeneity. The mythologies of nationhood in many nations also promoted—and often still promote—an idea of homogeneous cultures. David Theo Goldberg points out that monocultural assumptions influenced the notion of "high culture" in U.S. institutions of learning, a form of education that was intended to provide "the grounds for cohesion, the conditions of Americanness." After the civil rights movement, new forms of monoculturalism eventually created a situation of "integration" in which minorities were forced to be privately ethnic yet publicly American ("Introduction" 6).

MULTICULTURALISM AND THE "CULTURE WARS." Multiculturalism in the U.S. context started out as a debate about differing versions of pedagogy and education policy and turned eventually into what was called the "culture wars." For the Chicago Cultural Studies Group, multiculturalism is "a desire to rethink canons in the humanities—to rethink both their boundaries and their functions . . . to find the cultural and political norms appropriate to more heterogeneous societies within and across nations, including norms for the production and transmission of knowledges" (114). Henry Giroux suggests that multiculturalism has become a central discourse in the "struggle over issues regarding national identity, the construction of historical memory, the purpose of schooling, and the meaning of democracy" (325).

One of the most volatile debates in the history of U.S. multiculturalism concerned the curriculum of Stanford University's core Western culture course, a debate that has been said to have "set off" the culture wars. In early 1988 the university senate was debating whether to drop the requirement of the core reading list of fifteen works by "classic" thinkers such as Plato, Homer, Dante Alighieri, and Charles Darwin. This change to the core curriculum would have transformed the Western culture course into one called "Culture, Ideas, and Values," and it would have added the work of women, African Americans, Hispanics, Asians, and Native Americans to a "contracted core of the classics." An op-ed piece in the *Wall Street Journal* suggested that "the intellectual heritage of the West goes on trial at Stanford University today. Most predict it will lose" (cited in Gutmann 13). Not insignificantly, this debate dovetailed with a more fervent struggle over resources, such as admission to prestigious colleges and credentials for the elite labor market, and thus the accumulation of cultural capital. In short, what was at stake in the "culture wars" was not only how the canon would be defined but also who would have access to power, status, and influence.

Amy Gutmann suggests that "essentialists" dominated one side of this debate. They argued that diluting the core curriculum with new writings simply for the sake of including previously unheard voices and viewpoints would be to "forsake the standards of Western civilization for the standardness of relativism, the tyranny of the social sciences, lightweight trendiness, and a host of related intellectual and political evils" (13). The other side, often called the "deconstructionists," argued that preserving the core curriculum by excluding contributions of women, African Americans, Hispanics, Asians, and native Americans "as if the classical canon were sacred, unchanging and unchangeable would be to denigrate the identities of members of these previously excluded groups" (13). One of the key anti-multicultural texts that emerged at the time, Alan Bloom's *Closing of the American Mind* (1987), argued that college administrations during the 1960s and 1970s had given in to the demands of students, black power groups, and feminists, and had fatally compromised the standards of American higher education. The newer, and inferior, curriculum included works that were displacing the more valuable Western canon. The book incited many responses from people such as Dinesh D'Souza, William Bennett, Roger Kimball, and John Searle. There were also multiple critiques, such as those of Michael Bérubé and Cary Nelson, HENRY LOUIS GATES JR., Gerald Graff, and Peter N. Stearns. In 1996 Lawrence W. Levine published *The Opening of the American Mind*, a defense of Bloom's critics.

A key argument of the opponents of multiculturalism is that the point of education is to provide students with the very best of "culture," usually meaning "high culture" or "Western culture." Charles Taylor, in his oft-quoted and well-discussed essay "Multiculturalism and the Politics of Recognition," argues that his version of "recognition" deems that we should not assume that all cultures are equal but that we should give all cultures the "presumption" that they can provide something of value. Yet, he suggests, "the validity of the claim has to be demonstrated concretely, in the actual study of the culture. Indeed, for a culture sufficiently different from our own, we may have only the foggiest idea *ex ante* of in what its valuable contribution might consist" (67). Others might ask in response to this analysis and assertion of value, "contribution" to what? Is Taylor assuming a universal and supposedly objective notion of civilization, of progress? What are the assumptions and silences in this passage? Susan Wolf suggests that this line of thought takes us in an "unfortunate direction" because it leads away from one of the most crucial issues of multiculturalism. She suggests that Taylor's reason for studying cultures is based on some idea that it will "pay off" with a valuable aesthetic or intellectual contribution. Wolf contends that there are other, more important reasons to study such texts. The issue is not one of objective value; rather it concerns the transformative pedagogical nature of reading and learning about others. She argues that "by having these books and by reading them, we come to recognize ourselves as a multicultural community," and she suggests that "there is nothing wrong with allotting a special place in the curriculum for the study of our history, our culture. But if we are to study our culture, we had better recognize who we, as a community, are" (83–85).

The terrain and terminologies of multiculturalism are deeply contested. Joan Wallach Scott suggests that "political correctness" is the label attached to critical attitudes and behavior, whereas "multiculturalism" is the program it is said to be attempting to enact. According to Sneja Gunew, U.S. multiculturalists can include "ethnics (including Hispanics and Asians), Blacks (African-Americans who are united by the common history of slavery that has functioned as an excuse for occluding their contribution to the construction of the nation), indigenous peoples, feminists, gays and lesbians, ecologists, deconstructionists (usually meaning poststructuralists and postmodernists), and a generalized left" ("Multicultural" 55). Gunew suggests that these "motley groups are apparently united by their opposition to the West or Western values, also defined as Eurocentrism" ("Multiculturalism" 55). Other critiques of multiculturalism from more radical positions include those that see multiculturalism as a way of deflecting issues of racism, arguing that it becomes an apolitical smorgasbord of cultures where everyone is free to offer tidbits of culture or to taste them (see Gunew "Multicultural"). Indeed, as GAYATRI CHAKRAVORTY SPIVAK, Trinh T. Minh-ha, and Rey Chow have pointed out, even within universities or academic feminism, contexts that are supposedly more enlightened, it is common to witness the token "woman of color" being invited to conferences and similarly tokenistic forms of cross-cultural analysis, repeatedly uncovering the usual round of predictable stereotypes (Nnaemeka).

Further, multiculturalism's specific focus on culture, unless it includes a more nuanced and materialist analysis of the "politics of culture," often ignores or sidesteps structural issues, political activisms, and their histories. Hazel Carby argues in "The Multicultural Wars" (1992) that the literary-cultural emphasis on black women's texts also works as a substitute for the continuing work of desegregation and antiracism. Work in critical pedagogy has been central to the formulation and practice of a more critical multiculturalism. Some, most notably Giroux and Roger Simon, have developed an approach to critical pedagogy that critiques the very fundamental practices of power and authority both inside and outside the classroom. They call on educators as cultural workers to rethink education as an explicitly moral and political practice and to tie the production of forms of knowledge directly to the construction of a more just and therefore multicultural society.

MULTICULTURAL POLICY AND THE REGULATION OF DIFFERENCE. Multiculturalism is also a state policy developed to help deal with the contradictions of a society containing multiple cultural groups. Many have argued that the Canadian state founded the official policy of "multiculturalism" in response to a range of complex and potentially dangerous conflicts in the cultural politics of Canadian nationalism, as well as to serve the economic needs of nation building. Such risks included the threat of Québec separatism and demands for recognition by indigenous people, immigrants, and other minorities. The development of multicultural policy also intersected with the need, seen as a natural "evolution" of nationhood, to construct a unified and distinct national identity to differentiate Canada from the United States and Britain (Mackey). A similar official multicultural policy emerged in Australia. In Australia "the contention that culture and the study of culture are intimately linked to the political has not aroused the same kind of panic" (Gunew, "Multicultural" 59) that it did in the United States. Interdisciplinarity and cultural studies are also more respected in the Australian academy, and therefore anxieties about the "erasure of disciplinary borders" have less "emotional impact" (59).

Multicultural policy and ideology in Canada and Australia implicitly mobilize different definitions of "culture" for minority groups and for national culture. It has been argued that multiculturalism promotes the idea of minority cultures as fragments of cultures, constructed from folkloric and culinary remnants. In the multicultural model of culture, these cultural fragments become conceptually divorced from politics and economics and become commodified cultural possessions (Mackey). Kogila Moodley argues that Canadian multiculturalism promotes a "festive aura of imagined consensus," what Chris Mullard calls a "three Ss" model of culture. This model highlights "saris, samosas, and steel bands" in order to diffuse the "three Rs": "resistance, rebellion, and rejection" (320). However, a much broader definition of "mainstream" Canadian national culture is also implicit. The policy has been critiqued for maintaining the idea of British Canadians as the norm in relation to multicultural Canadians. In this construction of culture, a core Canadian national culture represents a "whole way of life" (in the sense discussed by RAYMOND WILLIAMS), and the "multicultures" exist as fragments of culture, only valued for the ways in which they contribute to the national culture (Mackey). In this sense, minority cultures in Canada are constructed through a "discourse of enrichment" similar to that found in accounts of Australian multiculturalism (Hage 31–32). Multiculturalism thereby positions Anglo-Canadians or Anglo-Celtic Australians in the center of the national "cultural map"; the difference between minority cultures and the dominant cultures is that dominant cultures simply exist, whereas minority cultures "*exist for* the latter" (32).

One of the key sites of struggle over multiculturalism has been literature, especially national literatures. Perhaps this is because the "multiracial and multiethnic nature" of nations is "made real to us," is "written into our consciousness" through writers (Hutcheon 5). Initially, in Canada, multicultural literature often referred to the work of ethnic minorities and was defined as the work of those born overseas. There has since been a shift to tackling broader questions of race and ethnicity in literatures rather than simply celebrating ethnic literature. Works in English by minority writers are now included as part of the multicultural field (Gunew, "Multicultural" 57). There is also an increasing awareness of and focus on racism (Hutcheon 7–10). In her introduction to the edited volume *Other Solitudes* (1990), Linda Hutcheon suggests that part of the impetus for the book is much more critical than the celebration of "others" of Canada. She points out that *all* Canadians, including the British and the French, should see themselves as ethnic. The fact that they do not indicates a hierarchy of social and cultural privilege that the collection intends to challenge.

Here multiculturalism is leaning toward a critique of "whiteness," another strand of current criticism that intersects with critical multiculturalism (see Dyer, Frankenberg, Morrison, Ware, Young).

In a more general way, a range of writers from various geographical locations and with complex links to literary theory and other related approaches from CULTURAL STUDIES, POSTCOLONIAL STUDIES, and critical race theory have influenced and helped define and contest multiculturalism and related issues. Some of the most influential writers are bell hooks, Stuart Hall, Spivak, Audre Lord, Adrienne Rich, Teresa de Lauretis, PAUL GILROY, and HOMI K. BHABHA. One of the key sites of inquiry that links up to multiculturalism concerns cultural diasporas and cultural hybridity. Work on "border" identities with respect to Latino/a studies, such as that of Guillermo Gómez-Peña and Gloria Anzaldúa, has been very important. Gilroy's and Bhabha's work has been particularly influential in its attempts to think about the concept of cultural hybridity. Bhabha has defined hybridity as "the construction of cultural authority within conditions of political antagonism or inequity. Strategies of hybridization reveal an estranging movement in the 'authoritative,' even authoritarian inscription of the sign" ("Culture's" 212). Others have noted that analyses in the name of hybridity are ultimately dependent on the very fixed and bounded categories they seek to cross or blur. One productive result of analytical approaches to multiculturalism has been the development of critical analyses of the subtleties of traveling signifiers, such as the replacement of overt biological racism with "cultural racism," including the continuing covert racism and flexible racisms at the heart of modernity, central to liberalism (Gilroy, There Ain't; Goldberg, Racist), and at the core of the nation-state (see especially Goldberg, Racial). One important caution regarding multiculturalism is that "minority perspectives are neither free of their own investments nor do they automatically retain a hold on some kind of privileged moral capital" (Gunew, "Postcolonialism" 11). It is here that a critique of identity politics such as that proposed by Gilroy ("End") is useful, as are analyses of the subtle co-optive nature of multiculturalism and the concept of "culture" in multicultural nations (Bannerji; Hage, White; Mackey). Multiculturalism remains a useful critical approach, adjacent to and partly overlapping with postcolonial theory, cultural studies, and critical race theory. Multicultural critical theory can serve to remind one of "both the local and the global in that it introduces minority perspectives as well as suggesting diasporic networks. It continues to be a way of situating subjectivities outside certain nationalist investments and hence may be used as a way of paying attention to minority perspectives, using them to critique dominant discourses and practices" (Gunew, "Postcolonialism" 12).

EVA MACKEY

See also CULTURAL STUDIES, NATIONAL LITERATURE, and POSTCOLONIAL STUDIES.

Benedict Anderson, *Imagined Communities: Reflections on the Origin and Spread of Nationalism* (1983, rev. ed., 1991); Gloria Anzaldúa, *Borderlands/La Frontera: The New Mestiza* (1987); Talal Asad, "Multiculturalism and British Identity in the Wake of the Rushdie Affair," *Genealogies of Religion: Discipline and Reasons of Power in Christianity and Islam* (1993); Himani Bannerji, *The Dark Side of the Nation: Essays on Multiculturalism, Nationalism, and Gender* (2000); Michael Bérubé and Cary Nelson, *Higher Education under Fire: Politics, Economics, and the Crisis of the Humanities* (1995); Homi K. Bhabha, "Culture's In Between," *Artforum* 32 (1993), *The Location of Culture* (1994), *Nation and Narration* (1990); Hazel Carby, "The Multicultural Wars," *Black Popular Culture* (ed. Gina Dent, 1992); Chicago Cultural Studies Group, "Critical Multiculturalism" (Goldberg); Rey Chow, *Woman and Chinese Modernity: The Politics of Reading between East and West* (1991); Dinesh D'Souza, *Illiberal Education* (1991); Richard Dyer, *White* (1997); Ruth Frankenberg, *White Woman, Race Matters: The Social Construction of Whiteness* (1993); Henry Louis Gates Jr., *Loose Canons* (1992); Ernst Gellner, *Nations and Nationalism* (1983); Paul Gilroy, *The Black Atlantic: Modernity and Double Consciousness* (1993), "The End of Anti-racism," *"Race," Culture, and Difference* (ed. James Donald and Ali Ratansi, 1990), *There Ain't No Black in the Union Jack* (1987); Henry A. Giroux, "Insurgent Multiculturalism and the Promise of Pedagogy" (Goldberg); Henry Giroux and Roger Simon, eds., *Popular Culture, Schooling, and Everyday Life* (1989); David Theo Goldberg, "Introduction: Multicultural Conditions" (Goldberg), *The Racial State* (2001), *Racist Culture: Philosophy and the Politics of Meaning* (1993); David Theo Goldberg, ed., *Multiculturalism: A Critical Reader* (1994); Guillermo Gómez-Peña, *Dangerous Border Crossers* (2000); Gerald Graff, *Beyond the Culture Wars* (1992); Sneja Gunew, *Framing Marginality: Multicultural Literary Studies* (1994), "Multicultural Multiplicities: US, Canada, Australia," *Cultural Studies: Pluralism and Theory* (ed. David Bennet, 1993), "Postcolonialism and Multiculturalism: Between Race and Ethnicity," www.english.ubc.ca/ffisgunew/race.htm (last accessed 12 August 2011); Amy Guttman, introduction (Taylor et al.); Ghassan Hage, "Locating Multiculturalism's Other: A Critique of Practical Tolerance," *New Formations* 24 (1994), *White Nation: Fantasies of White Supremacy in a Multicultural Nation* (2000); Stuart Hall, "Conclusion: The Multi-cultural Question," *Un/settled Multiculturalisms: Diasporas, Entanglements, Transruptions* (ed. Barnor Hesse, 2000), "Culture, Community, Nation," *Cultural Studies* 7 (1993), Linda Hutcheon, introduction, *Other Solitudes: Canadian Multicultural Fictions* (ed. Linda Hutcheon and Marion Richmond, 1990); Lawrence W. Levine, *The Opening of the American Mind* (1996); Eva Mackey, *The House of Difference: Cultural Politics and National Identity in Canada* (2000); Kogila Moodley, "Canadian Multiculturalism as Ideology," *Ethnic and Racial Studies* 6 (1983); Cherrie Moraga and Gloria Anzaldúa, eds., *This Bridge Called My Back: Writings by Radical Women of Color* (1981); Toni Morrison, *Playing in the Dark: Whiteness and the Literary Imagination* (1992); Obioma Nnaemeka, "Bringing African Women into the Classroom: Rethinking Pedagogy and Epistemology," *Borderwork: Feminist Engagements with Comparative Literature* (ed. Margaret R. Higonnet, 1994); Joan Wallach Scott, "Campus Communities beyond Consensus," *Beyond PC: Toward a Politics of Understanding* (ed. Patricia Aufderheide, 1992); Gayatri Chakravorty Spivak, *The Post-Colonial Critic: Interviews, Strategies, Dialogues* (ed. Sarah Harasym, 1990); Peter N. Stearns, *Meaning over Memory: Recasting the Teaching of History and Culture* (1993); Charles Taylor et al., *Multiculturalism and "The Politics of Recognition"* (ed. Amy Guttman, 1992, rev. ed., 1994); Trinh T. Minh-ha, *Woman, Native, Other: Writing Postcoloniality and Feminism* (1989); Vron Ware, *Beyond the Pale: White Women, Racism, and History* (1992); Susan Wolf, "Comment" (Taylor et al.); Robert Young, *White Mythologies: Writing, History and the West* (1990).

Nancy, Jean-Luc

Born in Bordeaux, France in 1940, Jean-Luc Nancy studied philosophy at the Sorbonne, where he took courses with Georges Canguilhem and Paul Ricoeur, the latter directing his master's thesis on the question of religion in G. W. F. Hegel. Nancy graduated in 1964 and began to teach at the University of Strasbourg in 1968. Thanks to Lucien Braun, who had invited him to Strasbourg the previous year to give a talk on structuralism, he met Philippe Lacoue-Labarthe. This was the beginning of a rare and lasting friendship, characterized by "an exceptional degree of sharing [*partage*]" ("D'une 'mimesis sans modèle'" 107), determining their decision not only to live in Strasbourg but also to share their personal lives and work.

Nancy has recalled that two names made this encounter possible: Martin Heidegger and Jacques Derrida, or "the question of being" and "'différance' as transformation of the ontological difference" (107). Their shared commitment to a new philosophical exigency, their common interest in German idealism, and their coming-of-age during the events of 1968 demanded a rupture with traditional conceptions of the history of philosophy. This exigency informs "a non-substantial but verbal ontology of being" that also opens toward "a metaphysics of the poem" (107). On the one hand, their intellectual proximity to one another originates in a questioning and displacement of the link that binds "being-substance-subject-subsistence" for Nancy or the link that binds "type-stele-Gestell-consistance/desistance-figure-model" for Lacoue-Labarthe (108). On the other, it originates in the philosophy-literature relation, which "engages less a 'philosophy of literature' than its inverse—a problematic of philosophical *Darstellung*, of philosophical writing as the suspension or disquietude of discourse" (108). While questions of philosophical presentation suggest why Friedrich Nietzsche remained a prominent reference for them in these early years, Lacoue-Labarthe and Nancy also turn to Immanuel Kant in rethinking the rapport between the literary and the philosophical.

Nancy and Lacoue-Labarthe have engaged in a number of collaborative projects, including *The Title of the Letter* (1973), a deconstructive reading of Jacques Lacan, as well as a series of texts on Sigmund Freud and psychoanalysis ("La panique politique" [1979], "Jewish People Don't Dream" [1980]); the translation and introduction to the principal texts of early German Romanticism in *The Literary Absolute* (1978; research into fascism and totalitarianism in *The Nazi Myth*, first published in 1981); a coedited volume on mimesis, *Mimesis of (Dis)Articulations* (1975); the creation of GRTST (Groupe de Recherches sur les Théories du Signe et du Texte) as well as the Center for Philosophical Research on the Political in Paris (*Replaying the Political* [1981]; *The Retreat of the Political* [1982]); and the organization of numerous other projects, both within and outside the university, including seminars, broadcasts, and translations. After ten years of intense collaboration, during which Nancy also published a number of monographs—on Hegel (*The Speculative Remark* [1973]), Kant (*The Discourse of the Syncope* [1975]), and René Descartes (*Ego sum* [1979])—Nancy and Lacoue-Labarthe decided to work in "mutual independence" ("D'une 'mimesis sans modèle,'" 109), a change which Nancy dates to 1981 when he published "Abandoned Being" in the literary review *Argiles*.

If the question of literature was closer to Lacoue-Labarthe's concerns at the outset of their collaboration, it is also clear that Nancy turned to literature with increasing attention. This shift is evident in a number of theoretical texts ("The Calculation of the Poet" [1997] and "The Resistance of Poetry" [1997]), as well as in the numerous essays that he has devoted to the relation between philosophy, literature, and the closely associated question of myth. Throughout Nancy's writings, literature is always present in his specific manner of addressing philosophy, taking into account the primordial importance of the (dis)articulation of discourse. Often finding itself today with no other legitimacy than that of the "political" or "ethical," literature, art, the work of art, "denies itself, in fact, all proper legitimacy"; "there can be only one legitimation for art, which is the sensuous attestation to and inscription of the overflowing of sense" (*Dis-Enclosure* 176). In other words, in its rapport with "transcendence" and the "sacred," art and literature for Nancy are the "excedence of sense" (176).

Nancy not only devotes several important theoretical texts to literature—including Friedrich Holderlin's poetics ("Calculation of the Poet"), the question of cutting and the "versement" of verse, of reciting "by heart," of the immemorial character of the *récit* and the voice of the poet ("Récit, récitation, récitatif" [2010])—but he has also written numerous critical essays (on Maurice Blanchot, Pascal Quignard, Michel Butor, Michel Leiris, and Michel Deguy, to name a few). He has also penned a number of texts that are more experimental in form, playing on several registers—recitatives for operas ("Dans ma poitrine, hélas, deux âmes . . ."), prose essays (*Corpus* [1992]; *The City in the Distance* [1999]; *Falling Asleep* [2007]); poems (*Anemone Traces* [2009]); *récits* ("There" [2007]); lectures and "accompaniments" (*Fortino Sámano: The Excesses of the Poem* [2010])—to which should be added "The Intruder" (2000), an extraordinary *récit* that marks itself off from Nancy's vast corpus by exploring the experience and ordeal of having a heart transplant in 1990, and a text that also resonates in unforgettable ways with the very beginnings of his philosophical writings, with questions of interruption, suspension, and the syncope. At once separation and conjunction, this disjunctive conjunction reopens and displaces itself incessantly throughout Nancy's writings.

If the "philoliterature" relation ("D'une 'mimesis sans modèle'" 109)—a relation that implies "an extremely complex sharing [*partage*] that remains itself in continual transformation" (*L'adoration* 62)—was always at the core of the collaborative work with Lacoue-Labarthe, each author has taken different paths in their own work.

Thus while Lacoue-Labarthe engages the question of mimesis and its relation to "ontotypology," Nancy turns (in the wake of Bataille and Blanchot) to motifs that he describes as "ontological and communal (or again of communal ontology)" ("D'une 'mimesis sans modèle'" 109). Left open in Heidegger's discussion of *Mitsein* and *Mitdasein*, this emphasis on the "cum" or "being-in-common" informs many of Nancy's most well-known works, including *The Inoperative Community* (1986), *The Appearance* (1991), and *Stolen Thought* (2001). Encumbered by "weighty" values and connotations, especially in relation to questions of gathering (of a people), the subject (sub-jectum, sup-position), and sense, all these philosophical concepts will be "reweighed" and reexamined in a number of books published in the late 1980s and 1990s, books which suggest how Nancy rethinks an increasingly broad range of philosophical topics—*The Gravity of Thought* (1986); *The Experience of Liberty* (1988); *A Finite Thinking* (1991); *The Sense of the World* (1993), and *Being Singular* (1996). If all these concepts are reevaluated less in order to "finish" with them than to instill a new circulation of sense, the question of the common or the "in-common" becomes increasingly foregrounded in Nancy's writings, drawing us toward a concept of the "coexistant" where "the 'with' that is constitutive of the existant must be understood in a way that is 'not categorical but existential.' Which means that [the with] is not a simple, extrinsic determination but an intrinsic condition of the very possibility of ek-sistence, which is to say nothing less than the display of the very sense of a being or of the sense of being" ("Mit-Sinn" 1). It is in terms of finite ek-sistence that Nancy's writings not only address questions of community, coexistence, communism, and being-in-common but also the conceptual underpinnings animating democracy as well as the revolutionary tradition of liberty, equality, and fraternity. In *The Inoperative Community*, Nancy extends this argument to the relation between myth and community, where literature or what he terms "literary communism" is the interruption of myth; writing thus becomes "the inscription of our finite resistance" (81) to all forms of completion, interiority, and closure. Retreating from this appeal to a "literary communism" in later work (see "Around the Notion of Literary Communism" in *Multiple Arts*) and the way it lends itself to the renewal of the myth of community, Nancy nowhere renounces the necessity of thinking the relation between politics and literature but turns increasingly to think "being-with" or the "in-common" in terms of sense.

Running parallel with these texts on the philosophy-literature relation, in which the most essential philosophical concepts are rethought to the point of exhausting their very essence, Nancy also addresses a wide range of artistic practices, including: the image (*The Ground of the Image* [2003]), painting (*The Gaze of the Portrait* [2000]), drawing (*More Ways Than One: Jacques Derrida* [2007]; *The Pleasure of Drawing*, 2009), music (*Listening* [2002]), photography (*Iconography of the Author* [2005]; *Wir* [2003]), sculpture (*Ardent Heart* [2003]), cinema (*The Evidence of Film* [2001]), and dance (*Outside Dance* [2001]). Across these various interventions with artists, writers, poets, filmmakers, musicians, and choreographers, Nancy encounters a singular world of thought and sensibility. Nancy turns to art and literature because they are the very site of the setting to work of difference. Each of the arts is unique and heterogeneous, isolated and exposed, forms that at once divide and mix distinct qualities (visual, sonorous, tactile, etc.), making them communicate, placing them in contact, and creating affects. In other words, it is not simply a question of recognizing that the work of art—whatever its support, medium, or syntax—implies a relation to the world but rather that the world itself comes to the work so as to form itself there: *forma formans*, the infinite forming of colors, touches, vibrations, densities, turnings, nuances, tones, reflections, shimmerings, and shadings. What attracts Nancy to these "work-worlds" is the laying hold of and acknowledging a world coming into existence, a birth to presence, a tracing out of a form that is never given in advance and remains unfixed—a form that, like a politics or democracy to come, "replays and revives the ex nihilo," which is the also, inescapably, "the sharing of the world" (*L'adoration* 61).

PHILIP ARMSTRONG AND GINETTE MICHAUD

See also Deconstruction: 2. The 1980s and After and French Theory
and Criticism: 1945 and After.

Jean-Luc Nancy, À l'écoute (2002, Listening, trans. Charlotte Mandell, 2007), À plus d'un titre: Jacques Derrida, sur un dessin de Valerio Adami (2007), L'adoration, vol. 2 of Déconstruction du christianisme (2010), Atlan: Les détrempes (2010), Au fond des images (2003, The Ground of the Image, trans. Jeff Fort, 2005), "Calcul du poète," Des lieux divins (1997, "The Calculation of the Poet," trans. Simon Sparks, The Solid Letter: Readings of Friedrich Hölderlin, ed. Aris Fioretos, 1999), La communauté désoeuvrée (1986, new. ed.1990, The Inoperative Community, trans. Peter Connor, 1991), La comparution (1991, "The Compearance," trans. Tracy B. Strong, Political Theory 20 [1992]), Corpus (1992, Corpus, trans. Richard Rand, 2008), "Dans ma poitrine, hélas, deux âmes . . . ," Claudio Parmiggiani: L'isola del silenzio (Italian trans. Alberto Panaro, 2007), La déclosion, vol. 1 of Déconstruction du christianisme (2005, Dis-Enclosure: The Deconstruction of Christianity, trans. Bettina Bergo, Gabriel Malenfant and Michael B. Smith, 2008), Le discours de la syncope, vol. 1, Logodaedalus (1976, The Discourse of the Syncope: Logodaedalus, trans. Saul Anton, 2008), "D'une 'mimesis sans modèle': Entretien avec Philippe Choulet au sujet de Philippe Lacoue-Labarthe," L'animal 19/20 (2008), Ego sum (1979), "L'être abandonné," L'impératif catégorique (1983, "Abandoned Being," trans. Brian Holmes, The Birth to Presence, 1993), Être singulier pluriel (1996, Being Singular Plural, trans. Anne E. O'Bryne and Robert D. Richardson, 2000), L'évidence du film / The Evidence of Film: Abbas Kiarostami (2001), L'expérience de la liberté (1988, The Experience of Freedom, trans. Bridget McDonald, 1993), L'impératif catégorique (1983), L'intrus (2000, rev. ed., 2005, "The Intruder," trans. Richard Rand, Corpus, 2008), "La jeune carpe," Haine de la poésie (ed. Mathieu Bénézet et al., 1979), "Là," Jean-Luc Nancy and Anne-Lise Broyer, Le ciel gris s'élevant (paraissait plus grand) (2007), "Mit-Sinn" (unpublished) (2010), L'oubli de la philosophie (1986, The Gravity of Thought, trans. François Raffoul and Gregory Recco, 1997), La pensée dérobée (2001), Une pensée finie (1990, A Finite Thinking, ed. Simon Sparks, 2003), "Philippe Lacoue-Labarthe à Strasbourg," Europe 973 (2010), Le plaisir au dessin (2007, rev. ed., 2009), "Les raisons d'écrire," Misère de la littérature (ed. Maurice Blanchot et al., 1979), "Récit, récitation, récitatif," Europe 973 (2010), Le regard du portrait (2000, "The Look of the Portrait," trans. Simon Sparks, Multiple Arts, 2006), La remarque spéculative (1973, The Speculative Remark, trans. Céline Surprenant, 2001), Résistance de la poésie (1997), Le sens du monde (1993, rev. ed., 2001, The Sense of the World, trans. Jeffrey S. Librett, 1997); Jean-Luc Nancy and Federico Ferrari, *Iconographie de l'auteur* (2005); Jean-Luc Nancy and Anne Immelé, *Wir* (2003); Jean-Luc Nancy and Philippe Lacoue-Labarthe, *L'absolu littéraire* (1978, *The Literary Absolute*, trans. Philip Bernard and Cheryl Lester, 1988), "Dialogue sur le dialogue," *Études théâtrales* 33 (2005), *Le mythe nazi* (1981, 2nd ed., 1991, 3rd ed., 1996, "The Nazi Myth," trans. Brian Holmes, *Critical Inquiry* 16 [1990]), "La panique politique," *Cahiers Confrontation* 2 (1979, "La panique politique," trans. Simon Sparks, *Retreating the Political*, 1997), "Le peuple juif ne rêve pas," *La psychanalyse est-elle une histoire juive?* (ed. Jean-Jacques Rassial and Adélie Rassial, 1980, trans. Brian Holmes, "The Unconscious Is Destructured Like an Affect" and "From Where is Psychoanalysis Possible?," *Stanford Literature Review* 6–8 [1989–1991]), *Rejouer le politique* (1981), *Le retrait du politique* (1983); Jean-Luc Nancy and Philippe Lacoue-Labarthe, eds., *Les fins de l'homme: À partir du travail de Jacques Derrida* (1981); Jean-Luc Nancy and Mathilde Monnier, *Dehors la danse* (2001); Jean-Luc Nancy and Claudio Parmiggiani, *Coeur ardent/Cuore ardente* (2003).

Narratology

Narratology is a specific way of understanding narrative that developed out of STRUCTURALISM and Russian formalism. While "narratology" is sometimes misleadingly used to describe any form of narrative analysis, the term properly refers to a particular period and type of such analysis. What characterizes narratology most clearly is a systematic and disinterested approach to the workings of narrative. This approach opposes interpretive models that observe or seek out "value" in certain narratives or provide hierarchies of narratives based on categories such as the author's "genius."

The ultimate historical ancestor of narratology is Aristotle (c. 384–322 BC), whose *Poetics* offers a prescriptive guide to the workings of poetry, including dramatic narrative poetry. While narrative is not considered explicitly in *Poetics*, it is implicitly embedded in Aristotle's forms of tragedy, comedy and epic. Although Western letters sporadically included observations on the forms of narrative during the next two thousand years, it is generally believed that the mode of literary theory retrospectively attributed to Aristotle did not reappear in concerted form until the twentieth century. The work of the Russian formalists in the 1920s, and especially that of folklorist Vladimir Propp, provided a more recent foundation for modern narratology. Emerging out of FERDINAND DE SAUSSURE's *Course in General Linguistics* (1916), structuralism began to infiltrate other areas of the human sciences, especially narrative theory. The procedure employed by structuralist anthropologist Claude Lévi-Strauss to interrogate the structure of myths, for example, provided a blueprint for narratology. The structuralist methods developed by literary analysts such as Algirdas Julien Greimas and Claude Bremond furthered this growing movement. As structuralism advanced within the human sciences in European and Anglo-American academia, so too did structuralist-orientated literary theory. ROLAND BARTHES's essay "Introduction to the Structural Analysis of Narratives" (1966) and Tzvetan Todorov's *Grammaire du Décaméron* (1969), the latter of which actually coined the term "narratologie," represented the birth of narratology proper, paving the way for thinkers such as Mieke Bal, Seymour Chatman, Dorrit Cohn, Gérard Genette, and Gerald Prince.

Encouraging the study of all modes of narrative, narratology grew out of the structuralist imperative to subject different forms to a "neutral" method of questioning. Narratology also drew inspiration from SEMIOTICS, an emergent field concerned with the nature of signs. Theoretically, narratology can identify the key structuring devices in narratives appearing in media as diverse as oral language, writing, mime, visual, audio and audiovisual media and electronic texts. Such analysis seeks to refer to core concepts translatable across media and forms, as well as to concepts developed to describe the specificities of particular forms within given media.

The tacit idea underpinning all narratology, however, is that narrative is part of the general process of *representation* that is embedded in human discourse. This view holds that the world is not given to humans in pure form but is instead always mediated or re-presented. STUART HALL suggests that there are three general approaches to the question of representation. The "reflective" approach sees meaning as residing in the person or thing in the real world, with a representation "reflecting" that meaning. The "intentional" approach sees meaning in the control exercised by the producer of a representation; she or he "uses" representation to make the world "mean." The "constructionist" approach locates meaning neither in the control of the producer nor in the thing represented. Instead, it identifies the thoroughly social nature of the *construction* of meaning. Narratology generally embraces the "constructionist" perspective as its guiding principle, seeing in narrative form the organization, possibility, and producer of narrative meaning.

In narratology, the most fundamental elements of representation are "story," "plot," and, indeed, "narrative" itself. While no narratological approach can proceed without some conception of each term, narratologists do not unanimously agree on precise definitions. Moreover, in common parlance, "story" and "narrative," as well as "story" and "plot" are constantly conflated. The effort to differentiate between "story" and "plot" began with the Russian formalists, in particular Viktor Shklovsky's influential distinction between *fabula* ("raw material of a story") and *sjuzet* ("the way a story is organized"). Anglophone narratologists generally translate these terms as "story" and "discourse" (Chatman). Genette, on the other hand, relies on the French terms "récit" and "discours" ("narrative" and "discourse") to distinguish between the events of a narrative and how these events are "arranged" by the devices and figures of narrative that are customarily identified by narratology. Ultimately, all these terms recognize that narratives consist of a "presentation" of something, which is always, in fact, a re-presentation. Alternatively, it might be said that *story* consists of "all the events that take place in a narrative"; *plot* consists of the "underlying causality that binds these events together"; and *narrative* is the manner by which "all these events with underlying causality are narrated" (Cobley).

These fundamental distinctions were developed by the immediate precursors of the main narratological enterprise that came after Russian formalism. Both Propp and Lévi-Strauss undertake analyses of narrative that focus on "story" or, in Lévi-Strauss's case, "semantic structure." In *Morphology of the Folktale* (1928) Propp examined one hundred Russian folk stories. Rather than attending to surface differences, Propp explored underlying commonalities, particularly the basic function of actions. Propp identified thirty-one functions characterizing the tales: for example, "An interdiction is addressed to the hero"; and "The hero marries and ascends the throne." Propp also isolated the seven basic roles of characters in his sample, identifying the particular sphere of action to which each—the hero, the villain, the princess and her father, the dispatcher, the donor, the helper, and the false hero—belonged.

Lévi-Strauss' method of myth analysis is often taken to be synonymous with that of Propp, despite the fact that, in 1960, Lévi-Strauss wrote a scathing assessment of the Russian's work (*Structural Anthropology*). Lévi-Strauss' approach to myth followed the model offered by his linguistic analysis, which examined the set of oppositions between the smallest possible elements of language. His celebrated dissection of the Oedipus story identifies various key events, actions, or relationships as fundamental elements of myth, or "mythemes." Lévi-Strauss then rearranges these elements in a table in order to demonstrate their identical functions in the narrative. Following this procedure for the Oedipus story, it is possible to see that mythemes such as "The Spartoi kill one another," "Oedipus kills his father, Laius" and "Eteocles kills his brother, Polynices" all go together as elements having to do with murder in this particular structure. The narrative, when isolated from a reader's surface involvement with its sequence, evinces just a small number of such repetitive relations that reveal the purpose of the story (Lévi-Strauss, "Structure and Form").

Equally crucial to narratology are the categories introduced by Greimas. Most importantly, Greimas emphasizes the functional nature of Propp's "dramatis personae" by referring, instead, to "actants." "Actants" or "actantial roles" are defined in relation to each other, in relation to their place in the narrative's "spheres of action" or "functions" and in relation to their place in the logic of a narrative. In Greimas's revision of the *roles* of dramatis personae, the actants comprise a set of *categories* such as "subject vs. object," "sender vs. receiver," and "helper vs. opponent." Narrative meaning in this formulation plays out through various functions: the "subject" *searches for* the "object"; the "sender" is on a quest, and so on. Additionally, Greimas explores the way in which narrative structure can be defined by the interaction of "positive" and "negative" functions, such as the opposition between a relationship designated A, consisting of "command/behest" (*a*) and "acceptance" (*non-a*), and a relationship designated A⁻ consisting of "violation" (*non-a⁻*) and "interdiction" (*a⁻*). Ultimately, Greimas posits a "semiotic square" of such coordinates as a tool for the analysis of narrative meaning.

In 1966, the same year that Greimas published *Structural Semantics*, the French journal *Communications* published a special edition containing essays by Barthes and Todorov. This edition adopted for a projected narratology the agenda set by Propp, Greimas, Lévi-Strauss, and others. In his "Introduction to the Structural Analysis of Narratives," Barthes proposes three *levels* of narrative: *functions* (following Propp), *actions* (citing Greimas) and *narration* (derived from Todorov). From Lévi-Strauss, Barthes also invokes the injunction to "dechronologize" narrative in a manner not dissimilar to the "synchronic" reworking of the Oedipus myth. "Both language and narrative," Barthes asserts, "know only a semiotic time, 'true' time being a 'realist,' referential illusion" (99). Barthes's treatment of narration, however, departs significantly from the fathers of narratology. Barthes's "narration" does not just include "content," "raw story matter," or the arrangement of *fabula* but also contemplation of what are now standard narratological foci, such as the role of the narrator and point of view.

While the question of "narrative levels" had been posed in literary criticism well before the advent of narratology, the systematization of issues pertaining to narration produced a sea change within literary theory. Before narratology, literary criticism frequently assumed that narratives were produced by authoritative individuals and consumed by painstaking readers. Narratologists such as Genette, Chatman, and Bal implicitly took Barthes's cue to problematize this view of narrative "transmission." Summarizing their work, Shlomith Rimmon-Kenan identifies the following participants in narrative, each of which might seem to aid the act of transmission but may equally "interfere" with it. Empirical entities named a "real author" and a "real reader" appear at each pole of the communication process (sending and receiving, respectively). These are placed in the company of other mediators in a narrative fiction, such as "implied author," "narrator," "narratee," and "implied reader" (Rimmon-Kenan 86; see also Gibson, "Authors"). As the organizing principle of the text, the implied author is responsible for the presentation of the text's materials: the ordering of scenes, the narration of certain objects and events, the structure of the plot, and so forth. The narrator is the "voice" that tells the story in the first or third person, sometimes as a character and, on occasion, "omnisciently." Theoretically, the narratee is the ideal entity to whom the text is narrated. The narratee is bracketed in this schema because, invariably, it is not possible to separate this entity from the implied reader (unless there is a represented audience in the text). Narratology's investigation of these textual coordinates demonstrates the complexity of narrative levels, dealing a blow to those in literary criticism who believe that the only impediment to "comprehension" of the "core meaning" of a narrative is a lack of cultured appreciation of canonical texts.

Questions pertaining to the discourse of the narrator or the implied author are logically connected to the issue of "point of view." Prior to the advent of narratology, arguments about this distinction in narrative revolved around the perceived efficiency of "showing" (by depicting story events through someone's point of view) vs. "telling" (through narratorial observations, sometimes made from an omniscient viewpoint). Narratology circumvents questions of value by formalizing analysis and focusing on what actually happens when events or objects in a narrative are "focalized" (Genette, *Narrative Discourse*) or "filtered" (Chatman, *Coming to Terms*) in a specific way. The exploration of issues of focalization reexamine in more detail those questions of authority raised by Émile Benveniste's protonarratological distinction between "histoire" and "discours."

Another area of concern to narratology is that of time or "duration." While its ultimate reference may be the movement of the clock, time in narrative does not necessarily unfold in linear fashion. Genette, for example, uses the term "analepsis" to describe the effect whereby a narrative moves backwards in time to depict events that have taken place *before* those most recently narrated. The reverse effect is "prolepsis" or "flash-forward." Both phenomena involve the narrative opting to choose some things or events rather than others, a method also employed by the features of narrative usually called "summary and scene." Summary within a narrative *tells* about events or people without directly presenting their speech. Scene, conversely, bears affinities with dramatic narrative: it *shows* the events and, more often than not, contains speech imitated through the use of quotation marks (Bal 104–5).

Criticisms of narratology can be boiled down to one ineluctable issue and several subsidiary ones. One of the most frequent subsidiary criticisms contends that narratological models are reductive and fail to apprehend the richness of narrative, neglecting, for example, the multifaceted nature of the characters. While there is some truth in this complaint, it should be noted that narratologists never explicitly deny such features of narrative. Further, it is clear that narratology is, in some senses, a self-consciously "general" exercise that attempts to account for *all* kinds of narrative. Another common subsidiary criticism is that the approach of narratology is static or that it provides a synchronic view of narrative without paying attention to the dynamic interaction of narrative elements. As with Saussurean linguistics, narratology appears constrained by a resolutely synchronic perspective. It has even been suggested that one handicap of narratology is that it is unable to think beyond the bounds of the "end" of narrative (Cobley).

It has also been argued that narratology neglects the pragmatics of narrative by failing to take into account the contextual factors that might govern the manner in which a narrative operates. Most narratives are accompanied by a relay indicating the mode and characteristics of the narrative enacted. Importantly, narratives also take place in specified situations; they are textually demarked as separate from ongoing discourse: the preliminary statement "I want to tell you a story" has a different bearing when addressed to a gathering around a campfire three thousand years ago, when appearing at the beginning of a nineteenth-century novel, and when uttered by a twenty-first-century stand-up comedian to an audience in a nightclub. Not only is it a relay indicating that a narrative will take place; it also operates in conjunction with the setting that tells what kind of narrative will take place and what kind of response should be elicited. A narratological analysis cannot examine all these factors: it can do no more than list the formal properties of the enacted narrative and attempt to show how its components interact.

One of the most noted criticisms of narratology appears in Paul Ricoeur's three-volume work *Time and Narrative* (1983). Ricoeur holds that time is not simply a part of the narrative apparatus but that narrative *is* the human relation to time. Ricoeur insists that the kind of temporality encountered in narrative has more to do with the interpretative mode of "expectation-memory-attention" than with the commonplace version of time as a series of instants arranged along a line. For Ricoeur, the end point of a narrative is crucial, and the anticipation of the conclusion dictates the understanding of successive actions, thoughts, and feelings ("Narrative Time"). From this perspective, the cornerstone of narrative structure is plot, or what Ricoeur, borrowing from Aristotle, calls "muthos" or "emplotment." Ricoeur chides narratology for the way it "dechronologizes" narrative and reduces it to a series of dominating "paradigmatic" functions, leaving sequence to the mercy of the linear interpretation of time.

Informing both Ricoeur's comments and the subsidiary criticisms of narratology is a deeper critique of the *text-centerdness* of narratology. Since the inception of narratology, there has been a growing awareness within literary theory of the need to consider how readers make meanings (see READER-RESPONSE CRITICISM). Furthermore, disciplines whose development has been influenced by narratology— such as media, communications, and CULTURAL STUDIES—have been dominated in the last twenty years by attempts to achieve an understanding of audiences' receptions of texts. Narratology's focus on textual constituents curtails its ability to explore readers' investment in semantic features of texts, how readers are engaged or moved by "muthos" or plot, how readers receive "cues" to their investments by the pragmatic aspects of texts, and how readers' perception in time is carried over into the very fabric of individual narratives.

Arguably, narratology represents a high point in the analytic turn that included Russian formalism, Prague structuralism, the Copenhagen school, and French structuralism and poststructuralism. As such, it attempts to take a *neutral* rather than prescriptive approach to textual analysis. Bal's vision of a "return" to narratology is just one indication that the narratological enterprise is still needed to help with the task of understanding the relatively limited number of reading *practices* that exist and the tendency of narratives to be understood as belonging to certain genres.

PAUL COBLEY

Aristotle, *Poetics* (trans. Malcolm Heath, 1996); Mieke Bal, *De Theorie van vertellen en verhalen* (1978, *Narratology: Introduction to the Theory of Narrative*, trans. Christine van Boheemen, 1985); Roland Barthes, "Introduction à l'analyse structurale des récits" *Communications* 8 (1966) ("Introduction to the Structural Analysis of Narratives," *Image-Music-Text*, ed. and trans. Stephen Heath, 1977), *S/Z* (1970, *S/Z*, trans. Richard Miller, 1974); Émile Benveniste, *Problèmes de linguistique générale* (1966–1974, *Problems in General Linguistics*, trans. Mary Elizabeth Meek, 1971); Wayne C. Booth, *The Rhetoric of Fiction* (1961); Edward Branigan, *Point of View in the Cinema: A Theory of Narration and Subjectivity in Classical Film* (1984), "Point of View in the Fiction Film," *Wide Angle* 8 (1986); Claude Bremond, *Logique du récit* (1973), "Morphology of the French Folktale," *Semiotica* 2 (1970); Peter Brooks, *Reading for the Plot: Design and Intention in Narrative* (1984); Seymour Chatman, *Coming to Terms: The Rhetoric of Narrative in Fiction and Film* (1990), *Story and Discourse: Narrative Structure in Fiction and Film* (1978); Paul Cobley, *Narrative* (2001); Dorrit Cohn, "Narrated Monologue: Definition of a Fictional Style," *Comparative Literature* 18 (1996); Dorrit Cohn and Gérard Genette, "A Narratological Exchange, " *Neverending Stories: Towards a Critical Narratology* (ed. Ann Fehn et al., 1992); Frank Collins and Paul Perron, eds. *Paris School Semiotics* (2 vols., 1989); Laurence Coupe, *Myth* (1997); Monika Fludernik, *Towards a "Natural" Narratology* (1996); Gérard Genette, *Figures*, vol. 3 (1972, partial trans., *Narrative Discourse: An Essay in Method*, trans. Jane E. Lewin, 1980), "Frontières du récit," *Communications* 8

(1966) ("Frontiers of Narrative," *Figures of Discourse*, trans. Alan Sheridan, 1982), *Nouveau discours du récit* (1983, *Narrative Discourse Revisited*, trans. Jane E. Lewin, 1988); Andrew Gibson, *Towards a Postmodern Theory of Narrative* (1996); Walker Gibson, "Authors, Speakers, Readers, and Mock Readers," *Reader-Response Criticism: From Formalism to Post-Structuralism* (ed. Jane P. Tompkins, 1980); Algirdas Julian Greimas, *Narrative Semiotics and Cognitive Discourse* (trans. Frank Collins and Paul Perron, 1990), *Sémantique structurale: Recherche de méthode* (1966, *Structural Semantics: An Attempt at Method*, trans. Danielle McDowell, Ronald Schleifer, and Alan Velie, 1983); Stuart Hall, "The Work of Representation," *Representation: Cultural Representations and Signifying Practices* (1997); Jeremy Hawthorn, *Studying the Novel* (1985, 4th ed., 2001); Michael Kearns, *Rhetorical Narratology* (1999); Claude Lévi-Strauss, *Anthropologie structurale* (1958, *Structural Anthropology*, 2 vols., trans. Claire Jacobson, Brooke Grundfest Schoepf, and Monique Layton, 1963–1977), "La structure et la forme: Réflexions sur un ouvrage de Vladimir Propp," *Cahiers de l'Institute de science economique appliquee* 99 (1960) ("Structure and Form: Reflections on a Work by Vladimir Propp," *Structural Anthropology*, vol. 2); David Lodge, *The Art of Fiction* (1992); Percy Lubbock, *The Craft of Fiction* (1926); Gerald Prince, *Narratology: The Form and Functioning of Narrative* (1982), "On Narratology: Criteria, Corpus, Context," *Narrative* 3 (1995); Vladimir Propp, *Morfologiia skazki* (1928, *Morphology of the Folktale*, trans. Laurence Scott, 1968); Paul Ricoeur, "Discussion: Ricoeur on Narrative," *On Paul Ricoeur: Narrative and Interpretation* (ed. David Wood, 1991), "Narrative Time," *On Narrative* (ed. W. J. T. Mitchell, 1981), *Temps et récit*, 3 vols. (1983–1985, *Time and Narrative*, 3 vols., trans. Kathleen McLaughlin and David Pellauer, 1984–1988); Shlomith Rimmon-Kenan, *Narrative Fiction: Contemporary Poetics* (1983); Marie-Laure Ryan, "Linguistic Models in Narratology: From Structuralism to Generative Semantics," *Semiotica* 28 (1979); Ferdinand de Saussure, *Cours de linguistique générale* (ed. Charles Bally and Albert Sechehaye, 1916, *Course in General Linguistics*, trans. Wade Baskin, 1959, trans. Roy Harris, 1983); Tzvetan Todorov, *Grammaire du Décaméron* (1969), "La grammaire du récit," *Langages* 12 (1968) ("The Grammar of Narrative," *The Poetics of Prose*, trans. Richard Howard, 1977), *Poétique* (1973, *Introduction to Poetics*, trans. Richard Howard, 1980).

National Literature

National literature as a concept emerged in close conjunction with modern nationalism in the late eighteenth century. Modern nationalism is distinctive from earlier forms of patriotism in defining the nation through the people as a whole, unified by the culture (language, customs, laws, the arts) and history they share, as well as the land on which they collectively live. National literature was both a synecdoche for that national culture and, through anthologies and institutionalized curricula, an efficient means by which it could be recirculated to domestic audiences to reinforce the national culture's unifying project. Organized historically, national literature also served as evidence of national maturity or advancement and was thus both a source of national pride and a register of national merit to international audiences.

Modern nationalism arose during the transition between the Enlightenment and Romantic eras, uncomfortably uniting disparate principles from the two philosophical movements (see Smith, "Neo-classicist"). Drawing on Enlightenment principles (such as John Locke's ideas of government), nationalism shifted the foundation of state's sovereignty from the monarch, authorized by divine right, to the people as a whole, based on their collective rights as sovereign subjects. While ideas of a sovereign subject who participates in a modern, bureaucratized nation-state were being developed and institutionalized, Romantic nationalism arose to argue for a feeling nation rather than a rational one. Johann Gottfried von Herder influentially suggested that the people and culture of the nation were tied ineluctably, even organically, to the land (climate, terrain, location). This privileging of organicism, origins, and emotional affect produced a Romantic nationalism that envisioned the people not as a collectivity of individuals working together (as Locke would have it) but as the naturally unified, even uniform, embodiment of distinctive national principles and characteristics.

The Enlightenment aspects of nationalism could facilitate anti-imperial movements, challenging the imperial power with the inherent rights of the indigenous population to govern themselves and their land. The Romantic aspects could generate a unifying and emotionally powerful sense of an "imagined community," to use Benedict Anderson's popular phrase, but could also lead nationalist movements in a fascist vein through the incipient racism of submerging individual variances in a singular national identity physiologically determined by the land. Hippolyte Taine's Herderian insistence on the centrality of "the race, the surroundings, and the era" (1:10) to the shaping of national culture is part of the wedding of literature to more racial ideas in the nineteenth century.

In literary study, when nationalist theory is invoked, Anderson's *Imagined Communities* has tended to dominate, partly because it has a relevant emphasis on print culture and the power of imagination. Nationalism theory is, however, much more diverse: key statements on nationalism include volumes and essays by Anthony D.

Smith, Ernest Gellner, Tom Nairn, and E. J. Hobsbawm, as well as Anderson's larger corpus. There is general consensus about what nationalism does: it defines the nation through the people as a whole in terms of a shared but distinctive language, culture, history, and territory, and it promotes strong emotional commitment to and even a desire to sacrifice oneself on behalf of, the nation. Consensus breaks down, however, on the question of how nationalism exerts such power—on whether nationalism itself is fundamentally populist (rooted in the people's authentic experience of and commitment to nationality) or a tool of hegemony—and, as a related problem, on how and why nationalism emerged in the late eighteenth century or whether it emerged much earlier.

In "Long-Distance Nationalism" first delivered as a lecture in 1992, Anderson builds on Lord Acton's 1862 pronouncement that "exile is the nursery of nationality" (59) to argue that nationalism emerges in response to GLOBALIZATION. Nationalism functions as a way of tying subjects firmly to the originating nation through culture and emotional affect on terms that do not require Herderian physical contact with the land and counteract the cultural mixings that the lowering price of print and travel technologies makes possible. Gellner, Hobsbawm, and others, coming out of a Marxist historical tradition, argue for nationalism as an interpellative tool of hegemony, soliciting the cooperation and standardization necessary to modernity. Smith's early work on the philosophical roots of nationalism generally avoid this question, but his recent books have insisted on affect as the ground of the ideology rather than the other way around (dismissing the work of Anderson and Hobsbawm as "social constructionism"). Interest in the transnational—Paul Gilroy's *Black Atlantic*, the emergence of transatlantic studies, multiculturalism, and, most significantly, POSTCOLONIAL STUDIES—has led to discussions of the limits of nationalism for grasping the myriad material and textual relations between individuals and peoples.

Given nationalism's requirement of a common national culture, it takes considerable effort to both define that culture and recirculate it as such to solicit popular knowledge of, and assent to its status as, the national culture. National literature—codified in anthologies, taught in schools, and invested with all the weight of cultural capital—has been a key part of this larger effort. As RAYMOND WILLIAMS notes, "the term *Nationalliteratur* began in Germany in the 1780s, and histories of 'national literatures' . . . were being written in German, French, and English from the same period in which there was a major change in ideas both of 'the nation' and of 'cultural nationality' " (53). National literature countered the long-standing dominance of classical culture, almost exclusively available to formally educated men of the upper classes in the eighteenth century, by sanctioning a vernacular culture in which all members of the nation, by definition, participate. Hence, it is a cliché of nineteenth-century writing that national literature reflects "the mind of a nation"—a phrase that appears in connection with national literature, for instance, in essays by

Harriet Martineau (3:206), William Johnson Fox (3:51), and Henry Wadsworth Long-fellow (377), and in anonymous contributions to *Blackwood's Edinburgh Magazine* (109) and *The Christian Reformer* (612). As such, it could also educate an international audi-ence on the nation's merits: "A country which has no national literature, or a litera-ture too insignificant to force its way abroad, must always be, to its neighbours, an unknown and misestimated country" (Carlyle 309). In Romanticism, national litera-ture also represents the land that defines the national subject, from Samuel Taylor Coleridge's apostrophe to Britain as his "Mother Isle"—"from thy lakes and mountain-hills, / Thy clouds, thy quiet dales, thy rocks and seas, / [I] Have drunk in all my intel-lectual life" (182, 184–86)—to Ralph Waldo Emerson's declaration that "America is a poem" (41).

In 1891, Walt Whitman declared that the United States consists of "forty-four Nations curiously and irresistibly blent and aggregated in ONE NATION, with one imperial language, and one unitary set of social and legal standards over all—and (I predict) a yet to be National Literature" (333), framing national literature as a late stage in the development of national culture—first comes a dominant (and dominat-ing) language, then laws, then literature. Thus, before *Nationalliteratur*, print was used to normalize language itself through the proliferation of dictionaries to stan-dardize language use. Samuel Johnson's 1747 *Plan* for his influential 1755 *Dictionary* sought to "preserve the purity" of English, partly by excluding professional jargons on the grounds that "they are generally derived from other nations" (4) and thus rely-ing on a conflation of national authenticity with uncontaminated derivation that would be significant in modern nationalism, especially in its more conservative forms. But, while national literature offered a vision of a unified national culture—in which, as Williams puts it, "the actually very diverse works of writers in English are composed into a national identity" (54)—from the start there were divisions in con-ceptualizations of that culture.

Most crucially, a distinction between the oral culture of the *volk* (songs, tales, beliefs) and the print culture of the literate, often urban, middle and upper classes was posited early on. Generally, the first was valorized as the remainder of an au-thentic ur-nationality and the second as evidence of cultural advancement and inter-national prestige. In England, they are exemplified by Bishop Percy's *Reliques of An-cient English Poetry* (1765) and Thomas Warton's *History of English Poetry* (1774): Percy stresses ballads and songs, insistently oral forms he grounds in a specifically English tradition of minstrelsy; Warton pays special attention to the sonnet and romances, both derived from non-English literatures and prevalent across much of Europe. Warton stresses civility and the march of progress, while Percy emphasizes authen-ticity. Percy helped to foster interest in the remote past as the ground of national identity. The division continues in the academic distinction between literary study and anthropology or folklore studies.

Defined as an advanced cultural form, (print) literature not only exemplified the national culture but also demonstrated its value and maturity in relation to other cultures, a distinction that David Lloyd has addressed in terms of ideas of "major" (universal, fully developed) and "minor" (idiosyncratic, underdeveloped) literatures, used to authorize the maturity of the metropole (and so its right to rule) by defining colonized nations as "juvenile"—an argument readily extended to cultures marginalized by the dominant "national" culture, such as working-class culture or regional cultures. The shift from an elite classicism to a more populist vernacular did not fully follow the theoretical politics of nationalism in transferring (cultural) power to the people as a whole or to the rural populations that were, by virtue of their connection to the land and disconnection from modernity (defined in terms of print literacy and cosmopolitanism), posited as remainders of an authentic national culture by such writers as Friedrich Schiller and William Wordsworth. National literature, as defined in print and in schools, remained largely the product of the elite who continued to work in the verse forms derived from classical and courtly cultures (ode, sonnet, epic, lyric, romance) or who mediated the oral forms of the past and rural culture for middle- and upper-class audiences through scholarly editions, complete with learned introductions and notes.

Positing a close correlation between a valuable national literature and a worthy nation was a key feature of early discussions of national literature. Thus, when new nations emerged from the European tradition in the Americas, the creation of a national literature became a nationalist imperative. In the United States, soon after Henry Clay offered his 1829 proposals for unifying the nation economically, diverse authors issued statements urging the creation and/or improvement of a distinctively American national literature. In his 1830 *The Importance and Means of a National Literature*, Clergyman William Channing defines national literature as a "public good" (4) for its "manifestation of a nation's intellect in the only forms by which it can multiply itself at home, and send itself abroad" (4) and for its role in the nation's "improvement" in "moral and intellectual power" (5). Serving this "public good" required not only essays urging the development of national literature—whether by avoiding certain genres, as Joseph Rocchietti argued, or breaking from foreign models, as former U.S. government official Peter Du Ponceau suggests in his 1834 *A Discourse on the Necessity and the Means of Making Our National Literature Independent of that of Great Britain*—but also its institutionalization through curricula in schools and, by the end of the nineteenth century, universities, as well as the continued publication of anthologies for home and school use. "National literature" became increasingly entrenched as a valuable—even necessary—branch of knowledge for the modern national subject, and that premise is still reflected not only in curricula but also in many nations' government funding of the arts. In the twentieth century, arguments for a national literature have often stressed this institutional dimension. Ngũgĩ wa Thiong'o's important essay "On the Abolition of the English Department" (1972), for instance, challenges the dominance of English studies in Africa on this basis, arguing for the placement of African literature at the center of African curricula.

About the same time, critiques of the institutionalization of national literature began drawing on Marxist cultural theory of the 1960s, especially ANTONIO GRAM-SCI's idea of hegemony. In 1968, Perry Anderson called for an "attack on the reactionary and mystifying culture inculcated in universities and colleges," particularly because "the Left has never truly questioned this 'national' inheritance which is one of the most enduring bonds of its subordination" (3, 4). Brian Doyle, in his account of the institutionalization of English literary study, critiques the ways the discipline, "by legitimizing only the study of 'valuable works,' . . . manufactured an essential and unbridgeable cultural distance between its own sphere of high art and the general domain of popular fiction and discourse" (6). Rarely invoking the term "nationalism," such critiques focus on class to argue that traditional literary study has failed to properly reflect the national culture precisely because it has represented the literature of the nation's elite. More recently, sociological analyses of national literature have emerged, such as Sarah Corse's *Nationalism and Literature*, understanding canon formation and the institutionalization of literary study as political processes through which nations are created under the guise of being represented.

Following the rise of postcolonial theory and the study of world literature in the West, the role of nationalism per se in the production of national literature came more to the fore. Christopher Clausen begins his 1994 essay polemically and tacitly drawing on multiculturalism: "The concept of 'national literatures' in English has outlived its usefulness and should be abandoned, both as a way of thinking about literary history and as a way of organizing curricula" (61). Clausen separates the study of national literature from the study of nationalism in literature, and contends that "to assert that literature in English is more profitably conceived as a variegated whole than subdivided along national lines is not to minimize the importance to a writer or reader of living in a specific place, a particular nation, or a distinct culture" (62), nearly echoing, though on different grounds, Taine's famous phrase. Such interrogations of the traditional study of national literature argue for the discarding of the modernist narrative of coherent national development for a postmodern one that is decentered, multifaceted, and particularized. But that historicizing move to particularity reiterates a Herderian emphasis on the determinisms of material surroundings ("the importance to a writer or reader of living in a specific place") even as it discards the national in favor of the transnational, the regional, and the liminal.

Despite these critiques, however, national literature remains deeply entrenched in institutionalized literary study; it is akin to MICHEL FOUCAULT's "author-function" in its persistence as a way of conceptually organizing a body of work and making claims for both its internal coherence and distinctness from other bodies of work. Classes, anthologies, categories of academic expertise, and government programs still rely on "American literature," "British literature," "Canadian literature," and so forth to define national cultures that are, if no longer so unreflectively or obviously tied to "the race" still yoked firmly to "the surroundings and the epoch."

JULIA M. WRIGHT

See also MARXIST THEORY AND CRITICISM, MULTICULTURALISM, POSTCOLONIAL STUDIES 2: 1990 AND AFTER, and RACE AND ETHNICITY.

Benedict Anderson, *Imagined Communities: Reflections on the Origin and Spread of Nationalism* (1983, rev. ed., 1991), "Long-Distance Nationalism," *The Spectre of Comparisons: Nationalism, Southeast Asia, and the World* (1998); Perry Anderson, "Components of the National Culture," *New Left Review* 50 (1968); F. M. Barnard, "National Culture and Political Legitimacy: Herder and Rousseau," *Journal of the History of Ideas* 44 (1983); David A. Bell, *The Cult of the Nation in France: Inventing Nationalism, 1680–1800* (2001); Thomas Carlyle, "State of German Literature," *Edinburgh Review* 92 (1827); William Ellery Channing, *The Importance and Means of a National Literature* (1830); Christopher Clausen, "'National Literature' in English: Toward a New Paradigm," *New Literary History* 25 (1994); Samuel Taylor Coleridge, "Fears in Solitude," *Coleridge: The Complete Poems* (ed. William Keach, 1997); Sarah M. Corse, *Nationalism and Literature: The Politics of Culture in Canada and the United States* (1997); Brian Doyle, *England and Englishness* (1989); Ralph Waldo Emerson, "The Poet," *Essays: Second Series* (1844); Michel Foucault, "Qu'est-ce qu'un auteur?," *Bulletin de la societe francaise de philosophie* 73 (1969) ("What is an Author?," trans. Josue V. Harari, *Foucault Reader*, ed. Paul Rabinow, 1984); William Johnson Fox, *Lectures Addressed Chiefly to the Working Classes* (4 vols., 1846); Ernest Gellner, *Nations and Nationalism* (1983); Paul Gilroy, *The Black Atlantic: Modernity and Double Consciousness* (1993); Arthur Henry Hallam, "On Some of the Characteristics of Modern Poetry, and On the Lyrical Poems of Alfred Tennyson," *Englishman's Magazine* 1 (1831); Johann Gottfried von Herder, *Idee zur Philosophie de Geschichte de Menschheit* (1784–1791, *Outlines of a Philosophy of the History of Man*, trans. T. Churchill, 1800); Eric J. Hobsbawm, *Nations and Nationalism since 1780: Programme, Myth, Reality* (1990); Samuel Johnson, *The Plan of a Dictionary of the English Language* (1747); David Lloyd, *Nationalism and Minor Literature: James Clarence Mangan and the Emergence of Irish Cultural Nationalism* (1987); John Locke, *Two Treatises of Government* (1689); Henry Wadsworth Longfellow, "Anglo-Saxon Literature" *North American Review* (July 1838); Harriet Martineau, *Society in America* (2nd ed., 3 vols., 1839); Ngũgĩ wa Thiong'o, "On the Abolition of the English Department," *The Post-Colonial Studies Reader* (ed. Bill Ashcroft, Gareth Griffiths, and Helen Tiffin, 1995); "Of a National Character in Literature," *Blackwood's Edinburgh Magazine* 3 (1818); "On the Gulistan of Sadi," *Christian Reformer* 9 (1853); Thomas Percy, *Reliques of Ancient English Poetry* (1765); Elizabeth Sauer and Julia M. Wright, eds., *Reading the Nation in English Literature: A Critical Reader* (2010); Friedrich Schiller, *Über naïve und sentimentalische Dichtung* (1795, *On the Naive and Sentimental in Literature*, trans. Helen Watanabe-O'Kell, 1981); Anthony D. Smith, *Chosen Peoples: Sacred Sources of National Identity* (2003), *The Nation in History: Historiographical Debates about Ethnicity and Nationalism* (2000), *National Identity* (1986), "Neo-Classicist and Romantic Elements in the Emergence of Nationalist Conceptions," *Nationalist Movements* (ed. Anthony D. Smith, 1976); Hippolyte Taine, *Histoire de la littérature anglaise* (4 vols., 1863–1864, *History of English Literature*, trans. H. Van Laun, 4 vols., 1864); Brook Thomas, ed., "National Literary Histories," special issue, *MLQ* 64 (2003); Thomas Warton, *The History of English Poetry, from the Close of the Eleventh to the Commencement of the Eighteenth Century* (4 vols., 1774); Walt Whitman, "Have We a National Literature?" *North American Review* 152 (1891); Raymond Williams, "Marxism, Structuralism and Literary Analysis," *New Left Review* 129 (1981); William Wordsworth, Preface to *Lyrical Ballads* (1802); Julia M. Wright, "'The Order of Time': Nationalism and Literary Anthologies, 1774–1831," *Papers on Language and Literature* 33 (1997).

Native Theory and Criticism

1. United States

Native American theory and criticism in its historical and theoretical practices is inevitably a contemporary phenomenon. The beginning of the field of Native American literary criticism can be approximately dated to the year 1977, when the Modern Language Association and the National Endowment for the Humanities held a joint curriculum development seminar in Flagstaff, Arizona. This first gathering of scholars and Native writers such as Paula Gunn Allen and Leslie Marmon Silko generated significant discussion and also launched books, scholarly articles, journals, and conference sessions. However, as the editors of a recent anthology of Native American literature, John Purdy and James Ruppert, point out, much of this early criticism was "impressionistic, personal, explanatory, laudatory, and unsophisticated" (3), which is understandable given the rather marginal status of Native American writing in the mainstream academy at the time. A significant shift would occur in the 1990s, when Native American literary criticism opened up to postmodern, poststructuralist, and deconstructivist theories.

As theories that are aimed at dismantling the totalitarian philosophical assumptions of Western civilization and that emphasize the creative power of language and discourse, postmodern and poststructuralist arguments provide a viable framework within which to approach Native American literature, a literature of resistance conceived as a political and politicized activity of writing back to the dominant center. Native and non-Native critics alike have pointed out the political dimension of Native American literary texts in their combining Native/indigenous epistemology with Western literary forms. Louis Owens, for example, characterizes this balancing act as "a matrix of incredible heteroglossia and linguistic torsions" (*Other* 15). And James Ruppert envisions the dialogical relation between Native and non-Native discourse fields as an effective tool to "disrupt the easy engagement of the dominant literary discourse" (x). Critics such as Kimberley Blaeser, Elaine Jahner, Karl Kroeber, Arnold Krupat, Alan Velie, and Gerald Vizenor, among others, have written abundantly about the usefulness of poststructuralist and postmodern theories in interpreting Native American literary texts. In 1989 Vizenor edited *Narrative Chance*, the only collection of critical essays that announces a postmodern approach to Native American writing. In his 1983 "Poststructuralism and Oral Literature" Krupat had linked JACQUES DERRIDA's infinite deferral of signification to the oral tradition of tribal people, who, as he puts it, seemed not to be concerned with fixed meanings at all. However, while these postmodern/poststructuralist interpretations of Native American literary works have been crucial to illustrating the commonality between contemporary discourse and tribal literatures, they have not been able to adequately and accurately explore the unique voice of Native American literature, a literature that, though written in English using conventional Western discursive modes, relies extensively on elements from Native epistemologies, specifically the reality of myth and ceremony of traditional oral literature.

More recently, critics such as Carlton Smith and Jace Weaver, along with Krupat and Owens themselves, have turned to the rhetorical strategies of postcolonial theory to elucidate the hybridized nature of Native American written narratives. As a phenomenon involving a dialectical relation between indigenous cultural traditions and Western European forms, postcolonial theory provides useful interpretative tools for discussing the cross-cultural aspect of Native American literature. Despite the historical, geopolitical, and ideological differences between Native American cultures and postcolonial communities around the world, and even though Native American populations remain, as Weaver points out, "a colonized people, victims of internal colonialism" ("From I-Hermeneutics" 13), critics have argued that both Native American and postcolonial writers are engaging in an intensely subversive ideological project. In The Turn to the Native (1996) Krupat adopts the notion of "anti-imperial translation" as used by Talal Asad to conceptualize the tension between Native American fiction and imperialist discourse. Similarly, in Mixedblood Messages (1998) Owens relies on Mary Louise Pratt's concepts of "contact zones" and "transculturation" to discuss the literary production of Native American authors. And Smith, in Coyote Kills John Wayne (2000), applies HOMI K. BHABHA's notion of "the third space" as an interpretive lens through which read to Louise Erdrich's Turtle Mountain series of novels. However, like postmodern and poststructuralist readings, such critical interpretations once again impose the discourse of the privileged, critical center (even when such a discourse presents itself in loyal opposition to that "center") on marginalized Native texts, ultimately silencing the Native/indigenous voice(s) out of which these texts arise.

In the past few years, Native and non-Native scholars alike have been arguing for a critical discourse that originates from the Native/indigenous cultural context of the texts themselves rather than from external critical methods. In a 1993 essay titled "Native Literature: Seeking a Critical Center," Blaeser launches a significant challenge to contemporary Native American authors, adamantly calling for "a critical voice and method which moves from the culturally-centered text outwards toward the frontier of 'border' studies, rather than an external critical voice and method which seeks to penetrate, appropriate, colonize, or conquer the cultural center, and thereby change the stories or remake the literary meaning" (53). Although it might be premature to talk about an established school or a movement envisioned as a response to such a critical appeal, Native American authors of the past generation have begun to provide the critical center Blaeser has been looking for. They have started to generate a Native American critical discourse that is very different from earlier interpretations of Native American literature. As an emergent critical discourse, Native American theory thus appears as a complex hybridized project, one that, while deeply

embedded within the narratives of Native American oral tradition and Native epistemology, inevitably conducts a dialogue with the larger critical discourse of contemporary theory.

Given the heterogeneity of voices, a heterogeneity all the more significant if we
consider the diverse cultural backgrounds of the various authors, it is inaccurate to
regard Native American critical theory as a monolithic form of discourse. Specifically, we can single out two main trends characterizing Native American theory and
criticism. The first argues for a separatist form of discourse (Allen, Robert Warrior,
and Craig Womack) and is aimed at legitimating concepts such as tribalism, sovereignty, and self-determination as crucial to the process of decolonization. The second considers a dialogical, cross-cultural perspective (Greg Sarris, Owens, and Vizenor) to be the most subversive way to challenge the authoritative discourse of Western
hermeneutics. Representatives of what might be called "tribalist discourse" adamantly argue for a cultural separatism rigidly based on a Native perspective. Envisioning a criticism rooted in the land and culture of Native American communities
and focusing on issues of Native sovereignty and nationalism, they attempt to create
a Native resistance movement against colonialism. On the other hand, acknowledging the complex level of hybridization and cultural translation already operating in
any form of Native discourse, the result of more than five hundred years of cultural
contact and interaction, critics who argue for a dialogical approach find the most
creative tool of resistance in language, a tool through which Native people can constantly reimagine themselves. In terms similar to those elaborated in the oral tradition of tribal cultures, in which words and narratives have the power to create and to
heal, they turn to language as the most powerful means for ensuring life and vital
energies in Native American writing and identity in opposition to the stasis and traps
created by the stereotypes and clichés of Euro-American imagination.

Regardless of the critical stance they end up taking, crucial to Allen, Warrior,
Womack, Sarris, Owens, and Vizenor is the necessity of generating a critical discourse that originates primarily from the culturally centered and epistemological
orientation of the texts themselves and that uses indigenous discursive modes as the
basic interpretive tools of analysis. Within this context, they do find some common
ground on a few specific premises. A first primary assumption is the importance of
inscribing the function and nature of the oral tradition onto the written page, revi-
talizing and reimagining a tradition too often reduced, in the Euro-American imaginary, to merely cultural artifact. In one degree or another, all of the aforementioned
authors suggest meaningful ways in which Native American rhetoric and epistemology can enter the discourse of First World ideology, dismantling the notion that theory is the exclusive product of Western discourse. A second assumption, clearly related to the first, is the importance of conveying in writing the dynamic quality of the
oral exchange, so that despite the confinement of the printed text, the vitality and
power of language of the oral traditions are maintained. The most significant result

of this cross-cultural "translation," which might constitute a further point of encounter among the writers involved in this revisionist critical project, is the multigeneric, heteroglot, and border quality of their texts; in such texts, the traditionally objective, authoritative stance of the Western critic is significantly dismantled, and the text itself becomes, much like a story, an open form, one involving the direct participation of the reader or listener. Shifting between third and first person, between scholarly argument and personal narrative, weaving bits and pieces of various discourses, including songs from traditional rituals and ceremonies, Allen, Womack, Sarris, Owens, and Vizenor in particular (Warrior's rhetorical strategies in *Tribal Secrets* follow more closely Western hegemonic patterns) elaborate new creative ways of doing theory, ultimately challenging the West to reconsider the meanings of its own cultural tradition.

The idea of cross-reading and cross-cultural communication as ways of opening up new ways of thinking while exploring differing epistemologies constitutes the central motif of Sarris's *Keeping Slug Woman Alive* (1993) and Owens's *Mixedblood Messages*. Both critics argue for a hybridized, multidirectional, and multigeneric discursive mode, one that reflects the cross-cultural nature of Native texts and that reinvents the discursive strategies of Western hegemonic theory. As critics implicated in the discourse of the metropolitan center, Sarris and Owens conceive of writing within and outside of the dominant discourse as a powerful, subversive tool with which to define a new sense of identity for Native people. At the same time, the methodology of these critics, in its polyvocality and heteroglot nature, deeply modeled on the richly layered world of the oral tradition, intends to challenge the authoritative, monologic stance of Eurocentric theory. According to Owens, for instance, ED-WARD W. SAID's extraordinary denigration of Native American cultures in *Culture and Imperialism* (1993), along with Bhabha's silencing of indigenous voices in his panoply of minority writers in *The Location of Culture* (1994), demonstrates the imperialist stance often adopted by postcolonial theorists. Even though Owens himself relies on the critical vocabulary of Bhabha, FRANTZ FANON, GAYATRI CHAKRAVORTY SPIVAK, and Trinh T. Minh-ha, among others, in discussing the work of Native American fiction writers, his gesture is ultimately a "catachrestic" one—to use Spivak's terminology—as he moves beyond the discursive strategies of postcolonialism and articulates the necessity of rethinking crucial concepts in postcolonial theorizing. By testing postcolonialism's ideas primarily against Native American problematics and predicaments, Owens suggests ways in which Native American literary texts are indeed accomplishing those acts of "(cross) cultural translation" (Bhabha 228) theorized within postcolonial discourse, bringing to the attention of the dominant culture differing epistemologies and discursive modes.

Gerald Vizenor's critical narratives represent possibly the most provocative and subversive challenge by a Native American author to the parameters of Western/Eurocentric theory. Both *Manifest Manners* (1994) and *Fugitive Poses* (1998) dissolve any fixed line between essay and story and forcefully employ trickster discourse in order to dismantle academic representations of Indianness. Crucial to Vizenor's work is the presence of the Native American trickster figure conceived, as it is, in absolutely linguistic terms. Like Nanaabozho, the mythic woodland tribal trickster of the Anishinaabe tales, the shape shifter who mediates between worlds, Vizenor's trickster discourse mediates between traditionally based ideas and Western hermeneutics, Vizenor's ultimate goal being that of challenging cultural beliefs and worldviews. In her groundbreaking text *Gerald Vizenor: Writing in the Oral Tradition* (1996), Kimberley Blaeser argues that Vizenor's writing begins in the traditional Chippewa/Anishinaabe tales of his ancestors, in which words have life, vibrancy, force, vitality, and power to create.

In both *Manifest Manners* and *Fugitive Poses*, as well as in virtually any of his other works, regardless of genre (Vizenor's eclectic production includes novels, short stories, drama, a screenplay, an autobiography, various collections of critical essays, haiku poetry, and journalistic pieces), Vizenor engages in a passionate deconstruction of age-old vexed representations of Indians. For more than five hundred years, Vizenor argues, the reality of tribal people has been simulated under this artifact known as *indian*, a misnomer that testifies more to the absence of Native people than to their presence. By insisting that the word be written with a lowercase i and italicized, Vizenor reflects his dissatisfaction with the problem of identity among tribal people, who have been burdened with names invented by the dominant society. Elaborating on Derrida's terminology, Vizenor applies the concepts of "absence" and "presence" to a discourse on Native American experience, conducting a penetrating critique of Euro-American colonialism in its construction of the *indian* as the absent other. Borrowing JEAN BAUDRILLARD's and Umberto Eco's ideas on the hyperreal and the absolute fake, Vizenor deconstructs simulations of Indianness that have defined and confined Native American cultures within animated museum walls.

Within such a mediative frontier zone of discourses, Native American theory and criticism appears to be facing ambiguities similar to those pointed out by HENRY LOUIS GATES JR. in his discussion of the relationship between black literature and literary theory. Rather than inventing black critical instruments and methodologies to explicate "signifying" black differences, Gates suggests ways in which the fused forms of African oral traditions and Western literary discourse can produce original ways of reading and interpreting black literary texts (9–10). Such a syncretic maneuver seems to characterize the nature and content of Native American criticism and theory as well. Closely paralleling the hybridized nature of Native American literature in its blending of oral and written forms, Native American theory and criticism from the outset thus appears as a mediative form of discourse. Regardless of the position that Native American theorists and critics end up taking, crucial to their texts is the presence of Native/indigenous rhetoric(s) and epistemology as the primary critical voice within which Western literary analysis is ultimately subsumed.

The result of the revisionist project that seeks to resist the imposition of external critical methods on Native texts is a form of discourse that challenges all of us to open up to ways of being in the world that are very different from the models of the Euro-centric hermeneutical tradition. On the border of various discourses, inside and out-side the West, always in the shifting and shimmering fluid zone of trickster, Native American theory and criticism calls for multidirectional boundaries that will con-tinue to be crossed as we as a community keep pursuing a cross-cultural dialogue.

ELVIRA PULITANO

See also POSTCOLONIAL STUDIES and RACE AND ETHNICITY.

Paula Gunn Allen, *Off the Reservation: Reflections on Boundary-Busting, Border-Crossing, Loose Can-ons* (1998), *The Sacred Hoop: Recovering the Feminine in American Indian Traditions* (1986); Homi K. Bhabha, *The Location of Culture* (1994); Kimberley Blaeser, *Gerald Vizenor: Writing in the Oral Tradition* (1996), "Native Literature: Seeking a Critical Center," *Looking at the Words of Our People: First Nations Analysis of Literature* (ed. Jeannette Armstrong, 1993); Henry Louis Gates Jr., *Black Literature and Liter-ary Theory* (1984); Elaine Jahner, "Allies in the Word-Wars: Vizenor's Use of Contemporary Critical Theory," *Studies in American Indian Literatures* 9 (1985), "A Critical Approach to American Indian Lit-erature," *Studies in American Indian Literature: Critical Essays and Course Designs* (ed. Paula Gunn Allen, 1983), "Metalanguages" (Vizenor); Karl Kroeber, "Deconstructionist Criticism and American In-dian Literature," *boundary 2* 7 (1979); Arnold Krupat, *Ethnocriticism: Ethnography, History, Literature* (1989), "Poststructuralism and Oral Literature," *Recovering the Word: Essays on Native American Litera-ture* (ed. Brian Swann and Arnold Krupat, 1987), *The Turn to the Native: Studies in Criticism and Culture* (1996), *The Voice in the Margin: Native American Literature and the Canon* (1989); Louis Owens, "As If an Indian Were Really an Indian: Native American Voices and Postcolonial Theory," *I Hear the Train: Reflections, Inventions, Refractions* (2001), *Mixedblood Messages: Literature, Film, Family, Place* (1998), *Other Destinies: Understanding the American Indian Novel* (1992); John Purdy and James Ruppert, eds., *Nothing but the Truth: An Anthology of Native American Literature* (2001); James Ruppert, *Mediation in Contemporary Native American Fiction* (1995); Greg Sarris, *Keeping Slug Woman Alive: A Holistic Approach to American Indian Texts* (1993); Carlton Smith, *Coyote Kills John Wayne: Postmodernism and Contemporary Fictions of the Transcultural Frontier* (2000); Alan Velie, *Four American Indian Literary Masters: N. Scott Momaday, James Welch, Leslie Marmon Silko, and Gerald Vizenor* (1982); Gerald Vizenor, *Fugitive Poses: Native American Indian Scenes of Absence and Presence* (1998), *Manifest Manners: Postindian Warriors of Sur-vivance* (1994, rpt., *Manifest Manners: Narratives on Postindian Survivance*, 1999); Gerald Vizenor, ed., *Narrative Chance: Postmodern Discourse on Native American Indian Literature* (1989); Robert A. Warrior, *Tribal Secrets: Recovering American Indian Intellectual Traditions* (1995); James Weaver, "From I-Herme-neutics to We-Hermeneutics: Native Americans and the Postcolonial," *Native American Religious Identity: Unforgotten Gods* (ed. Jace Weaver, 1998), *That the People Might Live: Native American Literatures and Native American Community* (1997); Craig S. Womack, *Red on Red: Native American Literary Separat-ism* (1999).

2. Canada

The conceptual distinction between scribal and print culture in the study of Native sign systems has been foundational to the development of the field of Native Cana-dian theory and criticism. Theories of writing by the First Peoples of Canada incorporate the study of myths, legends, tales, folklore, poetry, fiction, and drama to differentiate between storytelling traditions grounded in the transcription of speech and aboriginal writing systems that employ marks painted on, woven into, or carved on a material base to preserve and communicate information. Examples of aboriginal graphic texts include wampum belts, petroglyphs, pictographs, painted skins, and birch-bark scrolls. The distinction between language-based and pictographic Native sign systems in the study of aboriginal writing has precipitated a number of colonial assumptions that remain constitutive of the field, such as the notions that "aboriginal literacy" necessitates "competence with English or French writing systems," that "Native peoples lack a writing system and traditionally possess only a set of pictographic mnemonics," and that "pictography is not considered to be a form of writing because it does not literally transcribe speech . . . [and] cannot be deciphered without the knowledge of a live informant" (Olson 391). The conflation of writing with literacy has engendered, according to Germaine Warkentin, a "too easy classification" of Native peoples' sign systems as "oral cultures," a classification that overlooks a "rich legacy of material sign making attested to in the archaeological record, in the linguistic record, and in early North American history as Europeans have recorded it" (4). Calling for an engagement with the persistent and systematic relationship between "material base, social intention, and performance," Warkentin argues that the study of Native sign systems needs to be expanded not only to explore "the social function of writing and of books in general" but also to engage with the "sheer diversity" of writing composed within Native scribal culture so as to examine the "strengths and limits of European conceptions of writing" and the perception that Native sign systems represent a " 'primitive' level of human civilization" (14).

In A Native Heritage: Images of the Indian in English-Canadian Literature (1981), one of the first book-length studies to examine the "image of the Native in literature," Leslie Monkman explores texts by English Canadian writers to illuminate how Native peoples were characterized as "savage" and "primitive" with the aim of treating "the Indian as a doomed figure of the past" through which to assert "a lost heroic vitality" and "cultural eleg[y] of the new world" (5). Depicting the Indian as the antithesis of "white culture," these writers rehearsed the colonial fantasy of Native extinction by relegating the Indian to a literary-critical terrain generated through the "displacement, erosion, and death of indigenous cultures" (5). Focusing on the shifting historical contexts in which non-Native writers deploy "the Indian and his culture" either as a "stereotype" against which "to assert the values of his own culture" or as a site of culture and history appropriated "to concerns common to all cultures," Monkman concludes that Canada had neither "come to terms with the cultures of its native peoples" (161) nor avoided "exploiting the culture of a vanquished people" (163).

The problematic of ethnocentric literary practices and the marginalization of Native culture both have served as important sites of critique and intervention and have fostered a contestatory discourse that interrupts canonical norms of Canadian literary discourse, which situated Native culture as either "assimilat[ing] or vanish[ing]" (Fee, "Upsetting" 168). Such issues constitute the organizing framework for a collection of essays edited by Thomas King, Helen Hoy, and Cheryl Calver that inaugurated the cross-cultural, comparative study of Native literature in relation to settler-colony imaginative discourses, transcribed Native oral traditions, and contemporary Native influences. Emerging out of a conference held at the University of Lethbridge in Alberta in March 1985, the essays anthologized in The Native in Literature (1987) established the field of Native Canadian literature by invoking not only the "myths of native presence," which "marked the use of the Indian by Canadian writers," but also indigenous "oral story-telling techniques and traditional characters," which appear in "Indian oral stories" (12). The editors' purpose is to recognize both "Native and non-Native lines of influence in literature" (13).

The theoretical approach of many of the essays, informed by a view of literary pluralism, also undertakes to salvage writing by Native and non-Native authors so as to explore the political and cultural implications of the semiotic appropriation of the indigene. Kate Vangen claims in "Making Faces: Defiance and Humour in Campbell's Halfbreed and Welch's Winter in the Blood" that "defiance and humour blend in Native literature to mediate an otherwise tragic vision and to provide hope for further struggles against oppression" (189). In "An Intolerable Burden of Meaning: Native Peoples in White Fiction" Gordon Johnston argues that "Indian figures have been interesting, not in themselves, but as symbolic referents in a discourse about European civilization's virtues and vices, triumphs and failures" (50). Margery Fee's "Romantic Nationalism and the Image of Native People in Contemporary English-Canadian Culture" illustrates how the "ubiquitous presence" of Native characters "allows for the fulfilment of several ideology goals," including "the identity quest of the bourgeois individual" and a "white 'literary land claim' " (17). Terry Goldie's "Fear and Temptation," as well as his influential book-length study, Fear and Temptation: The Image of the Indigene in Canadian, Australian, and New Zealand Literature (1989), frames the indigene as a "semiotic pawn on a chessboard under the control of the white signmaker" (70). Drawing together deconstructivist and poststructuralist critical thinkers, Goldie's work examines the "inescapable, unchanging, and oppressive appropriation of the indigene," which unites settler colony cultures through "British imperialism's . . . need for [an] impossible process of indigenization" (78). While Goldie's text and the essays in The Native in Literature draw attention to the productive relationship between postcolonial theory and settler-colony imperialism, most notably conceptualized in EDWARD W. SAID's seminal text Orientalism (1978), they also disavow a recognition of the cultural autonomy of Native literary practices.

A turning point in Native Canadian criticism occurred during the late 1980s and early 1990s through a series of high-profile, public events involving Native writers that challenged the way Native literature had been ideologically contained by its positioning within a generalized, cross-cultural, comparative framework. These included the formation of the Committee to Reestablish the Trickster, a Toronto-based group of Native writers founded by John McLeod, Lenore Keeshig-Tobias, Tomson Highway, and Daniel David Moses, which organized workshops in Native cultural production and established publishing venues to "reclaim the Native voice" (Petrone, "Aboriginal" 17). Under the guidance of Native artists, participants explored techniques for adapting oral traditions to television, the stage, and paper so as to "dis/place and hybridize" traditional storytelling conventions (Godard 184). Sessions directed by Lenore Keeshig-Tobias and Daniel David Moses directly criticized the absence of Native texts in the Canadian canon and advanced an alternative principle of writing by Native cultural producers as a literature of resistance within the conventions of the dominant discourse. The centrality of the "appropriation of voice" debate also emerged at the Third International Feminist Book Fair, where Lee Maracle protested against non-Native peoples publishing Native stories. Claiming that non-Native appropriations of Native material disempower Native writers and distort the social relations through which oral traditions "convey knowledge, teachings, humour, and spirituality," Maracle argued for a recognition of the "material effects of imperialism in the dominant culture's ignorance of indigenous cultural practices and in their exclusion and denigration" (Emberley 94). Maracle also advocated against applying theory to Native texts, claiming that "the ridiculousness of European academic notions of theoretical presentation lies in the inherent hierarchy retained by academics, politicians, law makers, and law keepers. Power resides with the theorists so long as they use language no one understands" (90).

Debates involving what Barbara Godard identifies as the "appropriate form or appropriation" (185) in the formation of the field of Native Canadian theory and criticism have generated two approaches to study of the literature. Despite Maracle's opposition to the use of theory, critics such as Julia Emberley and Helen Hoy have drawn on postcolonial and poststructuralist methodologies to theorize questions of difference and displacement posed by aboriginal women's writing, though they do so in recognition of the power asymmetries and alternative cultural work facilitated through literary criticism. In *Thresholds of Difference: Feminist Critique, Native Women's Writings, Postcolonial Theory* (1993) Emberley argues for a "feminism of decolonization," examining the emplacement of Native women's writing within "ideological contradictions in dominant social formations" so as to illuminate "the various subjugated modes of resistance and alterity that emerge to combat patriarchal, capitalist, and colonial oppressions" (4). Helen Hoy's *How Should I Read These? Native Women Writers in Canada* (2001) undertakes a shifting, situated discourse that sets out to explore "the problematics of reading and teaching a variety of prose works by Native women writers in Canada from one particular perspective . . . that of a specific cultural outsider" (11). Incorporating feminist and First Nations theory, Hoy's study

engages with the politics of coimplication engendered through feminist and postcolonial scholarly work in order to examine mutually constitutive histories, relationships, and responsibilities (17).

The second approach to Native literary criticism theorizes the cultural autonomy
of the writing by privileging First Nations critical perspectives. Adopting a "separatist" approach, Jeannette Armstrong's anthology *Looking at the Words of Our People: First
Nations Analysis of Literature* (1993) insists on "listening to First Nations analysis"
while also contributing to "the dialogue on English literature and First Nations Voice
within literature itself" in order to "reconstruct a new order of culturalism and relationship beyond colonial thought and practise" (8). The collection features writers and
academics from Canada and the United States and includes essays by Kateri Damm,
Janice Acoose, Marilyn Dumont, Kimberly M. Blaeser, Duane Diatum, A. A. Hedge
Coke, Gerry William, Victoria Lena Manyarrows, Armand Garnett Ruffo, Greg Young-
Ing, and D. L. Birchfield. It also adopts a transnational indigenous perspective by
considering Native writing from both Canada and the United States (William, Ruffo,
Birchfield) while at the same time asserting the importance of a tribal-centered, his-
torical framework (Damm, Acoose, Blaeser, Ruffo).

This gesture toward the establishment of a countertradition within which to
locate aboriginal writing has also fostered a historicization of the field that privileges the literature's engagement with social and political contexts. Critics explaining the expansion in publishing by aboriginal authors since the 1960s have distinguished several definitive texts that in addition to affirming the cultural distinctiveness
of First Peoples' literary traditions also articulate common themes, such as loss of cultural cohesion, encounters with institutional racism, and renewal through homecom-
ing. In "Aboriginal Literature: Native and Métis Literature" (1997) Penny Petrone argues that contemporary publishing trends may be attributed to debates surrounding
the 1969 "Statement of the Government of Canada on Indian Policy," the "controversial 'White Paper'" that "recommended the abolition of special rights for Native
peoples" and "sparked a burst of literary activity" (9–10). Petrone suggests that this
"self-conscious, protest literature" arises out of a strident tone and political orientation that drew attention to the plight of aboriginal peoples in Canada (10). Maria
Campbell's *Halfbreed* (1973) is representative for Petrone of the harsh tone and "slo-
ganistic language" of these texts.

The significance of colonial government policy to the study of Native literature
has engendered a new direction within Native theory and criticism that recognizes
the literature's engagement with government legislation and colonial law. Thomas
King's *Truth about Stories: A Native Narrative* (2003) theorizes both literary and legislative contexts, illuminating the erosion of cultural communities through the relentless imposition of colonial policies by the Canadian government. In "What Is It about
Us That You Don't Like?" King explores the implications of Bill C-31 legislation and
Indian Act policy, which continue to affect Native communities, in order to illustrate

what he describes as "a montage of the horrors that legislative racism, judicial arrogance, and Native xenophobia can create" (*Truth* 150). In focusing on the implications of gender and race identity for Native peoples in connection with colonial law, King returns to the problematics of racism and imposed categories of identity and filiation, which inspired collections such as *Give Back: First Nations Perspectives on Cultural Practice* (1992) and *Enough Is Enough: Aboriginal Women Speak Out* (1987) to privilege the voice and experience of Native artists and women in their encounters with institutional racism and cultural marginalization.

Native literature remains imbricated in a history of colonial struggle to reassert the political, cultural, and intellectual integrity of aboriginal peoples and to secure the recognition of First Peoples communities as distinct nations within the geographical boundaries of Canada. Aboriginal writers examine these issues and participate in a process of cultural recovery and renewal by exploring the influences of colonial policy in their lives and by challenging a history of colonial occupation through their narrative interventions. Aboriginal issues in Canada include land claims, self-government, sovereignty, recognition of treaty rights, recognition of cultural diversity and renewal, and enhancement of educational and economic opportunities (Canada, Report). The acknowledgment by the Supreme Court of Canada that aboriginal oral histories may be submitted as evidence offers an important theoretical and methodological approach to the study of Native literatures because, as Germaine Warkentin suggests, an expanded conceptualization of aboriginal literacy and Native sign systems "may have significant legal results for the Canadian First Nations" (20). The increasing focus in Native criticism on law, legislation, and literature has important implications for the development of the field of Native Canadian theory and criticism.

CHERYL SUZACK

See also RACE AND ETHNICITY.

Jeannette Armstrong, ed., *Looking at the Words of Our People: First Nations Analysis of Literature* (1993); Maria Campbell et al., *Give Back: First Nations Perspectives on Cultural Practice* (1992); Julia Emberley, *Thresholds of Difference: Feminist Critique, Native Women's Writings, Postcolonial Theory* (1993); Margery Fee, "Romantic Nationalism and the Image of Native People in Contemporary English-Canadian Literature" (King, Calver, and Hoy), "Upsetting Fake Ideas: Jeannette Armstrong's *Slash* and Beatrice Culleton's *April Raintree*" (New); Len Findlay, "Re-Seeding Justice: Ron Benner's Native to the Américas," *Ron Benner: Gardens of a Colonial Present* (ed. Melanie Townsend, 2008); Barbara Godard, "The Politics of Representation: Some Native Canadian Women Writers," *Native Writers and Canadian Writing* (ed. W. H. New, 1990); Terry Goldie, *Fear and Temptation: The Image of the Indigene in Canadian, Australian, and New Zealand Literature* (1989), "Fear and Temptation: Images of Indigenous Peoples in Australian, Canadian, and New Zealand Literature" (King, Calver, and Hoy); Helen Hoy, *How Should I Read These? Native Women Writers in Canada* (2001); Gordon Johnston, "An Intolerable Burden of Meaning: Native Peoples in White Fiction" (King, Calver, and Hoy); Thomas King, *The Truth about Stories: A Native Narrative* (2003); Thomas King, Cheryl Calver, and Helen Hoy, eds., *The Native in Literature* (1987); Lee Maracle, "Oratory: Coming to Theory" (Campbell et al.); Leslie

Monkman, *A Native Heritage: Images of the Indian in English-Canadian Literature* (1981); W. H. New, ed., *Native Writers and Canadian Writing* (1990); David R. Olson, "Aboriginal Literacy," *Interchange* 25 (1994); Penny Petrone, "Aboriginal Literature: Native and Métis Literature," *The Oxford Companion to Canadian Literature* (ed. Eugene Benson and L. W. Connolly, 1997), *Native Literature in Canada: From the Oral Tradition to the Present* (1990); Royal Commission on Aboriginal Peoples, *Perspectives and Realities* (1996); Janet Silman, *Enough Is Enough: Aboriginal Women Speak Out* (1987); Kate Vangen, "Making Faces: Defiance and Humour in Campbell's *Halfbreed* and Welch's *Winter in the Blood*" (King, Calver, and Hoy); Germaine Warkentin, "In Search of 'The Word of the Other': Aboriginal Sign Systems and the History of the Book in Canada," *Book History* 2 (1999); Greg Young-Ing, "Aboriginal Peoples' Estrangement: Marginalization in the Publishing Industry" (Armstrong).

New Historicism

In 1982 STEPHEN GREENBLATT edited a special issue of *Genre* on Renaissance writing entitled "The Forms of Power and the Power of Forms," and he introduced the articles by identifying a joint enterprise, namely, an effort to rethink the ways that early modern texts were situated within the larger spectrum of discourses and practices that organized sixteenth- and seventeenth-century English culture. Many contemporary Renaissance critics had developed misgivings about two sets of assumptions that informed much of the scholarship of previous decades. Unlike the New Critics, Greenblatt and his colleagues were reluctant to consign texts to an autonomous aesthetic realm that dissociated Renaissance writing from other forms of cultural production, and unlike the prewar historicists, they refused to assume that Renaissance texts mirrored, from a safe distance, a unified and coherent worldview that was held by a whole population, or at least by an entire literate class. Greenblatt announced a new historicism that had appeared in the academy and would work from its own set of premises: Elizabethan and Jacobean society was a site in which occasionally antagonistic institutions sponsored a diverse and perhaps even contradictory assortment of beliefs, codes, and customs; authors who were positioned within this terrain experienced a complex array of subversive and orthodox impulses and registered these complicated attitudes toward authority in their texts; and critics who wished to understand sixteenth- and seventeenth-century writing must delineate the ways the texts they studied were linked to the network of institutions, practices, and beliefs that constituted Renaissance culture in its entirety.

While the term "New Historicism" quickly garnered considerable prestige, it also created expectations of a coherent theoretical program and set of methodological procedures that would govern the interpretive efforts. When the New Historicists failed to produce such position papers, critics began to accuse them of having a disingenuous relation to literary theory. Greenblatt's response, "Towards a Poetics of Culture" (1987), has profoundly affected the way academics understand the phenomenon of New Historicism. Via a shrewd juxtaposition of JEAN-FRANÇOIS LYOTARD's and FREDRIC JAMESON's paradigms for conceptualizing capitalism, Greenblatt attempts to show that the question regarding how art and society are interrelated cannot be answered by appealing to a single theoretical stance. Since New Historicists also pose this question, they should see the failure of Marxist and poststructuralist attempts to understand the contradictory character of capitalist aesthetics as a warning against any attempt to convert New Historicism into a doctrine or a method (see MARXIST THEORY AND CRITICISM). For Greenblatt, New Historicism is not and should not be a theory; it is an array of reading practices that investigate a series of issues that emerge when critics seek to chart the ways texts, in dialectical fashion, both represent a society's behavior patterns and perpetuate, shape, or alter that culture's dominant codes.

Most critics working in the field of cultural poetics agree that New Historicism is organized by a series of questions and problems, not by a systematic paradigm for interpreting literary works. In "The Poetics and Politics of Culture" (1989), for instance, Louis Montrose provides a list of concerns shared by New Historicists that agrees with and extends Greenblatt's commentary. Insisting that one aim of New Historicism is to refigure the relationship between texts and the cultural system in which they were produced, Montrose indicates that critics must problematize or reject both the formalist and reflectionist conceptions of literature in order to explain how texts not only represent culturally constructed forms of knowledge and authority but instantiate or reproduce in readers the very practices and codes they embody.

New Historicism also initiates a reconsideration of the ways authors specifically and human agents generally interact with social and linguistic systems. This second concern is an extension of the first, for if the idea that every human activity is embedded in a cultural field raises questions about the autonomy of literary texts, it also implies that individuals may be inscribed more fully in a network of social practices than many critics tend to believe. But Montrose suggests that the New Historicist hostility toward humanist models of freely functioning subjectivity does not imply social determinism. Instead, individual agency is constituted by a process he calls "subjectification": on the one hand, culture produces individuals endowed with subjectivity and the capacity of agency; on the other, it positions them within social networks and subjects them to cultural codes that ultimately exceed their comprehension and control.

Montrose adds a third concern: to what extent can a literary text offer a genuinely radical critique of authority or articulate views that threaten political orthodoxy? New Historicists' interest in delineating the full range of social work that writing can perform forces them to confront this issue, but Montrose sees no consensus regarding whether literature can generate effective resistance. Jonathan Dollimore and Alan Sinfield claim that Renaissance texts contest the dominant religious and political ideologies of their time, but other critics argue that the hegemonic powers of the Tudor and Stuart governments were so great that the state was able to neutralize all dissident behavior. Montrose insists that a willingness to explore the political potential of writing is a distinguishing mark of New Historicism.

Fourth, Montrose considers "the question of theory." He insists that cultural poetics is not itself a systematic paradigm for producing knowledge and that New Historicists must be well versed in literary and social theory and prepared to deploy various modes of analysis in their study of writing and culture. The emphasis borrowed from DECONSTRUCTION and poststructuralism on the discursive character of all experience and the position that every human act is embedded in an arbitrary system of signification that social agents use to make sense of their world allow New Historicists to think of past events as texts that must be deciphered. These poststructuralist theories often underlie such cryptically chiastic formulations as "the historicity of texts and the textuality of history." Other New Historicists invoke interpretive perspectives found in MICHEL FOUCAULT's and Clifford Geertz's writings. For virtually every New Historicist, theory is a potential ally.

The particularity of New Historicist studies means that its theory, or lack thereof, cannot be separated from the theoretical, historical, and aesthetic interests of its individual practitioners. In the introduction to *Practicing New Historicism* (2000) Catherine Gallagher and Greenblatt undertake a joint investigation of New Historicism's roots and evolution, providing a history of the reading group at the University of California at Berkeley that gave birth to the journal *Representations* in 1983 and casting light on some vantage points from which New Historicism's founders speak. The introduction notes the Berkeley group's debt to works of theory originating in Paris, Constance, Berlin, Frankfurt, Budapest, Tartu, and Moscow. Acknowledging New Historicism's debt to women's studies, the introduction makes explicit its commitment to including groups conventionally excluded from literary studies, as well as to the dismantling of aesthetic hierarchies.

Gallagher and Greenblatt identify four paradigm shifts that brought New Historicism's multifaceted practices into existence: from "art" to "representations," from materialism's objects to the history of the body and the human subject, from thematics to cultural "supplements," and from "ideology critique" to discourse analysis. Beyond these general principles, they maintain the "doggedly private, individual, obsessive, lonely" nature of New Historicist studies (18). The essays in *Practicing New Historicism* were authored individually, then rewritten as joint critical ventures. Despite their having been revised, the essays carry the imprint of their authors' distinctive voices and testify to the propensity for singularity, as well as demonstrate the truth of the introduction's closing remark that New Historicism is not "a repeatable methodology or a literary critical program" (19).

Like any influential movement in literary studies, New Historicist scholarship has received a good deal of critique. Its interest in the anecdote, or "anecdotalism" to use Gallagher and Greenblatt's term, has invited the charge of bad historiography. The New Historicist's extrapolation of large epistemological, historical, and political claims from a single text, this critique suggests, hangs a large weight on a small nail. Others have questioned anecdotalism's vague STRUCTURALISM, noting that the New Historicist use of the anecdote simultaneously implies and destabilizes a systematic analysis of culture. New Historicism has also been taken to task on ideological grounds. For some, it renders all discourse and history potentially literary, in that its approach to nonliterary texts ultimately frames those texts in literary and formalist terms. In this critique, not only are we not being historical yet but we are refashioning history into a domain for essentially ahistorical, literary analysis. Another kind of political critique attacks New Historicism's perceived adversarial relation to literature, in which critics read present-day political commitments into the literature of the past. Thus, the contemporary historicist reads the past dialectically in order to account for and criticize the political contests, inequalities, and injustices of our present age. Critics of this method (including New Historicists) point out that this assumes and essentializes a certain identity between the present and the past, an assumption that undermines the antiessentialist political premise of historicist inquiry and weakens the claim that representations are best understood only when considered in the context of their specific historical period. This refashioning of the past into the infancy of the present effectively reproduces an Enlightenment narrative of human development, one of the totalizing master narratives New Historicism putatively opposes.

These critiques aside, overestimating New Historicist method's impact on the professional study of English and American literature would be difficult. The practice has, for example, radically transformed the study of British Romanticism. Long celebrated for their achievements in English free-verse lyric poetry, the great male poets of the Romantic age were more or less coextensive, since the inception of English literary studies, with British Romantic literature itself, even after the poststructuralist intervention into the authority of that canon in the late 1970s and early 1980s. In New Historicist studies of British Romanticism these poets' commitment to individual consciousness and imaginative poetics has received careful attention. By insisting that class and economic conflict shadow the project of individual emotion recollected in tranquility, Marjorie Levenson's analysis of William Wordsworth's "Tintern Abbey" foregrounds the role of political life in the poetry of aesthetic individuation. Marginal authors are now more widely regarded as worthy in their own right. In addition to the traditional topics of Romanticist scholarship, New Historicism has brought new issues to the table, including the production of "Englishness," the relation of women's rights to revolutionary politics, the impact of slavery on the empire, sexual ambiguity and queerness, and Romanticism's long-ignored prose fiction tradition.

Beyond Renaissance and nineteenth-century fields of literary study, New Historicism has impacted every traditional period of English literary history, including medieval, Restoration and eighteenth-century, and twentieth-century and modernist studies. And its impact on American literary study has simultaneously shattered and revivified the field. Particularly because of the United States' complex racial history, New Historicism has promoted a revolutionary MULTICULTURALISM and postnationalism in the study of American literary and cultural institutions. American cultural studies (see CULTURAL STUDIES: 2. UNITED STATES) has, in its application of New Historicist techniques of discourse analysis and its interest in marginal textual productions, come to consider the fissures within American experience: the multiplicity of identity; the history of linguistic diversity and contest; the proliferation of nationalisms; the dissent of sexual others and nonnormative gender performances; and the permeable borders of its nation. The traditional canons of American literary scholarship in all of its historical subdisciplines—pre-1800, antebellum, postbellum, modernism, and POSTMODERNISM—have undergone substantial revision as a new generation of scholars have jettisoned the classic narratives of American literary history and identity in favor of newly conceptualized domains of American culture making.

In a 1989 essay, Hayden White highlighted New Historicism's ability to challenge the "reigning orthodoxies" of literary and historical studies in its insistence on naming textuality as the key to understanding representation, culture, and the past. Pointing out that all historical investigation is necessarily textual—historical events being "no longer directly accessible to perception"—White observes how different theories of textuality inform larger debates about the diachronic and synchronic elements at work in historical processes. New Historicism's tendency to read history as, according to Montrose, "the synchronic text of a cultural system" moves it away from conventional understandings of historical sequentiality and toward an account of the "poetic," rather than more "grammatical," codes of history, those aspects of history least inclined to conform to dominant modes of social organization and the stories they tell about themselves. While White perhaps underestimates the extent to which New Historicist practices have been influenced as much by early as by late Foucault, his analysis usefully highlights New Historicism's most enduring contribution to literary and historical studies: the attention it pays to objects, persons, and practices that, before it, had been understood as ephemera, secondary and inconsequential to the master narratives of Enlightenment historiography.

HUNTER CADZOW, ALISON CONWAY, AND BRYCE TRAISTER

See also bibliography for STEPHEN GREENBLATT.

Srinivas Aravamudan, *Tropicopolitans: Colonialism and Agency, 1688–1804* (1999); Carol Walker Bynum, *Holy Feast and Holy Fast: The Religious Significance of Food to Medieval Women* (1987); James Chandler, *England in 1819: The Politics of Literary Culture and the Case of Romantic Historicism* (1998); Catherine Gallagher, *Nobody's Story: The Vanishing Acts of Women Writers in the Marketplace, 1670–1820* (1994); Jonathan Goldberg, *James I and the Politics of Literature* (1983); Stephen Greenblatt, "Towards a Poetics of Culture" (Veeser); Sandra Gustafson, *Eloquence Is Power: Oratory and Performance in Early America* (2000); Steven Justice, *Writing and Rebellion: England around 1381* (1994); Marjorie Levinson, ed., *Rethinking Historicism: Critical Readings in Romantic History* (1989); Walter Benn Michaels, *The Gold Standard and the Logic of Naturalism* (1987); Louis A. Montrose, "The Poetics and Politics of Culture" (Veeser); Lee Patterson, *Chaucer and the Subject of History* (1991); Carolyn Porter, "Are We Being Historical Yet?" *South Atlantic Quarterly* 87 (1990); Brook Thomas, *The New Historicism and Other Old-Fashioned Topics* (1991); H. Aram Veeser, ed., *The New Historicism* (1989); Hayden White, "New Historicism: A Comment" (Veeser).

Phenomenology

Phenomenology is a philosophy of experience. For phenomenology, the ultimate source of all meaning and value is the lived experience of human beings. The task of the philosopher is to describe the structures of experience, particularly consciousness, the imagination, relations with other persons, and the situatedness of the human subject in society and history. The modern founder of phenomenology is the German philosopher Edmund Husserl (1859–1938), who sought to make philosophy "a rigorous science" by returning its attention "to the things themselves" ("zu den Sachen selbst"). He does not mean by this that philosophy should become empirical or that "facts" can be determined objectively and absolutely. Rather, Husserl proposes that reflection disregard all unprovable assumptions and describe what is given in experience. Philosophers should "bracket" the object world and, in a process he calls *epochéé*, or "reduction," focus their attention on what is immanent in consciousness itself, without presupposing anything about its origins or supports. Pure description of the phenomena given in consciousness would, Husserl believes, give philosophers a foundation of necessary, certain knowledge (see *Ideas* 95–105 and *Meditations* 11–23).

Partially due to Husserl's own analysis of the structure of knowledge, later phenomenologists have been skeptical of his contention that description can occur without presuppositions. According to Husserl, consciousness is made up of "intentional acts" correlated to "intentional objects." The "intentionality" of consciousness is its directedness toward objects, which it helps to constitute. Objects are always grasped partially and incompletely in "aspects" (*Abschattungen*) that are filled out and synthesized according to the attitudes, interests, and expectations of the perceiver.

Extrapolating from Husserl's description of consciousness, MARTIN HEIDEGGER (1889–1976) argues that understanding is always "ahead of itself" ("sich vorweg"), projecting expectations that interpretation then makes explicit. In *Being and Time* (1927), Heidegger argues that inherent in understanding is a "forestructure" ("Vorstruktur") of assumptions and beliefs that guide interpretation. His theory of understanding reflects his own assumptions about human existence, which he describes as a process of projection whereby we are always outside of and beyond ourselves as we direct ourselves toward the future. Heidegger extends Husserl's concern with epistemology into the domain of ontology and has been criticized for his perceived departure from phenomenology's original methodological rigor and cautious avoidance of speculation. *Being and Time* describes the structures of human existence (*Dasein*, or "being-there"), which can be seen as an application of Husserl's investigations of consciousness to other regions of experience, including relations with others, the meaning of death, and history. Heidegger's descriptions of existence as a "thrown project" ("geworfener Entwurf") and of "care" ("Sorge") are guided by his concern with "ontological difference": the relation between "beings" and "Being." He defines human being as that being for which Being is an issue, although he also finds that for the most part in everyday life the question of Being is neglected or forgotten.

Maurice Merleau-Ponty (1908–1961) retains many of Heidegger's existential analyses while rejecting his metaphysical speculations. He also corrects Husserl's tendency toward idealism by insisting on the primacy of perceptual experience and the ambiguities of the lived world. In *Phenomenology of Perception* (1945), Merleau-Ponty situates consciousness in the body. His notion of "perception" as the situated, embodied, unreflected knowledge of the world avoids divorcing the mind from the body or treating the body as a mere object. Consciousness is always incarnate, he argues, or else it would lack a situation through which to engage the world. The experience of embodied consciousness is also inherently obscure and ambiguous, he finds, and he consequently rejects the philosopher's dream of fully transparent understanding. For Merleau-Ponty, the primacy of perception makes philosophy an endless endeavor to clarify the meaning of experience without denying its density and obscurity.

Roman Ingarden (1893–1970), the founding father of phenomenological aesthetics, also rejects idealism. *The Literary Work of Art* (1931) and *The Cognition of the Literary Work of Art* (1937) seek to resolve the opposition between the real and the ideal. Unlike autonomous, fully determinate objects, literary works depend for their existence, he argues, on the intentional acts of their creators and of their readers. Because they have an intersubjective "life," however, they are not mere figments or private dream images. Yet their apparent ideal status as structures of consciousness does not make them like triangles or other mathematical figures, which are truly ideal objects without a specific moment of birth or a history of subsequent transformations (see *Literary* 331–55).

Ingarden describes a literary work as "an intersubjective intentional object" (*Cognition* 14). It has its origin in the acts of consciousness of its creator and these acts are then reanimated by the consciousness of the reader. Having a history that exceeds the consciousness of both reader and author, the existence of a work transcends any particular, momentary experience of it. Ingarden argues that the work has an "*ontically heteronomous* mode of existence" (*Literary* 362), because it is neither autonomous nor completely dependent on the consciousnesses of the author and the reader; rather, it is paradoxically based on them even as it transcends them. For Ingarden, the literary work consists of four related strata, each of which has its own characteristic "value qualities": (1) word sounds, (2) meaning units, (3) "schematized aspects" (the perspectives through which states of affairs are viewed), and

(4) represented objectivities. The work as a whole is "schematic," he argues, because the strata have "places of indeterminacy" that readers may fill in differently.

For Ingarden, the "aesthetic object" produced by the reader is correlated to, but also differs from, the "artistic object" of the author. Not only will readers respond differently to the possibilities left open by the work's indeterminacies or to the value qualities available in the various strata, but the cognition of a work is also an inherently temporal process. Like other objects that present themselves through aspects (*Abschattungen*), the work itself is available only "horizonally," that is, through an array of incomplete and perspectival views. Ingarden maintains, however, that "certain limits of variability" constrain a correct or adequate concretization, so that these limits are predetermined by the structure of the work (352).

While Ingarden has been extremely influential in the development of phenomenological reader-response theories, his views have also been subjected to extensive criticisms. Wolfgang Iser (1926–2007), for example, faults Ingarden for limiting the variability of permissible concretizations. Reading is a dynamic activity, Iser argues, and thus "a work may be concretized in different, equally valid, ways" (178). Iser also faults Ingarden for failing to appreciate the disruptions and dissonances through which many works achieve their effects.

Iser's appreciation of disjunction also led him to criticize Georges Poulet's (1902–1991) description of reading as a process of identification. While Poulet argues that reading overcomes the barriers ordinarily dividing selves, Iser maintains that "the real, virtual 'me'" never completely disappears even as "the alien 'me'" governing the text's world emerges (*Implied* 293). Reading entails a duplication of consciousnesses, which can give rise to new self-understanding as a result of the juxtaposition of habitual ways of thinking with those required by the text.

Phenomenology has also produced many studies of the imagination. Gaston Bachelard (1884–1962), for example, regards the poetic image as a privileged place in which new meaning emerges and through which being discloses itself. Bachelard asks that readers, in order to open themselves up to the revelations of the image, lay aside preconceptions and cultivate a capacity for wonder. Bachelard's attitude toward images, however, can be contradictory: while he regards images as evidence of the lived meaning of space, he also at times seeks the origins of images in the timeless, unconscious archetypes of Jungian psychology.

Interpretation and language have been the central themes of the most recent phase of phenomenology. Paul Ricoeur (1913–2005) calls on phenomenology to take a hermeneutic turn and to direct its attention toward cultural objects rather than individual consciousness. Because "the *cogito* can be recovered only by the detour of a decipherment of the documents of its life," reflection must become interpretation. Hermeneutic phenomenology must also explore the conflict of interpretations because the possibility of "very different, even opposing, methods" of understanding is a fundamental aspect of our experience as interpreting beings (99). A concern with new modes of understanding and expression leads Ricoeur to pay special attention to creativity in language. Phenomenology denies that structure alone can adequately explain language, as new ways of meaning can only be introduced through events of speech, which may extend or overturn the limits of existing conventions. Phenomenology also denies that language is self-enclosed. For phenomenology, language and interpretation are not stable, closed systems, because meaning, like experience, is endlessly open to new developments.

The inherent incompleteness of any moment of experience is the basis for JACQUES DERRIDA's (1930–2004) influential critique of Husserl's phenomenology. Questioning Husserl's dream of a presuppositionless philosophy, Derrida finds "a metaphysical presupposition" in the very assumption that a realm of "original self-giving evidence" can be found (4–5). Using Husserl's own theories about time and intersubjectivity, Derrida demonstrates that "nonpresence and otherness are internal to presence" (66). Because knowledge is always perspectival and incomplete, the present depends on memory and expectation to make sense of the world; elements of absence must consequently be part of presence for it to be meaningful. Furthermore, the assurance that self-reflections reveal generally shared structures of knowledge and existence rests on the tacit assumption that other consciousnesses share the same experience of a moment; this assumption is further evidence that the presence of the self to itself lacks the self-sufficiency Husserl sought in his quest for a solid foundation for philosophy. There is no getting beneath the repetitive, re-presentational structure of signification, Derrida argues, because supplementarity—the replacement of one sign or "trace" by another—is the structure of self-presence.

Contemporary phenomenology has for the most part abandoned Husserl's dream of a presuppositionless philosophy. His quest now seems an example of what Hans-Georg Gadamer (1900–2002) calls "the fundamental prejudice of the enlightenment," namely, "the prejudice against prejudice itself, which deprives tradition of its power" (270). Although some prejudices may be misleading, constricting, and oppressive, understanding is impossible without prejudgments (Vor-urteile) of the sort provided by cultural conventions and inherited beliefs. According to Gadamer, "the overcoming of all prejudices, this global demand of the enlightenment, will prove to be itself a prejudice, the removal of which opens the way to an appropriate understanding of our finitude" (276), including our belonging to history, culture, and language. Largely due to the influence of Gadamer, hermeneutic phenomenology and READER-RESPONSE CRITICISM have turned their attention to the role of customs, conventions, and presuppositions in the constitution of the human subject and its understanding of the world. What remains distinctive about phenomenology is its focus on human experience, but recent phenomenologists have stressed the inherent entanglement of experience in language, history, and cultural traditions.

PAUL B. ARMSTRONG

Gaston Bachelard, *Poétique de l'espace* (1958, *The Poetics of Space*, trans. Maria Jolas, 1964); Ludwig Binswanger, *Being-in-the-World* (ed. and trans. Jacob Needleman, 1963); Jacques Derrida, *La voix et la phénomène: Introduction au problème du signe dans la phénoménologie* (1967, *Speech and Phenomena, and Other Essays on Husserl's Theory of Signs*, trans. David B. Allison, 1973); Hans-Georg Gadamer, *Wahrheit und Methode: Grundzüüge einer philosophischen Hermeneutik* (1960, 5th ed., *Gesammelte Werke*, vol. 1, ed. J. C. B. Mohr, 1986, *Truth and Method*, trans. Garrett Barden and John Cumming, 1975, 2nd ed., trans. rev. Joel Weinsheimer and Donald G. Marshall, 1989); Martin Heidegger, *Sein und Zeit* (1927, *Being and Time*, trans. John Macquarrie and Edward Robinson, 1962), "Der Ursprung des Kunstwerkes," *Holwege* (1945, "The Origin of the Work of Art," *Martin Heidegger: Basic Writings*, ed. David Farrell Krell, 1977); Edmund Husserl, *Einleitung in die transzendentale Phänomenologie* (1950, *Cartesian Meditations: An Introduction to Phenomenology*, trans. Dorian Cairns, 1960), *Ideen zu einer reinen Phänomenologie und phänomenologischen Philosophie* (1913, *Ideas: General Introduction to Pure Phenomenology*, trans. W. R. Boyce Gibson, 1962); Roman Ingarden, *Das literarische Kunstwerk* (1931, *The Literary Work of Art*, trans. George Grabowicz, 1973), *Vom Erkennen des literarischen Kunstwerks* (1968, *The Cognition of the Literary Work of Art*, trans. Ruth Ann Crowley and Kenneth R. Olson, 1973); Wolfgang Iser, *Der Akt des Lesens: Theorie ästhetischer Wirkung* (1976, *The Act of Reading: A Theory of Aesthetic Response*, trans. Wolfgang Iser, 1978), *Der implizite Leser: Kommunikationsformen des Romans von Bunyan bis Beckett* (1972, *The Implied Reader: Patterns of Communication in Prose Fiction from Bunyan to Beckett*, trans. Wolfgang Iser, 1974); Hans Robert Jauss, *Toward an Aesthetic of Reception* (trans. Timothy Bahti, 1982); Maurice Merleau-Ponty, *Phénoménologie de la perception* (1945, *Phenomenology of Perception*, trans. Colin Smith, 1962); Georges Poulet, "Phenomenology of Reading," *New Literary History* 1 (1969); Paul Ricoeur, *The Philosophy of Paul Ricoeur* (ed. Charles E. Reagan and David Stewart, 1978).

Postcolonial Studies

1. Origins to the 1980s

Postcolonial studies constitutes a major intervention in the widespread revisionist project that has impacted academia since the 1960s. Postcolonial (mostly literary) studies is one of the latest "tempests" in a postist world replacing *Prospero's Books* (the title of Peter Greenaway's 1991 film) with a Calibanic viewpoint.

This new project's beginnings can be approximately dated to the early 1950s. The project of validating modernism, so heavily indebted to "primitive" (other) cultures and, directly or indirectly, to colonialism, was on the verge of being institutionalized. Since then, the connection between colonialism, modernism, and STRUCTURALISM has been fairly well established and has provoked a similar awareness of the considerably more problematical correlation between the postmodern, the poststructural, and the postcolonial.

A great shift occurred during the 1950s, the decade that saw the end of France's involvement in Indochina, the Algerian war, the Mau Mau uprisings in Kenya, and the dethroning of King Farouk in Egypt. Jean-Paul Sartre broke with Albert Camus over opposing attitudes toward Algeria. Fidel Castro gave his speech "History Will Absolve Me." Aimé Césaire's 1950 pamphlet *Discourse on Colonialism* appeared, and in 1952 FRANTZ FANON published *Black Skin, White Masks*. Fanon, Césaire, and Albert Memmi all published works that later became foundational critical texts of colonialist discourse. In London, Faber and Faber, where T. S. Eliot worked, published Nigerian Amos Tutuola's *The Palm Wine Drinker*, leading to "curiosity" about Anglo-African writing. In 1958 the Western narrative paradigm in which an author-anthropologist fabricates the other was seriously questioned in Chinua Achebe's novel *Things Fall Apart*, which clearly illustrates the sensationalism and inaccuracy of Western anthropology and history. French demographer Alfred Sauvy coined the term "Third World," a term scrutinized ever since as some (mainly in the English-speaking world) see it as derogative even as it became a staple in the French-, German-, and Spanish-speaking worlds.

The 1960s saw major developments in the critical formulation of the postcolonial problematic. The Caribbean novelist George Lamming published his Calibanic reading of a classical text, William Shakespeare's *The Tempest*, in *The Pleasures of Exile* (1960). In 1961, Fanon's *The Wretched of the Earth*, including Sartre's preface, legitimized for many the issues raised and postulated the Western "Manichean delirium" (good versus bad, black versus white, etc.). Fanon's book sees Western racism as a form of scapegoating that permits the West to cling to its power and leads to the colonized's violent reaction. The 1970s saw further growth in colonialist studies with Roberto Fernández Retamar's "Caliban" essays (1971 and 1986) and EDWARD W. SAID's *Orientalism* (1978), most likely the central text in the establishment of

postcolonial studies. While Said could still deplore the literary establishment's declaration of the serious study of imperialism off-limits, the 1980s established the centrality of the colonialist debate with its focus on how imperialism affected the colonies and how the former colonies wrote back in an attempt to correct Western views.

Memmi claims that "the most serious blow suffered by the colonized is being removed from history" (91). Postcolonial writing, then, is the slow, painful, and highly
complex means of fighting one's way into European-made history, a process of dialogue and necessary correction. That this writing back into history became institutionalized precisely at the moment when POSTMODERNISM was questioning the
category of history should make us think about the implications of postmodernism
in relation to the postcolonial.

The designation "postcolonial" has been used to describe writing and reading
practices grounded in colonial experience occurring outside of Europe but as a consequence of European expansion and exploitation of "other" worlds. Postcolonial
literature is constituted in counterdiscursive practices. Postcolonial writing is also
related to concepts that have resulted from internal colonialization, such as the repression of minority groups and to women voicing concern and frustration over colonialization by men, a "double" colonialization when women of color are concerned.
Among the large nomenclature, which includes so-called Third World literature,
minority discourse, resistance literature, response literature (writing back or rewriting the Western "classics"), subaltern studies, othering discourse, colonialist discourse, and so on, the term "postcolonial" (sometimes hyphenated, sometimes not)
gained prominence in the late twentieth century and replaced "Commonwealth literature" or "studies" and even "Third World literature" or "studies."

Postcolonial studies is not a discipline but a distinctive problematic that can be
described as an abstract combination of the problems inherent in newly emerging
fields that participated in the significant and overdue recognition that "minority"
cultures are actually "majority" cultures and that hegemonized Western (Euro-
American) studies have been unduly overprivileged for political reasons. The Australians Bill Ashcroft, Gareth Griffiths, and Helen Tiffin in their influential The Empire
Writes Back (1989) define "postcolonial" as "cover[ing] all the culture affected by the
imperial process from the moment of colonization to the present day" (2). This makes
postcolonial studies an enormously large field, particularly since literature offers
one of the most important ways to express these new perceptions. Postcolonial studies thus concerns the totality of "texts" (in the largest sense of "text") that participate in hegemonizing other cultures and the study of texts that write back to correct
or undo Western hegemony, what GAYATRI CHAKRAVORTY SPIVAK has called "our
ideological acceptance of error as truth" (In Other 109).

The emphasis is bound to be on the political and ideological rather than the aesthetic; thus postcolonial critics link definitions of aesthetics with the ideology of the
aesthetic, hegemony, and what Louis Althusser terms the ideological state appara-

tus. Connected with these issues is the problem of the genesis and content of the Western canon. Postcolonial studies is therefore instrumental in curricular debates and demands a multicultural curriculum. Perceiving former disciplines as participating in the colonizing process, it is bound to cross borders and be interdisciplinary. We cannot disconnect postcolonial studies from previous disciplines, nor can we attribute a definable core to such a "field." Like CULTURAL STUDIES, postcolonial studies is deliberately not disciplinary but rather names a field of inquisitive activities that question disciplinary studies; as Patrick Brantlinger has put it, they "discipline the disciplines."

By the late 1980s and 1990s, and largely due to Australian efforts, the terms "postcolonial literature" and "postcolonial culture" were well established along with such other postist constructions as "postindustrial," "poststructuralism," "postmodernism," "post-Marxism," and "postfeminism." Needless to say, the term has a jargonizing quality and lacks precision. Postist terminology in general is a signpost for new emphases in literary and cultural studies, reflecting the move from the margin (minorities) to the center that is also the major contribution of Derridean DECONSTRUCTION. Robert Young points out that it is significant that Sartre, Althusser, JACQUES DERRIDA, JEAN-FRANÇOIS LYOTARD, and HÉLÈNE CIXOUS were all either born in Algeria or personally involved with the events of the war (1).

Though seldom identical with postmodernism, postcolonial studies is nevertheless involved in a broad network of conflicting attempts at intervention into the master narrative of Western discourse. It is part of postal politics and a series of inventions and interventions that the Western post(al) network seems to be assimilating. Postmodernism's urge is to incorporate or co-opt almost everything, including its oppositional other. The postcolonial paradigm is not free of such absorption; one can speak of the postmodern colonialization of the postcolonial. To preserve some unitary sense in this multifarious network without falling prey to homogenizing tendencies that underlie most theories, postcolonial critics and writers claim that the term "postcolonial" basically covers the cultures affected by the imperial process; in other words, postcolonial critics inevitably homogenize as "imperialist" critics did before them. However, they typically profess an awareness of the problems entailed in this homogenization to a degree the others did not. Among various schools of postcolonial criticism, there are those who homogenize and see postcolonial writing as resistance and those who see no unitary quality to postcolonial writing. The key terms and main figures associated with postcolonial discourse include the following: "orientalism" (Said); "minority discourse" (JanMohamed); "subaltern studies" (Guha and Spivak); "resistance literature" (Harlow); "the empire writes back" (Ashcroft et al.); "Third World literature" (Nazareth); "hybridity," "mimicry," and "civility" (Bhabha).

Postcolonial studies is foremost a shift in emphasis, a strategy of reading, an attempt to point out what was missing in previous analyses, and an attempt to rewrite and to correct. Any account of postcolonial studies will have to come to terms with the (equally problematical) concept of postcoloniality. Kwame Anthony Appiah has said that "postcoloniality is the condition of what we might ungenerously call a *comprador* intelligentsia: a relatively small, Western-style, Western-trained group of writers and thinkers, who mediate the trade in cultural commodities of world capitalism at the periphery" (348). For Appiah, postcolonial studies is not really the province of those who have been colonized and gained problematical flag-independence, nor is it the discourse that pushes former marginalized subjects into the center, as is often assumed in the many canon debates. In other words, postcolonial studies does not necessarily imply the change that Western and non-Western intellectuals foresee but remains constituted in a particular class of well-educated people who should not confuse their theoretical insights with change. Though it is a correcting instrument that believes in facilitating change, no change is likely to occur from academic debates alone. Postcolonial discourse problematizes one face of the response to former Western hegemonic discourse paradigms, but it does not abolish anything; rather, it replaces one problematic with another. Well aware of this contradiction, numerous postcolonial critics have pushed for a radical rethinking of the field itself. As Benita Parry states, "The labour of producing a counter-discourse displacing imperialism's dominative system of knowledge rests with those engaged in developing a critique from outside its cultural hegemony" (55).

While postmodern literature tends to postulate the death of history, postcolonial writing insists on the historical as foundational and all embracing. Similarly, postmodernism refuses any representational quality, though the representational mandate remains strong in postcolonial writing and at times even relies on the topological. Postcolonial critical activity is "the de-imperialization of apparently monolithic European forms, ontologies, and epistemologies" (Ashcroft, Griffiths, and Tiffin 153). If postmodernism is identified with Jameson's "cultural logic of late capitalism," postcolonialism can be conceptualized as the last bulwark against an encroaching total capitalism. In a sense it is the only true counterdiscourse we are left with, truly "past the last post."

Despite apparent similarities between postmodern and postcolonial modes of writing (particularly in cross-cultural texts by, for example, Salman Rushdie, J. M. Coetzee, Wilson Harris, and Gabriel García Márquez), the postmodern aestheticization of politics only appears radical (a kind of radical chic-ism) but is essentially conservative and tends to prolong the imperial, while the postcolonial frequently appears conservative or is bound to use a conventional mimetic mode (related to realism and its many debates) but is essentially radical in the sense of demanding change.

GEORG M. GUGELBERGER

See also HOMI K. BHABHA, FRANTZ FANON, POSTMODERNISM, EDWARD W. SAID, and GAYATRI CHAKRAVORTY SPIVAK.

See also bibliographies for HOMI K. BHABHA, FRANTZ FANON, EDWARD W. SAID, and GAYATRI CHAKRAVORTY SPIVAK.

Kwame Anthony Appiah, "Is the Post- in Postmodernism the Post- in Postcolonial?" *Critical Inquiry* 17 (1991); Bill Ashcroft, Gareth Griffiths, and Helen Tiffin, *The Empire Writes Back: Theory and Practice in Post-Colonial Literatures* (1989); Patrick Brantlinger, *Crusoe's Footprints: Cultural Studies in Britain and America* (1990); Diana Brydon, "The White Inuit Speaks: Contamination as Literary Strategy," *Past the Last Post: Theorizing Post-Colonialism and Post-Modernism* (ed. Ian Adam and Helen Tiffin, 1990); Roberto Fernández Retamar, "*Caliban*" *and Other Essays* (trans. Edward Baker, 1989); Ranajit Guha and Gayatri Chakravorty Spivak, eds., *Selected Subaltern Studies* (1988); Barbara Harlow, *Resistance Literature* (1987); Abdul JanMohamed, "Humanism and Minority Literature: Toward a Definition of Counter-hegemonic Discourse," *boundary 2* 12/13 (1984); Albert Memmi, *Portrait du colonisé, précédé du portrait du colonisateur* (1957, *The Colonizer and the Colonized*, trans. Howard Greenfeld, 1965); Peter Nazareth, *The Third World Writer: His Social Responsibility* (1978); Benita Parry, "Problems in Current Theories of Colonial Discourse," *Oxford Literary Review* 9 (1987); Robert Young, *White Mythologies: Writing History and the West* (1990).

2. 1990 and After

Since 1990, postcolonial studies has consolidated its institutional profile through the publication of numerous introductions to the field, most of which continue to privilege literary theory, and anthologies of theory and criticism, which have begun to range more widely into CULTURAL STUDIES. National or area studies are the focus of more specialized anthologies and critical works, some of which widen the postcolonial to include areas previously excluded from consideration within this rubric (such as the United States and France), expand attention to imperialisms other than European (such as Japanese and Soviet), or examine the contested status of other nations within it. "Postcolonial" continues to describe particular cultures or certain aspects of cultures and to designate a historical period, but increasingly postcolonial theory describes "a set of questions and a style of thought which are made possible by colonialism and its aftermath, and which seek to rethink, and redescribe, its own enabling conditions" (Seth 214). Implicit in that agenda is the task of imagining what might make the postcolonial no longer necessary, possible futures beyond the unequal power relations that characterized the colonial period, a task that has persisted, often in exacerbated albeit changed form, into the neocolonial or globalized present. But postcolonial studies' modes often seem contradictory. In the most general sense, the focus has shifted from culture as context and literary texts toward an interest in the cultural production and circulation of identities, cultural representations, and commodities, although there has been little interest in the economics, management, or social structures that control, produce, and profit from these.

Institutionally, the field has expanded to the extent that some doubt whether a definable field can be systematically mapped. Whether or not it can be considered a field or a discourse like others, academic journals have been established in its name, some devoted to the full sweep of the postcolonial (*Interventions, Jouvert, Postcolonial Studies, Postcolonial Text, Third Text*), others dedicated to subspecializations, some of which—for example, diaspora studies, an area launched in dialogue with the postcolonial by Rey Chow's *Writing Diaspora*—have emerged as full-blown areas in their own right.

Along with many critical introductions, the provision of reference tools began with the region- and author-focused *Encyclopedia of Post-Colonial Literatures in English*, edited by Eugene Benson and L. W. Conolly (1994), the thematically organized *Companion to Postcolonial Studies*, edited by Henry Schwarz and Sangeeta Ray (2000), and the attempt to explore "the ramifications of different vectors of disciplinary and local conditions for thinking about the field" (xviii) in *Relocating Postcolonialism*, edited by David Theo Goldberg and Ato Quayson (2002). The reprinting of influential documents from the historical archive provides further resources for historical work (see collections by Braganca and Wallerstein, Brydon, and Harlow and Carter). Postcolonial thinking has adapted its vocabulary from work in various theoretical traditions, especially DECONSTRUCTION and Marxism (a borrowing many see as fraught with difficulties), and from a variety of disciplines. *Key Concepts in Post-Colonial Studies*, edited by Bill Ashcroft, Gareth Griffiths, and Helen Tiffin (1998), provides a helpful guide to the specialized use to which postcolonial theory has put various borrowed concepts.

Fuller examinations of concepts made prominent through postcolonial studies, such as orientalism or the subaltern, continue to be produced, while the lines separating postcolonial studies from critical race, diaspora, and whiteness studies or from border theory are often blurred. The dialogues between postcolonial studies and various areas of canonical literary study attest to the increasing influence of postcolonial approaches variously conceived. Studies of postcolonial fiction continue to dominate but have been joined by art, film, poetry, theater, and new media studies. Emerging fields, such as disability studies, queer studies, and Chicana or Chicano studies, often directly engage and redirect postcolonial work. Postcolonial studies engages such varied fields as architecture, international relations, geography, law, music, pedagogy, sport, religion, and urban studies and is also beginning to move beyond the humanities and social sciences into other forms of knowledge production. Sandra Harding argues that "postcolonial science and technology studies are beginning to create a second 'historiographic revolution'" (5). In short, few disciplines, areas of the world, and time periods now remain that have not received postcolonial reevaluations.

Yet those reevaluations continue to operate within competing systems of assumptions, with a large divide still separating those for whom the key concepts remain liberation, opposition, and resistance and those who prefer to explore concepts of creolization, hybridity, translation, and transformation. In the wake of Tejaswini Niranjana's *Siting Translation* (1992), which employs "the word *translation* not just to indicate an interlingual process but to name an entire problematic" (8), attention to the dominant role of English, both globally and within critical practice, has become an important dimension of the field. In their attention to "translated" persons, genres such as autoethnography and travel literature are achieving new prominence, and the long history of entanglement with science fiction is attracting new notice. Salman Rushdie's *Satanic Verses* (1988) has replaced the Calibanic metaphors of an earlier generation as the paradigmatic text for a certain brand of postcolonial theorizing focused on the question of how "newness enters the world."

If Ngũgĩ wa Thiong'o's phrase "decolonizing the mind" still describes the mandate of postcolonialism, that mandate has been interpreted in a variety of spheres and has been mobilized within an ever-widening set of sometimes conflicting agendas. A major gap continues between those who conceptualize postcolonial work as constituting a fundamental challenge to the very organization and assumptions of contemporary Western disciplinary structures and those who see it as merely another addition to the range of critical approaches brought to bear on literature, history, and culture, or more modestly yet, as merely adding to the range of literatures and cultures that may be studied quite adequately within conventional models. Another point of fracture separates those who see colonialism as structurally integral to capitalism and modernity and those who see it as incidental. For those who stress postcolonial theory's alliances with other activist political theories, such as feminism and Marxism, the contradictions of a radical movement dedicated to social change achieving institutional and professional success continue to preoccupy practitioners.

The theorist's institutional home department makes a difference because postcolonial studies is fundamentally interdisciplinary in its ambitions even if it is only "*appropriatively* interdisciplinary" (Goldberg and Quayson, preface xvi) or just multidisciplinary in its practice. Robert Fraser, Peter Hallward, and many others seek to reclaim the field for literary studies, but David Scott and others believe it should engage more fully with concerns traditionally considered the domain of the social sciences. Teresa Ebert notes divisions between "two fundamentally different ways of understanding postcoloniality," either as a "cultural politics" or as "the articulation of the international division of labor" (204–5). The ways in which critics seek to bridge, privilege, or supplement these divisions cannot easily be reduced to a binary choice, and self-critique comes with the territory.

Work in postcolonial studies has expanded far beyond the influence of the three thinkers in literary studies whom Robert Young once labeled "the holy trinity" of the field: HOMI K. BHABHA, Edward W. Said, and Gayatri Chakravorty Spivak. Young's own work exemplifies these changing patterns to some degree. His *White Mythologies* (1990) provides one of the earlier introductions to European theoretical backgrounds, and *Colonial Desire* (1995) traces the complicated genealogy of postcolonial theory's fascination with hybridity. *Postcolonialism: An Historical Introduction* (2001) "in many ways rewrites *White Mythologies*" (427), reflecting some of the major shifts in the field, including movement toward (1) embedding accounts of literary and philosophical theory within material and historical contexts in an attempt to reconcile the activism of anticolonial movements with the deconstructive energies of high theory; (2) turning away from debates with postmodernism toward a reconsideration of modernity, alternative modernities, and countermodernities; (3) rethinking historicism as an enabling condition of Western history; (4) widening and complicating the domain of the postcolonial beyond the dominance of the English empire, the English language, and the privileging of colonial discourse analysis; and (5) expressing discontent with the term "postcolonial," which continues to generate dissatisfaction among practitioners and detractors alike and which some (most notably those who equate postcolonial studies with postmodernism) now suggest may have outlived its usefulness.

Throughout the 1990s, work critical of the concept "postcolonial," and especially of the role of the prefix "post-," continued to appear. Theorists sought to move the field back toward material reality and the consequences of oppression for ordinary people's lives, especially in the Third World. The critiques are now part of the orthodox understanding of the field's dimensions, with subsequent work seeking to recast the terms of the debate, to shift it toward a more extensive analysis of the kind of thinking that underlies the debate and provides it with its terms of reference or to examine more intensively the potential of a subfield, such as subaltern studies, within it (see, for example, Vinayak Chaturvedi's anthology *Mapping Subaltern Studies and the Postcolonial* [2000]).

Subaltern studies, too, is characterized by change and disputation. When the nine-volume *Subaltern Studies: Writings on South Asian History and Society* began in 1982, the project defined itself as a historiographic intervention in the writing of Indian history, undertaken out of dissatisfaction with elite forms of history and their failure to address the politics of the people and especially the paradigm of peasant insurgency. By 1986, though, some had turned away from the project's roots in the theories of ANTONIO GRAMSCI and E. P. Thompson toward a dialogue with notions of discourse from MICHEL FOUCAULT or Said. In 1988, subaltern studies entered the U.S. academy as an intervention into postcolonial theory rather than through its initial engagements with historiography, Marxism, and peasant studies. Scholarship developing the culturalist emphasis has been most influential within postcolonial studies. Gyan Prakash noted in 1994 that "we have several accounts of the resistance of the colonized, but few treatments of their resistance as theoretical events" (5). This stream of subaltern studies locates that theorization within the conjunction of the social sciences and the humanities in order to rethink conditions of class, relations of cultural production, historicism, and the idea of the political. Dipesh Chakrabarty argues that "European thought is at once both indispensable and inadequate in helping us to think through the experiences of political modernity in non-Western nations" (16). European theory is not rejected but recontextualized within and beside other systems of thought.

Scholarship continues to elaborate and redirect the foundational insights of many thinkers whose work is seen as indispensable in consolidating the field as an influential revisionist project in the early 1990s and in providing it with its distinctive vocabulary. Spivak, for example, brought the work of the Subaltern Studies Collective to the attention of North Americans and eventually to those working in diverse locations around the world, albeit in a critical and revisionary fashion. Yet despite their significant differences and the complexity of their individual work, Bhahba, Spivak, and Said are associated with a brand of postcolonialism that valorizes exilic, cosmopolitan, and diasporic perspectives and with literary modes of reading the world as text. Bhabha's essays, first published throughout the 1980s but collected in revised form in *The Location of Culture* (1994), established his focus on the "transnational and translational sense of the hybridity of imagined communities" (5) as the dominant image of postcolonial studies in this period. Readers have tended to take from his work his interest in cultural difference, migrant sensibilities, performances of identity, and the "unhomely" as "a paradigmatic colonial and post-colonial condition" (9). Bhabha's later work affiliates itself with border, diasporic, and cosmopolitan theories that sometimes seem to blur the distinctions between postcolonialism and U.S. MULTICULTURALISM, even as his notion of the "politics of location" animates contradictory positions on these matters.

Spivak's *Critique of Postcolonial Reason* (1999) collects revisions of much of her earlier work, reorganized into "a practitioner's progress from colonial discourse studies to transnational cultural studies" (ix–x). In seeking to address "the 'sanctioned ignorance' of the theoretical elite" (x), she works through chapters dedicated to the major disciplinary configurations of philosophy, literature, history, and culture in an attempt to "reconstellate" or "mis-take" their theoretical foundations (128) and to ask the fundamental postcolonial question, "In what interests are differences defined?" (357). Such a question enables her to reconceive the relations between the literary and other spheres without abandoning her belief in literature as an imperiled "cultural good" (*Death* 71). Spivak's influence can be traced within most developments in the field, from the pedagogic to the highly theoretical, from translation theory to engagement with the ethical turn.

Bhabha and Spivak bring deconstructive reading practices to the cultural texts of imperialism and postcolonialism, whereas Said's work retains strong affinities with the European humanist tradition of twentieth-century comparative literature, but they agree in assigning a privileged role to the cultural analysis of strategies of representation. Said's description in *Culture and Imperialism* (1993) of cultural identities as "contrapuntal ensembles" has been readily assimilated to the hybrid antiessentialisms of the other two. Said adds to his continuing articulation of the legacy of orientalism his influential notion of the autonomous intellectual, always "out of place" (as he named his 1999 autobiography), with a duty to "speak truth to power," a belief articulated in *Representations of the Intellectual* (1993) and his essays in *Reflections on Exile* (2000). Because of Said's tireless work analyzing representations of Islam and arguing the Palestinian case for self-determination, only FRANTZ FANON has received more commentary and generated more dispute in this always contentious field.

Depending on one's perspective, postmodernist theories seemed either to energize or to threaten the field throughout the 1980s, but a renewed dialogue with modernity and ideas of the modern, and especially with modernist engagements with Marxism, emerged to preoccupy theorists at the end of the twentieth century. In its redirection of attention from India toward the Caribbean, Black Britain, and the Americas and from the confines of national study toward multiple diasporic formations, Paul Gilroy's *Black Atlantic* (1993) struck many chords within the shifting postcolonial studies field, as did Timothy Brennan's *At Home in the World* (1997) and James Clifford's *Routes* (1997).

There was a beleaguered sense to much Marxist critique of postcolonial studies throughout the 1990s, but renewed engagements with traditions of cultural critique, cultural materialism, and Marxist theories characterize the most energetic refocusings within the field, as in the essays in Crystal Bartolovich and Neil Lazarus's *Marxism, Modernity, and Postcolonial Studies* (2002) and Lazarus's *Nationalism and Cultural Practice in the Postcolonial World* (1999), the latter of which, along with Asha Varadharajan's *Exotic Parodies* (1995), suggests that the THEODOR W. ADORNO of *Negative Dialectics* and the FRANKFURT SCHOOL could prove pivotal.

The strain of postcolonial studies devoted to theorizations of resistance continues as it updates the language and focus for a different constituency. Eduardo Duran and Bonnie Duran's suggestion that "we should not be tolerant of the neocolonialism that runs unchecked through our knowledge-generating systems" (7) continues to motivate postcolonial studies across many fields of endeavor, yet the dialogue between indigenous studies and postcolonial studies remains fragmentary, tentative, and often contentious.

Postcolonial studies research within colonial and transnational feminisms and women's studies has generated several important anthologies, as well as many influential individual studies. A substantial number of theoretically focused analyses engaging colonial and postcolonial feminisms, gender studies, and queer studies in specific locations continue to appear, enriching and complicating theoretical developments within each domain. Following Fanon's problematic lead in "Algeria Unveiled" (1959) feminist critics have analyzed the function of the veil in Muslim societies from variously nuanced postcolonial perspectives. Spivak's meditations on sati have sparked a similar spate of reexaminations of this practice and its signifying functions in India and beyond. Octavio Paz's influential essay "The Sons of La Malinche" (1950) has prompted attempts to rethink this problematic paradigm within Chicana/o and Latin American cultures. These examples serve as reminders that, as Sanjay Srivastava argues, "it seems of continuing importance to conceptualise globalisation also from the perspective of non-metropolitan societies" (192). Such work constitutes the traditional and continuing strength of postcolonial studies, to such an extent that Graham Huggan argues that "postcolonial studies might better be seen as an analytical attempt to *globalise* the already wide scope of cultural studies" (240).

India continues to be a major site of investigation for postcolonial exploration, especially in the field of gender studies, history, and colonial discourse analysis, but its formerly dominant position within the field is increasingly being complemented by work retrieving earlier anticolonialist thinking in other parts of the world, in languages other than English, and by work that addresses colonialist discourse within other locations. Postcolonial approaches are used to unify and differentiate study of the geopolitical organization of the francophone world in Kamal Salhi's *Francophone Post-Colonial Cultures* (2003). Thinkers such as the Argentinian Enrique Dussel, the Uruguayan Eduardo Galeano, the Peruvian José Carlos Mariátegui, and the Brazilian Roberto Schwartz are receiving new attention within the context of postcolonial studies. In the Caribbean, writing by Edouard Glissant has been translated into English and analyzed for its contributions to postcolonial theory, and some of Wilson Harris's essays have been republished for a newly attentive audience. In *Caliban's Reason* (2000) Paget Henry validates a tradition of Afro-Caribbean philosophy in an effort that parallels work undertaken earlier by Kwame Anthony Appiah and Emmanuel Chukwudi Eze for African philosophy. These and other works pose Gaurav Desai's question, "What happens when Africa, for so long the great aporia of postcolonial thought, takes center stage?" (8).

Traditional fields of English literary study previously untouched by postcolonial studies—early modern, eighteenth century, Romanticism—are beginning to identify different gaps within a field that continues to expand its range. This is part of a major shift in the field: self-consciousness about methodology and potential limits to postcolonial reading strategies persists but with less focus on the term "postcolonial" and more attention to the institutional constraints and complicities that attend its practice. Just as cultural studies can no longer be located within a few metropolitan locations, so postcolonial studies is increasingly diversified across African, Asian, Caribbean, Indian, Latin American, and Pacific locations and reverberates through First World cultural and historical studies.

Simon Gikandi suggests that "at the bare bottom, postcolonial theory is the assertion of the centrality of the literary in the diagnosis and representation of the social terrain that we have been discussing under the sign of globalization" (647). While such a focus on literary modes of knowing may indicate obscurantist idealism to those who deplore what they see as the inflation of literary modes of understanding within postcolonial studies, to many others such work, albeit in necessarily altered form due to postcolonial interventions, remains essential to the field's decolonizing agenda, with implications for every field of human endeavor. Thus, the problem STUART HALL identified in "When Was 'The Post-colonial?' " (1996) remains the fundamental challenge facing postcolonial studies in the twenty-first century: "These two halves of the current debate about 'late modernity'—the post-colonial and the analysis of the new developments in global capitalism—have indeed largely proceeded in relative isolation from one another, and to their mutual cost" (257–58). Postcolonial studies is still struggling to find a way to bridge that gap effectively, but the strengths it brings to this debate are considerable.

DIANA BRYDON

See also HOMI K. BHABHA, CULTURAL STUDIES, FRANTZ FANON, GLOBALIZATION, MULTICULTURALISM, RACE AND ETHNICITY, EDWARD W. SAID, and GAYATRI CHAKRAVORTY SPIVAK.

See also bibliographies for HOMI K. BHABHA, EDWARD W. SAID, and GAYATRI CHAKRAVORTY SPIVAK.

Kwame Anthony Appiah, *In My Father's House: Africa in the Philosophy of Culture* (1992); Bill Ashcroft, Gareth Griffiths, and Helen Tiffin, *Key Concepts in Post-Colonial Studies* (1998); Crystal Bartolovich and Neil Lazarus, eds., *Marxism, Modernity, and Postcolonial Studies* (2002); Eugene Benson and L. W. Conolly, eds., *Encyclopedia of Post-Colonial Literatures in English* (1994); Aquino de Braganca and Immanuel Wallerstein, eds., *The African Liberation Reader: Documents of the National Liberation Movements* (1982); Timothy Brennan, *At Home in the World: Cosmopolitanism Now* (1997); Diana Brydon, ed., *Postcolonialism: Critical Concepts in Literary and Cultural Studies* (2000); Dipesh Chakrabarty, *Provincializing Europe: Postcolonial Thought and Historical Difference* (2000); Vinayak Chaturvedi, ed., *Mapping Subaltern Studies and the Postcolonial* (2000); Rey Chow, *Writing Diaspora: Tactics of Intervention in Contemporary Cultural Studies* (1993); James Clifford, *Routes: Travel and Translation in the Late Twentieth Century* (1997); Gaurav Desai, *Subject to Colonialism: African Self-Fashioning and the Colonial Library* (2001); Eduardo Duran and Bonnie Duran, *Native American Postcolonial Psychology* (1995); Teresa L. Ebert, "Subalternity and Feminism in the Moment of the (Post)modern: The Materialist Return," *Order and Partialities* (ed. Kostas Myrsiades and Jerry McGuire, 1995); Emmanuel Chukwudi Eze, ed., *Postcolonial African Philosophy* (1997); Robert Fraser, *Lifting the Sentence: A Poetics of Postcolonial Fiction* (2000); Simon Gikandi, "Globalization and the Claims of Postcoloniality" *South Atlantic Quarterly* 100 (2001); Paul Gilroy, *Black Atlantic: Modernity and Double Consciousness* (1993); Edouard Glissant, *Le discours antillais* (1981, *Caribbean Discourse*, trans. J. Michael Dash, 1989), *Poétique de la relation* (1990, *Poetics of Relation*, trans. Betsy Wing, 1997); David Theo Goldberg and Ato Quayson, preface, *Relocating Postcolonialism* (Goldberg and Quayson); David Theo Goldberg and Ato Quayson, eds., *Relocating Postcolonialism* (2002); Stuart Hall, "When Was 'The Post-Colonial?,' " *The Post-colonial Question: Common Skies, Divided Horizons* (ed. Iain Chambers and Lidia Curti, 1996); Peter Hallward, *Absolutely Postcolonial: Writing between the Singular and the Specific* (2001); Sandra Harding, *Is Science Multi-Cultural? Postcolonialism, Feminism, and Epistemologies* (1998); Barbara Harlow and Mia Carter, eds., *Imperialism and Orientalism: A Documentary Sourcebook* (1999); Paget Henry, *Caliban's Reason* (2000); Graham Huggan, *The Post-Colonial Exotic: Marketing the Margins* (2001); Neil Lazarus, *Nationalism and Cultural Practice in the Postcolonial World* (1999); Tejaswini Niranjana, *Siting Translation: History, Post-Structuralism, and the Colonial Context* (1992); Gyan Prakash, ed., *After Colonialism: Imperial History and Its Postcolonial Displacements* (1994); Kamal Salhi, ed., *Francophone Post-Colonial Cultures* (2003); Henry Schwarz and

Sangeeta Ray, eds., *A Companion to Postcolonial Studies* (2000); David Scott, *Refashioning Futures: Criticism after Postcoloniality* (1999); Sanjay Seth, "A 'Postcolonial World'?" *Contending Images of World Politics* (ed. Greg Fry and Jacinta O'Hagen, 2000); Sanjay Srivastava, *Constructing Post-Colonial India: National Character and the Doon School* (1998); Asha Varadharajan, *Exotic Parodies: Subjectivity in Adorno, Said, and Spivak* (1995); Robert Young, *Colonial Desire: Hybridity in Theory, Culture, and Race* (1995), *Postcolonialism: An Historical Introduction* (2001), *White Mythologies: Writing History and the West* (1990).

Postmodernism

The term "postmodernism" was first used in reference to architecture as early as 1947 and then by the historian Arnold Toynbee in the 1950s. Literary critics, most notably Harry Levin, Irving Howe, Leslie Fiedler, and Ihab Hassan, began to use the term in the 1960s to distinguish post–World War II experimental fiction from the classics of high modernism. The term spurred skepticism (had not James Joyce, Franz Kafka, and the various avant-gardes already performed all the tricks now called postmodern?) and antagonistic evaluation. The Old Left (Howe) and the critical establishment (Levin) deplored the new writers' lack of high seriousness, their apparent contempt for the well-made, unified literary work, and their addiction to popular culture.

For many post-war critics the linchpin of modernism was art's autonomy from the sordid daily concerns of commercial culture. The artist (almost always male in this modernist vision of heroic alienation) exiled himself from ordinary life to create a useless, disinterested art object that was potentially revolutionary in the purity of its contempt for the given. Only the distance afforded by exile and autonomy maintained art's critical and oppositional edge. Postmodern art seemed to capitulate to the dominant culture, which various writers now designated "postindustrial" or "postmodern." Thus, discussions of postmodernism began to debate not only changes in artistic style but also whether society itself had changed. Had the West entered some new historical period—and, if so, had that change ushered in a new relation between the arts and society?

Fiedler's slogan "Cross the border, close the gap" (17) exemplified the determination of postmodernism's champions to pull art back into the maelstrom of daily life. Literary criticism, along with its new colleague literary theory, began focusing on the complex relations between the artwork and its social contexts. Generally speaking, the formal analysis of the artwork in isolation yielded to an exploration of the work's social determinants and to its ideological or political impact on its audience. (This shift took some twenty years, 1965–1985 being the key period of transition.) The postmodernists argued that the belief that intellectuals and artists can enjoy an artistic and political autonomy from capitalism is both illusionary because the very materials of their work (language, images) come from the culture and sterile because the purity of the alienated artist forecloses access to the energies and disputes that are lived in the culture while also severing any connection to an audience beyond the artistic elite. The modernist artist is left high and dry.

A cultural politics accompanied this shift in critical paradigms. Against the traditional Marxist emphasis on economic issues and the liberal concern with legally guaranteed equality, the New Left and the liberation movements it inspired (feminism, gay and lesbian activism, post–civil rights racial politics) insisted that cultural practices—common linguistic usage, media images, educational curricula and techniques—were crucial sites of oppression and of potentially transformative struggle. The exuberant valuing of heterogeneity over unity in 1960s radicalism foreshadowed postmodern theory's later concern with "difference" and postcolonial theory's interest in "hybridity." The new art and the new politics ignored the distinction between high and low art, tapping into the affective power of popular culture. This postmodern populism opened the door to heterogeneous voices, mixed genres (like the New Journalism), and other breaches of decorum.

The rise of literary theory, particularly that inspired by the French poststructuralists, brought postmodernism from the streets and the novel into the academy. Theory was not associated with postmodernism at first, but JEAN-FRANÇOIS LYOTARD'S *The Postmodern Condition* in 1979 made the two nearly synonymous. Defining "*postmodern* as incredulity toward metanarratives" (xxiv), Lyotard emphasizes the antifoundational and antiholistic aspects of French theory, tied to its hostility to eternal, metaphysical truths and to grand explanatory narratives. He proposes a postmodern world in which decisions are made on the basis of local conditions and are applicable only in that limited context. Individuals participate in a multitude of such localities, and the lessons, beliefs, and practices of one site are not transferable to any other. Lyotard celebrates this multiplicity of "language games" (xxiv) and offers ceaseless experimentation in all these games as the highest good.

A counterattack against Lyotard was led by Jürgen Habermas and FREDRIC JAMESON, who employed arguments reminiscent of Levin's and Howe's earlier worries. Habermas insists that a complete immersion in the local gives us no way to judge it and is thus doomed to accommodation with the given. Jameson similarly laments a lack of distance between postmodern art and theory and the capitalist society that generates it. While Habermas believes we must retain modernity's dream of emancipation through Reason, Jameson argues that we need an art capable of representing the complex realities of a global economic order that exploits the majority. The debate here focuses on the political consequences of French theory, on whether it actually disrupts Western society by advocating local, varied, heterogeneous "difference" against the unifying, identity—obsessed practices of the massive states and transnational corporations that organize life in the contemporary West and, increasingly, around the world. What the French writers and their leftist critics (EDWARD W. SAID and TERRY EAGLETON, as well as Jameson) share is a conviction that language, images, and other cultural phenomena are as central to the production of contemporary social order as economic or political processes, if not more central. French sociologist JEAN BAUDRILLARD argues that we enter a postmodern world once the production of images and information, not the production of material goods, determines who holds power. Such arguments make cultural politics central and lead directly to the interest on the part of CULTURAL STUDIES in identity formation and collective action through signifying practices. But there still remains the question how to move from art's rewording of the world to measurable social impact, and the leftist critics of French theory almost always accuse it of having no model of political action beyond anarchistic linguistic play, while its rightist critics accuse it of cynicism and nihilism.

Given this contested relation of postmodern (French) theory to politics, relations between more directly political forms of criticism (such as feminism, ethnic studies, or gay and lesbian studies) have been wary. Nonwhite and nonmale critics have often been impatient with abstruse philosophical arguments surrounding epistemological foundations and have been suspicious of postmodern deconstructions of the subject, concentrating instead on more historically informed studies of the social origins of various marginalized groups and of the biases that shape how those groups have been treated and (mis)represented. This work is recognizably postmodern in its focus on local conditions and its denial of universal standards for the judgment of all cases. And this work also distantly echoes JACQUES DERRIDA's account of Western thought's hostility to and fascination with the Other and MICHEL FOUCAULT's work on the social constitution and discipline of identity. But insofar as they use history and memory to strengthen group and personal agency, these critics advocate an "identity politics" that goes against the hostility toward identity, the insistence that it is a trap, found in much poststructuralist thought. The battles over identity's usefulness as a matter of political strategy have been particularly pronounced in feminism, with JUDITH BUTLER's influential work arguing for the abandonment of a disenabling attachment to subjection.

1980s discussion of postmodernism in the arts focused especially on issues of style and periodization. Critics such as Hassan, Charles Jencks, Linda Hutcheon, and Brian McHale attempt to describe the stylistic hallmarks of postmodernism. Artists and critics influenced by Baudrillard show a concern with the images in circulation in the culture and their recoding, reuse, and recycling in art. Unlike the heroic modernist, who created works out of pure imagination, the postmodern artist works with cultural givens, trying to manipulate them in various ways (parody, pastiche, collage, juxtaposition) for various ends. The ultimate aim is to appropriate these materials in such a way as to avoid being utterly dominated by them.

These matters all became muddier after the 1980s. By 1995 the debate over postmodern theory had lost most of its steam, while the practices of contemporary artists and writers no longer appeared similar enough to justify using a single term like "postmodernism" to characterize them. We appear to be in a pluralistic, eclectic moment in which both artists and critics use bits and pieces of various theories and cultural materials without being concerned about allegiance to one side or the other in some central debate. Just as one does not need to be either a Derridean or an anti-Derridean, so one does not have to choose whether to be modern or postmodern. In the early 1990s, Jameson and David Harvey tried to link the stylistic features of contemporary art to a more general account of the current social order, adopting a fairly traditional notion that art reflects the material realities of the day. But they also had to adopt the Hegelian and Marxist notion that every era has an essential unity, one that they associated with GLOBALIZATION. Critics of their view, especially those working in POSTCOLONIAL STUDIES, objected to the notion that globalization meant the eclipse of meaningful local differences. What globalization really entails, they insisted, is the struggle of capitalist economic forces with the traditions and values in various locales. The results of these struggles are always mixed, unpredictable in advance, and different from place to place. These kinds of arguments echo an earlier view, expressed most forcefully by Andreas Huyssen, that the widespread use of the term "postmodern" leads to a crisis in the whole notion of historical and artistic periods. Totalizing accounts of an era generate skepticism because distinctive features of that era can always be discovered in other eras, while noncharacteristic features will be found in the era in question. Periodization is a rhetorical creation, a way of constructing a historical "other" that allows us to define a desirable present by contrasting it to an inferior past, or vice versa. In this view, what is distinctive about postmodernism is not something new but our attention to and interest in features of the past that until now were most often ignored. Postmodernism, then, is just part of the very complex rereading of history taking place in the current climate of a critical questioning of the Western tradition. Paradoxically, many of the materials for a radical questioning can be found in the tradition itself if we look in different places (noncanonical works) or in familiar places with new eyes. But there is also a concomitant interest in non-Western voices that offer different perspectives on the West's image of itself and its past.

During the postmodernism debates' heyday a stark choice was often presented: modernist or postmodernist, jettisoning the whole Western tradition or buying it wholesale. Such dramatic options can generate clarity and intensity but do not encourage nuance. Oddly enough, the term "postmodern" tempted critics toward the kind of grand narrative moves that Lyotard claimed he was trying to avoid and made them rather shy of using the term, although it can remain a useful heuristic for the study of contemporary fiction. The term is still widely used as a convenient catch-all reference to the sea change in critical practices and artistic mood that followed the political upheavals of the 1960s and the arrival of French theory.

In retrospect, postmodernism is probably best understood as marking the site of several related, but not identical, debates among artists and intellectuals during the last four decades of the twentieth century. These conflicts revolved around the relation of artworks to social context, art and theory to political action and the dominant social order, cultural practices to the transformation or maintenance of society in all its aspects, the collapse of traditional philosophical foundations to the possibility of critical distance from and effective critique of the status quo, and an image-dominated consumer society to artistic practice, and around the future of a Western tradition that appears more heterogeneous than previously thought at the same time that it appears insufficiently tolerant of (open to) multiplicity. At the very least, post-modernism signals the multiplication of voices, questions, and conflicts that shattered what seemed to be (without ever really being) the placid unanimity of the great tradition and the West that gloried in it.

JOHN MCGOWAN

See also JEAN BAUDRILLARD, FEMINIST THEORY AND CRITICISM: 5. 1990 AND AFTER, FRENCH THEORY AND CRITICISM: 1945 AND AFTER, FREDRIC JAMESON, JEAN-FRANÇOIS LYOTARD, MARXIST THEORY AND CRITICISM: 2. STRUCTURALIST MARXISM, and MARXIST THEORY AND CRITICISM: 3. 1989 AND AFTER.

See also bibliographies for JEAN BAUDRILLARD, JUDITH BUTLER, and FREDRIC JAMESON.

Leslie A. Fiedler, *What Was Literature? Class Culture and Mass Society* (1982); Hal Foster, ed., *The Anti-Aesthetic: Essays on Postmodern Culture* (1983); Jürgen Habermas, *Der Philosophische Diskurs der Moderne* (1985, *The Philosophical Discourse of Modernity*, trans. Frederick G. Lawrence, 1987); David Harvey, *The Condition of Postmodernity: An Inquiry into the Origins of Cultural Change* (1989); Ihab Hassan, *The Postmodern Turn: Essays in Postmodern Theory and Culture* (1987); Linda Hutcheon, *A Poetics of Postmodernism: History, Theory, Fiction* (1988); Andreas Huyssen, *After the Great Divide: Modernism, Mass Culture, Postmodernism* (1986); Charles Jencks, *The Language of Post-Modern Architecture* (1977, 4th ed., 1984); Jean-François Lyotard, *La condition postmoderne: Rapport sur le savoir* (1979, *The Postmodern Condition: A Report on Knowledge*, trans. Geoff Bennington and Brian Massumi, 1984); Brian McHale, *Postmodernist Fiction* (1987).

Psychoanalytic Theory and Criticism

1. Traditional Freudian Criticism

Several of SIGMUND FREUD's contemporaries as well as later writers produced studies of literary figures and literary works that established elementary models of psychoanalytic criticism along the lines of Freud's own forays into literary criticism, such as his remarks on the Oedipal scheme in *Hamlet* (1899), his theoretical essay "Creative Writers and Day-dreaming" (1908), and his psychobiographical essay "Dostoevsky and Parricide" (1928). Such models typically assumed relative transparency between the fictional product and the creative artist: read psychoanalytically, the literary work disclosed the author's unconscious fantasies. The aim of this criticism was typically psychobiographical; the exact, manifest terms of the narrative were subordinated to those patterns of wish and defense revealed by analytic discovery of "latent content." The best examples of this style of criticism (still in practice) refuse to subordinate art to neurosis and deploy the tools of psychoanalysis to explore precise terms of language, metaphor, and character.

After Freud, the best-known pioneer of traditional psychoanalytic criticism is probably Ernest Jones (1879–1958). Jones authored almost two hundred essays in theory and applied psychoanalysis, including articles on dreams, literature, religion, war neuroses, female sexuality, Ireland, chess, ice skating, and the common cold. He was instrumental in introducing Freud to the English-speaking world and presided over the origins of the British psychoanalytic establishment. He was the author of the first full biography of Freud (1957), the standard account until later biographies were produced by Ronald W. Clark (1980) and Peter Gay (1988). Jones's early monograph *On the Nightmare* (1910) demonstrates a bold effort to apply psychoanalytic perspectives to history and legend, sketching analyses of witches, vampires, and Druids, and engaging in speculative etymology (mares, horses, and the linguistic m[a]r root). (Jones himself suffered throughout his life from vivid nightmares [see Brome].) His essay "The Theory of Symbolism" (1916) is an energetic and shrewd effort to regularize Freud's ideas as stated in *The Interpretation of Dreams* (1900) and elsewhere: to articulate elementary structures of symbolic representation in dream and literature. Jones connects symbols with primitive sensorial residues of "primary process" mentation anchored in repressed, unconscious representations of the body, sexual life, family relations, and death: a reservoir of images common to human development and liable to regressive attention during periods of stress, dreaming, or creative activity. He is especially attentive to the linguistic, etymological origins of symbols. (JACQUES LACAN, in his insistence on the *letter* rather than the *corpus* in symbolism, still gives a substantial nod to Jones's essay ["Function" 81].)

Another of Freud's first-generation followers, Otto Rank (1884–1939), covered more literary and theoretical ground. *The Myth of the Birth of the Hero* (1909) is a remarkably erudite compilation of core motifs in cultural myths: the hero, the double, and the theme of incest. Rank's essay on the "The Double" (1914) uses literary examples from E. T. A. Hoffman, Fyodor Dostoevsky, Robert Louis Stevenson, Oscar Wilde, Guy de Maupassant, and Edgar Allan Poe, aligning brief biographical sketches with theoretical emphasis on narcissism and projection: the double is both a reflection of self-love and a rival. His massive work on the incest-motif, *The Incest Theme in Literature and Legend* (1912), is a broad survey of Oedipal dynamics in European and world literature and mythology.

Less well known than Jones or Rank, Ella Freeman Sharpe (1875–1947) deserves mention because of her unique attention to language, especially metaphor. Her essay "The Impatience of Hamlet" (1929) extends Jones's study (the early version published in 1910) and deepens it to consider pre-Oedipal issues, as well as the therapeutic functions of art: "The poet is not Hamlet. Hamlet is what he might have been if he had not written the play of *Hamlet*" (205). At her death she was working on a large treatment of Shakespeare's late career, a portion of which was published as "From *King Lear* to *The Tempest*" (1946). This fragmented essay is full of brilliant speculations and amplifies Freud's identification of the tripartite mother-imago in *Lear* (see Freud, "The Theme of the Three Caskets" [1913]). Sharpe's literalism opens her to charges that she writes the worst sort of psychoanalytic criticism, as when she speaks of "child Lear" howling in rage at his mother's pregnancy, or the king's retinue of knights as a symbol for feces, or the Bard himself as an angry, defecating infant (246). Yet her criticism is sharper than its reductions. She was well aware of the problem of treating characters as people or patients. At its best her own critical language marries the metaphors of Shakespeare and psychoanalysis to construct provocative readings of particular passages.

One of the fullest early developments of Freudian analysis of a single author was produced by Marie Bonaparte (1882–1962). Perhaps best known for her largess in helping Freud and his family escape the Nazis in 1938, Princess Bonaparte wrote an immense study of Edgar Allan Poe (1933). Freud wrote a brief preface to the work, which is a thorough effort to relate biographical details to all aspects of the artist's literary production. Bonaparte relies heavily on Freud's theoretical relation of the poet to the dreamer ("Creative Writers and Day-dreaming" [1908]) and translates backward from literature to unconscious wishes and fears, producing reductive psychosexual allegories. Hers is a primary-process criticism that seeks to collapse conventional forms of literary representation in favor of regressive translations to unconscious origins. She views Poe as a writer who transformed private traumata into fiction, principally the death of his mother when he was two, and argues that his artistic goal was to resurrect a living bond to a dead woman, a project simultaneously thrilling and terrifying. Bonaparte's Poe is a pathological, "sadonecrophilist" genius haunted by obsessive fantasies he could not comprehend but only repeat. More recent psychoanalytic approaches to the mystery of Poe, studies that essentially rely on

Bonaparte even as they deride her apparent crudeness, are Daniel Hoffman's *Poe Poe Poe Poe Poe Poe Poe* (1972) and Lacan's "Seminar on 'The Purloined Letter'" (1956). This style of psychobiography achieved more sophisticated application in works by Phyllis Greenacre on Jonathan Swift and Lewis Carroll and by Leon Edel on Henry James.

Probably the best contemporary illustration of traditional Freudian criticism is the early work of Frederick Crews (b. 1938). His seminal book on Nathaniel Hawthorne (1966) rescues that writer from conventional moralistic allegory and attends seriously to the dark landscape of sexual ambivalence that energizes his fiction. "The form of [Hawthorne's] plots," writes Crews, "often constitutes a return of the repressed" (17). Hawthorne's fascination with Puritans and the cultural history of guilt reflects his own unconscious impulses, which tend primarily to be Oedipal (79). Crews offers finely tuned analyses of metaphor, image, and character, which he presses toward psychobiographical conclusions about Hawthorne's "incomplete resolution of early Oedipal feelings" (241). For the most part, Crews's Hawthorne is carried by his fantasies rather than being the master of them. Beginning in the mid-1970s, Crews developed a radical disaffection with psychoanalysis. Although he came to reject the claims of psychoanalysis to scientific or interpretive validity, Crews retained a relatively generous attitude toward his book on Hawthorne. Instead of using Freud to explain Hawthorne's sexual fascinations, however, Crews later pointed to similar themes in both writers and located each in a zeitgeist of "the psychological atmosphere of Romanticism" (*Skeptical* xiii–xiv).

DAVID WILLBERN

See also SIGMUND FREUD.

Marie Bonaparte, *Edgar Poe, étude psychanalytique* (1933, 2 vols., *The Life and Works of Edgar Allan Poe: A Psychoanalytic Interpretation*, trans. John Rodker, 1971); Richard Boothby, *Freud as Philosopher: Metapsychology after Lacan* (2001); Victor Brome, *Ernest Jones: Freud's Alter Ego* (1982); Norman O. Brown, *Love's Body* (1966); Ronald W. Clark, *Sigmund Freud: The Man and the Cause* (1980); Frederick Crews, *Out of My System: Psychoanalysis, Ideology, and Critical Method* (1975), *Psychoanalysis and Literary Process* (1970), *The Sins of the Fathers: Hawthorne's Literary Themes* (1966), *Skeptical Engagements* (1986); Leon Edel, *Henry James* (5 vols., 1953–1972), *Henry James: A Life* (1985); Anton Ehrenzweig, *The Hidden Order of Art: A Study in the Psychology of Artistic Imagination* (1967); Otto Fenichel, *The Psychoanalytic Theory of Neurosis* (1945); Graham Frankland, *Freud's Literary Culture* (2000); Peter Gay, *Freud: A Life for Our Time* (1988); Phyllis Greenacre, *Swift and Carroll: A Psychoanalytic Study of Two Lives* (1955); Daniel Hoffman, *Poe Poe Poe Poe Poe Poe Poe* (1972); Frederick J. Hoffman, *Freudianism and the Literary Mind* (1945); Ernest Jones, *Hamlet and Oedipus* (1949), *The Life and Work of Sigmund Freud* (3 vols., 1957), *On the Nightmare* (1931), *Psycho-Myth, Psycho-History: Essays in Applied Psychoanalysis* (1974), "The Theory of Symbolism," *Papers on Psycho-Analysis* (5th ed., 1916); Ernst Kris, *Psychoanalytic Explorations in Art* (1952); Julia Kristeva, *La révolte intime* (1997, *Intimate Revolt: The Powers and Limits of Psychoanalysis*, trans. Jeanine Herman, 2002); Jacques Lacan, "Fonction et champ de la parole et du langage en psychanalyse," *La psychanalyse* 1 (1956) ("The Function and Field of Speech and Language in Psychoanalysis" ["The Rome Discourse"], *Écrits: A Selection*, trans. Alan Sheridan, 1977), "Le seminaire sur 'La lettre volee'" *La psychanalyse* 2 (1956) ("Seminar on 'The Purloined Letter,'" *Écrits*, John Muller and William Richardson, eds., *The Purloined Poe: Lacan, Derrida, and Psychoanalytic Reading* (1988); Otto Rank, *Der Doppelgänger* (1914, *The Double: A Psychoanalytic Study*, trans. Harry Tucker Jr., 1925), *Das Inzest-Motiv in Dichtung und Sage* (1912, *The Incest Theme in Literature and Legend: Fundamentals of a Psychology of Literary Creation*, trans. Gregory C. Richter, 1992), *Der Künstler und andere Beiträge zur Psychoanalyse der dichterischen Schaffens* (4th ed., 1925, *Art and Artist: Creative Urge and Personality Development*, trans. Charles Francis Atkison, 1932), *Mythus von der Geburt des Helden* (1909, *The Myth of the Birth of the Hero*, trans. F. Robbins and Smith Ely Jelliffe, 1914); Ella Freeman Sharpe, *Collected Papers on Psycho-Analysis* (ed. Marjorie Brierley, 1950); Elizabeth Wright, *Psychoanalytic Criticism: A Reappraisal* (1984, 2nd ed., 1998).

2. Reconceptualizing Freud

Melanie Klein, Simon O. Lesser, Norman N. Holland, and Norman O. Brown reconceptualized classical Freudianism, arguing that the content of psychic fantasy was relevant to literary study as well as to therapy. For Klein, literature and fantasy reflect the drive; for Lesser and Holland, texts evoke in readers intrapsychic struggles characterized chiefly by strategies of defense; for Brown, such struggles are also observable in history. The impact of these theorists' writings challenged the postwar hegemony of New Criticism; their work continues to be invoked in contemporary literary debates, including those that concern DECONSTRUCTION.

Melanie Klein (1882–1960) was a prominent member of the interwar "English school" of psychoanalysis in London. Following through on her intuition of a parallel between dreams and children at play, Klein undertook the first serious and extensive analyses of young children, work that culminated in *The Psycho-Analysis of Children* (1932). There Klein hypothesized the existence of a pre-Oedipal phase (or "position" in her terminology) in which children introject their first object, the breast, splitting it into ideal and persecutory (or "good" and "bad") modes, an action that corresponds to the genesis of ego and superego. This introjection and splitting presupposes the existence of a nonlibidinous aggressive drive. Children later experience "the depressive position," in which the final loss of the good object becomes the prototype of all subsequent mourning. Psychic life consists of symbiotic anxieties (at the prospect of annihilation or loss) and defenses (expressed in mature love as alternations between guilt and reparation). In challenging the supremacy of the Oedipus complex, Klein presented an alternative psychoanalytic account of feminine sexuality. Rather than conceiving of girls as arriving at sexuality through deprivation or lack, Klein redefined penis envy as a defense against a more primordial fear, the attack from either parent (as introjected in the nascent superego).

In *Revolution in Poetic Language* (1974) JULIA KRISTEVA draws on the Kleinian theory of the drive to argue that such pre-Oedipal processes correspond to the semiotic (27, 151–52). Toril Moi argues that HÉLÈNE CIXOUS's mother figure may be based in part on Klein's "Good Mother" (115). Kleinian theory is invoked by Margery Durham in her explication of Samuel Taylor Coleridge's "Christabel," and Simon

Stuart applies Klein's theories to Romantic poets, especially William Blake and William Wordsworth. Alison Sinclair studies the literary theme of cuckoldry from a Kleinian perspective, arguing that deceived husbands both deny and reenact the childhood experience of dispossession; she concludes that literature itself may be understood as a continuation of that denial.

Like Klein, whom he cites with approval, Simon O. Lesser (1909–1979) was one of the first American critics to argue that the experience of reading and interpreting literature should be understood psychoanalytically as a function of the ego's defenses against prohibited impulses, especially as these impulses are stimulated by fantasies evoked by the text. Relying on the work of Klein, Ernst Kris, and Otto Fenichel, Lesser asserted, in articles written between 1952 and 1976, collected in *Fiction and the Unconscious* (1957) and in *The Whispered Meanings* (1977), that formalist criticism (e.g., that of Cleanth Brooks and Robert Penn Warren) was naïve in its misunderstanding of the source of the reader's identification with the narrators and protagonists of fiction. Lesser's best-known demonstration of his case is his reading of Nathaniel Hawthorne's "My Kinsman, Major Molineux." He contends that readers implicitly identify with Robin's unconscious quest for sexual adventure and his fantasy of escape from authority even while consciously denying any such identification. Lesser accuses New Criticism and other formalisms of evading the powerful instinctual drives expressed in literature at the latent level, as in Elder Olson's interpretation of W. B. Yeats's "Sailing to Byzantium," which he faults for ignoring the speaker's duplicity and ambivalence about sexuality.

Lesser's influence on Norman N. Holland (b. 1927) has been explicitly acknowledged: the younger critic recognized his predecessor's innovation in using the tenets of psychoanalysis to understand the act of reading literature. In *Psychoanalysis and Shakespeare* (1966) his criticism became overtly Freudian, although his objectives were still text centered, but in *The Dynamics of Literary Response* (1968) Holland developed a reader-response criticism that drew on psychoanalytic and psychological traditions of ego development (see READER-RESPONSE CRITICISM). The continuity between his earliest and latest work is in his concern to elaborate some fundamental human identity in and through the study of literature. Holland's argument in *Dynamics* is close to Lesser's in *Fiction and the Unconscious*: readers experience literature as a transformation of unconscious fantasy materials. However, in works since *Five Readers Reading* (1975) he has exchanged his earlier text-centered model for a wholly interactive one that defines text as promptuary and the experience of reading as part of infinitely recursive feedback loops in which readers are located. Holland sees this interactive model as part of a twentieth-century tradition that includes Ernst Cassirer, Edmund Husserl, and John Dewey and that "bridged the gap" of Cartesian dualism.

Holland's work has accorded increasing importance to individual variations in interpretation. In "The Delphi Seminar," coauthored with Murray Schwartz (1975), and in later works, Holland advocates a pedagogy according to which diversity of interpretation is never divorced from individual psychology. He advocates and exemplifies the view that critics must acknowledge their own anxieties, defenses, and even sociopolitical biases in dealing with texts. In his most recent work he calls for reader-response criticism to become conscious of such unacknowledged presuppositions by learning from questions raised by feminist, Third World, and gay critics. A complete account of his critical position, together with his assessment of related ones, is available in Holland's *Guide to Psychoanalytic Psychology and Literature and Psychology* (1990).

Among these attempts to rethink Freud, Norman O. Brown's is the most idiosyncratic; Brown (1913–2002) made two principal contributions to contemporary criticism: *Life against Death* (1959) and *Love's Body* (1966). Brown argued that Freud's importance lay in his depiction, in *Civilization and Its Discontents* (1930), of a universal neurosis, that the institution of repression implied the seemingly permanent human subjugation to a life of illusion and sublimation, and that the only chance for some "way out" of this dilemma was to be found in Freud's metapsychological speculations on Eros and Thanatos, the life and death drives (or libido and *Todestrieb*). The "way out" that Brown adumbrates is set forth in the last chapter of *Life against Death*, "The Resurrection of the Body." There he argues that psychoanalysis must situate itself inside the larger tradition of occidental and oriental mysticism, which he valorizes in works of Christian gnosticism, Jewish kabbalism, Taoism, Jacob Boehme, Blake, Rainer Maria Rilke, and dissident psychoanalytic theorists. Brown interprets Freud's "oceanic feeling"—from *The Future of an Illusion* (1928)—as denoting a desire for union between self and world that, once recovered, can heal the divisions created by repression. Brown's intent in *Love's Body* is to pursue to its logical conclusion this "way out," beginning with a perception of separateness and the repression of political society. Brown paraphrases and quotes directly from more than three hundred works in the mystical tradition he celebrates, but apart from free association and a general relevance to his chapters' broad rubrics, these excerpts are not otherwise connected. The result is a mosaic in which the intellectual affinities of various authors are asserted through juxtaposition.

CHRISTOPHER D. MORRIS

See also SIGMUND FREUD and READER-RESPONSE CRITICISM.

David Bleich, *Subjective Criticism* (1978); Norman O. Brown, *Apocalypse and/or Metamorphosis* (1993), "Apocalypse: The Place of Mystery in the Life of the Mind," *Harper's* (May 1961), *Closing Time* (1973), "Daphne, or Metamorphosis," *Myths, Dreams, and Religion* (ed. Joseph Campbell, 1970), *Hermes the Thief* (1947), *Hesiod's Theogeny* (1953), *Life against Death* (1959), *Love's Body* (1966); Janice Doane and Devon Hodges, *From Klein to Kristeva: Psychoanalytic Feminism and the Search for the "Good Enough" Mother* (1992); Margery Durham, "The Mother Tongue: Christabel and the Language of Love," *The (M)other Tongue: Essays in Feminist Psychoanalytic Interpretation* (ed. Shirley N. Garner, Claire Kahane, and Madelon Sprengnether, 1986); Elizabeth A. Flynn and Patrocinio P. Schweickart, eds.,

Gender and Reading: Essays on Readers, Texts, and Contexts (1986); Phyllis Grosskurth, *Melanie Klein: Her World and Her Work* (1986); Norman N. Holland, *The Dynamics of Literary Response* (1968), *Five Readers Reading* (1975), *Holland's Guide to Psychoanalytic Psychology and Literature and Psychology* (1990), *The I* (1985), *Laughing: A Psychology of Humor* (1982), "The Nature of Psychoanalytic Criticism," *Literature and Psychology* 12 (1962), "The New Paradigm: Subjective or Transactive?" *New Literary History* 7 (1976), "The Prophetic Tradition," *Studies in Romanticism* 21 (1982), *Psychoanalysis and Shakespeare* (1966), "Twenty-five Years and Thirty Days," *Psychoanalytic Quarterly* 55 (1986), "Unity Identity Text Self," *PMLA* 90 (1975); Norman N. Holland and Murray Schwartz, "The Delphi Seminar," *College English* 36 (1975); Norman N. Holland and Leona F. Sherman, "Gothic Possibilities" (Flynn and Schweickart); Melanie Klein, *The Writings of Melanie Klein* (4 vols., 1984, vol. 1, *Love, Guilt, and Reparation and Other Works, 1921–1945*; vol. 2, *The Psycho-Analysis of Children*; vol. 3, *Envy and Gratitude and Other Works, 1946–1963*; vol. 4, *Narrative of a Child Analysis*); Julia Kristeva, *La révolution du langage poétique: L'avant-garde à la fin du XIXe siècle, Lautréamont et Mallarmé* (1974, *Revolution in Poetic Language*, trans. Margaret Waller, 1984); Simon O. Lesser, *Fiction and the Unconscious* (1957), "The Image of the Father," *Five Approaches of Literary Criticism* (ed. Wilbur Scott, 1963), "The Language of Fiction," *A College Book of Modern Fiction* (ed. Walter B. Rideout and James K. Robinson, 1961), "Some Unconscious Elements in Response to Fiction," *Literature and Psychology* 3 (1953), *The Whispered Meanings: Selected Essays of Simon O. Lesser* (ed. Robert Sprich and Richard Nolan, 1977); Toril Moi, *Sexual/Textual Politics: Feminist Literary Theory* (1985, 2nd ed., 2002); Michael Rustin, *The Good Society and the Inner World: Psychoanalysis, Politics, and Culture* (1991); Alison Sinclair, *The Deceived Husband: A Kleinian Approach to the Literature of Infidelity* (1993); Simon Stuart, *New Phoenix Wings: Reparation in Literature* (1979).

3. The Post-Lacanians

In the late 1930s JACQUES LACAN began challenging a number of conclusions long advanced by many psychoanalytic theorists and analysts. Lacan not only inveighed against the approach of American ego psychologists and their emphasis on the stability of the ego as a betrayal of Freudian thought but he also redefined the ego in relation to the "subject" of structural linguistics and SEMIOTICS. In his "return to Freud," Lacan attempts to find rigorously psychoanalytic explanations for the ego's relation to the unconscious, which Lacan reconceives in semiotic terms and claims was "structured like a language."

In the 1970s and 1980s a new wave of French theorists argued that Lacan did not go far enough in probing precisely the areas characterizing his discourse: the psychoanalytic dimensions of the "subject"; psychoanalysis as both a clinical practice and a cultural institution; and psychoanalysis as ideologically committed and engaged. JULIA KRISTEVA, for instance, has followed Lacan in her conception of the subject and in her approach to the woman question: "A woman cannot 'be'; it is something which does not even belong in the order of *being*" (Marks and de Courtivron 137). As for writing, Kristeva sees women as facing two alternatives: either valorizing "phallic dominance, associated with the privileged father-daughter relationship, which gives rise to the tendency toward mastery," or valorizing "a silent underwater body," which entails the choice of marginalization (Marks and de Courtivron 166). The alternative she proposes is that women assume a negative function, one that would reject whole structures and explode social codes. Likewise, Michèle Montrelay, who sees her writing as a contribution to a better understanding of the laws, structure, and dynamic of the unconscious, is convinced that "in our civilization, psychoanalysis, as theory and as treatment, is one of the most precious, highest, most symbolic forms of freedom" (Jardine and Menke 254) and emphasizes the political aspect of her work. In *The Shadow and the Name* (1977) she attempts to probe psychoanalytic concepts, such as the assumption of woman as a "dark continent" and others concerning gender relations that continue to function within Freudian discourse. Often close to representing femininity in traditional terms—the feminine as the shadow and the outside that supports culture—Montrelay is concerned with exposing the phallocentric bias in the Lacanian ethical hierarchy that privileges the symbolic over the imaginary. Rather than attempting to reverse the hierarchy, she proposes to shift the emphasis away from a hierarchy of values and to regard the imaginary not as "the poor relative" but as necessary to give consistency to the symbolic (155–56).

Contrarily, feminists such as JUDITH BUTLER question whether such a return is even possible and instead seek other strategies for destabilizing structures that reify phallic privilege in the symbolic. In *Gender Trouble: Feminism and the Subversion of Identity* (1990) Butler criticizes Lacan's theoretical construction of the symbolic on the grounds that it is too deterministic and does not account for the variations, imperfections, and alterations that can take place in the signifying structures defining gender and reinforcing phallic privilege: "The alternative perspective that emerges from psychoanalytic theory suggests that multiple and coexisting identifications produce conflicts, convergences, and innovative dissonances within gender configurations which contest the fixity of masculine and feminine placements with respect to paternal law" (67). In *Bodies That Matter: On the Discursive Limits of "Sex"* (1993), contending that there is no inside or outside to culture, no a priori state of being, prediscursive reality, or pre-Oedipal state, Butler also reworks Lacan's ideas about the mirror stage and the symbolic to demonstrate how universal applications of Lacan's theories fail to describe a number of complications—that identification and desire are not always separate, mutually exclusive developments and that heterosexist assumptions underlie the Oedipal narrative in psychoanalysis.

Similarly committed to a more radical strategy, Shoshana Felman explores literary and cultural criticism in relation to what she frequently calls the force of Lacan's teaching, his "revolutionary" pedagogy. Her work indicates the movement of Lacanian studies in the 1980s toward an appreciation of Lacanian *practice* as actively engaged with postmodern and avant-garde modes of thought. For Felman, Lacan's great contribution to contemporary culture is his teaching about rhetorical "performance" and "cognition," doing and knowing. She draws on speech act philosopher J. L. Austin's definition of the "performative" as rhetorical enactment, language use as separate as possible from what it conveys, a pure doing. The "constative," or cognitive, is what rhetoric creates, meaning as pure sense conveyed apart from how it came to be. The "revolutionary" dimension of Lacan's pedagogy for Felman is the dialogism of the performative and constative, how in practice they undermine, deconstruct, and yet inform each other. The interactions of doing and undoing form the dynamic basis, Felman says, of psychoanalysis's "ineradicable newness" (*Literary* 12), its evergreen vitality and unceasing "revolutionary" nature.

In *Jacques Lacan and the Adventure of Insight* (1987) Felman wants to bring pedagogy into psychoanalysis and to show that a pedagogue should teach in relation to the student's "unmeant knowledge" (77), the unconscious as it is inscribed but at the same time hidden in teaching as a kind of text; the "unmeant" is of paramount importance because "teaching, like analysis has to deal not so much with lack of knowledge as with resistances to knowledge" (79). Felman's rendition of Lacan is an implicit plea for adoption of a complex and subtle response to pedagogic discourse: respect for the Other conceived as the unconscious within language, respect given through the performative enactment of reading the unconscious text by actively recognizing resistances and absences and "unmeant" knowledge. Felman argues in her discussions of literature, criticism, and education that humans must read and interpret psychoanalytically so as to respond to the radical alterity of the impossibilities posed by the Other. In actual practice, her reading of literature focuses on the rhetorical dimension of hiddenness in texts, that which emerges when one reads the patterns of rhetorical strategy in a text as well as the achieved effects of rhetoric.

GILLES DELEUZE AND FÉLIX GUATTARI also critique psychoanalysis in order to transform it altogether by unmasking its ideological foundation in the values of bourgeois culture. Their works *The Anti-Oedipus* (1972) and *A Thousand Plateaus* (1980) expose repression and castration as fundamental to psychoanalytic machinery, critique the psychoanalytic characterization of the unconscious as an ideal of static being rather than active production, and outline the hegemonic constraints of the Oedipal narrative. By rejecting the notion of repression and castration as "molar"—blanket conceptions, a cluster of suppressed assumptions united in an ideologically motivated pattern that is taken mistakenly to be "scientific" and "naturally" the way humans function—Deleuze and Guattari argue that in psychoanalysis, "there is finally only one sex, the masculine, in relation to which the woman, the feminine, is [also] defined as a lack, an absence" (*Anti-Oedipus* 294). By contrast, the "molecular," nonessentialist conception of the unconscious, like the repression that engenders it, "knows nothing of castration," precisely because castration as such is an ideologically motivated construct not attributable to the operation of repression (295). Deleuze and Guattari seek to explode the concept of castration as a form-giving and unifying concept and speak instead of the unconscious producing positive "multiplicities" and "flows" (295), potentially not just "two sexes, but n sexes," perhaps "a hundred thousand" (296).

What allows the constitution of such "molar" conceptions of castration to begin with is Freud's conception of the unconscious as a static *representation*. The fact of the unconscious as such is not objectionable, and to a certain point Freud conceived of the unconscious as the site of the "production of desire." Deleuze and Guattari, without irony, call this conception the "great discovery of psychoanalysis" (*Anti-Oedipus* 24). The problem comes, rather, in Freud's attempt to bury the unconscious "beneath a new brand of idealism" and to associate it with the *representation* (rather than *production*) of "a classical theater" of "myth, tragedy, [and] dreams" (24). In short, Freud, and Lacan after him, connects the unconscious, in a detour through Greek myth, inextricably with the family and the ideological investments inherent to the West. Oedipus is thus a construct "more powerful . . . than psychoanalysis, than the family, than ideology, even joined together" (122) and encompasses the whole of the hegemonic regime that is "Western culture"; it is "Oedipus" at this encompassing level that Deleuze and Guattari oppose in their fervor to be "anti-Oedipal."

Lacanian critics that emerged in the 1990s have expressed less interest in questioning the way sexual difference structures subject formation in Lacan's work than in exploring Lacan's ideas about the Real in order to reinvigorate metaphysics—in particular the philosophy of Immanuel Kant, G. W. F. Hegel, Karl Marx, and Friedrich Engels. A group of intellectuals often referred to as the "Slovenian Lacanians" falls into this category. Among the better known of these intellectuals is SLAVOJ ŽIŽEK, who rereads Hegel's philosophy through Lacan and resituates Lacan as a philosopher. In *Tarrying with the Negative: Kant, Hegel, and the Critique of Ideology* (1993), for example, Žižek builds a case for considering Lacan as a transcendental philosopher, arguing that Lacan's psychoanalytic theory offers a sort of "critique of pure desire" as it probes the question "how desire is possible" (3). Žižek's elaboration of Lacan's thought has not been without some controversy, however. In *Contingency, Hegemony, Universality* (2000) Butler, Ernesto Laclau, and Žižek debate the viability of the Real, as well as whether the Lacanian view of subject formation is compatible with ANTONIO GRAMSCI's notion of hegemony. More recently, Alenka Zupančič has followed in Žižek's path, combining psychoanalytic theory and social philosophy by interpreting Kant through Lacan, and vice versa, in *Ethics of the Real: Kant, Lacan* (2000).

Finally, scholars such as Lawrence A. Rickels and Todd Dufresne have made specific aspects of Lacan's theory a less prominent feature of their work; they critique instead the development of psychoanalytic theory as an institutional discourse. In Rickels's three-volume *Nazi Psychoanalysis* (2002), for example, he illuminates the ways that psychoanalysis gained legitimacy as it was co-opted to advance the war causes of the German and American military during World War II. Todd Dufresne takes a similarly historical approach in reevaluating the ideas of Sigmund Freud and Lacan by tracing the cultural influences on psychoanalytic thought.

SHARLA HUTCHISON, CHIARA BRIGANTI,
AND ROBERT CON DAVIS-UNDIANO

See also JUDITH BUTLER, HÉLÈNE CIXOUS, GILLES DELEUZE AND FÉLIX GUATTARI, FRENCH THEORY AND CRITICISM: 1945 AND AFTER, LUCE IRIGARAY, JULIA KRISTEVA, JACQUES LACAN, and SLAVOJ ŽIŽEK.

See also bibliographies for JUDITH BUTLER, HÉLÈNE CIXOUS, GILLES DELEUZE AND FÉLIX GUATTARI, LUCE IRIGARAY, JULIA KRISTEVA, and SLAVOJ ŽIŽEK.

Alain Badiou, Deleuze: La clameur de l'être (1997, Deleuze: The Clamor of Being, trans. Louise Burchill, 1999), L'ethique: Essai sur la conscience du mal (1993, Ethics: An Essay on the Understanding of Evil, trans. Peter Hallward, 2001), Manifeste pour la philosophie (1989, Manifesto for Philosophy, trans. Norman Madarasz, 1999); Judith Butler, Ernesto Laclau, and Slavoj Žižek, Contingency, Hegemony, Universality: Contemporary Dialogues on the Left (2000); Hélène Cixous, Angst (1977, Angst, trans. Jo Levy, 1985); Gilles Deleuze, The Deleuze Reader (ed. Constantin V. Boundas, 1992), Empirisme et subjectivité (1953, Empiricism and Subjectivity: An Essay on Hume's Theory of Human Nature, trans. Constantin V. Boundas, 1991), La philosophie critique de Kant (1963, Kant's Critical Philosophy: The Doctrine of the Faculties, trans. Hugh Tomlinson and Barbara Habberjam, 1984); Todd Dufresne, Tales from the Freudian Crypt: The Death Drive in Text and Context (2000); Todd Dufresne, ed., Freud under Analysis: History, Theory, Practice (1997), Returns of the "French Freud": Freud, Lacan, and Beyond (1996); Shoshana Felman, Jacques Lacan and the Adventure of Insight: Psychoanalysis in Contemporary Culture (1987), Le scandale du corps parlant: Don Juan avec Austin; ou, La séduction en deux langues (1980, The Literary Speech Act: Don Juan with J. L. Austin; or, Seduction in Two Languages, trans. Catherine Porter, 1983, rpt., The Scandal of the Speaking Body: Don Juan with J. L. Austin, or Seduction in Two Languages, 2003); Alice Jardine and Anne Menke, "The Politics of Tradition: Placing Women in French Literature," Yale French Studies 75 (1988); Jacques Lacan, Écrits (1966, Écrits: A Selection, trans. Alan Sheridan, 1977, trans. Bruce Fink, Héloise Fink, and Russell Grigg, 2002), Le séminaire livre XX: Encore, 1972–1973 (ed. Jacques Alain Miller, 1975, On Feminine Sexuality: The Limits of Love and Knowledge, 1972–1973, trans. Bruce Fink, 1998); Elaine Marks and Isabelle de Courtivron, eds., New French Feminisms: An Anthology (1980); Michèle Montrelay, L'ombre et le nom: Sur la féminité (1977); Laurence A. Rickels, Nazi Psychoanalysis (3 vols., 2002, vol. 1, Only Psychoanalysis Won the War; vol. 2, Crypto-fetishism; vol. 3, Psy fi); Slavoj Žižek, Culture (2003), For They Know Not What They Do: Enjoyment as a Political Factor (1991), Philosophy (2003), Society, Politics, and Ideology (2003); Alenka Zupančič, Ethics of the Real: Kant, Lacan (2000).

Queer Theory and Criticism

1. Gay Male

Like second-wave feminism and African-American studies, the queer academic proj-ect originated in the liberation movements of the 1960s and 1970s, and like its fellow travelers on the political left, it contributed to and benefited from the broad culture of liberalism intent on fostering a more just society. At the outset, "homosexuality" as a descriptive category was both criminalized and pathologized by every institu-tion in government, church, and medicine, and the discursive residues of the McCar-thy trials of the 1950s linked homosexuality with communism in the national imagi-nary as enemies of the state, a form of prejudice that was interlined with the prescriptive veneration of the white, heterosexual, reproductive couple as the norma-tive economic unit of postwar American prosperity. Moreover, gay liberation suffered from its own belatedness: while the political aspirations of feminists and black activ-ists appealed to large and visible populations, "homosexual" society had no broad existence because "homosexuals" lived under the regime of the closet by which indi-viduals might purchase uncertain safety by silence and invisibility. (For a full histori-cal narrative of the preliberationist era, see John D'Emilio's *Sexual Politics, Sexual Com-munities: The Making of a Homosexual Minority in the United States, 1940–1970* [1983]).

Therefore, while antihomophobic advocates would share the goals and learn from the strategies of the feminists and African Americans who preceded them, they began without a cohesive community or clear historical sensibility. The goals of ac-tivism, then, like all liberationist movements, were twofold: to galvanize the urgency of an identity politics through celebratory reclamation of cultural space, cultural production, and history and to begin a thorough and rigorous analysis of the matrix of homophobic discrimination. Queer historiography conventionally locates the real origin of the movement in the Stonewall riot in New York in 1969, when the rather diverse patrons of a gay tavern fought back against a police raid. Stonewall reveals much about the ad-lib strategies of the early days of gay-lib: improvisation, public spectacle, and tactical displays of anger enabled activists to invent the move-ment as they went along, consolidating an identity and a history of resistance as they proceeded.

The tactics of resistance and the strategies of public theatrics remain central to the queer project. They survive, and indeed flourish, in Pride festivals across the world, in activist groups that continue to struggle for full civil rights, in the lives of gay men and lesbians who have renounced the closet for visibility and dignity. They had a powerful renaissance in the ACT UP movement (the AIDS Coalition to Unleash

Power) in the 1980s and early 1990s that resisted the demonization of gay men at the outset of the epidemic and fought governments and pharmaceutical companies for sufficient and timely medical care. As gay identity morphed into "queer" cultural possibility among younger, more privileged and sophisticated gays and lesbians in the 1990s, outrageous acts became the commonplace of everyday rebellion, even though gay cultural sites, gay studies programs, and antihomophobic affirmation had become a real, if tenuous, feature of the academic "institution."

Although it is a somewhat arbitrary exercise to mark the onset and culmination of theoretical schools, it is certainly possible to speak of a golden age of queer literary studies in the decade between 1985, with the publication of EVE KOSOFSKY SEDGWICK's *Between Men: English Literature and Homosocial Desire*, and 1995, which saw the last of the major books that remap the field, David Halperin's *Saint Foucault: Towards a Gay Hagiography*. The most influential theorists of this period—who, in addition to Sedgwick and Halperin, include D. A. Miller, Lee Edelman, JUDITH BUTLER, and Ed Cohen—bring together the historical paradigms of MICHEL FOUCAULT and sharp deconstructive praxis to explore sexual identification and desire as a fundamental category of historical understanding and discursive representation. Collectively, their work interrogates the regulation of the sexual subject and the disciplining of desire through the homophobia that circulates through patriarchal culture.

Dellamora's *Masculine Desire: The Sexual Politics of Victorian Aestheticism* (1990) consolidates his extensive mapping of the homoerotic contours of nineteenth-century masculine textualities: in the historical stretch from Tennyson to Wilde, he examines the multiple discourses of "an aesthetic-cultural space in which men could contest conventional gender coding while expressing the worth of male-male desire" (167). His deft articulation of the ways in which the Victorians deployed oblique homoerotic images to challenge hegemonic masculinities culminates in a theory of homophobia circulated in the wake of the Oscar Wilde trials, when scandal resulted in a conservative reaffirmation of "the naturalness of gender norms, of manly men and womenly women" (216). If Stonewall is the mythic origin for the politics of activist resistance, then the Wilde trials has served as a rich historical locus for theorizing the essential modernity of media-generated, scandalous homophobia. Dellamora's work is congruent with Ed Cohen's *Talk on the Wilde Side: Toward a Genealogy of a Discourse on Male Sexualities* (1993), which traces how the unspeakable sexuality became highly marketable. Cohen demonstrates how "the newspapers necessarily developed a compensatory set of signifying practices to invoke the unprintable signifier without naming it directly" (144); the homosexual becomes, in the popular symbolic, a recognizable type through the episteme of scandal, which grafted "a highly visible set of critically nonnormative public behaviours"—aestheticism and effeminacy—onto "an obscure but apparently transgressive set of sexual practices" (181). The opposition between fascination and repulsion is undone in modern surveillance and diagnostics in direct proportion to the traceability of the unseen from the seen, with the consequent production of the "homosexual" as a monstrous specter that haunted the fin de siècle.

The gap between censuring discourse and illicit sexual actuality is central, too, in the argument of Alan Bray's *Homosexuality in Renaissance England* (1982). Bray contends that prior to the early eighteenth century, theological and juridical reprobation of same-sex activity was barely distinguishable from the philosophical language of general disorder and dissolution. Homosexuality emerged liminally as "part of a universal potential for disorder which lay alongside an equally universal order. It was part, in a word, of its shadow" (26).

Foucault's three-volume *History of Sexuality* (1976–1984) quickly became the authoritative poststructuralist guide to analyzing the discourses of knowledge production in the historical field. The first and most general volume, *The Will to Knowledge* (1976), argues that from the eighteenth century onward, "sex" became increasingly mystified in direct proportion to the incitement to ideologically motivated discourses of sexuality, a cultural domain that linked knowledge to power in the regulation and surveillance of the subject. By the end of the nineteenth century and the rise of Freudian psychoanalysis, "sex" became "an imaginary point determined by the deployment of sexuality that each individual has to pass in order to have access to his own intelligibility, to the whole of his body, and to his identity." Hence, Foucault argues, "the importance we ascribe to it, the reverential fear with which we surround it, the care we take to know it" (155–56). Central to Foucault's theory is that there is no binary division to be sustained between the power that watches and the pleasure that is watched: rather, "power lets itself be invaded by the pleasure it is pursuing; and power asserts itself in the pleasure of showing off, scandalizing, or resisting [the gaze]" (45). Moreover, if the proliferating taxonomies of perversion resulted in greater institutional control and oppression of homosexuals—for the transformation of the early modern sodomite into the nineteenth-century homosexual yielded "a personage, a past, a case history and . . . a species" (43)—then the production of knowledge also permitted what Foucault terms a "reverse discourse," by which homosexuality began to speak on its own behalf (101).

It is precisely in this reverse discourse—the complex and oblique forms in which homosexuality engaged speech—that Foucault's totalizing theory of sexuality as knowledge production determined the poststructuralist disposition of subsequent queer theory and criticism, its fascination with the erotics of textual secrecy. For the truth of texts, like that of sex, requires a sophisticated hermeneutic approach to the domains that harbor and are organized around the imperative of a fundamental secret. The crux of the matter is expressed more succinctly by Sedgwick: "Where would the whole, astonishing and metamorphic Western romance tradition (I include psychoanalysis) be if people's sexual desire were even momentarily assumed to be transparent to themselves?" (*Epistemology* 26).

Consolidating the historiographical work of Foucault and a prehensile deconstructive analytics, Sedgwick reconceptualizes the sex/gender system, initiating startling approaches to sexual anxieties and opacities in canonical literature. Sedgwick's program originates in her conceptualization of the regulatory power of "homosexual panic" in *Between Men: English Literature and Male Homosocial Desire*: if male bonds in patriarchal culture can be understood as a "homosocial continuum" extending from the most normative and prescribed modes of affiliation to the most reprobated and proscribed homosexual bonds, then a certain space of undecidability is opened on the spectrum in which "no man must be able to ascertain that he is not (that his bonds are not) homosexual" (*Between* 88–89).

Sedgwick's point is that ubiquitous homosexual panic is a universal regulatory economy rather than a localized means of persecuting the homosexual minority; therefore, the discourses of anxious indeterminacy constitute a traceable impulse and institute a queer hermeneutic imperative, in literature. Sharpening Foucault's precept that, after the eighteenth century, knowledge and sex became conceptually inseparable, Sedgwick notes that sexual epistemology was increasingly structured by its pointed refusal of same-sex possibility: in proportion "as knowledge meant sexual knowledge, and secrets sexual secrets, there . . . developed one particular sexuality that was distinctly constituted *as* secrecy . . . whose accessibility to knowledge is uniquely preterited" (*Epistemology* 73–74).

The narrative function of secrecy is conceptualized as isomorphic with the novel itself in the elegantly lucid writing of D. A. Miller; if Sedgwick inquires into what secrecy covers, Miller asks what covers secrecy (that is, what "takes secrecy as its field of operation" [*Novel* 207]). And while Sedgwick's master critical trope is preterition and its refusals and diffusions, Miller's is paradox. In *The Novel and the Police* (1988), Miller reasons that because fictional characters strike compromises between disclosure and concealment, expression and repression, "the secret subject is always an open secret" (205). While the subject can take recourse to secrecy in order to conceive of himself as resistant to social control—to maintain the boundaries between private and public, inside and outside—the phenomenon of the open secret does not "bring about the collapse of these binarisms, but rather attests to their fantasmatic recovery," for although "we know perfectly well that the secret is known, we must persist, however ineptly, in guarding it" (207). Like Sedgwick, Miller is broadly concerned with secrecy as an epistemological dimension of closetedness: writing is a form of encryption that seeks neither to know secrets nor to make them known.

Miller's subsequent work turns from literature to film, theater, and other forms of cultural production. His essay on Hitchcock, "Anal *Rope*" (in Diana Fuss's *inside/out: Lesbian Theories, Gay Theories* [1991]) is an indispensable account of how homosexuality emerges obliquely in the field of vision through the oblique signifying practices of connotation. In contrast to the immediate self-evidence of denotation, connotation "will always manifest a certain semiotic insufficiency," which allows homosexual meaning, paradoxically, "to be elided even as it is also being elaborated" (123–24). Miller's concise diagnostics are supremely helpful to any reader attempting to negotiate a homosexual possibility that riffles through the textual regime of the closet that holds homosexuality "definitionally in suspense" (125). As he argues, while connotation might produce an "essentially insubstantial homosexuality," it nonetheless tends "to raise this ghost all over the place." In addition to its conceptual rigor, Miller's writing is remarkable for its playful, witty engagement with its subject; his best moments deploy a tart campiness that cuts to the chase in short order. Thus he concludes, "Connotation tends to light everywhere, to put all signifiers to a test of their hospitality . . . [;] like an arriviste who hasn't arrived, it simply can't stop networking" (125).

The enormous amount of scholarship produced in literary, historical, and cultural studies fields since 1990 would suggest that queer studies, too, can't stop networking. The methodological expansion of gay studies into the queer-theoretical project has been driven by a new generation of graduate students intent on challenging homophobia in direct ways, by, following Sedgwick, exposing the universalizing tendency of homophobia to regulate the sex/gender system, and, most importantly, by extending literary-analytical methodologies to the furthest reaches of cultural production, high and low. Much recent work has been enabled by Butler's demonstration that gender is a matter of performative citations of morphological ideals, its artificiality exposed and discerned by the transgressive practices of cross-dressing and impersonation. It follows that the performatives of gender have been analyzed in the field of performance itself, most notably in cinema. A spectrum of Butlerian approaches appears in Ellis Hanson's edited collection *Out Takes: Essays on Queer Theory and Film* (1999). More recently, Hanson has surveyed the recent history of the queer studies project and observed that "in the past decade, queer theory, the deconstruction of sexual rhetoric, has revolutionized the field simply by conceiving sexuality as a story we tell ourselves about ourselves, a story that changes with every telling, that is written as much by the audience as by the ostensible author, and that figures the very incoherence, artificiality, and slipperiness of language itself" (2072). This arriviste, it would seem, has arrived.

ERIC SAVOY

Leo Bersani, Homos (1995); Joseph Bristow, *Effeminate England: Homoerotic Writing after 1885* (1995); Alan Bray, *Homosexuality in Renaissance England* (1982); Steven Bruhm, *Reflecting Narcissus: A Queer Aesthetic* (2001); Gregory W. Bredbeck, *Sodomy and Interpretation: Marlowe to Milton* (1991); George Chauncey, *Gay New York: Gender, Urban Culture, and the Making of the Gay Male World, 1890–1940* (1994); Steven Cohan, *Masked Men: Masculinity and the Movies in the Fifties* (1997); Ed Cohen, *Talk on the Wilde Side: Toward a Genealogy of a Discourse on Male Sexualities* (1993); William A. Cohen, *Sex Scandal: The Private Parts of Victorian Fiction* (1996); James Creech, *Closet Writing / Gay Reading: The Case of Melville's "Pierre"* (1993); Douglas Crimp, ed., *AIDS: Cultural Analysis, Cultural Activism* (1988); Louis

Crompton, *Byron and Greek Love: Homophobia in 19th-Century England* (1985); Richard Dellamora, *Apocalyptic Overtures: Sexual Politics and the Sense of an Ending* (1994), *Masculine Desire: The Sexual Politics of Victorian Aestheticism* (1990); John D'Emilio, *Sexual Politics, Sexual Communities: The Making of a Homosexual Minority in the United States, 1940–1970* (1983); Jonathan Dollimore, *Sexual Dissidence: Augustine to Wilde, Freud to Foucault* (1991); Alexander Doty, *Making Things Perfectly Queer: Interpreting Mass Culture* (1993); Lee Edelman, *Homographesis: Essays in Gay Literary and Cultural Theory* (1994); Diana Fuss, *Inside/Out: Lesbian Theories, Gay Theories* (1991); Jonathan Goldberg, *Sodometries: Renaissance Texts, Modern Sexualities* (1992); David Halperin, *One Hundred Years of Homosexuality and Other Essays on Greek Love* (1990), *Saint Foucault: Towards a Gay Hagiography* (1995); Ellis Hanson, "Looking Backward, Looking Forward: MLA Members Speak," *PMLA* 15 (2000), Ellis Hanson, ed., *Out Takes: Essays on Queer Theory and Film* (1999); Wayne Koestenbaum, *The Queen's Throat: Opera, Homosexuality, and the Mystery of Desire* (1993); Robert K. Martin, *The Homosexual Tradition in American Poetry* (1979); Moe Meyer, ed., *The Politics and Poetics of Camp* (1994); D. A. Miller, *Bringing Out Roland Barthes* (1992), *The Novel and the Police* (1988); Michael Moon, *A Small Boy and Others: Imitation and Initiation in American Culture from Henry James to Andy Warhol* (1998), David Savran, *Taking it Like a Man: White Masculinity, Masochism, and Contemporary American Culture* (1998); Eve Kosofsky Sedgwick, *Between Men: English Literature and Male Homosocial Desire* (1985), *Epistemology of the Closet* (1990), *Tendencies* (1993); Eric Savoy and David Bergman, ed., *Camp Grounds: Style and Homosexuality* (1993); Simon Watney, *Practices of Freedom: Selected Writings on HIV/AIDS* (1994); Jeffrey Weeks, *Against Nature: Essays on History, Sexuality, and Identity* (1991).

2. Lesbian

At the beginning of the 1970s, a scholar interested in lesbian issues and images in literature could have turned to only two reference works: Jeannette Foster's privately printed 1956 study, *Sex-Variant Women in Literature*, and a compendious bibliography collected by Barbara Grier (under the pseudonym Gene Damon) titled *The Lesbian in Literature*. This situation would change dramatically, as social, cultural, and political forces began to supplant the New Criticism with the politically grounded theories found in African American, feminist, Marxist, gay, and lesbian criticism.

The origins of lesbian criticism lie specifically in the political theories and movements that gave rise to lesbian feminism, itself the outgrowth of the women's liberation, gay liberation, and New Left movements of the 1960s. Frustrated by the homophobia of heterosexual feminists, the sexism of gay men in the "homophile" movement, and the subordination of gender to class analysis in the New Left, lesbians began to form their own political organizations and collectives. Groups such as the Furies and Radicalesbians shaped the theoretical position of lesbian feminism.

Some participants in the new movement developed an even more rigorous critique of heterosexuality that came to be known as lesbian separatism. Separatist theory proposed that lesbianism was more a political than sexual identity and that abandoning heterosexuality was a prerequisite to destroying male supremacy. Accordingly, separation from heterosexual women, all men, and even nonseparatist lesbians was seen as a political necessity.

Lesbian criticism developed rapidly in this climate and was supported by the growth of women's studies programs in colleges and universities, and the advance of lesbian fiction and poetry, the authors of which—particularly Judy Grahn, Audre Lorde, and Adrienne Rich—were often critics and professors themselves. Much of this early criticism and theory moved easily between the boundaries of community and campus, which were far more permeable then than they are now. For example, lesbian panels at the meetings of the Modern Language Association of America attracted hundreds of women in and outside academia. The earliest compilations of lesbian literary theory were found in special issues of *Margins*, a small press journal, and *Sinister Wisdom*, a lesbian journal with wide community readership. Lesbian literary theory initially constituted itself as a stream of thought separate from either heterosexual feminist or gay male thought, although it bore some relationship to both. Most, although not all, lesbian feminist critics identify along the axis of gender (female/male or feminine/masculine) rather than that of sexuality (homosexuality/ bisexuality/heterosexuality). It would be over a decade before significant numbers of lesbian critics developed theoretical and institutional connections to gay male and bisexual critics.

Early theoretical constructions can be seen, first, as attempts to challenge the erasure of lesbian existence from the feminist literature of the time and to oppose the deviance model of lesbianism, in which lesbians were portrayed as unnatural, monstrous, "unsexed" creatures or pathetic victims of biology, and replace it with one stressing the normality, indeed desirability, of lesbian life. Adrienne Rich, for example, in her influential essay "Compulsory Heterosexuality and Lesbian Existence" (1979), coined the term "lesbian continuum" to describe what she saw as similarities, not differences, among various expressions of love between women. Female friendship, familial relationships, partnership, commitment, and sexuality all exist along the same continuum.

In early lesbian criticism, there was little focus on issues of race, ethnicity, and class. Scant attention was paid to writers of color, since the lesbian movement then, as now, was predominantly white. However, in the late 1970s and early 1980s the creative work, political writing, and scholarship of lesbians of color would emerge as a powerful influence on the evolution of lesbian criticism and theory. The poetry of Pat Parker, Audre Lorde's "biomythography" or blending of autobiography, novel, and personal mythology into a hybrid literary form in *Zami: A New Spelling of My Name* (1983), and Gloria Hull's work on figures of the Harlem Renaissance provided the foundation for a lesbian theory more alert to the multiple differences that condition lesbian identity, producing contradictory bases of social identity and shifting axes of political identification (see Allen, Gomez, Moraga, and Shockley). One of the most influential pieces of lesbian criticism from this period, Barbara Smith's "Toward a Black Feminist Criticism" (1977), originally published in *Conditions*, another community-based literary journal, contains a much-debated lesbian reading of Toni Morrison's *Sula*. In many ways, Smith's provocative essay marked a turning point not only for African American feminist criticism but also for lesbian and feminist criticism in general.

"Classic" lesbian theory, then, proceeded from the assumptions that one could (with difficulty perhaps) define a category called lesbian; that lesbians shared certain experiences and concepts, and that discursive practices—literary texts, critical analyses, political theories—proceed from lived experience. The critical debates of the 1980s called most of these assumptions into question, rendering established notions of lesbian identity, history, and culture both unstable and problematic. Experience, authenticity, voice, writer—even the category "lesbian" itself—were scrutinized, qualified, and sometimes abandoned by theorists trained in DECONSTRUCTION and poststructuralist methodologies. Social construction theory, which many literary critics adopted from the social sciences, also provided tools for questioning the coherence of any essentialist, universal, or transhistorical positing of identity such as "lesbian." Psychoanalytic criticism, much of it based on feminist critiques of classic Freudian narratives of lesbianism and the poststructuralist theories of JACQUES LACAN, sought to affirm the psychic processes involved in the formation of lesbian subjectivity and desire. The "turn to theory," as it is sometimes euphemistically referred to, placed a greater emphasis on intellectual abstraction and European philosophical influence than the more practically engaged critical practices and political strategies that had been at the root of Anglo-American lesbian-feminist criticism in the 1970s. This, in turn, produced debates among lesbian scholars, intellectuals and political activists that would transform lesbian criticism and theory.

The reconfiguration of lesbian criticism in the 1980s arose in part from the rejection of a perceived lesbian-feminist orthodoxy. By the end of the 1970s this orthodoxy had generated its own opposite position, and lesbians began to openly, if acrimoniously, debate sexuality, power, and gender roles. The 1982 conference at Barnard College, "The Scholar and the Feminist," brought these debates to public attention, thus marking the emergence of the "sex wars." Here, feminists opposed to pornography and lesbians who defined themselves as "sex radicals" clashed over the politics of lesbian sexual practices believed by some to corroborate the patriarchal oppression of women. Writers, critics, and activists such as Pat Califa articulated a "sex-radical" position that emphasized the personally and politically liberating potential of lesbian sadomasochism as a refusal of women's disenfranchisement from arenas of power and pleasure. In contrast to the gender inclusiveness of earlier lesbian feminism, the "sex wars" produced distinct tensions between lesbian and feminist modes of critical analysis. Butch-femme role-playing and sadomasochistic sexual practices, both historical and contemporary, became especially rich topics for discussions of lesbian self-presentation in literature, film, theater, and performance art. Esther Newton, for example, argued that the mythic figure of the "mannish lesbian" permitted early twentieth-century women to embrace explicit sexuality as part of their self-definition as lesbians.

The AIDS crisis and the resurgence of right-wing conservative activism in the 1980s produced a new cultural and political coalition of lesbians and gay men who began to identify with one another's theoretical commitments. This contributed to new modes of theorization that relocated the specificity of lesbianism along the axis of sexuality, thus linking lesbian criticism to gay male and bisexual criticism. This did not mean that lesbian critics abandoned their analyses of gender or treated gender and sex as utterly divided from one another; rather they began to explore and debate the complex connections between gender, sex, and sexuality. Of course, many lesbian critics continued to envision lesbian existence and textuality as ontologically separate from that of gay men and continued to work within a lesbian "perspective" and "tradition" that granted formal coherence and presence to the lesbian subject. However, the categories that had organized earlier lesbian critical methods and models became less distinct and their boundaries blurred as lesbian critics intensified their efforts to contribute intellectually to the understanding of the diversity of lesbian existence.

The 1990s saw a rapid expansion of lesbian criticism that was largely the result of the new courses, programs, and conferences for lesbian and gay studies that were established at colleges and universities. At the same time, the ongoing critique of identity categories and the formation of new political and critical alliances both inside and outside the academy, led to the introduction of a much debated and controversial term: "queer theory." Originally coined by Teresa de Lauretis, "queer theory" was proposed as a means of getting around the universalist presumptions and assimilationist politics thought to be inherent in the categories "lesbian" and gay, "homo" and "hetero," "black" and "white." "Queer," as a corrective, was intended to be more inclusive of a wide range of nonconforming subject positions, including bisexuality, transsssexuality, and transgender. The term drew fire from many lesbian critics: some claimed that "queer" simply restored the primacy of patriarchy by implicitly privileging the interests of gay men. Others argued that the appeal of queer lay in its function as a ubiquitous corporate logo, a means of assimilating lesbian and gay politics into the logic of consumer capitalism. Other lesbian critics, however, found it useful. Like deconstructive critical practice, queer theory contests lesbian essentialism. In this way, the lesbian becomes one manifestation of what Teresa de Lauretis calls the "eccentric" subject, not a unique and special category in a world marked exclusively by gender dualism. Queer theorists, many influenced by the work of the French counterenlightenment philosopher Michel Foucault, offer antiessentialist, rigorously historicized analyses of nonnormative sexual and cultural practices that animate a discursive construct called "lesbian." One of the influential works of this period was Judith Butler's *Gender Trouble*. Butler's argument challenges the idea that gender is expressive of biological sex, instead emphasizing the performative and parodic nature of gender.

New international research in the new century is focusing attention on lesbian communities in local and global contexts, a development that promises to deepen our critical awareness of the roles that cultural tradition, race, ethnicity, nation, and globalization play in shaping lesbian identities (see Burgin; Roberston). The current interest in transnational feminism has realigned lesbian-feminist theories and post-colonial theories in an examination of interactions between "lesbian" and "nation." Such research usefully demonstrates that the globalization of gay and lesbian movements is always belied by specific forms of gender and sexual identification, strategies of representation, and practices of cultural subversion that are motivated by specific concepts of nationhood. Related to much of this work are analyses of new communications technologies in connection with developing modes of articulating the lesbian subject. For example, the notion of "virtual" lesbianism has become necessary to consider as more lesbians create identities and communities in cyberspace and as online forms of writing widen the possibilities for lesbian cultural and political participation (see Case). In the academy, in addition to departments and programs of lesbian and gay studies, the interdisciplinary influence of lesbian criticism and theory is more apparent than ever in cultural studies, media and film studies, gender and ethnic studies, and area studies programs. In fact, it often seems that these programs have absorbed much of the work that was earlier performed under the rubric of women's studies. While this may appear to undermine the visibility of lesbian criticism, we might also say that lesbian studies—as queer activists have been wont to claim for themselves—is everywhere. Lesbian criticism can only be the better for that.

BONNIE ZIMMERMAN AND DANA HELLER

Paula Gunn Allen, The Sacred Hoop: Recovering the Feminine in American Indian Traditions (1986); Dorothy Allison, Skin: Talking About Sex, Class, and Literature (1994); Gloria Anzaldúa, Borderlands / La Frontera: The New Mestiza (1987); Lauren Berlant and Elizabeth Freeman, "Queer Nationality," Fear of a Queer Planet: Queer Politics and Social Theory (ed. Michael Warner, 1993); Nicole Brossard, La lettre aérienne (1995, The Aerial Letter, trans. Marlene Wildeman, 1988); Diana Lewis Burgin, Sophia Parnok: The Life and Work of Russia's Sappho (1994); Judith Butler, Gender Trouble: Feminism and the Subversion of Identity (1990); Mary Carruthers, "The Re-Vision of the Muse: Adrienne Rich, Audre Lorde, Judy Grahn, Olga Broumas," Hudson Review 36 (1983); Sue-Ellen Case, "Toward a Butch-Femme Aesthetic," Making a Spectacle: Feminist Essays on Contemporary Women's Theatre (ed. Lynda Hart, 1989), The Domain Matrix: Performing Lesbian at the End of Print Culture (1996); Danae Clark, "Commodity Lesbianism," Camera Obscura 25/26 (1991); Blanche Wiesen Cook, "'Women Alone Stir My Imagination': Lesbianism and the Cultural Tradition," Signs 4 (1979); Gene Damon [Barbara Grier], Jan Watson, and Robin Jordan, The Lesbian in Literature: A Bibliography (1967, 2nd ed., 1975); Teresa de Lauretis, "Eccentric Subjects: Feminist Theory and Historical Consciousness," Feminist Studies 16 (1990); Teresa de Lauretis, ed., "Queer Theory: Lesbian and Gay Sexualities," special issue, Differences 3 (1991); Laura Doan, ed., The Lesbian Postmodern (1994); Lillian Faderman, Odd Girls and Twilight Lovers: A History of Lesbian Life in Twentieth-Century America (1992), Surpassing the Love of Men: Romantic Friendship and Love Between Women from the Sixteenth Century to the Present (1981); Jeannette H. Foster, Sex Variant Women in Literature (1956, rpt., 1985); Diana Fuss, Essentially Speaking: Feminism, Nature, and Difference (1989); Jewelle Gomez, "Imagine a Lesbian . . . A Black Lesbian . . . ," Trivia: A Journal of Ideas 12 (1988); Judy Grahn, The Highest Apple: Sappho and the Lesbian Poetic Tradition (1985); Judith Halberstam, Female Masculinity (1998); Dana Heller, ed., Cross-Purposes: Lesbians, Feminists, and the Limits of Alliance (1997); Gloria T. Hull, Color, Sex, and Poetry: Three Writers of the Harlem Renaissance

(1987); Annamarie Jagose, *Lesbian Utopics* (1994); Karla Jay, *The Amazon and the Page: Natalie Clifford Barney and Renée Vivien* (1988); Karla Jay and Joanne Glasgow, eds., *Lesbian Texts and Contexts: Radical Revisions* (1990); Jill Johnston, *Lesbian Nation: The Feminist Solution* (1973); Elizabeth Lapovsky Kennedy and Madeline D. Davis, *Boots of Leather, Slippers of Gold: The History of a Lesbian Community* (1994); Audre Lorde, *Zami: A New Spelling of My Name* (1983), *Sister Outsider: Essays and Speeches* (1984); Elaine Marks, "Lesbian Intertextuality," *Homosexualities and French Literature: Cultural Contexts, Critical Texts* (ed. George Stambolian and Elaine Marks, 1979); Biddy Martin, *Femininity Played Straight: The Significance of Being Lesbian* (1997), "Lesbian Identity and Autobiographical Difference[s]," *Life/Lines: Theorizing Women's Autobiography* (ed. Bella Brodzki and Celeste Schenck, 1988); Cherríe Moraga, *Loving in the War Years* (1983); Cherríe Moraga and Gloria Anzaldúa, eds., *This Bridge Called My Back: Writings By Radical Women of Color* (1984); Sally Munt, ed., *New Lesbian Criticism: Literary and Cultural Readings* (1992); Esther Newton, "The Mythic Mannish Lesbian: Radclyffe Hall and the New Woman," *Signs* 9 (1984); Sharon O'Brien, "'The Thing Not Named': Willa Cather as a Lesbian Writer," *Signs* 9 (1984); Radicalesbians, "The Woman-identified Woman," *Radical Feminism* (ed. Anne Koedt, Ellen Levine, and Anita Rapone, 1973); Adrienne Rich, "Compulsory Heterosexuality and Lesbian Existence," *The Signs Reader: Women, Gender, and Scholarship* (ed. Elizabeth Abel and Emily K. Abel, 1983); Jennifer Ellen Robertson, *Takarazuka: Sexual Politics and Popular Culture in Modern Japan* (1998); Judith Roof, *A Lure of Knowledge: Lesbian Sexuality and Theory* (1991); Barbara Smith, *The Truth That Never Hurts: Writings on Race, Gender, and Freedom* (2000); Carroll Smith-Rosenberg, "The Female World of Love and Ritual," *Signs* 1 (1975); Bonnie Zimmerman, *The Safe Sea of Women: Lesbian Fiction, 1969–1989* (1990), "What Has Never Been: An Overview of Lesbian Feminist Criticism," *Feminist Studies* 7 (1981).

3. Queer Theory

Queer theory is the radical deconstruction of sexual rhetoric. It has sought to develop links between various forms of progressive activism (the lesbian and gay movement, the women's movement, HIV/AIDS activism, and movements for racial justice, among others), and the analytical rigor of poststructuralism (especially that of MICHEL FOUCAULT, ROLAND BARTHES, JACQUES DERRIDA, and PAUL DE MAN). It interrogates the binaristic thinking that has traditionally characterized sexual politics, in particular such familiar oppositions as heterosexuality/homosexuality, masculine/feminine, sex/gender, closeted/out, center/margin, conscious/unconscious, nature/culture, and normal/pathological, to name a few.

On or about 1991, the term "queer theory" burst into academic consciousness with the force of a revelation. Teresa de Lauretis is credited with coining the term in a special issue she edited in 1991 for the feminist journal *differences*, though she was not otherwise an avid or exemplary proponent of its methods. Nearly all definitions of queer theory share the paradoxical tendency of eschewing definition, even though they all say much the same thing and focus on much the same list of foundational texts. As these definitions implicitly reveal, queer theory is no more haunted by the impossibility of definition than any other theoretical term; rather, its political value, its conceptual coherence, its flexibility, and its novelty lie in its peculiar deployment of deconstructive methods, which have resulted in an extraordinarily wide-ranging applicability.

Queer theory was, from the moment of its inception, an oddly retrospective designation that came to be applied to a group of more or less poststructural texts that had already been written—indeed, the word "queer" is, paradoxically, infrequent in them and in some cases altogether absent. These important early texts include Foucault's writings on sexuality, Gayle Rubin's "Thinking Sex" (1984), Eve Kosofsky Sedgwick's *Between Men* (1985) and *Epistemology of the Closet* (1990); Gloria Anzaldúa's *Borderlands* (1987), D. A. Miller's *The Novel and the Police* (1988), Douglas Crimp's *AIDS: Cultural Analysis, Cultural Activism* (1988), Judith Butler's *Gender Trouble* (1990), Diana Fuss's *Essentially Speaking* and *Inside/Out* (1989), David Halperin's *One Hundred Years of Homosexuality* (1990), Lee Edelman's "Homographesis" (1994) and "The Plague of Discourse" (1994), James R. Kincaid's *Child-Loving* (1992), Jonathan Dollimore's *Sexual Dissidence* (1991), and the essays of Monique Wittig.

Queer theory emerged in part from Foucauldian social constructionism, and it theorized sexuality as a mode of performativity through which subjectivity is not only enacted but also imperiled. Although it is deeply indebted to lesbian and gay studies and women's studies (in which social constructionism was already quite common), it challenged those fields by being radically anti-identitarian and taking such categories as "lesbian," "gay," and "woman" not as the self-evident foundation for knowledge but rather as indeterminate signifiers whose instability and contradictions can serve as a volatile site for political negotiation and struggle. The epithet was embraced by sex radicals in the 1990s precisely because it was so richly pejorative that it could scarcely fail to communicate the sense of anger that activists felt at being unjustly shamed and discriminated against for their unconventional sexual practices. Furthermore, the term "queer" was thought to preserve a persistent ambiguity that figured the very indeterminacy of desire and language and the contingency, the instability, the ultimate impossibility of sexual identity. Queer theory proved uniquely useful in deconstructing the very category of the sexual, rendering it more flexible, opening its definitional boundaries to explore its other discursive affinities, both historical and potential.

Queer theory asks what we think sex is or ought to be, how we came to think that way, for whose profit we think that way, and how, for the sake of social justice, we might think and act differently. This deconstructive impetus is the most controversial, but also the most political, dimension of queer theory. Some of its opponents consider queer theory to undermine the foundational claims for political action, especially those of identity-based movements and to promote an elitist language of analysis rather than a "street language" of action. This critique tends to devalue intellectual rigor in political movements and overlook the political activism of the theorists themselves; furthermore, as Lee Edelman, has pointed out, "to remain enchanted by the phantom of a political engagement outside and above an engagement with issues of rhetoric, figuration, and fantasy is to ignore the historical conceptualization of homosexuality in a distinctive relation to language" (21). Because of this focus on rhetoric, queer theory has proved a boon to politically engaged literary critics, and it is no coincidence that virtually all of its earliest proponents were employed by university departments of literature or rhetoric. Queer theory has a profound investment in formalism, close reading, and style, in that it is concerned primarily with the figuration of desire and sexuality as they are ideologically constituted in and through language.

Besides deconstruction, feminism, and gay studies, the intellectual trend that has most influenced queer theory is psychoanalysis, though that influence has been persistently controversial. Part of the appeal of queer theory, especially in its more Foucauldian spirit, is its challenge to the hegemony of psychoanalysis (also psychiatry and biology) in the study of sexuality in the humanities. Some queer theorists have also been inspired by psychoanalysis's invention of the unconscious, its rich interpretive strategies, and its sophisticated theorization of connections between desire and language. Some theorists have opposed themselves to psychoanalysis or set it aside to pursue other approaches (Halperin, Rubin, and Sedgwick, for example), while others (most notably Butler, Edelman, and Fuss) have sought to appropriate and rethink psychoanalysis, especially the more rigorously psycholinguistic work of Jacques Lacan. Another controversial source of inspiration for queer theory has been postcolonial and critical race theory, though a number of critics in these fields have taken queer theory to task for having a predominantly white and Western frame of reference. At its most sensitive to racial and ethnic politics, queer theory questions the purity of the very category of sexuality and "illuminates how various dimensions of social experience—race, sexuality, ethnicity, diaspora, gender—can cut across or transect one another, resulting in their potential mutual transformation" (Harper et al., 1).

Beyond the massive deployment of queer theory in literary studies, some particularly innovative developments in the field since the coining of the term have included Marjorie Garber's magisterial studies of cross-dressing and bisexuality; Sandy Stone's posttranssexual manifesto; Michael Warner's critique of the politics of "normal" in debates over public sex, gay marriage, and gay media; José Esteban Muñoz's theorization of racial and sexual "disidentification"; Jonathan Goldberg's analysis of the rhetoric of "sodomy"; Joseph Litvak's reading of "sophistication"; the further expansion of queer theory into visual studies (for example, the group of critics in Out Takes, edited by Ellis Hanson), into musicology (for example, the group of critics in Queering the Pitch, edited by Philip Brett et al.), and into sociology and law (for example, the work of Steven Seidman and William B. Turner); Jane Gallop's "anecdotal theory" and her writings on the erotics of pedagogy; and Sedgwick's theorization of shame dynamics and reparative reading in Touching Feeling.

ELLIS HANSON

See also bibliography for EVE KOSOFSKY SEDGWICK.

Gloria Anzaldúa, *Borderlands/La Frontera: The New Mestiza* (1987); Philip Brett, Gary Thomas, and Elizabeth Wood, eds., *Queering the Pitch: The New Gay and Lesbian Musicology* (1994); Douglas Crimp, *AIDS: Cultural Analysis, Cultural Activism* (1988); Teresa de Lauretis, "Queer Theory: Lesbian and Gay Sexualities," *differences* 3 (1991); Lee Edelman, *Homographesis: Essays in Gay Literary and Cultural Theory* (1994); Michel Foucault, *Ethics: Subjectivity and Truth* (trans. Robert Hurley, et al., 1997), *Histoire de la sexualité*, vol. 1, *La volonté de savoir* (1976, *The History of Sexuality*, vol. 1, *An Introduction*, trans. Robert Hurley, 1978), vol. 2, *L'usage des plaisirs* (1984, vol. 2, *The Use of Pleasure*, trans. Robert Hurley, 1986), vol. 3, *Le souci de soi* (1984, vol. 3, *The Care of the Self*, trans. Robert Hurley, 1986); Diana Fuss, *Essentially Speaking* (1989), *Identification Papers* (1995); Diana Fuss, ed., *Inside/Out: Lesbian Theories, Gay Theories* (1991); Jane Gallop, *Anecdotal Theory* (2003), *Feminist Accused of Sexual Harassment* (1997); Marjorie Garber, *Vested Interests: Cross-Dressing and Cultural Anxiety* (1992), *Vice Versa: Bisexuality and the Eroticism of Everyday Life* (1995); Jonathan Goldberg, *Sodometries: Renaissance Texts, Modern Sexualities* (1992); David Halperin, *One Hundred Years of Homosexuality and Other Essays on Greek Love* (1990); Ellis Hanson, ed., *Out Takes: Essays on Queer Theory and Film* (1999); Phillip Brian Harper, Anne McClintock, José Esteban Muñoz, and Trish Rosen, "Queer Transexions of Race, Nation, and Gender: An Introduction," *Social Text* 15 (1997); James R. Kincaid, *Child-Loving: The Erotic Child and Victorian Culture* (1992); Joseph Litvak, *Strange Gourmets: Sophistication, Theory, and the Novel* (1997); D. A. Miller, *The Novel and the Police* (1988); José Esteban Muñoz, *Disidentifications: Queers of Color and the Performance of Politics* (1999); Gayle Rubin, "Thinking Sex," *Pleasure and Danger* (ed. Carol S. Vance, 1984); Steven Seidman, ed., *Queer Theory/Sociology* (1996); William B. Turner, *A Genealogy of Queer Theory* (2000), Michael Warner, *Fear of a Queer Planet: Queer Politics and Social Theory* (1993), *Publics and Counterpublics* (2002), *The Trouble with Normal* (1999); Monique Wittig, *The Straight Mind and Other Essays* (1992).

Race and Ethnicity

The 1960s witnessed an upheaval of grassroots movements determined to bring social justice to the minority communities of the United States. Activist groups and movements such as the American Indian movement, the Chicana/o movement, the Asian American movement, and the Black Panthers, to name but a few, sought self-determination for their communities, as well as federal, state, and local programs to ameliorate the social inequities these communities faced. Fought on a number of fronts, these struggles always included education as a key site for positive social change. Activists demanded, for instance, that college curricula be redesigned to address the history and culture of their too-often neglected communities. Thus, ethnic studies programs, either individually or comparatively focused, took root in colleges and universities across the nation, and these curricular changes also shaped programs of study in already established departments such as those of history, English, philosophy, anthropology, geography, and the like. While scholars had been working on matters of race prior to these social movements, institutional structures were now being set in place to grant greater legitimacy to research examining not only sociological aspects of race and racism but also how race and culture informed each other.

Rather than merely descriptive signifiers, "race" and "ethnicity" chart a history of practices to quantify intelligence, measure moral worth, and establish the superiority of the Caucasian race. One continues to be struck by the prescience of W. E. B. Du Bois's assertion in *The Souls of Black Folk* (1903) that "the problem of the twentieth century is the problem of the color line—the relation of the darker to the lighter races of men in Asia and Africa, in America and the islands of the sea" (45). In the founding document of biological taxonomy, *Systema naturae* (1758), Linnaeus proposed dividing *Homo sapiens* into four categories based mainly on cartography, though he also considered color, temperament, and posture. His four groups were *Americanus*, *Europeus*, *Asiaticus*, and *Afer* (i.e., African). Linnaeus's student, Johann Friedrich Blumenbach, in the third edition of his *On the Natural Variety of Mankind* [1775]), then offered a five-race schemata with Caucasians at the top of the list. The key distinction between the eighteenth-century racial hierarchies and nineteenth-century racial thinkers (whom Kwame Anthony Appiah has aptly identified as biological racialists) is how the latter set out to show that racial distinctions were innate, permanent, and biological rather than transcendent. Unlike in Blumenbach's model, race could not be transcended. Identified by Gould as the "granddaddy of modern scientific racism" (49), Comte Arthur de Gobineau figures prominently in this transition. In his *Essay on the Inequality of the Human Races* (1853–1855) Gobineau asserted the fundamental inequality of the races and was terrified that interracial mixing would dilute the white race's superiority, a theme that ran throughout the remainder of the nineteenth and into the twentieth century.

In the decades since the 1960s, pioneering work in literary and CULTURAL STUDIES by critics such as Barbara Christian, Ramón Saldívar, Hazel Carby, Américo Paredes, José Limón, Elaine Kim, Frank Chin, Nelly McKay, HENRY LOUIS GATES JR., Ward Churchill, and Winona Laduke, to name but a few scholars, has addressed such issues as how black vernacular was used as a signifying practice in African American culture, how race and gender factor into the construction of the African American subject, how Mexican and Mexican American ballads (*corridos*) addressed social unrest along the U.S.-Mexico border, how the "yellow peril" figured as a trope for the dehumanization and marginalization of Asian immigrants, and how racist stereotypes of Native Americans contributed to the genocidal practices carried out against them in the United States. Scholars have also combined various theoretical approaches such as NEW HISTORICISM, Marxism, postcolonialism, feminism, and queer studies with investigations into how race and ethnicity are represented, constructed, and performed in a variety of cultural formations.

The most heated debates concerning race and culture have been those around the very idea of the meaning of "race." The debates have been carried out by Anthony Appiah, Cornel West, bell hooks, Lucius T. Outlaw, PAUL GILROY, Frank H. Wu, Richard Rodriguez, and Patricia Williams, among others. Whether one considers race to be a biologically determined or socially constructed category, one must understand how race has played itself out in the United States if its articulation to cultural formations is to be understood and elucidated. The practices of racializing subjects are not universal; rather they are historically specific. To examine the intersections of race and culture thus requires a historical understanding of how race has developed as both signifier and lived reality.

While "ethnic" appeared as early as the fifteenth century in English, "ethnicity" in its definition as denoting ethnic character or peculiarity did not surface in the English lexicon, according to the *Oxford English Dictionary*, until 1953, when David Riesman used it in an essay in the *American Scholar*, referring to "The groups who, by reason of rural or small-town location, ethnicity, or other parochialism, feel threatened by the better educated upper-middle-class people." As Nathan Glazer and Daniel P. Moynihan make clear in the introduction to their influential edited collection *Ethnicity: Theory and Experience* (1975), ethnicity emphasized the process of group formation based on culture and descent. Like Du Bois, the ethnicity school took a social approach to race and understood it as one of a number of determinants of ethnicity.

In *Racial Formation in the United States* (1986) Michael Omi and Howard Winant delineate three distinct stages of the ethnicity approach. The first was a pre-1930s stage, when the ethnic-group view was seen as a direct challenge to the biological racialists. The second, a liberal stage from the 1930s to 1965, centered on assimilationism and cultural pluralism. Omi and Winant argue that it was during the second stage that ethnicity became the dominant paradigm for understanding race in the United States, and they point to Gunnar Myrdal's 1944 study *An American Dilemma: The Negro Problem and Modern Democracy* as the catalyst for the dominance of this paradigm. The third stage of the ethnicity approach was post-1965, a neoconservative backlash against the struggle for group rights. Ultimately, Omi and Winant reject this paradigm because it reduces race to an element of ethnicity. They want to keep race as a discrete and central category because when it becomes a mere feature of ethnicity, it fails to comprehend the specific characteristics of racial minority groups.

Omi and Winant propose to accentuate race through what they call "racial formation." In their stress on the social, economic, and political constructions of race, they represent a diverse group of critical race theorists such as Appiah, Gates, and David Theo Goldberg, who since the mid-1990s have similarly highlighted the social construction of race. Given the influence of Omi and Winant's work and the paradigm it represents, their definition bears quoting at length:

> The meaning of race is defined and contested throughout society, in both collective action and personal practice. In the process, racial categories themselves are formed, transformed, destroyed and reformed. We use the term *racial formation* to refer to the process by which social, economic and political forces determine the content and importance of racial categories, and by which they are in turn shaped by racial meanings. Crucial to this formulation is the treatment of race as a *central axis* of social relations which cannot be subsumed or reduced to some broader category or conception. (61)

Race must be a fundamental element, and we must understand the processes whereby racial formations are constructed. Variants on this idea continue to shape the debate in current race theory. The emergence of whiteness studies is especially salutary. Drawing on the idea that race is a social construction, theorists such as Alexander Saxton, Richard Dyer, Ruth Frankenberg, and David Roediger began in the early 1990s to problematize the idea of white as an unmarked racial category, as an axiomatic norm against which all races could be measured. They investigate the multiple ways in which radically different groups of people have been colligated under the supposedly homogenous signifier "white" and thereby reveal its social and political construction.

Certainly, in the early years of the twenty-first century the book that has stirred the most critical debate on the topic of race is Gilroy's *Against Race: Imagining Political Culture beyond the Color Line* (2000). Reviewing the atrocities fascists and ultranationalists have committed in the name of race, Gilroy recommends that we renounce race because that renunciation "seems to represent the only *ethical* response to the conspicuous wrong that raciologies continue to solicit and sanction" (41). He summarily rejects the assertion that "ethnicity" and "culture" offer greater precision than "race" for marking social divisions among people. Unlike Omi and Winant, who reject ethnicity because it subsumes the centrality of race, Gilroy finds race itself no less a useless and fictitious category than ethnicity. Advances in molecular biology and nanotechnology offer Gilroy the means to delegitimize racial thinking. He deploys what the medical industry and sciences have learned from nanotechnology and genomics to trump any biological arguments that there are such things as races. He writes that "we can draw an extra measure of courage from the fact that the proponents of the ideas of 'races' are further than ever from being able to answer the basic question that has confounded them since the dawn of raciology: if 'race' is a useful way of classifying people, then how many 'races' are there? It is rare nowadays to encounter talk of a 'Mongoloid race'" (*Against* 37).

Recognizing that groups who have been able to bond together around racial identifications to effect social change will have a hard time renouncing race and that they will have to be persuaded that there is something worthwhile to gain from their renunciation of race, Gilroy asserts that "they will have to be reassured that the dramatic gestures involved in turning against racial observance can be accomplished without violating the precious forms of solidarity and community that have been created by their protracted subordination along racial lines. The idea that action against racial hierarchies can proceed more effectively when it has been purged of any lingering respect for the idea of 'race' is one of the most persuasive cards in this political and ethical suit" (12–13). Ultimately, Gilroy wants to leave the century of the color line behind for a more future-oriented, cosmopolitan, planetary humanist approach to political culture. Gilroy's proposed political project requires, to paraphrase STUART HALL, that we be prepared to work without guarantees. Strategies and their attendant results cannot be known in advance. Moreover, racist practices may best be undercut by refusing to grant their fundamental premise, namely, that race is a viable way to subdivide humankind.

If we think along with Gilroy in renouncing race, we must ask a series of questions that ramify into curricular, scholarly, and sociopolitical concerns. First, what are the implications for the distribution of material resources? While race may be an illusory fiction, racism is a powerful reality. We live in a racist world, and racism affects lives in material ways—in the zoning of neighborhoods, the quality of public education, access to equitable pay and employment, and so forth. If as scholars we abandon race and the government abandons it as well, what will be the implications for these material concerns? If the idea of race is abandoned, what might it mean for the way scholars compile anthologies, teach classes, organize disciplines, and build programs? If race is a fiction to be renounced, can we even have anthologies of or courses on Latina/o, African American, Asian American, or Native American culture, politics, and so on? If we answer in the negative, what then will be the rubrics under which we organize our research and teaching? What will become of ethnic studies programs? These questions are merely illustrative, not exhaustive, of the issues we must think through if we pursue the avenue Gilroy has laid out for us. The answers are not easy to come by, but the questions must be asked and thought through.

RALPH E. RODRIGUEZ

See also AFRICAN AMERICAN THEORY AND CRITICISM, FRANTZ FANON, GENDER, MULTICULTURALISM, NATIVE THEORY AND CRITICISM, and POSTCOLONIAL STUDIES: 2. 1990 AND AFTER.

K. Anthony Appiah, "Race" (Frank Lentricchia and Thomas McLaughlin), "The Uncompleted Argument: Du Bois and the Illusion of Race" (Gates); K. Anthony Appiah and Amy Gutmann, Color Conscious (1998); Mario Barrera, Race and Class in the Southwest: A Theory of Racial Inequality (1979); W. E. B. Du Bois, "The Conservation of the Races," American Negro Academy Occasional Papers 2, (1897), The Souls of Black Folk (1903, ed. David W. Blight and Robert Gooding-Williams, 1997); Richard Dyer, White (1997); Michael Eric Dyson, Race Rules: Navigating the Color Line (1997); Gerald Early, ed., Lure and Loathing: Essays on Race, Identity, and the Ambivalence of Assimilation (1993); Yen Le Espiritu, Asian American Panethnicity: Bridging Identities and Institutions (1992); Frantz Fanon, Peau noire, masques blancs (1952, Black Skin, White Masks, trans. Charles Lan Markmann, 1967); Ruth Frankenberg, White Women, Race Matters: The Social Construction of Whiteness (1993); Henry Louis Gates Jr., ed., "Race," Writing, and Difference (1985); Paul Gilroy, Against Race: Imagining Political Culture beyond the Color Line (2000), The Black Atlantic: Modernity and Double Consciousness (1993), "There Ain't No Black in the Union Jack": The Cultural Politics of Race and Nation (1987); Henry Giroux, Fugitive Cultures: Race, Violence, and Youth (1996); David Theo Goldberg, Racist Culture: Philosophy and the Politics of Meaning (1993); David Theo Goldberg, ed., Anatomy of Racism (1990); Thomas F. Gossett, Race: The History of an Idea in America (1965); Stephen Jay Gould, The Mismeasure of Man (1981, rev. ed., 1996); Jorge J. E. Gracia and Pablo De Greiff, eds., Hispanics/Latinos in the United States: Ethnicity, Race, and Rights (2000); Carl Gutiérrez-Jones, Critical Race Narratives: A Study of Race, Rhetoric, and Injury (2001); Thomas C. Holt, The Problem of Race in the Twenty-First Century (2000); bell hooks, Black Looks: Race and Representation (1992); Reginald Horsman, Race and Manifest Destiny: The Origins of Racial Anglo-Saxonism (1981); Noel Ignatiev, How the Irish Became White (1995); Robin D. G. Kelley, Yo' Mama's Dysfunctional! Fighting the Culture Wars in America (1997); Frank Lentricchia and Thomas McLaughlin, eds., Critical Terms for Literary Study (1990, 2nd ed., 1995); Arnoldo de León, They Called Them Greasers: Anglo Attitudes toward Mexicans in Texas, 1821–1900 (1983); George Lipsitz, The Possessive Investment in Whiteness: How White People Profit from Identity Politics (1998); Lisa Lowe, Immigrant Acts: On Asian American Cultural Politics (1996); Wahneema Lubiano, ed., The House That Race Built (1998); Scott L. Malcolmson, One Drop of Blood: The American Misadventure of Race (2000); Charles W. Mills, The Racial Contract (1997); David Morley and Kuan-Hsing Chen, eds., Stuart Hall: Critical Dialogues in Cultural Studies (1996); Toni Morrison, Playing in the Dark: Whiteness and the Literary Imagination (1992); Suzanne Oboler, Ethnic Labels/Latino Lives: Identity and the Politics of (Re)presentation in the United States (1995); Michael Omi and Howard Winant, Racial Formation in the United States: From the 1960s to the 1980s (1986); Lucius T. Outlaw, On Race and Philosophy (1996); Clara Rodriguez, Changing Race: Latinos, the Census, and the History of Ethnicity in the United States (2000); David R. Roediger, The Wages of Whiteness: Race and the Making of the American Working Class (1991); Edward W. Said, Orientalism (1978); E. San Juan Jr., Racial Formations/Critical Transformations: Articulations of Power in Ethnic and Racial Studies in the United States (1992); Alexander Saxton, The Rise and Fall of the White Republic: Class Politics and Mass Culture in

Nineteenth-Century America (1990); Bart Schneider, ed., Race: An Anthology in the First Person (1997); Shawn Michelle Smith, American Archives: Gender, Race, and Class in Visual Culture (1999); Werner Sollors, Beyond Ethnicity: Consent and Descent in American Culture (1986), "Ethnicity," Lentricchia and McLaughlin); William Stanton, The Leopard's Spots: Scientific Attitudes toward Race in America, 1815–1859 (1960); Mary C. Waters, Ethnic Options: Choosing Identities in America (1990); Cornel West, Race Matters (1993); Patricia Williams, The Alchemy of Race and Rights (1991); Howard Winant, The World Is a Ghetto: Race and Democracy since World War II (2001).

Rancière, Jacques

It is difficult to categorize the work of Jacques Rancière (b. 1940) or to definitively capture his influence on contemporary theory and criticism. Having published texts on subjects as wide-ranging as Marxist theory, working-class politics and literature, the history of philosophy, democratic theory, and the politics of aesthetics, Rancière's work does not sit comfortably within any single academic discipline. For rather than adopting the postulates of any particular field, discipline, or system of thought, Rancière's scholarship demonstrates a forthright and even rebellious determination to occupy the intermediary spaces between discourses without opting for any of them in the end. Like the work of MICHEL FOUCAULT, Rancière's scholarship is best understood as a consistent deconstructive effort that challenges the formative boundaries of academic thought itself.

Rancière first came to prominence in the 1960s when, as a student of the French philosopher Louis Althusser, he contributed to the influential book *Reading Capital* (1965) with another of Althusser's students, Étienne Balibar. After the Parisian student revolt of May 1968, Rancière broke ranks with Althusser on the grounds that his former teacher's work, influenced as it may have been by Althusser's partisan affiliation with the French Communist Party, had become overly rigid and was no longer hospitable to spontaneous popular dissent. Methodologically, Rancière's split with Althusser (which he outlines in his 1974 publication *Althusser's Lesson*) can be traced to the theoretical centrality that Althusser afforded to FERDINAND DE SAUSSURE's linguistic demarcation between *langue* and *parole*, which, once applied outside the study of language, has a tendency of reducing all social, cultural, and political phenomena to the status of passive "reflections" issuing from an underlying structure. For Rancière, the centrality of this distinction, whether as a psychoanalytically conceived unconscious or the Marxian notion of the economic infrastructure or "base," robbed political actions of their critical force and produced a highly formulaic conception of politics. In his future work, Rancière would still opt for a linguistically inflected theory of political action but one that conceives of all political interventions as socially effective forces in their own right—or, in linguistic terms, as illocutionary acts fully capable of reconfiguring their emergent systemic conditions. In this regard, Rancière's modified approach more closely resembles the theory of SPEECH ACTS associated with J. L. Austin than much of the theoretical work derived from Saussurean structuralism.

In the years following his departure from the mainstream of French Marxism, Rancière published a number of texts that brought critical scrutiny to the assumptions that had structured and animated European Marxist and leftist thought. In *The Nights of Labor* (1981), Rancière revealed that the political attitudes of the French working class were often much more diverse and fragmented than many of France's intellectuals had a tendency to claim. Essentially a book of social history constructed from extensive archival research, The Nights of Labor argues that working peoples in France rarely considered their class status as "noble" and more often desired the comfort and security that defined bourgeois life. In the subsequent The Philosopher and His Poor (1983) Rancière broadened the scope of his previous work to consider more generally why philosophy has so consistently thought it necessary to speak on behalf of the downtrodden and how this tacit silencing of the poor by a philosophy that claimed to speak for those unable to speak for themselves has shaped the history of class conflict and struggle. In 1987, Rancière published the rather eclectic The Ignorant Schoolmaster: Five Lessons in Intellectual Emancipation, a focused examination of the historical figure Joseph Jacotot, an unorthodox nineteenth-century school teacher whose radical methods of pedagogy lead him to assert that all students were equally intelligent and that their seeming intellectual inequalities were largely the product of social and institutional practices.

The Ignorant Schoolmaster marks Rancière's increasing distance from the narrow concerns of class stratification and conflict and his growing interest in the larger and more diffuse processes by which the ordering of the social (or rather the "sensible") comes to appear as self-evident and how different forms of political intervention are able to modify this hegemonic order. Accordingly, Rancière's work throughout the 1990s and into the first decade of the twenty-first century questioned received wisdom in a wide range of scholarly fields by demonstrating the multifaceted character of what he would come to call the "distribution of the sensible." Yet rather than outline these efforts in a strictly chronologically fashion, it would be truer to the intent of Rancière's work and a better illustration of the critical efficacy of his antidisciplinarity to jump among them through a discussion of some of the central themes that weave these books together. Arguably Rancière's most influential contribution to contemporary theory and criticism has been his reconfiguration of the relationship between equality and politics. It was the central concern of almost all of his work in the 1990s, including On the Shores of Politics (1992), The Names of History (1992), and Disagreement: Politics and Philosophy (1995). Equality, for Rancière, is neither a means nor an end but rather the structuring principle from which the political community itself emerges. Rancière's engagement with the concept of equality does not, therefore, attempt to understand how politics deals with problems of material or symbolic inequality; instead it attempts to understand what sorts of "inequality" give rise to the political community in the first place.

Rancière follows Aristotle in understanding the human as a zoon politikon—a "political animal"—in the fundamental sense that all humans are capable of speech and reasoned dialogue: humans qua speaking beings share a primordial linguistic or cognitive equality prior to the constitution of the political community, as it is through the exercise of this singular capacity that politics are possible. However, this simple equation quickly becomes paradoxical, as the political community tends to cancel out this underlying dialogical equality by excluding and silencing some segment of the populous as one of its founding gestures. Through this definition of politics, Rancière diverges sharply from Aristotle, for whom the normal functioning of politics is an agonistic process of negotiation between various sectors of the political community. For Rancière, however, the distribution of a delegated citizenry is a second-order process that merely proceeds from the more fundamental division of the society into those worthy of political subjectivity and those who are excluded. Politics is not therefore a process of negotiation performed within an already proscribed political arena but a performative enunciation by the excluded segment of the society—what he calls the "part of no part"—in their demand for political recognition. Put differently, politics is never really about any superficial material grievance, but rather always involves the contestation of the limits of the political sphere itself.

In his most recent publications, Rancière applies his previous work in political philosophy to the field of aesthetic criticism. In particular, he extends his dualistic conception of political philosophy, in which politics is the name given to the clash between an established order and an excluded element, to the study of the politics of aesthetics. Yet unlike this earlier work, his political aesthetics are not based on an explicitly topological framework of inside/outside but are more methodologically immanent. This is clear enough once one considers Rancière's definition of the "distribution of the sensible": "I call the distribution of the sensible the system of self-evident facts of sense perception that simultaneously discloses the existence of something in common and the delimitations that define the respective parts and positions within it . . . it can be understood in a Kantian sense as the system of *a priori* forms determining what presents itself to sense experience" (*Politics of Aesthetics* 12–13). In this sense, the "politics" of aesthetics cannot involve a process whereby an excluded element is permitted access into the realm of the sensible, for what is outside the very perception of the senses cannot really exist as an "excluded element" that makes illocutionary demands. Instead, Rancière's notion of political aesthetics involves the alteration or modification of the coordinates of the sensible's distribution from within: it is the attempt to shift the framework of perception in order to disrupt the received order of things, create dissensus within consensus, and permit the emergence of new ways of doing and making in the world.

While there are many benefits to working from such a broad conception of political aesthetics, it is not without its shortcomings. For instance, it becomes unclear how exactly art exerts political agency once the links that previously permitted one to endow artistic production with political meaning have been completely severed. How can art make competent political decisions without any solid ground on which to stand? In *The Emancipated Spectator* (2008), Rancière responds to these criticisms, though no definite resolution is reached. Cautious of artistic attempts to fabricate a new political community through the direct engagement of the audience (Bertolt Brecht) but equally critical of a consumer society in which political resistance itself seems to be little more than an aesthetic style, Rancière seriously considers art's impotence for critiquing a commodity world largely defined by artistic innovation. Rancière's response is careful and moderate. Reciting the postulates of poststructuralism, Rancière observes that the aesthetics of mass-consumer society are subject to the same undefinable and wandering excess inherent to all modes of signification, including new artistic forms mobilized through global communications technologies and capital flows. In this way, Rancière shows how even critical art that has been wholly incorporated into the flows of capital is never fully stripped of its latent critical edge and thus it remains a force for heterogenesis and redistribution. Yet it is difficult to view this intervention as squarely confronting the problem of art's waning political charge: for insofar as the politics of aesthetics is understood as primarily a function of its excessive signification, then all manner of aesthetics becomes political by definition, and the vicissitudes of aesthetics and politics suffer from increasing tautology. The interrelation between aesthetics, politics, and global capitalism thus remains largely an open question in Rancière's work, and it is far from certain whether the all-encompassing character of his theoretical apparatus will be suited to the task.

MATTHEW MACLELLAN

See also FRENCH THEORY AND CRITICISM: 1945 AND AFTER and MARXIST THEORY AND CRITICISM: 3. 1989 AND AFTER.

Jacques Rancière, *Aux bords du politique* (1992, *On the Shores of Politics*, trans. Liz Heron, 1995), *La chair des mots: Politiques d'ecriture* (1998, *The Flesh of Words*, trans. Charlotte Mandell, 2004), *Chroniques des temps consensuels* (2005, *Chronicles of Consensual Times*, trans. Steven Corcoran, 2010), *Le destin des images* (2003, *The Future of the Image*, 2009), *Dissensus* (trans. Steven Corcoran, 2010), *La fable cinématographique* (2001, *Film Fables*, trans. Emiliano Battista, 2006), *La haine de la démocratie* (2005, *Hatred of Democracy*, trans. Steve Corcoran, 2006), *L'inconscient esthétique* (2001, *The Aesthetic Unconscious*, 2010), *La maître ignorant: Cinq leçons sur l'émancipation intellectuelle* (*The Ignorant Schoolmaster: Five Lessons in Intellectual Emancipation*, trans. Kristin Ross, 1991), *Malaise dans l'esthétique* (2004, *Aesthetics and its Discontents*, 2009), *La mésentente: Politique et philosophie* (1995, *Disagreement: Politics and Philosophy*, trans. Julie Rose, 1999), *Les noms de l'histoire: Essai de poétique du savoir* (1992, *The Names of History: On the Poetics of Knowledge*, trans. Hassan Melehy, 1994), *La nuit des prolétaires* (1981, *The Nights of Labor: The Workers' Dream in Nineteenth-Century France*, trans. John Drury, 1989), *La partage du sensible: Esthetique et politique* (2000, *The Politics of Aesthetics*, trans. Gabriel Rockhill, 2004), *Le philosophe et ses pauvre* (1983, *The Philosopher and his Poor*, trans. John Drury, Corinne Oster, and Andrew Parker, 2004), *Le spectateur émancipé* (2008, *The Emancipated Spectator*, trans. Gregory Elliott, 2009).

Reader-Response Criticism

Reader-response criticism maintains that the interpretive activities of readers, rather than the author's intention or the text's structure, explain a text's significance and aesthetic value. Biographical accounts of how a writer responds to his or her critics initiated this kind of criticism. That is, since a writer may respond to commentary provided by friends, reviewers, or critics, biographers assumed that the study of these responses helps to explain how and why the style, ideas, aims, or forms of the writer evolved (see, for example, McGann 24). Modern versions of this criticism emerged in the 1970s, in reaction against the hegemonic New Criticism, which reduced accounts of the reader's responses to the infamous "affective fallacy" and treated the devices and structures of the text as purely objective. The modern versions include psychological and theoretical accounts of the reader's activity and sociohistorical accounts of a text's interpretations or an author's reception. The psychological and theoretical accounts preserve the scientific objectivity of the critic or the transformative force of textual or aesthetic norms, whereas the historical accounts of literary reception limit or repudiate aesthetic norms and examine the reader's social or institutional context, what STANLEY FISH terms his or her "interpretive community."

Trained in psychoanalysis, Norman Holland engages in a psychological criticism that considers interpretation a function of a reader's personal identity. For example, Holland claims that while readers' responses to William Faulkner's "A Rose for Emily" may show remarkable differences, the critic does not evaluate the responses; instead, the critic discerns each reader's characteristic traits, including defensiveness, indifference, aggressiveness, or vulnerability (123–24). For Holland, once the facts of a text have satisfied the ego defenses of the reader, he/she readily projects his fears and wishes onto it. Through this process, which Holland labels "DEFT" ("defense, expectation, fantasy, transformation"), the text frees the reader to reexperience his or her self-defining fantasies and to grasp their significance (Holland and Sherman 217). And the same personal response goes for the critic, who exhibits neither the reader's self-determination nor self-improvement but rather his or her unconscious defenses and fantasies. However, while the critic's interpretation reveals his or her identity, the interpretive power of the critic depends on the ability to maintain scientific objectivity.

Very few reader response critics have focused so directly on individual readers as Holland. Since the late 1960s, Wolfgang Iser, a cofounder of Germany's influential school of Constance, has argued that the reader's activity is not self-reflexive but rather explains textual interpretation more generally; however, he considers scientific objectivity a "classical," "absolute" norm concealing "hidden meanings" and stifling the reader's imagination. In *The Implied Reader* (1972) and *The Act of Reading* (1976), Iser construes the text as a many-layered structure through which readers wander, constructing projections ("protentions") of new experience and reinterpretations ("retentions") of past experience. Influenced by the phenomenological critic Roman Ingarden, who argues that the literary text works as an only partially determined structure concretized but not fully realized by the reader's activity, Iser believes that a "potential" of the text admits other readings, which represent other potentials. Iser assumes that the text establishes norms that guide and limit readers, but he maintains that the text's potentials, which include indeterminate gaps, blanks, discrepancies, and absences, disturb its structure and stimulate the reader's activity (Act 98–99). Readers synthesize "perspectives" deriving from the text's narrator, characters, and plot, but the text still signals, guides, and manipulates these perspectives, moving them to reinterpret the text and, more importantly, to produce what it cannot—the experience of a coherent, living whole growing out of "the alteration or falsification of that which is already ours" (Act 98–99, 132). In other words, the text's indeterminate structures acquire a negative force, prodding readers to construct their own text and change their lives. Although schools, parents, and churches may have taught readers to read, Iser maintains that their "controlled observation" of themselves allows them to escape this "fallen" world and to improve their lives. Paradoxically, the indeterminate negativity of the text can provoke the reader not only to produce a coherent text but also to adopt positive and redemptive values.

In *The Fictive and the Imaginary* (1993), Iser acknowledges that literature has lost the capacity to guide or improve the reader because the horrors of two world wars and competition from music, film, and other media have rendered literature marginal. To restore literature's "all-encompassing" function, Iser adopts a general aesthetic theory in which fiction and the imaginary support activities that are relevant in everyday life. He argues that philosophy has recently accorded both fiction and the imaginary a positive role in understanding and even constituting reality; at the same time, the activity of play—whereby fiction and the imaginary determine each other—enables fiction and the imaginary to escape cognitive discourses and to break the boundaries between thought and reality. While all discourses foster this play between the fictive and the imaginary, Iser claims, literature provides the paradigmatic case. While he still dismisses the influence of schools and other everyday cultural institutions, Iser claims that literature's negativity, which undermines established beliefs and fixed practices, and literature's doubling, which overcomes the opposition of fiction and reality or self and other, enables literature to reveal the plasticity or new human possibilities described by a literary anthropology. Similarly, in *The Range of Interpretation* (2000), Iser argues that, like the interplay of the fictive and the imaginary, literary forms of cultural translation or interpretation explain the practices of psychological, sociological, and theological systems and by envisaging new possibilities expose their limits and transcend them.

Like Holland and Iser, Fish claims that the irreducible effects of language move readers to produce interpretations, so that, as a normative force, the author teaches or fashions the reader. In the early "Affective Stylistics" (1970), Fish positions reading as a temporal process in which the reader constructs interpretations and repudiates them in favor of new ones. For Fish, while the reader's first interpretation may contradict subsequent interpretations, this does not invalidate either reading. If readers are competent, such inconsistency only shows that they are experiencing a certain kind of text, not that they are misconstruing its true structure or its author's intention. In later work, Fish abandons the assumption that competent readers discover one "deep structure" or normative intention, arguing that this view did not explain why some readers interpret a text one way and others interpret it another. He also rejects the belief that aesthetic theory ensures a reader's self-consciousness or governs interpretive practice. He admits that theorists may examine the rhetorical figures of a text, the unifying intention of its author, its play of gender differences, or its critiques of ideology; however, he considers these diverse interpretive practices a matter of local, Derridean, authorial, feminist or Marxist beliefs rather than of valid theory, whose general rules cannot determine correct interpretations ("Consequences" 433–38; see also Knapp and Michaels 738–40).

Adopting the pragmatist's belief that the community of inquirers establishes the truth of a theory, Fish claims, moreover, that what determines an interpretation's validity is not the identity of the reader nor the norms of aesthetic theory but the ideals and methods of the reader's "interpretive community" (Is There 171). New Critics, authorial humanists, phenomenologists, structuralists, Derrideans, feminists, and Marxists represent diverse interpretive communities whose ideas institutions disseminate, students master, scholars judge, and journals and publishing houses distribute. To reject the absolute ground of an author's intention or a text's structure is not to consider any interpretation as good as any other or to lapse into a vacuous relativism, as some critics say; rather, since the community of similar interpreters judges an interpretation, some interpretations are believed to be better or worse than others, at least, for that community.

Like Holland and Iser, Steven Mailloux, a scholar of American literature, pragmatist philosophy, and literary theory, maintains that authors communicate meanings to readers and thereby teach readers how to read. Like Fish, he claims that different readers produce different interpretations and even different texts because diverse rhetorical conventions govern their interpretive practices. In *Reception Histories*, he sees interpretation as an act of translation whereby a formal reader seeks to approximate the words of the text, while an authorial reader uses textual, biographical, or historical evidence to clarify the intentions of the author (46). He objects that the empiricist Fish consigns too much to the reader's beliefs and too little to theory, which, Mailloux says, has at least unexpected consequences—it directs research, precludes unacceptable views, and exposes concealed interests (*Rhetorical* 151–66). Mailloux repudiates theoretical ideals but does not dismiss universal theory in favor of local beliefs, as Fish does; instead, he rejects the metaphysical quest for ultimate grounds, irrefutable arguments, or foundational truths, as Richard Rorty does. For Mailloux, to reject theory is to focus "on the rhetorical dynamics among interpreters within specific cultural settings" and to recognize that "theory soon turns into rhetorical history" (*Rhetorical* 144–45). Furthermore, while Fish insists that interpretation is professional, Mailloux, adopting Foucault's notion of power, characterizes interpretation as a "politically interested act" that "participates in . . . a politics embedded in institutional structures and specific cultural practices" (*Power* 149). Mailloux's antifoundational "rhetorical hermeneutics" explains the changing history and politics of a text's many readings more effectively than does Fish's account of interpretive communities or Iser's account of the reader's transformations.

Other political critics have developed a feminist reader-response criticism and gendered and Marxist histories of reception. For instance, Patrocinio Schweickart defends literature's transformative power but complains that because the main proponents of reader-response criticism have been highly privileged males and its main texts male texts, it has ignored differences of gender ("Reading" 35). To overcome this "androcentric" bias, reader-response criticism should, Schweickart argues, address women readers and women's texts in order to communicate with the female presence in them. Criticism should also, Schweickart maintains, resist the patriarchal inculcation of masculine perspectives, especially the process of "immasculation," whereby women come to consider themselves the other. In other words, Schweikart believes that a feminist reader-response critic reads male and female texts differently. In Iser's fashion, the feminist critic recognizes that since the immasculation produced by the male text is a result of her own response, she can resist it. As with Fish and Mailloux, the critic expects the feminist community to validate her account of a female author if it shows her subjective engagement rather than the text's structure or the author's intention.

Janice Radway, a scholar of the history of literacy and reading in the United States, also defends feminist reader-response criticism but avoids theoretical accounts of engaged feminist reading and instead undertakes objective, empirical studies of modern women's responses to texts. For example, in *Reading the Romance*, Radway examines the responses of approximately forty women to the contemporary romance novels recommended by Dorothy Evans, a local bookstore clerk. She shows that these women's genre conceptions, preferences, and reading habits are "tied to their daily routines, which themselves are a function of education, social role, and class position" (50). Radway effectively demonstrates, moreover, that, contrary to formal criticism's labeling of popular culture as mere escapist or mindless entertainment, romance reading allows women to distance themselves from their everyday activities and reflect on their habits and lives.

Jane Tompkins also defends popular culture but favors historical studies of literary reception rather than empirical accounts of contemporary women's responses. In "The Reader in History" (1980), she argues that reader-response critics mistakenly adopt the New Critical faith in textual interpretation, arguing that "although New Critics and reader-oriented critics do not locate meaning in the same place, both schools assume that to specify meaning is criticism's ultimate goal" (201). Like Radway, she fears that the formal emphasis on meaning renders critics unable to appreciate popular literature. Moreover, she complains that a formal emphasis is inimical to literature's broad sociopolitical interests, which are, she insists, pressing and urgent and not merely theoretical (see "Indians").

Tony Bennett, a British scholar of Marxist theory and cultural policy, also justifies the study of popular culture and of broad social policies based on reader's responses. He maintains, for example, that literature's canonical genres and texts and opposition to nonliterary discourses have changed markedly, especially in the twentieth century when the media comes to heavily influence the reader's practices (15). He claims, moreover, that literature does not exclude popular culture; on the contrary, like high art, popular literature employs intertextuality, figural forms, and other literary devices. In *Bond and Beyond*, he and Janet Woollacott argue, for example, that when the Bond novels and films became popular in the 1960s and the 1970s, they effectively subverted the older spy fiction in which a prudish but gentlemanly British agent wards off threats to Britain's national integrity (83). Like Fish and Mailloux, Bennett critiques foundational aesthetic or textual norms and examines the reader's interpretive community or, in his terms, "reading formation." He and Woollacott show in their book that established "reading formations" situate and construct the reader's norms and ideals (59–60). To interpret a text is to contest its terrain, to vindicate one's methods and ideologies, and, by implication if not by explicit assertion, to debunk opposed methods and ideologies. Rhetorical practices have sociopolitical import, but this is limited in part by the governmental policies or technologies of power regulating cultural institutions. Bennett shows, for example, that during the nineteenth century, when the schools turned literature into a "moral technology," the ideal teacher and, subsequently, the many-layered text made the reader's interpretive activity the basis of his/her unending ethical improvement (*Outside* 177–80). The aesthetic negativity of the text does not transform the reader, as Iser says; rather, a text provides "a space in which to exhibit not correct readings but a *way* of reading" (188) because literary study's authoritative mechanisms or "reading formations" impose on the reader indeterminate norms capable of "endless revision."

Schweikart complains that, established as common sense, reader-response criticism has not changed much since its origins in the 1980s ("Action" 70), although important methodological differences have emerged. Unlike Radway, Holland, and Iser, she faults the masculinist bias of reader-response criticism; these critics all assume, nonetheless, that, while the subjective beliefs, ideals, and paradigms of readers explain their interpretations of a text, critics preserve their objectivity and the text or aesthetic theory, its transcendent norms. By contrast, despite the many differences of Bennett, Fish, Mailloux, and Tompkins, their reception studies critique the foundational norms of aesthetic theory and situate the diverse interpretations of a text's many readers within their "interpretive communities," "rhetorical practices," or "reading formations," acknowledging, thereby, how deeply criticism is implicated in its sociohistorical life.

PHILIP GOLDSTEIN

Tony Bennett, *Culture: A Reformer's Science* (1998), *Formalism and Marxism* (1979), "Marxism and Popular Fiction," *Literature and History 7* (1981), *Outside Literature* (1990), "Texts in History: The Determinations of Readings and Their Texts," *Post-Structuralism and the Question of History* (ed. Derek Attridge, Geoff Bennington and Robert Young, 1989); Tony Bennett and Janet Woollacott, *Bond and Beyond: The Political Career of a Hero* (1987); Stanley Fish, "Consequences," *Critical Inquiry 11* (1985), *How Milton Works* (2001), *Is There a Text in this Class? The Authority of Interpretive Communities* (1980), "Literature in the Reader: Affective Stylistics" (Tompkins), *Professional Correctness: Literary Studies and Political Change* (1995); Roman Ingarden, *Das Literarische Kuntswerk* (1931, *The Literary Work of Art*, trans. George Grabowicz, 1973); Wolfgang Iser, *Der Akt des Lesens: Theorie ästhetischer Wirkung* (1976, *The Act of Reading: A Theory of Aesthetic Response*, trans. Wolfgang Iser, 1978), "Fictionalizing: The Anthropological Dimension of Literary Fictions," *New Literary History 21* (1990), *Fiktive und das Imaginäre* (1991, *The Fictive and the Imaginary*, trans. Wolfgang Iser, 1993), *Prospecting: From Reader Response to Literary Anthropology* (1993), *The Range of Interpretation* (2000); Norman N. Holland, "Unity Identity Text Self" (Tompkins); Norman N. Holland and Leona F. Sherman, "Gothic Possibilities," *New Literary History 8* (1977); Steven Knapp and Walter Benn Michaels, "Against Theory," *Critical Theory 8* (1982); Steven Mailloux, *Reception Histories: Rhetoric, Pragmatism, and American Cultural Politics, Rhetorical Power* (1998); Jerome J. McGann, *The Beauty of Inflections: Literary Investigations in Historical Method and Theory* (1985); Toby Miller, *Technologies of Truth: Cultural Citizenship and the Popular Media* (1998); Janice A. Radway, *Reading the Romance: Women, Patriarchy, and Popular Literature* (1991); Patrocinio P. Schweickart, "Reading as Communicative Action," *Reader 43* (2000), "Reading Ourselves: Toward a Feminist Theory of Reading," *Courage and Tools* (ed. Joanne Glasgow and Angela Ingram, 1990); Jane P. Tompkins, "'Indians': Textualism, Morality, and the Problem of History" *Critical Inquiry 13* (1986), "The Reader in History" (Tompkins), *Sensational Designs: The Cultural Work of American Fiction 1790–1860* (1986); Jane Tompkins, ed., *Reader-Response Criticism* (1981).

Reception Theory

Reception theory, the approach to literature that concerns itself primarily with a reader's actualization of the text, is based on a collective enterprise. Hans Robert Jauss, with his University of Constance colleagues Manfred Fuhrmann and Wolfgang Iser and with philosophers, historians, and critics such as Rainer Warning, Karlheinz Stierle, Dieter Henrich, Günther Buck, Jürgen Habermas, Péter Szondi, and Hans Blumenberg are part of a loosely organized group that during the second half of twentieth century gathered regularly at colloquia and contributed to the multivolume *Poetik und Hermeneutik.*

The group's first and most provocative pronouncements were two inaugural addresses at the University of Constance: Jauss's in 1967, later published as "Literary History as a Challenge to Literary Theory," and Iser's "The Appeal Structure of Texts" delivered in 1970. Whereas Iser's work is based more on the German phenomenological tradition, Jauss's explicit aim is to reintroduce the issue of history into the study of literature. Jauss reacts against three different conceptions of history in literary studies: an idealist one that represents history as a teleology, a positivist one derived from nineteenth-century historicism, which has to forgo questions of relevance in order to save objectivity, and one based on an irrationalist aesthetic (*Geistesgeschichte*). Instead, Jauss sees MARXIST THEORY AND CRITICISM and Russian formalism as the two most influential methodologies that attempt to come to terms with the relationship between history and aesthetics. The two schools react strongly against the blind empiricism of positivism and against an aesthetic metaphysics, but they attempt to solve the problem in opposite ways.

Jauss criticizes Marxist thinkers such as GEORG LUKÁCS both for their naïve view of literature as a passive reflection of the real world and for basing their aesthetic on a classical canon. A new and more valid history of literature must take into account both the Marxist insistence on mediation and Russian formalist findings about how literary works are perceived. This alternative is an aesthetics of reception, which shifts the critic's attention away from the producer of the text and from the text itself toward a dialectic of production and consumption. The central notion Jauss uses to accomplish this task is the "horizon of expectations," or *Erwartungshorizont*, a term that derives from a number of German philosophical and historical traditions and that refers, in general, to the set of expectations against which readers perceive the text.

In the early 1970s he repeatedly defended and adjusted his theories, particularly in a confrontation with the aesthetics of the FRANKFURT SCHOOL, especially the posthumously published work of THEODOR W. ADORNO. Unlike Adorno in his *Aesthetic Theory* (1970), Jauss believes that literature and art can play a role in our society that is both progressive and affirmative, and he points to the elitist consequences of positing an autonomy of art that cannot do justice to the role of art in the preautono-mous period. In response, Jauss replaces the horizon of expectations with the aes-thetic experience—the aesthetic as a dialectic of self-enjoyment in the enjoyment of something other—as the new cornerstone of his aesthetic theory. Reception theory came under attack from critics in the German Democratic Republic in the early 1970s, when influential theoreticians such as Robert Weimann diagnosed it as the logical result of a refusal to confront the Marxist answers to contradictions inherent in a bourgeois society. Jauss especially was targeted in these attacks because he had attempted to reintroduce a subjective concept of history in literary studies.

Jauss's work in the late seventies, gathered in his *Aesthetic Experience and Literary Hermeneutics* in 1982, moved toward a more hermeneutical interest in the aesthetic experience itself. He distinguishes three basic experiences: a productive aesthetic praxis (*poiesis*), a receptive praxis (*aisthesis*), and a communicative praxis (*katharsis*). Central in this new phase of Jauss's thinking is the third praxis, which is defined as "the enjoyment of the affects as stirred by speech or poetry which can bring about both a change in belief and the liberation of his mind in the listener or the spectator" (92). The aesthetic experience can have three functions in society: it can create norms, simply pass on existing norms, or refuse to conform to the existing norms. Both bourgeois and (neo-) Marxist literary theories have failed to see the continuum between a progressive change of horizons and the adaptation to existing norms.

Whereas Jauss seems to have moved closer to Iser's insistence on the role of the individual reader, many of his younger colleagues in Germany have concentrated on the sociological considerations of his early essays. On the basis of a "constructive functionalism," Norbert Groeben and Siegfried J. Schmidt have developed a theory of literature that opposes to the hermeneutical schools an empirical and functional view of literature. Hermeneutics can at best have a heuristic function: its findings must be tested intersubjectively before they can claim validity. Work in this field is truly interdisciplinary and employs concepts and methods from social psychology, text theory, pragmatics, communication theory, linguistics, and philosophy.

Reception theory has initiated a new interest in the historical dimension and the communicative aspects of the literary text, but its impact seems to have been limited for the most part to Germany and Western Europe.

GEERT LERNOUT

Elizabeth Freund, *The Return of the Reader: Reader-Reception Criticism* (1987); Gunter Grimm, *Rezeptionsgeschichte: Grundlegung einer Theorie* (1977); Norbert Groeben, *Rezeptionsforschung als em-pirische Literaturwissenschaft: Paradigma-durch Methodendiskussion an Untersuchungsbeispielen* (1977); Robert C. Holub, *Reception Theory: A Critical Introduction* (1984); Hans Robert Jauss, *Ästhetische Erfah-rung und literarische Hermeneutik* (1977, rev. ed., 1982, partial trans., *Aesthetic Experience and Literary Hermeneutics*, trans. Michael Shaw, 1982, partial trans., *Question and Answer: Forms of Dialogic Under-standing*, trans. Michael Hays, 1989), "Der Leser als Instanz einer neuen Geschichte der Literatur," *Poetica* 7 (1975), *Literaturgeschichte als Provokation der Literaturwissenschaft* (1967, "Literary History As a

Challenge to Literary Theory," in *Toward an Aesthetic of Reception*), *Toward an Aesthetic of Reception* (trans. Timothy Bahti, 1982); Manfred Naumann et al., *Gesellschaft, Literatur, Lesen: Literaturrezeption in theoretischen Sicht* (1973); Siegfried Schmidt, *Grundriss der empirischen Literaturwissenschaft* (2 vols., 1980–1982); Steven Tèotèosy de Zepetnek and Irene Sywenky, eds., *The Systemic and Empirical Approach to Literature and Culture as Theory and Application* (1997).

Said, Edward W.

In *The World, the Text, and the Critic* (1983), a diverse collection of essays written between 1969 and 1981, Edward Said (1935–2003) writes that "texts are worldly, to some degree they are events, and, even when they appear to deny it, they are nevertheless a part of the social world, human life, and of course the historical moments in which they are located and interpreted" (4). He further notes that "my position is that theory has to be grasped in the place and time out of which it emerges as a part of that time, working in and for it, responding to it; then, consequently, that first place can be measured against subsequent places where the theory turns up for use" (242). Said's essay "Traveling Theory" (1982) examines the academization of GEORG LUKÁCS's revolutionary Marxism. Lucien Goldmann "as an expatriate historian at the Sorbonne . . . degrades [Lukács's] theory, lowers it in importance, domesticates it somewhat to the exigencies of a doctoral dissertation in Paris" (*World* 236). When RAYMOND WILLIAMS, situated in the tradition of Cambridge University English, rereads both Lukács and Goldmann, Said sees "an extraordinary virtue to the distance" in time and space, "even the coldness of his critical reflections" (240). Paul Bové notes that Williams's "virtue" proves to Said that "responsible methods can be developed to judge the efficacy of the various 'misreadings' or 'misinterpretations' whenever a theory is recast by a successor in a different cultural-historical context" (212).

These ideas of how to approach knowledge (formation) as an academic intellectual and how to write and speak as a public person developed into key motives of all of Said's work. In *Beginnings* (1975) he declares that "the writer's life, his career, and his text form a system of relationships whose configuration in real human time becomes progressively stronger" (227). Intimately intertwining his work as a literary and cultural critic with his life as a dislocated Palestinian, he shaped an academic position for himself that was worldly and thus relevant to the public. In the figure of Said, the academic and the political became enmeshed and inseparable. In addition to having a distinguished career in English and comparative literature at Columbia University, Said was an active supporter of the Palestinian cause. Moreover, he distinguished himself as an opera critic, pianist, public speaker, and essayist. He also wrote regularly for Arab newspapers.

In *Out of Place*, his memoir prompted by a leukemia diagnosis in 1991, Said asserts that his cultural and social placelessness always made him feel on the margins. From his singular perspective of displacement, marginality, and hybridity he develops an influential type of cultural and literary criticism. Linking his essays and books, which vary greatly in subject matter and scope, is their claim to oppositional or counterhegemonic intellectualism that is committed to global social justice and that recognizes its own historical and cultural limitations and ideological interpellations.

Broached as a problem of authorship in the early *Joseph Conrad and the Fiction of Autobiography* (1966), the issue of taking responsibility for the uses to which one puts the knowledge conferred by privilege and power reappears in *Beginnings* as the problem of the authority of a "beginning intention." *Beginnings* mediates the need "to reverse oneself" and "to accept thereby the risks of rupture and discontinuity" (34), that is, to begin again and again in a process of reading as action, a process Said probes in a revisionist reading of the history of the modern European novel. European literature and culture have helped to construct idiosyncratic non-Western "imagined communities," in Benedict Anderson's phrase, that are transparent, accessible, and knowable to Western readers or consumers.

Said's groundbreaking *Orientalism* (1978) is a highly politicized contrapuntal reading of imperial discourse about the non-Western Other. The book offers a revisionist account of Western imperialism and colonization from a non-Western, non-imperial perspective. Original and highly controversial is *Orientalism*'s combination of poststructuralism (MICHEL FOUCAULT's discourse analysis) and Western Marxism (ANTONIO GRAMSCI's theory of the intersections of political and civil society) as a means of directing attention to the discursive and textual coproduction of imperial and colonial hegemony. The book unmasks the orientalist claims of objective knowledge of non-Western peoples as hegemonic rhetorical conventions and stereotypical notions embedded in Western "desires, repressions, investments, and projections" (8). Retelling the history of orientalism, it intercedes decisively in its discursive formation.

The book's particular contribution to cultural criticism consists in its analysis of the reciprocal and intimate relationship of imperial knowledge, culture, and power. *Orientalism* has been widely established as *the* pioneering work of colonial discourse analysis—the systemic study and critique of the Eurocentric process of production of knowledge about the silent Other, the Orient, and its inhabitants. Widespread critical consensus holds that together with GAYATRI CHAKRAVORTY SPIVAK's subaltern studies and HOMI K. BHABHA's writing on hybridity, ambivalence, and mimicry, *Orientalism* moved POSTCOLONIAL STUDIES to center stage in North America in the late 1970s and 1980s. It marks the point at which Western academic institutions started to formally recognize Foucauldian imperial and ideological study and also colonial discourse as an area of study.

Said's threefold approach to orientalism—as an academic discipline, a Eurocentric style of thought based upon binary notions of Orient/Occident or West/East, and a discourse that confirms the need for colonial power, domination, and hegemony—exposes the complicity of Western scholarship and writing with imperial power. In the essay "Secular Criticism" (1983), Said posits an alternative for the critic in the form of a secular, worldly critical consciousness that shows an "acute sense of what political, social, and human values are entailed in the reading, production, and transmission of every text" (*World* 26). He introduces Erich Auerbach, the German Jewish refugee from European fascism in "oriental" exile in Istanbul, as an example of secular critical consciousness and claims that an Auerbachian kind of "cooperation between filiation and affiliation . . . is located at the heart of critical consciousness" (16). Said sees a form of critical affiliation lacking in most poststructuralist criticism (and its postcolonial strands), which is enmeshed in a "process of representation, by which filiation is reproduced in the affiliative structure" (22). By this, Said means a process of ethnographic, personalizing representation that, as he denounces in "The Politics of Knowledge" (1991), affirms existing power structures with its "fetishization and relentless celebration of 'difference' and 'otherness'" (*Reflections* 183), replacing or realigning Eurocentrism with Afrocentrism, Islamocentrism, nativism, and other essentialisms.

While celebrated as an outstanding introduction to colonial discourse analysis, *Orientalism* has also been widely criticized for its homogenizing and totalizing approach to orientalist and more generally colonial discourse. As Said himself conceded in subsequent works, colonial discourse is neither homogeneous nor an entity but has created diverse narratives of anti-imperial resistance and imperial critique from both non-Western and Western sources. It has especially served in the construction of anticolonial nationalist and antimodernist narratives. Said emphasizes the many narratives of subaltern anti-imperial resistance in his subsequent works, including a series of Palestinian resistance or counternarratives: *The Question of Palestine* (1979), *After the Last Sky* (1986), *Blaming the Victims* (1988), and *Covering Islam* (1981).

Culture and Imperialism (1993) extends the project of *Orientalism* to the level of global imperial culture, discourse, and anti-imperial resistance, which means to European (canonical) literature of and counterliterature from Asia, the Middle East, Africa, Ireland, and the Caribbean. Said follows a more general academic trend of situating the local within the context of GLOBALIZATION. By juxtaposing culture and imperialism, that is, texts and histories, he develops a complex web of relations between the two without ever reducing the one to the other. The book's first part takes to task the American mass media, including its way of depicting non-Western "natives" as a residue of neoimperialism, and engages in a contrapuntal reading of Verdi's *Aida* (1871) and several canonized realist novels. It confirms Said's continuing resolute devotion to secular criticism as the opposite of processes of canon formation, which he claims dangerously resemble a religious consciousness, a mystical mode (masked as objectivity and realism) of regarding social reality. The second part is devoted to anti-imperial resistance discourses that have arisen out of formerly colonized countries. Said comments on Ali Mazuri's TV series *The Africans* (1986) on PBS: "Here at last was an African on prime-time television, in the West, daring to accuse the West of what it has done, thus reopening a file considered closed" (39). He also refers to various literary works as prominent examples of fictional counternarratives.

Tropes of spatiality come to supplement the modernist emphasis on time. Said appeals to the postcolonial intellectual to write back to both Western (neo)imperialism and postcolonial nationalism. As his discussion of Iraq and the United States in *Culture and Imperialism* shows, he is not against the West per se but against all imperial powers that restrict the freedom of people, especially by means of an oppressive nationalist rhetoric and practice. In "Yeats and Decolonization" he suggests that there are two moments of nationalist revival in the Third World and its literature: a first moment of "nationalist anti-imperialism," which reaches from World War I to the 1950s, and a second moment of "liberationist anti-imperial resistance," which starts in the 1950s. The first moment's literature is primarily concerned with the geographical idea of nation space, while the second's engages in a liberatory discourse that attempts to exceed Eurocentric parameters.

Critics have accused Said of neglecting two important aspects of postcolonial nationalism: different Third World countries have been faced with different historical, spatial, and temporal conditions of decolonization and nationalism, and, more important, the postwar period has generated diverse non-Eurocentric postcolonial concepts of the nation. Though Said shows sympathy for the desire of cultural rootedness (filiation), he insists on the priority of cultural routedness (affiliation), which he exemplified in his life and intellectual positionings. In this regard, he reflects the tendency in Western postcolonial theory and criticism to overstate the living in between of cultures and languages as a positive potential for integrative, cross-cultural dynamics at the meeting ground of Western academe and society. Similarly reflective is his apotheosis of the trope of intellectual marginality and minority existence as a vantage point for worldly, secular criticism. In his essays "Intellectuals in the Post-Colonial World" (1986) and "Third World Intellectuals and Metropolitan Culture" (1990) the protagonist of the struggle for decolonization is not the reified revolutionary but the anti- or postcolonial intellectual as distanced, self-critical academic.

In *Representations of the Intellectual* (1994), insisting on the political necessity of individualized critical consciousness, Said regrounds the oppositional intellectual in a humanistic critical practice that prioritizes individual subject authority and intellectual freedom. He has in many instances pronounced his disillusionment with collective oppositional approaches, which manifest themselves too often as domination, culpability, and/or torpor. *Representations* can be read as a treatise on the contemporary intellectual's responsibility as a marginal, Auerbachian minority figure who analyzes the prevailing cultural system of representation and intervenes in its discursive formation by retelling its history. It is a responsibility mapped along the contours of nationalism, exile, and a contradistinction between professional and amateur. Whereas the professional intellectual interacts in the enclosed and exclusionary circles of specialization, privilege, and power, the amateur, in spite of institutional affiliations and constraints, professional specialization, and ideological interpellation, takes a position at the margin that seeks to criticize and disturb. Passionately committed to social justice and public exchange, the amateur's approach is comparative and interdisciplinary. As an example Said introduces the figure of the exiled thinker—THEODOR W. ADORNO, Constantine Cavafy, Jonathan Swift, C. L. R. James. The Pen and the Sword (1994), The Politics of Dispossession (1994), and Peace and Its Discontents (1996), which followed Representations of the Intellectual within two years, demonstrate Said's practice of critical, committed engagement as amateur intellectual in the Palestinian struggle.

Said's literary and cultural criticism is firmly, even if critically, based in European, liberal humanist philosophy and policy. It is characterized by an uneasy relationship with Marxism—that is, with its epistemological and ontological claims and totalities, which seem unable to answer to the problems and needs of formerly colonized, Third World countries. Yet Said also distances himself from the poststructuralist disruptions of dominant, totalizing discursive structures articulated by figures such as Foucault, JACQUES DERRIDA, or JEAN-FRANÇOIS LYOTARD. He has repeatedly argued that poststructuralism overlooks resistance, "the role of classes, the role of economics, the role of insurgency and rebellion" (World 244). His major criticism of Foucault and Derrida is their destruction of "intention" and "will" in the interest of "infinite substitution," which makes resistance, in particular subaltern resistance, impossible (see "Criticism between Culture and System" in World). For Said, deconstructive interpretive strategies relinquish the critic's responsibility for texts and hence for what becomes of culture; they indulge in an unworldly practice of literary and cultural criticism as a form of professional intellectualism. Marxist and poststructuralist theories share a Eurocentrically myopic perspective of the Third World.

Said sees worldly, secular intellectualism and criticism as being grounded in the universal humanist values of justice, freedom, democracy, and human rights. Rejecting postmodernist claims of the death of the intellectual as the bearer and purveyor of the grand narratives of the Enlightenment, he maintains liberal humanist ideals as the worldly critic's toolkit and burden. Oppositional, secular criticism needs to proceed from liberal humanist values—not, however, because they once were lived experiences and need to be reclaimed as such but because these liberal ideals have served intellectuals as a reminder of the tensions, contradictions, and fine balance between the promises and limited realities (injustices, nondemocratic practices, unfreedoms) of liberal humanist forms of political and social order in this world. Like Foucault, Said is sensitive to the oppositional critic's positional dilemma—her or his highly ambivalent inscription within the genealogy of power knowledge—but counters the latter's "political quietism" and antihumanism with his commitment to work within humanism and make it responsive to its avowed ideals and promises.

SABINE MILZ

See also CULTURAL STUDIES: 2. UNITED STATES, MULTICULTURALISM, and POSTCOLONIAL STUDIES.

Edward W. Said, *After the Last Sky: Palestinian Lives* (1986), *Beginnings: Intention and Method* (1975), "Between Chance and Determinism," *Times Literary Supplement* (6 February 1976), *Blaming the Victims: Spurious Scholarship and the Palestinian Question* (1988), *Covering Islam: How the Media and the Experts Determine How We See the Rest of the World* (1981, rev. ed., 1997), *Culture and Imperialism* (1993), "Edward Said," *Criticism in Society: Interviews* (by Imre Salusinszky, 1987), *The Edward Said Reader* (ed. Moustafa Bayoumi and Andrew Rubin, 2000), *Humanism and Democratic Criticism* (2004), "Intellectuals in the Post-Colonial World," *Salmagundi* 70–71 (1986), *Joseph Conrad and the Fiction of Autobiography* (1966), *Musical Elaborations* (1991), *On Late Style: Music and Literature Against the Grain* (2006), "Opponents, Audiences, Constituencies, and Community," *The Politics of Interpretation* (1983), *Orientalism* (1978), "Orientalism Reconsidered," *Race and Class* 27 (1985), *Out of Place: A Memoir* (1999), *Peace and Its Discontents: Essays on Palestine in the Middle East Peace Process* (1996), *The Pen and the Sword: Conversations with David Barsamian* (1994), *The Politics of Dispossession: The Struggle for Palestinian Self-Determination, 1969–1994* (1994), *Power, Politics, and Culture: Interviews with Edward W. Said* (ed. Gauri Viswanathan, 2001), *The Question of Palestine* (1979), *Reflections on Exile and Other Essays* (2000), *Representations of the Intellectual: The 1993 Reith Lectures* (1994), "Third World Intellectuals and Metropolitan Culture," *Raritan* 9 (1990), *The World, the Text, and the Critic* (1983), "Yeats and Decolonization," *Nationalism, Colonialism, and Literature* (1990); Paul Bové, *Intellectuals in Power: A Genealogy of Critical Humanism* (1986).

Saussure, Ferdinand de

The Swiss linguist Ferdinand de Saussure (1857–1913) is widely considered to be the founder of modern linguistics. Owing to his attempts to describe the structure of language rather than the history of particular languages and language forms, his work forms the major starting point at the turn of the twentieth century for the method of structuralism in linguistics and literary studies and a significant branch of SEMIOTICS. During the early twentieth century, Saussure's work in linguistics and interpretation participated in widespread transformations in understanding across a range of intellectual disciplines, including literary modernism, psychoanalysis, and philosophy. In particular, Saussure's work and methodological approach dramatically affected literary theory and criticism in the last decades of the twentieth century.

Algirdas Julien Greimas and Joseph Courtés locate the emergence of a precise, "scientific" model of interpretation, identified with Saussurean linguistics, Husserlian PHENOMENOLOGY, and Freudian psychoanalysis, at the start of the twentieth century. According to this model of interpretation, form and content are not distinct: every "form" is alternatively a semantic "content," a "signifying form." Consequently, interpretation offers an analogical paraphrase of something that *already* signifies within some other system of signification.

Such a reinterpretation of form and understanding is implicit in Saussure's posthumous *Course in General Linguistics* (1916). In his lifetime, Saussure published relatively little, and his major work, the *Course*, was the transcription by his students of several courses in general linguistics he offered between 1907 and 1911. In the *Course*, Saussure called for the "scientific" study of language to counter the work in historical linguistics that had been done in the nineteenth century. Historical (or "diachronic") linguistics took particular words to be the building blocks of a language and used them to trace the origin and development of Western languages from a putative common language source. It was precisely this study of the unique occurrences of words, with the concomitant assumption that the basic "unit" of language is, in fact, the *positive* existence of "word-elements," that Saussure questioned. The "comparative school" of nineteenth-century philology, Saussure says in the *Course*, "did not succeed in setting up the true science of linguistics" because "it failed to seek out the nature of its object of study" (Baskin trans. 3). That "nature," he argues, is to be found not simply in the "elemental" words that a language comprises—the seeming "positive" facts (or "substances") of language—but in the *formal* relationships that give rise to those "substances."

Saussure bases his systematic reexamination of language on four assumptions. First, he argues that the scientific study of language must examine the *system* rather than the history of linguistic phenomena. For this reason, he distinguishes between the particular occurrences of language—its particular "speech events," known as *parole*—and the proper object of linguistics: the system (or "code") governing those events, which he called *langue*. This systematic study requires the "synchronic" examination of the relationship between elements of language at a particular instant rather than the "diachronic" study of the development of language through history.

This assumption gave rise to the school of thought known as STRUCTURALISM, a term coined by Roman Jakobson in 1929. As described by Jakobson, structuralism maintains that "any set of phenomena examined by contemporary science is treated not as a mechanical agglomeration but as a structural whole [in which] the mechanical conception of processes yields to the question of their function" (711). Here, Jakobson points to the second foundational assumption in Saussurean linguistics: the view that the basic elements of language can only be studied in relation to their *functions* rather than their *causes*. Instead of focusing exclusively on unique events and entities, those events and entities must be *situated* within a systemic framework in which they are related to other events and entities. As Greimas and Courtés note, this is a radical reorientation that reconceives "interpretation" and thus reconfigures notions of explanation and understanding. Rather than being understood as an "effect" subordinate to a phenomenon's causes, explanation here consists in subordinating a phenomenon to its future-oriented "function" or "purpose." Explanation is no longer independent of human intentions or purposes (even though those intentions can be impersonal, communal, or, in Freudian terms, "unconscious").

In his linguistics, Saussure accomplishes this transformation specifically through the functionalist redefinition of the "word" as the "sign." The sign, he argues, is the union of "a concept and a sound image," which he calls "*signified* [*signifié*] and *signifier* [*signifiant*]" (66–67; Roy Harris's 1983 translation offers the terms "signification" and "signal" [67]). The "combination" of the two terms is "functional" in that neither the signified nor the signifier is the "cause" of the other; rather, "each [derives] its values from the other" (8). In this way, Saussure defines the basic element of language, the sign, in *relational terms* and subjects the basic assumption of historical linguistics, the *identity* of the elemental units of language and signification (i.e., "words"), to rigorous analysis. For Saussure, we recognize different occurrences of the word "tree" as the "same" word not because the word is defined by inherent qualities, but because it is defined as an element in the "structural whole" of language.

A relational or "diacritical paradigm" governs the conception of all elements of language in structural linguistics. This approach can be most clearly seen in the Saussurean concept of "phonemes" and "distinctive features" of language. The smallest articulated and signifying units of a language, phonemes, are not the sounds that occur in language but the "sound images" that are *phenomenally* apprehended by speakers as conveying meaning. Drawing on this model, the leading spokesperson for Prague school structuralism, Jan Mukařovský, noted in 1937 that "structure . . . is a phenomenological and not an empirical reality; it is not the work itself, but a set of functional relationships which are located in the consciousness of a collective (generation, milieu, etc.)" (cited in Galan 35).

Phonemes, then, are not *positive* objects but a "phenomenological reality." In English, for instance, the phoneme /t/ can be pronounced in multiple ways, but in all cases an English speaker will recognize it as *functioning* as a /t/. An aspirated t (i.e., a t pronounced with an h-like breath after it), a high-pitched or low-pitched t sound, an extended t sound, and so on will all function in the same manner in distinguishing the meaning of "to" and "do" in English. Moreover, the differences between languages are such that phonological variations in one language can constitute distinct phonemes in another. In every natural language, the vast number of possible words is a combination of a small number of phonemes. English, for instance, possesses fewer than forty phonemes that combine to form over a million different words.

The phonemes of language are themselves systematically organized *structures* of features. In the 1920s and 1930s, drawing inspiration from Saussure, Jakobson and Nikolai S. Trubetzkoy isolated the "distinctive features" of phonemes. These features are based on the physiological structure of the speech organs—tongue, teeth, vocal chords, and so on—that Saussure mentions in the *Course* and that Harris describes as "physiological phonetics" (Harris trans. 39). These features combine in "bundles" of binary oppositions to form phonemes. In this way, phonology is a specific example of a general rule of language described by Saussure:

> In language there are only differences. Even more important: a difference generally
> implies positive terms between which the difference is set up; but in language there
> are only differences *without positive terms*. Whether we take the signified or the
> signifier, language has neither ideas nor sounds that existed before the linguistic
> system. (Baskin trans. 120)

In this framework, linguistic identities are determined not by inherent qualities but by systemic ("structural") relationships.

In the *Course*, Saussure articulates the direction and outlines of a functional analysis of language. His only extended published work, the 1878 *Memoir on the Primitive System of Vowels in Indo-European Languages*, was fully situated within the project of nineteenth-century historical linguistics. Yet even within this work, as Jonathan Culler has argued, Saussure demonstrates "the fecundity of thinking of language as a system of purely relational items, even when working at the task of historical reconstruction" (*Saussure* 66).

The conception of the relational or diacritical determination of the elements of signification suggests a third assumption governing structural linguistics: "the arbitrary nature of the sign." Saussure argues that the relationship between the signifier and signified in language is never necessary (or "motivated"): one could just as easily use the sound signifier "arbre" as the signifier "tree" to unite with the concept of tree. Further, Saussure equally insists on the arbitrary nature of the signified: one could as easily define the concept of tree by its woody quality (which would exclude palm trees) as by its size (which excludes the low woody plants we call shrubs).

Rather than reflecting a hierarchy of priority, each of Saussure's assumptions derives its value from the others. In other words, Saussurean linguistics understands the phenomena it studies according to overarching relationships of *combination* and *contrast*. Consequently, language is both the *process* of articulating meaning (signification) and its *product* (communication), and these two functions of language are neither identical nor fully congruent (see Schleifer, *Analogical* ch. 2). Here, we see the alternation between form and content perceived by Greimas and Courtés in modernist interpretation: language presents contrasts that *formally* define its units, and these units combine on succeeding levels to create the signifying *content*. Thus, in language, distinctive features combine to form contrasting phonemes on another *level* of apprehension: phonemes combine to form contrasting morphemes, morphemes combine to form words, words combine to form sentences, and so on. In each instance, the whole phoneme, or word, or sentence is greater than the sum of its parts.

The fourth assumption of Saussure's *Course*, which stipulates that language is primarily a "social activity," can be seen as both the most radical and least developed element of his system. Reflecting a dramatic turn from simple physicality or mentalism, Saussure "socializes" language at every level. Individual language acts, he notes, are "merely language in embryo" (13) and language itself "exists perfectly only within a collectivity" (14). In many ways, the dualities of the first three assumptions of Saussure's nascent science of language are all reconfigured and resolved socially. In this schema, diachroncity is not so much negated as situated alongside a synchronic system that subsumes the evolutionarily informed artifacts of language under the larger framework of their functionality. Similarly, both the "relational determinism" of linguistic entities and the arbitrary nature of the sign itself are situated within a social context. In the former, the nonpositive object of study emerging from progressively more complex levels of combination and contrast is a socially determined object, intimately implicated in the "form-contents" of institutions, conventions, and other facets of culture. The arbitrariness of the sign, on the other hand, is resolved by social contingency: the signified and signifier are socially coupled, from the acquisition of language in preverbal children to the exchange of the complex utterances between adult members of a linguistic community.

In conjunction with the first three assumptions of the *Course*, the reframing of all levels and aspects of language as functions of social activity led Saussure to call for a new science that could transcend linguistic science and study "the life of signs within society." Saussure named this science "semiology" (from the Greek *semeîon*, "sign") (16). The "science" of semiotics, as it came to be practiced in Eastern Europe in the 1920s and 1930s and Paris in the 1950s and 1960s, widened the study of language and linguistic structures to include the *literary* artifacts constituted (or articulated) by those structures. Throughout the later part of his career, Saussure pursued his own "semiotic" analysis of Latin poetry in an attempt to discover concealed anagrams of proper names. The method of study was in many ways the opposite of the functional rationalism of his linguistic analyses: it attempted to examine the problem of "chance," which "becomes the inevitable foundation of everything" (cited in Starobinski 101). Such a study, as Saussure himself claims, focuses on "the material fact" of chance and meaning (cited in Starobinski 101), so that the "theme-word" whose anagram Saussure seeks, is, as Jean Starobinski argues, "an *instrument*, and not a vital germ of the poem. The poem is obliged to *re-employ* the phonic materials of the theme-word" (45). In this regard, Saussure's work demonstrates a desire to evade all the problems arising from *consciousness*: "Since poetry is not only realized *in* words but is something born *from* words, it escapes the arbitrary control of consciousness to depend solely on a kind of linguistic legality" (121).

Saussure's attempt to discover proper names in Latin poetry emphasizes his view of the arbitrary nature of the sign. As Tzvetan Todorov argues,

> Saussure's work appears remarkably homogeneous today in its refusal to accept symbolic phenomena [phenomena that have *intentional* meaning]. . . . In his research on anagrams, he pays attention only to the phenomena of repetition, not to those of evocation. . . . In his studies of the *Nibelungen*, he recognizes symbols only in order to attribute them to mistaken readings: since they are not intentional, symbols do not exist. Finally in his courses on general linguistics, he contemplates the existence of semiology, and thus of signs other than linguistic ones; but this affirmation is at once limited by the fact that semiology is devoted to a single type of sign: those which are arbitrary. (269–70)

If Todorov's claim is true, it is because Saussure could not quite conceive of "intention" without a subject; that is, he could not completely escape the opposition between form and content that his work so called into question, resorting instead to "linguistic legality."

Saussure's work occupies the space between, on the one hand, nineteenth-century conceptions of history, subjectivity, and causal modes of interpretation and, on the other hand, twentieth-century "structuralist" conceptions of what Lévi-Strauss called "Kantianism without a transcendental subject" (cited in Connerton 23): conceptions that erase the opposition between form and content (or subject and object) and the hierarchy of foreground and background in full-blown structuralism, psychoanalysis, and even quantum mechanics. Saussure's systematic approach circumscribes a signal moment in the study of meaning and culture.

GABRIEL RUPP AND RONALD SCHLEIFER

Ferdinand de Saussure, *Cours de linguistique générale* (ed. Charles Bally and Albert Sechehaye, 1916, *Course in General Linguistics*, trans. Wade Baskin, 1959, trans. Roy Harris, 1983); Paul Connerton,

The Tragedy of Enlightenment: An Essay on the Frankfurt School (1980); Jonathan Culler, Saussure (1976); F. W. Galan, Historical Structures: The Prague School Project, 1928–1946 (1985); Roman Jakobson, "Retrospect," Selected Writings, vol. 2 (1971); Ronald Schleifer, Analogical Thinking: Post-Enlightenment Understanding in Language, Collaboration, and Interpretation (2000); Jean Starobinski, Les mots sous les mots: Les anagrammes de Ferdinand de Saussure (1971, Words upon Words: The Anagrams of Ferdinand de Saussure, trans. Olivia Emmett, 1979); Tzvetan Todorov, Théories du symbole (1977, Theories of the Symbol, trans. Catherine Porter, 1982).

Science Studies

While universities and funding institutions continue to promote interdisciplinarity in research and teaching, at the beginning of the twenty-first century a political valuation of training in the sciences over training in the humanities is increasingly rearing its head in the form of severe cuts in public funding to the humanities announced alongside large endowments for research chairs and institutes in the sciences. This shift in valuation away from the humanities and toward the sciences is not new, but is symptomatic of the ideological and institutional entrenchment of a nineteenth-century division between science and culture in the West. That this divide has never been adequately bridged, despite multifarious attempts to do so, is attested to by the controversial emergence of the field of science studies, an unwieldy field of study whose parameters, research methods, and proper objects of study remain subjects of great debate both within the field and without. The public reception of scholarly work in science studies points to the persistence of the science-culture divide underpinning understandings of both the production of knowledge and the function of the university. Science has been understood as an infallible instrument through which knowledge is produced and solutions to problems are developed, whereas culture continues to be valued as that through which we obtain nourishment for the mind and soul—an escape from the harsh reality of everyday life. This conception of culture, which continues to produce such demand as exists for a liberal arts education even today, reveals the indefatigability of a valuation of "high culture."

To understand why the very existence of science studies—the field of study that examines the practices, paradigms, and cultural mores through which science produces knowledge—has unsettled political categories and boundaries within literary studies, the university, and the public, one has to begin with the oft-shifting function and valuation of science and the humanities in the university in the debates that took place in the United Kingdom in the 1880s.

In the late 1870s, an educational reform was proposed that suggested that the classical humanities curriculum taught in British universities be replaced with ones featuring training in both the humanities and the natural sciences, with an emphasis on the sciences. Matthew Arnold became a vocal defender of the classical humanities education, delivering multiple lectures on the subject of the state of culture in Britain, human nature, and the function of literary criticism in the intellectual formation of British citizens. In response to proclamations made by reformers concerning the waning relevance of a classical humanities education, Arnold argues that classically trained humanists can offer much-needed historical perspective to prevent scientists from falling prey to a variety of errors that could result from short-sightedness and a lack of informed contemplation of the possible social and political repercussions of their actions. In 1880, the British biologist Thomas Henry Huxley delivered a lecture entitled "Science and Culture" at a new science college in Birmingham in which he challenged Arnold's claim that the properly moral education can be obtained solely through training in the classical humanities. Huxley proclaims that "the free employment of reason, in accordance with scientific method, is the sole method of reaching truth" (148) and, further, that this "unhesitating acceptance of reason is the supreme arbiter of conduct" (152). The debate between Arnold and Huxley continued in the form of Rede lectures at Cambridge, speeches at the Royal Academy of the Arts in London, and a written correspondence that continued throughout the 1880s. This debate concerning the merits of academic training in the humanities versus the sciences has taken place—albeit in different forms and in different contexts—countless times since the 1880s and continues to inform the parameters of debate for the field of science studies as well as the basic form of its public reception.

In 1959, the British novelist and physicist C. P. Snow delivered the Rede Lecture at Cambridge University, entitled "The Two Cultures." In this talk, Snow laments an increasing tendency toward disciplinary compartmentalization in British universities. The lack of communication, mutual understanding, "hostility and dislike" between what he calls "literary intellectuals" and scientists had become so severe that the division between humanists and scientists was now "a gulf of mutual incomprehension" (4). Snow stresses that if the British universities were to continue to favor the humanities and fail to recognize the merits of an education in the sciences, Britain would face political challenges given the geopolitics of the cold war. Due to a lack of funding, Britain was lagging behind both Europe and the United States, where funding for scientific research was rapidly expanding, and Snow believed that this disparity needed to be remedied urgently. An expanded version of this talk, *The Two Cultures and the Scientific Revolution* (1959), describes each of the two cultures in detail, arguing that the terrain of "culture" does not belong solely to the humanities. Instead, Snow insists, research in the sciences constitutes a culture unto itself, and the humanists' lack of comprehension of this culture is the result of their own hermeticism and ignorance. While Snow believes that scientists are also guilty of their own form of ignorance, he argues that the literary intellectuals' ignorance is more pernicious because this discipline, as the training ground of the elite, has been endowed with the institutional authority through which to define what constitutes culture. The narrowness of this definition, Snow argues, is no longer tenable.

Suggesting that the sciences hold the potential to break down class barriers that continue to be upheld by the elite tradition of a liberal arts education, Snow argues that an institutional unwillingness to promote the meritocracy of the sciences reflects just how much the elite British stand to lose if the "literary intellectuals" are shaken from their pedestal. Writing that "this polarization is a sheer loss to us all," Snow seeks to redefine what counts as culture. Emphasizing the counterproductivity of an educational system that produces a nation of scholars at odds with one another—indeed unable to agree on the very terms of the debate—Snow advocates a rapprochement between the two cultures. While Snow himself approaches this debate with a balanced perspective as a literary intellectual and a physicist, he does not value the humanities and the sciences equally. The normative claim implicit in his narration of the social and political function of each of the two cultures—that scholarship in the humanities doesn't hold a candle to the potential of the sciences to address social and political problems of urgency—was echoed by many other prominent figures in the "two cultures" debate, which raged on for decades following Snow's lecture.

Though the perceived ideological differences dividing the two cultures continue to animate much popular and academic debate even today, the notion of an academic distinction between the sciences and the humanities is actually relatively recent. As Stefan Collini notes, the term "scientist" was coined in 1834 in reference to those who had previously been described as "students of the knowledge of the material world" (Collini qtd. in Snow, ix). Indeed, universities did not distinguish between the natural and human sciences until the mid-nineteenth century when J. S. Mill's concept of the "moral sciences" assumed an institutional form in universities. In Germany, G. W. F. Hegel's concept of *Geist* informed the name bestowed on the newly invented field of *Geisteswissenschaften*, or the human sciences. The German philosopher Wilhelm Dilthey intended to extend Immanuel Kant's work on the natural sciences to this newly established field of the human sciences, asserting that scholarship in the human sciences is normative in form while scholarship in the natural sciences is empirical, even though both disciplines share the aim of representation and explanation. Though the parameters and function of these two separate disciplines were just beginning to be defined and worked out in the late nineteenth century, the imagined opposition between the sciences and the humanities has been naturalized to such a degree that it is difficult to imagine that the two disciplines had once been indissociable from one another, in both name and methodology.

Science studies scholars offer critical commentary on the cultural production of scientific knowledge in a particular context. Science has often been understood as an autonomous, self-contained, and even mechanical entity that deduces data and knowledge from the natural world uninfluenced by the subjective concerns that plague the production of other forms of knowledge (including those offered by literary and cultural texts). Snow's two cultures thesis clearly informs this perception of science, reinforcing the conception of science as a bias-free form of knowledge. The very concept of bias, which simply refers to the context-specific perspective from which we engage with knowledge or a set of theories, is understood to belong to the sphere of the humanities and culture and to be entirely absent from the sphere of science. As many science studies scholars have argued, both scientific and literary accounts of the world are historically and culturally specific. These scholars do not argue that this insight renders scientific knowledge any less valuable but rather that the conditions of its production and public reception are quite different than they are popularly imagined to be.

In order to understand the character of the convergences and divergences between literary studies and science studies, it is important to be attentive to the intellectual legacies against which each field of study is formed. For science studies, the field's forbearers were divided into two main intellectual camps based at the University of Vienna: the first was the Vienna circle, proponents of logical positivism, and the second was Karl Popper's splinter group of "critical rationalism" and falsifiability. The key tenets of each of these schools of thought continue to be debated by scholars working in the field today. The positivists believe that science produces fact and knowledge through the translation of carefully collected data from a particular site into a universal truth applicable to heterogeneous sites according to the principle of induction. Popper's falsificationism, on the other hand, maintains that scientific fact is not derived from data alone and that because seemingly nonscientific considerations inform the character of scientific fact, it is imperative to develop a method through which true science can be distinguished from all pseudosciences. Popper names a particular quality shared by all true scientific theories: these theories must make predictions that could potentially be proven false in a particular context. Marxism and Freudianism (see MARXIST THEORY AND CRITICISM and PSYCHOANALYTIC THEORY AND CRITICISM), according to Popper, are categorized as pseudosciences because their theories are expansive and flexible enough, he argues, to explain away any new evidence that might disprove the theories. In other words, these theories are not falsifiable. For Popper, then, all scientific theories are merely provisional. Any particular theory is given a chance to govern the method undertaken in a set of experiments until the theory is proven false, at which point a new theory replaces it (until this theory is proven false, and so on). Popper's theory, which suggests that any conception of science that understands this method of inquiry to be following a trajectory toward ever greater knowledge and truth is naïve, anticipates the much more well-known work of Thomas Kuhn, developed three decades later at the University of California, Berkeley.

For better or for worse, Kuhn's polemic against positivism, *The Structure of Scientific Revolutions* (1962), remains the most frequently cited work in the field now known as science studies. Indeed, the concept of the "paradigm" popularized by Kuhn, has transformed the way in which the practice of science is understood for both science studies scholars and the general public. Kuhn was strongly influenced by the work of Michael Polanyi; in fact, Kuhn was accused of plagiarizing Polanyi's ideas. Polanyi, like Kuhn, rejected positivism as well as the notion of science's objectivity and disinterestedness, arguing that objective truth cannot possibly be produced by science as a discipline considering the personal, economic, and political stakes of this type of research. The popularity of Kuhn's ideas, quickly eclipsing that of Polanyi's work, can possibly be explained by the accessible and controversial nature of his writing.

The significance of Kuhn's concept of the paradigm—apart from providing a convenient shorthand name for the distinct ideological clusters from which scientific knowledge is produced—is that it revolutionized the form of disciplinary critique in science studies. Kuhn's claim that scientific theories and methods belonging to a particular paradigm are "incommensurable" with one another to such a degree that scientists attempting a dialogue from within distinct paradigms were "talking past each other" or "speaking different languages" meant that the proper focus of the critique of science was now relegated to particular sites, labs, or paradigms.

For Kuhn, the impetus for scientific change is a shift in the collective will of the scientists working within a particular paradigm. Against Popper, Kuhn argues that a particular theory is deemed false and ceases to direct research in a particular paradigm not once it ceases to predict and explain patterns found in data collected but instead once the group of researchers lose faith in its merits and a new theory is proposed to take its place. Before Kuhn, it was widely believed that scientific research taking place in different contexts diverged only in content—that is, according to the particular objects of study under scrutiny—and that research projects were all animated by an identical set of theoretical tenets. Kuhn's insight that an entire theoretical "worldview," or paradigm, can be deemed inadequate and replaced by a contradictory paradigm rather than a complementary paradigm that would build on the knowledge produced under the previous paradigm points to a general trajectory of discontinuity and theoretical incoherence that complicates the study of science. Thus, knowledge produced by science is understood by followers of Kuhn to exemplify contingency rather than progress toward truth. The insight that science lacks the ability to distinguish the "most true" theory from a group of competing theories that inform scientific research at any particular moment and that instead one particular theory gains prominence for "subjective," "nonscientific" reasons is taken up by many science studies scholars in the subsequent decades.

Perhaps the most significant convergence between literary theory and science studies occurs around concepts of universal truth, essentialism, and progress (see POSTMODERNISM, DECONSTRUCTION: 1. DERRIDA, DE MAN, AND THE YALE CRITICS, and DECONSTRUCTION: 2. THE 1980S AND AFTER); questions concerning these concepts were raised in both fields and fiercely debated during the three decades between the 1960s and the 1990s. Literary theorists disillusioned with teleological conceptions of science, truth, and progress were inspired by the most radical implications of Kuhn's arguments: first, that scientific fact only registers as true in one particular paradigm, that is, for those who share the same set of economic and political values or interests, thus dismissing the concept of a universal truth; and second, that there is no overarching form of progress or forward trajectory that organizes the direction of scientific discovery. That is, according to Kuhn, our situatedness in our particular paradigm structures our thoughts and blinds us to the "big picture" to such an extent that it is impossible to determine whether any particular paradigm offers the theoretical capacity to direct a program of research to produce knowledge that contributes in a cumulative, rather than destructive, manner in relation to knowledge amassed thus far.

Unfortunately, the aspect of science studies that remains most familiar to those who do not work within the field is a widely misunderstood and oft-parodied notion of relativism. An important concept in science studies is that of contingency: this concept offers significant explanatory power in the context of the production of scientific objects and knowledge because it emphasizes a lack of evidence of necessity within the study of scientific research practices. The role occupied by scientific knowledge in Western society, coupled with an unwavering faith in the objectivity of the scientific method, has meant that dominant scientific theories, especially when endorsed by institutions such as respected scholarly journals or professional associations, are received as nothing less than the sole and inevitable truth of the natural world. Science studies scholars aim to show that the production of scientific knowledge is contingent in the sense that what eventually emerges as knowledge is not a straightforward, objective reflection of data obtained during testing but rather a reflection of the data selected for analysis for a number of social and political reasons. Contingency describes the way in which social and political factors thought to be external to scientific research are in fact central to and determinant of the knowledge that eventually gets produced, from the question of which research projects receive grant money up. The concept of contingency in no way suggests that the phenomena described by the scientific knowledge produced are thus phantasmal or do not have consequences, merely that they do not constitute something akin to capital "T" truth.

While Kuhn's ideas certainly anticipated it, the concept of social construction did not come to dominate debate in science studies until a decade following the publication of The Structure of Scientific Revolutions. This concept performed an important function in the early work of Bruno Latour and it retains explanatory power today, but it also engendered several unproductive debates and dichotomies, temporarily robbing science studies of much of its credibility as a field. The concept of social construction in Latour's early writing offers a way of understanding how some scientific theories and facts gain acceptance as the correct and true theories and facts (he offers the example of the way in which Louis Pasteur's theory gained prominence for political reasons rather than because it had any proven scientific merit), while others are discarded, rarely to be debated in the public realm. Although many scholars today view a particular form of constructivism as taking a realist stance, constructivism and realism were considered to be at odds with one another for decades. The conspiratorial quality that has come to be associated with the concept of social construction is the result of misinterpretation rather than the authors' intention. As Gordon McOuat writes, the debate has wrongly been understood as one of naturalness versus constructedness (nature here is understood as a space void of human impact or manipulation) or reality versus unreality. As McOuat notes, the word "constructed" does not refer to an entity that is imagined or unreal but rather one that is analyzed by critics to gain understanding of its origins and function in a particular context. Citing Gaston Bachelard's argument that *facts are made* ("une fait est fait"), McOuat writes that the concept of construction does not refer to a notion of unreality; rather the claim is that facts do not originate in an ideological or cultural vacuum, nor do they signify into an ideological or cultural vacuum (306). Instead, scientific facts are constructed in the sense that they are "fabricated, made to work, made to perform" (306). Thus, objects and knowledge can be *both* real *and* socially constructed (rather than *either* real *or* socially constructed): "The more closely we examine a thing as constructed, the more we see it as real" (306).

Many science studies scholars have directed critical attention to the forms of exclusion on the basis of gender, race, and class that have been endemic to the production of scientific knowledge. Sandra Harding's work attends to the consequences of the fact that scientific knowledge produced through these gendered, raced, and classed mechanisms supports existing social hierarchies and modalities of oppression, reflecting the way scientific knowledge is informed by the interests of those in power. Feminist epistemologists ask important questions concerning how identity, perspective, and a particular set of material conditions determine not only the mechanisms through which knowledge is produced but also the content of this knowledge itself. Evelyn Fox Keller discusses the consequences of science's valuation of what is understood as a specifically masculine capacity for objective inquiry at the expense of feminine subjectivity; her groundbreaking book *A Feeling for the Organism* (1983) argues that a persistent valuation of a masculine epistemology over all other forms of epistemology impedes the production of scientific knowledge, as was the case when structural sexism prevented Barbara McClintock from contributing her important research on genetic transposition to the field of biology. Keller argues that the opposition between masculine and feminine epistemology understood as a distinction between "rational, distant objectivity" and subjective affect or attachment impoverishes science as a result of an unwarranted focus on objectivity. Many crucial insights and discoveries can only arise out of a subjective attachment to the object of study, and a science that disallows this form of study will fail to progress in the manner that a more epistemologically heterogeneous science could progress, she argues. The study of science as an androcentric practice continues to animate a number of feminist interventions in the field today, including that of DONNA HARAWAY.

One of the many important insights Haraway offers to science studies is that language—and metaphor in particular—plays a crucial role in circulating intrinsically unstable constructions in a seemingly stable form. Her essay "A Cyborg Manifesto: Science, Technology, and Socialist-Feminism in the Late Twentieth Century," first published in 1985, puts forth the figure of the cyborg as that which unsettles a number of dichotomies, oppositions, and boundaries that needlessly perpetuate both academic factionalism and modalities of oppression beyond the university. Re-solving debates between realism and constructivism (or nature versus culture) initi-ated by Lysenkoism and a quest for a "nonideological" form of epistemology, Har-away insists that scientific practice resides somewhere in between the maligned "ideological" science and the irreproachable "objective" science, insofar as these poles are imagined as in opposition to one another. She argues that the persistence of an idealized concept of nature and a fallacious opposition between nature and technology has thwarted the best political attempts made by scholars in literary and science studies, and she proposes the stance of techno-realism in place of this pho-bic and moralistic naturalism. Exceeding the category of the human, the cyborg stands in for the possibility of a new form of epistemology and productive politics that would transform scholarship beyond tired rehearsals of the same debates bounded by false oppositions. The figure of the cyborg is theorized as an entity that unsettles the code through which we understand science and technology and one that reveals the discourses and metaphors that structure this understanding as re-flecting particular interests rather than a natural or eternal truth. For Haraway, the critical analysis of discursive constructions in science is crucial to narrowing the per-ceived gap between the humanities and the sciences, and it is only at the intersection of disciplines and disparate systems of thought, she argues, that we can adequately address the multitude of urgent problems that require analysis on the part of not just one of the two disciplines but both the humanities and the sciences together.

Many of the public confrontations between the humanities and the sciences have unfortunately worked to reentrench conceptions of literary critics as hopelessly impractical, divorced from reality, and irrelevant while creating the impression that scientists have the public good in mind as they redirect the focus of debates to issues of wider relevance. One particular example of such a confrontation, now known as the "Sokal affair," instigated a decade of debate surrounding the perceived "anti-intellectualism" of the scholarship being carried out in the humanities during the heyday of postmodernism; this debate was dubbed the "Science Wars." In 1996, phys-icist Alan Sokal submitted a satirical article entitled "Transgressing the Boundaries: Toward a Transformative Hermeneutics of Quantum Gravity" to a special issue on the Science Wars to be published by the journal *Social Text*. In his article, Sokal de-vised an argument he felt was certain to appeal to the editors of the special issue: identifying himself as a physicist alienated from his colleagues, Sokal argued that both quantum gravity and "physical reality" in general are merely social constructs. The article contained numerous outrageous statements that Sokal believed would sound alarm bells for any editor—whether in the sciences or the humanities—and he later defended himself against accusations of academic dishonesty by arguing that his prank merits a fraction of the concern that should be directed toward the type of scholarship that would accept and publish such a nonsensical piece of writing.

The publication of Sokal's article brought to the fore many of the same questions and debates that followed C. P. Snow's "Two Cultures" lecture given forty years earlier. Sokal echoes Snow's incommensurability thesis; however, he goes even further: Sokal believes that literary criticism tends toward irrelevancy in a way that is not only naïve but actually dangerous (particularly in its capacity to undermine the institutional authority of science). Sokal argues that science should be seen as an emancipatory tool rather than an inherently oppressive one. As a discipline of pragmatism and empiricism, science possesses the capacity to diagnose and develop solutions to social and political problems, he argues, while the humanities' tendency to contemplative thought and criticism is not only useless but can hinder the progress of the sciences. Max Horkheimer and THEODOR W. ADORNO and other members of the FRANKFURT SCHOOL, on the other hand, have argued that pragmatism and empiricism in the absence of critical philosophy has created a set of conditions that has turned out to be politically catastrophic.

The political climate of the early twenty-first century is one of a populist surge of anti-intellectualism in which academic work that lacks "real world application" is deemed self-indulgent. This is a climate in which scientific research receives more generous funding than that allocated to literary studies. Scientific research and technological development are endowed with a new sense of importance and urgency as this mode of inquiry is marshaled to do political work—for instance, science is hailed as the inevitable savior from multiple threats, including global warming, nuclear war, epidemic disease, poverty, and more. While the field of science studies has been widely misunderstood as one that aims to denounce the authority of scientific discourse, the field is more properly understood as a project that seeks, in good faith, to bring together the disciplinary strengths of the humanities and the sciences in the name of a common goal. The original impetus for critical social theory, described by Horkheimer as the elaboration of a properly scientific method for the study of culture, through which scholars trained in different fields could avoid the pitfalls that plague each of the disciplines when carried out in isolation as well as the tendency toward divisive critique or factionalism, is a conception of scholarship that is as urgently required today as it was when it was initially proposed in 1931. Horkheimer writes that

> the question today is to organize investigations stimulated by contemporary philosophical problems in which philosophers, sociologists, economists, historians, and psychologists are brought together in permanent collaboration to undertake in common that which can be carried out individually in the laboratory in other fields. In short, the task is to do what all true researchers have always done: namely, to pursue their larger philosophical questions on the basis of the most precise scientific methods, to revise and refine their questions in the course of their substantive work, and to develop new methods without losing sight of the larger context. (9)

As a field of inquiry into the mechanisms through which science produces knowledge, the interests served by these practices, and the modes through which this knowledge gets circulated, science studies is uniquely positioned to bridge this gap between the humanities (perceived as irrelevant) and science (perceived as indispensable) by showing that the literary analysis of science remains just as urgent as, and indissociable from, the technical breakthroughs being made in labs.

SARAH BLACKER

Matthew Arnold, "Literature and Science," *The Nineteenth Century* (August 1882); Gaston Bachelard, *The New Scientific Spirit* (1984); Georges Canguilhem, *Le normal et le pathologique* (1943, *On the Normal and the Pathological* trans. Carolyn R. Fawcett, 1978); Harry Collins and Trevor Pinch, *The Golem: What Everyone Should Know About Science* (1993); Ludwik Fleck, *Entstehung und Entwicklung einer wissenschaftlichen Tatsache* (1935, *Genesis and Development of a Scientific Fact*, ed. Thaddeus J. Trenn and Robert K. Merton, trans. Fred Bradley and Thaddeus J. Trenn, 1979); Ian Hacking, *The Social Construction of What?* (2000); Donna Haraway, "Manifesto for Cyborgs: Science, Technology, and Socialist Feminism in the 1980s," *Socialist Review* 80 (1985); Sandra Harding, *The "Racial" Economy of Science* (1993), *Whose Science? Whose Knowledge?* (1991); David Hess, *Science and Technology in a Multicultural World: The Cultural Politics of Facts and Artifacts* (1995); Max Horkheimer, "Die gegenwärtige Lage der Sozialphilosophie und die Aufgaben eines Institut für Sozialforschung," *Frankfurter Universitätsreden* (1931) ("The Present Situation of Social Philosophy and the Tasks of an Institute for Social Research," *Between Philosophy and Social Science. Selected Early Writings*, trans. G. Frederick Hunter, Matthew S. Kramer, and John Torpey, 1993); Thomas Henry Huxley, "Science and Culture," *Collected Essays of Thomas H. Huxley* (1899); Evelyn Fox Keller, *A Feeling for the Organism: The Life and Work of Barbara McClintock* (1983), *Reflections on Gender and Science* (1985); Thomas S. Kuhn, *The Structure of Scientific Revolutions* (1962); Bruno Latour, *Laboratory Life: The Construction of Scientific Facts* (1986), *We Have Never Been Modern* (1993); Gordon McOuat, "The Latest Latour: Realism and Hope in Science Studies," *Canadian Journal of History* 36 (2001); Barbara Herrnstein Smith, *Scandalous Knowledge: Science, Truth and the Human* (2006); C. P. Snow, *The Two Cultures and the Scientific Revolution* (1959); Alan Sokal, "A Physicist Experiments with Cultural Studies," *Lingua Franca* 6 (1996), "Transgressing the Boundaries: Toward a Transformative Hermeneutics of Quantum Gravity," *Social Text* 46/47 (1996).

Sedgwick, Eve Kosofsky

Eve Kosofsky Sedgwick (1950–2009) was among QUEER THEORY's most formative and distinguished thinkers. Her postidentitarian conception of "queer" is original in its insights and its methodologies, and her history of "homosocial desire" is comparable in contemporary intellectual significance and impact only to the accounts and analyses in the first volume of MICHEL FOUCAULT's *History of Sexuality* (1976–1984). Sedgwick's books have played a decisive role in the creation, development, and persistence of queer presence in contemporary critical thought. Any account of them will tell a story of what she calls "the queer moment," the temporal dimensions of which are disclosed in her work as they are shaped by it, and also of the queer movement, whose activist impulses her work exemplifies.

Between Men: English Literature and Male Homosocial Desire (1985), which attends to the sexual politics of British culture between, roughly, 1750 and 1850 (the "Age of Frankenstein"), offered unprecedented resources for studying the history and theory of sexuality and helped consolidate the institutionalization of lesbian and gay studies in the United States. *Epistemology of the Closet* (1990) explores the more recent history of sexuality from the late 1800s to the present (the "Age of Wilde"), while palpably present in *Tendencies* (1993) is another history comprising the emergency of AIDS and the particular forms of activism it summoned into being, which Sedgwick herself considers key to the emergence of queer theory.

Sedgwick's refusal to disengage activism from thought is clear from her writings on AIDS and cancer. Given the unyielding uniqueness of her critical modes, however, the notion of an "application" of theory must be questioned. Her exegeses are irreducible to any established hermeneutic. If her theoretical sources can be readily identified—DECONSTRUCTION, the work of Foucault, STRUCTURALISM, feminism, psychology, and Buddhism—her relationship to each is characteristically interventionist and original. This reflective indocility is no less evident in Sedgwick's relationship to genre. Her writing has been compared (sometimes negatively) with that of Henry James and Marcel Proust but remains inimitable, each text differing from the others not only in ambition and argument but also in a continuously renewed experimentation with thought and genre. "A Poem Is Being Written" (an essay in *Tendencies*), for instance, combines autobiography, theory, and Sedgwick's own poetry in such a manner that a concept of "queer" is at once described and enacted. The force and originality of Sedgwick's concepts prove inconceivable without the formal and stylistic innovations that underwrite them.

Born in Dayton, Ohio, Sedgwick earned a BA in English in 1971 from Cornell and a PhD in 1975 from Yale. From 1988 to 1998 she taught at Duke University, and after that she was Distinguished Professor of English at the City University of New York Graduate School.

Sedgwick's doctoral dissertation, revised as The Coherence of Gothic Conventions (1980), augurs much of the work that follows in its demonstration of the crucial operation of the gothic's conventions and gestures in modern Western culture. Between Men argues further that during the Age of Frankenstein a fundamental change in power and cognition transpired, crystallizing at once in the modern, capitalism-marked Oedipal family and in the gothic constellation of homophobia (fear and hatred of homosexuality), paranoia (which Sedgwick condenses into the formulation "homosexual-homophobic knowing"), and epistemology (how we know what we know). Epistemology investigates the consequences of the uneasy and incomplete transition from the "male paranoid Gothic," in which homophobia functions in the absence of a (yet-to-be-consolidated) homosexual culture, to the homophobic project of "homo/heterosexual definition" that marks the Age of Wilde, whereby "every given person, just as he or she was necessarily assignable to a male or female gender," was by the first decade of the twentieth-century "considered necessarily assignable as well to a homo- or hetero-sexuality" (1–2).

Sedgwick's history depends centrally on male "homosocial desire," her term describing the affectively charged cognitive, psychical, physical, and political bonds that obtain between men in even the least ostensibly cathexis-marked of intersubjective relations. Between Men offers readings of British texts demonstrating that the erotic rivalry immanent to the literary plot of triangulated desire comprises a mediation that renders a socially unacceptable form of male-male desire into one of heterosexual heroism.

Sedgwick calls the period of the paranoid gothic the Age of Frankenstein because Mary Shelley's novel hinges on a tableau whose iconography of two men chasing each other across a landscape vividly displays the homoerotophobic/homoerotic project that Sedgwick discerns as the bedrock of Romantic and much later nineteenth-century thought. The undecidability displayed by the Frankenstein tableau hinges doubly on whether the two men represent two consciousnesses or only one and on whether their bond is murderous or amorous. The spectrum of relations between men during this period is organized around this culturally ubiquitous homophobic/paranoid image, accepted as immemorial human nature, of male solipsism and male threat.

Sedgwick defines the Age of Wilde by reference to a homosocial spectrum now marked by a "gaping and unbridgeable homophobic rift" (Between Men 201), a rift opened during the mid- to late nineteenth century by a proliferation of public discourses on homosexuality culminating in, but also extending far beyond, the trials of Oscar Wilde. Wilde's novel The Picture of Dorian Gray (1890) enacts the epochal shift from the gothic to the modern(ist) in its use of such conventional gothic gestures as the double alongside the introduction of a distinctly new gay minoritarian rhetoric of the "glass closet" or "open secret" (a codification legible to "those in the know"), as well as a distinctly new public rhetoric of the "empty secret" closely associated with (male high) modernism. The latter "serves a purpose of universalizing, naturalizing, and thus substantively voiding—depriving of content—elements of a specifically and historically male homosexual rhetoric" (Epistemology 165).

Epistemology of the Closet demonstrates the need for an awareness, in any critical enterprise, of the epistemological operations of homophobia and forcefully dissolves the perimeters that could otherwise be thought to circumscribe the field of lesbian and gay studies. The seven axioms that it formulates have changed the way we think about sexuality and proved indispensable to contemporary critical theory. One, "People are different from each other" (22), states a fact whose apparent simplicity is belied by the absence of intellectual tools for speculation on it, an absence Sedgwick's own work significantly redresses. Another is a methodological point initiated in Between Men and emboldened by Epistemology: "The study of sexuality is not coextensive with the study of gender; correspondingly, antihomophobic inquiry is not coextensive with feminist inquiry. But we can't know in advance how they will be different" (27). If Between Men seems primarily concerned with the specifically male homosocial continuum, its central argument—historical changes in that continuum are bound, often causally, to changes in economic, ideological, and gender arrangements— provides important leverage to feminist inquiry and activism.

In Epistemology, Sedgwick elaborates two contradictory models for understanding homosexuality (20): "minoritizing" perceives the homo/heterosexual definition as "an issue of active importance primarily for a small, relatively fixed homosexual minority"; "universalizing" perceives that definitional process as "an issue of continuing, determinative importance in the lives of people across the spectrum of sexuality" (1). Tendencies examines two other contradictory gender models: the inversion trope, "in which a gay man represents 'a woman's soul trapped in a man's body,' " and the trope of gender separatism, the idea "that people of the same gender, people grouped together under the single most determinate diacritical mark of social organization, people whose economic, institutional, emotional, physical needs and knowledges may have so much in common, should bond together also on the axis of sexual desire" (viii). Sedgwick resists adjudicating between these conceptual antagonisms, choosing instead "to find new ways to think about lesbian, gay, and other sexually dissident loves and identities in a complex social ecology where the presence of different genders, different identities and identifications, will be taken as a given" (ix).

Throughout her writings, Sedgwick investigates paranoia as an epistemological mode that determines, no less than it is an effect of, social relations. In "Shame in the Cybernetic Fold: Reading Silvan Tomkins" (in Shame and Its Sisters [1995]) and "Paranoid Reading and Reparative Reading: or, You're So Paranoid, You Probably Think This Introduction Is about You" (in Novel Gazing [1997]), she explores the cognitive paranoia that she discerns as the diacritical mark of much recent literary and cultural criticism and develops a pointedly alternative "reparative" practice of reading. Even in her late work with and on Buddhism, her appreciation of the activity of "realization" versus knowledge acquisition can be seen as analogous to "reparative" reading.

Sedgwick proposes four important definitions of "queer" in *Tendencies*. One is "the open mesh of possibilities, gaps, overlaps, dissonances and resonances, lapses and excesses of meaning when the constituent elements of anyone's gender, of anyone's sexuality aren't made (or *can't* be made) to signify monolithically" (7). Second, queer denotes "same-sex sexual object choice, lesbian or gay, whether or not it is organized around multiple criss-crossings of definitional lines" (8). Third, especially significant for Sedgwick, is "the ways that race, ethnicity, postcolonial nationality criss-cross with [gender and sexuality] *and* other identity-constituting, identity-fracturing discourses" (see *Gary in Your Pocket* [1996] and "Socratic Raptures, Socratic Ruptures: Notes toward Queer Performativity" [1993]). The notion of performativity, language that does what it says, precisely informs her fourth definition, obliquely and importantly at odds with the second: " 'Gay' and 'lesbian' still present themselves (however delusively) as objective, empirical categories governed by empirical rules of evidence (however contested)." But, she concludes, " 'Queer' seems to hinge much more radically and explicitly on a person's undertaking particular, performative acts of experimental self-perception and filiation. A hypothesis worth making explicit: that there are important senses in which 'queer' can signify only *when attached to the first person*. One possible corollary: that what it takes—all it takes—to make the description 'queer' a true one is the impulsion to use it in the first person" (8).

STEPHEN M. BARBER

See also QUEER THEORY AND CRITICISM and GENDER.

Gary Fisher, *Gary in Your Pocket: Stories and Notebooks of Gary Fisher* (ed. Eve Kosofsky Sedgwick, 1996); Andrew Parker and Eve Kosofsky Sedgwick, eds., *Performativity and Performance* (1995); Eve Kosofsky Sedgwick, *Between Men: English Literature and Male Homosocial Desire* (1985), *The Coherence of Gothic Conventions* (1980), *A Dialogue on Love* (1999); *Epistemology of the Closet* (1990), *Fat Art, Thin Art* (1994), "Socratic Raptures, Socratic Ruptures: Notes toward Queer Peformativity," *English Inside and Out: The Places of Literary Criticism* (ed. Susan Gubar and Jonathan Kamholtz, 1993), *Tendencies* (1993), *Touching Feeling: Affect, Pedagogy, Performativity* (2003); Eve Kosofsky Sedgwick, ed., *Novel Gazing: Queer Readings in Fiction* (1993); Eve Kosofsky Sedgwick and Adam Frank, eds., *Shame and Its Sisters: A Silvan Tomkins Reader* (1995).

Semiotics

Semiotics can be defined broadly as a domain of investigation that explores the nature and function of signs as well as the systems and processes underlying signification, expression, representation, and communication. Numerous cultural traces (verbal, pictorial, plastic, spatial artifacts, etc.) indicate that the constitution of signs, the laws that govern them, and their role in human life have been ongoing concerns over the ages. The history of investigation into the nature of signs is an important aspect of the history of philosophy in general, and contributions to the theory can be noted from the Greeks onward. The twentieth century witnessed a revival of interest in the principles of sign systems and processes inherited from this long tradition of intellectual activity, mainly because of the pioneering work of FERDINAND DE SAUSSURE and Charles Sanders Peirce, who are recognized as the founders of the modern European and Anglo-American traditions of semiotics.

Literary semiotics can be seen as a branch of the general science of signs that studies a particular group of texts within verbal texts in general. Although it describes what is characteristic of literary texts or discourse, it is founded on the same principles and analytic procedures as the semiotics of verbal discourse. There exists no generally accepted definition of the scope and object of literary semiotics. For one thing, the boundaries of literary discourse seem to have been established more by tradition than by objective, formal criteria. Contrary to other semiotic discourses (for instance, legal discourse), literary discourse cannot be characterized by a specifically distinctive content as the literariness of a text varies according to culture and epoch (a text identified as religious in the Middle Ages is seen as literary today). Also, a wide-ranging debate continues regarding the status of the verbal sign and the nature of the signifying process based on whether semioticians adopt an intentional, or meaning-oriented, description of a sign system or the codes correlating a given expression with a given content or else a more extensional, truth-condition-oriented one that concentrates on the processes of communication by which signs are used to designate, to refer to "things or states of the real or of some possible world" (Sebeok, *Encyclopedic* 937).

Charles Morris, who drew his inspiration from Peirce, provides a conceptual framework for situating various approaches to the semiotics of literature in relationship to one another. Defining "semiosis" as a process in which signs function as vehicles, interpretants, and interpreters, Morris determines three areas of complementary investigation: syntactics, which studies the relation of sign-vehicles within sign systems; semantics, the relation of signs to objects they represent; and pragmatics, the relation of signs to interpreters. Hence, if one considers literary texts in terms of semiosis, they can be defined as syncretic sign systems encompassing a syntactic dimension that can be analyzed on the phonological level (e.g., the specific sound patterns organizing the text) and on the level of narrative syntax, on the semantic level (the text's content elements), and in terms of the pragmatic or communicative context (addresser and addressee). The first two dimensions stress the structural features of texts and are concerned with their expression and content forms, whereas the third stresses the signifying process and concentrates on analyzing texts' generative processes and interrelations with other texts (Sebeok, *Encyclopedic* 453–54). Far from being exclusive, the different methodological approaches to each of these domains of investigation are complementary.

Peirce adopted a philosophical and logical perspective to the study of signs and proposed a general theory of semiotics in which linguistic signs had an important but by no means essential role, but Saussure worked out the foundations of a general linguistic theory in which he considered language as a system of signs. Linguistics was considered to be part of the general science of semiology, which he defined as "*a science that studies the life of signs within society*. . . . Semiology would show what constitutes signs, what laws govern them" (16). Saussure's writings were instrumental in the development of literary semiotics in Europe, especially with respect to the study of the syntactic and semantic dimensions of texts. Yuri Tynianov and Roman Jakobson openly acknowledge the impact Saussurean linguistics had on the theoretical work undertaken by the Russian formalists during the first three decades of the twentieth century, the heuristic value of the synchronic/diachronic opposition, of the notion of system, of the distinction between speech and language: "To apply these two categories (the existing norm and individual utterances) to literature and to study their relation," they write, "is a problem that must be examined in detail" (101–2).

In a major review of the formalists' goals and accomplishments, Boris Eikhenbaum stressed the importance of theory in uncovering the systematic nature of literary facts and, following Roman Jakobson in "On Realism in Art" (1921), of focusing not on literature but on "literariness," on the pertinent features of literary texts that distinguish them from other discourse. The formalists used contemporary linguistic theory to compare spoken language with literary language and to consolidate the principle of specification. Victor Shklovsky (*Theory of Prose* [1929]) made great progress in analyzing the short story and the novel when he linked processes inherent to composition with general stylistic processes and related the variable and permanent aspects of the artistic form of a work with those of other works, thereby setting out the possibilities for a history of forms, one that still remains to be written. Other fundamental concepts, such as motivation, basically concerned with plot construction, led to the distinction between elements in the construction of a work (subject) and those that make up its material (fable) and laid the groundwork for Vladimir Propp's discovery of function in the plot analysis of folktales, one of the most important innovations of the formalists. Later Soviet semioticians, such as MIKHAIL BAKHTIN were influential in extending the boundaries of literary semiotics and reorienting the domain from a more scientistic bent to a semiotics of culture.

Whether imported directly from America and Geneva or indirectly via Russia or Vienna, both Peirce's "semiotic" and Saussure's "semiology" were influential in the studies of the verbal arts undertaken by the members of the Prague circle. In his programmatic article "Art as Semiotic Fact" (1934) Jan Mukařovský establishes the semiotic framework for the study of art and suggests that the work of art should be considered as a sign composed of "(1) a perceivable signifier, created by the artist, (2) a 'signification' / = aesthetic object / registered in the collective consciousness and (3) a relationship with that which is signified, a relationship which refers to the total context of social phenomena" (Matejka and Titunik 6). Other critics made important advances in the study of visual semiotics as applied to folk art, songs, and theater. Jakobson in "What Is Poetry?" (1933) and Mukařovský in "Poetic Reference" (1936) (both in *Semiotics of Art*) further the study of poetic language by investigating the problem of poetic reference from the point of view of internal reference and its oblique but essential relationship to the extralinguistic context.

French semiotics, which developed directly from Russian formalism and Prague structuralism and arrived in Paris via New York thanks to Roman Jakobson's influence on Claude Lévi-Strauss during World War II, made a critical contribution to the study of literary texts during the mid-1960s. A special issue of *Communications* edited by ROLAND BARTHES in 1966 and devoted to the structural analysis of narrative contains articles by the leading European semioticians who had a profound impact on the future and evolution of literary semiotics. In his introduction, which owes a great deal to Louis Hjelmslev's rethinking and development of Saussure's concepts of sign, system, and process, to Lévi-Strauss for the study of the paradigmatic notion of structure, and to Émile Benveniste for the concept of level of analysis, Barthes ascertains that narrative analysis must be based on deductive procedures and must construct hypothetical models patterned on structural linguistics. He proposes a multilevel model of analysis in which each level stands in a hierarchical relationship to the others and narrative elements have both distributional (if relations are situated at the same level) and integrative relationships (if situated at different levels). In turn, levels are defined as operations or systems of symbols and rules. Barthes then delimits three linked levels of description—"functions," "actions," and "narration"—in which a function has meaning only within the field of action of an actant, and action is meaningful only when narrated.

The other authors in this volume propose alternate and complementary solutions to some of the problems raised by Barthes. Claude Bremond's contribution, on the logic of narrative possibilities, is situated at the most abstract level and examines the logical constraints (sequences of functions) on the organized events of any narrative. Algirdas Julien Greimas's text focuses on the more anthropomorphic level of representation, actions, where primary logical functions take on meaning. Umberto Eco's article, analyzing Ian Fleming's James Bond novels, deals with narrative combinatories, whereas Tzvetan Todorov, in his study of the categories of literary texts, proposes a more global and more integrated theory of narrative that not only takes into account functions and actions but also concentrates heavily on the level of narration. The volume closes with an important article by Gérard Genette on the boundaries of narrative that establishes distinctions between diegesis and mimesis, narration and description, and narrative and discourse and lays the groundwork for his influential work on the structure of time (i.e., the relation between the form of expression and the form of content of time) in Marcel Proust's *In Search of Lost Time*.

Two major tendencies in France evolve from the intellectual activity of the mid-1960s. The first, founded on the Saussurean-Hjelmslevian legacy, best represented by Greimas's work, has become known as the "Paris school" of semiotics. It concentrates on syntactic and semantic domains of the discipline and adopts an immanentist attitude to texts. (See Greimas, *On Meaning*, as well as Schleifer and Broden, for an overview of Greimas's semiotic theory.) In later books, Greimas explores the possibility of constructing a discursive syntax based on aspectualities (states of a temporal process—inchoateness, duration, termination—that allow for the representation of temporality as process) and attempts to give a semiotic interpretation of traditional theories of passions. The study of the passional dimension of numerous literary texts is accompanied by a disengagement with Peirce's semiotic and an engagement with PHENOMENOLOGY and catastrophe theory.

The second tendency is represented by the large number of works that draw their inspiration from a radical questioning of the structural principles defining semiosis. JULIA KRISTEVA and especially Barthes were instrumental in this respect. Barthes begins his study S/Z (1970) by challenging the very possibility of structural analysis to account for any text's specificity or individuality. He then shifts the problematic from science and ideology to writing and rewriting—in short to a semiotics of addressers and addressees, of signs and interpreters. He also substitutes a semiotics of codes for a semiotics of signs and processes and, without structuring or hierarchizing them, determines five codes under which all the textual signifiers can be grouped: hermeneutic (enigma), semic, symbolic, proairetic (actions), and cultural (references to a science or body of knowledge).

In his innovative work, Eco attempts to overcome some of the dramatic oppositions that exist between the Saussurean (Hjelmslevian-Greimassian) and Peircean theories of semiosis, which originate from very different epistemological contexts and traditions. In *The Role of the Reader* (1979) he integrates the three domains of semiotics identified by Morris and works out an elaborate theory of the reader as an active principle of interpretation in the generative process of text. Introducing operative notions such as model reader and closed and open texts, he integrates concepts dealing with discursive and narrative structures, topics, isotopies, textual levels, and intertextual competence into a general semiotic theory of narrative.

Robert Scholes, whose work deals with particular texts and ways in which they may be read and interpreted, does not concentrate on the syntactic or semantic dimension of narrative per se but adopts a semiotic approach based on the study of codes. Other critics, including Terence Hawkes, Jonathan Culler, TERRY EAGLETON, and FREDRIC JAMESON, have offered both a critique and discussion of the limits of the semiotic project. In an attempt to go beyond the paradigm of structural semiotics, Jackson Barry in the innovative *Art, Culture, and the Semiotics of Meaning* (1999) examines how the perception of the artistic form, including verbal texts, can contribute to the emergence of meaning—how the form of art, its signifier, literally helps "make" meaning.

Semiotic theory has been refined and modified progressively through the investigation of various literary genres and specific domains. Semiotic medieval studies, for instance, have been "as much oriented toward studying the discursive consciousness of medieval intellectual life" as "toward the documentation of events" (Vance 725). Michael Riffaterre has advanced poetic theory more generally by integrating a theory of intertextuality with semiotic theory and by providing a flexible definition of the notion of intertext. Numerous monographs and articles have been published on the semiotics of the theater and the novel, much of the work on the novel concentrating on synchronic semiotic structures. Other semiotic work makes important contributions to the semiotic analysis of film texts, often employing psychoanalytic models, and other studies extend the theoretical boundaries of literary semiotics into a domain of sociosemiotics and contribute to the redefinition of an important area of CULTURAL STUDIES focusing on feminist theory and practice. A number of studies attempt to focus and refocus semiotics on the literary work in general and its apprehension through the reading process by working out a semiotic theory of reading and examining the mediating function of the literary sign between symbolic forms and the materiality of the world.

A major school of semiotics represented by Greimas and his collaborators seems to be disengaging its work from Peirce and embracing phenomenology and catastrophe theory, but other semioticians are reexamining Peircean theory and demonstrating its heuristic value in the study of literary texts, taking up such varied topics as time and poetic metaphor. Most of the semioticians currently working in the Peircean paradigm to some degree or other support the need, through the dynamics of semiosis, to open up the study of text onto the social environment. Jean Fisette notes that these works raise important epistemological questions about the concept of texts, their mode of existence in a given culture, and their contribution to the issue of symbolic productions in general and could herald a "renewal of studies in literary semiotics which, this time, would be free of all the canons inherited from structuralism" (184).

PAUL PERRON

See also ROLAND BARTHES, NARRATOLOGY, FERDINAND DE SAUSSURE, and STRUCTURALISM.

See also bibliography for ROLAND BARTHES.

Jackson Barry, *Art, Culture, and the Semiotics of Meaning* (1999); Roland Barthes, ed., "Recherches sémiologiques: L'analyse structurale du récit," special issue, *Communications* 8 (1966); Paul Bouissac, ed., *Encyclopedia of Semiotics* (1998); Thomas Broden, "A. J. Greimas (1917–1992): Commemorative Essay," *Semiotica* 105 (1995); John Deely, *Introducing Semiotic: Its History and Doctrine* (1982); Umberto Eco, *The Role of the Reader: Explorations in the Semiotics of Texts* (1979); Jean Fisette, "Compte rendu," *RS/SI (Canadian Journal of Semiotics)* 11 (1991); Gérard Genette, *Figures*, vol. 3 (1972, partial trans., *Narrative Discourse: An Essay in Method*, trans. Jane E. Lewin, 1980); Algirdas Julien Greimas, *De l'imperfection* (1987), *On Meaning: Selected Writings in Semiotic Theory* (trans. Paul J. Perron and Frank H. Collins, 1987); Algirdas Julien Greimas and Jacques Fontanille, *Sémiotique des passions* (1991, *The Semiotics of Passions*, trans. Paul J. Perron and Frank H. Collins, 1992); Roman Jakobson, "O realismu v umĕni," *Červen* 4 (1921) ("On Realism in Art," *Readings in Russian Poetics: Formalist and Structuralist Views*, ed. Ladislav Matejka and Krystyna Pomorska, 1962); Ladislav Matejka and Irwin R. Titunik, eds., *Semiotics of Art: Prague School Contributions* (1976); Charles Morris, "Foundations of the Theory of Signs," *Foundations of the Unity of Science* 1 (1938); Vladimir Propp, *Morfologiia skazki* (1928, *Morphology of the Folktale*, trans. Laurence Scott, 1958, 2nd ed., ed. Louis A. Wagner, 1968); Michael Riffaterre, *Semiotics of Poetry* (1978); Ferdinand de Saussure, *Cours de linguistique générale* (ed. Charles Bally and Albert Sechehaye, 1916, *Course in General Linguistics*, trans. Wade Baskin, 1959); Ronald Schleifer, introduction, *Structural Semantics* by Algirdas Julien Greimas (1987); Robert Scholes, *Semiotics and Interpretation* (1982); Thomas Sebeok, ed., *Encyclopedic Dictionary of Semiotics* (3 vols., 1986); Tzvetan Todorov, *Théories du symbole* (1977, *Theories of the Symbol*, trans. Catherine Porter, 1982); Yuri Tynianov and Roman Jakobson, "Problemy izucheniia literatury i iazyka," *Novyi Lef* 12 (1928) ("Problems in the Study of Literature and Language," *Readings in Russian Poetics: Formalist and Structuralist Views*, ed. Ladislav Matejka and Krystyna Pomorska, 1962); Eugene Vance, "Chaucer's Pardoner: Relics, Discourse, and Frames of Propriety," *New Literary History* 20 (1989).

Speech Acts

In its current form, speech act theory is associated with a series of lectures given at Harvard University in 1955 by the Oxford philosopher J. L. Austin (1911–1960) and published posthumously in 1962 as *How to Do Things with Words*. The ideological roots of speech act theory in Western thought go back, however, to the pre-Socratic philosophers and the Hebrew Scriptures and have remained a peripheralized yet powerful force in the margins of the dominant Platonic-Christian-scientific-intellectual tradition.

At issue in the debate over speech acts is whether language is to be conceived as a system of structures and meanings or as a set of acts and practices. As such, the debate replicates the ancient Western debates between logic and rhetoric, transcendence and immanence, description and persuasion; between Plato and the Sophists; between the rabbinical tradition and the kabbalists; and between St. Augustine and the gnostics. It might even be thematized, as Harold Bloom suggests in *A Map of Misreading* (1973), as a clash between the Greek logos ("word"), with its associations of static visual structure, and the Hebrew "davhar" ("word"), with its associations of dynamic human action (42).

Unacknowledged antecedents of modern speech act theory can be located in late eighteenth-century epistemology and political philosophy, especially in the response to Immanuel Kant's account of the mental faculties. Johann Georg Hamann, Johann Gottfried von Herder, Friedrich Schleiermacher, and especially Wilhelm von Humboldt recognized language as the process by which the mind articulates and conceptualizes elements of the material world. The act that takes place on uttering a word, according to Humboldt, is an "act of spontaneous positing by bringing-together (synthesis)," through which the mind creates an object (184). While these philosophers defined cognition as essentially verbal, they also defined verbalization as essentially communicative. "I cannot think the first human thought, I cannot align the first reflective argument without dialoguing in my soul or without striving to dialogue," writes Herder (128). In England, John Horne Tooke, Jeremy Bentham, and William Godwin drew on a strong tradition of social contract theory and highlighted the role of speech acts in enacting authority and constructing the social order. Samuel Taylor Coleridge synthesized political, theological, and German idealist frames of reference into a philosophy of language centered on the "I am" (Greek "eimi" or Latin "sum") as the "verb-substantive" that expresses the identity of noun and verb, of being and act. For Romantic philosophers, then, verbal utterances typically enact the speaker's cognitive process; they act on a dialogic partner and seek that person's response. This revisionary understanding of language can be traced onward through the German philosophical tradition from G. W. F. Hegel to Hans-Georg Gadamer, who in *Truth and Method* (1960) rereads the history of medieval Christianity so as to find a dynamic, creative, active logos in St. Augustine and St. Thomas Aquinas (sec. 3.2.A).

Austin's specific formulation of speech act theory opens with a distinction between what he calls the "constative," an utterance used for stating things or conveying information, and the "performative," an utterance used for doing things or performing actions. The phrases "I now pronounce you man and wife" (when uttered by the presiding minister at a wedding), "I christen this ship the *Joseph Stalin*" (when uttered by an authorized official), "I promise I'll be there," and "I bet you five dollars" convey no information, Austin notes, and therefore are neither true nor false; instead, they perform the action referred to in the phrase (marrying, christening, promising, betting).

Later in *How to Do Things with Words*, Austin grows disenchanted with the constative-performative distinction, saying that it is finally impossible to make the distinction stick in analyses of specific utterances—all constatives perform actions too, and performatives do convey information—and so he suggests a new framework. He proposes that we call the utterance itself—the words artificially divorced from their social context—a "locution" and then explore the locution as a complexly relational speech act: as an "illocution"—what we intend to do—and as a "perlocution"— the effect on our listener that we want to have. Thus, for example, the adult who says to a child, "I'd love to see your drawing," might be describing (or "constating") a state of mind (locution), promising to look at the drawing (illocutionary force), and building the child's self-esteem (perlocutionary effect). This allows the linguist to explore the operation of language in the give-and-take of real interpersonal speech-use situations.

This approach to language is ideologically deviant in the West, where the transcendental logos (linguistic structure in the mind of God) has always taken precedence over fallen human speech, what people actually say and hear. It is important to note this deviance, because the next stage of speech act theory entailed an attempt to assimilate Austin's insights to the dominant tradition of linguistic philosophy. In 1969 the American philosopher John Searle published *Speech Acts*, an analytical application of Austin's lectures to a single speech act: promising. Searle worried that his work on speech acts would be seen as dealing with what Ferdinand de Saussure called *parole*, actual speech, the tabooed periphery of Western linguistics at least since Aristotle (17a1–7). "I am arguing, however," Searle writes, "that an adequate study of speech acts is a study of *langue*" (17), or of transcendental structure. He states explicitly what an "adequate study of speech acts" must consist of in order to qualify as a study of *langue*:

> Certain forms of analysis, especially analysis into necessary and sufficient conditions, are likely to involve (in varying degrees) idealization of the concept analyzed. In the present case, our analysis will be directed at the center of the concept of promising. I am ignoring marginal, fringe, and partially defective promises. (55)

This attempt to abstract or idealize out of actual speech acts a conceptual "center" formalizes Austin's own indication, early in *How to Do Things with Words*, that he will exclude from consideration any nonserious uses of language, "special circumstances," and "etiolations of language" that fall outside of "ordinary circumstances" (22). Searle's analysis recuperates speech act theory for transcendental linguistics by eliminating the dangerous variability of interpersonal communication. Eight years later, the Chomskyan linguist Jerrold Katz went further and recuperated the constative-performative distinction for analytical philosophy, specifically in terms of Chomsky's distinction between competence (our possession of an idealized transformational system) and performance (our actual speech), arguing that it should be possible to analyze performatives and constatives in terms of a decontextualized competence (the "null context") (184–85).

An idealized analysis is also the goal of the sociologist Jürgen Habermas, who adapts Anglo-American speech act theory as one part of his attempt to develop a "universal pragmatics," a sociological theory of communicative processes based on the assumption that speakers share basic norms of rational behavior. These formalistic revisions of Austin speak strongly of the continuing ideological dominance of logic in Western thought; in different ways, Searle, Katz, and Habermas attempt to rescue Austin's philosophical insights by discovering the logical core of his work. In another reading, however, such as is offered by French thinkers such as JACQUES DERRIDA, Shoshana Felman, and GILLES DELEUZE AND FÉLIX GUATTARI, what Austin was in fact doing was playing a different game, a game that Derrida associates with deconstruction, Felman with psychoanalysis, and Deleuze and Guattari with "order-words" and a language's "becoming-minoritarian" (77ff., 104ff.). In an expansion of Austin's own terms that Felman and Derrida hint at, Austin was attempting to displace traditional "constative linguistics" with a new "performative linguistics," a concern with language as performance.

However, as Derrida shows in his deconstruction of Austin in "Signature Event Context" (1972), there is a "constative" or logical exclusion within Austin's own argument that undermines the explanatory power of speech act theory. Austin treated figurative or poetic language as extrinsic to his concerns:

> A performative utterance will, for example, be in a peculiar way hollow or void if said by an actor on the stage, or if introduced in a poem, or spoken in soliloquy. . . .
> Language in such circumstances is in special ways—intelligibly—used not seriously, but in ways parasitic upon its normal use—ways which fall under the doctrine of the etiolations of language. All this we are excluding from consideration. (*How* 22)

"Walt Whitman," Austin says later, "does not seriously incite the eagle of liberty to soar" (104). But Derrida inverts and displaces Austin's serious/parasitic hierarchy, arguing that problematic factors such as iteration and alterity intervene in any representational system. Moreover, every speech act must be "iterable," capable of being repeated in an infinite number of different and nonexhaustible contexts. Far from being the "ditch or external place of perdition" that Austin tried to exclude from his theory, parasitism and the risk of failure are the conditions of possibility for the performative; it must be "citable" in order to have a chance of being effective.

The issue of whether theory should begin with an idealized model and gradually work to incorporate marginal cases or start with the realization that every case is impure became a turning point of the Derrida-Searle debate of the late 1970s. Prompted by Derrida's deconstruction of Austin, Searle wrote a "reply," assuming that Derrida was attacking Austin. Derrida then wrote a hundred-page deconstruction of Searle's reply ("Limited Inc a b c . . ." [1977]), seeking to demonstrate both that Searle is way out of his league philosophically, and that methodologically Searle, Austin, and Derrida are not so very far apart; Derrida also reiterated the importance, and the implications, of iterability:

> A standard act depends as much upon the possibility of being repeated, and thus potentially [éventuellement] of being mimed, feigned, cited, played, simulated, parasited, etc., as the latter possibility depends upon the possibility said to be opposed to it. And both of them "depend" upon the structure of iterability which, once again, undermines the simplicity of the oppositions and alternative distinctions. (91–92)

This would suggest that there is no substantial difference between promising on stage and promising in "real life": both are performances of speech acts that the speaker/actor has witnessed and internalized. MIKHAIL BAKHTIN's theory of internal dialogism is relevant here: every word we hear and speak is a repetition or reenactment of previous uses that is both saturated with earlier dialogues and inclined toward a specific situational response from a real listener.

To put it simply, one implication of the deconstructive interpretation of speech act theory is that we are always acting, in both senses of the word, whether we have memorized our lines from a specific script or, more generally, from "life," from previous speech encounters; our acting always relies on a socially regulated pattern for our behavior. Barbara Johnson notes that "the performative utterance thus automatically fictionalizes its utterer when it makes him the mouthpiece of a conventionalized authority" (60); similarly, Mary Louise Pratt stresses in her critique of essentialism in speech act theory that "people always speak from and in a socially constituted position," a position that is constantly shifting (62–63).

Persuasive as Derrida's deconstruction of Austin is, he does not offer a methodological alternative to Austin's serious-parasitic distinction. One influential solution to the problem is suggested by H. Paul Grice in his 1975 article "Logic and Conversation." Grice asks how it is possible for us to imply things. This has been a recurrent problem for "constative" linguists, since their systemic model requires that communication be possible only if it obeys the rules, but various evasive speech acts fail to do so and yet succeed as speech acts. Grice argues that implied speech acts do in fact break the rules but in a controlled fashion. It is possible for us to manipulate the expectations and assumptions we bring to speech situations so as to make ourselves understood indirectly. More problematically, Grice wants to formalize these assumptions (tacit "rules" or "maxims") for all human speech. He assumes, for example, that all conversation will naturally strive to be both rational and cooperative. To accept Grice's model as universal, as his "constative" followers (linguistic pragmaticians, notably Deirdre Wilson and Dan Sperber) have done, requires that we ignore the ethnic, gender, and class biases supporting this supposedly universal principle, and ignore as well our own irrational and uncooperative speech acts, blind rages, oneiric discourse, deliberate attempts to disrupt conversations, lies and cons, and pouting silences.

Charles Altieri, moreover, shows that the very choice to speak indirectly has implications for interpretation: "What B says is fairly clear; why he puts his statement this way and what the choice itself may mean is tantalizing" (86). Altieri offers the term "expressive implicature" to describe speech acts "where aspects of tenor or mode are foregrounded" (88). This modification of Grice is particularly useful, Altieri argues, in the stylistic analysis of literature: it allows the critic to explore the significance of the writer's stylistic self-presentation. All of Grice's examples deal with implicit constatives, or what might be called "locutionary implicature": speech acts that convey information in a roundabout way. But when Walt Whitman incites the eagle of liberty to soar, in Austin's example, he is not conveying implicit information; he is doing something, attempting to sway his readers in certain ways. He might be thought of as urging his readers to carry the banner of democracy (illocutionary implicature) and attempting to goad those readers into action (perlocutionary implicature). A more demystificatory Marxist reading might see Whitman as urging his readers to have a certain aesthetic experience of liberty (illocutionary implicature), which has the effect of passivizing those readers, making them uncritical of the actual infractions of liberty all around them (perlocutionary implicature).

Another important influence on literary applications of speech act theory is the work of the structuralist linguist Émile Benveniste, who independently developed ideas similar to Austin's in the course of his analysis of utterance, dialogue, and the position of the speaker within discourse. Unlike Austin, Benveniste believes it is important to maintain the performative-constative distinction by identifying the performative more rigorously as a unique, self-referential utterance that has the quality of "referring to a reality that it itself constitutes by the fact that it is actually uttered in conditions that make it an act" (236). For Benveniste, performativity derives from subjectivity as it emerges in and through language, as a speaker locates himself or herself in the present instance of discourse by using such deictic words as "this," "here," or "now" or even posits his or her subjectivity by appropriating the resources of language in saying "I" and "you." This definition of the performative has a range of possible applications to fiction and poetry. Literary critics have frequently commented, too, on John Searle's attempt to analyze literary speech acts in his essay "The Logical Status of Fictional Discourse" (1975) by postulating that writers of fiction implicitly invoke a set of "horizontal conventions" that temporarily suspend the "vertical rules" linking everyday speech acts to reality.

Indeed, there is no one way to "apply" speech act theory to literary texts, but the concepts and problems that speech act theories entail open up a host of new perspectives on literature and fiction. In the broadest sense, every literary text is a speech act, an utterance in an ongoing speech situation ("literary tradition," dialogically conceived) that is shaped by successive acts of reading, by the writer's directedness toward interpretation, and various background factors that affect all speech situations, such as purpose (what drives the writer to write and the reader to read and what brings them together), medium (the technologies of voice, print, digital storage and transmission; the economics of acquisition, production, and distribution), and historical moment. From this perspective, a speech act approach shades into sociology and cultural critique. On another level, every reading of a text is a speech situation in which the reader both constitutes and responds to the text as speech act; this approach shades into psychology, PHENOMENOLOGY, and READER-RESPONSE CRITICISM. From a still narrower perspective, every utterance within a literary text is a speech act, analyzable along Bakhtinian lines in terms of who is speaking to whom and how many (and whose) voices it polyphonically transforms; this shades speech act theory back toward formalism (see Mikhail Bakhtin).

Besides literary theory, other discourses—sociopolitical theory, legal theory, gender studies, and cultural critique—have been significantly influenced by speech act theory. In the 1970s, PIERRE BOURDIEU acknowledged that Austin's work was important because it called attention to the social acts performed by language and speech. He argued, however, that Austin and most of his followers were wrongly seeking to locate the criteria of performativity inside the linguistic system. Instead, the performative is effective only when, and because, it is authorized by a power that comes from outside language. Referring frequently to authoritative speech acts, as instances of "social magic," Bourdieu shows that authorized speakers mask their appropriation of power by disguising their performative utterances as descriptive statements. More recently, a parallel reading of the performative as necessarily "misrecognized" has been suggested by SLAVOJ ŽIŽEK, who begins from an entirely different framework derived from Hegelian idealism and Lacanian psychoanalysis. In Žižek's version, authority is explained as the impossibility of the "pure performative": in order to be effective, to achieve "verbal magic," the performative must assume the form of its opposite, the constative (epitomized here by the statement "It is like that").

JUDITH BUTLER's influential theories of social discourse and performativity build on Derrida and Bourdieu. The notion of a "sovereign subject" who creates and takes responsibility for his or her utterances is merely a fantasy of our desire to attribute agency; instead, the subject who cites a performative is, for Butler, "temporarily produced" as the "belated and fictive" origin of it (*Excitable Speech* 49). The effects of power, produced by iteration itself, include the infliction of pain by hate speech, the maintenance of "norms" of race, gender, and sexuality, and the very phenomenon of gendering. For many contemporary theorists, as for Butler, the deconstructive reading of speech act theory has turned Austin's assumption of an intending speaker inside out: the individual speaker has been replaced by social discourse, and the individual speech act has given way to a generalized performativity.

If speech act theory has morphed into performativity theory in many literary and cultural contexts, in linguistic and some philosophical circles it has evolved into pragmatics. Speech act theory provides inroads into the problematic of language not as transcendental structure but as social behavior. As such, it offers one of the twentieth century's most persuasive methodological alternatives to the mainstream linguistic tradition from Aristotle and Augustine to Saussure and Chomsky. Despite attempts to assimilate it back into that tradition, it continues to inspire oppositional approaches to language.

ANGELA ESTERHAMMER AND DOUGLAS ROBINSON

Charles Altieri, *Act and Quality: A Theory of Literary Meaning and Humanistic Understanding* (1981); J. L. Austin, *How to Do Things with Words* (ed. J. O. Urmson and Marina Sbisà, 1962, 2nd ed., 1975); Émile Benveniste, *Problèmes de linguistique générale* (1966–1974, *Problems in General Linguistics*, trans. Mary Elizabeth Meek, 1971); Harold Bloom, *A Map of Misreading* (1975); Pierre Bourdieu, *Ce que parler veut dire: L'économie des échanges linguistiques* (1982, partial trans., *Language and Symbolic Power*, ed. John B. Thompson, trans. Gino Raymond and Matthew Adamson, 1991); Kenneth Burke, *A Grammar of Motives* (1945), *Language as Symbolic Action: Essays on Life, Literature, and Method* (1966); Judith Butler, *Bodies that Matter: On the Discursive Limits of "Sex"* (1993), *Excitable Speech: Contemporary Scenes of Politics* (1997); Gilles Deleuze and Félix Guattari, *Mille plateaux*, vol. 2 of *Capitalisme et schizophrénie* (1980, *A Thousand Plateaus: Capitalism and Schizophrenia*, trans. Brian Massumi, 1987); Jacques Derrida, "Limited Inc a b c . . . ," *Glyph* 2 (1977) ("Limited Inc a b c . . . ," trans. Samuel Weber, 1977), "Signature evenement context," *Marges de la philosophie* (1972, "Signature Event Context," trans. Samuel Weber and Jeffrey Mehlman, 1977); Angela Esterhammer, *The Romantic Performative: Language and Action in British and German Romanticism* (2000); Shoshana Felman, *Le scandale du corps parlant: Don Juan avec Austin; ou, La séduction en deux langues* (1980, *The Literary Speech Act: Don Juan with J. L. Austin; or, Seduction in Two Languages*, trans. Catherine Porter, 1983, rpt., *The Scandal of the Speaking Body: Don Juan with J. L. Austin, or Seduction in Two Languages*, 2003); Hans-Georg Gadamer, *Wahrheit und Methode: Grundzüge einer philosophischen Hermeneutik* (1960, 5th ed., *Gesammelte Werke*, vol. 1, ed. J. C. B. Mohr, 1986, *Truth and Method*, trans. Garrett Barden and John Cumming, 1975, 2nd ed., trans. rev. Joel Weinsheimer and Donald G. Marshall, 1989); H. Paul Grice, "Logic and Conversation," *Syntax and Semantics*, vol. 3, *Speech Acts* (ed. Peter Cole and Jerry Morgan, 1975); Jürgen Habermas, *Theorie des kommunikativen Handelns* (1981, *The Theory of Communicative Action*, trans. Thomas McCarthy, 1984); Johann Gottfried Herder, *Abhandlung über den Ursprung der Sprache* (1772, *On the Origin of Language*, trans. Alexander Gode, 1966); Wilhelm von Humboldt, *Über die Verschiedenheit des menschlichen Sprachbaues und ihren Einfluss auf die geistige Entwicklung des Menschengeschlechts* (1835, *On Language: The Diversity of Human Language-Structure and Its Influence on the Mental Development of Mankind*, trans. Peter Heath, 1988); Barbara Johnson, "Poetry and Performative Language: Mallarmé and Austin," *The Critical Difference: Essays in the Contemporary Rhetoric of Reading* (1980); Jerrold Katz, *Propositional Structure and Illocutionary Force* (1977); Mary Louise Pratt, "Ideology and Speech-Act Theory," *Poetics Today* 7 (1986), *Toward a Speech Act Theory of Literary Discourse* (1977); Sandy Petrey, *Speech Acts and Literary Theory* (1990); Douglas Robinson, "Metapragmatics and Its Discontents," *Journal of Pragmatics* 10 (1986); John R. Searle, "The Logical Status of Fictional Discourse," *New Literary History* 6 (1975), "Reiterating the Differences: A Reply to Jacques Derrida," *Glyph* 2 (1977), *Speech Acts: An Essay in the Philosophy of Language* (1969); Valentin N. Voloshinov, *Marksizm i filosofiia iazyka* (1929, *Marxism and the Philosophy of Language*, trans. Ladislav Matejka and Irwin R. Titunik, 1973); Deirdre Wilson and Dan Sperber, *Relevance: Communication and Cognition* (1986); Ludwig Wittgenstein, *Philosophische Untersuchungen* (*Philosophical Investigations*, trans. G. E. M. Anscombe, 1953, 3rd ed., 1967); Slavoj Žižek, *Enjoy Your Symptom!: Jacques Lacan in Hollywood and Out* (1992, 2nd rev. ed., 2001).

Spivak, Gayatri Chakravorty

Gayatri Chakravorty Spivak (b. 1942) is one of "the holy trinity" of postcolonial theorists named in Robert Young's *Colonial Desire* (1995), the others being EDWARD W. SAID and HOMI K. BHABHA. Brought up and educated in Kolkata, Spivak migrated to the United States in 1962 for postgraduate studies in comparative literature at Cornell University. In 1991 she became Avalon Professor in the Humanities at Columbia. Her translation of JACQUES DERRIDA's *Of Grammatology* (1967) in 1976 established her as one of the most influential cultural critics in the humanities, with her impact extending far beyond her base in POSTCOLONIAL STUDIES.

Spivak's first book was a conventional, biographically oriented academic monograph on W. B. Yeats (1974), but she has characteristically been much more interested in discourse than in literature and literary criticism per se. "Literature" is the shortest of the four sections in *A Critique of Postcolonial Reason* (1999), a gathering of her most important essays. (The other parts are "Philosophy," "History," and "Culture.") Nonetheless, the pieces in this section have proved extremely influential among feminist and postcolonial literary critics in particular, offering radically new and productive, if controversial, modes of reading both canonical and noncanonical writers. Linking these essays, as well as Spivak's work on literature to that in other areas, is her attention to the discursive techniques and tropes by which the identity of the (neo)colonial subject is constructed in both hegemonic and counterhegemonic forms of representation and to the epistemological and political implications of the relationship between such discursively constructed figures and their "real" historical referents.

The sometimes formidable challenge of Spivak's work as a whole derives partly from the effortless and eclectic way that she draws on discourses as diverse as feminism, psychoanalysis, DECONSTRUCTION, and (neo-)Marxist forms of political economy. She brings these various kinds of critical theory together to demonstrate their respective limits and incompatibilities, as well as their mutual points of interrogation.

Whereas Said is generally dismissive of deconstruction and skeptical about Marxism, and Bhabha is sympathetic to the former but hostile to the latter, Spivak embraces both in a largely affirmative manner. Insofar as she insists on the continuing importance of Marxism as a form of politics and intellectual critique, she can be linked back to an older strand of postcolonial criticism represented by such figures as Aimé Césaire, FRANTZ FANON, and Amilcar Cabral. Spivak is also the only one of the "trinity" to consistently inflect postcolonialism with a feminist agenda. While focusing primarily on the colonized female and her heirs in the neocolonial era, she also recognizes the agency of white women in colonialism ("Three Women's Texts and a Critique of Imperialism" [1985]) and addresses the symbolic roles they perform in colonial discourse ("Imperialism and Sexual Difference" [1986]).

Said and Bhabha characteristically focus on the discourses of the dominant orders of Western society or the relatively empowered figure of the (post)colonial critic or artist, but Spivak is concerned with less privileged constituencies. In "Can the Subaltern Speak?" (1988), arguably her most important essay, she extends the scope of ANTONIO GRAMSCI's term and applies it to the "Third World" to signify "subsistence farmers, unorganized peasant labor, the tribals and communities of zero workers on the street or in the countryside" (84). In her later work she extends it again to disadvantaged sectors within the contemporary Western metropolis, particularly to describe involuntary economic migrants represented by the "urban homeworker." Her analysis is directed especially at the predicament of the female subaltern, whom she represents as doubly marginalized no matter where she is located.

Spivak's principal concern is whether the subaltern can speak for him- or herself or can only be represented and spoken for in distorted or "interested" fashion by others. Her particular target is the contemporary Western "radical" intellectual who is, ostensibly, the champion of the oppressed but who characteristically announces the death of the (Western, liberal, bourgeois, sovereign, male) subject in the postmodern episteme while retaining a conception of the self-knowing, unified subject in respect of marginalized groups, including those she defines as subaltern. This methodological critique underpins a more important political objection to the apparent "benevolence" of some Western "high" theory. Spivak accuses figures such as Gilles Deleuze and MICHEL FOUCAULT of believing that they are able to stand outside the general system of exploitation of the Third World in order to intervene on the subaltern's behalf (see GILLES DELEUZE AND FÉLIX GUATTARI). In ascribing to the subaltern a subjectivity from which the latter is then presumed to be capable of speaking, such Western intellectuals come to represent (in the sense of speaking for or standing in for) the subaltern. Spivak sees this gesture as continuous with the history of the construction of the subjectivity and subject positions for the colonized—and the ventriloquistic articulation of their voice—in the era of formal Western imperialism, a process illustrated with great force in both "The Rani of Sirmur" (1985) and "Can the Subaltern Speak?"

Spivak advances her argument in the latter essay by interposing in her analysis of Foucault and Deleuze an account of the debates over the prohibition of sati (the immolation of Hindu widows) in early nineteenth-century India. The colonizers constructed the figure of a subaltern female that called out for protection, thus assenting to the imposition of the "modernizing," "liberating," and "progressive" regime of empire. This consolidated imperial Britain's self-image as "civilized" in comparison with her "barbaric" local male oppressors, the Indian men who supposedly enforced the custom of sati. The counterdiscourse of the indigenous Indian male, by contrast, has the voice of the sexed subaltern articulate her voluntary assent to sati in the name of a defense of tradition against colonialism. In both interpretations of the issue of sati the voice of the subaltern is ventriloquized; "spoken for" as the women are, one "never encounters the testimony" of their own "voice-consciousness" ("Can" 93).

Spivak's affiliations with feminism are clear, but her work presents a persistent criticism of Western feminism for its failure to "dehegemonize" its own guiding presuppositions. Preeminent among these is that "woman" is implicitly understood as being white, heterosexual, and middle class, to the same extent that in liberal humanism "man" is constructed in practice in narrowly patriarchal and ethnocentric terms. Spivak's essays "French Feminism in an International Frame" (1981) and "Three Women's Texts and a Critique of Imperialism" criticize the (self-)interested intervention on behalf of the subaltern woman by Western feminism and the latter's complicity in the dominant discourses of the world's privileged societies and thus anticipate her critique of some Western "radical" theory.

Spivak offers JULIA KRISTEVA's interest in the subaltern Chinese woman as an example par excellence of "benevolent" First World feminists exploiting the Third World in the process of their own self-constitution. Kristeva's work expresses above all else the disillusioned debate among Western "radicals" over the way forward after the 1968 Paris *événements*. This suggests to Spivak the essential irrelevance of Kristeva's work to a genuinely internationalist feminism. Kristeva's shortcomings are repeated in Anglo-American feminism as well, as "Three Women's Texts" demonstrates forcefully. Here Spivak concludes that "the academic [Western] feminist must learn to learn from [Third World women], to speak to them, to suspect that their access to the political and sexual scene is not merely to be corrected by our superior theory and enlightened compassion" (135).

Yet there is (ostensibly) no question of her supporting "the tired nationalist claim" that only the native can know the native. She argues that some contemporary Western theory, especially Derrida's work, is necessary to postcolonialism because it both encourages scrupulous vigilance toward the terms of engagement with the non-Western Other and undermines foundational models of identity, which might encourage reverse ethnocentrism. Despite her collaboration in, and sympathy for, the counterhegemonic historiography of the Indian Subaltern Studies Group, Spivak argues in "Subaltern Studies: Deconstructing Historiography" (1985) that the project is flawed by its mistaken assumption of a "pure" or "essential" form of subaltern consciousness, the "truth" of which can be retrieved independently of the determinations of (neo)colonial forms of knowledge and discursive practice. She argues that these have in fact precipitated an "epistemic fracture" that makes impossible the recovery of an original, or originary, subaltern consciousness. The failure of the group sufficiently to factor in this "fracture" could lead to a reinscription of bourgeois and humanist models of both identity and agency. Spivak concludes that one must see in such practices a repetition of, as well as a rupture with, (neo)colonial epistemologies.

This problem of "repetition in rupture" also applies to Spivak's own work, demonstrating the central theme of the difficulty of escaping the gravitational pull of the forms of knowledge that the "radical" critic presumes to criticize. Insofar as Spivak asserts that the subaltern cannot speak, she is repeating the gesture of constituting and speaking for, or in place of, the subaltern—the very maneuver for which she criticizes Foucault and Deleuze. If her account of subaltern muteness were true, there would be only the West (and the native elite, perhaps) to write about. Moreover, Spivak leaves herself no option but to address the West and in practice to focus not so much on the subaltern as on the Western intellectual as her privileged object of investigation. Her polemics on the importance of "unlearning one's privilege" are clearly directed at Western colleagues, and, ironically, the prescriptions of "French Feminism in an International Frame" function just as much as Kristeva's own *About Chinese Women* (1974) as "a set of directives for class- and race-privileged literary women" (*In Other* 136). In Spivak's scheme, the "benevolent" Western would-be ally of the subaltern is left with the seemingly impossible demand of opening up to the other without in any way "assimilating" that other to his or her own ethics, subject position, and identity. Spivak is brilliantly persuasive in her analysis of "the itinerary of silencing" endured by the subaltern, but she pays very little attention to the process by which the subaltern's "coming to voice" could be achieved. In this respect, for all its highly productive impact on postcolonial cultural studies—and other intellectual fields—Spivak's work might be considered to be unnecessarily deterministic and politically pessimistic.

BART MOORE-GILBERT

See also FEMINIST THEORY AND CRITICISM, GLOBALIZATION, MARXIST THEORY AND CRITICISM: 3. 1989 AND AFTER, MULTICULTURALISM, and POSTCOLONIAL STUDIES.

Mahasweta Devi, *Imaginary Maps* (trans. Gayatri Chakravorty Spivak, 1994); Gayatri Chakravorty Spivak, "Can the Subaltern Speak?," *Colonial Discourse and Post-colonial Theory* (ed. Patrick Williams and Laura Chrisman, 1993), *A Critique of Postcolonial Reason: Toward a History of the Vanishing Present* (1999), *Death of a Discipline* (2003), *In Other Worlds: Essays in Cultural Politics* (1987), *Other Asias* (2004), *Outside in the Teaching Machine* (1993), *The Post-Colonial Critic: Interviews, Strategies, Dialogues* (ed. Sarah Harasym, 1990), *The Spivak Reader* (ed. Donna Landry and Gerald MacLean, 1996).

Structuralism

Structuralism in linguistics and literary studies found its major starting point in Swiss linguist FERDINAND DE SAUSSURE's work at the turn of the twentieth century. But it was more fully realized—in fact, the term "structuralism" was coined—in Roman Jakobson's ongoing work in linguistics, SEMIOTICS, and literary analysis. (In this development, structuralism should be seen as a subdivision or a methodological field in the larger area of semiotics that finds its origins in both Saussure's and Charles Sanders Peirce's work.) In *Course in General Linguistics* (1916), the transcription by his students of several courses in general linguistics he offered between 1907 and 1911, Saussure calls for the "scientific" study of language to replace the nineteenth century's historical linguistics. His work attempts to reduce the huge number of facts about language to a manageable number of propositions based on the *formal* relationships defining and existing between language's elements.

Saussure's reexamination of language is based on four assumptions: that language is *systematic* (the whole is greater than the sum of its parts), that its elements are *relational* (linguistic "entities" are defined in relationships of combination and contrast to one another), that the nature of linguistic elements is *arbitrary* (they are defined in terms of the function and purpose they serve rather than in terms of their inherent qualities), and that language has a *social* nature (the larger context for analysis, determination, and realization of language's structure).

In 1929 Jakobson designated as "structuralism" the treatment of "any set of phenomena . . . not as a mechanical agglomeration but as a structural whole." He describes the focus of study as "the internal premises of the development: now the mechanical conception of processes yields to the question of their function" ("Retrospect" 711). By focusing on the "structural whole," Jakobson articulates the first three of Saussure's assumptions. First, he demonstrates that the scientific study of language needs to examine the system, or "code," of language rather than its particular "speech events," an approach that calls for a "synchronic" conception of the relationships among language's elements at a particular moment of time rather than the "diachronic" study of the development of language through history. Second, in abandoning a "mechanical conception of processes" he assumes that the basic elements of language are arbitrary and can only be studied in relation to their functions rather than their causes. Third, Jakobson implies that the social nature of language, its articulation and communication of meanings, cannot be ignored in pursuit of mechanical reduction.

Such a structural analysis governs the conception of all elements of language in linguistics, from the "distinctive features" that combine to form phonemes to sentences, paragraphs, and more extended segments of language that combine to form discourse insofar as discourse creates a "meaningful whole" (Greimas, *Structural*

59). Literary structuralism aims to extend structural analysis's method of focusing rigorously on binary oppositions to discover overarching relationships of *combination* and *contrast* in language to discourses beyond the limit of the sentence—poetry, narratives (including the anonymous narratives of folktales Vladimir Propp studies in *Morphology of the Folktale* [1928] and the myths Claude Lévi-Strauss's examines in *Structural Anthropology* [1958]), film, social formations (including gender and class relations), and wider areas of "semantics" and meaning. Such analyses are based on the fact that language and systems of signification are structured as "both *energeia* and *ergon*"—"as creation and as oeuvre" (Jakobson, "Signum" 179). Language is thus both the *process* of articulating meaning (signification) and its *product* (communication), functions neither identical nor fully congruent. Since language's elements are arbitrary, moreover, neither contrast nor combination are "basic." Distinctive features combine to form contrasting phonemes on another level of apprehension, phonemes combine to form contrasting morphemes, morphemes combine to form words, words combine to form sentences, sentences form paragraphs, paragraphs form (or are) discourses, discourses embody or imply ideologies, and so forth. At each level, the "structural whole" is greater than the sum of its parts—just as water, H_2O, is more than the mechanical agglomeration of hydrogen and oxygen (*Course*, Baskin trans. 103).

Saussure's first three assumptions lead him to call for a new science that would study "the life of signs within society," his fourth assumption. He names this science "*semiology* (from Greek *semeîon* 'sign')" (Baskin trans. 16). The "science" of semiotics, as it came to be practiced in Eastern Europe in the 1920s and 1930s and Paris in the 1950s and 1960s widened the study of language and linguistic structures to literary artifacts constituted (or articulated) by those structures. Prague school structuralism and French structuralism came to examine meaningful cultural phenomena from the viewpoint of the conditions that make such phenomena possible, including the structures that give rise to that meaning. But even before the term "structuralism" was coined, many principles of structural linguistics (if not the rigorous definitions of structure articulated by Jakobson, Jan Mukařovský in Prague and Lévi-Strauss in Paris) influenced Russian formalism's study of literature's particular "effects" produced by the "elements" of literature and narrative. In all these areas, Jakobson is a central figure: he participated in Russian formalism, helped organize the Prague circle, and opened Lévi-Strauss to the structural study of myth and cultural anthropology by introducing him to structural linguistics.

Russian formalism is important to literary structuralism's development in Prague and Paris because in focusing on the formal "devices" that create literary effects it attempted to produce a "science" of literature parallel to Saussure's effort in linguistics. However, Russian formalism's assumption that "literature" could be legitimately—"scientifically"—isolated from other cultural phenomena led Jakobson, Mukařovský, and Lévi-Strauss to oppose "structure" to "form" as the central concept of understanding. That is, the opposition, implicit in formalism, between form and content does not allow for a conception of literature as a *social* and *cultural* as well as an aesthetic phenomenon.

Structuralism, in contrast, offers a framework of understanding in which what is structured in not simply "content" but rather phenomena *already structured* on a different "level" of apprehension, so that the isolated content implicit in literary "formalism"—New Critical as well as Russian—betrays the dynamic relational nature of meaning. In 1921, Jakobson described scientific formalism's object of study as "literariness," those isolated forms that make an utterance characteristically "literary," avoiding anything "extraliterary" (e.g., psychology, politics, or philosophy). In 1933, as a member of the Prague circle, Jakobson modified this position in arguing that the poetic function, or "poeticity," can be viewed as only one constituent part of poetry's complex structure. "Poeticity" (unlike "literariness") is a relational rather than an absolute element of a poetic work. When the poetic function is dominant, "the word is felt as a word and not a mere representation of the object being named or an outburst of emotion" ("What?" 378).

In emphasizing the existence of "literature" within configurations of cultural significance, Jakobson and Prague semiotics more generally emphasize literary discourse's global cultural existence. French structuralism in the 1950s and 1960s also emphasizes the relationship between structuralism and cultural institutions. Lévi-Strauss studies a wide range of myths, mostly Amerindian, and attempts to discover the structure—the grammar—of mythological narrative. He applies structural linguistics' methods to narrative, with the result that structural anthropology analyzes narrative discourse as linguistics analyzes sentences. In 1964 he articulated the ambition of structuralism and semiotics as "to transcend the contrast between the tangible and the intelligible by operating from the outset at the sign level. The function of signs is, precisely, to express the one by means of the other" (*Raw* 14). Like the Prague structuralists, he attempts to isolate and define the conditions of meaning in culture, to articulate the relationship between nature's tangible entities and culture's intelligible meanings.

Lévi-Strauss, in his anthropological work and such important methodological essays as "The Structural Study of Myth" (1955) and "Structure and Form: Reflections on the Work of Vladimir Propp" (1960) attempts to describe the nature of the "human mind" through a kind of structural "algebraic matrix of possible permutations and combinations" (Leach 40). This work initiated a literary movement that became a watershed in modern criticism, causing a major reorientation in literary studies, marked most notably in the United States in 1975 when Modern Language Association of America gave its annual award for an outstanding book of criticism to Jonathan Culler's *Structuralist Poetics*. French structuralism attempts to explain literature as a system of signs and codes and of the conditions that allow that system to function in a way that emphasizes the essential intelligibility, as Lévi-Strauss says, of the phenomena it studies. In *Structural Semantics* (1966), for instance, Algirdas Julien Greimas attempts to "account for" meaning (including literary meaning) as fully and objectively as Saussure's linguistic science attempts to account for the phenomenon of language.

ROLAND BARTHES attributes the power of structuralism to its being "essentially an *activity*" that could "reconstruct an 'object' in such a way as to manifest thereby the rules of functioning" ("Structuralist" 214). Structuralism, according to Barthes, focuses on a text's synchronic dimension (the system of *langue* as opposed to its individual speech events, *parole*), the specific ways in which a text is like other texts. The structural comparison of texts is based on similarities of function (character development, plot, theme, and so forth, as well as the functional definitions of linguistic elements such as finite verbs, pronouns, tenses, and so forth), relationships that Lévi-Strauss calls "homologies." The predominantly synchronic analysis of homologies "re-creates" the text as a "paradigm," a system of structural possibilities. Following these precepts, Greimas attempts to reduce the thirty-one functions of Propp's *Morphology of the Folktale* to axes of knowledge, desire, and power. In more specific studies of literature, Tzvetan Todorov attempts to describe the "grammar" of narratives (*The Poetics of Prose* [1971]) and to position relationally the "fantastic" as a genre within a configuration of other literary genres (*The Fantastic* [1970]). The genre of the fantastic is an "entity" of literature precisely because it relates to other so-called entities (themselves functions of other relationships). Perhaps the clearest examples of structuralist analyses of literary texts—in their pretense to scientific objectivity they most fully seem to avoid the social and temporal contexts of discourse—are Jakobson's analyses of a Shakespeare sonnet and short lyrics by several poets. Barthes's structuralist analysis of a biblical narrative, "Introduction to the Structural Analysis of Narratives" (1966) and Greimas's book-length study of a single short story by Guy de Maupassant (*Maupassant: The Semiotics of Text* [1976]) are also examples of structural analyses of anonymous and nonanonymous narratives.

For Jakobson and Lévi-Strauss in their structuralist analysis of Charles Baudelaire's "Les chats" ("'Les chats' de Charles Baudelaire" [1963]) binary oppositions demonstrate that "phenomena of formal distribution obviously have a semantic foundation" (218). The analysis closely examines the structural oppositions of parts of speech, poetic forms, semantic features (e.g., animate versus inanimate nouns), and so forth, demonstrating that "the different levels . . . blend, complement each other or combine to give the poem the value of an absolute object" (217). Such an "absolute" object is what Greimas calls "the still very vague, yet necessary concept of the *meaningful whole* [*totalité de signification*] set forth by a message" (*Structural* 59). Jakobson and Lévi-Strauss assume that meaning is present, unified, and reasonably the object of scientific analysis. At the end they present (in narrative form) the "experience" of the poem, the appearance of "Les chats" as "a closed system" of grammatical forms and semantic meanings and, simultaneously, "the appearance of an open system in dynamic progression" that aims to "resolve" the poem's felt grammatical/semantic oppositions (218–19).

Structuralism expanded the areas subject to rigorous analysis beyond literary studies to discursive and social-cultural phenomena. Barthes, for example, illuminates semiotic theory, the system of fashion, narrative structure, textuality, and many other topics. Claude Bremond attempts to trace the "logic" of narrative. Paris school semiotics, following Greimas, expands structural analysis to such divergent areas as gestural language, legal discourse, and social science. Further, Michael Riffaterre, Umberto Eco, Jonathan Culler, and others have done significant work in semiotic approaches to semantic theory, closely allied to structuralism. Here again structuralism has tended to focus on the fixity of relations within synchronic paradigms at the expense of temporality, or the "diachronic" dimension, which involves history.

This tendency to avoid dealing with time and social change, a tendency much less pronounced in Prague structuralism, concerned many critics of structuralism from its beginning and ultimately became a main component of the "poststructuralist" critique of the scientific goals of structuralism, in which structuralism's strength as an analytic technique is connected to what many see as its major weakness. Its self-imposed limitations, especially its lack of concern with diachronic change and its focus on general systems rather than on individual cases, became increasingly evident in the late 1960s. JACQUES DERRIDA's decisive critique of Lévi-Strauss in "Structure, Sign, and Play in the Discourse of the Human Sciences" (1966) (in *Writing and Difference*) and *Of Grammatology* (1967) makes the case that the attempt to investigate structure implies the ability to stand outside and apart from it, which is similar to the methods of Russian formalism that both Prague and French structuralism criticized. Derrida specifically critiques Lévi-Strauss's privileging of the opposition between "nature" and "culture," arguing that since one never transcends culture, one can never examine it from the "outside." There is no standing free of structure, no so-called natural state free of the structural interplay that, in the structuralist analysis, constitutes meaning, and therefore there can be no objective examination of structure. The attempt to "read" and "interpret" cultural structures cannot be adequately translated into exacting scientific models.

Structuralism and semiotics have learned from the critique of the structuralist enterprise and its enabling assumption of the opposition between the tangible and the intelligible, nature and culture. The work of JULIA KRISTEVA, like that of later Barthes (e.g., S/Z), both utilizes and goes beyond "structuralism," combining the "poststructural" work of JACQUES LACAN and Barthes and the earlier critiques of formalism and structural linguistics by MIKHAIL BAKHTIN with the achievements of structuralism and semiotics. But the poststructuralist critique of structuralism can be "accounted for" within the methodological framework of structuralism first fully articulated by Saussure. The relational and arbitrary nature of signifying phenomena both call for and also breach the first assumption of structuralism, its systematicity. Moreover, this structural account of poststructuralism again implies the fourth assumption, the social nature of language. Arbitrariness itself, as the structural linguist Émile Benveniste argues, is arbitrary from the outside, but from the inside—within the society and culture in which languages function—the sign's arbitrary nature seems necessary; since meaning's elements are relationally defined and arbitrary, they demand a structural system for their realization. But those very features of relationality and arbitrariness also continually unweave the structural system. Since language can use anything to articulate its meanings, any "structure" can be recontextualized (relationally and arbitrarily). As Greimas notes, the "edifice" of language "appears like a construction without plan or clear aim" (Structural 133) because "discourse, conceived as a hierarchy of units of communication fitting into one another, contains in itself the negation of that hierarchy by the fact that the units of communication with different dimensions can be at the same time recognized as equivalent" (82). In ways like this, then, structuralism in its scientific study of language and meaning anticipates and articulates the terms of its own "poststructuralist" critique.

RONALD SCHLEIFER AND GABRIEL RUPP

See also FRENCH THEORY AND CRITICISM: 1945 AND AFTER, NARRATOLOGY, FERDINAND DE SAUSSURE, and SEMIOTICS.

See also bibliographies for ROLAND BARTHES and JACQUES DERRIDA.

Roland Barthes, "L'activité structuraliste," Les lettres nouvelles 32 (1963) ("The Structuralist Activity," Critical Essays, trans. Richard Howard, 1972), "Introduction à l'analyse structurale des récits" Communications 8 (1966) ("Introduction to the Structural Analysis of Narratives," Image—Music—Text, ed. and trans. Stephen Heath, 1977); Claude Bremond, Logique du récit (1973); Algirdas Julien Greimas, Maupassant: La sémiotique du texte (1976, Maupassant: The Semiotics of Text, trans. Paul Perron, 1988), Sémantique structurale: Recherche de méthode (1966, Structural Semantics: An Attempt at Method, trans. Daniele McDowell, Ronald Schleifer, and Alan Velie, 1983); Roman Jakobson, "Co je poezie?," Volné smery 30 (1933–1934) ("What Is Poetry?," trans. Michael Heim, Language and Literature, ed. Krystyna Pomorska and Stephen Rudy, 1968), "Retrospect," Selected Writings, vol. 2 (1971), "Úvahy o básnictví doby husitské," Slovo a slovesnost 3 (1936) ("Signum et Signatum," trans. Michael Heim, Semiotics of Art: Prague School Contributions, ed. Ladislav Matejka and Irwin R. Titunik, 1976); Roman Jakobson and Claude Lévi-Strauss, "'Les chats' de Charles Baudelaire," L'homme 2 (1963) ("Charles Baudelaire's 'Les Chats,'" trans. Katie Furness-Lane, Introduction to Structuralism, ed. Michael Lane, 1970); Edmund Leach, Lévi-Strauss (1970, rev. ed., 1974); Claude Lévi-Strauss, "L'analyse structurale du mythe" (1955, "The Structural Study of Myth," Structural Anthropology), Anthropologie structurale (1958, Structural Anthropology, 2 vols., trans. Claire Jacobson and Brooke Grundfest Schoepf, and Monique Layton, 1963–1977), Mythologiques, vol. 1, Le cru et la cuit (1964, The Raw and the Cooked, trans. John Weightman and Doreen Weightman, 1975), "La structure et la forme: Réflexions sur un ouvrage de Vladimir Propp," Cahiers de l'Institute de science economique appliquee 99 (1960) ("Structure and Form: Reflections on a Work by Vladimir Propp," Structural Anthropology, vol. 2); Richard

Macksey and Eugenio Donato, eds., *The Structuralist Controversy: The Languages of Criticism and the Sciences of Man* (1970); Ferdinand de Saussure, *Cours de linguistique générale* (ed. Charles Bally and Albert Sechehaye, 1916, *Course in General Linguistics*, trans. Wade Baskin, 1959, trans. Roy Harris, 1983); Tzvetan Todorov, *Introduction à la littérature fantastique* (1970, *The Fantastic: A Structural Approach to a Literary Genre*, trans. Richard Howard, 1973), *Poétique de la prose* (1971, *The Poetics of Prose*, trans. Richard Howard, 1977).

Williams, Raymond

The most important legacy of Raymond Williams (1921–1988) is CULTURAL STUD-
IES, the interdisciplinary field that he, more than anyone else in the English-speaking
world since the late 1940s, pioneered and consolidated. Williams exemplifies the social figure of the politically committed writer. Confident that "all kinds of writing
produce meaning and value" (*Politics* 326), he wrote over 650 publications—27 academic books, 5 novels, 3 plays, 7 pamphlets, 60 magazine columns on television, and
more than 500 articles and reviews—as critic, theorist, historian, journalist, political commentator, pamphleteer, dramatist, and novelist and in a variety of styles
(conversational, high academic, technically condensed, literary, polemical).

Williams was born into a working-class family in Wales and was educated at
Trinity College, Cambridge. The foundations of his prolific intellectual career were
set down after World War II during a period of employment with the Oxford University Extra-Mural Delegacy and active involvement with the Workers Educational
Association. He taught drama and fiction, putting an increasing emphasis on their
political and social contexts and also stressing the theme of a democratic and permanent education. His important early books move from criticism (*Reading and Criticism* [1950]) and drama (*Drama from Ibsen to Eliot* [1952], *Drama in Performance* [1954]) to
film (*Preface to Film* [1954]) and culture and communications (*Culture and Society, 1780–
1950* [1958], *The Long Revolution* [1961]). The last two, in particular, formed his contributions to the radical cultural milieu that was emerging in postwar England.

In *Culture and Society*, now a humanities classic, Williams breaches the narrow
confines of the prevailing definitions that separate literature, culture, and politics.
Through a close reading of Edmund Burke, John Stuart Mill, Matthew Arnold, and
other late eighteenth- to mid-twentieth-century writers, he reconstructs the newly
active sense of "culture" that emerged around the time of the Industrial Revolution
as a critique of industrialization and mechanization. The book found warm response
in the cultural politics of the 1960s. By studying culture in the context of its relationships with the four terms ("class," "industry," "democracy," and "art") with which it
had been associated structurally in the "culture and society" tradition that he was
organizing and making visible, Williams breaks further new ground. He stresses
connection and interaction in support of the claim that important social and historical processes occur *within* language and, indeed, that the active meanings and values
embodied in language and in the changing patterns of language exert a formative
social force. *Keywords* (1976), developed as an appendix to this earlier text but not
published until much later, offers a selective vocabulary of culture and society within

this theoretical framework. A recognizable trademark of Williams's writings is its continual recourse to keyword analysis.

The Long Revolution, another of Williams's most important and enduring works, provides evidence that the changes and conflicts of a whole way of life are deeply implicated in its systems of learning and communication, with the result that cultural history is far from being a mere province of idle aesthetic interest. Theoretical work and historical scholarship combine to restore both conceptual terms ("creativity," "culture," "individual," "society") and instituted forms (education, literacy, the press, standardization of the language, conventions of drama and fiction) to the real historical networks of active social relationships that give them meaning. The book contributed substantially to the production of modern cultural studies in general as well as to the advance of a politically committed current within it. For Williams's argument weds together culture and democracy. *Culture and Society* looks backward, but *The Long Revolution* looks forward to the next decade and, in contrast with the cultural conservatism of F. R. Leavis and T. S. Eliot, offers a program for the radical democratic reform of cultural institutions. Its theoretical perspective, one of the most generous political creeds of our times, maintains that we are living through a long revolution that is simultaneously and in connected ways economic, political, and cultural and that transforms people and institutions in the process of extending the transformation of nature, the forms of democratic self-governance, and the modes of education and communication. Uneven and conflicted as this process may be, enhancing its development is the main criterion of intellectual, moral, and political value.

In *Communications* (1962), Williams deepens his fieldwork in cultural studies, reviewing the contents and methods of cultural media and finding supports for the contention that relationships of power, property, and production are no more fundamental to a society than relationships in describing, learning, modifying, exchanging, and preserving experiences. He asserts that these latter are "a central and necessary part of our humanity" (11). Later, in *Television* (1974), he investigates one particular cultural institution in historical depth, with the intention of refuting Marshall McLuhan's arguments of technological determinism and instead situating television and its effects within a critical sociology of society as a totality, analyzing both its achievements in extending public education and its falling short of the possibilities for democratic broadcasting controlled by the cultural producers.

From 1961 to his early retirement in 1983, Williams worked at Cambridge University. During the first half of the 1960s he was active on the left of the Labour Party and then in the extraparliamentary New Left, indicting capitalism in the *May Day Manifesto* (1968), coedited with E. P. Thompson and STUART HALL. Meanwhile, cultural studies was finding its first institutionalized form as a graduate unit of the English department at the University of Birmingham, with Richard Hoggart as the founding

director of the Centre for Contemporary Cultural Studies (1964) and Hall as his successor (1969–1979) and with Williams as a major intellectual influence during the
first decade.

In such books from this time as *Modern Tragedy* (1966), *Drama from Ibsen to Brecht*
(1968), *The English Novel from Dickens to Lawrence* (1970), and *The Country and the City*
(1973), Williams produced major revaluations of both the dramatic and fictional traditions by reading texts as the scenes of historical meanings and transformations.
He is most actively concerned here with the aesthetic access to historical (lived) form
and with the historical form's relationships to recorded forms and their conventions,
and he also most fully works two of his best-known categories: "the knowable community" (contrasting with both the unknowable and the known and thus incorporating a certain dynamic potentiality that links the object-community and the
subject-observer) and "structure of feeling" (the distilled residue of the organization
of the lived experience of a community over and above the institutional and ideological organization of the society).

In the 1970s a widely increasing international theoretical sophistication, converging with a period of renaissance of intellectual Western Marxism, offered Williams new opportunities, audiences, and confirmations, both validating, however
indirectly, his own long-standing efforts to argue for a more complex world of relationships between literature, criticism, and other forms of writing and social practice and also inviting him, as a longtime critic of the crude anticultural Marxism of
the received orthodox traditions, to take up residence as a respected innovator in the
renewed house of Marxism. By the end of the decade most of Williams's writing refers itself to Marxism, testifying to a change of address if not of opinion, although he
never ceases to engage oppositionally with the established culture. His works now
appear as initiatives within the development of a general Marxist theoretical culture.
The remarkable *Politics and Letters* (1979) represents an innovation in form: through
hundreds of pages of exacting interview, Williams reviews with four editors of *New
Left Review* the frames and details of his life's work and repeatedly tests himself
against that journal's view of Marxism. In the earlier "Notes on Marxism in Britain
since 1945" (in *Problems in Materialism and Culture* [1980]) he defines his current
position—by which many will want to identify his legacy—as "cultural materialism"; this is a theory of culture as a productive process and a theory of specific cultural practices or "arts" as social uses of the material means of production (including language and the technologies of writing and other communications media).

This position is elaborated further in *Contact: Human Communication and Its History* (1981) and *Culture* (1981). Against Williams's earlier anthropological sense of
culture as a whole way of life, he now distinguishes manifestly signifying institutions, practices, and works within modern society (including language, fashion, and
advertising) from others in which signification, though present, is "more or less

completely" dissolved into other substantial needs and actions (just as these latter, in turn, are reciprocally in solution in manifestly signifying activities).

Marxism and Literature (1977), though rather schematic and compressed, is perhaps the best and most fully coherent of this Marxist theoretical series. It conducts a characteristically coded struggle against French STRUCTURALISM and poststructuralism, taking issue with the language paradigm and the notion of the arbitrary sign. It is also a rewarding encounter with all the elements of a Marxist cultural and literary theory, on which numerous improvements are convincingly worked. The most important contributions here may be the revisions in the categories of "hegemony" and "structure of feeling." The concept of hegemonic cultural domination, based in selective systems of inclusion and exclusion, provides for both social reproduction and resistance and for both connectedness and a determinate order among social practices. In the 1980s, Williams's refinements provided renewed points of contact between his work and the program of cultural studies at Birmingham (which became an independent department in 1988). "Structure of feeling," now redefined with greater categorical precision to mark the generative border country between the lived and the fully articulated as a structured social experience in solution, effective but still semantically preemergent, may be Williams's important contribution to that striving in contemporary cultural thought that has produced a family of undefinable yet operative categories, among which should be included PIERRE BOURDIEU's habitus, JACQUES DERRIDA's *différance*, MICHEL FOUCAULT's procedures, JULIA KRISTEVA's *chora*, and GILLES DELEUZE AND FÉLIX GUATTARI's plane of consistence.

In all his cultural work, Williams wrote against two traditions: "one which has totally spiritualized cultural production, the other which has relegated it to secondary status" (*Politics* 352–53). He was committed to the view that "the categories of literature and criticism were so deeply compromised that they had to be challenged *in toto*" (326). He was led in the 1980s to issues of feminism, ecology, and North-South relations. The possibilities of democratic cultural innovation and an alternative social order continued to win his confidence far more readily than the cultural pessimism in light of which only the past is to be won and a high culture is to be preserved and extended. He opted for "making hope practical, rather than despair convincing" (240).

Few books and articles have been addressed specifically to his work, but nearly everything in the increasingly voluminous literature on cultural studies makes some reference to Williams. In the sharpening struggles for a definition of cultural studies, there is some risk that Williams's legacy may be diminished to a narrow political sociology, cut to a measure that ill suits the richer dimensions both of his own concerns and of the potentialities of the field. At the same time, his pronounced *parti pris* with Marxism and modernism is bound to bring the paradigm-bound aspects of his work under increasingly sharp scrutiny and criticism from a post-Marxist or postmodernist site of inquiry. Stocktaking, like the long revolution for which Williams struggled, is yet at an early stage.

JOHN FEKETE

See also CULTURAL STUDIES, TERRY EAGLETON, ECOCRITICISM, MARXIST THEORY AND CRITICISM, and EDWARD W. SAID.

Raymond Williams, *Border Country: Raymond Williams in Adult Education* (ed. John McIlroy and Sallie Westwood, 1993), *Communications* (1962, 3rd ed., 1976), *The Country and the City* (1973), *Culture* (1981), *Culture and Society, 1780–1950* (1958), *Drama from Ibsen to Eliot* (1952, rev. ed., *Drama from Ibsen to Brecht*, 1968), *The English Novel from Dickens to Lawrence* (1970), *Keywords: A Vocabulary of Culture and Society* (1976, rev. ed., 1983), *The Long Revolution* (1961, rev. ed., 1966), *Marxism and Literature* (1977), *Modern Tragedy* (1966), *Politics and Letters: Interview with "New Left Review"* (1979), *Problems in Materialism and Culture: Selected Essays* (1980), *The Raymond Williams Reader* (ed. John Higgins, 2001), *Television: Technology and Cultural Form* (1974), *Towards 2000* (1983).

Žižek, Slavoj

Since the publication of his first major work in English, *The Sublime Object of Ideology* (1989), the Slovene scholar Slavoj Žižek (b. 1949) has become a prominent thinker in the field of cultural criticism. Žižek's interdisciplinary approach incorporates and adapts theories derived from Lacanian psychoanalysis, German idealist philosophy, and Marxism. His use of dialectical psychoanalysis to rethink modern philosophical and political systems is further characterized by the hallmarks of his writing: densely associative prose illuminated by examples taken from a broad range of cultural objects (such as Wagnerian opera, cyberspace, courtly love, contemporary nationalist movements, and the films of Alfred Hitchcock and David Lynch). Žižek, who holds doctoral degrees in both philosophy and psychoanalysis, describes his project as an "endeavour to use Lacan as a privileged tool to reactualize German idealism" (see the preface to *Žižek Reader*). Contesting the way JACQUES LACAN has been grouped with "deconstructive" thinkers such as JACQUES DERRIDA, Žižek situates Lacan as the true heir to an Enlightenment tradition that includes René Descartes, Immanuel Kant, G. W. F. Hegel, and Friedrich Wilhelm Joseph von Schelling. An important aspect of Žižek's project is to juxtapose the Western philosophical tradition and Lacanian psychoanalysis in order to decipher the ways in which Lacan effectively rewrites the unconscious structures of thought guiding these earlier philosophers.

In his work to date, Žižek adopts and develops Lacan's concept of the Real as the unsymbolizable kernel of enjoyment that disrupts our understanding of mundane reality as it is structured by the symbolic. The tension between the symbolic and the Real is the central dialectic operating throughout Žižek's work. Shared cultural fantasies perpetuated by capitalist social organization conceal this fundamental antagonism between the symbolic and the Real even as they animate and structure the subject's desire and protect against excessive enjoyment. By arguing for the unconscious operations of the Real, Žižek's approach involves "an effort to unearth, to render visible again, this constitutive violence whose 'repression' is coextensive with the very existence" of the [symbolic] order (*Metastases* 205). Rather than enabling further repression by seeking resolutions to fundamental antagonisms, Žižek advocates "tarrying" with their negativity.

In contrast to the postmodernist emphasis on the radical contingency of all phenomena, Žižek claims to decipher the ubiquitous, transhistorical dimensions of subjectivity: "Historicity proper involves a dialectical relationship to some unhistorical kernel that stays the same—not as an underlying Essence but as a rock that trips up every attempt to integrate it into the symbolic order" (*Metastases* 199). Žižek thus situates himself in opposition to "constructionist" explanations of subjectivity as well as to Althusser's theory of interpellation, both of which fail to consider the subject prior to subjectivization. Žižek remains loyal to Lacan's model of divided subjectivity, whereby the traumatic entry into language coincides with a splitting of the subject. In other words, identification with signifiers provided by the symbolic order allows individuals to live out their subject positions while masking the original void, which is paradoxically the positive condition of the subject's existence. The subject derives further phantasmatic support for the illusion of its own coherence from the pursuit of an imaginary or "sublime" object (the Lacanian *objet a*) that fills out the empty place at the core of the subject and the symbolic order. As a fantasy that "gives body" to the hole of unsymbolizable Real, the *objet a* traps the subject in a closed circuit of desire; it is both the object that the subject desires so as to conceal its constitutive lack and the lack itself, which causes the subject's desire. In contrast to the practices of ego psychology, which affirm the stability and integrity of the subject, the psychoanalytic "cure" preferred by Žižek is "subjective destitution," whereby the subject foregoes both defensive responses and dependence on symbolic supports and identifies with *le sinthome*, or the singular part of the meaningless Real that demands an uncompromising resistance to the symbolic.

Despite criticisms that Žižek's psychoanalytic approach is politically indeterminate or impractical, one dimension of his ongoing work remains committed to the interrogation and development of radical democracy. The combination of Lacanianism and socialism in Žižek's work serves two functions: first, it politicizes and popularizes psychoanalysis by addressing broad cultural phenomena, and second, it critiques the hermeneutical assumptions and goals of classical Marxism. By going back to the Hegelian roots of Marx's thought, Žižek challenges the economic determinism of classical Marxism, questioning its consideration of exclusively "material" causes and its relegation of fantasy to the realm of mere illusion and asserting instead that social organization depends on underlying psychosocial forms that throughout history have been internalized and acted out by subjects. Ideology critique, for instance, traditionally presupposes naïve subjects who are deluded but who can be brought to envision society as a rationalized totality. According to Žižek, this view of ideology tends to efface fundamental antagonisms that cannot be resolved since their very existence is a necessary condition for the emergence of the symbolic order. Žižek reconceptualizes ideology as a specter, with no ontological substance, which nevertheless supplements the account of reality offered by the symbolic and prevents recognition of the "preideological kernel" of failed symbolization denoted by the Real (*Mapping* 1–33). Not only does classical Marxism ignore the role of fantasy in constituting and sustaining our object world, but its desire for a socialist utopia actually supports the thoroughly ideological fantasy of a unified and stable social order. Žižek further argues that one of the central notions of Marxism—class struggle—is better understood as an effect rather than a cause of constitutive antagonisms at the core of modern capitalist society. He interprets the plurality of particular social struggles as diverse symbolizations of the same traumatic kernel of the Real. For example, sexual difference, far from being ontologically determined or simply an effect of discursive practices, is a manifestation of the internal conflicts that plague every subject, conflicts that are themselves produced by inconsistencies in the symbolic process (*Metastases* 137–64).

According to Žižek, modern ideological systems operate through a built-in distance between structure and subject whereby the subject knows precisely what he or she is doing but does it anyway (*Sublime* 29). Thus, subjects regard ideology and authority from a cynical position, but their actions nevertheless do the work of believing for them. While the ruling ideology expects its subjects to maintain this cynical distance, the most dangerous threat is actually posed by those persons who take ideology too seriously and whose excessive actions inadvertently expose the contradictions that underlie the illusion of a harmonious, nonantagonistic social structure. Consistent with Žižek's dialectical analysis of modernity is his claim that the proliferation of discourses such as liberal MULTICULTURALISM, identity politics, and DECONSTRUCTION—similar in their ethical position of unconditional respect for alterity—in fact depoliticize the social by accommodating marginal groups and neutralizing their potential for effective resistance. To further a program of opposition to the social and economic disparities generated by global capitalism, Žižek marshals ideas from a wide variety of philosophical and political thinkers. For instance, *The Ticklish Subject* (1999), arguably Žižek's most sustained and sophisticated challenge to contemporary critical theory, calls for a return to the "subversive core" of the Cartesian subject in the interests of a genuinely emancipatory leftist politics. Elsewhere, Žižek refers to himself as a "Paulinian materialist," locating revolutionary potential in St. Paul's militant defense of universal truth (*The Fragile Absolute* [2000]). Žižek's work in the early twenty-first century resumes the strategy of resurrecting "dead" thinkers by calling for a return to Lenin, attributing to him an uncompromising commitment to radical politics regardless of the consequences. Žižek contrasts Lenin's rigid pursuit of revolutionary goals, which freed him from the constraints imposed by the established order, with the current activities of a consensus-driven liberal Left, which merely chooses from among already entrenched modes of symbolization. A genuinely radical intervention (the Lacanian *passage à l'acte*) "chooses the impossible," so that the choice itself effects a shift in the coordinates of the symbolic network (*On Belief* 113–27). According to Žižek, a transposition of a theory from its original context to another historical moment (such as Lenin's return to Marx or Lacan's return to Freud) can undermine the symbolic efficiency of a totalizing system. Therefore, for Žižek, confronting global capitalism from the standpoint of universal truth at the moment when it denies the possibility of such a stance would constitute a truly transformative act.

GRACE POLLOCK

See also MARXIST THEORY AND CRITICISM: 3. 1989 AND AFTER.

Slavoj Žižek, The Abyss of Freedom: Ages of the World (1997), The Art of the Ridiculous Sublime: On David Lynch's Lost Highway (2000), Did Somebody Say Totalitarianism? Five Interventions in the (Mis)Use of a Notion (2001), Enjoy Your Symptom! Jacques Lacan in Hollywood and Out (1992), Everything You Always Wanted to Know about Lacan (But Were Afraid to Ask Hitchcock) (1992), First as Tragedy Then as Farce (2009), The Fragile Absolute; or, Why the Christian Legacy Is Worth Fighting For (2000), The Fright of Real Tears: Krzysztof Kieslowski between Theory and Post-Theory (2001), The Idea of Communism (2010), In Defense of Lost Causes (2008), The Indivisible Remainder: An Essay on Schelling and Related Matters (1996), Living in the End Times (2010), Looking Awry: An Introduction to Jacques Lacan through Popular Culture (1991), The Metastases of Enjoyment: Six Essays on Woman and Causality (1994), The Monstrosity of Christ: Paradox or Dialectic? (2009), On Belief (Thinking in Action) (2001), Organs without Bodies: On Deleuze and Consequences (2003), The Parallax View (2006), The Plague of Fantasies (1997), The Sublime Object of Ideology (1989), Tarrying with the Negative: Kant, Hegel, and the Critique of Ideology (1993), The Ticklish Subject: The Absent Centre of Political Ontology (1999), Welcome to the Desert of the Real (2002), The Žižek Reader (1999, ed. Elizabeth Wright and Edmond Wright); Slavoj Žižek, ed., Cogito and the Unconscious (1998); Mapping Ideology (1994); Revolution at the Gates: Selected Writings of Lenin from 1917 (2002); Slavoj Žižek, Judith Butler, and Ernesto Laclau, Contingency, Hegemony, Universality: Contemporary Dialogues on the Left (2000); Slavoj Žižek and Mladen Dolar, eds., Opera's Second Death (2002); Slavoj Žižek and Renata Salecl, Gaze and Voice as Love Objects (1996).

CONTRIBUTORS

Paul B. Armstrong, Brown University:
Phenomenology

Philip Armstrong, Ohio State University:
Jean-Luc Nancy

Ian Balfour, York University: Walter
Benjamin

Eve Tavor Bannet, University of Oklahoma: Georg Lukács

Stephen M. Barber, University of Rhode
Island: Eve Kosofsky Sedgwick

Lindon Barrett, late of University of
California, Riverside: African-
American Theory and Criticism:
3. The 1990s

Jon Beasley-Murray, University of British
Columbia: Pierre Bourdieu

Robert de Beaugrande, late of Universi-
dade Federal de Paraíba, Brazil:
Discourse: 1. Discourse Analysis

Davina Bhandar, Trent University:
Donna Haraway

Guyora Binder, University at Buffalo
Law School: Law and Literature

Sarah Blacker, University of Alberta:
Science Studies

Chiara Briganti, Arcadia University:
Hélène Cixous; Luce Irigaray;
Psychoanalytic Theory and Criticism:
3. The Post-Lacanians

Gerald L. Bruns, University of Notre
Dame: Martin Heidegger

Diana Brydon, University of Manitoba:
Postcolonial Studies: 2. 1990 and
After

Ian Buchanan, University of Wollongong:
Gilles Deleuze and Félix Guattari

Hunter Cadzow, independent scholar:
New Historicism

Susan R. Carlton, independent scholar:
Simone de Beauvoir

Cynthia Chase, Cornell University: Paul
de Man

Michael P. Clark, University of California, Irvine: Jacques Lacan

Paul Cobley, London Metropolitan
University: Narratology

Alison Conway, University of Western
Ontario: New Historicism

John Corr, Wilfrid Laurier University:
Paul Gilroy

Reed Way Dasenbrock, University of
Hawaii at Manoa: Stanley Fish

Robert Con Davis-Undiano, University
of Oklahoma: Hélène Cixous; Luce
Irigaray; Psychoanalytic Theory and
Criticism: 3. The Post-Lacanians

George L. Dillon, University of Washington: Discourse: 2. Discourse Theory

Leland de la Durantaye, Harvard
University: Giorgio Agamben

Marlo Edwards, Okanagan College:
Gender

Diane Elam, independent scholar:
Feminist Theory and Criticism:
3. Poststructuralist Feminisms

Caryl Emerson, Princeton University:
Mikhail Bakhtin

Angela Esterhammer, University of
Zurich: Speech Acts

Grant Farred, Cornell University: Stuart
Hall

John Fekete, Trent University: Raymond
Williams

Robert Elliot Fox, Southern Illinois
University, Carbondale: Henry Louis
Gates Jr.

Gary Genosko, Lakehead University:
Jean Baudrillard

Christina Gerhardt, Pacific University,
Oregon: Theodor W. Adorno

Andrew Gibson, Royal Holloway,
University of London: Ethics

Philip Goldstein, University of Dela-
ware: Reader-Response Criticism

Andrew Griffin, University of California, Santa Barbara: Stephen
Greenblatt

Georg M. Gugelberger, University of
California, Riverside: Postcolonial
Studies: 1. Origins to the 1980s

M. A. R. Habib, Rutgers University,
Camden: Marxist Theory and
Criticism: 1. Classical Marxism

Ellis Hanson, Cornell University: Queer
Theory and Criticism: 3. Queer
Theory

Robert Harvey, State University of New
York, Stony Brook: Jean-François
Lyotard

Dana Heller, Old Dominion University:
Queer Theory and Criticism:
2. Lesbian

Jacqueline Henkel, University of Texas at
Austin: Linguistics and Language

Ben Highmore, University of Sussex:
Michel de Certeau

Peter Hitchcock, City University of New
York: Marxist Theory and Criticism:
3. 1989 and After

Julian Holland, McMaster University:
Marxist Theory and Criticism:
2. Structuralist Marxism

Dana Hollander, McMaster University:
Emmanuel Levinas

Linda Hutcheon, University of Toronto:
Sigmund Freud

Sharla Hutchison, Fort Hays State
University: Hélène Cixous; Luce
Irigaray; Psychoanalytic Theory and
Criticism: 3. The Post-Lacanians

Caren Irr, Brandeis University: Frankfurt School

Zubeda Jalalzai, Rhode Island College:
Frantz Fanon

Biodun Jeyifo, Harvard University:
Frantz Fanon

Tim Kaposy, George Mason University:
Franco Moretti

Thomas Keenan, Bard College: Walter
Benjamin

Douglas Kellner, University of California, Los Angeles: Fredric Jameson

J. Douglas Kneale, University of Western Ontario: Deconstruction: 1. Derrida, de Man, and the Yale Critics

Cassandra Laity, Drew University: Modernist Theory and Criticism

Donna Landry, University of Kent: Feminist Theory and Criticism: 4. Materialist Feminisms

Marcia Landy, University of Pittsburgh: Antonio Gramsci

Vincent B. Leitch, University of Oklahoma: Cultural Studies: 2. United States

Geert Lernout, University of Antwerp: Reception Theory

Mitchell R. Lewis, Elmira College: Cultural Studies: 2. United States

Gregory Lucente, late of University of Michigan: Antonio Gramsci

Eva Mackey, Carleton University: Multiculturalism

Gerald MacLean, Wayne State University: Feminist Theory and Criticism: 4. Materialist Feminisms

Matthew MacLellan, University of Alberta: Jacques Rancière

Vicki Mahaffey, University of Illinois at Urbana-Champaign: Modernist Theory and Criticism

Theodore O. Mason Jr., Kenyon College: African American Theory and Criticism: 1. Harlem Renaissance to the Black Arts Movement; African American Theory and Criticism: 2. 1977 to 1990

John McGowan, University of North Carolina at Chapel Hill: Postmodernism

Ellen Messer-Davidow, University of Minnesota: Feminist Theory and Criticism: 1. From Movement Critique to Discourse Analysis

Ginette Michaud, Université de Montréal: Jean-Luc Nancy

Anne Milne, University of Guelph: Ecocriticism

Sabine Milz, Fanshawe College: Edward W. Said

Sourayan Mookerjea, University of Alberta: Cultural Studies: 4. Canada

Bart Moore-Gilbert, Goldsmiths College, University of London: Homi K. Bhabha; Gayatri Chakravorty Spivak

Christopher D. Morris, Goldsmiths College, University of London: Homi K. Bhabha; Psychoanalytic Theory and Criticism: 2. Reconceptualizing Freud

Gary Saul Morson, Northwestern University: Mikhail Bakhtin

Jeffrey T. Nealon, Pennsylvania State University: Judith Butler

Kelly Oliver, Vanderbilt University: Julia Kristeva

Vincent P. Pecora, University of Utah: Frankfurt School

Andrew Pendakis, University of Alberta: Alain Badiou

James Penney, Trent University: Jacques Lacan

Paul Perron, University of Toronto: Semiotics

Jan Plug, University of Western Ontario: Deconstruction: 2. The 1980s and After

Grace Pollock, independent scholar: Slavoj Žižek

Mark Poster, University of California, Irvine: Michel Foucault

Elvira Pulitano, University of Geneva: Native Theory and Criticism: 1. United States

Jean-Michel Rabaté, University of Pennsylvania: Roland Barthes; Jacques Derrida

Herman Rapaport, Wake Forest University: French Theory and Criticism: 1945 and After

Marc Redfield, Brown University: Georges Bataille; Maurice Blanchot

Stephen Regan, Durham University: Terry Eagleton

Douglas Robinson, Lingnan University: Speech Acts

Ralph E. Rodriguez, Brown University: Race and Ethnicity

Gabriel Rupp, University of Central Oklahoma: Ferdinand de Saussure; Structuralism

Eric Savoy, Université de Montréal: Queer Theory and Criticism: 1. Gay Male

Ronald Schleifer, University of Oklahoma: Ferdinand de Saussure; Structuralism

Bonnie Kime Scott, San Diego State University: Feminist Theory and Criticism: 2. Anglo-American Feminisms

Richard Stingle, professor emeritus, University of Western Ontario: Northrop Frye

John Storey, University of Sunderland: Cultural Studies: 1. United Kingdom

Justin Sully, University of Alberta: Étienne Balibar

Cheryl Suzack, University of Toronto: Native Theory and Criticism: 2. Canada

Imre Szeman, University of Alberta: Globalization

Bryce Traister, University of Western Ontario: New Historicism

Graeme Turner, University of Queensland: Cultural Studies: 3. Australia

Chris Weedon, Cardiff University: Feminist Theory and Criticism: 5. 1990 and After

Gary Wihl, Washington University in St. Louis: Marxist Theory and Criticism: 2. Structuralist Marxism

David Willbern, University at Buffalo,
    State University of New York:
    Psychoanalytic Theory and Criticism:
    1. Traditional Freudian Criticism

Julia M. Wright, Dalhousie University:
    National Literature

Bonnie Zimmerman, professor emeri-
    tus, San Diego State University:
    Queer Theory and Criticism:
    2. Lesbian

INDEX OF NAMES

INDEX OF TOPICS